Regional Variation in
Indian Ocean Coral Reefs

SYMPOSIA OF THE ZOOLOGICAL SOCIETY OF LONDON

NUMBER 28

Regional Variation in Indian Ocean Coral Reefs

(The Proceedings of a Symposium, organized jointly by the Royal Society of London and the Zoological Society of London, held at The Zoological Society of London on 28 and 29 May, 1970)

Edited by

D. R. STODDART

Department of Geography,
University of Cambridge,
Cambridge, England

SIR MAURICE YONGE

Department of Zoology,
University of Edinburgh,
Edinburgh, Scotland

Published for

THE ZOOLOGICAL SOCIETY OF LONDON

BY

ACADEMIC PRESS

1971

ACADEMIC PRESS INC. (LONDON) LTD

Berkeley Square House

Berkeley Square

London, W1X 6BA

U.S. Edition published by

ACADEMIC PRESS INC.

111 Fifth Avenue,

New York, New York 10003

Library of Congress Catalog Card Number: 72-141728
ISBN: 0-12-613328-X

PRINTED IN GREAT BRITAIN BY
J. W. ARROWSMITH LTD., BRISTOL

CONTRIBUTORS

BARNES, J., *Department of Botany, The University of Durham, Durham, England* (p. 87)

BELLAMY, D. J., *Department of Botany, The University of Durham, Durham, England* (p. 87)

BRAITHWAITE, C. J. R., *Department of Geology, Dundee University, Dundee, Scotland* (p. 39)

BRANDER, K. M., *Marine Science Laboratories, Menai Bridge, Anglesey, Wales** (p. 397)

CAMPBELL, A. C., *Department of Zoology, Oxford University, Oxford, England* (p. 433)

DREW, E. A., *Department of Botany, University of St. Andrews, St. Andrews, Fife, Scotland* (p. 87)

FARROW, G. E., *Department of Geology, University of Hull, Hull, England†* (p. 455)

FLEISSNER, G., *Zoologisches Institut der Universität Frankfurt/M, Siesmayerstr. 70, West Germany* (p. 535)

FLEISSNER, H., *Unterwasser und Dokumentarfilm für Wissenschaft und Bildung, Bad Nauheim, Steinfurther Str. 33, West Germany* (p. 535)

GOPINADHA PILLAI, C. S., *Central Marine Fisheries Research Institute, Mandapam Camp, India* (p. 301)

GUILCHER, A., *Institute of Geography, University of Paris, Paris, France‡* (p. 65)

HUMPHREYS, W. F., *Department of Zoology, University College of North Wales, Bangor, Wales§* (p. 397)

JONES, D. J., *Department of Botany, The University of Durham, Durham, England* (p. 87)

KENYON, L., *Chelsea Arts Club, Chelsea, London, England* (p. 87)

LOYA, Y., *Department of Biological Sciences, State University of New York at Stony Brook, New York, U.S.A.* (p. 117)

LYTHGOE, J. N., *Medical Research Council, Vision Research Unit, University of Sussex, Brighton, Sussex, England* (p. 87)

McKENZIE, K. G., *British Museum (Natural History), London, England* (p. 543)

* Present address: Fisheries Laboratory, Ministry of Agriculture, Fisheries and Food, Lowestoft, England.
† Present address: Department of Geology, University of Glasgow, Glasgow, Scotland.
‡ Present address: Faculté des Lettres, B.P. 860, 29N Brest, France.
§ Present address: Department of Zoology, Australian National University, Canberra, Australia.

McLeod, A. A. Q. R., *Marine Science Laboratories, Menai Bridge, Anglesey, Wales* (p. 397)

Mergner, H., *Lehrstuhl für Spezielle Zoologie an der Ruhr-Universität Bochum, West Germany* (p. 141)

Ormond, R. F. G., *Physiological Laboratory, University of Cambridge, Cambridge, England* (p. 433)

Pichon, M., *Station Marine d'Endoume et Centre d'Océanographie, Marseille, France* (p. 185)

Rosen, B. R., *Department of Geophysics and Planetary Physics, School of Physics, The University, Newcastle-upon-Tyne, England* (p. 87, p. 163, p. 263)

Scheer, G., *Hessian State Museum, Darmstadt, Germany* (p. 329)

Sigee, D. C., *Department of Botany, University College of Wales, Cardiff, Wales* (p. 217)

Slobodkin, L. B., *Department of Biological Sciences, State University of New York at Stony Brook, New York, U.S.A.* (p. 117)

Spencer Davies, P., *Department of Zoology, University of Glasgow, Glasgow, Scotland* (p. 217)

Stoddart, D. R., *Department of Geography, University of Cambridge, Cambridge, England* (p. 3, p. 217, p. 549)

Taylor, J. D., *Department of Zoology, British Museum (Natural History), London, England* (p. 501)

Thomassin, B. A., *Station Marine d'Endoume et Centre d'Océanographie, Marseille, France* (p. 371)

Whitton, B. A., *Department of Botany, The University of Durham, Durham, England* (p. 87)

ORGANIZERS AND CHAIRMEN

ORGANIZERS

D. R. STODDART and SIR MAURICE YONGE *on behalf of The Zoological Society of London*

CHAIRMEN OF SESSIONS

A. GUILCHER, *Institute of Geography, University of Paris, Paris, France*

D. R. STODDART, *Department of Geography, University of Cambridge, Cambridge, England*

SIR MAURICE YONGE, *Department of Zoology, University of Edinburgh, Edinburgh, Scotland*

FOREWORD

This Symposium is concerned with coral reefs but exclusively those from the Indian Ocean, indeed confining attention to those in its western areas. This geographical restriction is fitting both because of the importance of Indian Ocean reefs in the history of coral reef studies and because of the great proliferation of work in these areas of recent years.

As a source of knowledge to western man about coral reefs, the Indian Ocean takes undoubted precedence. Although specific reference to corals in classic literature appears to be confined to the red coral of commerce (*Corallium rubrum*) found in the Mediterranean, the Greeks of Alexandria encountered true scleractinian corals at the head of the Gulf of Suez where the canal of their day entered the Red Sea. There was connexion by the land route to the Persian Gulf and to India before Portuguese, Dutch, British and French navigators reached there by sea, sailing subsequently to Malaya and the Indonesian Islands. It was somewhat later that Columbus discovered the coral reefs of the Atlantic in the Caribbean and the Gulf of Mexico. Later still the Pacific was crossed, initially by Magellan, and Spanish joined hands with Portuguese exploration at the Philippines, in the very centre of coral diversity.

During the seventeenth and eighteenth centuries many Indian Ocean reef areas such as Zanzibar, Mauritius, Seychelles, the Maldives and, much further east, many islands of the Indonesian Archipelago were settled, if only as trading posts, and increased knowledge about reefs and their exotic fauna, notably of shells and fishes, reached Europe. The knowledge and interest of naturalists increased although it was not until the mid-eighteenth century that the completely animal nature of corals was established independently by Peysonnel in France and John Ellis in England. Amongst navigators increased knowledge led to increased respect, the hazards of reef navigation almost terminated Cook's first voyage when, just two hundred years ago, H.M.S. *Endeavour* was wrecked in the central region of the Great Barrier Reef of Australia.

Science begins to come into the picture with Chamisso who accompanied von Kotzebue during his Pacifc voyage of 1815–18. The Indian Ocean reappears in the centre of the stage with the voyage of H.M.S. *Beagle* in 1831–36. Although Charles Darwin set off on that voyage with the idea of wide scale subsidence as the universal cause of atoll and barrier reef formation already in his mind, he crossed the Pacific making singularly little contact with coral reefs. Not until the Indian Ocean did he make personal encounter with the reefs of Cocos–Keeling atoll and then with the fringing reefs of Mauritius, the former later to be the site of highly personal and stimulating studies by Wood–Jones in the early years of this century.

The nineteenth, and the early years of the twentieth, century are largely associated with Pacific studies and the inauguration of deep drilling through atolls, beginning at Funafuti and culminating in Eni-wetok. This period saw the two Indian Ocean expeditions of Stanley Gardiner, the first to the Laccadives and Maldives in 1899–1900, the second, on H.M.S. *Sealark* in 1905, to the Chagos and the Seychelles, together with the work of Seymour Sewell in Indian waters when Director of the Zoological Survey. The Dutch were subsequently to establish a marine laboratory in the coral reef waters at the Bay of Batavia, and the Egyptians at Al-Ghardaqa at the north end of the Red Seas.

It was not, however, until after the last war that the Indian Ocean and particularly its western regions again became the scene of wide and intensive studies on corals and coral reefs. In the Red Sea, reefs have been studied by French, German, Israeli, Egyptian and British workers. The French have also been very active in the waters around Madagascar, the Comoros Archipelago and Mauritius, Indian workers have studied reefs and reef corals in the waters around the southern coasts of their country, and there have been British Expeditions to the Maldives and the Seychelles. The Royal Society has also become involved due to its interest in the fauna of Aldabra, earlier studied by Fryer in the course of the *Sealark* Expedition, where, in association with the U.S. National Academy, a biological station is now being erected. The Israelis have recently built a marine laboratory at Eilat.

We shall hear a good deal about these activities from the representatives of five countries who contribute to this Symposium. Items of discussions that have been printed are those which the authors made themselves and they are necessarily incomplete. Most of these discussion items are printed at the end of the papers to which they refer, the only exception being the longer and more general contribution by Dr. K. G. McKenzie on pp. 543–547.

On p. 535 reference is made to the film shown at the Symposium by Herrn. H. and G. Fleissner who contributed this short interesting description.

July 1971   C. M. YONGE

CONTENTS

GEOLOGY AND MORPHOLOGY OF REEFS
Environment and History in Indian Ocean Reef Morphology

D. R. STODDART

CONTENTS

Seychelles Reefs: Structure and Development

C. J. R. BRAITHWAITE

Mayotte Barrier Reef and Lagoon, Comoro Islands, as compared with other Barrier Reefs, Atolls and Lagoons in the World

ANDRÉ GUILCHER

Morphology and Ecology of the Reef Front of Aldabra

J. BARNES, D. J. BELLAMY, D. J. JONES, B. A. WHITTON, E. A. DREW, L. KENYON, J. N. LYTHGOE and BRIAN R. ROSEN

REGIONAL STUDIES OF REEFS

The Coral Reefs of Eilat (Gulf of Eilat, Red Sea)
YOSSEF LOYA and LAWRENCE B. SLOBODKIN

Structure, Ecology and Zonation of Red Sea Reefs
(in comparison with South Indian and Jamaican Reefs)
HANS MERGNER

Principal Features of Reef Coral Ecology in Shallow Water Environments Mahé, Seychelles
BRIAN R. ROSEN

Comparative Study of the Main Features of some Coral Reefs of Madagascar, La Réunion and Mauritius
MICHEL PICHON

Reef Forms of Addu Atoll, Maldive Islands
P. SPENCER DAVIES, D. R. STODDART and D. C. SIGEE

DISTRIBUTION OF CORALS
The Distribution of Reef Coral Genera in the Indian Ocean
BRIAN R. ROSEN

Composition of the Coral Fauna of the Southeastern Coast of India and the Laccadives
C. S. GOPINADHA PILLAI

CONTENTS

Coral Reefs and Coral Genera in the Red Sea and Indian Ocean

GEORG SCHEER

OTHER REEF INVERTEBRATE COMMUNITIES

Les Faciès d'Epifaune et d'Epiflore des Biotopes Sédimentaires des Formations Coralliennes dans La Région de Tuléar (Sud-Ouest de Madagascar)

BERNARD A. THOMASSIN

Comparison of Species Diversity and Ecology of Reef-Living Invertebrates on Aldabra Atoll and at Watamu, Kenya

K. M. BRANDER, A. A. Q. R. McLEOD and W. F. HUMPHREYS

Observations on *Acanthaster planci* and other Coral Reef Echinoderms in the Sudanese Red Sea

R. F. G. ORMOND and A. C. CAMPBELL

Back-reef and Lagoonal Environments of Aldabra Atoll distinguished by their Crustacean Burrows

GEORGE E. FARROW

Reef Associated Molluscan Assemblages in the Western Indian Ocean
JOHN D. TAYLOR

The Coral Gardens of Shadwan
HELMUT FLEISSNER and GUENTHER FLEISSNER 535

CONCLUSION

Remarks

K. G. McKENZIE 543

2*

Problems and Prospects in Indian Ocean Reef Studies
D. R. STODDART

(Photograph by Fritz Goreau)

THOMAS F. GOREAU:
A TRIBUTE

by

C. M. YONGE

University of Edinburgh,
Edinburgh, Scotland

The programme of this Symposium contains the name T. F. Goreau who was to have contributed a paper on the reefs of the Gulf of Eilat. An account of work in that area is given by a fellow-worker, Dr. Y. Loya. But, as will be known to most of you, Tom Goreau died on April 22, 1970. His work on corals and on coral reefs over a period approaching twenty years was supremely outstanding and his death at the tragically early age of 45, at the very height of his powers, is a devastating loss to science and to all of us who knew him an equally great personal loss.

To those concerned with the organization of this Symposium it appeared appropriate that the volume containing the contributed papers should constitute a memorial to him, that it should contain his portrait with some account of his work with appreciations from some of those most intimately concerned with him and his work on coral reefs. No one, certainly in the lifetime of anyone here present, has contributed more and so many different ways to the fundamental understanding of the nature, growth and maintenance of coral reefs.

Tom Goreau was born in 1924 in Berlin, from which his parents later moved to Munich, but left Germany when Hitler came into power in 1933 and the magazine publishing house in which his father was an editor was taken over by the Nazis. By way of Vienna and Switzerland the family made its way to Paris where they remained until January 1936 when they moved to the United States. Thus his elementary education was divided between Munich, Vienna, Zurich, and Paris while in New York he attended the well known High School of Music and Art. His parents tell of his early gift for drawing, well developed even before he could write, although artistic interests were later to be overshadowed by increasing preoccupation with biology. His first contact with fossils was made at the age of five in the collections of Ralph von Koenigswald, then a young graduate student at Munich.

He graduated Bachelor of Arts at Clark University, Worcester, Mass., and then proceeded to medical studies at Philadelphia with a period at Chicago, notable because it was there he met his wife, Nora. But, under the compelling influence of Professor Evelyn Hutchinson, he abandoned medicine to become a graduate student in the Zoology Department at Yale. His first professional contact with marine biology appears to have been as an assistant oceanographer in the U.S. Navy and the Scripps Institution during the summer of 1947 when he worked at Bikini. His vivid scientific imagination was fired by the problems presented by coral reefs, questions particularly of their formation, constitution, maintenance and recent history.

Such matters formed the subject matter of his doctor's thesis, "A study of the biology and histo-chemistry of corals" which was not, however, presented until 1956, five years after he had been appointed lecturer in physiology in the then University College, later University, of the West Indies at Kingston, Jamaica. He had gone there primarily to work on corals and coral reefs but remained a devoted teacher of medical physiology until his appointment as Professor of Marine Science in 1967. He enjoyed teaching and to as varied a range of students as could be encountered anywhere in the world. After long experience he told the writer he had failed to find the slightest correlation between intelligence and racial origin.

Professor Ivan Goodbody, his colleague in zoology over many years, writes of these early years that "Laboratory facilities were still being built and there were none on the sea coast when he first arrived in Jamaica, but Tom's energy and enthusiasm enabled him to overcome any such handicaps. With an outboard engine and a borrowed boat he began to explore the Jamaican reefs while at the same time beginning his important laboratory experiments on the growth and calcification of corals. Before Scuba had become generally available Tom had built for himself an oxygen breathing apparatus which enabled him to make his first explorations into the deeper parts of the reef and subsequently with Scuba he developed his exploration to the point where his diving ability became almost legendary. Convinced early on that the north coast reefs offered better opportunities for study than those on the south coast, but tied by his teaching duties to a working week in Kingston, Tom commuted almost every weekend across the island to the north shore to explore and to study the reef community. Slowly over the years with the use of aeroplanes, helicopters, boats and Scuba he mapped and charted the north coast reefs and developed his ideas on their growth and structure, the production and movement of sediments, and the nature of the ancient shorelines."

Following completion of his Ph.D. in 1956, Tom became associated with the New York Zoological Society in a "Coral reef project—Jamaica" during the course of which, and it continued until 1967, the greater part of his later research was carried out. He had, however, grants from other sources including the Office of Naval Research, Washington.

While his first published work on corals appears to have been on an electronmicrographical examination of their flagellated epithelia and on phosphomonoesterases, the first general intimation that a major figure had appeared in the field of experimental study of reef-building corals was contained in the series of papers on the physiology of skeleton formation in corals published in 1959 and 1960 in the *Biological Bulletin*. Here, in frequent collaboration with his wife, Nora, a highly skilled histologist, he produced conclusive evidence that the endozoic algae (zooxanthellae) which are invariably contained within the endoderm (gastroderm) of all hermatypic corals are responsible for the exceptionally high rates of calcification found in these, as compared with ahermatypic, corals. These rates are essential for the maintenance of shallow water reefs against so many adverse physical and biological factors. What had been at the best no more than speculation now became scientific evidence based on accurate measurement of calcification rates by the use of radioactive calcium-45 as tracer. By use of this elegant method, he was able to measure skeletal growth within a few hours of initial exposure. He did so *in situ* on the reefs by the use of weighed and sealed glass jars containing corals with the tracer in the water, the corals being subsequently sampled by the use of a hollow steel core punch. Experiments in light and in darkness and also after removal of the zooxanthellae by keeping corals in darkness for 6 weeks revealed that, in the fourteen species studied, growth was on average ten times faster in sunlight when zooxanthellae were present. By simultaneous use of ^{45}Ca and ^{14}C-carbonate he was able to present a picture of the possible pathways of both calcium and carbonate during calcification which, subject to some modifications, provides the probable basis for the final elucidation of these fundamental processes.

Growth, of course, involves increase of the tissues, themselves responsible for formation of the polyps and mesenterial filaments— the means of feeding and digestion—no less than of the skeleton. The form of growth characteristics of any species he revealed as dependent on properties inherent in the tissues. As he wrote, "In corals with determinate colony shapes, the amount of living tissue is directly proportional to the surface area and the skeletal mass is proportional to the volume, the two parameters are related by a constant which varies according to the species". In branching colonies such as *Acropora* spp., calcification rates are up to ten times greater in apical than lateral or basal areas whereas in massive rounded corals, e.g. *Colpophyllia* or *Goniastrea*, there is little difference from one area to another. With development of his deep water studies, he found that important reef-builders such as *Montastrea annularis* and *Porites astreoides*, which occur as hemispherical masses near the surface, become flattened and plate-like in the dim light of greater depths; this is a consequence of reduction in zooxanthellae with consequent effects on calcification, the tissues being unaffected.

On the long vexed question of the status of the zooxanthellae in the nutrition of hermatypic corals (they are absent in ahermatypes) Tom held firmly to the view that, unlike the octocorallian Xeniidae, these corals are not autotrophs. He believed that they were carnivorous although extending the range of their food to include suspended or deposited organic detritus. He found support in the results of his early work on enzymes and electron-microscopy. This would provide a solution for the problem of the nutrition of small polyped corals, with vestigial tentacles but with, if anything, hypertrophied mesenterial filaments.

Scleractinian corals, with the hydrozoan *Millepora* and the octocorallians, *Heliopora* and *Tubipora*, are only some, if the most spectacular, of hermatypic organisms responsible for the formation of reefs. Plants are as important as animals and Tom Goreau paid equal attention to their powers of calcification and the relation to these to photosynthesis. In one of the most important of his papers he divides all reef producers to primary hermatypes which are frame-builders and include corals and lithothamnioid algae, secondary hermatypes which are framefillers and framecementers and comprise other types of both corals and calcareous red algae with some molluscs, and also sand formers which include many kinds of red and green calcareous algae and a wide range of invertebrates. The ubiquitous calcareous green *Halimeda*, comprising many species, particularly interested him and his collaborator Eileen Graham.

Ivan Goodbody has referred to Tom's preoccupation with the north coast where his studies of the reefs around Ocho Rios are the most comprehensive ever undertaken in the Atlantic.   They reveal a complexity hitherto unsuspected in this ocean and challenge comparison with the most elaborate of those described in the Indo-Pacific. Proceeding shoreward from deep water he described 7 to 9 zones which he named according to their significant features and which included a buttress zone superficially resembling that described on the windward side of Pacific atolls. Here, however, they are primarily composed of the coalescence of heads of *Montastrea annularis* and other massive reef builders. He was of the general opinion that these buttresses represent a stage in the growth of a young and vigorous reef.

He found effectively all the species of corals hitherto described from Jamaica but, with deeper exploration over the years, encountered many undescribed species. Further ecological work was held up until the entire assemblage, which began to rival the wealth of species in the Indo-Pacific, could be described in collaboration with his close friend Professor J. W. Wells of Cornell. The British Museum has agreed to publish the monograph and Tom talked of beginning joint work in the autumn of 1970. It remains most fortunate that this unique collection is in the expert custody of John Wells and that this project will proceed.

With the co-operation of Dr. Willard D. Hartman, formerly a fellow graduate student at Yale, the nature and biological significance of the sponge fauna came under review. The importance of the boring clionids which penetrate the attaching areas of coral colonies below the level of the tissues was emphasized. Subsequently the rounded heads may break away and fall into the soft bottom sediments. Although the lighter, plate-like colonies of deeper water are similarly attacked, these tend to remain in place indicating an adaptive significance for a form of growth associated with lower light intensity and reduced content of zooxanthellae.

Another discovery was made, of such significance that it should be related in this account, slightly abbreviated, sent by Dr. Hartman. He relates how, in 1964, "Tom set before us a curious calcareous

organism that had been found on the lower surface of a coral at a depth of
70 m on the Discovery Bay reefs. The mound-shaped skeleton, 14 cm ×
8 cm across and 7 cm deep, was formed of solid $CaCO_3$ and its surface
was indented with regularly spaced pits, 1 mm deep and 0·2 and 0·5 mm
in diameter. From the walls of the pits thin spicules protruded, and a
thin membrane bearing a central hole stretched across the top of each
pit. After considerable discussion Dr. Frederick M. Bayer recalled that
the British zoologist, Hickson, had described a supposed relative of the
blue coral, *Heliopora*, which fitted the description of the organism,
which he had named *Ceratoporella nicholsoni*. But the spicules, unlike
those of Tom's creature, were untouched by acid and assumed to be
siliceous. This brought to mind the curious sponges, *Astrosclera* and
Merlia, described by Lister and Kirkpatrick as having a skeleton made
up of calcium carbonate with siliceous spicules."

"Further research revealed that the organism was indeed Hickson's
Ceratoporella nicholsoni, which had been dredged off Cuba at a depth
of 200 m by the U.S. Coast and Geodetic Survey Steamer "Blake" in
1878. Tom soon discovered more specimens and his underwater photographs revealed a surface pattern of stellate excurrent canal systems
each of which converge upon a central osculum in the living state. With
fresh material we were able to demonstrate the existence of choanocyte
chambers in the thin veneer of tissue that covers the massive calcareous
skeleton, and to show that the openings into the pits on the surface of
the skeleton are indeed ostia. We were then certain that the organism
belongs with the *Porifera*."

"Inspired by a suggestion of Kirkpatrick that *Astrosclera* and *Merlia*
are similar to stromatoporoids, we noted the remarkable similarity
between the stellate impressions in the calcareous skeleton of *Ceratoporella* and the astrorhizae of stromatoporoids. We became convinced
that the presence of astrorhizae in this group of fossils proves that they
were sponges."

"Tom's continued explorations of overhangs and caves turned up
six additional species of coralline sponges including three new genera
and a species of the previously known genus *Merlia*. All share a compound skeleton of siliceous spicules, organic fibers and a basal mass of
aragonite. Although we have suggested that these coralline sponges are
descendants of the stromatoporoids and a group of Mesozoic organisms
previously thought to be relatives of the tabulate corals and have set
up a new class, the Sclerospongiae, to receive all these groups, un-
equivocal evidence remains to be obtained. The mutual presence of
astrorhizae is the strongest argument for our hypothesis."

"During the last year of his life, Tom had the opportunity of exploring underwater caves and grottoes in Micronesia and again found a remarkable fauna of sponges, several of which appear to throw light on still other groups of enigmatic fossils. We had only begun our studies of these forms at the time of Tom's death."

"Although we have interpreted the recent coralline sponges as relics of what was an abundant group of animals in Paleozoic and Mesozoic seas, Tom was impressed with their common occurrence on the deeper parts of modern reefs and regarded them as important elements in the formation and consolidation of the basal reef framework. He would often remark about his sense of excitement while exploring reef caves and overhangs, saying that he felt as though he were swimming in a Paleozoic or Mesozoic sea populated by stromatoporoids, lithistid sponges, encrusting foraminiferans, solitary corals, serpulid polychaetes, and thecidioid brachiopods."

It was while studying calcification in *Fungia scutaria* at Eilat in Israel during 1963 that Tom found that many of these corals contained one or more specimens of an unsuspected type of mytilid bivalve. Unlike the distantly related species of *Lithophaga* (date mussels) which bore into dead coral rock, these bivalves were truly symbiotic, opening by enlarged siphons into the coelenteron. Although the writer, attracted by his work on corals, had already met Tom, the discovery of this delightful bivalve brought us into the closest contact. Dr. Soot-Ryen of Norway, as the leading authority on mytilids, kindly agreed to identify and to name and describe the genus and species, now *Fungiacava eilatensis* gen. n., sp. n. Soot-Reyen. It proved to be uniquely adapted while the symbiotic relations, involving the zooxanthellae as well as coral and bivalve, were three-fold constituting what Tom described as a "Troika". Two papers have happily been completed while a third, dealing with the mode of penetration, which must be chemical because the excessively delicate shell is everywhere covered by a thin "pallial envelope", is now being published. The fascinating story of settlement and post-larval penetration will be followed by the Israelis in their marine laboratory at Eilat.

After he encountered them in the Indo-Pacific, initially no doubt at Bikini, Tom became interested in the bivalve Tridacnidae species, of which he later kept specimens living at Discovery Bay. Association with zooxanthellae is there even more far-reaching than in hermatypic corals. After exposure of *Tridacna elongata* in light to the presence of $^{14}CO_2$, with Nora Goreau he demonstrated by radio-autography the almost immediate labelling of the zooxanthellae which are "farmed" in the thickened, deeply pigmented siphonal tissues. Within 10 min this was followed by the appearance of striking carbon-14 activity in secreting surfaces, notably the pallial mucous glands, byssus gland and strip of secretory epithelium in the style sac. Here also the writer became associated and the brief note so far published will be followed by a detailed account in collaboration with Nora Goreau.

Latterly, in papers given at Symposia held at Koror in the Palau Isles in 1968 and at Bikini in the following year, he presented his views on the recent history of coral reefs, all of which, as we now know them, must have come into being since the sea attained its present level only about 5000 years ago and so actually within historic times. So much of modern reefs are built on the foundations of Pleistocene reefs with the gradual rise from the lowest levels in the last glacial period interrupted by a series of temporary halts approximately 14 000, 11 000 and 8500 years ago indicated by benching at -60, -40 and -25 m levels. Tom felt strongly that present conditions were largely provisional and owe much to chance which alone would seem to have determined whether any community came to consist of no more than scattered coral patches or attained the density and diversity of population needed for framework formation. In this connection he noted the presence in corals of eco-variants associated with environmental factors and other variations characterized by differences in characters such as colour, size of calices, etc. which do appear to be genetically controlled. (There is more than a hint here of the long controversy between the relative significance in corals of growth forms and species.) But he also considered that the physiological differences which exist between zooxanthellae living in shallow and in deep water might influence the phenotype of the animal, concluding that these different types of variations, existing alone or in combination, might well have saved the reef systems during the stresses imposed by no less than five major Pleistocene glaciations. Where he confessed himself baffled, leaving the solution to those who followed, was why coral associations should have diversified so widely during the stable and warm conditions of the Tertiary whereas these recent periods of stress have also been periods of stability.

It will be perceived that, after initial establishment there, Tom's activities were by no means confined to Jamaica. He worked, and taught, at Puerto Rico and elsewhere in the West Indies while he paid a further visit to Pacific reefs at Eniwetok in the summer of 1957. Of particular interest in connection with this Symposium, he joined the Israeli South Red Sea Expedition in the spring of 1962. Working in the Dahlak Archipelago, some 50 km SSE of Massawa, Ethiopa, he was the first, after Mortensen, to study the feeding behaviour of the crown of thorns starfish, *Acanthaster planci*, which spreads over and consumes reef corals and has now become notorious because of the population explosion which has led to widespread damage to Indo-Pacific reefs. He made various subsequent visits to the Israeli Red Sea coast at Eilat (where *Fungiacava* was discovered), the last in 1969 when he was one of a party, including Yossef Loya, which surveyed the coast of the Sinai Peninsula. Further experience of Pacific reefs was made in 1967, when, with the writer, he was a guest on the Belgian *De Moor* Expedition to the Great Barrier Reef of Australia. He was able to dive on the inner side of the outer barrier reefs and in the channels between the outer reefs as well as at Low Isles and on other inner reefs. His general impression was of a greater diversity, but not of a significantly greater wealth, of coral than he knew at Jamaica. Here, and later in Micronesia, he was impressed by the greater depth to which Caribbean reefs extend. In the following year we were again jointly concerned, together with John Wells, with meetings on the conservation of Pacific islands and reefs held under the auspices of the International Biological Programme at Guam and at Koror (Palau) in Micronesia. He was to return to that area in the summer of 1969 as Team leader for the Saipan survey of *Acanthaster* conducted under the auspices of the U.S. Department of the Interior and the Office of Naval Research. He produced a characteristically penetrating report which is about to be published. This was to be his last overseas enterprise.

But to return to Jamaica. As Ivan Goodbody reports, "Commuting across the island was time-wasting and tiring and, with the help of the Kaiser Bauxite Company, Tom started the Discovery Bay Marine Laboratory in the small cottage on the beach which became so well known to marine biologists from all over the world". This was in 1965 and it is amazing what was done in these primitive conditions and with what enthusiasm by workers of all ages from graduate students (and younger) to elderly professors. But clearly something better was needed, a suitably planned permanent laboratory devoted to the study of every aspect of coral reefs. A grant from the Wolfson Foundation to the University of the West Indies brought realization nearer and success was assured with the provision of a like sum from the University of the West Indies. At the same time that Tom was appointed Professor of Marine Sciences in the University of the West Indies, he had also become Professor of Biological Sciences in the State University of New York at Stony Brook which assumed major financial responsibilities in connection with the running of the laboratory at Discovery Bay. During the last two years of his life, Tom was largely preoccupied with plans for the building of the new laboratory which proceeded with the customary delays and frustrations that he found hard to bear. But it *was* completed to be officially opened by H.R.H. Princess Alice, Chancellor of the University of the West Indies, on March 24, 1970. Tom was present and spoke about his plans for the future. On the very edge of coral reefs, this is a perfect site for intensive, long term work on corals and coral reefs. It came into being solely as the result of his work, in the course of which, with Nora and his family, he sacrificed much comfort. What comes from it will be his best memorial.

It is impossible to sum up Tom Goreau's career solely in terms of his scientific achievements and the final building of the permanent laboratory. He was a most remarkable human being. His scientific knowledge and technical competence were impressive. He was an outstanding biologist—which includes zoology, botany, physiology and biochemistry—with tremendous interest in geology (going back perhaps to his early encounter with fossils at Munich) and was a more than competent chemist and physicist. He was a superb diver and underwater photographer (in the latter he had the guidance of Fritz, his father; Tom used to say that he had been brought up in a darkroom). He had a compelling enthusiasm which carried everyone with him. Something of his personality may be conveyed by the tributes of some of those most closely associated with him. Ivan Goodbody writes that "Tom will be remembered not only for his enormous patience and generosity towards students and colleagues alike. In a world where scientists have become increasingly specialized Tom was almost unique in the breadth of his scientific knowledge. His laboratory at Mona was a "mecca" for student, staff and visitor alike and no matter how busy he may have been he never failed to listen, to advise and to criticize where necessary. Tom demanded of himself and sought in others excellence in scientific research and thought, and set an example and inspiration which is hard to match".

Norman Newell of the American Museum of Natural History refers to his "extraordinary breadth of comprehension . . . . His interest in physiology of marine organisms, especially the physiology of lime secretion, led him to reinforce his laboratory experiments by direct field observations ingeniously recorded. His scholarship in this area was highly original and earned for him an impressive reputation for outstanding leadership. His ultimate goal in research was not simply refined and controlled observations and experiments, he was concerned with causes. Goreau characteristically wished to learn all about coral reefs and this obsession led him into unaccustomed paths: regional photographic mapping and shallow-water echo profiling in and around the Jamaican reefs. And as an extension of these studies he drew many

original conclusions about the origins of reef morphology, the environmental regimen and the post-glacial history of his reefs. The Jamaican
reefs emerge as the best developed in the tropical Atlantic".

John Wells, perhaps his closest associate, writes of how hard it is
"for me and his other friends here in Cornell to realize that Tom has
gone. He was the kind of person once met never forgotten. He had so
much more to do even though he had already accomplished enough for
a normal lifetime. I hope I and his various co-workers can at least
finish in some way the projects he had underway". In a subsequent
statement he adds that "The field work in Jamaica dealt with the reef
tracts down to about 15 m, but with increasing use of SCUBA equipment, Goreau and his collaborators extended surveys down to 100 m,
recording nearly every meter of descent by photography, and making
extensive collections of corals and associated organisms from a number
of transects especially along the north coast of the island, revealing
an elaborate pattern of coral assemblages, including those of dark
caverns, previously not known in the Caribbean. Goreau had opened
an almost wholly new world by extending direct observation down the
reef slopes to the lowest limits of hermatypic coral growth. In the
depths below 15 m there appeared not only recognizable ecovariants
of shallow water forms but also other types, often in great abundance
("supercolonies"), that were specifically distinct. The large collections
made necessary extensive taxonomic revisions. At least 10 new species
were found plus several previously known only from one or two specimens collected fortuituously in the 18th Century and thought to be
extremely rare but actually common in deep water. A summary of the
nature of these deeper zones and a tentative revised list of the corals
was published in 1967 in advance of descriptions of the new species, and
for several years Goreau had been engaged in preparation of an elaborate
monograph of the reefs and reef corals of Jamaica. Other papers coming
out of these intensive reef surveys described the great buttresses, the
canyons through which sediments from the back reef environments are
conveyed down slope by density currents, the rate of reef growth,
composition and lithification of reef sediments, the role of sponges in
coral breakdown and reef maintenance and the relation of existing
reefs to those of the Pleistocene."

"In spite of the many published results, new discoveries and new
concepts came faster than even Goreau and his collaborators could
cope with, and at his untimely death in 1970, there remained many
unpublished reports, manuscripts, preliminary drafts, and vast amounts
of data, hopefully yet to be worked up by his many friends and associates. These included such things as the description and interpretation

of the extraordinary new groups of calcareous sponges, Pleistocene
raised reefs, calcareous algae, new concepts of reef physiology and
ecology, West Indian ahermatypic corals, "chimaeras" or "neoplasms"
in corals, coral histology, and the economy of coral reefs."

From the standpoint of a graduate student who first met him at
Stony Brook and then was a fellow member of an expedition with him,
Yossef Loya was to speak, during the Symposium, of Tom "as a close
friend and an inspiring teacher. He never made any of the distinctions
that normally exist between student and professor. He treated everyone
with equal dignity, respect and concern . . . . I will always remember
the great impact he had on me personally when we spent last summer
studying the coral reefs along the Gulf of Eilat. Many long nights
were passed lying on the ground, gazing at the stars and talking. He
obviously enjoyed every minute of the trip and frequently expressed
his joy to all of us. His limitless enthusiasm and enormous energy was
transmitted to the entire group, so that we worked 16 hours a day
willingly. It was this characteristic, his moving spirit, that describes
everything he did in his tragically short lifetime".

In a letter to Fritz Goreau, Harry S. Ladd, whose name looms so
large in the literature of coral reefs and who first met Tom at Bikini, says
how, to initial admiration and respect, was speedily added affection and
later, as he read his research papers, there went with it "a secret feeling
of satisfaction—I know this young man and he is wonderful . . . , In my
opinion, Fritz, your son was the most talented and the most productive
of all that large group now studying reefs and reef ecology". Willard
Hartman, at the conclusion of his letter about their joint work on
sponges, writes that "Tom's important contributions to the study of
coral reef ecology sprang from his insatiable curiosity, lively intellect,
boundless energy and broad knowledge of science. He was an expert
SCUBA diver and underwater photographer and through his use of
these techniques brought to the attention of the scientific world an
extraordinary spectrum of biological and geological phenomena on
the deeper parts of coral reefs . . . . Those of us who have been influenced
by Tom intellectually and personally can pay no better tribute to him
than to continue the work which he helped us begin and which, alas,
he can no longer share with us".

It remains for the writer to add that the six years of scientific
collaboration with Tom Goreau, starting and ending at Jamaica but
ranging from Europe across the Pacific to Australia in the years
between, and with continually increasing friendship, were deeply
memorable. The difference between our ages seemed to disappear
while our interests were entirely complementary. Tom's name will en-

dure indefinitely as amongst the greatest of workers on coral reefs—in all aspects of their wide diversity—and the memory of him will persist throughout the lifetimes of all who knew him as that of a striking personality and of a most lovable man.

Acknowledgements are rendered for much of the information contained in this article to all whose names have been given. Fritz Goreau has kindly supplied the following list of Tom's papers:

1947. (with Austin, T. S.) Ecological studies on the reef and waters of Bikini Atoll. *Rep. Comm. Treatise mar. Ecol. Paleoecol.* **1946–1947**: 8–9.

1953. Phosphomonoesterases in reef building corals. *Proc. natn. Acad. Sci. Wash.* **39**: 1291–1295.

1955. (with Bowen, V. T.) Calcium uptake by a coral. *Science, N.Y.* **122**: 1188–1189.

1956. (with Philpott, D. E.) Electromicrographic studies of flagellated epithelia in madreporarian corals. *Expl. Cell Res.* **10**: 552–556.

1956. Histochemistry of the mucopolysaccharide-like substances and alkaline phosphatases in the Madreporaria. *Nature, Lond.* **177**: 1029–1030.

1957. Calcification in reef building corals. Abstr. *Proc. Assoc. Isl. Mar. Labs.* No. 1. La Parguara, Puerto Rico.

1958. Calcification and growth in reef-forming corals. *Int. congr. Zool.* **15**: 248–250.

1958. Buttressed reefs in Jamaica, British West Indies. *Int. congr. Zool.* **15**: 250.

1959. The ecology of Jamaican coral reefs. I. Species composition and zonation. *Ecology* **48**: 67–90.

1959. The physiology of skeleton formation in corals. I. A method for measuring the rate of calcium deposition by corals under different conditions. *Biol. Bull. mar. biol. Labs., Woods Hole* **116**: 59–75.

1959. Further studies on the buttress zone of Jamaican coral reefs. *Int. oceanogr. Congr.* No. 1. United Nations, New York.

1959. (with Goreau, N. I.) The physiology of skeleton formation in corals. II. Calcium deposition by hermatypic corals under various conditions in the reef. *Biol. Bull. mar. biol. Labs, Woods Hole* **117**: 239–250.

1960. On the physiological ecology of the coral *Meandrina braziliensis* (Milne-Edwards and Haime). *Proc. Assoc. Isl. Mar. Labs* No. 3. U.C.W.I., Jamaica.

1960. (with Goreau, N. I.) The uptake and distribution of labelled carbon in reef building corals with and without zooxanthellae. *Science, N.Y.* **131**: 668–669.

1960. (with Goreau, N. I.) The physiology of skeleton formation in corals. III. Calcification rate as a function of colony weight and total nitrogen content in the reef coral: *Manicina areolata* (Linnaeus). *Biol. Bull. mar. biol. Labs, Woods Hole* **118**: 419–428.

1960. (with Goreau, N. I.) The physiology of skeleton formation in corals. IV. On isotonic equilibrium exchanges of calcium between corallum and environment in living and dead reef corals. *Biol. Bull. mar. biol. Labs, Woods Hole* **119**: 416–427.

1961. On the relation of calcification to primary productivity in reef building organisms. In *The biology of Hydra and some other coelenterates*: 269–285. Lenhoff, F. M. and Loomis, W. F. (eds), Univ. Miami Press.

1961. Problems of growth and calcium deposition in reef corals. *Endeavour* **20**: 32–40.

1961. Recent investigations on the growth of coral reefs in Jamaica. *Bull. Sci. Res. Council, Jamaica* **2**: 41–44.

1961. The structure of the Jamaican reef communities: geological aspects. Final Progress Report. Biology Branch. Office of Naval Research. Under Contract Nonr (G)-003-60 (MR 104-556).

1961. Reminiscences of V. A. Zans. *Geonotes* **4**: 44–46.

1963. Calcium carbonate deposition by coralline algae and hermatypic corals in relation to their roles as reef builders. *Ann. N.Y. Acad. Sci.* **109**: 127–167.

1963. (with Hartman, W. D.) Boring sponges as controlling factors in the formation and maintenance of coral reefs. In *Mechanisms of hard tissue destruction*: 25–54, Sognnaes, R. F. (ed). Washington: A.A.A.S. Publication No. 75.

1964. On the predation of coral by the spiny starfish *Acanthaster planci* (L) in the Southern Red Sea. Proc. Israel South Red Sea Expedition, 1962. *Bull. Sea Fish. Res. Stn. Israel* **35**: 23–26.

1964. Mass expulsion of zooxanthellae from Jamaican reef communities after hurricane "Flora". *Science, N.Y.* **145**: 383–386.

1964. Fore-reef slope: structure, sediment and community relationships. Abstr. *A. Meeting geol. Soc. Am.*, **1964** Miami.

1965. (with Goreau, N. I., Yonge, C. M.) Evidence for a soluble algal factor produced by the zooxanthellae of *Tridacna elongata* (Bivalvia, Tridacniidae). Abstract. *Int. Conf. Trop. Oceanogr.* Miami.

1966. (with Hartman, W. D.) Sponge: effect on the form of reef corals. *Science, N.Y.* **151**: 343–344.

1966. (with Kevin Burke) Pleistocene and Holocene geology of the island shelf near Kingston, Jamaica. *Mar. Geol.* **4**: 207–225.

1966. (with Hartman, W. D.) *Ceratoporella*, a living sponge with stromatoporoid affinities. Abstract. *Am. Zool.* **6**: 262.

1967. (with Graham, E. A.) A new *Halimeda* from Jamaica. *Bull. mar. Sci. Gulf Caribb.* **17**: 432–441.

1967. (with Wells, J. W.) The shallow-water Scleractinia of Jamaica: revised list of species and their vertical distribution range. *Bull. mar. Sci. Gulf Caribb.* **17**: 442–453.

1968. (with Yonge, C. M.) Coral community on muddy sand. *Nature Lond.* **217**: 421–423.

1968. (with Goreau, N. I., Neumann, Y. and Yonge, C. M.) *Fungiacava eilatensis* n. gen., n. sp. a boring bivalve commensal in reef corals. Abstract. *Am. Zool.* **8**: 799.

1969. Post Pleistocene urban renewal in coral reefs. *Micronesica*, **5**: 323–326.

1969. (with Goreau, N. I., Soot-Ryen, T., Yonge, C. M.) On a new commensal mytilid (Mollusca: Bivalvia) opening into the coelenteron of *Fungia scutaria* (Coelenteratea). *J. Zool., Lond.* **158**: 171–195.

1969. (with Hartman, W. D.) New classes of Porifera from the tropical Atlantic and Indo-Pacific Oceans. Abstr. *Proc. Assoc. Isl. Mar. Labs* No. 8.

1970. (with Goreau, N. I., Yonge, C. M., Neumann, Y.) On feeding and nutrition in *Fungiacava eilatensis* (Bivalvia, Mytilidae), a commensal living in fungiid corals. *J. Zool., Lond.* **160**: 159–172.

1970. (with Hartman, W. D.) Jamaican coralline sponges: their morphology, ecology and fossil relatives. *Symp. zool. Soc. Lond.* No. 25: 205–243.

1970. (with Land, L. S.) Submarine lithification in Jamaican reefs. *J. sed. Petrol.* **40**: 457–462.

Geology and Morphology of Reefs

Symp. zool. Soc. Lond. (1971) No. 28, 3–38.

ENVIRONMENT AND HISTORY IN INDIAN OCEAN REEF MORPHOLOGY

D. R. STODDART

Department of Geography, University of Cambridge, Cambridge, England

INTRODUCTION

Until recent years, following the International Indian Ocean Expedition, the coral reefs of the Indian Ocean have been comparatively neglected and current reef generalizations derive largely from work in the Pacific. I have elsewhere reviewed studies of the surface features of Indian Ocean reefs and islands (Stoddart, 1969a), revising some of the conclusions of Sewell (1935) and Gardiner (1936), and this paper considers the significance of environmental factors, broadly defined, in Indian Ocean reef morphology. In explaining modern reefs we need to consider not only the effects of present-day environmental factors, but also to what extent the reefs have been affected by environmental changes during Pleistocene and earlier times. Reefs as geological structures are markedly resistant to erosional changes over time scales of 10^3–10^5 years (Stoddart, 1969b), and many modern Indian Ocean reef communities only veneer much older reef structures.

Darwin (1842) himself was among the first to study Indian Ocean reefs, at Cocos-Keeling and Mauritius in 1836, and his theory of subsidence accounts satisfactorily for the gross geological relations of reef limestones and their foundations in the Indian Ocean. The paucity of modern reef growth, however, particularly over large areas of older reef limestones, makes it necessary to pay particular attention to relative movements of land and sea level during the Pleistocene. As will become apparent, in explaining reef variation in the Indian Ocean it is at least as important to consider cases where modern reefs do not grow as it is to consider those where they do.

PREVIOUS WORK

Apart from the early work in the Red Sea of Ehrenberg (1834), Klunzinger (1877–1879), Walther (1888) and von Marenzeller (1907), on the East African coast by Ortmann (1892) and Werth (1901), and at Cocos-Keeling and Mauritius by Darwin (1842), the reefs of the Indian Ocean were made known largely by two men: J. Stanley Gardiner and R. B. Seymour Sewell. Gardiner's first expedition in 1899–1900 took him from Minikoi through the Maldive Islands to Addu Atoll (Gardiner, 1903–1906); his second, the Percy Sladen Trust Expedition, in 1905 and 1908, covered the Chagos Archipelago, Seychelles, Amirantes, Coetivy, Cargados Carajos, Farquhar, Providence, St. Pierre and Mauritius (Gardiner, 1907–1936). Gardiner's collections covered both marine and terrestrial fauna and flora, and for many reefs his results form the only or the latest data available. Sewell worked in the Maldive, Andaman and Nicobar Islands, and led the John Murray Expedition of 1933–1934. Both Gardiner (1931, 1936) and Sewell (1935) published summary accounts of the reefs they had studied. Alexander Agassiz (1903) also cruised through the Maldives in 1901–1902, but his voluminous account is of little value.

Other reef studies before 1945 were generally unrelated to Gardiner's and Sewell's work in the western and central Indian Ocean. Cocos-Keeling was studied by Forbes (1879), Guppy (1889, 1890), Wood-Jones (1910) and Gibson-Hill (1948, 1950), all workers with Malaysian rather than Indian Ocean experience. Collections were made at Christmas Island in 1897–1898 (Andrews, 1900), the Amirantes in 1882 (Coppinger, 1884), Aldabra in 1908–1909 (Fryer, 1911), and in the Laccadives (Oldham, 1895). Apart from Sewell's work (1932) on the Indian coast, that of Ortmann (1889) and Walther (1891) in Ceylon, of Coutière (1898) and Gravier (1911) in the Gulf of Aden, and of Crossland (1902, 1904, 1907) in East Africa and the Red Sea, there were almost no studies of mainland reefs around the Indian Ocean.

With notable exceptions such as Guppy, Crossland and Sewell, these earlier workers were less concerned with the structure of reef communities and their physiographic expression than with the taxonomy and biogeography of the reef biota. Hence much of the data accumulated contributed little to the development of coral reef studies which took place after 1945. Apart from the work on Cocos, Addu, Goifurfehendu, Salomon, Minikoi and Aldabra, it is often difficult to construct coherent accounts of Indian Ocean reefs from this earlier literature.

RECENT STUDIES

Recent Indian Ocean studies have been carried out largely by French and British workers. Guilcher's (1955) work on Banc Farsan, Red Sea, was followed by geomorphic studies in northwest Malagasy (Guilcher, 1956, 1958; Guilcher et al., 1958) and at Mayotte, Comoro

Islands (Guilcher *et al.*, 1965). Guilcher's geomorphic and sedimento-logical work has been supplemented in Madagascar and at Europa by that of Battistini (1964, 1966a; Berthois and Battistini, 1969) and also by the extensive ecological work at the Tuléar marine station in southwest Madagascar (Pichon, 1964; Vasseur, 1964; Blanc, Chamley and Froget, 1966) and by reconnaissance studies in Mauritius (Pichon, 1967). British workers have studied marine geomorphology and ecology at Addu Atoll, Maldive Islands (Stoddart, 1966), Diego Garcia Atoll, Chagos Archipelago (Stoddart and Taylor, 1971), Aldabra Atoll and neighbouring islands north of Madagascar (Stoddart, 1967, 1970a; Stoddart *et al.*, 1971), and the fringing reefs of Mahé, Seychelles (Taylor, 1968; Lewis, 1968, 1969; Taylor and Lewis, 1970). The Royal Society of London, which initiated work on Aldabra in 1967, has now established a research station there for both land and marine studies.

There have also been brief visits to the Maldives and other reefs by the Yale Seychelles Expedition (Kohn, 1964, 1967, 1968), by the *Xarifa*, the *Anton Bruun*, and the *Te Vega*; to Cocos-Keeling, Mauritius and the Seychelles by members of the Coastal Studies Institute, Baton Rouge; and to parts of the Red Sea by Israeli expeditions. Little work has been published on African reefs (Boshoff, 1958; Talbot, 1965), and that on the reefs of western Australia (Fairbridge, 1948a), Houtman's Abrolhos (Teichert, 1947; Fairbridge, 1948b), and the Sahul Shelf (Teichert and Fairbridge, 1948) remains largely unrelated to Indian Ocean studies. In spite of the further work reported at this Symposium, large gaps remain: most of the Maldives and Laccadives have not been visited since Gardiner and Sewell: there are no modern accounts of the reefs of the Amirantes, Tromelin, Agalega, Cargados Carajos, Coetivy and other western Indian Ocean islands (though see Baker, 1963), or of Christmas Island, the Andamans and Nicobars; the Chagos Archipelago remains largely unknown: and apart from Pillai's (1967) work, no further studies have been made of the reefs of the Asian mainland.

TYPES AND ORIGINS OF INDIAN OCEAN REEFS

Indian Ocean reefs include sea-level atoll, fringing and barrier reefs, elevated reefs, and reef platforms now submerged. Reefs are poorly developed or absent on the continental coasts of Somalia, the Indian sub-continent, and Malaya, but are well-developed in parts of the Persian Gulf, the Red Sea, the coasts of Kenya and Tanzania, western Madagascar, and parts of Sumatra and northwest Australia (Fig. 1).

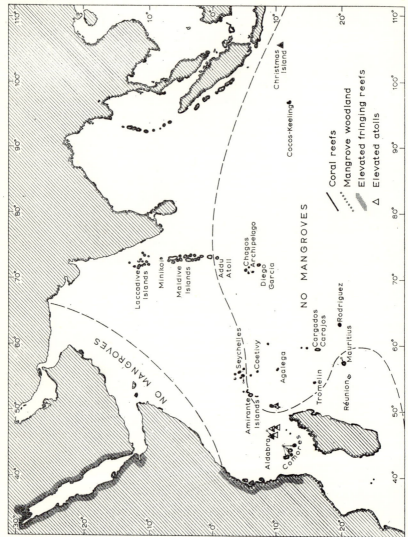

Fig. 1. The Indian Ocean, showing the distribution of sea-level and elevated reefs and of major mangrove communities. After Stoddart (1969a).

Sea-level reefs

Barrier reefs are absent on continental shores, except for a discontinuous submerged barrier in northwest Madagascar; Mayotte, a volcanic island in the Comoros, has a fine barrier reef. Reefs of continental coasts are mostly fringing reefs, and this type is also developed round the granitic Seychelles, the volcanic Comoros and Mascarenes, and the sedimentary Andamans and Nicobars. After continental fringing reefs, atolls are the dominant reef type of the Indian Ocean, represented in the Maldives and Chagos archipelagoes, at Cocos, Farquhar, Cosmoledo and other reefs. Suvadiva Atoll, Maldives (length 70 km, breadth 53 km, area 2250 km^2) is one of the largest atolls in the world. Other open-ocean reefs lack the typical atoll form, and are best described as linear patch or table reefs (e.g. Coetivy, Agalega, Cargados Carajos, Tromelin); many show well-developed lagoonal meshing, in Maxwell's (1968) terminology.

Emerged reefs

Elevated coral reefs are widely distributed on the coasts of East Africa (Werth, 1901; Ortmann, 1892; Crossland, 1902, 1904; Alexander, 1968) and the Red Sea (Walther, 1888; Macfadyen, 1930; Guilcher, 1955). They are known from Christmas Island in the eastern Indian Ocean (Andrews, 1900; Trueman, 1965) and from Aldabra and the neighbouring islands of Assumption, Astove, Cosmoledo and St. Pierre in the western Indian Ocean (Baker, 1963; Stoddart, 1967, 1970a). They are also found, though less well developed, on Madagascar and islands of the Mozambique Channel, and in the Seychelles and the Mascarenes. The extent of elevation varies from 360 m at Christmas Island to 10 m or less in the southwest Indian Ocean and along the African coast. The degree of preservation varies from that of entire elevated atolls such as Aldabra, with little-altered reef faunas, to the altered limestones of former fringing reefs on Mauritius and neighbouring Ile aux Aigrettes, and to the small inconspicuous residual fragments of former fringing reefs on Mahé, Seychelles.

In addition to these clearly elevated reefs, both Gardiner and Sewell have claimed elevation of varying amounts throughout the Chagos and the Maldives, largely on the basis of the existence of patches of reef-derived sediments, in some cases with corals said to be in the position of growth, slightly above present sea level. Re-examination of Gardiner's examples at Addu and Diego Garcia Atolls suggests that most such outcrops are of lithified island sediments not indicating any sea-level change, and this may also be true of Gardiner's classic site at Minikoi Atoll (Gardiner, 1901). The evidence for eustatic sea-level changes is considered in the section on pp. 24–30.

Submerged reefs

Platforms of reef limestone which fail to reach present sea-level are among the most remarkable reef features of the Indian Ocean. The total area of such banks in the western Indian Ocean (Fig. 2) is approximately 140 000 km^2, compared with 155 000 km^2 for the Bahama Banks. Some of the banks are of great size: the Seychelles Bank covers 43 000 km^2, Saya de Malha 40 000 km^2, Nazareth Bank 26 000 km^2, and the banks of the Chagos Archipelago 13 500 km^2. The banks have general maximum depths of 33–90 m, and most have a shallower rim round at least part of their periphery, at 8–20 m depth. Such banks are quite widespread in the reef seas, though Davis (1918) was the last to investigate them systematically: thus maximum depths and rim depths of banks in the China Sea are 30–110 m and 7–26 m respectively, and the mean depths of thirteen banks in the Caribbean range from 20 to 42 m. Great Chagos Bank (Fig. 3), measuring 150 × 100 km, is one of the best known bathymetrically: the central basin is about 70 m deep; it has a rim 1·6 km wide at 10–18 m, and a very pronounced terrace within this rim, 8–20 km wide and 30 m deep. The Seychelles Bank is the only one of these banks to have been investigated in any detail (Matthews and Davies, 1966; Lewis and Taylor, 1966), and on this, as on the others, modern coral growth appears to be insignificant.

Ocean structure and reef origins

The distribution and size of Indian Ocean coral reefs must be viewed in the perspective of the development of the Indian Ocean itself. The bottom topography, especially of the western Indian Ocean, is now reasonably well known (Heezen and Tharp, 1965, 1966; Fisher, Engel and Hilde, 1968), and the bathymetry shown in Fig. 4 is highly generalized. Most of the ocean floor lies at depths of 4–5 km. Rising from this floor are linear ridges (the Chagos-Laccadive ridge; the Ninetyeast Ridge), arcuate plateaus and ridges (Mid-ocean Ridge; Mascarene Plateau), and isolated islands (e.g. Aldabra, Mascarenes, Cocos-Keeling). The Chagos-Laccadive Ridge, the Mascarene Plateau, and the isolated islands are, in addition to continental coasts, the main sites of reef limestone development; no sea-level islands are present on the Mid-Ocean and Ninetyeast Ridges.

From geological and paleomagnetic data on the surrounding continents it is apparent that the Indian Ocean began to form in Mesozoic

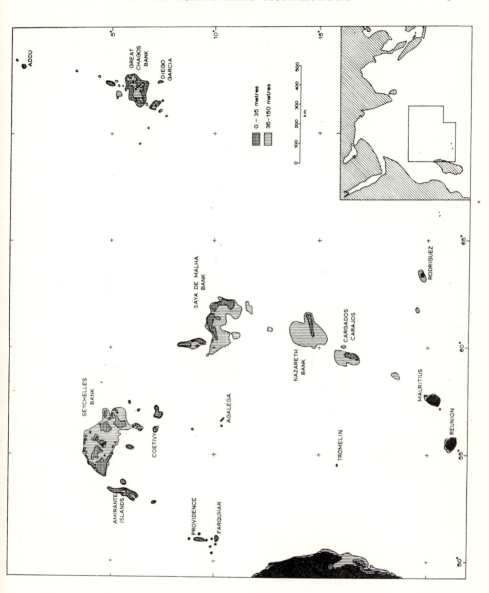

FIG. 2. Submerged reefs of the western Indian Ocean. Bathymetry from Fisher, Johnson and Heezen (1967), with additions reproduced from British Admiralty charts 2899 and 2900 with the sanction of the Controller, H.M. Stationery Office and of the Hydrographer of the Navy.

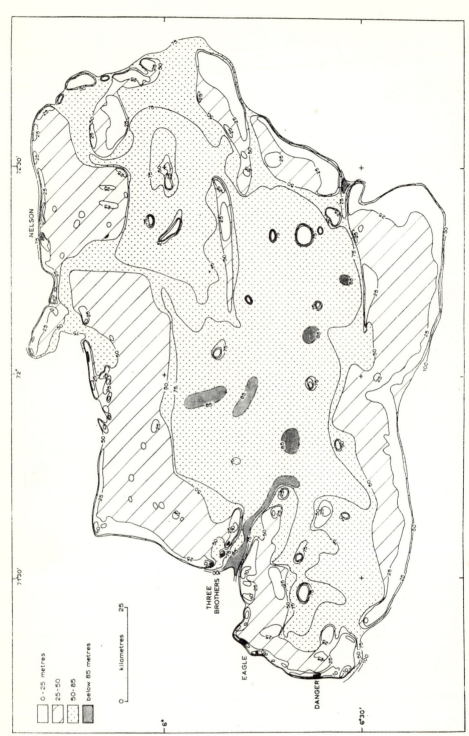

FIG. 3. Great Chagos Bank: bathymetry. Reproduced from British Admiralty chart No. 3 with the sanction of the Controller, H.M. Stationery Office and of the Hydrographer of the Navy.

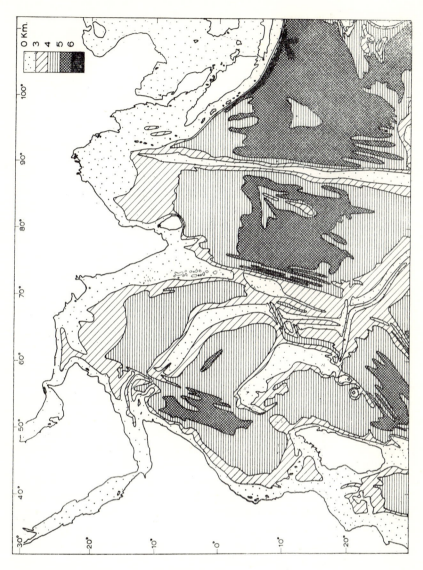

Fig. 4. The Indian Ocean: generalized bathymetry. After Le Pichon and Heirtzler (1968), based on Heezen and Tharp (1965). Major features northeastwards from Madagascar include the arcuate Mascarene Plateau between the Seychelles and Mauritius; the Mid-Ocean (Carlsberg) Ridge; the Laccadives–Maldives–Chagos Ridge; and the Ninetyeast Ridge.

time. Much of the evidence for its early development is inferential, but it is likely that its main lineaments existed by the early Tertiary, when the foundations of the present reefs were formed and when much reef growth probably began. Basalts dredged from the ocean floor have been dated radiometrically, and associated sediments paleontologically. Foraminifera in a volcanic agglomerate dredged from the slopes of Providence at 1350 m depth are Eocene–Oligocene (or possibly late Cretaceous) in age (Wiseman, 1936). Basalts from the Amirante Ridge north of Alphonse have been dated at $82 \pm 16 \times 10^6$ yr (middle-late Cretaceous) (Fisher *et al.*, 1968), others from the Chain Ridge in the Somali Basin at 90×10^6 yr (Cretaceous) (Bunce *et al.*, 1967), and others from the southern end of the Ninetyeast Ridge at 60×10^6 yr (Eocene) (Bezrukov, Krylov and Cernishev, 1966). Bottom sediments of Eocene-Oligocene age are widely distributed over the floor of the ocean (Le Pichon and Heirtzler, 1968), and thick sequences of sedimentary rocks are found near some continental margins (Francis, Davies and Hill, 1966). Magnetic lineations parallel with the Mid-Ocean Ridge suggest continued widening over at least the last 20×10^6 yr, at half-rates of 1–$2 \cdot 2$ cm yr^{-1} within the present reef seas (Le Pichon and Heirtzler, 1968).

The structure of the main island groups may be related to these developments. The Mascarene Plateau is of diverse origin. The Seychelles Bank in the north is an isolated "micro-continent" of Upper Pre-Cambrian age (650×10^6 yr) (Baker and Miller, 1963), presumably formerly connected with the microcontinent of Madagascar, though some doubt exists over the earlier relationships of Madagascar and Africa and the status of the Mozambique Channel (Flower and Strong, 1969). Silhouette in the Seychelles is formed by an early Tertiary syenite-microgranite, and the main granites are intruded by both late Pre-Cambrian and Tertiary basic dykes, the latter broadly contemporary with the dated ocean-floor basalts and with massive volcanic outpourings in India and Madagascar (Davies, 1968). Granites similar to those of the Seychelles, with dykes, are inferred on geophysical grounds to underlie the Mascarene Plateau between the Seychelles Bank and Saya de Malha (Matthews and Davies, 1966). Saya de Malha and Nazareth Banks are thought to consist of coral-capped volcanic rocks (Shor and Pollard, 1963; Francis and Shor, 1966), while Cargados Carajos bank is underlain by either granitic or volcanic rocks at shallow depth and is capped with coral (Shor and Pollard, 1966; Bunce, *et al.*, 1967).

The separate Mascarene Islands at the southern end of the Mascarene Plateau are young volcanoes with correspondingly reduced reef development. Surface volcanoes on Rodriguez, which has raised reef limestones, are dated at $1 \cdot 3$ and $1 \cdot 5 \times 10^6$ yr (McDougall, Upton and Wadsworth, 1965). Flows on Mauritius are dated $7 \cdot 8$–$6 \cdot 8 \times 10^6$ yr (Early Pliocene) and $3 \cdot 5$–$0 \cdot 17 \times 10^6$ yr, and the whole complex, measuring 60×45 km, may have been built in 12×10^6 yr, i.e. since the late Tertiary (McDougall and Chamalaun, 1969). On the volcanically active reefless island of Réunion, dates range from 2 to $0 \cdot 1 \times 10^6$ yr, with an older undated series of flows (Upton and Wadsworth, 1965).

After the Mascarene Plateau, the most extensive reef limestone province in the Indian Ocean is formed by the Chagos, Maldive and Laccadive Archipelagoes. This interrupted, linear, aseismic ridge, 3000 km long, appears from seismic refraction and gravity anomalies to consist of coral limestone capping massive volcanics (Glennie, 1936; Francis and Shor, 1966). It has been suggested that the volcanism responsible for this ridge moved northwards over time to culminate in the outpourings of the Deccan Traps, which are largely Paleocene-Eocene (Wellman and McElhinny, 1970); if so, the southernmost volcanics, in the Chagos, could be as old as Cretaceous, and the Chagos-Laccadive Ridge could mark the track taken by the Indian sub-continent as it moved northwards away from Africa (Francis and Shor, 1966).

There is less information on the history of isolated islands which now exist only as surface reefs. The bathymetry of many (e.g. Aldabra, Cosmoledo, Europa, Tromelin, Cocos-Keeling), rising from depths of 4–5 km, suggests a volcanic basement, and this is partially confirmed by dredging of basalts from their slopes (e.g. on Providence). From the structure of the ocean floor itself, as already outlined, it can be inferred that these volcanoes are unlikely to be older than Eocene. The volcanoes which are still above sea-level and are reef-fringed, such as the Mascarenes and Comoros, are undoubtedly younger than those now drowned and have absolute dates ranging from Pliocene to Quaternary; two, Réunion and Grand Comore, are still active (Lacroix, 1936; Battistini, 1967). Corals and limestone with *Lepidocyclina* from the summit of a guyot at $0 \cdot 7$ km depth near Cocos-Keeling indicate a Miocene age for sediments on the summit of a cone $3 \cdot 3$ km high (Niino and Oshite, 1966): more investigations are needed of guyots elsewhere in the Indian Ocean, e.g. in the Mozambique Channel.

No deep drilling has yet been carried out on open-ocean reefs in the Indian Ocean, and data on reef thicknesses are hence limited. Geophysical data indicate thicknesses of reef limestones of 1 km plus $0 \cdot 2$–$0 \cdot 5$ km lagoonal carbonate sediments on Saya de Malha (Shor and

Pollard, 1963), of less than 1 km in the Amirantes (Matthews and Davies, 1966), of 0·6–1·7 km under 1 km of water near Great Chagos Bank (Francis and Shor, 1966), and of less than 0·5 km on Seychelles Bank (Davies and Francis, 1964). These thicknesses compare with 1·25 km on Eniwetok Atoll in the Pacific, where paleontological evidence from cores shows that reef growth began in the Eocene, and with 0·4 km on Mururoa and 0·2 km on Midway, other cored atolls.

Reef histories are undoubtedly more complex in non-oceanic areas peripheral to the Indian Ocean basin. These include particularly the Red Sea and Gulf of Aden, which have characteristics of embryonic widening oceans and extensive fringing and elevated reefs (Laughton, 1966); Madagascar, particularly the northwest coast (Battistini, 1965); and the islands and coastlands of the tectonically active Andaman Sea (Rodolfo, 1969; Weeks, Herbison and Peter, 1967).

We may conclude that the reefs of the Indian Ocean have been built almost entirely during Tertiary and Quaternary times; that the thicker reef sequences cap older, mainly volcanic, structures, forming the great atoll and submerged reef-bank chains; and that fringing reefs and barriers have formed on younger volcanoes such as the Mascarenes and Comoros in Pliocene and Pleistocene times. The main Indian Ocean reefs had reached their approximate distribution, extent and form by the end of the Tertiary, and their present surface features record the erosional and depositional consequences of Pleistocene and Holocene sea-level fluctuations. These consequences and their chronology are considered in detail in the Section on pp. 24–30.

DISTRIBUTION OF REEF COMMUNITIES

Corals

Remarkably little is known of the distribution of coral communities in the Indian Ocean, though Rosen (this volume, pp. 263–299) has reviewed the distribution of scleractinian coral genera. Taylor (1968) in the Seychelles distinguished an *Acropora* community on exposed seaward reefs and a *Porites* community in protected reefs and channels, and a similar distinction has been recognized by Talbot (1965) at Tutia, Tanzania, and by Sewell (1922, p.987) in the Nicobar Islands. Pichon (1967) found a *Pavona* and an *Acropora* community in Mauritius. At Addu Atoll the reefs are dominated by *Acropora* and other branching, foliaceous and unattached species (Stoddart, 1966). The lack of massive corals at Addu is noteworthy, and the dominance of the faster-growing branching forms may result from the lack of destructive cyclones in this equatorial belt. Unfortunately we have no comparable data from cyclone areas.

Lack of reef coral diversity is probably not a limiting factor in reef development on open-ocean reefs, though diversity gradients are found on continental shores. The southernmost coral reef on the African coast is at Inhaca, Mozambique (Macnae and Kalk, 1958), though scattered hermatypic corals occur as far south as Port Elizabeth in latitude 34°S. (Day, 1969). Corals are also poorly represented in north India (Cutch) and the Persian Gulf, though more investigations are needed of these areas.

The Alcyonarian coral *Heliopora* is widespread in the Indian Ocean, though apparently absent in Houtman's Abrolhos (Thorpe, 1928), and is in places an important reef builder, as is the hydrozoan *Millepora*. The Alcyonarian soft corals *Sarcophyton* and *Lobophytum* are unimportant in the Maldives, Chagos and western Indian Ocean reefs, but are numerous in the Nicobars and Andamans and are present in the Seychelles, perhaps indicating an important difference in the ecology of isolated reefs and of reefs adjacent to high islands.

Calcareous algae

Reef-edge ridges of encrusting melobesioid algae are less prominent in the Indian Ocean than in the central and western Pacific. Low algal ridges with surge channels are found locally on Addu, Peros Banhos and Diego Garcia Atolls, comparable in extent to Pacific examples, and Taylor (1968) reports similar ridges from exposed reefs on Mahé, Seychelles. Both Crossland (1902, pp. 497–498) and Gardiner (1906, p. 456) commented on the sparse development of encrusting algae on western Indian Ocean reefs, but the latter was wrong in reporting their absence in the Seychelles. Though ridges are generally not prominent, encrusting reef-edge algae are widespread, though Setchell (1930) was equally misleading in his over-emphasis on the role of algae in the Maldives and Chagos. The atolls where ridges have so far been described are all in the equatorial belt marginal to the Trades. More data are needed from areas of constant surf on Trade-wind reefs, though observations on Aldabra, Farquhar and Cosmoledo have so far not revealed extensive algal ridges.

Marine angiosperms

In spite of their importance in sediment-stabilization, little is known of the distribution of marine angiosperms on Indian Ocean reefs, and Den Hartog's (1970) recent monograph is based on collections made before the present expansion of scientific work. Rich sea-grass communities of the genera *Cymodocea*, *Thalassodendron*, *Diplanthera*, *Syringodium*, *Halophila*, *Thalassia* and *Enhalus* are known from the East African coast, Madagascar, the Seychelles and Aldabra. Extensive beds are found in south India and elsewhere on the Asian coast. Sea-grasses are, however, poorly represented on central Indian Ocean reefs. Only two species have been reported from the Maldives, both for the first time in 1966. Gardiner (1907) referred to the absence of sea-grasses in the western Indian Ocean, but his statement needs revision and in the case of Diego Garcia is certainly incorrect. At least three genera are important on Mauritius reefs (Pichon, 1967).

Taylor and Lewis (1970) have discussed the sediments and faunas of marine sea-grass communities on Mahé, Seychelles. Taylor notes that *Thalassodendron ciliatum* (= *Cymodocea ciliata*) is apparently absent from reef flats around granitic islands in the Seychelles, where it is replaced by *Thalassia hemprichii*; *T. ciliatum* is, however, common on the coral island of Coetivy, as well as on the East African coast, and the possibility of a sediment or substrate control on the distribution of sea-grasses needs further study.

Mangroves

Mangrove communities are widespread on continental coasts round the Indian Ocean and Madagascar, and are particularly well developed in East African estuaries and on the mainland and high island coasts east of the Ganges delta. The limits of mangrove communities shown in Fig. 1 refer to high mangrove woodland of geological significance: mangroves are found outside these limits, for example in the Red Sea (Kassas and Zahran, 1967), the Persian Gulf (Kendall and Skipworth, 1969) and the Makran coast (Snead, 1967), but generally as scattered stunted trees. Even on the Indian coast, as near Bombay and Mandapam, mangrove communities may be replaced by salt marsh communities.

Away from the continental coasts, mangroves are generally less well represented, though nine species were represented in the now largely destroyed mangrove forests of the Seychelles (Sauer, 1967). Mangroves are also well developed on Aldabra, and in the Andamans and Nicobars. No mangroves are recorded from the Laccadives, five species from the Maldives (forming "great groves" on some atolls, according to Gardiner, but certainly unimportant on Addu), and two from the Chagos, where they are very uncommon, or, as on Diego Garcia, non-existent. Two species are known from Mauritius (Sauer,

1961). Mangroves are absent on Cocos-Keeling, Christmas, and most of the smaller western Indian Ocean islands, including the Amirantes. In this respect the central oceanic atolls compare with the more remote Pacific groups, such as the Tuamotus. The mangrove communities have so far been only studied in detail on the continental coasts and on Aldabra (Macnae, 1968), and more work is needed of their role in promoting sedimentation on reefs and in chemically weathering reef limestones.

PHYSICAL ENVIRONMENT

Variations in environmental factors over the Indian Ocean clearly affect the form of coral reefs: the study of these variations is important in explanatory studies of particular reef features, but since so little is known of many Indian Ocean reefs, the study of environmental factors itself has predictive value in suggesting the probability of specific features being present. Reefs are adapted to and themselves modify environmental factors, and it is therefore important to distinguish between factors which show wide regional differences, and those which may show high but local variability dependent on reef morphology itself. Thus both temperature and salinity distributions show broad gradients over the ocean, but in the area covered by Fig. 1 they nowhere constitute factors limiting reef growth, except possibly in areas of upwelling such as the Somali coast: extreme values are found (e.g. salinities as high as $48\%_0$ in the Persian Gulf and as low as $26\%_0$ at Mandapam) but these are purely local phenomena without regional significance.

Much information on physical oceanography has been collected during the International Indian Ocean Expedition, and general models have been proposed relating wind stress and sea state over the Indian Ocean (Cox, 1970). For several reasons these new data are not yet directly applicable to the study of reef variation, and in this section we consider the influence of physical factors on reefs in terms of wind systems, storms, tides and rainfall.

Wind

Wind is important primarily through the action of wind waves and swell: the adjustment of reefs to these factors has been clearly shown in the Marshall Islands (Munk and Sargent, 1954). Because of the smaller size and monsoonal circulation of the Indian Ocean, adjustments of reefs to the Trade-wind circulation patterns is less marked

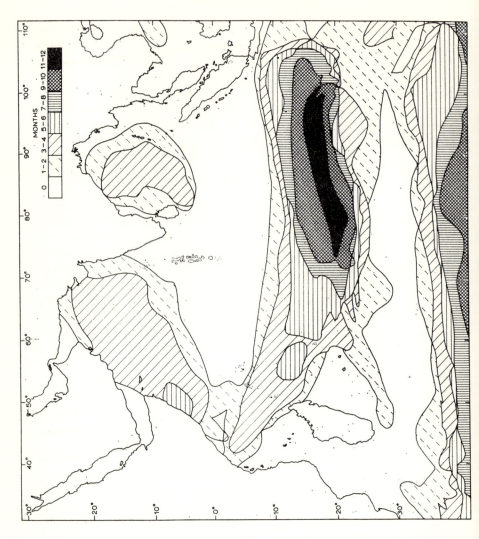

FIG. 5. Constancy of wind in the Indian Ocean. The map shows the number of months in the year in which the frequency of winds greater than Beaufort Force 4 (approximately 7 m sec^{-1}) exceeds 70%. Based on *Monthly meteorological charts of the Indian Ocean* (M.O. 470, 1949) by permission of the Controller, Her Majesty's Stationery Office.

than in the open Pacific. North of the equator the monsoonal circulation is dominant, with seasonal reversal and often inequality of winds. The Seychelles and the Chagos in the equatorial zone experience the Southeast Trades for part of the year and calms for the rest, and only the reefs south of 10°S are dominated by the Trades. North of the equator one would not therefore expect the marked variation between windward and leeward reefs characteristic of Pacific Trade-wind reefs, while further south, as on Aldabra, Assumption, and Farquhar, such a distinction can be made.

Figure 5 illustrates these patterns by showing the number of months in each year in which the frequency of winds greater than Beaufort force 4 (7 m sec^{-1}) exceeds 70%. The core of the Trade-wind belt in the southern hemisphere is clearly marked (Agalega has 11 months), and the seasonal extension towards the west and northwest is also apparent. The areas of constant moderately high winds north of the equator, in the Arabian Sea and the Bay of Bengal, are purely seasonal and occur during the northern summer season. Within the areas covered by the Trades the wind blows with great constancy and a speed of 6–9 m sec^{-1}. Figure 5 is clearly highly approximate: it suggests, for example, that Aldabra is affected by the Trades for only five months of the year, which is an underestimate, and other modifications could be suggested. Nevertheless it clearly distinguishes the seasonal monsoonal, the equatorial calm, and the seasonal and permanent Trade-wind areas, and thus serves as a useful substitute for a map of sea surface conditions. One important reservation must be made: wind-generated waves, as swell, travel outside their area of generation, and morphologically significant sea conditions are not restricted to the areas shown in Fig. 5. Swell from the southeast is certainly important on reefs in the equatorial zone, and it is likely that swell from the southern Westerlies also reaches some reefs: the Indian Ocean, however, is much narrower than the Pacific, and because of the shadow effect of Africa and Madagascar swell from the Westerlies is only likely to affect reefs in the eastern part of the ocean.

Tropical storms

Equally important in reef physiography is the distribution of tropical cyclones (Fig. 6). These are almost absent from the zone between 6°N and 5°S, and are strongly concentrated in the Bay of Bengal, the Arabian Sea, and the southwest Indian Ocean. Most of the Maldives and the Chagos atolls lie outside cyclone areas, as do the Seychelles, the Amirantes, and (marginally) Aldabra and Coetivy. The Laccadives and Minikoi, the Andamans and Nicobars, Comoros,

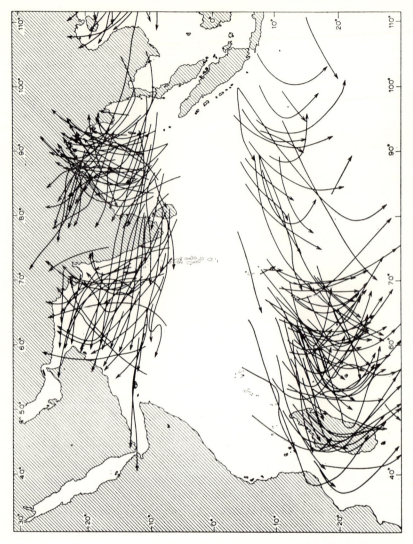

Fig. 6. Distribution of tropical storms in the Indian Ocean. From Stoddart (1969a). Based on *Monthly meteorological charts of the Indian Ocean* (M.O. 470, 1949) by permission of the Controller, Her Majesty's Stationery Office.

Madagascar, the Mascarenes, Agalega, Cargados Carajos, Tromelin, Cocos-Keeling and Christmas Island are affected. Cyclones are an important control of coral growth, reef morphology and sediment accumulation, though their destructive effects may be less marked on isolated reefs than on the shores of high islands and mainland coasts (Stoddart, 1970b; Sauer, 1962; McIntire and Walker, 1964).

Tides

Tidal information is reasonably full for mainland coasts, but is inadequate for most Indian Ocean islands; the following information is based on predictions in *Admiralty Tide Tables 1970*. The tides themselves are not well understood, though it is thought that there is an amphidromic point in the Arabian Sea, another off the coast of southeast Africa, and a third west of Australia. Most Indian Ocean tides are semidiurnal or mixed, mainly semidiurnal. Figure 7 shows types of tides and spring tidal range at selected Indian Ocean stations.

Tides with a range at springs of 0·3–1·0 m, which may be classified as microtidal, are experienced in the Laccadives, Maldives, south India and Ceylon, Cocos-Keeling, Agalega, Mauritius and Réunion. Mesotidal areas, with a spring tidal range of 1·0–2·0 m, are found in the Andamans, the Nicobars, the Chagos Archipelago, Christmas Island, the Seychelles, the Amirantes, and eastern Madagascar. A macrotidal springs range of more than 3·0 m, unusually large for reef areas, is experienced in the southwest Indian Ocean: on the coast of East Africa (Zanzibar, Pemba, Tutia) and northwest Madagascar, but also on the islands of the Comoros and the Aldabra group. Such extreme tides on atolls have no counterpart in other oceans. High tidal ranges are also found over small areas elsewhere in the Indian Ocean, particularly in the Mergui Archipelago (more than 5 m) and in the Gulf of Cambay (8·78 m). High tidal ranges are important in reef areas because reef corals normally only grow up to neap tide levels, and because desiccation and exposure to the atmosphere limit the growth of corals, algae and other organisms on intertidal flats.

Precipitation

Finally, precipitation is an important environmental parameter, as an ecological control of coral growth in areas of high tidal range, because of its contribution to outflowing groundwater on shores on reef flats in areas of heavy rainfall, and because of the limiting effect of low rainfall on shoreline vegetation. Schott (1935) prepared a rainfall map of the Indian Ocean, using mainly mainland and high island records, and this has been brought up to date in Fig 8 (Stoddart,

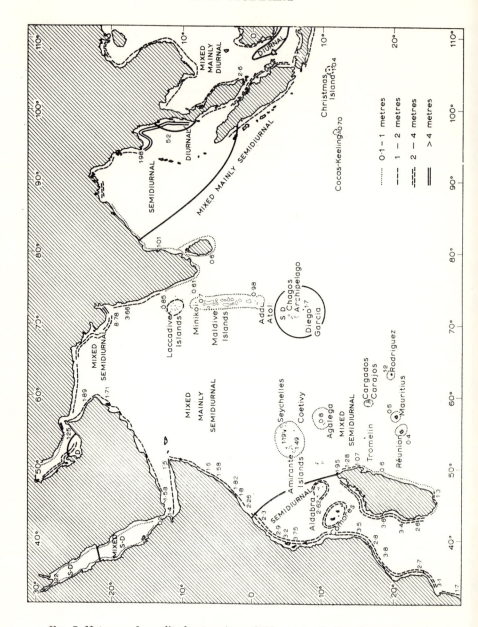

FIG. 7. Nature and amplitude at springs of tides in the Indian Ocean. Reproduced from data extracted from *Admiralty Tide Tables, volume II, 1970 edition*, with the sanction of the Controller, H.M. Stationery Office and the Hydrographer of the Navy.

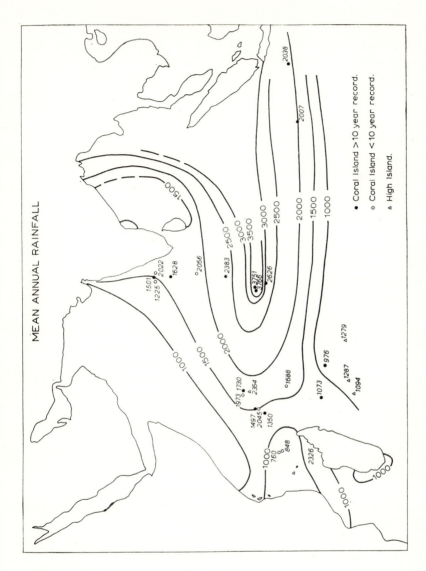

FIG. 8. Rainfall over the Indian Ocean. Isohyets based on coral island records of more than 10 years duration. From Stoddart (1970c).

1970c) using coral island records. Major regional differences are found with maximum atoll rainfalls at Peros Banhos and Salomon, Chagos Archipelago, of 3750 m, falling to 2626 mm at Diego Garcia and 2420mm at Addu, and to 1500–2000 mm in the Seychelles, at Minikoi, Cocos-Keeling and Christmas Island. Lowest atoll rainfalls (less than 1000 mm) are those in the Aldabra group north of Malagasy. Much lower rainfalls, of less than 200 mm per annum, are experienced on the coasts of Somalia, the Red Sea and the Persian Gulf. Since it is based on coral island records, Fig. 8 probably closely approximates the distribution of rainfall over the oceans: because of orographic effects the rainfalls of high islands may be up to one third or one half greater than the rainfall of the surrounding ocean, and drainage from rivers becomes an important local control of reef growth.

INDIAN OCEAN REEFS AND PLEISTOCENE SEA LEVELS

Although over extended time scales reef growth can be placed in the context of the geological evolution of the Indian Ocean basin, and although at the present time specific reef features can be shown to be in adjustment with currently operating physical and biological processes, these taken together cannot provide a complete explanation of the surface features of modern reefs. This is so for two reasons: (a) the existence of anomalous features on modern reefs, and (b) the known instability of sea level during the Pleistocene, and particularly the brevity of the present still-stand of the sea.

Anomalous reef features

Three sets of features may be considered anomalous in terms of present reef growth and processes: elevated reefs, submerged reefs, and certain features of reef surfaces now close to present sea level.

Elevated reefs are well developed in the southwest Indian Ocean (at Aldabra and neighbouring islands, in the Seychelles and Mascarenes), at Madagascar, the Tanzania and Kenya coasts, and along the margins of the Red Sea. They are absent from the central Indian Ocean (except for a very recent raised reef in south India), but raised reefs and reef-associated sediments are found in the eastern Indian Ocean, in the Andamans (Sewell, 1925), Nicobars (Sewell, 1922; Gee, 1926), western Australia, Houtman's Abrolhos, and Christmas Island. Though widely developed, their absence from the central Indian Ocean throws doubt on any purely eustatic explanation of their origin. Elevated intertidal notches in reef limestones have also been described from the Red Sea by Guilcher (1955) and correlated with similar features described by

Fairbridge (1948a, 1948b) from western Australia: raised notches are, however, also absent from other limestone coasts, for example at Aldabra and in East Africa, which makes eustatic explanations suspect.

The main submerged reefs are the extensive submarine banks of the Mascarene Plateau and the Chagos Archipelago, which commonly show marked bevellings at levels of 33–90 m and 8–20 m depth. Platforms beneath modern reefs are also very evident in the northern Maldives at depths of 50–75 m, and minor bevels have been described elsewhere, e.g. at 8–15 and 18–22 m in the Seychelles (Lewis, 1968).

Anomalous features of reef flats include drying intertidal surfaces too high for modern coral growth and of probably erosional origin; emerged and lithified coral conglomerates, some of which have been described as emerged reef rocks; and reef islands and raised beaches. In spite of their ambiguity, all of these have been used as evidence of former slightly higher sea levels, and workers such as Fairbridge (1948a) in Houtman's Abrolhos and Weydert (1969) at Tuléar, Madagascar, have interpreted them in terms of eustatic sea level changes. Gardiner (1931) and Sewell (1935) both assumed that raised reefs and reef islands indicate emergence following a post-glacial high stand of the sea, but in general little attention has been paid to the widespread submerged features. In discussing their origins and significance we need to consider (1) the course of the last glacial regression and subsequent rise of the sea to its present level, since the latter will define the period during which present reef growth has been effective; and (2) the variations of sea level and their effects on reefs over the Pleistocene as a whole.

Holocene sea level and the last regression

The history of the most recent rise in sea level is now well established with the aid of radiocarbon dating. From 15 000 to 8000 years B.P. sea level rose throughout the world at approximately $1 \cdot 0$–$1 \cdot 25$ cm yr^{-1}. There is growing evidence for a continued but slower rise of sea level, at from $0 \cdot 03$ to $0 \cdot 08$ cm yr^{-1}, over the last 4000 years (Scholl, Craighead and Stuiver, 1969; Redfield, 1967). There is little confirmation in recent work for the proposed series of Holocene high sea levels and still-stands, at up to 5 m above the present level, originally defined from the southeast Indian Ocean and later applied throughout the world by Fairbridge (1961). Fairbridge's scheme is, however, often used to explain anomalous features of reefs (e.g. Weydert, 1969; Lewis, 1968), generally without consideration of the process rates involved.

D. R. STODDART

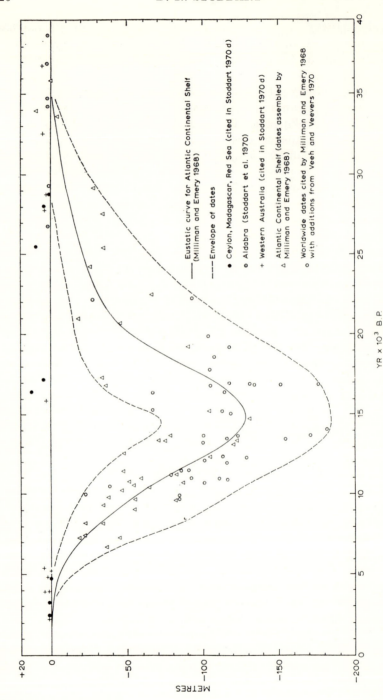

Fig. 9. Eustatic change in sea level over the last 40 000 years.

Figure 9 is based on a compilation of radiocarbon dates for sea level samples published by Milliman and Emery (1968), with some additions. It shows that the last glacial low sea level reached −120 m at 15 000 years B.P., and that the sea then rose fairly rapidly to −20 m at about 7000 years B.P. The scatter of dates is considerable and these values are only approximate: thus Veeh and Veevers (1970) report evidence for a fall to −175 m during the last regression. From this curve it is clear that modern reef growth related to present sea level must have begun about 5000 years ago. Figure 9 shows nine dates for Indian Ocean samples which suggest slightly higher sea levels than the present during this period: of these, six are those originally published by Fairbridge from western Australia. The others are from a sea level deposit in the Red Sea, dated at 4770 years B.P.; one at 0·6–1 m in Ceylon, dated at 2990 years B.P.; and the third, at 1·1–1·4 m in Madagascar, dated at 2250 years B.P. (Friedman, 1966; Shepard, 1963; Battistini, 1963).

Still-stand near 30 000 years ago

Figure 9 also shows the fall in sea level preceding the last glacial low, from a level close to that of the present level and dated about 30 000 years ago. Indian Ocean reef dates assignable to this still-stand span a period of about 12 000 years and are mostly for samples between present sea level and +5 m. They include five radiocarbon dates for Aldabra Atoll, four from western Australia, and three from the Red Sea (for details, see Stoddart, 1970d). In addition, not shown in Fig. 9, is a series of five dates between 26 750 and 34 400 years B.P. for raised reefs on the Tanzania coast, for which elevations have not been published but which are for deposits clearly affected by warping (Alexander, 1968; see also Battistini, 1966b; Temple, 1970). Several further dates (two from the Red Sea, one from Australia, and four from Tanzania) lie within the period of the glacial low sea level, and thus must indicate local movements.

In interpreting these dates and the evidence for a 30 000 year still-stand, two points must be made. First, many of the dates are close to the limit for ^{14}C dating, and even slight contamination could produce misleading dates; in the case of several Red Sea samples, for example, discrepancies have been revealed between ^{14}C dates and those obtained by other radiometric methods. Second, the elevation thus dated may result from local tectonic movements rather than eustatic sea level changes, and in this connection the absence of similar elevated reef deposits from the central Indian Ocean may be significant. Conversely, as Milliman and Emery (1968) have shown, the evidence for a 30 000 year still-stand is by no means limited to the Indian Ocean.

It is therefore probable that about 30 000 years ago sea level in the reef seas of the Indian Ocean stood at or slightly above its present level for substantially longer than the present still-stand has so far lasted. This, rather than Holocene high stands, could account for the existence of planed-rock reef flats, the existence of islands on them, and other slightly elevated reef features.

Earlier Pleistocene fluctuations

The last glacial sea level shift, though well documented in Fig. 9, covers only a fraction of Pleistocene time. Furthermore, ^{14}C dating of many reef samples from Aldabra, Tanzania, the Red Sea and western Australia has yielded indeterminate ages, mostly greater than 32–39 000 years. The development of uranium-series dating methods has yielded further data on these elevated reefs. Seychelles raised reefs, at $+6$ m on Praslin and at $+9$ m on Mahé, are dated at $140 \pm 30 \times 10^3$ years, and a similar reef on Gabriel Island, Mauritius, at $+2$ m, is dated at $160 \pm 40 \times 10^3$ years. That these dates are reasonable is shown by the fact that the Mauritius raised reefs overlie lavas which have been dated by the K-Ar method at 170×10^3 years (McDougall and Chamalaun, 1969). Samples from western Australia at $+4$ m are dated at 100 ± 20 and $140 \pm 30 \times 10^3$ years. Samples from raised Red Sea reefs at $+2$ to $+9.5$ m cluster between 70 and 92×10^3 years (Veeh and Giegengack, 1970), and from tectonically deformed reefs in Ethiopia at 80, possibly 100–120, and 200×10^3 years (Lalou et al., 1970).

Similar studies in other parts of the world have resulted in a variety of estimates of the date and duration of late Pleistocene high sea levels; some of these are shown in the inset in Fig. 10, which also plots the available uranium-series age determinations for the Indian Ocean. There is little agreement between the inferred high sea levels reported from Barbados, New Guinea and elsewhere and the Indian Ocean dates, but it is reasonable to conclude that sea level stood at or slightly above its present level for much of the period $70–190 \times 10^3$ years B.P.; this period includes the last main interglacial. Figure 10 also places in perspective the length of the period of present reef growth during the Holocene: it is a priori unlikely that reef features formed during the last 5000 years could compare in magnitude with those formed during late Pleistocene high sea levels. It must also be emphasized that Fig. 10 covers only one-tenth of the time-span of the Pleistocene: most discussions of the effects of Pleistocene changes concentrate almost exclusively on Wisconsin and Holocene time, largely because

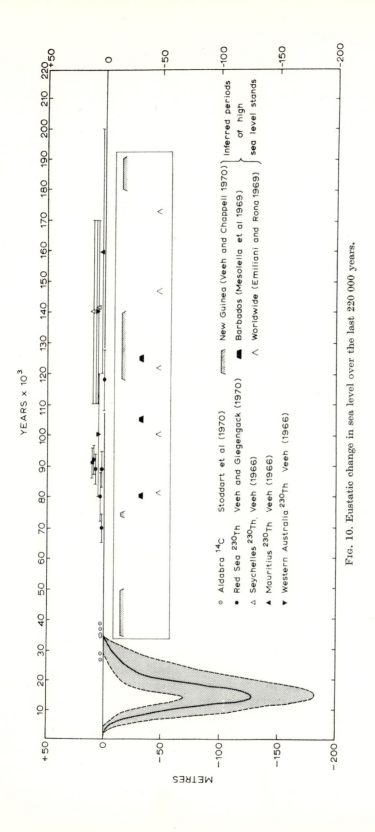

FIG. 10. Eustatic change in sea level over the last 220 000 years.

of the lack of information for earlier periods. If the conclusions from the last 200 000 years are extended over the last 2 million it is clear that very extensive reef growth could have taken place at a variety of levels above, at and below the present level throughout this period. The complexity of the Pleistocene in the reef seas is thus only now being appreciated. Further, though bevelling by marine erosion can take place on a small scale during glacial low sea levels, we know that reefs are in general resistant to major erosional modification by both subaerial and marine erosion, and that once they have been formed, coral reefs are remarkably persistent geomorphic features (Stoddart, 1969b).

CONCLUSION

The major features of reef structure and distribution in the Indian Ocean can be explained in largely Darwinian terms in the context of the Tertiary evolution of the Ocean itself. Reef morphology is, however, more complex: we must consider how far morphologic features reflect modern conditions of reef growth as influenced by waves, storms, tides and other factors, and to what extent they are inherited from features formed during the long and complex period of the Pleistocene. In analysing Pleistocene events we tend to structure the data in terms of eustatic sea level fluctuations, largely because of their generality, but we must also consider the possibilities of local tectonic movements. We have seen that there is a major province of elevated reefs in the western Indian Ocean and the Red Sea, and another, less extensive, in the southeast. Between the two are the submerged banks of the Mascarene Plateau and the Chagos Archipelago. These distributions raise the major questions of Indian Ocean reef studies. Why are there distinct areas of raised and submerged reefs? Why were the late Pleistocene and earlier reefs, which now form the raised reefs and submerged banks, so much more extensive than those of the present? Why were many banks not colonized by corals during the last rise of sea level? Why do most modern Indian Ocean reefs only thinly veneer much older structures?

To answer these questions requires a much more detailed knowledge of the reefs in the Pleistocene. Palaeotemperature data from deep sea cores suggest that in the equatorial zone of the Indian Ocean, as elsewhere, sea temperatures did not fall sufficiently during glacial maxima to inhibit reef growth (Oba, 1969), though the reef zone presumably contracted at its latitudinal limits. Thus reef communities probably maintained themselves in their present positions though at lower levels during the recurrent crises of sea level change. We do not know why these communities were unsuccessful during the Holocene in colonizing many banks submerged as the sea level rose.

It is, moreover, clear that it is no longer reasonable to explain problematic features of modern reefs by reference only to the rather uncertain high stands of the sea in Holocene times. In total these high still-stands (assuming their reality) were of insignificant duration by comparison with similar stands throughout the Pleistocene. Nor can studies of morphology alone (Biewald, 1964) lead to reliable conclusions on the history of specific features. The outstanding problems are thus partly geological and partly ecological. We need data from deep borings to supplement the present inadequate picture of the reefs in the Pleistocene; and we need ecological studies, both of areas where reefs are now growing, and, equally important, of areas like the Mascarene Plateau banks where they are not, to determine the status and geological potential of reef growth at the present day.

ACKNOWLEDGEMENTS

I thank the Royal Society and other bodies for supporting field studies at Addu Atoll, Maldive Islands (1964), Diego Garcia Atoll, Chagos Archipelago (1967), Aldabra Atoll (1966–1970), and in South India (1969), and for making possible shorter visits to the Seychelles, Mauritius, Comoros, Madagascar, atolls near Aldabra and in the Amirantes, and the Kenya coast, during 1966–1970.

REFERENCES

Agassiz, A. (1903). The coral reefs of the Maldives. *Mem. Mus. comp. Zool. Harv.* **29**: 1–168.

Alexander, C. S. (1968). The marine terraces of the northeast coast of Tanganyika. *Z. Geomorph.* (N.F.) Supplbd. **7**: 133–154.

Andrews, C. W. (1900). *A monograph of Christmas Island (Indian Ocean), physical features and geology, with descriptions of the fauna and flora by numerous contributors.* London: Trustees of the British Museum (Natural History).

Baker, B. H. (1963). Geology and mineral resources of the Seychelles Archipelago. *Mem. geol. Surv. Kenya* **3**: 1–140.

Baker, B. H. and Miller, J. A. (1963). Geology and geochronology of the Seychelles Islands and structure of the floor of the Arabian Sea. *Nature, Lond.* **199**: 346–348.

Battistini, R. (1963). L'age de l'encoche de corrosion marine flandrienne de 1–1·3 m de la Baie des Galions (extrême-sud de Madagascar). *C. r. somm. Séanc. Soc. geol. Fr.* **1963**: 16.

Battistini, R. (1964). *Etude géomorphologique de l'Extrême-Sud de Madagascar.* Paris: Editions Cujas.

Battistini, R. (1965). Problèmes géomorphologiques de l'extrême nord de Madagascar. *Madagascar Rev. Géog.* **7**: 1–61.

Battistini, R. (1966a). Le morphologie de l'ile Europa. *Mém. Mus. natn. Hist.
nat., Paris* N.S. (A) **41**: 7–18.

Battistini, R. (1966b). Le Quaternaire littoral des environs de Dar-es-Salam
(Tanzanie): essai de corrélations avec le Quaternaire littoral malgache.
Bull. Assoc. fr. Ét. quat. **3**: 191–201.

Battistini, R. (1967). Le volcan actif de la Grande Comore. *Madagascar Rev.
Géog.* **10–11**: 41–77.

Berry, L., Whiteman, A. J. and Bell, S. V. (1966). Some radiocarbon dates and
their geomorphological significance, emerged reef complex of the Sudan.
Z. Geomorph. (N.F.) **10**: 119–143.

Berthois, L. and Battistini, R. (1969). Etude sédimentologique de l'ile Europa.
Madagascar Rév. Géog. **15**: 7–52.

Bezrukov, P. L., Krylov, A. J. and Cernishev, V. I. (1966). Petrography and
absolute ages of basalts from the bottom of the Indian Ocean. *Oceanologia*
6: 261.

Biewald, D. (1964). Die Ansatztiefe der rezenten Korallenriffe im Indischen
Ocean. *Z. Geomorph.* (N.F.) **8**: 351–361.

Blanc, J. J., Chamley, H. and Froget, C. (1966). Sédimentation paralique et
récifale à Tuléar. *Recl. Trav. Stn. mar. Endoume fasc. hors-série,* Suppl.
5: 24–69.

Boshoff, P. H. (1958). Development and constitution of the coral reef. In *A
natural history of Inhaca Island, Moçambique,* (W. Macnae and M. Kalk,
eds). Johannesburg: Witwatersrand University Press, 49–56.

Bunce, E. T., Langseth, M. G., Chase, R. L. and Ewing, M. (1967). Structure of
the western Somali Basin. *J. geophys. Res.* **72**: 2547–2555.

Coppinger, R. W. (1884). *Report on the zoological collections made in the Indo-
Pacific Ocean during the Voyage of H.M.S. "Alert" 1881–1882.* London: Trustees of the British Museum (Natural History).

Coutière, H. (1898). Notes sur les récifs madréporiques de Djibouti. *Bull. Mus.
natn. Hist. nat., Paris* **4**: 87–90, 155–157.

Cox, M. D. (1970). A mathematical model of the Indian Ocean. *Deep Sea Res.*
17: 47–75.

Crossland, C. (1902). The coral reefs of Zanzibar. *Proc. Camb. phil. Soc. math.
phys. Sci.* **11**: 493–503.

Crossland, C. (1904). The coral reefs of Pemba Island and of the East African
mainland. *Proc. Camb. phil. Soc. math. phys. Sci.* **12**: 36–43.

Crossland, C. (1907). Reports on the marine biology of the Sudanese Red Sea.
IV. The recent history of the coral reefs of the mid-west shores of the Red
Sea. *J. Linn. Soc.* (Zool.) **31**: 14–30.

Darwin, C. R. (1842). *The structure and distribution of coral reefs.* London: Smith,
Elder and Co.

Davies, D. (1968). When did the Seychelles leave India? *Nature, Lond.* **220**:
1225–1226.

Davies, D. and Francis, T. J. G. (1964). The crustal structure of the Seychelles
Bank. *Deep Sea Res.* **11**: 921–927.

Davis, W. M. (1918). Coral reefs and submarine banks. *J. Geol.* **26**: 198–223,
289–309, 385–411.

Day, J. H. (1969). *A guide to marine life on South African shores.* Cape Town: A. A. Balkema.

Den Hartog, C. (1970). *The sea-grasses of the world.* Amsterdam: North-Holland Publishing Co.

Ehrenberg, C. G. (1834). Uber die Natur und Bildung der Corallenbänke des rothen Meeres und über einen neuen Fortschritt in der Kenntniss der Organisation im Kleinsten Raume durch Verbesserung des Mikroscops von Pistor und Schick. *Abh. K. Akad. Wiss. Berl.* (phys. Kl.) **1832**: 381–432.

Emiliani, C. and Rona, E. (1969). Caribbean cores P. 6304–8 and P. 6304–9: new analysis of absolute chronology: reply. *Science, N.Y.:* **166**: 1551–1552.

Fairbridge, R. W. (1948a). Notes on the geomorphology of the Pelsart Group of the Houtman's Abrolhos Islands. *J. Proc. R. Soc. West. Aust.* **33**: 1–43.

Fairbridge, R. W. (1948b). The geology and geomorphology of Point Peron, Western Australia. *J. Proc. R. Soc. West. Aust.* **34**: 35–72.

Fairbridge, R. W. (1961). Eustatic changes in sea level. *Physics Chem. Earth* **4**: 99–185.

Fisher, R. L., Engel, C. G. and Hilde, T. W. C. (1968). Basalts dredged from the Amirante Ridge, western Indian Ocean. *Deep Sea Res.* **15**: 521–534.

Fisher, R. L., Johnson, G. L. and Heezen, B. C. (1967). Mascarene Plateau, western Indian Ocean. *Bull. geol. Soc. Am.* **78**: 1247–1266.

Flower, M. F. J. and Strong, D. F. (1969). The significance of sandstone inclusions in lavas of the Comores Archipelago. *Earth Plan. Sci. Lett.* **7**: 47–50.

Forbes, H. O. (1879). Notes on the Cocos or Keeling Islands. *Geogrl. J.* **1**: 777–784.

Francis, T. J. G., Davies, D. and Hill, M. N. (1966). Crustal structure between Kenya and the Seychelles. *Phil. Trans. R. Soc.* (A) **259**: 240–261.

Francis, T. J. G. and Shor, G. G. Jr. (1966). Seismic refraction measurements in the northwest Indian Ocean. *J. geophys. Res.* **71**: 427–449.

Friedman, G. M. (1966). A fossil shoreline reef in the Gulf of Eilat (Aqaba). *Israel J. Earth Sci.* **14**: 86–90.

Fryer, J. C. F. (1911). The structure and formation of Aldabra and neighbouring islands—with notes on their fauna and flora. *Trans. Linn. Soc. Lond* (2) **14**: 397–442.

Gardiner, J. S. (1901). The atoll of Minikoi. *Proc. Camb. phil. Soc. math. phys. Sci.* **11**: 22–26.

Gardiner, J. S. (1903–6). *The fauna and geography of the Maldive and Laccadive Archipelagoes, being the account of the work carried on and of collections made by an expedition during the years 1899 and 1900.* Cambridge: University Press. 2 volumes.

Gardiner, J. S. (1906). The Indian Ocean, being results largely based on the work of the Percy Sladen Expedition in H.M.S. "Sealark", Comm. B. T. Sommerville, 1905. *Geogrl. J.* **28**: 313–332, 454–465.

Gardiner, J. S. (1907). Description of the expedition. *Trans. Linn. Soc. Lond.* (2) **12**: 1–55, 111–175.

Gardiner, J. S. (1907–36). Reports of the Percy Sladen Trust Expedition to the Indian Ocean in 1905. *Trans. Linn. Soc. Lond.* (2) **12–19**.

Gardiner, J. S. (1931). *Coral reefs and atolls: being a course of lectures delivered at the Lowell Institute at Boston, February 1930.* London: Macmillan.

Gardiner, J. S. (1936). The reefs of the western Indian Ocean. I. Chagos Archipelago. II. The Mascarene Region. *Trans. Linn. Soc. Lond.* (2) **19**: 393–436.

Gee, E. R. (1926). The geology of the Andaman and Nicobar Islands, with special reference to Middle Andaman Island. *Rec. geol. Surv. India* **59**: 208–232.

Gibson-Hill, C. A. (1948). The island of North-Keeling. *J. Malay. Brch. R. Asiat. Soc.* **21**: 68–103.

Gibson-Hill, C. A. (1950). Papers on the fauna of the Cocos-Keeling Islands. *Bull. Raffles Mus.* No. 22: 1–298.

Glennie, E. A. (1936). Report on the value of gravity in the Maldive and Laccadive Islands. *Scient. Rep. John Murray Exped. 1933–1934*, **1**: 95–107.

Gravier, C. (1911). Les récifs de coraux et les madréporaires de la Baie de Tadjourah (Golfe d'Aden). *Annals. Instn. océanogr. Monaco* 2 (3): 1–99.

Guilcher, A. (1955). Géomorphologie de l'extremité septentrionale du Banc Farsan (Mer Rouge). *Annals. Inst. océanogr. Monaco* **30**: 55–100.

Guilcher, A. (1956). Etude géomorphologique des récifs coralliens du nord-ouest de Madagascar. *Annals. Inst. océanogr., Monoco* **33**: 64–136.

Guilcher, A. (1958). Mise au point sur la géomorphologie des récifs coralliens de Madagascar et dépendances. *Mém. Inst. scient. Madagascar* (F) **2**: 89–115.

Guilcher, A. (1971). Mayotte barrier reef and lagoon, Comoro Islands, as compared with other barrier reefs, atolls and lagoons in the world. *Symp. zool. Soc. Lond.* No. 28: 65–86.

Guilcher, A., Berthois, L., Battistini, R. and Fourmanoir, P. (1958). Les récifs coralliens des Iles Radama et de la Baie Ramanetaka (Côte nord-ouest de Madagascar). Etude géomorphologique et sédimentologique. *Mém. Inst. scient. Madagascar* (F) **2**: 117–199.

Guilcher, A., Berthois, L., Le Calvez, Y., Battistini, R. and Crosnier, A. (1965). Les récifs coralliens et le lagon de l'Ile Mayotte (Archipel des Comores, Océan Indien). *Mém. ORSTOM* **11**: 1–210.

Guppy, H. B. (1889). The Cocos-Keeling Islands. *Scott. geogr. Mag.* **5**: 281–297, 457–474, 569–588.

Guppy, H. B. (1890). The dispersal of plants as illustrated by the flora of the Keeling or Cocos Islands. *J. Trans. Vict. Inst.* **24**: 267–306.

Heezen, B. C. and Tharp, M. (1965). Physiographic diagram of the Indian Ocean. *Spec. Publs. geol. Soc. Am.*

Heezen, B. C. and Tharp, M. (1966). Physiography of the Indian Ocean. *Phil. Trans. R. Soc.* (A) **259**: 137–149.

Kassas, M. and Zahran, M. A. (1967). On the ecology of the Red Sea littoral salt marsh, Egypt. *Ecol. Monogr.* **37**: 297–316.

Kendall, C. G. St. C. and Skipworth, P. A. d'E. (1969). Geomorphology of a recent shallow-water carbonate province: Khor al Bazam, Trucial Coast, southwest Persian Gulf. *Bull. geol. Soc. Am.* **80**: 865–892.

Klunzinger, C. B. (1877–1879). *Die Korallthiere des rothen Meeres*. Berlin: Verlag der Gutmann'schen Buchhandlung.

Kohn, A. J. (1964). Notes on Indian Ocean atolls visited by the Yale Seychelles Expedition. *Atoll. Res. Bull.* **101**: 1–12.

Kohn, A. J. (1967). Environmental complexity and species diversity in the gastropod genus *Conus* on Indo-West Pacific reef platforms. *Am. Nat.* **101**: 251–259.

Kohn, A. J. (1968). Microhabitats, abundance and food of *Conus* on atoll reefs in the Maldive and Chagos Islands. *Ecology* **49**: 1046–1062.

Lacroix, A. (1936). *Le volcan actif de l'île Réunion et ses produits*. Paris: Gauthier-Villars.

Lalou, C., Nguyen, H. V., Faure, H. and Moreira, L. (1970). Datation par la méthode uranium-thorium des hauts niveaux de coraux de la depression de l'Afar (Éthiopie). *Revue Géogr. phys. Géol. dyn.* (2) **12**: 3–8.

Laughton, A. S. (1966). The Gulf of Aden. *Phil. Trans. R. Soc.* (A) **259**: 150–171.

Le Pichon, X. and Heirtzler, J. R. (1968). Magnetic anomalies in the Indian Ocean and sea-floor spreading. *J. geophys. Res.* **73**: 2101–2117.

Lewis, M. S. (1968). The morphology of the fringing coral reefs along the east coast of Mahé, Seychelles. *J. Geol.* **76**: 140–153.

Lewis, M. S. (1969). Sedimentary environments and unconsolidated carbonate sediments of the fringing coral reefs of Mahé, Seychelles. *Mar. Geol.* **7**: 95–127.

Lewis, M. S. and Taylor, J. D. (1966). Marine sediments and bottom communities of the Seychelles. *Phil. Trans. R. Soc.* (A) **259**: 279–290.

Macfadyen, W. A. (1930). The undercutting of coral reef limestone on the coasts of some islands in the Red Sea. *Geogrl. J.* **75**: 27–34.

Macnae, W. (1968). A general account of the flora and fauna of mangrove swamps and forests in the Indo-West-Pacific region. *Adv. mar. Biol.* **6**: 73–270.

Macnae, W. and Kalk, M. (eds) (1958). *A natural history of Inhaca Island, Mocambique.* Johannesburg: Witwatersrand University Press. Second edition 1969.

Marenzeller, E. von. (1907). Riffkorallen des Roten Meeres. *Denkschr. Akad. Wiss., Wien* **80**: 27–97.

Matthews, D. H. and Davies, D. (1966). Geophysical studies of the Seychelles Bank. *Phil. Trans. R. Soc.* (A) **259**: 227–239.

Maxwell, W. G. H. (1968). *Atlas of the Great Barrier Reef.* Amsterdam: Elsevier.

McDougall, I. and Chamalaun, F. H. (1969). Isotopic dating and geomagnetic polarity studies on volcanic rocks from Mauritius, Indian Ocean. *Bull. geol. Soc. Am.* **80**: 1419–1442.

McDougall, I., Upton, B. G. J. and Wadsworth, W. J. (1965). A geological reconnaissance of Rodriguez Island, Indian Ocean. *Nature, Lond.* **206**: 26–27.

McIntire, W. G. (1961). Mauritius: river-mouth terraces and present eustatic sea-stand. *Z. Geomorph.* (N.F.) Suppl. **3**: 39–47.

McIntire, W. G. and Walker, H. J. (1964). Tropical cyclones and coastal morphology in Mauritius. *Ann. Ass. Am. Geogr.* **54**: 582–596.

Mesolella, K. J., Matthews, R. K., Broecker, W. S. and Thurber, D. L. (1969). The astronomical theory of climatic change: Barbados data. *J. Geol.* **77**: 250–274.

Milliman, J. D. and Emery, K. O. (1968). Sea levels during the past 35 000 years. *Science, N.Y.* **162**: 1121–1123.

Munk, W. H. and Sargent, M. C. (1954). Adjustment of Bikini Atoll to ocean waves. *Prof. Pap. U.S. geol. Surv.* **260–C**: 275–280.

Nesteroff, W. D. (1959). Age des derniers mouvements du graben de la mer Rouge déterminé par la méthode du C^{14} appliquée aux récifs fossiles. *Bull. Soc. géol. Fr.* (7) **1**: 415–418.

Niino, H. and Oshite, K. (1966). Geologic survey by the Umitakamaru International Indian Ocean Expedition in the winter of 1962–1963. *Rec. oceanogr. Wks Japan* N.S. **8**(2): 27–30.

Oba, T. (1969). Biostratigraphy and isotopic paleotemperatures of some deep-sea cores from the Indian Ocean. *Scient. Rep. Tohoku Univ.* (2) **41**: 129–195.

Oldham, C. F. (1895). Natural History notes from H.M. Marine Survey Steamer 'Investigator'', Commander C. F. Oldham, R.N., commanding. Series II, No. 18.i. The topography of the Arabian Sea in the neighbourhood of the Laccadives. ii. The physical features of some of the Laccadive Islands, with suggestions as to their mode of formation. *J. Asiat. Soc. Beng.* **64**: 1–14.

Ortmann, A. E. (1889). Beobachtungen an Steinkorallen von der Südküste Ceylons. *Zool. Jb.* (Syst.) **4**: 493–590.

Ortmann, A. E. (1892). Die Korallriffe von Dar-es-Salaam und Umgegend. *Zool. Jb.* (Syst.) **6**: 631–670.

Pichon, M. (1964). Contibution à l'étude de la répartition des Madréporaires sur le récif de Tuléar. *Recl Trav. Stn. mar. Endoume fasc. hors-série*, Suppl. **2**: 79–203.

Pichon, M. (1967). Caractères généraux des peuplements benthiques des récifs et lagons de l'ile Maurice (Océan Indien). *Cah. ORSTOM, sér. océanogr.* **5**(4): 31–45.

Pillai, C. S. G. (1967). *Studies on South Indian corals.* Ph.D. thesis, University of Kerala.

Redfield, A. C. (1967). Postglacial change in sea level in the western North Atlantic Ocean. *Science, N.Y.* **157**: 687–692.

Rodolfo, K. S. (1969). Bathymetry and marine geology of the Andaman Basin, and tectonic implications for southeast Asia. *Bull. geol. Soc. Am.* **80**: 1203–1230.

Sauer, J. D. (1961). *Coastal plant geography of Mauritius.* Baton Rouge: Louisiana State University Press.

Sauer, J. D. (1962). Effects of recent tropical cyclones on the coastal vegetation of Mauritius. *J. Ecol.* **50**: 275–290.

Sauer, J. D. (1967). *Plants and man on the Seychelles coast: a study in historical biogeography.* Madison: University of Wisconsin Press.

Scholl, D. W., Craighead, F. C., Sr. and Stuiver, M. (1969). Florida submergence curve revised: its relation to coastal sedimentation rates. *Science, N.Y.* **163**: 562–564.

Schott, G. (1935). *Geographie des Indischen und Stillen Ozeans.* Hamburg: Verlag von C. Boysen.

Setchell, W. A. (1930). Nullipore reef control and its significance. *Proc. Pacif. Sci. Congr.* **4**(3): 265–296.

Sewell, R. B. S. (1922). A survey season in the Nicobar Islands on the R.I.M.S. "Investigator", October 1921 to March 1922. *J. Bombay nat. Hist. Soc.* **28**: 970–989.

Sewell, R. B. S. (1925). The geography of the Andaman Sea basin. *Mem. Asiat. Soc. Beng.* **9**: 1–26.

Sewell, R. B. S. (1928). A study of recent changes of sea level based largely on a study of coral growths in Indian and Pacific seas. *Int. Revue ges. Hydrobiol. Hydrogr.* **20**: 89–102.

Sewell, R. B. S. (1932). The coral coasts of India. *Geogrl J.* **79**: 449–465.

Sewell, R. B. S. (1935). Studies on coral and coral formations in Indian waters. *Mem. Asiat. Soc. Beng.* **9**: 461–540.

Sewell, R. B. S. (1936a). An account of Addu Atoll. *Scient. Rep. John Murray Exped. 1933–1934*, **1**: 63–93.

Sewell, R. B. S. (1936b). An account of Horsburgh or Goifurfehendu Atoll. *Scient. Rep. John Murray Exped. 1933–1934*, **1**: 109–125.

Shepard, F. P. (1963). Thirty-five thousand years of sea-level. In *Essays in marine geology in honor of K. O. Emery*: 1–10. Collins, T. (ed.) La Jolla: University of Southern California.

Shor, G. G., Jr. and Pollard, D. D. (1963). Seismic investigations of Seychelles and Saya de Malha Banks, northwest Indian Ocean. *Science, N.Y.* **142**: 48–49.

Snead, R. E. (1967). Recent morphological changes along the coast of West Pakistan. *Ann. Ass. Am. Geogr.* **57**: 550–565.

Stoddart, D. R. (1966). Reef studies at Addu Atoll, Maldive Islands: preliminary results of an expedition to Addu Atoll in 1964. *Atoll. Res. Bull.* **116**: 1–122.

Stoddart. D. R. (1967). Ecology of Aldabra Atoll, Indian Ocean. *Atoll Res. Bull.* **118**: 1–141.

Stoddart, D. R. (1969a). Regional variation in Indian Ocean coral reefs. *Symp. Corals and Coral Reefs mar. Biol. Assoc. India.*

Stoddart, D. R. (1969b). Ecology and morphology of Recent coral reefs. *Biol. Rev.* **44**: 433–498.

Stoddart, D. R. (1970a). Coral islands of the western Indian Ocean. *Atoll. Res. Bull.* **136**: 1–224.

Stoddart, D. R. (1970b). Coral reefs and islands and catastrophic storms. In *Applied coastal geomorphology*: 155–197; Steers, J. A. (ed.). London: Macmillan.

Stoddart, D. R. (1970c). Rainfall of Indian Ocean coral islands. *Atoll Res. Bull.* **147**: 1–21.

Stoddart, D. R. (1970d). Sea-level change and the origin of sand cays: radiometric evidence. *J. mar. biol. Ass. India.*

Stoddart, D. R. and Taylor, J. D. (1971). Geography and ecology of Diego Garcia Atoll, Chagos Archipelago. *Atoll Res. Bull.* **149**: 1–237.

Stoddart, D. R., Taylor, J. D., Fosberg, F. R. and Farrow, G. E. (1971). Geomorphology of Aldabra Atoll. *Phil. Trans. R. Soc.* (B) **260**: 31–65.

Talbot, F. H. (1965). A description of the coral structure of Tutia Reef (Tanganyika Territory, East Africa), and its fish fauna. *Proc. zool. Soc. Lond.* **145**: 431–470.

Taylor, J. D. (1968). Coral reef and associated invertebrate communities (mainly molluscan) around Mahé, Seychelles. *Phil. Trans. R. Soc.* (B) **254**: 129–206.

Taylor, J. D. and Lewis, M. S. (1970). The flora, fauna and sediments of the marine grass beds of Mahé, Seychelles. *J. nat. Hist.* **4**: 199–220.

Teichert, C. (1947). Contributions to the geology of Houtman's Abrolhos, Western Australia. *Proc. Linn. Soc. N.S.W.*: 145–196.

Teichert, C. and Fairbridge, R. W. (1948). Some coral reefs of the Sahul Shelf. *Geogrl Rev.* **38**: 222–249.

Temple, P. H. (1970). Aspects of the geomorphology of the Dar-es-Salaam area. *Tanzania Notes Rec.* **71**: 21–54.

Thorpe, L. (1928). Alcyonaria of the Abrolhos Islands, Western Australia. *J. Linn. Soc.* (Zool.) **36**: 479–531.

Trueman, N. A. (1965). The phosphate, volcanic and carbonate rocks of Christmas Island (Indian Ocean). *J. geol. Soc. Aust.* **12**: 261–283.

Upton, B. G. J. and Wadsworth, W. J. (1965). Geology of Réunion Island, Indian Ocean. *Nature, Lond.* **207**: 151–154.

Vasseur, P. (1964). Contribution à l'étude bionomique des peuplements sciaphiles infralittoraux de substrat dur dans les récifs de Tuléar, Madagascar. *Recl Trav. Stn mar. Endoume, fasc. hors-série*, Suppl. **2**: 1–77.

Veeh, H. H. (1966). Th^{230}/U^{238} and U^{234}/U^{238} ages of Pleistocene high sea-level stand. *J. geophys. Res.* **71**: 3379–3386.

Veeh, H. H. and Chappell, J. C. (1970). Astronomical theory of climatic change: support from New Guinea. *Science, N.Y.* **167**: 862–865.

Veeh, H. H. Giegengack, R. (1970). Uranium-series ages of corals from the Red Sea. *Nature, Lond.* **226**: 155–156.

Veeh, H. H. and Veevers, J. J. (1970). Sea level at −175 m off the Great Barrier Reef 13 600–17 000 year ago. *Nature, Lond.* **226**: 536–537.

Walther, J. (1888). Die Korallenriffe der Sinaihalbinsel: geologische und biologische Beobachtungen. *Abh. sachs. Akad. Wiss.* **14**: 437–506.

Walther, J. (1891). Die Adamsbrucke und die Korallenriffe der Palkstrasse. *Petermanns Mitt.* (Erganzungsheft) **102**: 1–40.

Weeks, L. A., Herbison, R. N. and Peter, G. (1967). Island arc system in Andaman Sea. *Bull. Am. Ass. petrol. Geol.* **51**: 1803–1815.

Wellman, P. and McElhinny, M. W. (1970). K-Ar age of the Deccan Traps, India. *Nature, Lond.* **227**: 595–596.

Werth, E. (1901). Lebende und jungfossile Korallenriffe in Ost-Afrika. *Z. Ges. Erdk. Berl.* **36**: 115–144.

Weydert, P. (1969). Les variations récentes du niveau marin et leurs influences sur la morphologie récifale dans la Baie de Tuléar (sud-ouest de Madagascar). *C. r. hebd. Séanc. Acad. Sci., Paris* (D) **268**: 482–484.

Wiseman, J. D. H. (1936). The petrography and significance of a rock dredged from a depth of 744 fathoms, near to Providence Reef, Indian Ocean. *Trans. Linn. Soc. Lond.* (2) **19**: 437–443.

Wood-Jones, F. (1910). *Coral and Atolls: a history and description of the Keeling-Cocos Islands, with an account of their fauna and flora, and a discussion of the method of development and transformation of coral structures in general.* London: L. Reeve.

Symp. zool. Soc. Lond. (1971) No. 28, 39–63.

SEYCHELLES REEFS: STRUCTURE AND DEVELOPMENT

C. J. R. BRAITHWAITE

Department of Geology, Dundee University, Dundee, Scotland.

SYNOPSIS

The reefs of the Seychelles appear to be poorly developed in respect of both coral density and lateral extent when compared to other areas. The reasons for this are probably more complex than the obvious suggestions of unfavourable salinities or water turbidity. The reefs are fringing in Darwin's sense and the combination of physical and biological processes leads at the present day to the construction of three distinctive forms which are partly a reflection of ecology and are often spatially related. These are characterized by an *Acropora* assemblage, a *Porites* assemblage, and a third, basically calcrudite accumulation. They are not necessarily mutually exclusive. With them are associated constructional forms which are probably relict.

There seems to be no close correlation between areas currently recognized as reefs and those with the most prolific coral growth. It is clear that there are both "reefs" with essentially no corals and areas of high coral productivity which would not be so called. Descriptions of both of these are given together with an outline of the main structural features of contemporary accretions.

It is shown that, as in other areas, the simplified model of reef growth as a continuous progression of upwards growth to sea level, followed by seawards accretion, with or without subsidence is a mis-statement. An attempt is made to produce a more reasonable explanation applicable to other modern reefs and to geologically ancient structures thought to be of reef origin.

INTRODUCTION

The Seychelle Islands are situated at approximately 55° 30′ east 4° 40′ south on the Seychelles Bank, an area of shallower water (generally less than 60 m depth) of some 31 000 sq. km, surrounded by oceanic deeps. There are over one hundred granitic and coralline islands in the group, but this study relates particularly to Mahé, the largest, and to those islands immediately adjacent to it. Elongate in a NNE–SSW direction, Mahé's greatest dimensions are about 24 × 8 km, while offshore Cerf reaches 1·7 and St. Anne 2·3 km in length (see map, Fig. 1). Geologically these are part of a Pre-Cambrian granite mass cut by Tertiary minor intrusions, and these old hard rocks contribute to the impressive relief of the islands, rising on Mahé to 905 m in places. It seems likely that this geological background has provided tectonic stability to the area over something greater than

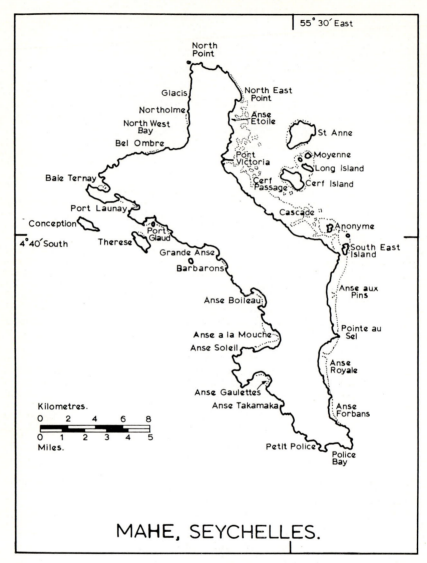

FIG. 1. Sketch map of Mahé showing positions of the localities mentioned in the text.

ten million years, and this provides an interesting contrast with many other reef areas.

By comparison with descriptions of other areas the reefs of Mahé seem to be poorly developed in respect of both coral density and lateral extent. Darwin would probably have classified them as "fringing", but this description is really only applicable to the east coast since along the western shore reefs in the popular sense are narrow or absent. One might, therefore, justifiably divide the reefs into windward and leeward types, the dominant wind direction being that of the south-east monsoon, and perhaps add to these specialized forms in sheltered areas on the east coast or within channels. This would reflect real morphological differences but would in some ways be a misleading division and it is more profitable to consider in the first instance not the gross shape, but the kinds of accumulation taking place at present. That is to say, what organisms, assemblages or processes are contributing to a possible reef growth, what structures do they produce, and how are these related to each other and to what one might call the physico-chemical aspects of the system, current activity, salinity, temperature, suspended matter and similar factors.

The present account, being brief, can only partially answer these questions, but it does add an additional one: are the structures which we see today a reflection of the environment in which we find them and, if not, what other processes have been involved in their formation? Such a question is perhaps only of academic interest to the biologist, concerned more with the existence and character of a substrate than with its origin, but it is of fundamental importance geologically.

There are a number of relevant published observations on this area, the more recent being Lewis and Taylor (1966); Taylor (1968); Lewis (1968, 1969) and Rosen (1971). Of these Taylor and Rosen have concentrated on biological aspects and Lewis sedimentological. The author's own work commenced in 1964 and has included three field seasons on Mahé (1965–1966, 1967–1968 and 1969–1970) and one on Aldabra (1969). It is proposed first to describe the constructional forms present and second, to outline the general morphology of the reefs around Mahé, showing how the constructional forms are related to them. Finally, an attempt will be made to relate these features to the history of development of the reefs.

DESCRIPTIONS OF CONSTRUCTIONAL FORMS

In order to clarify the discussion it seems desirable to define "reef." This is here understood as a rocky eminence at or near sea level. It may be an isolated pinnacle or bank of a size measured in tens of metres or greater, or extend as a shelf from the shore having a steep seaward margin. In the latter case three important descriptive areas can be recognized, fore-reef, reef-edge and back-reef.

The interaction of physical, chemical and biological processes leads at the present day to the construction of three distinctive forms which are partly a reflection of ecology and are often spatially related. These are characterized by an *Acropora* assemblage, a *Porites* assemblage and a third basically calcrudite accumulation. These are not necessarily mutually exclusive; they will be described in turn and brief comments made on their distribution. The associations can be readily identified in Taylor's (1968) and Rosen's (1971) work and detailed ecological information can be gained from these sources. Faunal comments here should be treated as abbreviated and for the purpose of definition only.

The Acropora *assemblage*

As the name suggests, this assemblage is dominated by species of *Acropora*. It is regarded as a series, one end of which is characterized by species of *Acropora* of the *A. formosa/A. pharaonis* type which are conveniently called "stagshorn" and the other by *A. humilis, A. digitifera* and related forms with *A. irregularis.*

Stagshorn corals generally are known to have high growth rates (Vaughan and Wells, 1943; Goreau, 1961) and, given suitable environments, give rise to extensive thickets metres or tens of metres in diameter which may consist exclusively of this morphospecies.

They appear in general to be sensitive species, requiring high light intensities and access to open waters with free circulation. Their success in such areas might be attributed to their high rate of ground-covering growth effectively swamping competition, but this is not certain. As the basal portions of the colony die they become brittle, their strength being further reduced by the activities of boring algae and sponges. Breakage under gravity or wave-induced pressures results in the production of coarse debris partly interlocking the living frame and becoming encrusted with calcareous algae where circulation is good. The net effect of these processes is the growth of a bank, rising above the sea floor, with a slope generally less than 30°, by an amount proportional to the time interval over which growth has taken place. These structures seem incapable of growth in areas of high wave impact since the corals themselves, being by nature fragile, cannot become established under such conditions.

The largest area falling into this category is probably on the north-western side of Cerf Island where prolific growth occurs on a broad gently sloping surface rising to a depth of only 1–2 m. Similar growth is also present along rather limited sectors of "reef front" on the western margin of Cerf Passage a probable difference in the initial surface being reflected in a steeper slope (Fig. 2). Stagshorn growths

FIG. 2. *Acropora* assemblage: a stagshorn-clothed reef front on the western side of Cerf Passage south-west of Port Victoria lighthouse. Depth approximately 4 m.

are not, however, confined to such areas, they are found on the west coast off Anse Soleil in approximately 8 m, at Port Launay in 3·5–4 m and in North-West Bay and similar open water areas. Comparable, though smaller, structures occur in a number of other localities growing on a variety of bases and seeming to differ in no important respect from patches which may be individual colonies of *A. pharaonis* found in shallow water back-reef environments on, for example, the Anse aux Pins reef flat.

Within a general *Acropora* assemblage patches of stagshorn may decrease in size and frequency, their place being taken by a varied association including *Acropora humilis*, *A. diversa*, *A. digitifera*, *A. irregularis* and *A. hyacinthus*. This is a more tolerant association and some forms such as *A. humilis* can withstand emersion, forming the edge fauna in more sheltered areas. With increasing wave impact their place is taken by *Pocillopora* of the *danae-meandrina* group and, in rough water environments, by *Millepora*, with *Tubipora* and other alcyonarians. Here the *Acropora* spp. are forced back a little from the edge to less vulnerable sites. In areas of very high impact only calcareous algae grow.

The tolerance of this group extends towards the cloudier and more variable situations occupied by the *Porites* association and in what can be called intermediate areas there is a certain amount of overlap.

Generally this *Acropora* assemblage can be regarded as more typical of open waters on slopes commonly of 20° or less to depths in excess of 20 m (North-West Bay). Some growths, particularly of *A. irregularis* are clearly adjusted to water movements and show a strong lineation of major and minor branches parallel to the surface on which they grow and to the direction of wave approach. This association occurs on a number of reef fronts south of North-East Point and elsewhere on which corals may be found growing either on loose debris, on material bound by calcareous algae, or as the upper fringe of a growth frame the basis of which is formed by *in situ* and overturned colonies of earlier generations. This last situation is perhaps best seen in banks off Anse aux Pins and east of St. Anne and Cerf Islands. In these areas ridges occur up to 20–30 m wide and 70–100 m long rising 6 m from a floor which is commonly almost flat and essentially bare of corals. These banks appear to be the direct result of the interdependent growth of successive generations of colonies of the corals concerned (Fig. 3).

Fig. 3. *Acropora* assemblage: a view of the face of an *Acropora* ridge extending at right angles to the reef front east of Anonyme. Depth about 5 m. Fish in this and later photographs (approximately 10 cm in length) give an indication of scale.

The Porites *assemblage*

This is dominated by massive colonies of *Porites lutea*. In some areas it consists almost exclusively of this coral but elsewhere these may be accompanied by *Porites nigrescens* and species of *Psammocora, Echinopora, Galaxea, Lobophyllia* and others. This community flourishes best in waters which are generally calm and characterized by extreme or erratic temperature and salinity conditions, sometimes combined with turbidity or depth-induced low light intensity. They seem in general unable to tolerate wave impact and grow only as small colonies or not at all where circulation is good.

These predominantly massive colonies, growing one upon another, have a tendency to produce steep-walled or cliff-like reef-edges. Such massive growth frames have been recognized in a number of areas, occurring in two main situations. First, as pure free standing growth pinnacles which may be ten metres or more in diameter and rising a similar amount from the sea floor (see Fig. 4) and second as a growth frame superimposed on a bank of some other origin.

A number of pinnacles are to be found on the east coast in the Port Victoria area, generally within embayments wholly or partly separated from the open sea. Smaller, though structurally identical pinnacles, have been noted in an embayment off the east coast of Cerf Island (in 8 m), at Port Launay (in 4 m), at Anse Soleil (8 m) and at various other localities where they have a direct relationship with isolated colonies growing free on the sea floor. Allied to the latter are colonies growing on and ultimately covering banks of loose coral debris (a good example off Anse Etoile) or other origin. It is clear that difficulties arise in the interpretation of *Porites*-lined channel margins such as those north of Port Victoria where one cannot, by direct observation, be certain that the edge is or is not a result of the growth of colonies similar to those now forming its face. Some evidence is available and will be discussed below.

Calcrudite accumulations

These include any bank-like features produced by the mechanical accumulation of coarse fragments of corals, algae, molluscs, echinoderms and others, generally of a size measured in centimetres. Such bioclastic debris will, of course, occur in any area of prolific coral growth, intermingled and to a large extent interlocked, with growth frame, and commonly crusted with calcareous algae. These occurrences are, however, excluded from this category which is reserved for accumulations where coral growth is seen as an addition to rather than

Fig. 4. *Porites* assemblage: a general view of a cliff-like face of *Porites* edge on the north-western margin of the channel to Port Victoria inner harbour. Depth about 8 m.

the basis of the structure (Fig. 5). Two examples will serve to illustrate the point. A bank of approximately 400 × 250 m lies off Anse Etoile. The outer surface of this slopes to the north-east at about 10–15° to depths of greater than 10 m and though it bears local sparse growths of the *Acropora humilis/digitifera* assemblage the bulk of it consists of loose coral debris among which fragments taken to be stagshorn *Acropora* are prominent. Moreover, at the upper end of the slope towards sea level, a number of shallow channels (1–1·5 m deep) are

Fig. 5. Stick *Acropora* debris forming a bank on a level floor adjacent to the narrow reef on the north-east side of Port Launay (depth 3–4 m). Calcrudite accumulations on the Anse au Pins platform, off Anse Etoile, or elsewhere look essentially similar.

cut into this material which appears to be loose and unconsolidated. Large areas in shallow water are covered by dense growths of *Sargassum* so that accretion does not appear to be active. The bank top is flat, a little below low-water springs, and much of it is cavernous, debris being bound by calcareous algae, while the nearshore slope, though steeper (40°) than the seaward is again loose and bears scattered colonies of *Porites*. The second occurrence concerns almost the entire length of the Anse aux Pins edge. Here much of the back-reef area lies up to a metre or more below low water springs. It is notable, however, that at the seaward margin there is a more or less abrupt step up to this level formed by the landward spread of coral debris. This is always encrusted by calcareous algae and along its seaward margins is bound into place by them to form a continuous cavernous frame. The inner margin of this, however, which may be 10 or more than 100 m to landward, is commonly loose and it grades into isolated shingle banks which are aligned parallel to the dominant current direction.

These are not the only examples of calcrudite accumulations and others are morphologically and texturally similar. In most cases there

is little doubt that the debris has been derived from the area to seaward
and yet there are few of them in which the seaward slopes now bear
coral growths likely to form a suitable source area for the sediment.
This is obviously an anomalous situation and it therefore seems worth
considering whether these accumulations are contemporary or are
relicts from an earlier phase in the present accumulation cycle. However,
before attempting this it seems necessary to describe the Seychelles
reefs as a whole.

MORPHOLOGY OF SEYCHELLES REEFS

In this section it is proposed to summarize briefly the morphological features of Seychelles reefs as they now are and show the extent
to which the structures described above contribute to them. To this
end it is convenient to define four broadly based and overlapping groups
of structures.

1. Exposed reefs
2. Sheltered reefs
3. Rocky platforms
4. Non-reef coral and algae growths

The characteristics of each of these will be described together with
some of their more general implications. It is important to note that
observations have for the most part been restricted to superficial
aspects of the reefs and that little is known as yet of the substructure.

Exposed reefs

These are best and most typically developed on the east coast,
particularly on the north-south section which occupies the southern
half of the island. This is made up of two principal bays, Anse aux Pins
in the north and Anse Royale in the south, together with minor embayments.

Anse aux Pins, taken as an example, is about 6 km in length and
at its widest point the reef edge is about 650 m from the shore. The
edge is almost continuous, roughly parallel to the coast and broken
only by one major channel. Along the length of the reef and with
minor variations also parallel to the coast, a series of major ecological
and sedimentological zones can be recognized. These are well known
on many comparable reefs and have been described in some detail for
Mahé by Taylor (1968). With some modification in nomenclature they
are here defined as:

a) The beach

b) Rippled sand zone
c) Grass beds (principally *Thalassia* and *Syringodium*)
d) Open sands with cobble ridges clothed in *Sargassum* and *Turbinaria*
e) The reef edge (a composite zone with several subdivisions defined principally by corals)
f) The fore-reef slope
g) The floor in front of the reef.

Each of these zones is characterized by a particular faunal and floral assemblage and, to some extent, by characteristic sediment and sedimentary structures. Their general layout can be seen in Fig. 6.

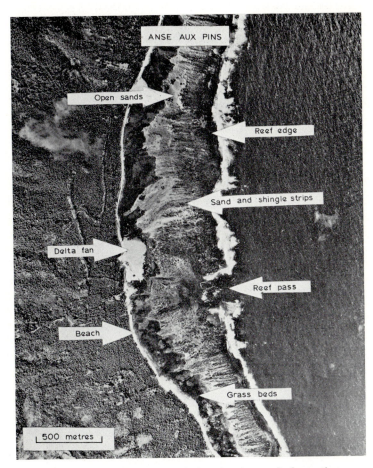

FIG. 6. Anse aux Pins: aerial view showing marked zonation.

Since the present account is concerned largely with structural features little comment will be made on the back-reef areas, though it is to be noted that the cobble ridges have been referred to under calcrudite accumulations (above).

In the reef edge environments, bioconstruction, principally by corals and encrusting calcareous algae, dominates other processes. Given that these areas fall broadly within the *Acropora* assemblage described above, the detailed structure is controlled by local ecological factors. At the shoreward margin of the edge-zone a low platform is built up by expanded plate-like growths of *Acropora humilis*. To seaward of these in some areas inclined columns of *Pocillopora* of the *P. danae-meandrina* series form a distinctive unit. This coral apparently thrives in active surf and yet does not seem able to tolerate direct wave impact. Hence, in areas subject to such impact, colonies are seen on the land-ward end of oblique columns formed by the directed growth of succes-sive colonies in similar positions.

On the seaward margin of the edge the dominant forms are usually alcyonarians, species of *Millepora* together with occasional *Heliopora*. The growth forms of these emphasize vertical sheets and the structures produced in the resultant rock body are quite different from those of the inner sub-zones.

Throughout the edge-zone coral densities are highly variable and there are in some areas few or none. Many surfaces bear soft corals and zoanthids which contribute little to the structure, but dead corals and all other available surfaces are crusted with calcarious algae resembling *Lithophyllum*.

The critical point about all such edges is that they are *higher* than the general level of the reef flat. Their upward growth is limited by the ability of the component corals to withstand emersion and the apparent lack in this area of any spray-zone growth of calcareous algae (Fig. 7).

The edge, therefore, does not show evidence of a progressive sea-ward migration, but has apparently originated close to its present site. The back reef areas are veneered with sediment, thickest in the cobble, grass zone and deltaic areas where accumulation rates are higher, but apparently based on some existing platform. Indeed, beneath the sediment surface on Anse aux Pins, Bel Ombre and a number of other localities corals and coralgal blocks (not representative of an edge zone fauna) can be found with smooth planated surfaces of erosional origin.

All of the reefs exposed to the open sea on the east coast have a structure approximately similar to this; where they become narrower,

FIG. 7. Anse aux Pins: a general view of the emersed edge at low water springs, showing its elevation in relation to the general level of the platform. Note the density of the coral cover and the absence of an algal rim.

the innermost zones are the first to disappear, producing situations as at Anse Forbans where rippled sand and grass zones are absent. Conversely, with increasing shelter, as for example off Anse Etoile, the outer sub-zones disappear and the seaward margin of the edge is made up of colonies of *Acropora humilis*.

The reef edge on Anse aux Pins is broken into by a number of narrow surge channels (a few up to about 2 m deep) the deeper of which are floored with small amounts of loose sand and other, coarser, debris. The walls of these channels form comparatively sheltered environments for the growth of corals not normally found in areas subject to direct wave impact. The growth of these corals, together with calcareous algae, particularly along the rim of the channel in the zone of maximum water movement, can be expected to lead ultimately to a roofing over of the channel which, as it becomes progressively more restricted, provides a trap for any loose debris moving over the surface of the reef.

The reef-front and its facing floor are commonly variable. Detailed examination of the southern half of the Anse aux Pins reef shows that much of the front is a bare "rocky" surface crusted with calcareous algae with few or no living corals, those present having the appearance of being a late addition to, rather than an integral part of, the structure. The slope is commonly between 25° and 30° and is marked in some areas by a series of grooves 1–2 m deep and 2–4 m apart. At the southernmost end, however, opposite Pointe au Sel village the edge is breaking up under wave impact and joint defined blocks are separated by deeper (about 3 m) gullies floored with coarse sand and rounded blocks of well cemented limestone. Surfaces are almost devoid of corals, which again appear as late additions. Because of surface crusts of algae and the nature of the components it is difficult to be sure that the larger masses are limestone, but it seems probable that they are. Smaller masses of coral and algae material have been detached and thrown up onto the reef edge in this area.

The floor in front of the reef lies at between 8 and 10 m, sloping gently and apparently flattening to seawards. This is also variable, but along the section examined coral growth is the exception rather than the rule. Much of the surface is bare and rocky, the "rock" being algally crusted carbonate debris which may or may not be lithified. On this there may be loose cobbles of coralgal debris aligned in some cases to form a well marked lineation parallel to wave directions. Locally there are patches of *Sargassum* and *Turbinaria* and larger sand bodies whose strongly rippled surfaces suggest that they are mobile. These become particularly frequent close to the Anse aux Pins channel. Isolated corals or small patches do occur at intervals, but the bulk of growth and what are undoubtedly the most prolific areas of coral growth are confined to a comparatively small number (three south of the channel) of *Acropora* assemblage ridges, described in an earlier section and extending at right angles to the shore. These are the only areas, leaving aside the edge zone, in which active accretion appears to be taking place. There is no evidence that the reef itself is particularly active or that it is riding forwards over a talus slope, which in these areas does not exist (Fig. 8).

This description is broadly true for floors off Cerf, St. Anne and Anonyme. All of these islands have been extended laterally by accretion of coralgal fragments and some *in situ* growth. Anonyme in particular has on its northern side a wide lateral extension and it is clear that this is higher on the seaward side where a narrow ridge has been built up to the level of low-water spring tides by a calcrudite accumulation firmly bound by calcareous algae. The landward sides of these islands vary. For Anonyme there is a comparatively wide sandy shelf, clothed with *Syringodium* and bordered by a *Porites* association. On the south western shore of Cerf the reef is narrow and is clearly a growth frame,

Fig. 8. Anse aux Pins: a general view showing the level floor at approximately 12 m depth off the reef edge. Note to the left (looking south) the abrupt termination of one of the *Acropora* assemblage ridges (here including Faviids and *Porites*). Much of the floor adjacent to the reef platforms along the eastern shore has this general appearance.

although much of it is dead. Its maximum elevation is only about 2 m and in front of it a sandy floor slopes gently away towards the centre of Cerf Passage. The area north of Cerf and around Moyenne is a more open sandy environment with *Porites* knolls.

Sheltered reefs

The most interesting area of modification on this coast is that around Port Victoria harbour. The reefs in this area are in a sense sheltered from any but a weakened, refracted, wave attack by the offshore islands of the Cerf and St. Anne group. It is to this that they owe some of their peculiarities, others will emerge in the description following.

At their widest point the reefs in this area extend nearly 2 km from the shore, but they are divided by channels and hollows, and their outermost margins tend to be represented by isolated flat-topped banks and pinnacles. A number of streams flow onto the reef flats and the inshore margins in many areas are thus characterized by contamination with terrigenous quartz and clay minerals, and by structures associated with deltaic deposition. In the past some of these areas were clothed with mangroves, but they have been cleared and now contain a faunal association in which *Uca* and *Gafrarium* are prominent.

The back-reef areas away from these influences are wide and sandy with local clumps of grass (*Enhalus* north of Port Victoria) and isolated coral colonies (*Galaxea, Favia* spp. and others) appearing towards the edge of the bank, whether this is open sea or a channel. There is commonly only a narrow fringe of thalloid algae corresponding in a loose sense to the wider brown algal and cobble zone on Anse aux Pins. The channels and hollows within the boundaries of the reef extend to depths of 10–15 m, generally increasing seawards. They are normally steep-sided and floored with a poorly sorted sediment which is always veneered with mud when examined (calm weather). This is typically marked by large numbers of mounds produced by burrowing crustacea. Two end members in a series of reef-front types can be recognized. The faces open to the sea, with a freer circulation, are generally of lower slopes (about 45°) and bear an *Acropora* assemblage, while in the more restricted areas there is first a loss of corals such as *A. irregularis* and then the appearance of *Porites, P. nigrescens* and *Psammocora*. These are initially accompanied by digitate *Acropora* species but in the inner channels massive colonies of *Porites* (up to 4 m diameter) and its associates dominate cliff-like faces. Parallel faunal changes may also occur downslope so that the same edge may bear *Acropora* spp. along its upper margin and *Porites* below. At about 15 m depth coral density has commonly decreased to leave a slope of about 45° mantled with mud or small amounts of coral debris and bearing scattered large colonies of *Favia* spp., *Porites* and *Pachyseris*. Corals growing at or near the level of low water spring tides in these areas are commonly flat-topped. This could be either the result of an active planation or simply a reflection of the corals' inability to grow above this level. In spite of its considerable tolerance for extreme conditions generally *Porites* seems unable to survive emersion.

Behind the coral-bearing edges the reef flats tend to be 1–1·5 m below the coral-defined surface. Within the area close to the edge smaller *Porites* and other corals grow towards their limiting level and are often themselves flat-topped. They are accompanied by cavernous rocky pinnacles rising to the same level and consisting of dead coral and algal frame clothed in *Sargassum* and bearing few living corals. These are separated by open sandy floors with isolated clumps of a large-leaved *Halimeda* and extensively burrowed by shrimps. In this area, therefore, as on Anse aux Pins, the edge is in fact higher than the reef flat.

The sediment on channel floors is highest and apparently thickest at their landward ends, but leaving aside any terrigenous debris there is no compelling reason for assuming that it is derived either from landward or seaward. There are in fact certain problems in a landward derivation since the reef edge is the highest point. Examination suggests that it is unlikely that sediment often finds its way over this living barrier, hollows between corals are often entirely free of sediment. Instead of a general movement to and cascading over edges, there appears to be a comparatively small number of gaps, generally near channel heads, through which sediment moves, principally under the influence of stronger ebb-tide currents.

Edge zones are narrow and channel floors have few corals, these being generally near to the walls, probably having simply fallen off and continued growing. One sees at this time no evidence of a history of progressive closure of these areas by forward migration of channel walls, and there is some evidence to support a contrary view from excavations made in connection with airfield construction. These are in the area behind Anonyme and South East Island and extend up to 20 m below sea level. They were at the time of examination (January, 1970) some hundreds of metres in length, and in none of those examined was there any indication of a continuous coral frame. Unpublished data from more than a hundred boreholes also show that corals occur in pinnacles, and debris, and strongly suggest that edges have formed approximately where they stand and do not represent an end-point in a series of forward migrations from a palaeo-front.

Non-reef growth areas

It has been noted that areas of prolific coral growth are not habitually linked with morphological features called reefs, and it is the purpose of this section to examine such occurrences.

Offshore from the main reef front throughout the Port Victoria area are scattered pinnacles and banks, some of them within channels, others making up the "edge" facing open water. They include growth frame and mechanical accretion features, but in addition to these there are high points on the floor well away from surface reefs. Some of these rise to within 5–6 m of the surface, others are somewhat deeper. All have margins with low slopes and taper out gently into a smooth predominantly sandy floor. Many of these banks bear corals, which are sometimes a *Porites* and sometimes an *Acropora* assemblage, but there is little evidence to suggest that they are or are not the product of coral growth. Geophysical surveys have shown that the lower limiting granite surface is an irregular one, and in general it seems quite probable that these are simply high points in the floor, perhaps underlain by granite, which just happen to have been colonized by corals. There are similar areas of prolific coral growth on a level floor of about 10 m depth north west of St. Anne.

Such coral patches also occur on the west coast. They have been found in North-West Bay at depths of from 4 m to more than 25 m. Some do occur on convenient high points, but others may be found on otherwise level floors. Small reefs are developed in this area on the north-south coast south of Northolme. These are very narrow and are in many cases debris accumulations with erosional channels cut into their margins. Coral faunas are of low density, in contrast to the high density and diversity of fauna found in shallow water (4–5 m) clear of the reef front (Fig. 9). The east-west section east of Bel Ombre has

Fig. 9. Non-reef prolific growth area. This example is in about 4 m depth off Anse Soleil. Note the high density cover of living corals and compare this with Fig. 10.

no true reef, but composite colonies grow at frequent intervals along the margin of a sandy shelf which supports a narrow grass zone. Such areas have a gradational relationship with steeper granitic coasts many of which support quite rich coral faunas either actually on the granite (west of Bel Ombre) or on a flat floor at the foot of the granite slope. These may form banks as at Anse Soleil, or may simply be sparse patches. The granite surfaces are particularly interesting in that many of them do plunge directly into waters of 5—10 m depths and that flutes and grooves on them, which are believed to be subaerial in origin, also extend to these depths with little modification by features ascribable to present sea level.

Rocky platforms

It has already been noted that coral growth on Mahé, and particularly on the reefs, is poor in comparison to other areas. To emphasize this point, there are a number of "reefs" on which there is little or no coral growth.

At Police Bay, at the extreme southern tip of the island, a narrow platform some 20 m wide is developed in the eastern half of the bay. Throughout its width this is divided by prominent spurs and grooves, the latter up to about a metre wide and deepening seawards. Most of the visible surface is crusted with calcareous algae, but beneath this cover corals are also present even though the platform itself is almost devoid of living corals. Some of the grooves are floored with sand, but the walls are a dense scoured limestone surface, stained grey. There is no doubt that this is a cemented rock extending for several metres below present low water. The reef-front in this area has a low slope (15° in places) and is predominantly "rocky", surfaces being crusted with algae. Living corals are generally rare or absent, and observation suggests that the rock extends for *at least* 5–6 m below sea level (Fig. 10).

At Petit Police the beach is fringed with extensive developments of hard, well-cemented, beach-rock. To seaward of this there is a platform some 20 m wide with a near vertical seaward edge. The rock throughout this platform is a hard, well-cemented, calcarenite, differing in no important respect from adjacent beach-rocks. Limited coral growth does take place along the edge of this platform, although corals tend to be stunted as a result of exposure to waves where they do not occupy protected sites such as joint-controlled fissures. Serpulids form minor constructive mounds rising from the surface of the platform towards its northern end. It is concluded that this platform is entirely erosional in origin.

Rocky surfaces of similar appearance but unknown structure are also present at Port Glaud.

There are still a number of distinctive areas which have not so far been considered, including some of the larger bays on the west coast. In some of these such as Grande Anse the shore is wholly sandy and

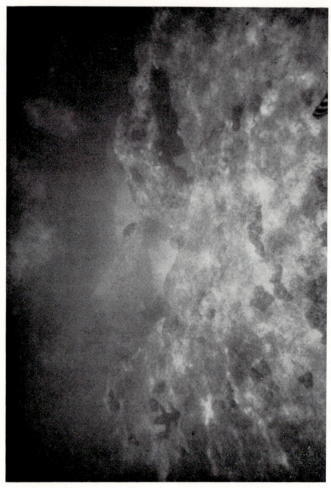

Fig. 10. General view of rocky floor in 3–4 m depth off Police Bay platform. Note the absence of corals and the fact that this surface is an algally crusted carbonate rock. This general appearance is typical also of much of the southern end of the Anse aux Pins "reef front" and other areas noted in the text.

there seems to be no significant coral growth within the immediate area. At Anse la Mouche and Anse Boileau on the other hand shelves are developed up to 500 m or more in width. At Anse la Mouche there is a distinction between a sandy shelf on the southern side of the bay, with a wide grass zone and coral patches developed along its steeper seaward slope, and a "reef" along the northern side with a well defined edge. In several bays on this coast, notably Anse Takamaka, Anse Gaulettes and Barbarons, there are narrow reefs, apparently built mainly by debris accumulation and bearing little or no coral growth. These are presumed to have a gradational relationship with structures bearing coral growths of higher density.

DISCUSSION AND SPECULATION

From the foregoing account it seems that physical and biological processes lead at the present day to the construction of three distinctive forms which are partly a reflection of ecology and are often spatially related. These are, the *Acropora* assemblage, the *Porites* assemblage and calcrudite accumulation. They are not mutually exclusive, and they have a gradational relationship with areas of low accumulation, gravel patches too small to be called banks, and coral thickets with relief no greater than that of individual colonies. It is important to note that there seems to be no close correlation between areas currently recognized as "reefs" and those with the most prolific coral growth. It is clear that there are both "reefs" with essentially no corals and areas of high coral productivity which would not be so called.

For those to whom "reef" and "coral reef" are synonymous this does seem to be an anomalous situation but, as has been indicated, relationships are often such as to suggest that contemporary growth and accumulation is an addition to some previous structure which may have looked quite different. It is not part of a continuing process of unvarying accumulation such as, for example, continuous coral growth. Structures have been described on which there is little or no contemporary accumulation and it therefore seems reasonable to suggest that similar platforms or banks may also be present beneath areas where accumulation is taking place.

How could such banks be formed? It is well known (e.g. Fairbridge, 1950) that reef-like shapes are capable of being developed by erosion upon rocks which are not essentially of reef origin. Over a number of years authors have further drawn our attention to the possibility, and indeed probability, that in certain reefs current growth is a superficial development upon an antecedent base which has previously been modified by erosion. The idea clearly owes something to Daly (1915) but among more recent proponents of variations we may list MacNeil, 1950, 1954; Cloud, 1959; Goreau and Burke, 1966; Hoffmeister and Multer, 1968; and Moberly, 1968. Emersion seems to be a necessary corollary to such erosion and is probably accompanied by some cementation (see Dunham, 1969; Braithwaite, 1968). One imaginative view of the kind of sub-aerial events suggested is that of Flint *et al.* (1953), while it is to MacNeil (1954) that we owe the transference of this idea (with due acknowledgement to his predecessors Asano, 1942; Yabe, 1942) to its present form and application to reefs.

The reefs of the Seychelles rest upon an irregular granite surface which, however, is very probably benched. There are few absolute ages available for any of the carbonate material at the moment. Veeh (1966) using Th^{230}/U^{238} and U^{234}/U^{238} ratios has put ages of 140 ± 30 ($\times 10^3$) and 80 ± 40 ($\times 10^3$) years on certain raised limestones in the Seychelles. These occurred at heights of 6–9 m above present datum and are clearly pre-glacial. The world-wide emergence corresponding to the Würm–Wisconsin glacial probably resulted in the removal of much of the limestone deposited at this high level and we have no knowledge of how much of it might have remained in areas now occupied by reefs. It is clear, however, that no carbonate deposition can have taken place within this area for some considerable time if one assumes (as seems reasonable) stability of the land. The post-glacial submergence, taking place around 9000 B.P. and corresponding as it probably did with a general rise in temperatures of tropical surface waters, almost certainly resulted in the growth of corals. Had the sea level rise been continuous 0nd regular one might have expected these corals to have formed reefs after the classic Darwinian pattern, but there is good evidence that this was not the case. Submergence throughout the world was an erratic process and though the net movement of sea level may have been upwards there were times when it was stationary or falling.

Chronologies are available, Fairbridge (1961) lists "the Bahama Event" (4500 years B.P.) and "the Crane Key Emergence" (3300 years B.P.) among others, while Bloch (1965) gives a number of more recent fluctuations. Many of these might be applicable to features on Mahé, but it is not necessary to accept them to appreciate how comparable changes might influence the processes of reef formation.

Low sea levels are critical since they would be expected, by lowering base level, to have initiated a new cycle of erosion. One might reasonably expect that any emergence would bring about a rapid cementation of the unstable aragonite-bearing sediments, but this seems not to have been the case. Some superficial cementation may have occurred, taking the form of a "case hardening" such as that on Aldabra, where tight well cemented limestone is almost confined to erosion surfaces. Areas of cement have been noted on Anse aux Pins and at Petit Police, but sediment might equally have remained uncemented as are the sub-recent "plateau" deposits on Mahé.

In any event, it seems probable that erosion of newly emergent reefs took place producing channels and hollows. Once a channel was determined by such run-off the pattern of water circulation would help to maintain the feature even though corals would re-establish along its margins as sea level once more rose (cf. Moberly, 1968).

Unpublished borehole evidence suggests that sediments in any one location have changed fairly abruptly on a number of occasions, and it is tempting to suggest that these changes are to be linked with sea level changes, though they are not in fact correlatable among themselves.

Using figures only half of those estimated by Vaughan (1919) (but see also Goreau, 1961) on growth rates, a reef some 200 m thickness could have been produced in the time available or, alternatively, one stretching further from the shore. In fact there is probably less than about 30 m maximum thickness of carbonates in the reef areas and in many places there are no reefs at all.

In conclusion it seems probable that growth of the reefs has been in a series of comparatively small increments, each being followed by emersion and a period of erosion during which thickness was reduced. Probably none of these was greater than 2–3 m and contemporary accretion is probably on a surface about 2 m below present low water (pure speculation) and has only reached sea level where growth or sediment accumulation rates have been sufficiently fast; principally on the reef edges.

Though they are commonly linked, coral growths and reefs are separate phenomena. For the fringing reefs of Mahé, morphology and structure are functions of history rather than of present coral growth and ecology, and it seems likely that this may also be true for other reefs and coral growth areas.

ACKNOWLEDGEMENTS

Work was begun in the Seychelles in 1962 by a group headed by the late Professor J. H. Taylor, and it was tragic that his first visit to the Seychelles with the author in 1967–1968 should have resulted in his untimely death. The author would like to acknowledge the debt he owes to Professor Taylor both on a personal level and from the point of view of the project.

The work was supported initially by the Royal Society and the Department of Scientific and Industrial Research. Expenses for the author's 1965–1966 field season were met by the Carnegie Trust for the Universities of Scotland and since 1967 the project has been financed by a Natural Environment Research Council Grant.

Leave of absence was generously granted to the author by the Universities of Dundee and St. Andrews.

Unpublished information on site investigations was made available by Mr. G. G. Pickton (Ministry of Public Building and Works), and Mr. Van der Hof (Costain–Blankevoort) granted access to dredging operations.

Laboratory and transport facilities were provided by Mr. G. Lionnet (Director, Department of Agriculture, Seychelles) and other assistance by Mr. K. Jivan Shah.

Mr. B. R. Rosen and Mr. M. R. Talbot both assisted in the field over complete field seasons and contributed to the results.

The author gratefully acknowledges the help given to him by all of these and others involved in the work.

References

Asano, D. (1942). Coral reefs of the South Sea Islands. *Rep. Tôhoku Imp. Univ. Geol. Palaeont. Inst.* **39**: 1–19. (In Japanese, see Burke, H. W. 1951).

Bloch, M. R. (1965). A hypothesis for the change of ocean levels depending on the Albedo of the Polar Ice Caps. *Palaeogeog., Palaeoclimatol., Palaeoecol.*, **1**: 127–142.

Braithwaite, C. J. R. (1968). Diagenesis of phosphatic carbonate rocks on Remire, Amirantes, Indian Ocean. *J. sedim. Petrol.* **38**: 1194–1212.

Burke, H. W. (1951). Contributions by the Japanese to the study of coral reefs. *Memo. for record, Military Geol. Branch U.S. Geol. Surv.*: 43 pp. (English summaries of papers in Japanese).

Cloud, P. E. (1959). Geology of Saipan, Mariana Islands: Submarine topography and shoal water ecology. *Prof. Pap. U.S. geol. Surv.*, **280**-K: 362–445.

Daly, R. A. (1915). The Glacial Control Theory of coral reefs. *Proc. Am. Acad. Arts Sci.* **51**: 157–251.

Dunham, R. J. (1969). Early vadose silt in Townsend mound (reef), New Mexico. *Publs. Soc. econ. Palaeont. Miner., Tulsa* **14**: 139–181.

Fairbridge, R. W. (1950). The geology and geomorphology of Point Peron, Western Australia. *J. Proc. R. Soc. West. Aust.* **34**: 35–72.

Fairbridge, R. W. (1961). Eustatic changes in sea level. *Physics Chem. Earth*, **4**: 99–185.

Flint, D. E., Corwin, G., Dings, M. C., Fuller, W. P., MacNeil, F. S. and Saplis, R. A. (1953). Limestone walls of Okinawa. *Bull. geol. Soc. Am.* **64**: 1247–1260.

Goreau, T. (1961). Problems of growth and calcium deposition in reef corals. *Endeavour* **20**: 32–39.

Goreau, T. and Burke, K. (1966). Pleistocene and Holocene geology of the island shelf near Kingston, Jamaica. *Mar. Geol.* **4**: 207–225.

Hoffmeister, J. E. and Multer, H. G. (1968). Geology and origin of the Florida Keys. *Bull. geol. Soc. Am.* **79**: 1487–1502.

Lewis, M. S. (1968). The morphology of the fringing coral reefs along the east coast of Mahé, Seychelles. *J. Geol.* **76**: 140–153.

Lewis, M. S. (1969). Sedimentary environments and unconsolidated carbonate sediments of the fringing coral reefs of Mahé, Seychelles. *Mar. Geol.* **7**: 95–127.

Lewis, M. S. and Taylor, J. D. (1966). Marine sediments and bottom communities of the Seychelles. *Phil. Trans. R. Soc.* (A) **259**: 279–290.

MacNeil, F. S. (1950). Planation of recent reefs in Okinawa. *Bull. geol. Soc. Am.* **61**: 1307–1308.

MacNeil, F. S. (1954). The shape of atolls: an inheritance of sub-aerial erosion forms. *Am. J. Sci.* **252**: 401–427.

Moberly, R. (1968). Loss of Hawaiian littoral sand. *J. sedim. Petrol.* **38**: 17–34.

Rosen, B. R. (1971). Coral communities of Mahé, Seychelles. *Symp. zool. Soc. Lond.* No. **28**, 163–183.

Taylor, J. D. (1968). Coral reef and associated invertebrate communities (mainly molluscan) around Mahé, Seychelles. *Phil. Trans. R. Soc.* (B.) **254**: 129–206.

Vaughan, T. W. (1919). Corals and the formation of coral reefs. *Rep. Smithson. Instn.* **1917**: 189–276.

Vaughan, T. W. and Wells, J. W. (1943). Revision of the sub-orders, families and genera of the Scleractinia. *Spec. Pap. geol. Soc. Am.* **44**: 1–363.

Veeh, H. H. (1966). Th^{230}/U^{238} and U^{234}/U^{238} ages of Pleistocene high sea level stand. *J. geophys. Res.* **71**: 3379–3386.

Yabe, H. (1942). Problems of the coral reefs. *Rep. Tôhoku Imp. Univ. Geol. Palaeont. Inst.* **39**: 1–6. (In Japanese, see Burke, H. W. 1951).

Symp. zool. Soc. Lond. (1971) No. 28, 65–86.

MAYOTTE BARRIER REEF AND LAGOON, COMORO ISLANDS, AS COMPARED WITH OTHER BARRIER REEFS, ATOLLS AND LAGOONS IN THE WORLD

ANDRÉ GUILCHER

Institute of Geography, University of Paris, Paris, France*.

SYNOPSIS

Mayotte barrier reef seems to be the only feature of this kind in the Indian Ocean. Comparisons are made with similar structures in Polynesia, Melanesia and Micronesia, and with other reefs, especially atolls, in the Indian marine space. The following points are examined: number of passages connecting the lagoon with the open sea as related to density of former subaerial valleys; low islands, or sand cays, on the barrier, located near outlets, infrequent as on the Queensland and New Caledonia barriers, unlike those occurring in the Society Islands and at Madagascar; absence of pink algal ridge as in the greater part on the Indian Ocean, unlike Micronesia and Polynesia; occurrence of faroes as barrier elements, related to wave refraction at outlets and compared with similar features in New Caledonia and in the Maldives; calcium carbonate content in the recent deposits of the lagoon, intermediate between the content in Bora Bora and Southern New Caledonia lagoons, and in Tahiti and Eastern New Caledonia lagoons; explanation of these differences by the ratio between the area covered by the central islands and the lagoons.

INTRODUCTION

This paper consists of comparative remarks about the Mayotte reef and lagoon, which were described previously in detail (Guilcher *et al.*, 1965; see also Guilcher, 1963, 1965b). Mayotte barrier reef is certainly the best feature of this kind in the Indian Ocean. It even seems, as Davis (1928: 372) already noticed, that no other true barrier reef exists in that ocean, in opposition with the Pacific Ocean, where such structures are widespread in Queensland, the Gambier Islands, the Society Islands, Wallis, the Fijis, New Caledonia, the Solomons, Bougainville, Bismarck Archipelago, Eastern New Guinea, the Carolines, Indonesia, etc.

Mayotte barrier reef (Fig. 1) is built around an extinct, complex volcano, 660 m high, 38 km long and 21 km wide in its emerged part. It covers an area of 370 sq. km. De Saint Ours (1958) considers that this volcano is possibly Miocene (but no absolute datings seem to have been made so far). The barrier is clearly related to a subsidence of the volcano, and this subsidence itself was complex since a double barrier is found in the southwest, extending for 18·5 km. The larger, outer barrier extends over a total length of 140 km. Volcanic eruptions much

---

* Present address: Faculté des Lettres, B.P. 860, 29N Brest, France.

5

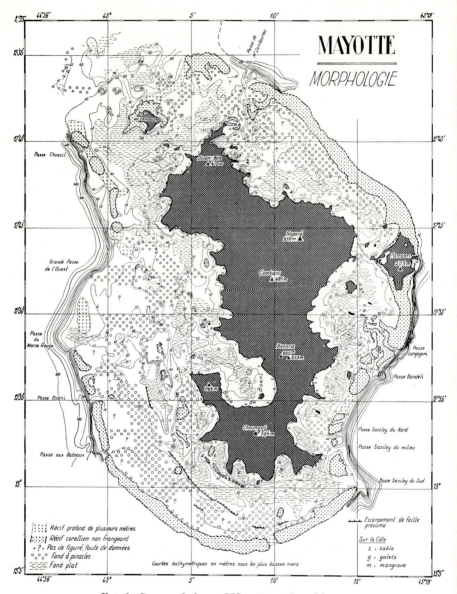

FIG. 1. Geomorphology of Mayotte reefs and lagoon.

younger than those which built the mainland (Lower or Middle
Pleistocene?) have cut across the eastern portion of the barrier, thus
creating Pamanzi Island in which ashes are mixed with broken pieces
of corals. This fact demonstrates that the barrier existed well before

Holocene times. The width of the lagoon varies from 3 to 15 km; its depth exceeds 30 m in most places and reaches approximately 80 m in the West-South-West.

PASSAGES AS RELATED TO FORMER VALLEYS AND TO AREA COVERED BY THE CENTRAL ISLAND

A first fact of interest is the number of passages connecting the lagoon with the open sea. At least nine passages cut across the barrier, and most of them can accommodate ships. In addition, the western and the northern sections of the barrier are discontinuous and more or less drowned in several places, thus contrasting with the southern and the eastern sections. Two passages at least, Longogori Passage (Fig. 2) and M'Zambourou Passage (Fig. 1), are clearly occupied by drowned valleys, as deep as 50–60 m (Longogori) and 80 m (M'Zambourou). Longogori Passage meanders typically as a subaerial valley. The upper parts of these valleys have been recognized in the lagoon by echo-sounding. Other passages seem to have also been initially true valleys, but sand bars were subsequently built by the surf across their outer ends, and corals grew on the sediment, thus obscuring the initial shape. Such is the case of Bandeli Passage, and probably North Saziley Passage and South Saziley Passage. It may be that other passages in the West had the same evolution and were filled by recent coral sedimentation, since the author has discovered in the northwestern part of the lagoon another submarine valley, 60–70 m deep, the outlet of which has not been found.

Another evidence for former subaerial erosion in the lagoon is the occurrence of several depressions, 60–70 m deep, with steep sides and flat floors, which seem to be closed depressions and are thought to have a karstic origin. Pinnacles raising in one of them point to the same interpretation as they seem to be former "hums".

Accordingly, we come to the conclusion that the large number of passages across the barrier is related to an erosive phase which occurred during the low sea level connected with the last glaciation (and during older glaciations?). Radiating valleys starting from the central volcano were incised into the calcareous deposits of the lagoon, in which a karstic morphology also came into existence. These radiating valleys escaped from the lagoon across the barrier. It is possible that the rainfall was larger than now, favouring a more efficient erosion by rivers. Modifications in drainage and in positions of passages may have resulted from successive fillings during high sea levels. So far, however,

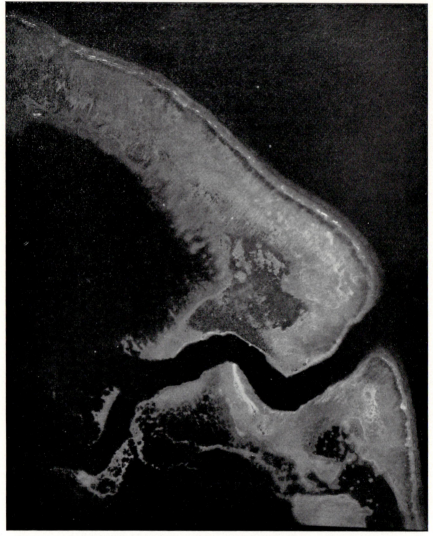

Fig. 2. Longogori Passage in Mayotte eastern barrier. Institut Géographique National, Paris, Copyright.

no local evidence has been found for older high sea levels, perhaps because the subsidence has been going on slowly until the present time.

Now, if barrier reefs in the Pacific are considered for comparison, it will be seen that the number of passages is often large in these areas, even if we exclude very shallow gaps, called *hoa* in Polynesian language, which allow the surf to spread over the reef into the lagoon, and if we consider only passages at least several metres deep (*ava* in Polynesian). At Ponape, Caroline Islands, the number of passages is 19, and most of them lie off drowned valleys (Tayama, 1952: 238). At Palau and at Truk in the same group, many passages also exist: several are connected with drowned valleys at Palau; the relation is more obscure at Truk, which is an almost-atoll (Tayama, 1952: 238, 242, and charts). The barrier along the southeastern side of Bougainville Island is cut by numerous wide gaps. According to charts, the situation is the same around the northwestern part of Gazelle Peninsula, New Britain; on the north coast of Manus Island, Bismarck Archipelago; around Southeastern and Eastern New Guinea and Tagula Island (Davis, 1928: 363–368); etc. The relation of passages with valleys in lagoons and on dry land is often evident in these islands (e.g. at Tagula: Davis, 1928: 365), and the same is true in New Georgia, Solomon Islands (Stoddart, 1969a: 393), and in New Caledonia where drowned valleys have been described off Tuo (Guilcher, 1965a: 184, 193), and in Saint Vincent Bay (Avias, 1965). Off Queensland (Fairbridge, 1950: 366, 379), the northern portion of the barrier, lying off Cape York Peninsula and at the East of Torres Strait, consists of reefs much more continuous than in the South, off Cairns and Townsville, where isolated, widely scattered patches occur at the outer edge of the shelf, as if the density of passages would be related to the density and size of the continental rivers. In the Society Islands, there is generally a connection between the size of the central islands and the number of the passages. The smallest islands, Maupiti and Bora Bora (26 and 38 sq. km) have only one passage in their barriers: three passages exist at Huahine (70 sq. km); nine (closely related to the main valleys) are found around the twin volcanoes of Raiatea and Tahaa (260 sq. km); and about thirty around Tahiti, the largest and highest island in the group (1042 sq. km). Wallis near Western Samoa, where the central island Uvea is approximately the same size as, but much lower than, Huahine, has one deep passage connected to a submarine valley system in the lagoon, and three shallow ones (Doumenge, 1961, and charts).

So far as the number of passages is concerned, Mayotte thus seems to be representative of what occurs on barrier reefs in general. The most enclosed lagoons are found around the smallest central islands, because passages are generally outlets of river systems and such systems are stunted when islands are very small. With its moderate or inter-mediate size, Mayotte has a number of passages intermediate between dwarf islands as Maupiti and much larger islands with many radiating valleys as Tahiti. Sub-continents or continents such as New Guinea and Australia amplify the case for large islands.

It appears that these remarks on passages could not be extended to atolls. If shallow gaps, or *hoa*, are excluded, as they were for barrier reefs, the number of passages, although variable in detail, is much smaller as an average around atolls than around barriers. A fairly large number of atolls have no passage allowing navigation: this situation is general in the eastern Tuamotus, and is not unknown in Micronesia (Tayama, 1952: 248). In the Society Islands, only one atoll, Mopelia, has one passage, and the four others have none. Rangiroa, western Tuamotus, which is the second atoll in size in the world (79 km × 30), has only two passages, and Kaukura (44 km × 13), in the same group, has no passage (Guilcher *et al.*, 1969: 40). Examples of atolls with many passages can be found, of course: Kwajalein, Marshall Islands, the largest atoll in the world, is described as having 28 passages (Tayama, 1952: 249). The common scarcity of passages around atolls, even large, in contrast with that occurring in barriers, is probably due to the lack of mountain standing in the middle of the structure: when the lagoon dried during glaciation, there was no reason for the formation of a radiating drainage, and the waters collecting in the lagoon could easily escape through only one or two gaps (although multiple outlets across the atoll rim can be equally understood). When an atoll lagoon has no passage at all, it must be supposed that a gap existed formerly and was subsequently closed by coral growth, as is shown in the present time in some passages around Mayotte. There is evidence for such an evolution in the closed atolls of Micronesia (Tayama, 1952: 248). In any case, if passages are generally an inheritance of former valleys, as they are thought to be by the writer, they often must have been more or less filled since the post-glacial rise in sea level, because passages as deep as the deepest parts of the adjoining lagoons are not frequent.

LOW ISLES, OR SAND CAYS, ON THE BARRIER

In spite of its length of 140 km, the barrier reef around Mayotte bears only four small sand cays. Two of them are located in the southeast, on both sides of South Saziley Passage; the other ones are in the northwest, at the South of Choazil Passage. All are immature, unconsolidated sand cays, apparently devoid of beach-rock, and submerged at high spring tide. Consequently, they bear no vegetation and their shape is subject to variation. Nevertheless, two of them at least are old enough to be mapped on French chart No. 1046, which was surveyed in 1841.

Two problems related to these sand cays will be discussed here: location, and scarcity.

Location

The four sand cays around Mayotte are situated near gaps in the barrier. The cays on both sides of South Saziley Passage (Fig. 3) are typical in this respect. The other ones occur on the margin of shallower interruptions of the reef flat. Such a location is of common occurrence. As Davis (1928: 13), Stoddart (1962a: 100), and others quoted by Stoddart pointed out, it is related to wave refraction. As Davis said, "the longshore drift of the sand on the reef-front beaches is there halted, from whichever way it comes, by the waves that are refracted as they

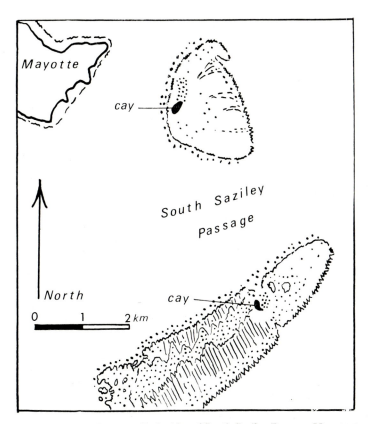

FIG. 3. Immature sand cays on both sides of South Saziley Passage, Mayotte barrier.

sweep into the pass, so that they beat upon both of its transverse shore lines". This principle is well illustrated by many other cays on barrier reefs in the world, especially on the barrier around Raiatea and Tahaa, Society Islands, where five couples of cays are beautifully developed at five passages, at Bora Bora and Maupiti, where the unique passage is also bordered by two sand cays, and in several places around Tahiti.

Scarcity

The problem of the number of cays on barriers is more difficult to solve. There are barrier reefs other than the Mayotte barrier, which are very poor in cays. This is the case in New Caledonia, where the only well-developed, permanent cay on the barrier (1000 km long, northern extensions excluded) is the Grand Tenia Cay at the passage leading to Saint Vincent Bay. It is a permanent feature, including massive beach-rock and covered with bushes, although it is frequently reworked on its sides by waves, as proved by unconformities in the beach-rock. It was recently used as the site of a boring hole. Eight other very small sand cays are mapped on the New Caledonian barrier: two in the West, six in the East. Most of them are immature or even temporary features. However, one mature cay at least has existed near Tuo, East coast (Guilcher, 1965a: 190). Its name is Ain Cay, and it was destroyed by a hurricane in 1932. Its remnants consisted in 1960 of residual beds of beach-rock and of two new small, sandy islets bearing a low, sparse, herbaceous vegetation.

Another barrier poor in sand cays is the barrier extending for more than 300 km off the southeastern coast of New Guinea from Port Moresby eastwards. So far as the writer is aware, it bears only two cays, Great Daugo Island and Little Daugo Island, situated off Port Moresby and located as usual at a passage. They consist of loose sand dunes and consolidated sand and gravel resting upon reef-rock, and are cut at sea level by visors of the tropical type. The outer reefs of the Great Barrier of Queensland are also devoid of sand cays (Stoddart, 1965: 132).

In contrast to such barriers, however, numerous sandy islands, more or less consolidated into beach-rock, cover large parts of other barriers. This is the usual situation in the Society Islands, for example at Bora Bora (Guilcher et al., 1969: 61, plate II), and at Maupiti (idem, plate III), where the islands are mostly located on the wind-ward side, illustrating a general rule also valid for atolls. Similarly in the Gambier Islands, the incomplete barrier surrounding Mangareva and smaller volcanic islands bears several long, wooded, low islands in its windward section. The eastern side of the barrier around Wallis Island bears also six sand cays. Tahiti may be considered as intermediate between these two types, since its barrier bears only seven small cays in spite of its rather great extent (approximately 170 km).

However, in areas where cays are almost absent on outer barriers, cays may be found on inner barriers or on reefs isolated in lagoons. Examples of forested cays are numerous in the New Caledonia lagoon (Guilcher, 1965a); and cays in the lagoon off Queensland are famous and a few have been studied with great accuracy (Steers, 1929, 1937; other references in Fairbridge, 1950, and Stoddart, 1965).

One explanation for the frequency or scarcity of sand cays on reefs has been proposed by Stoddart (1962a: 101). This author has thought that a very small tidal range is an important factor in cay growth. Speaking of reefs bearing many sand cays off the British Honduras, where the tidal range does not exceed one foot, he says: "without such a small range many sand cays on exposed reefs simply could not exist, for the large waves crossing the reefs at high tide would wash all debris into the lagoon. Hence on the Australian Great Barrier Reef, where the tidal range may be over 10 feet, there are very few cays indeed on the outer reefs".

This remark may be applied to the Mayotte reefs, since at Mayotte the tidal range can be as large as 3·50 m during spring tides. In the writer's opinion, the tidal range is certainly a factor of considerable importance at Mayotte, and perhaps the chief explanation of the scarcity and immature character of sand cays on the outer reefs. It may also explain why no sand cay is found even on the inner barrier, because at high spring tide the oceanic waves are able to travel over the outer reefs into the lagoon and to keep a sufficient energy to break on the coast of the mainland. At Port Moresby, New Guinea, the tidal range normally reaches 1·70 m at spring tides; and 1·50 m at Noumea, New Caledonia. Although these figures are much smaller than at Mayotte, one may consider that they are large enough to allow the waves to wash the cays at high spring tides, and to account for their scarcity on outer reefs if Stoddart's views are accepted. In New Caledonia, it seems that the range is sufficient to wash the outer reefs, but not the inner reefs, at which the oceanic swell does not arrive without a considerable loss of energy when it has travelled over reefs covered by only 1·50 m of water. In contrast, the tidal range in the Society Islands is less than 0·50 m, a factor which could explain the large development of sand cays on the barriers (Guilcher et al., 1969). Another similar example is the great number of sand cays of eastern

Guadalcanal, Solomon Islands, where the tidal range does not exceed 1 m at spring tides (Stoddart, 1969b: tidal range p. 410).

However, it must be noticed that the sand cay distribution in the tropical world does not always fit with the tidal range. One region where well-developed, numerous sand cays occur on outer reefs is the northwestern and western coast of Madagascar (Guilcher, 1956, 1958a; Battistini, 1964b). A part of these cays, known as the Barren Islands (off Maintirano), lie on the so-called "drowned barrier", of unknown origin, just on the edge of the Malagasy shelf in the Mozambique Channel. Many cays have grown sufficiently to be vegetated, in spite of the tidal range which exceeds 4 m at spring tides in most places of this coast. Some of them are wholly mature. Another region of the same type is the lagoon off Queensland, where a tidal range reaching more than 3 m, combined with wide gaps between the outer reefs, has not prevented many cays from growing (Steers, 1929, 1937).

These discrepancies show that factors other than the tidal range must certainly be taken into account (just in the same way as wave refraction at passages does not explain everything in sand cay location, as Stoddart (1962a: 102) himself pointed out. Another element must be the frequency of hurricanes, or of periods of heavy surf of extra-tropical origin, which are able to counteract the sand cay evolution towards a mature stage. Evidence for such an action is the destruction, previously mentioned in this paper, of Ain Cay by a hurricane off the east coast of New Caledonia. But the waves generated by hurricanes cannot be so destructive on inner sand cays, situated in a lagoon more or less protected by an outer barrier, as around Queensland and New Caledonia. At Mayotte, hurricanes are rather frequent, and they cannot be neglected in an explanation of the poor sand cay development in that area. Stoddart (1962b, 1963) has reported the catastrophic effects of Hurricane Hattie (1961) on sand cays off British Honduras, and similar actions have been described after the 1958 typhoon at Jaluit Atoll in the Marshall Islands (Blumenstock, 1961). These phenomena are not so efficient, however, as to prevent many sand cays from existing in these two areas. In the Society Islands, where hurricanes are extremely rare, although not completely unknown, periods of heavy swell generated in the Southern Ocean and travelling for thousands of kilometres to the reefs can account for absence of sand cays on the southwestern side (Newell's (1956) and Stoddart's (1969c) swellward side) of barriers and atolls such as Bora Bora, Mopelia, Scilly, and the western Tuamotus (Guilcher et al., 1969: 25, 27, 29, 40), while low isles are found on the eastern side which is subject to moderate, constant swell generated by the Trade-winds. This fact tends to show that, so far as cays are concerned, the occasional heavy swell deriving from the westerlies might be more destructive, in some regions at least, than tropical storms. It is also possible that the presence of many sand cays off the northwestern and western coasts of Madagascar, in spite of the large tidal range, is partly related to the very moderate waves typical of that area except during occasional hurricanes.

An area in which neither low tidal range nor absence of heavy swell can explain the presence of sand cays on outer reefs is the southwestern coast of Madagascar. Battistini has shown (1959, 1960, 1964a) that mature sand cays are not infrequent in this region between the mouths of the Mangoky River and the Onilahy River (approximately 21° to 24°S), although the tidal range reaches 3 m at spring tides at Tulear, and the coast is beaten by swell coming from the Southern Ocean more frequently than in the Society Islands.

The conclusion is that these two factors in location are probably able to explain many particularities in sand cay distribution, but not all the observed facts. The sand cays around Mayotte can be reasonably understood in this way, but something else must probably be taken into consideration in some other areas. Stoddart's opinion (1962a: 102), that exposure and grain-size of available sediment also play a part, is certainly true in explaining locations within small areas, but probably not in accounting for regional distribution. Further research seems to be needed.

ABSENCE OF ALGAL OUTER RIDGE AT MAYOTTE

Since the American studies in the Marshall Islands (Taylor, 1950; Emery, Tracey and Ladd, 1954), the algal ridge, which is made essentially of *Porolithon*, is often considered as a typical feature of oceanic reefs. It has been reported from many reefs in the Pacific Ocean, as Funafuti Atoll, Ellice Islands; Rose Atoll, American Samoa; the Society Islands; the Tuamotu Islands; etc. (Kuenen, 1950: 430; Davis, 1928: 516; Guilcher, Denizot and Berthois, 1966; Guilcher *et al.*, 1969; Chevalier *et al.*, 1968; other references in these papers).

Around Mayotte, however, this beautiful pink ridge is absent, in spite of the oceanic position of the island, and this absence is not peculiar to Mayotte in the Indian Ocean. The writer has never noticed it on the reefs off the northwestern coast of Madagascar. It is not mentioned in Battistini's description of Europa Atoll, Mozambique Channel (1966), nor in Stoddart's description of Aldabra Atoll, British Indian Ocean Territory (1968): but these atolls are slightly emerged features, apparently built during the last interglacial, and have no extensive present-time reef flats. Speaking of Mauritius, Pichon says (1967: 40): "we have observed no typical formation of algal ridge, in spite of the presence of *Porolithon onkodes* which was recognized with certainty". On Tulear outer reef, southwestern coast of Madagascar, Pichon (1964: 118) describes with accuracy the outer reef flat and mentions several species of algae on it, but no typical algal ridge as in the Pacific; *Porolithon* is absent in the list. The present writer has not seen any *Porolithon* ridge on the reefs around La Réunion. In Gardiner's book on the Maldive and Laccadive Islands (1903), this feature seems also not to have been mentioned. In the Seychelles, Lewis (1968; 1969: 104) found an algal ridge on the windward reefs of Mahé Island, but he comments on it as follows: "even on these windward reefs it may be absent. Few of the spectacular features of the algal ridges of Pacific reefs are seen around Mahé". As a matter of fact, the algal ridge seems to be well-developed only in the northeastern Indian Ocean, where it has been mentioned long ago by Darwin (1842) at Cocos-Keeling Atoll (French translation, 1878: 13–15) and more recently by Kuenen on the south coast of Java and the west coast of Sumatra (1950: 431). According to Kuenen (1933; 1950: 431) it is absent in the inland waters of Indonesia (i.e. outside the oceanic environment).

The problem is thus to explain the absence or very poor development of the algal ridge in the greater part of the Indian Ocean, in spite of the presence of *Porolithon onkodes* at least as testified by Pichon at Mauritius (the other pink lithophylloid alga on the algal ridge in the Pacific being *Porolithon craspedium*). It has been repeated by many authors that these calcareous algae, which live mostly a little above mean sea level, need to be constantly washed by surf and swash, so that their sites of predilection are the windward side of the structures and the places strongly beaten by oceanic swells. This adaptation is evident. When the writer visited Tarawa and the nearby atolls in the Gilbert Islands (Guilcher, 1967), he failed to observe any typical *Porolithon* ridge, and he tried to explain this absence by the situation of the Gilberts just under the Equator in the doldrums and very far from the origin of swells generated in the westerlies, whereas the Marshalls in the North, and the South Pacific atolls on the other side, lie in the trade winds and receive foreign swells which still keep a large part of their initial energy. Such an explanation, however, cannot account for the facts observed in the Indian Ocean. Mauritius, La Réunion and Southwest Madagascar receive heavy swells, and even at Mayotte the breakers are distinctly higher as an average than in the

Gilberts. The problem of the *Porolithon* ridge at Mayotte and in the Indian Ocean seems thus to remain open.

FAROES AND FARO-LIKE REEFS ON THE MAYOTTE BARRIER

The examination of the Mayotte barrier provides a good approach to the problem of faro origin.

The name faro is taken from the Maldive Islands, Indian Ocean, where faroes are chains of small atolls forming larger atolls. The latter may also include faroes not only on their outer rims but also in their lagoons (Guilcher, 1958b: 127). Other faroes are reported from the Tagula Barrier in the Louisiade Archipelago, and from the Vanua Levu Barrier, Fiji Islands, both in the South Pacific. This shows that a part of the faroes are found on barriers, and not only on (and in) atolls.

In several places around Mayotte, faro-like reefs occur as components of the barrier, and their origin is clear. The two best examples are Boeni Reef in the western portion of the barrier, and the northern end of the eastern barrier near M'Zambourou Passage (Fig. 4A and B, and Fig. 5). At both places the reef faces the oceanic swell and bears on its lagoonside two distal ends or wings which are recurved so as to enclose a body of water, 20 m deep. Coral patches grow on the sheltered side and tend to fill the small lagoon. It seems evident that the formation of such structures is related to wave refraction in the outlets of the barrier. The influence of refraction at Boeni Faro is testified by two recurved sand spits in the northern part of the feature. At a more advanced stage, the sheltered body of water can be completely cut from the general lagoon, at low tide at least. This stage is represented at the North Reef, on the east side of M'Zambourou Passage (Fig. 4C). The residual lagoons are 3–8 m deep. This more advanced stage is to be explained by the fact that the North Reef receives swells on two sides, northeast and south, because waves travel in the lagoon on a fetch long enough to create, at a lesser scale, a second morphological zonation on the south side. Mayotte lagoon includes also a circular reef, which may be compared with the faroes inside the lagoons of the Maldives (Fig. 4D). This feature is the result of the growth of two coral "arms" which have enclosed a part of the general lagoon.

The investigations carried out around New Caledonia during the Singer–Polignac Expedition have shown that many faroes of the same origin occur in that region too (Guilcher, 1965a,b). The difference is that most faroes (with two exceptions near Tuo) are situated not on the barrier, but inside it. These lagoon-faroes are located in the Great

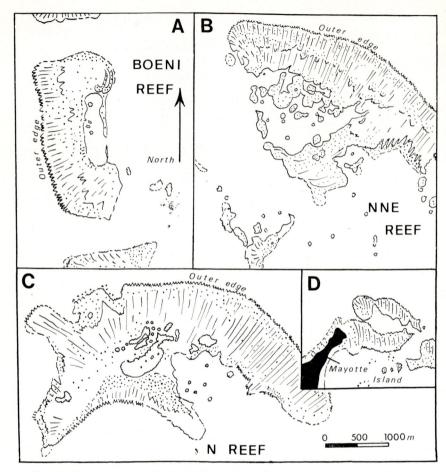

FIG. 4. Three faroes (A, B, C) at different stages in development on Mayotte barrier, and a fourth faro (D) in the lagoon at the northernmost tip of Mayotte Island.

Southern Lagoon. They are horseshoe-shaped features, closely adapted to the southeast Trade-winds prevailing in that area. Most of them are still open on their leeward side; a few are almost entirely closed, but even there the rim of the faro remains thinner on the leeward side as an evidence of the process of formation, thus resembling Boeni Faro (Fig. 4A).

Let us now examine whether the faroes of the Maldives may be explained in the same way as the faroes around Mayotte and New Caledonia. Although the writer has never visited the Maldives, he

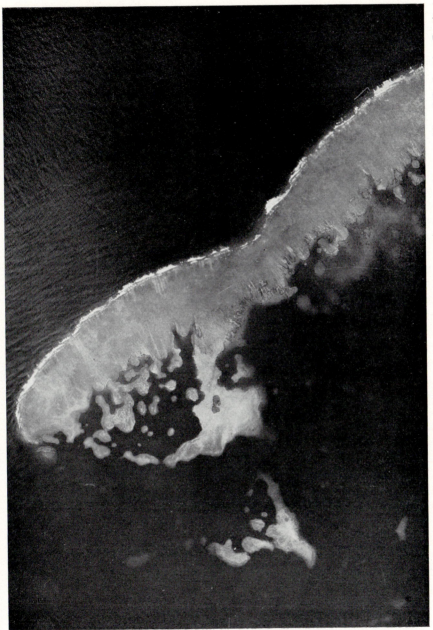

FIG. 5. Faro at the north end of Mayotte eastern barrier. Contrast between inner and outer sides of the barrier. Institut Géographique National, Paris, Copyright.

thinks, after an examination of Admiralty charts, Nos. 66a, 66b and 66c, which give an accurate picture of this archipelago at the scale of 1 : 292 000, that there is a good possibility for a positive answer. It is well-known (Ramanathan, 1966–1969) that the Maldives lie in the Indian monsoon belt, with alternating winds from southwest in Summer and from northeast in Winter, the former travelling on a longer fetch than the latter and generating a much heavier surf. Therefore, it will be expected that the best faroes are 1) found on the west sides of the atolls, which are exposed to the southwestern monsoon; 2) that these faroes are quite often asymmetric, the west side of the rim being much thicker than the east side; 3) that they are not unfrequently horseshoe-shaped, the lagoon of the faro communicating sometimes freely in the east with the general largoon and 4) that the best examples are found not close to the equator at Suvadiva Atoll and Kolumadulu Atoll, but between 3° 30′N and 7°N, at Ari Atoll, Malosmadulu Atoll and Tiladummati Atoll, where the fetch of the southwestern monsoon is longer and consequently the surf more efficient. At places where faroes are well developed on the east side of the atolls, they show a reverse asymmetry, with a thicker rim (and often islands) in the east, certainly related to the swell generated by the northeast monsoon which is prevalent in wave generation on that side (good examples at Tiladummati Atoll and Male Atoll). As to the faroes located inside the lagoons of the large atolls (the best ones being in South Malosmadulu Atoll, Ari Atoll and Male Atoll), they are, in contrast, almost symmetric, and could be explained as two opposite horseshoes built under the influence of the alternating monsoons, as Krempf (1927) proposed for the Paracels in the South China Sea. Krempf's theory is certainly not valid for atolls in general; but, so far as the Maldives are concerned, the writer's opinion is that, if large Maldive atolls have a structural origin, there is some evidence for a climatic origin of Maldive faroes. The comparison with the observations at Mayotte seems fruitful in this respect.

Another possible explanation of faro-like reefs is the influence of oceanic water entering the lagoon through a passage and favouring the growth of coral arms on both sides of the inlet. If the incoming current flows for some reason along the inner side of the barrier, the consequence may be the enclosure of small lagoons between the barrier and the coral extensions stretching along it. Such a process seems to have acted near Longogori Passage (Figs 2 and 6). It has also been suggested by Tayama (1952: 256, 110) for features observed in Micronesia. The "subsidiary lagoons" mentioned by Wiens (1962: 2–7) in Pacific atolls could perhaps be explained in the same way.

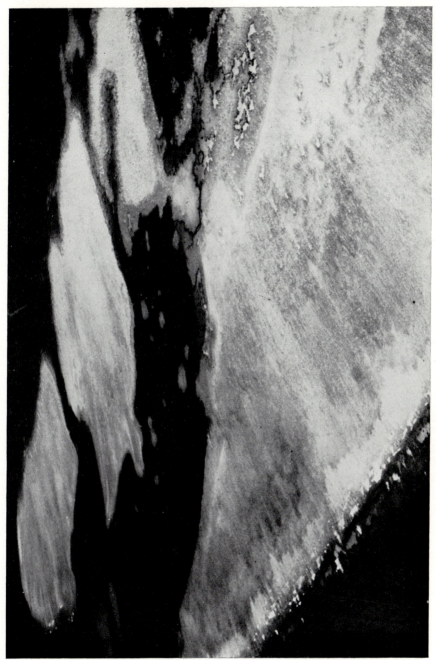

FIG. 6. Faro-like reef near Longogori Passage. Photo. A. Guilcher.

It seems wise not to extend these interpretations to Vanua Levu and Tagula barriers. Since these regions are affected by recent, strong tectonic warping or tilting, accurate studies in the field are needed before any conclusion is proposed. Apparent faroes may prove to be small atolls, or double barriers, or even single barriers around rocky islets.

CALCIUM CARBONATE CONTENT IN THE RECENT DEPOSITS
OF THE LAGOON

Calcium carbonate content measurements are useful as a test of terrigenous versus organogenic origin of lagoon sediments. The investigations which were made in this respect in the Mayotte lagoon were a part of a more general research which extended also to lagoons behind barrier reefs around New Caledonia, Bora Bora, and Tahiti. The comparison of the results in these various lagoons leads to the following general conclusion (Guilcher, Saint-Requier and Doumenge, 1966; Guilcher, 1968; Guilcher et al., 1969).

In humid and semi-humid tropical countries, the percentages of terrigenous and skeletal particles in lagoons behind barrier reefs depend chiefly on the ratio between the area covered by the central, not corallian, islands and the area covered by the surrounding lagoons. The other factors are subsidiary.

Mayotte lagoon represents intermediate conditions. The calcium carbonate content, which was determined on 200 samples distributed in all parts of the lagoon, lies between 98 and 100% in the outer and middle areas, and close to the coast in the northwest. In the inner area especially in the west, but also in the northeast, the east, and the south, it is between 94 and 47%. The terrigenous fraction, which is fine, is supplied by rivers during the rainy season. It is remarkable that such fine particles settle at less than 5 km from the coast, and that, regardless of the relief energy, the calcareous sedimentation predominates in all but three samples.

Tahiti, where the mountain is larger (1042 sq. km) and higher (2241 m in the larger volcano, 1332 m in the smaller one), and the lagoon comparatively narrow (2 or 3 km as an average in areas where it is best developed), has a lagoon much more influenced than around Mayotte by sediments deriving from the land: the medium calcium carbonate content is only 55% and it exceeds 90% in only 6 samples out of 72. The sediments are more terrigenous around the larger volcano than around the smaller one. Another lagoon where the terrigenous fraction is considerable is the Tuo Lagoon on the east coast of New Caledonia, where the calcareous content falls below 50% in a strip as wide as 9 km in the eastern part of the lagoon. The influence of the large, mountainous mass of the mainland is obvious.

In contrast, the Great Southern Lagoon of New Caledonia has a sedimentation almost entirely calcareous throughout (more than 90% in 84 samples out of 88; everywhere more than 87%). This is because it projects into the sea and is bordered by land only for a very short distance in its northern part. Similarly, at Bora Bora 51 samples out of 52, equally distributed throughout the lagoon and comprising some beach samples, contain more than 98% of calcium carbonate. Although the mountain is high (727 m), its influence is negligible because the rocks are pervious, the area is too small (38 sq. km) to permit a true drainage pattern to exist, and the lagoon is comparatively wide.

It must be noticed that all these islands receive an abundant rainfall, reaching for example 80 in. (2 m) at Bora Bora meteorological station, a figure particularly significant with regard to the very small terrigenous influence.

These results, which started in the Indian Ocean and were later extended to the Pacific Ocean, tend to show that the influence of the central islands on lagoon sedimentation is smaller than one could have expected *a priori*. It may be supposed that in almost-atolls (wide lagoons with small central islands) as Truk and the Gambiers, the terrigenous influence is probably almost nil; and that in the Queensland lagoon, which is wide compared to the catchment area of the Queensland rivers flowing to the Coral Sea, the terrigenous influence probably does not extend far from the continent. Precise data for these lagoons, and for others such as the Wallis lagoon, would be welcomed.

True barrier reefs are not found in arid areas such as the Red Sea. Such areas would evidently be less favourable to terrigenous sedimentation than humid areas.

The Mayotte barrier reef and lagoon, although unique of their kind in the Indian Ocean, provide from various points of view useful data for comparison with the coral belt as a whole. Still further aspects could have been considered and compared, such as the double barrier, the spur and groove system, the zonation on the barrier, the sea-grass meadows: providing material for another paper.

REFERENCES

Avias, J. (1965). Sur l'origine du gête de chrome de l'Île Hugon (Baie de Saint-Vincent, Nouvelle-Calédonie). *C. r. somm. Séanc. Soc. géol. Fr.* 301–303.

Battistini, R. (1959). Observations sur les récifs coralliens du Sud-Ouest de Madagascar. *Bull. Soc. géol. Fr.* (7) **1**: 341–346.

Battistini, R. (1960). Quelques aspects de la morphologie du littoral Mikea (côte sud-ouest de Madagascar). *Cah. océanogr.* **12**: 548–571.

Battistini, R. (1964a). *Etude géomorphologique de l'Extrême-Sud de Madagascar.* Thesis, Paris, 636 pp.

Battistini, R. (1964b). Une reconnaissance aérienne des Îles Barren (côte ouest de Madagascar). *Madagascar Rev. Géog.* **5**: 105–115.

Battistini, R. (1966). La morphologie de l'Île Europa. In: Mission Scientifique à l'Île Europa. *Mém. Mus. natn. Hist. nat., Paris* n. sér., A, **41**: 7–18.

Blumenstock, D. I. (ed.) (1961). A report on typhoon effects upon Jaluit Atoll. *Atoll Res. Bull.* **75**: 105 pp.

Chevalier, J. P., Denizot, M., Mougin, J. L., Plessis, Y. and Salvat, B. (1968). Etude géomorphologique et bionomique de l'atoll de Mururoa (Tuamotu). *Cah. Pacif.* **12**: 1–144.

Darwin, C. (1842). *The structure and distribution of coral reefs.* London (2nd ed.: 1874; 3rd ed.: 1889; French translation of the 2nd ed., Paris, Baillière, 1878).

Davis, W. M. (1928). The coral reef problem. *Spec. Publs Am. geogr. Soc.* **9**: 596 pp.

De Saint-Ours, J. (1958). *Etudes géologiques dans l'Extrême-Nord de Madagascar et l'archipel des Comores.* Thesis, Strasbourg (mimeogr.), 205 + 110 pp.

Doumenge, F. (1961). Observations à propos des formations coralliennes de lÎ'le Wallis. *Bull. Ass. Géogr. fr.* 301–302: 186–196.

Emery, K. O., Tracey, J. I. Jr., and Ladd, H. S. (1954). Geology of Bikini and nearby atolls. *Prof. Pap. U.S. geol. Surv.* 260A: 1–265.

Fairbridge, R. W. (1950). Recent and Pleistocene coral reefs of Australia. *J. Geol.* **58**: 330–401.

Gardiner, J. S. (1903). *The fauna and geography of the Maldive and Laccadive Archipelagoes.* **1**. Cambridge Univ. Press: 471 pp.

Guilcher, A. (1956). Etude géomorphologique des récifs coralliens du Nord-Ouest de Madagascar. *Annls. Inst. océanogr., Monaco* **30**: 65–136.

Guilcher, A. (1958a). Mise au point sur la géomorphologie des récifs coralliens de Madagascar et dépendances. *Mém. Inst. scient. Madagascar*, F, **2**: 89–115.

Guilcher, A. (1958b). *Coastal and Submarine Morphology.* London and New York, Methuen and Wiley: 274 pp.

Guilcher, A. (1963). Quelques caractères des récifs-barrières et de leurs lagons. *Bull. Ass. Géog. fr.* 314–315: 2–15.

Guilcher, A. (1965a). Grand Récif Sud, Récifs et Lagon de Tuo. *Expéd. Fr. Récifs Corall. Nouv. Caléd., Fond. Singer-Polignac, Paris*, **1**: 135–240.

Guilcher, A. (1965b). Coral reefs and lagoons of Mayotte Island, Comoro Archipelago, Indian Ocean, and of New Caledonia, Pacific Ocean. In: *Submarine Geology and Geophysics. Proc. Symp. Colston Res. Soc.*, Bristol **7**: 21–45 (London, Butterworths).

Guilcher, A. (1967). Les Îles Gilbert comparées aux Tuamotus. *J. Soc. Océan.* **23**: 103–113.

Guilcher, A. (1968). Les conditions d'écoulement dans trois Îles tropicales d'après les apports terrigènes à leurs lagons coralliens. *Maurice Pardé Commemor. Vol.*, 257–261.

Guilcher, A., Berthois, L., Le Calvez, Y., Battistini, R. and Crosnier, A. (1965). Les récifs coralliens et le lagon de l'Île Mayotte. *Mém. Off. Rech. Sci. Techn. Outremer*, **11**: 210 pp.

Guilcher, A., Berthois, L., Doumenge, F., Michel, A., Saint-Requier, A. and Arnold, R. (1969). Les récifs et lagons coralliens de Mopelia et de Bora-Bora (Îles de la Société) et quelques autres récifs et lagons de comparaison (Tahiti, Scilly, Tuamotu occidentales). *Mém. Off. Rech. Sci. Techn. Outremer*, **38**: 107 pp.

Guilcher, A., Denizot, M. and Berthois, L. (1966). Sur la constitution de la crête externe de l atoll de Mopelia ou Maupihaa (Îles de la Société) et de quelques autres récifs voisins. *Cah. Océanogr.* **18**: 851–856.

Guilcher, A., Saint-Requier, A. and Doumenge, F. (1966). Les teneurs des sédiments en carbonate de calcium dans le lagon de Tahiti, et dans les lagons derrière les barrières coralliennes en général. *C. r. hebd. Séanc. Acad. Sci., Paris* **263**: 25–27.

Krempf, A. (1927). La forme des récifs coralliens et le régime des vents alternants. *Trav. Serv. océanogr. Pêch. Indoch.* **2**: 33 pp.

Kuenen, P. H. (1933). Geology of coral reefs. *Snellius Exped. Eastern Part Netherl. East Indies*, 1929–1930, 5, geol. results, part 2. Utrecht, 126 pp.

Kuenen, P. H. (1950). *Marine Geology.* New York, Wiley, 568 pp.

Lewis, M. S. (1968). The morphology of the fringing coral reefs along the east coast of Mahé, Seychelles. *J. Geol.* **76**: 140–153.

Lewis, M. S. (1969). Sedimentary environments and unconsolidated carbonate sediments of the fringing coral reefs of Mahé, Seychelles. *Mar. Geol.* **7**: 95–127.

Newell, N. D. (1956). Geological reconnaissance of Raroia Atoll, Tuamotu Archipelago. *Bull. Am. Mus. nat. Hist.* **109**: 311–372.

Pichon, M. (1964). Contribution à l'étude de la répartition des Madréporaires sur le récif de Tuléar (Madagascar). *Recl. Trav. Stn. mar. Endoume*, hors sér., suppl. **2**: 81–203.

Pichon, M. (1967). Caractères généraux des peuplements benthiques des récifs et lagons de l'Île Maurice (Océan Indien). *Cah. O.R.S.T.O.M.*, (Océanog.) **5**: 31–45.

Ramanathan, K. R. (1966–1969). Some meteorological results of the International Indian Ocean Expedition. *Morning Rev. Lectures*, 2nd. Oceanog. *Congr. Moscow*, 1966 (UNESCO, Paris, 1969): 227–238.

Steers, J. A. (1929). The Queensland coast and the Great Barrier reefs. *Geogr. J.* **74**: 232–257; 341–370.

Steers, J. A. (1937). The coral islands and associated features of the Great Barrier reefs. *Geogr. J.* **89**: 1–28; 119–146.

Stoddart, D. R. (1962a). Three Caribbean atolls: Turneffe Islands, Lighthouse Reef, and Glover's Reef, British Honduras. *Atoll Res. Bull.* **87**: 151 pp. (also as *Contrib.* 62–63, *Louisiana State Univ., Coastal Studies Inst.*, Baton Rouge).

Stoddart, D. R. (1962b). Catastrophic storm effects on the British Honduras reefs and cays. *Nature, Lond.* **196**: 512–515.

Stoddart, D. R. (1963). Effect of Hurricane Hattie on the British Honduras reefs and cays, October 30–31, 1961. *Atoll Res. Bull.* **95**: 142 pp.

Stoddart, D. R. (1965). British Honduras cays and the low wooded island problem. *Trans. Inst. Br. Geogr.* **36**: 131–147.

Stoddart, D. R. (1968). The conservation of Aldabra. *Geogr. J.* **134**: 471–486.

Stoddart, D. R. (1969a). Geomorphology of the Marovo elevated barrier reef, New Georgia. *Phil. Trans. R. Soc.* (B) **255**: 383–402.

Stoddart, D. R. (1969b). Sand cays of eastern Guadalcanal. *Phil. Trans. R. Soc.* (B) **255**: 403–432.

Stoddart, D. R. (1969c). Reconnaissance geomorphology of Rangiroa Atoll, Tuamotu Archipelago. *Atoll Res. Bull.* **125**: 31 pp.

Tayama, R. (1952). Coral reefs in the South Seas. *Bull. hydrogr. Dep., Tokyo* **11**, 941: 292 pp. (English text: 181–292, and 2 vols. photos. and charts).

Taylor, W. R. (1950). *Plants of Bikini and other Northern Marshall Islands.* Univ. of Michigan Press, 227 pp.

Wiens, H. J. (1962). *Atoll environment and ecology.* Yale University Press, 532 pp.

DISCUSSION

SCHEER: Professor Guilcher has explained the shape of faros in the northern Maldives through the influence of winds from different directions. I will draw your attention to another point. We have in one and the same atoll patch reefs with rounded top, patch reefs with flattened top, patch reefs with a depression at the surface, then mini-atolls, and finally faros, faros with accumulated sand in their lagoon, faros with sand cays, and faros with islands. Could not a faro be the natural result of a patch reef increasing in size?

STODDART: From work in progress on the morphometry of atolls in the Maldives, it is clear that not only does the frequency of faros change systematically from north to south through the Maldive Islands, but so does the maximum and mean depths of the atoll lagoons and also the percentage of the lagoon circumference occupied by reefs which reach the surface. These systematic differences must probably be explained by differences in the rates of reef growth resulting either from environmental gradients at the present day or lags towards the north in the rate of resumption of reef growth following glacial low sea levels. The scale of the variations found suggests that the latter explanation is more likely than the former. It is also important to define what is meant by faro rather precisely: some of the examples shown by Prof. Guilcher from, for example, Mayotte, are not sufficiently like Maldivian faros to merit the same name. They more closely resemble elongate reefs in the British Honduras barrier reef lagoon, which Dr. E. G. Purdy has demonstrated are features which inherit the features of tectonically-determined forms in the underlying older rocks.

Symp. zool. Soc. Lond. (1971) No. 28, 87–114.

MORPHOLOGY AND ECOLOGY OF THE REEF FRONT OF ALDABRA

J. BARNES, D. J. BELLAMY, D. J. JONES, B. A. WHITTON

Department of Botany, The University of Durham, Durham, England

E. A. DREW

Department of Botany, University of St. Andrews, St. Andrews, Fife, Scotland

L. KENYON

Chelsea Arts Club, Chelsea, London, England

J. N. LYTHGOE

Medical Research Council, Vision Research Unit, University of Sussex, Brighton, Sussex, England

and

BRIAN R. ROSEN

Department of Geophysics and Planetary Physics, School of Physics, The University, Newcastle-upon-Tyne, England

SYNOPSIS

This paper sets out the findings of a systematic Scuba diving survey of the reef front of Aldabra, an elevated atoll situated at 46° 20′E and 9° 25′S. In the absence of any other strictly comparable data of this type from the Indian Ocean it does not pretend to discuss regional variation but simply attempts to set down a base line for future comparative work.

The paper describes:

1. The general morphology of the reef front, relating the main features to the degree of exposure to the action of waves and onshore winds. Certain problems concerning the dynamics of reef growth in relation to hurricane force winds are discussed.

2. The general zonation of hard corals on the reef front is described. Zones are tentatively defined using the basic methodology of the Zurich–Montpellier School of Sociology (Braun-Blanquet, 1951). Zones are delimited on the basis of growth forms, restricted species of hermatypic corals, as well as the presence of other taxonomic groups of sessile benthos.

3. The effects of major reef channels on the above zonation is detailed. Striking effects on the distribution with depth and the morphology of certain genera and species are shown. The importance of careful site selection when studying transects for comparative work is emphasized.

THE MORPHOLOGY OF THE REEF FRONT

Figure 1 shows the distribution of transects studied around the atoll. (For exact details of survey methods, see Barnes *et al.* (1970) and

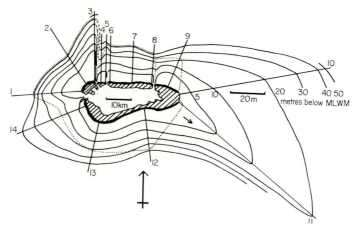

Fig. 1. Map showing the position of the survey transects and approximate contours
of the reef front. Note the difference between the scale of the atoll and the reef front.
MLWM—mean low water mark.

Bellamy, Drew, Jones and Lythgoe (1970)). Study of the transects showed
that the hermatypic corals are most abundant at depths between -10
and -25 m, although isolated colonies can be found from high water
mark to 55 m deep. It also showed that the activity of the reef,
assessed as areas supporting the growth of hermatypic coral, is correlated with Stoddart's (1967) classification of shore types according to
exposure. The system, however, needs to be expanded and we propose
four categories, based on a subjective estimate of exposure to wind
and wave action derived from the position of the atoll in relation to the
Trade-winds. The four categories (see Fig. 2) are detailed below, together
with information about the relevant sublittoral reef phenomena.

   The first type of shore (transects 10 and 11) is the most severely
exposed; neither reef ridge nor reef flat is present. The elevated reef
rock which is deeply eroded into knife-like plates and pinnacles, slopes
gradually into the sea. The reef front itself slopes almost imperceptibly
to a depth of 30 m, below which there is a marked break of slope.
No hermatypic corals are present, the substrate being composed of
compacted coral sand and aggregations of calcareous red algae, "rhodoliths".

   The second type of shore (transects 12 and 13) is less exposed;
a reef flat is present but it is not delimited by a marked ridge. The
elevated reef rock slopes into the sea except at the head of pocket
beaches where there are undercut cliffs. The reef front is characterized
by large areas of dead coral which vary greatly in extent. Sometimes

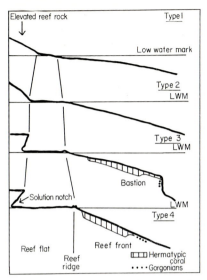

FIG. 2. The principal morphological features of each reef type. The various parts of the reef front are not drawn to scale, the maximum height of the elevated reef rock is 4 m, for the scale of the sublittoral parts see Figs 1 and 3.

the entire reef front consists of dead, but intact, "stagshorn" coral (e.g. transect 12). At the other extreme there are simply dead, eroded and/or partly concreted zones and patches (e.g. transect 13). These observations suggest that non-synchronous catastrophic events have caused massive mortalities.

The third type of shore (transects 4 to 9) is moderately exposed, the reef flat is wide, exposed at most low tides and is delimited by a marked reef ridge. Cliffs undercut by solution are a constant feature of the coast. Hermatypic corals are abundant and the reef front is characterized by deep water bastions. These are massive structures composed of coral rock, protruding up to 100 m out from the general reef front, they are separated from each other by sloping channels which are partly infilled from the landward end by coral, sand and talus. The seaward peak of each main bastion is approximately 25 m below low water mark. Their seaward faces slope steeply, some vertically, others undercut, to a maximum depth of 45 m. Although the bastions were too large to be accurately surveyed by free swimming divers, they were examined as follows. The diving team submerged opposite a fixed land mark to a depth at which the peaks of the bastions were clearly visible. Swimming at a fixed speed, one diver timed the "occurrence" of the bastions, while the other sketched the relevant

features of each. Regular surfacing to allow time checks against fixed
land marks helped to reduce the inaccuracies inherent in the survey
method. Results for part of the series adjacent to transect 6 are given
in Fig. 3. It must be noted that the dimensions given are accurate
only within the limitations of the survey method used. Transects 4
to 8 were all laid down gullies, the profiles of two of the bastions are
shown in the figure.

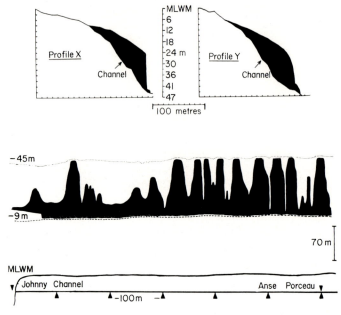

FIG. 3. Details of the deep water bastions adjacent to transect 6.

The fourth type of shore (transects 1 and 2) is the least exposed.
It has the widest type of reef flat and a raised and almost continuous
reef ridge. Cliffs undercut by deep solution notches are a dominant
feature and extensive beaches are present. The reef front slopes more
steeply than in any of the other areas and supports a continuous and
diverse benthic fauna and flora over large sectors.

The observations indicate that the reef is today growing actively
only along the most sheltered shores of the atoll, which is therefore
growing west across the opposing trade winds. This is contrary to
the view that the windward side of atolls provides the best conditions
for coral, and hence for reef growth (Yonge, 1951; Emery, Tracey
and Ladd, 1954; Wiens, 1962).

Aldabra is situated within the northern limit of the hurricane belt, and it is suggested that the direction of growth of the atoll can be explained as an effect of occasional contact with a hurricane. The upwelling of cold water caused by onshore hurricane force winds could account for the large-scale kills described above. After heavy onshore winds, divers saw large areas of the living reef covered with a veneer of freshly deposited sand. It is suggested that massive deposition of sand during hurricanes along the southern shore (which is characterized by large dunes on raised beaches), could also account for the large-scale death of the coral with subsequent erosion and regeneration taking place between such catastrophies.

On the severely exposed coasts such regeneration could be precluded by continuous erosion of the shallower parts of the reef and more regular deposition of sand and talus. Comparative study of a range of reefs passing northwards out of the hurricane belt should help to clarify these correlations and problems. It is interesting to note that the richest growth of coral on Mahé in the Seychelles, which are situated north of the hurricane belt, is also on the more sheltered shores (see Rosen, pp. 163–183, in this volume).

The overall pattern of the contemporary reef front can therefore be explained adequately, the origin of the bastions alone remaining in doubt. It is unlikely that the massive coral growth necessary to form such structures could have taken place below 30 m, and, if so, it seems safe to conclude that the bastions represent an old reef front erosion feature, formed when the sea level was lower, perhaps during the last glacial period. (A hypothetical formation sequence is shown in Fig. 4.) They have a direct analogy in the deep water cliffs described on the western reefs of certain of the Marshall Islands (Wiens, 1962), which, although continuous, have the same depth range as the Aldabra bastions. It must be stressed that they are not analogous to the spurs and grooves nor the buttresses described in many accounts of atolls (Goreau, 1959; Wiens, 1962), which are structures developed in shallow water and are themselves much smaller.

ZONATION OF THE SESSILE BENTHOS

Transect number 1 was studied in great detail using a photographic technique developed by one of us (E. Drew). Full details of the method will be published elsewhere. However, in essence it consists of making a complete photographic record of a marked transect, metre by metre. Analysis of the photographs allows a detailed picture of the structure of the reef front communities to be built up.

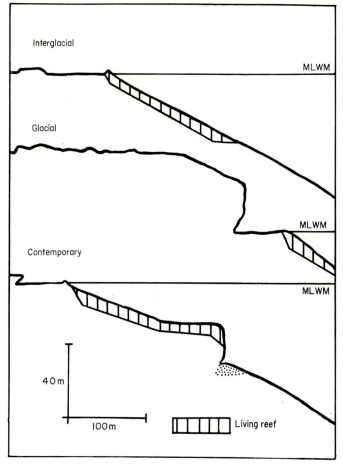

F<small>IG</small>. 4. Hypothetical sequence for the formation of the bastions. Stage 1, interglacial reef forming. Stage 2 glacial, interglacial reef being eroded away, producing a wave cut platform and an undercut cliff. Stage 3 contemporary, the remains of the glacial cliff represents the face of the bastion. The wave cut platform is covered by material eroded from above which has obliterated most of the undercut. The dissection of the reef front into bastions could be explained by fresh water erosion while exposed during the glacial period. N.B. the contemporary reef cliff is not drawn to scale. MLWM —mean low water mark.

Figure 5 shows the distribution of the sessile benthos divided into the main types of organism and the main growth forms of the hermatypic corals with depth. The following ten type/growth form categories are easily recognizable.

1. Honeycomb growth form of upright intersecting plates designated H on the diagrams and tables.

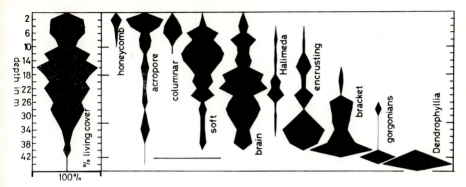

Fig. 5. Distribution of the sessile benthos in relation to depth below mean low water mark, based on the data from the photo-transect 1.

2. Branching growth form typical of the acropore corals, designated A.

3. Columnar growth form of massive upright stalagmite-like columns, designated AC.

4. Soft corals mainly alcyonacians, also including anthozoans and hydrozoans.

5. Brain growth form designated B; these are all small colonies, and hence the term "massive" is not used.

6. Calcareous macrophytes, mainly *Halimeda* spp.

7. Growth form producing extensive encrustations, designated E.

8. Growth forms producing outgrowths resembling bracket fungi, designated Br.

9. Gorgonians, sea fans and sea whips designated G.

10. *Dendrophyllia* spp. designated D.

Study of the distribution of these categories indicates the presence of six distinct zones.

Zone 1. Mean low water mark 6 m depth, a community dominated by honeycomb, branching and columnar forms.

Zone 2. 6 m to 14 m deep, a closed community dominated by soft corals.

Zone 3. 14 m to 28 m, a more or less closed community dominated by brain corals with abundant *Halimeda*.

Zone 4. 28 m to 38 m; open communities dominated by encrusting forms.

Zone 5. 38 m to 42 m; a mixture of bracket encrusting corals and gorgonians.

Zone 6. 42 m to 44 m; a very sparse zone of the ahermatypic coral, *Dendrophyllia micrantha*.

Greatest difficulty was found in distinguishing the boundary between Zones 3 and 4. Reference to collections of corals from the transect, see below, helped greatly in this respect.

The zonation would appear to be related to two main environmental factors which vary with depth. In the shallowest zones decrease in surf action could account for the gradual replacement of the "shock resistant" honeycomb and columnar forms by more delicate colonies of acropores. A constant feature of the reef front on the most sheltered shore at depths in excess of 12 m were large table-like colonies of *Acropora* sp. No. 4. Some of these were more than 1·5 m in diam and were easily destroyed, for example, if they were leaned upon. This fact alone shows that there is a rapid reduction in the effects of wave action, even at these moderate depths. Deeper, the attenuation of light, acting through the dependence of the hermatypic corals on their algal symbionts, could account for the replacement of the self-shading branching corals successively by brains, encrusting, bracket forms, and finally by ahermatypic corals.

VARIATION IN THE ZONATION OF THE REEF FRONT

Once zonation had been established it was not a difficult task to determine the presence and the extent of each zone while diving. The results of the survey of zonation on the 14 transects and at the mouths of each reef channel are shown in Fig. 6. It is at once evident that the zonation is a constant feature of the whole reef front, except along the most exposed shore, and that the main factor affecting the zonation is the presence of the reef channels.

Apart from the main reduction in extent of each zone due to the fan of sand deposited over the reef front below and adjacent to the channel entrance, the channels have two main effects. Firstly, the loss of the gorgonian and soft coral zones and a gradual amalgamation of all the hermatypic coral zones. Secondly, the displacement of the ahermatypic zone into the channel where *Dendrophyllia* spp. can be found almost up to mean low water mark. Within the channels *Dendrophyllia* occurs as a small bush-like growth form (max. 30 cm high), which branches in all directions. This is in marked contrast to the deep water form which consists of large (up to 90 cm high), almost pectinate colonies branching in one plane. It is interesting to note that as the zone swings up into the channel the growth form gradually changes.

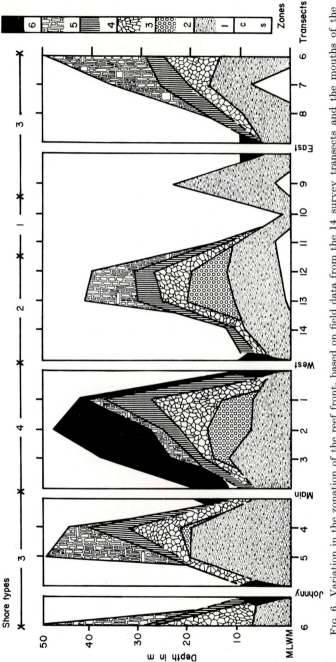

Fig. 6. Variation in the zonation of the reef front, based on field data from the 14 survey transects and the mouths of the channels which are labelled Main, Johnny, East and West, see Fig. 1. C—*Cymodocea*, S—*Sargassum*, Eulittoral species.

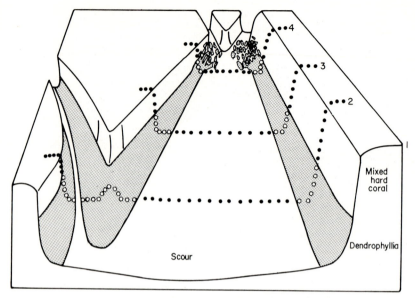

Fɪɢ. 7. Diagrammatic representation of the zonation within the Main Channel.

Figure 7 shows the zonation within Main Channel, which was studied by means of 4 transects. Here a distinct zonation is maintained with *Dendrophyllia* confined to a lower zone. The shallower hermatypic zone includes an admixture of all types of growth form. There is some tendency for the brain corals, which include the largest colonies found on the atoll, to be localized along the lip of the channel. In the shallower waters at the lagoon end of the channel, all zonation is lost and a complete intermingling takes place.

A similar zonation occurs within East Channel, *Dendrophyllia* being present even though it is absent from the adjacent reef front. Zonation in the smaller channels is never well marked, intermingling of all zones taking place from just within the channel entrance.

The rapid flow of water, which characterizes the channel environment must have a main formative effect on the biota present. This is probably reflected by the abundance of the rounded brain forms and the lack of branched colonies, except those typical of the surf zone. However, tidal flow has other than purely mechanical effects, namely, maintaining matter in suspension which cuts down light penetration and represents an abundant supply of food. The interaction of these factors, together with the rapid attenuation of light down the vertical channel sides, could well give the non-symbiotic *Dendrophyllia* some advantage in these shallow water zones. The relevance of the change in growth form is more obscure and the fragility of the *Dendrophyllia*, even in locations subject to currents well in excess of 5 knots, must be noted. Table I gives a list of the deep water corals which are displaced from their normal zones into the channels.

TABLE I

Species displaced from depths into channels

Dendrophyllia micrantha	*Pachyseris laevicollis*
Goniastrea incrustans	*Podabacia sp.*
Leptoseris mycetoserioides	*Porites lichen*
Montipora sp. 2.	*Seriatopora hystrix*

It is therefore clear that the zonation phenomena described are striking features of sublittoral Aldabra, features which must form a basis for future comparative work. However, it is also abundantly clear that when planning any such comparative study, care must be taken in the location of all transects whether surveyed by diving or dredging. Also that all depths recorded for the zone boundaries have only strictly local meaning.

THE ZONATION OF CERTAIN REEF FISH (J. Lythgoe)

A routine count of some 30 species of fish was made on each transect. These species were chosen early in the study chiefly by virtue of their abundance or ease of recognition. From 3–6 counting stations were chosen on each transect, the exact locations depending upon terrain and diving time available. The number of each species visible at one time was recorded. The actual number was counted if there were less than 50 individuals in sight, where there were more the number was estimated to the nearest order of magnitude.

This simple counting technique does not give the actual number of individuals within a known volume of water, partly because some individuals are hidden from view and partly because the visible range depends upon the turbidity of the water and the optical properties of the fish themselves. Nevertheless the technique gives a fair measure of relative abundance, especially for a particular species on a single transect. Counting was generally confined to the reef front itself

6

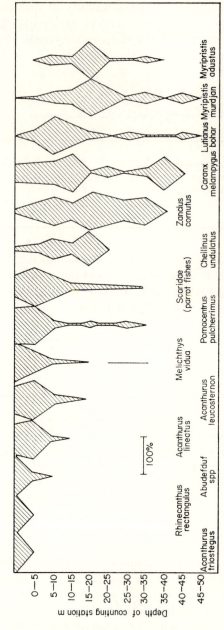

Fɪɢ. 8. Distribution of 14 common reef fish with depth. The count at the depth where each species was most abundant is shown as 100%, all other counts being expressed as a percentage of that figure.

since deeper excursions onto the sand were prevented by limitations of diving. The results for 14 species of fish are presented in Fig. 8.

It is not very meaningful to explain the distribution of fishes in terms of depth alone. Some species such as the garden eels which make burrows in the sand or the trigger fish, *Odonus niger* (Rupp.), which lives under large boulders surrounded by sand probably need the relatively still conditions of deeper water if they are not to be buried or exposed by wave action. Other species such as the Squirrel fishes *Myripristis murdjan* (Forsk.) and *M. adustus* (Blkr.) are associated with table-like coral growth forms which are themselves restricted to depths exceeding 12 m.

There is however, a clearly defined group of fishes that are virtually confined to Zone 1. At least three of these species are surgeon fishes (Acanthuridae) which Hiatt and Strasburg (1960) consider to be exclusively herbivores. *Rhinecanthus rectangulus* (Schn.) is considered by the same authors to be a grazer which forages away from living coral and which feeds chiefly on algae and crustacea. Other Zone 1 fish are *Pomacentrus pulcherrimus* Smith and *Abudefduf* spp. (chiefly *A. sexfasciatus* (CetV.) and *A. septemfasciatus* (Lac.)) which are omnivores sometimes scraping algae from the bottom. A good indicator species for Zone 1 is *Acanthurus leucosternon* (Benn) since it inhabits most of Zone 1 and is one of the most conspicuous fishes in the sea, see Fig. 9A. Gosline (1965) also reports that this is a shallow water species in Hawaii and it would be interesting to study its vertical distribution in other areas. At first glance it is tempting to speculate that the restricted downward distribution of these Zone 1 fishes results from the lack of suitable algal food at greater depths. However algae were observed at all depths visited and one genus (*Halimeda*) was particularly abundant between 15 and 25 m.

On Aldabra the dead alga-covered coral in shallow water is liberally scored by the "beak" marks of parrot fishes. They are known as important grazers (Suyehiro, 1942; Hiatt and Strasburg, 1960; Bakus, 1964). Most of the parrot fishes sighted on Aldabra (see Fig. 9B) were feeding and since more than 60% of the parrot fishes were seen in water shallower than 10 m their destructive effect on the shallow reef must be considerable. *Rhinecanthus rectangulus* is another grazer of the very shallow reef that feeds away from living coral (Hiatt and Strasburg, 1960) whilst the last coral grazer (Randall, 1955) that we have consistently studied, the Giant Humphead Wrasse *Cheilinus undulatus* Rupp., lives somewhat deeper.

Most of the common species were seen all round the island with the exception of the very exposed Point Hodoul transect 10 where we

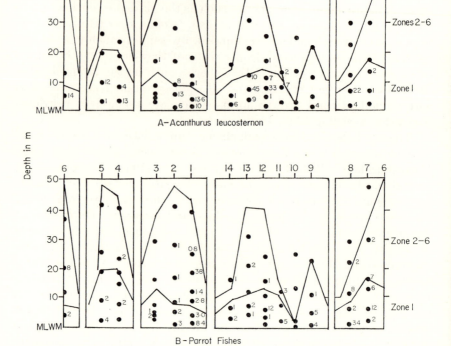

Fig. 9. Actual counts at each depth station on each transect for A—*Acanthurus leucosternon* and B—Parrot fishes. Data for Transect 1 are the means of a number of counts.

found no coral rock at all and the fish fauna was very impoverished. There is an indication that *Acanthurus leucosternon* and *Melichthys vidua*, both shallow water species, live in slightly deeper water off the more exposed coasts. The channels support a very rich fish population both in numbers and species but no fishes were noted that are confined to them except possibly the large trigger fish *Pseudobalistes flavimarginatus* (Rupp.) which makes a hollowed out nest in the sand on the margins, or at the seaward end, of the channels.

FURTHER ANALYSIS OF THE ZONATION OF THE HERMATYPIC CORALS

More detailed analysis of the zonation on the most sheltered shore was made possible by systematic collection of all sessile benthos taken from contiguous 2 m sections of transect 1, at 10 m intervals.

Table II gives the results of the study, data being given for the hard corals only. The Table is arranged in order of distance from the reef ridge and depth, and is structured in the manner of an association table of classic phytosociology (Braun-Blanquet, 1951). The results of a number of random quadrats collected within the general area of transect 1 are included in their respective positions in the Table with relation to depth.

Although it is impossible to draw firm conclusions based on data from a single transect studied in this way, the marked zonation shown by over 50% of the species would appear to indicate that a true sociologic zonation does exist.

Two further growth forms are shown on the table:

1. Designated S, solitary corals of the family Fungiidae.
2. Designated BL, large brain forms with deep surface markings. These are large calice meandroid forms which are often very distinct underwater, due to a brick red fluorescence. Unfortunately, when the polyps are expanded it is impossible to distinguish them from the ordinary brain corals in the photo transect.

Table III shows further analysis of the distribution of species with depth. Figures for the percentage number of species in each growth form and the percentage number of species in each family, are given for each depth studied. This analysis links the growth form and the sociologic data together, and indicates that the boundary between Zones 5 and 6 may be difficult to distinguish.

A tentative series of sociologic groupings are proposed. These complement, enhance and subdivide the growth form, benthos type zonation described above. It is suggested that if these sociologic groupings have anything more than local significance, then certain species and, or species groups could be used as markers for future comparative work. The composite data relating to each zone are summarized below.

Zone 1. Branching and columnar zone. This zone can be subdivided into two parts.

(a) A shallow water form in close proximity to the reef edge, which is poor in species and is dominated by members of the Acroporidae. *Acropora glochiclados* and *Stylophora mordax* could be regarded as marker species.

(b) Slightly deeper and further from the reef ridge, members of the Acroporidae share dominance with members of the Faviidae. Marker species are *Astreopora myriophthalma*, *Porites andrewsi* and *Millepora exaesa*.

TABLE II

Sociological Table based on Data from Transect 1

Depth in metres		1	1	1	2	2	3	2	2	2	5	5	6	7	8	9	11	10	12	15	17	18	18	20	21	22	27	28	33	35	39	41	43	43	44
Quadrat sample number		1	2	3	4	R	5	6	7	8	9	10	R	11	12	13	14	15	R	16	17	18	19	R	20	21	22	23	R	24	25	R	R	R
Species showing Zonation																																		
Acropora irregularis	A	×	·	×	×	·	×	×	·	·	·	·	·	·	·	·	·	·	·	·	·	·	·	·	·	·	·	·	·	·	·	·	·	·
A. glochiclados	A	·	·	×	×	×	·	·	·	·	·	·	·	·	·	·	·	·	·	·	·	·	·	·	·	·	·	·	·	·	·	·	·	·
Stylophora mordax	A	·	×	×	×	×	·	·	·	·	·	·	·	·	·	·	·	·	·	·	·	·	·	·	·	·	·	·	·	·	·	·	·	·
Acropora sp. 2	A	·	×	×	×	·	×	·	·	·	·	·	·	·	·	·	·	·	·	·	·	·	·	·	·	·	·	·	·	·	·	·	·	·
Acropora palifera	A	×	×	×	×	×	×	×	×	×	×	·	·	·	·	·	·	·	·	·	·	·	·	·	·	·	·	·	·	·	·	·	·	·
Millepora platyphylla	H	×	×	·	×	×	×	×	·	·	×	×	×	·	·	·	·	·	·	·	·	·	·	·	·	·	·	·	·	·	·	·	·	·
Montipora tuberculosa	E	·	·	·	×	·	×	×	×	×	×	×	×	×	·	·	·	·	·	·	·	·	·	·	·	·	·	·	·	·	·	·	·	·
Leptoria phrygia	B	·	·	×	·	·	·	×	·	×	×	×	×	·	×	·	·	·	·	·	·	·	·	·	·	·	·	·	·	·	·	·	·	·
Porites lutea	B	·	·	·	·	×	×	×	×	×	×	×	×	×	·	×	·	·	·	·	·	·	·	·	·	·	·	·	·	·	·	·	·	·
Favites abdita	B	·	·	·	·	×	×	×	×	×	×	×	×	×	×	×	·	·	·	·	·	·	·	·	·	·	·	·	·	·	·	·	·	·
Platygyra lamellina	B	·	·	·	×	×	×	×	×	×	×	×	×	×	×	×	×	×	×	×	×	×	×	×	×	×	×	×	×	×	×	×	×	×
Echinopora gemmacea	B/E	·	·	·	·	·	×	×	·	×	×	×	×	×	×	×	×	×	×	×	×	×	×	×	×	×	×	×	×	×	×	×	×	×
Galaxea fascicularis	E/B	·	·	·	·	×	×	×	×	×	×	×	×	×	×	×	×	×	×	×	×	×	×	×	·	·	·	·	·	·	·	·	·	·
Favia pallida	B	·	·	·	·	×	×	×	·	×	×	×	×	×	×	×	×	×	×	·	·	·	·	·	·	·	·	·	·	·	·	·	·	·
Astreopora myriophthalma	E	·	·	·	·	·	×	×	×	×	×	×	×	×	×	×	×	×	×	×	×	·	·	×	·	×	·	×	·	×	·	·	·	·
Porites andrewsi	A	·	·	·	·	·	·	×	×	×	×	×	×	·	·	·	·	·	·	·	·	·	·	·	·	·	·	·	·	·	·	·	·	·
Montipora verrucosa	E	·	·	·	·	×	×	×	×	×	×	×	×	×	×	×	×	×	·	·	·	·	·	·	·	·	·	·	·	·	·	·	·	·
Millepora exaesa	E	·	·	·	·	·	·	·	·	·	×	·	·	·	·	·	×	×	·	·	·	·	·	·	·	·	·	·	·	·	·	·	·	·
Pocillopora eydouxi	A	·	·	·	·	·	·	·	·	·	·	·	·	·	·	×	×	·	×	×	×	×	×	·	·	·	·	·	·	·	·	·	·	·
Fungia (Pleuractis) paumotensis	S	·	·	·	·	·	×	×	·	×	×	×	×	×	·	·	·	·	·	·	·	·	·	·	·	·	·	·	·	·	·	·	·	·
Fungia (Pleuractis) scutaria	S	·	·	·	×	×	×	×	·	·	·	·	·	·	·	·	·	·	·	·	·	·	·	·	·	·	·	·	·	·	·	·	·	·
Porites nigrescens	A	·	·	·	·	·	·	·	·	·	·	·	·	·	·	·	·	×	×	·	×	×	×	×	×	×	×	×	×	×	×	×	×	×
Lobophyllia corymbosa	BL	·	·	·	·	·	·	·	·	·	·	·	·	·	·	·	·	·	·	·	·	·	×	·	·	·	·	·	·	·	·	·	·	·
Goniastrea pectinata	B	·	·	·	·	·	·	·	·	·	·	·	·	·	·	·	·	·	·	×	·	×	·	×	×	×	×	×	×	×	×	×	×	×
Leptastrea purpurea	E	·	·	·	·	·	·	·	·	·	·	·	·	·	·	·	·	·	·	×	×	×	×	×	×	×	×	×	·	×	·	·	·	·

Table II (continued)

		12	14	15	17	12	19	17	12	9	7	12	17	5	11	11	5	12	14	17	15	14	13	8
Pavona varians	E/B		×	×					×	×	×		×											
Montipora erythraea	E		×	×					×	×			×											
Physogyra sp.	BL/E		×				×	×	×	×	×	×	×	×										
Pachyseris laevicollis	BR				×																			
Hydnophora exesa	E				×				×	×	×	×	×	×										
Gyrosmilia interrupta?	BL/E						×	×		×		×	×	×										
Mycedium tubifex	E						×						×	×										
M. tenuicostatum	E						×	×		×		×												
Porites lichen	E/BR						×	×	×	×	×	×	×	×										
Acanthastrea echinata	E/B						×	×	×	×	×	×	×	×										
Pocillopora danae	A												×	×										
Echinophyllia aspera	E									×			×	×										
Herpolitha limax	S									×			×	×										
Symphyllia valenciennesi	BL	×	×				×	×		×		×	×	×										
Turbinaria sp.	BR		×				×	×		×		×	×	×										
Lobophyllia hemprichii	BL											×	×	×										
Podabacia sp.	BR											×												
Seriatopora hystrix	A											×		×										
Leptoseris mycetoseroides	BR/E											×	×	×										
Goniastrea incrustans	E/B											×	×	×										
Agariciella ponderosa	BR											×	×	×										
Plesiastrea sp.	E													×					×	×		×		×
Montipora sp. 2	E													×					×	×	×	×		×
Dendrophyllia micrantha	D																				×			×
Total number of species		8	5	6	6	0	6	5	8	7	13	15	14	15	11	5	12	14	17	15	14	13	8	7

Acropora cf. diversa No. 1 A 7, 14; A. cf. diversa No. 2 A 6; A. monticulosa A 8; A. spicifera A 1, 10, 11, 20, 23, A. sp. No. 4 A 4, 18; A. variablis A 17, 23R; Anomastraea irregularis? B 15R; *Cyphastrea chalcidicum* B 9, 12, 21, 23; *Coscinaraea* sp. No. 1 E 15, 23; *Distichopora fisheri* A 7; *Favites* cf. *pentagona* B/E 9, 12, 21; *F.* sp. B/E II; *Cycloseris cyclolites* S 10R, 15; *Favia stelligera* E/B 14; *Favia* sp. E/B 12; *Hydnophora exesa* E/B 8; *Leptastrea immersa* E/B 7, 15R; *Montipora elschneri* E 15; *Pectinia lactuca* B/E 16, 19R; *Pocillopora damicornis* A 1; *Porites (Synaraea) iwayamaensis* A 3; *Stylophora pistillata* A 8, 15R; *Tubipora musica* B 1; *Pectinia* sp. BL/E 22; *Goniastrea retiformis* B/E 15; *Coscinaraea monile* E/B 15, 23R; *Pavona explanulata* E 16; *Montipora* cf. *punctata* E 16; *Seriatopora* sp. A 16; *Acropora* sp. No. 3 A 16; *Pavona Pseudocolumnastrea)* sp. 20. Sample quadrats are numbered consecutively, R denotes a random sample not on the transect. The occurrence of all species which exhibit no zonation, or for which there is only one record are shown as a running head below the table, e.g. *Acropora* cf. *diversa* No. 1 A, present in samples 7 and 14. These are included in the species totals given at the bottom of the main table.

TABLE III

Analysis of Sociological Zones based on Data from Table II

Depth in metres	% Number of species present in each growth form								% Number of species present in each family														
	Honeycomb	Acropore + Columnar	Brain	Encrusting	Solitary	BL. Meandroid	Bracket	Dendrophyllia	Acroporidae	Pocilloporidae	Milleporidae	Tubiporidae	Faviidae	Poritidae	Stylasteridae	Oculinidae	Fungidae	Mussidae	Siderastreidae	Agariciidae	Caryophylliidae	Pectinidae	Dendrophyliidae
1	18	70	10	·	·	·	·	·	48	22	15	5	5	5	·	·	·	·	·	·	·	·	·
2	·	22	56	22	·	·	·	·	38	8	8	·	30	10	3	3	·	·	·	·	·	·	·
3	·	18	35	35	12	·	·	·	33	7	7	·	26	7	·	7	13	·	·	·	·	·	·
5	7	20	40	26	7	·	·	·	23	6	6	·	30	16	·	3	10	6	·	·	·	·	·
6	6	18	35	35	·	6	·	·	34	·	13	·	34	13	·	·	·	6	·	·	·	·	·
7	·	14	50	36	·	·	·	·	27	·	9	·	46	9	·	9	·	·	·	·	·	·	·
8	·	60	20	20	·	·	·	·	20	20	·	·	20	40	·	·	·	·	·	·	·	·	·
9	·	21	43	29	7	·	·	·	8	8	8	·	60	8	·	·	8	·	·	·	·	·	·
10	·	11	36	36	6	11	·	·	19	13	·	·	26	·	·	7	7	7	7	7	7	·	·
11	·	6	41	41	12	·	·	·	14	·	·	·	44	7	·	·	14	·	14	7	·	·	·

TABLE III (continued)

12	5	20	25	40	5	5	7	7	·	23	12	6	23	6	6	12	6	6
15	·	22	35	22	7	7	·	8	8	8	12	·	8	·	8	8	8	·
17	·	34	22	22	11	11	·	26	12	12	·	12	·	·	12	19	19	·
18	·	21	27	30	8	10	4	·	·	32	12	·	6	·	·	12	19	19
19	·	10	30	30	·	30	·	·	·	29	14	14	·	·	·	·	29	14
20	·	20	27	34	·	6	13	16	·	44	16	·	·	16	·	16	8	·
21	·	9	34	29	5	14	19	·	6	28	12	6	18	6	6	·	6	18
22	·	6	25	44	·	6	19	8	·	35	17	·	8	·	8	8	8	8
27	·	8	19	38	4	19	12	5	10	22	·	10	22	·	10	5	16	16
28	·	7	15	56	·	15	7	8	·	35	8	8	8	8	8	8	8	17
33	·	13	30	39	·	5	13	6	12	40	·	6	6	6	12	12	6	12
35	·	·	·	50	50	50	·	·	·	·	50	50	·	·	·	·	·	·
39	·	·	·	33	33	33	·	·	34	·	33	33	33	·	·	·	·	34
41	·	·	·	·	·	·	·	·	100	·	·	·	·	·	·	·	·	100
43	·	·	·	50	50	50	·	·	·	·	50	50	50	·	50	·	·	·
44	·	·	·	·	·	·	·	100	100	·	·	·	·	·	·	·	·	100

Zone 2. Soft coral zone. Members of the Faviidae are the dominant hermatypic corals, the zone shows high diversity of both species and families. No true marker species are present.

Zone 3. Brain corals. The zone is dominated by members of the Faviidae and is distinguished from Zone 2 by the lack of *Millepora platyphylla*. Marker species include *Echinophyllia aspera, Herpolitha limax, Pachyseris laevicollis, Symphyllia valenciennesi, Porites lichen* and *Podabacia* sp.

Zone 4. Encrusting corals. Large diversity of both species and families. Defined only by the presence of *Agariciella ponderosa* and *Plesiastrea* sp.

Zone 5. Gorgonian zone. This is below the lower limit of the Faviidae and co-domination is shared by the Poritidae and *Dendrophyllia*.

Zone 6. Ahermatypic zone of *Dendrophyllia*.

DISCUSSION

Most accounts of the zonation of reef benthos deal with shallow water phenomena and especially with the eulitorral. Accounts of deep water communities built up from dredging are also quite common (see summaries in Yonge, 1963; Stoddart, 1969). Due mainly to the danger of working from boats near the surf zone, data relating to the immediate sub-littoral are scant.

Wells (1954) describes three zones from the seaward reef front of Bikini. The *Echinophyllia* zone from 18 m to 91 m, the *Leptoseris* zone from 91 m to 146 m and the *Sclerhelia-Dendrophyllia* zone below 146 m. There seems little doubt that the ahermatypic zones from Bikini and Aldabra are analogous. If any further analogies can be drawn it would seem that Zone 3 Aldabra corresponds to the *Echinophyllia* zone and perhaps the more or less ahermatypic *Leptoseris* zone to Zone 5 described above. Although this is pure speculation it is interesting to note that even with the enormous difference in overall depth, the lowest zone in each case consists of ahermatypic non symbiotic species. The role of diminishing light intensity as a factor determining the zonation, at least in part, must therefore be accepted.

Pichon (1964) also describes three zones from the seaward reef slope of Madagascar. These are:

1. L'horizon supérieur from 0–5 m typified by a variety of Acropores and the presence of *Millepora platyphylla*.

2. L'horizon intermédiaire from 5–10 m depth, the fauna includes *Leptoria phrygia* and *Millepora platyphylla* and is dominated by alcyonacians.

3. L'horizon inférieur, 10–15 m, the zone includes many members of *Favia* and *Favites*.

It would appear that the zones do correspond to Zones 1, 2 and 3 described above for Aldabra. In fact almost the exact depth zonation described by Pichon could be found on Aldabra between transect 1 and West Channel, see Fig. 4. Lack of the same marker species could be due to zoogeographical or reef type differences or simply due to incompleteness of one or both lists. However, the overall similarity cannot be dismissed simply as pure coincidence. In both cases Zone 1 is dominated by members of the Acroporidae, Pocilloporidae and Faviidae; Zone 2 by soft corals; Zone 3 is dominated by members of the Faviidae with representatives of numerous families, it lacks *Millepora platyphylla* and includes the shallowest occurring meandroid form namely *Lobophyllia corymbosa*. It must be noted that the hermatypic complement of Pichon's Zone 2 is dominated by encrusting and bracket forms. When considered as the percentage of hermatypic species in each growth form, Zone 2 on Aldabra is co-dominated by brain and encrusting forms. Bracket forms only attain importance as members of the Aldabra reef front at depths in excess of 24 m, except in the channels. It would appear therefore that the two reef fronts do differ in this respect. However, it is again emphasized that uniformity in the location of all sample stations and even in the method of handling the data is of great importance if such comparison between sites is to be meaningful.

On the basis of the similarities described above, it is suggested that the sociological zonation described is of more than local significance. It is suggested that at this preliminary stage of investigation, it is best to regard the zones as an alliance group. A series of very tentative names based on the dominant families each with the suffix ion denoting alliances (*sensu* Braun-Blanquet, 1951) are given below.

Zone 1. Euacroporion.   Zone 4. Favio-Pectinion.
Zone 2. Alcyonacion.   Zone 5. Gorgonacion.
Zone 3. Eufaviidion.   Zone 6. Dendrophyllion.

If on further study this is found acceptable then difference in marker species such as those between Aldabra and Madagascar would give divisions at the association level (suffix etum). For example the Euacroporion is represented on Aldabra by the associations *Acroporetum glochiclados* and the *Milleporetum exaesa* and on Madagascar by the *Acroporetum pharaonis*.

CONCLUSIONS

Systematic Scuba survey of the Aldabra reef front has indicated that the following features are of importance and could form a basis for any future comparative studies.

1. The presence of the four reef front types with respect to exposure to wave and storm action.

2. The distribution of the areas of active reef growth and catastrophic and erosional phenomena in relation to exposure, especially to hurricane force winds.

3. The distribution and structure of the bastions.

4. The presence of six zones based on the distribution of types of benthos and growth forms of hard corals and their relation to the zonation of reef fish and other mobile fauna.

5. The effects of reef channels, exposure and any other main reef features on the above zonation.

6. The presence of biotic (sociological) zonation and its relevance and constancy locally and geographically.

As Stoddart (1969) has pointed out that "many of the difficulties in comparing reefs stems from the lack of uniformity of surveying method", it is suggested that the methods used in this study could form a useful basis for all studies of sub-littoral reef phenomena. It is emphasized that the first step in any such study must be to ascertain and map the zonation. This must be completed before even simple distribution with depth data can have any real ecological value. Sociological study of the type described must be supplemented by the systematic recording of as many quadrats as possible from known depths and known positions within the zonation pattern. Only when this has been carried out on a large enough scale will meaningful comparative study be possible. Computer programmes have already been developed for structuring raw data of the type described into formal association tables (Moore, 1964).

The work opens up the exciting possibilities of combined sociologic, behavioral and trophic dynamic study of the total reef community. It shows above all that coral reefs are complex ecosystems in which the energy used and stored in the accretion of the living reef is of equal importance to that actually flowing through the reef food webs.

REFERENCES

Bakus, G. J. (1964). The effect of fish grazing on invertebrate evolution in shallow tropical waters. *Publ. Allan Hancock Foundation* **1**. No. 27. Univ. California Press.

Barnes, J., Bellamy, D. J., Drew, E., Jones, D. J., Lythgoe, J. and Whitton, B.A. (1970). Sub-littoral reef phenomena of Aldabra. *Nature, Lond.* **225**: 268–269.

Bellamy, D. J., Drew, E., Jones, D. J. and Lythgoe, J. (1970). A preliminary report of the work of Phase VI of the Royal Society Expedition to Aldabra. *Rep. underwat. Ass.* **4**: 100–104.

Braun-Blanquet, J. (1951). *Pflanzensoziologie*, 2nd ed. pp. 620. Vienna: Springer.

Emery, K. O., Tracey, J. I. Jr. and Ladd, H. S. (1954). Geology of Bikini and nearby atolls. Geology. *Prof. Pap. U.S. geol. Surv.* **260**-A: 1–265.

Goreau, T. F. (1959). The ecology of Jamaican coral reefs 1. *Ecology* **40**: 67–90.

Gosline, W. A. (1965). Vertical zonation of inshore fishes in the upper water layers of the Hawaiian Islands. *Ecology* **46**: 823–831.

Hiatt, R. W. and Strasburg, D. W. (1960). Ecological relationships of the fish fauna on coral reefs of the Marshall Islands. *Ecol. Monogr.* **30**: 65–127.

Moore, J. J. (1964). A classification of the Bogs and Wet Heaths of Northern Europe. *Int. Symp. vegetationskunde*, pp. 310.

Pichon, M. (1964). Contribution à l'étude de la répartition des Madréporaires sur la récif de Tuléar. *Recl Trav. Stn mar. Endoume* (Fasc. Hors-Séries) Suppl. **2**: 79–203.

Randall, J. E. (1955). Fishes of the Gilbert Islands. *Atoll Res. Bull.* **47**: 243 pp.

Stoddart, D. R. (1967). Ecology of Aldabra atoll, Indian Ocean. *Atoll Res. Bull.* **118**: 1–141.

Stoddart, D. R. (1969). Ecology and morphology of Recent coral reefs. *Biol. Rev.* **44**: 4, 433–498.

Suyehiro, Y. (1942). A study on the digestive system and feeding habits of fish. *Jap. Zool.* **10**: 303 pp.

Wells, J. W. (1954). Recent corals of the Marshall Islands. *Prof. Pap. U.S. geol. Surv.* **260**-I, 385–486.

Wiens, H. J. (1962). *Atoll Environment and Ecology*. pp. 1–532. New Haven: Yale University Press.

Yonge, C. M. (1951). The form of coral reefs. *Endeavour* **10**: 136–144.

Yonge, C. M. (1963). The biology of coral reefs. *Adv. mar. Biol.* **1**: 209–260.

Appendix

Provisional check list of corals collected during
The Royal Society Expedition to Aldabra, phase 6

BRIAN R. ROSEN

The corals on which this list is based are being examined more fully in conjunction with other material from the same region.

   class Anothoza Ehrenburg
   subclass Zoantharia de Blainville
   order Scleractinia Bourne
   suborder Astrocoeniina Vaughan and Wells
   family Thamnasteriidae Vaughan and Wells
genus *Psammocora* Dana
subgenus *Psammocora* Dana
   Psammocora (Psammocora) nierstraszi van der Horst

family Pocilloporidae Gray
genus *Stylophora* Schweigger
   Stylophora mordax (Dana)
   Stylophora pistillata (Esper)
genus *Seriatopora* Lamarck
   Seriatopora cf. *hystrix*
   Seriatopora sp.
genus *Pocillopora* Lamarck
   Pocillopora damicornis (Linnaeus)
   Pocillopora danae Verrill
   Pocillopora eydouxi Milne-Edwards and Haime

family Acroporidae Verill
genus *Acropora* Oken
   Acropora monticulosa (Brueggemann)
   Acropora palifera (Lamarck)
   Acropora irregularis (Brook)
   Acropora cf. *diversa* (Brook) No. 1
   Acropora cf. *diversa* (Brook) No 2
   Acropora spicifera (Dana)
   Acropora variabilis (Klunzinger)
   Acropora glochiclados (Brook)
   Acropora sp.—No. 1
   Acropora sp.—No. 2
   Acropora sp.—No. 3
   Acropora sp.—No. 4
genus *Astreopora* de Blainville
   Astreopora myriophthalma (Lamarck)
genus *Montipora* Quoy and Gaimard
   Montipora verrucosa (Lamarck)
   Montipora elschneri (Vaughan)
   Montipora cf. *tuberculosa* (Lamarck)
   Montipora cf. *punctata* Bernard
   Montipora cf. *erythraea* von Marenzeller
   Montipora sp.–No. 1
   Montipora sp.–No. 2

suborder Fungiina Verrill
superfamily Agariciidae Gray
family Agariciidae Gray
genus *Pavona* Lamarck
subgenus *Pavona* Lamarck
   Pavona (Pavona) praetorta (Dana)
   Pavona (Pavona) frondifera Lamarck
   Pavona (Pavona) cf. *minor* Brueggemann
   Pavona (Pavona) varians Verrill
   Pavona (Pavona) clivosa Verrill
   Pavona (Pavona) explanulata Lamarck
   Pavona (Pavona) gardineri van der Horst

subgenus *Pseudocolumnastraea* Yabe and Sugiyama
    Pavona (*Pseudocolumnastraea*) sp.
genus *Leptoseris* Milne-Edwards and Haime
    Leptoseris columna Yabe and Sugiyama
    Leptoseris tubulifera Vaughan
genus *Leptoseris?* Milne-Edwards and Haime
    Leptoseris? mycetoseroides Wells
genus *Agariciella* Ma
    Agariciella ponderosa (Gardiner)
genus *Pachyseris* Milne-Edwards and Haime
subgenus *Pachyseris* Milne-Edwards and Haime
    Pachyseris (*Pachyseris*) *laevicollis* (Dana)
    Pachyseris (*Pachyseris*) *rugosa* (Lamarck)

family Siderastreidae Vaughan and Wells
genus *Anomastraea* von Marenzeller
subgenus *Anomastraea* von Marenzeller
    Anomastraea (*Anomastraea*) *irregularis* von Marenzeller
genus *Coscinaraea* Milne-Edwards and Haime
    Coscinaraea monile (Forskål)
    Coscinaraea sp.—No. 1
    Coscinaraea sp.–No. 2

superfamily Fungiicae Dana
family Fungiidae Dana
genus *Cycloseris* Milne-Edwards and Haime
    Cycloseris cyclolites (Lamarck)
genus *Fungia* Lamarck
subgenus *Pleuractis* Verrill
    Fungia (*Pleuractis*) *paumotensis* Stutchbury
    Fungia (*Pleuractis*) *scutaria* Lamarck
subgenus *Danafungia* Wells
    Fungia (*Danafungia*) sp.
genus *Herpolitha* Eschscholtz
    Herpolitha limax (Esper)
genus *Podabacia* Milne-Edwards and Haime
    Podabacia sp.

superfamily Poriticae Gray
family Poritidae Gray
genus *Porites* Link
subgenus *Porites* Link
    Porites (*Porites*) *lutea* Milne-Edwards and Haime
    Porites (*Porites*) *andrewsi* Vaughan
    Porites (*Porites*) *nigrescens* Dana
    Porites (*Porites*) *lichen* Dana
subgenus *Synaraea* Verrill
    Porites (*Synaraea*) *iwayamaensis* Eguchi

suborder Faviina Vaughan and Wells
superfamily Faviicae Gregory
family Faviidae Gregory
subfamily Faviinae Gregory
genus *Plesiastrea* Milne-Edwards and Haime
Plesiastrea versipora Lamarck
Plesiastrea sp.
genus *Favia* Oken
Favia stelligera (Dana)
Favia pallida (Dana)
Favia sp.
genus *Favites* Link
Favites abdita (Ellis and Solander)
Favites cf. *pentagona* (Esper)
genus *Goniastrea* Edwards and Haime
Goniastrea retiformis (Lamarck)
Goniastrea pectinata (Ehrenberg)
Goniastrea incrustans Duncan
genus *Platygyra* Ehrenberg
Platygyra lamellina Ehrenberg
genus *Leptoria* Milne-Edwards and Haime
Leptoria phrygia (Ellis and Solander)
genus *Hydnophora* Fischer
Hydnophora microconos (Lamarck)
Hydnophora exesa (Pallas)

subfamily Montrastreinae Vaughan and Wells
genus *Diploastrea* Matthai
Diploastrea heliopora (Lamarck)
genus *Leptastrea* Milne-Edwards and Haime
Leptastrea purpurea (Dana)
Leptastrea immersa Klunzinger
genus *Cyphastrea* Milne-Edwards and Haime
Cyphastrea chalcidicum (Forskål)
genus *Echinopora* Lamarck
Echinopora gemmacea (Lamarck)

family Rhizangiidae d'Orbigny
genus *Oulangia* Milne-Edwards and Haime
Oulangia sp.

family Oculinidae Gray
subfamily Galaxeinae Vaughan and Well¹
genus *Galaxea* Oken
Galaxea fascicularis (Lamarck)

family Mussidae Ortmann
genus *Blastomussa* Wells
Blastomussa merleti (Wells)
genus *Acanthastrea* Milne-Edwards and Haime
conanthastrea echinata (Dana)

genus *Lobophyllia* de Blainville
subgenus *Lobophyllia* de Blainville
    Lobophyllia (Lobophyllia) corymbosa (Forskål)
    Lobophyllia (Lobophyllia) hemprichii (Ehrenberg)
genus *Symphyllia* Milne-Edwards and Haime
    Symphyllia nobilis (Dana)
    Symphyllia valenciennesi Milne-Edwards and Haime

            family Pectiniidae Vaughan and Wells
genus *Echinophyllia* Klunzinger
    Echinophyllia aspera (Ellis and Solander)
genus *Mycedium* Oken
    Mycedium tenuicostatum Verrill
    Mycedium tubifex (Dana
genus *Physophyllia* Duncan
    ? *Physophyllia ayleni* Wells
genus *Pectinia* Oken
    Pectinia lactuca (Pallas)
    Pectinia sp.

            suborder Caryophylliina Vaughan and Wells
            superfamily Caryophylliicae Gray
            family Caryophylliidae Gray
            subfamily Eusmiliinae Milne-Edwards and Haime
genus *Physogyra* Quelch
    Physogyra sp.
genus *Gyrosmilia* Milne-Edwards and Haime
    ? Gyrosmilia interrupta (Ehrenberg)

            suborder Dendrophylliina Vaughan and Wells
            family Dendrophylliidae Gray
genus *Dendrophyllia* de Blainville
    Dendrophyllia micrantha (Ehrenberg)
    Dendrophyllia cf. florulenta van der Horst
genus *Turbinaria*
    Turbinaria sp.

            subclass Octocorallia Haeckel
            order Stolonifera Hickson
            family Tubiporidae Ehrenburg
genus *Tubipora* Linnaeus
    Tubipora musica Linnaeus

            order Coenothecalia Bourne
            family Helioporidae Moseley
genus *Heliopora* de Blainville
    Heliopora coerulea (Pallas)

7

class Hydrozoa Owen
order Milleporina Hickson
family Milleporidae Fleming
genus *Millepora* Linnaeus
Millepora platyphylla Hemprich and Ehrenberg
Millepora exaesa Forskål

order Stylasterina Hickson and England
family Stylasteridae Gray
subfamily Distichoporinae Stechow
genus *Distichopora* Lamarck
Distichopora violacea (Pallas)
Distichopora fisheri Broch forma *alpha* Wells

NOTE: Certain zoogeographic aspects of this important collection are discussed elsewhere in this volume, pp. 263–299.

Regional Studies of Reefs

Symp. zool. Soc. Lond. (1971) No. 28, 117–139.

THE CORAL REEFS OF EILAT (GULF OF EILAT, RED SEA)*

YOSSEF LOYA and LAWRENCE B. SLOBODKIN

Department of Biological Sciences, State University of New York at Stony Brook, New York, U.S.A.

SYNOPSIS

This paper, the first of a series, is intended to serve as a preliminary systematic list of the corals of Eilat and presents the results of a study on the structure and zonation of scleractinian corals at the reefs of Eilat. The study was carried out by means of line transects run underwater with Scuba apparatus. The transects were run along depth contours, parallel to the shore, at fixed intervals, from the back-reef region through the reef-flat to a depth of 30 m. Each transect was 10 m long. Any coral that underlay the transect was recorded and its projected length on the line was measured to the nearest centimeter. A total of 84 transects were surveyed, in three stations, at the natural reserve of the Eilat coral reefs.

The reefs of Eilat are of the fringing type with scleractinian corals as the most important hermatypic organisms. Profile transverses at Eilat demonstrate five main regions: (a) the back-reef, (b) the reef-crest, (c) the upper fore-reef, (d) the patch reef, and, (e) the lower fore-reef. These in turn are divided into different zones named according to their most important faunal or structural features. *Stylophora pistillata* is the dominant species in the lagoon, rear-reef and reef-flat zones. *Millepora dichotoma*, although a hydroid coral, is the most important hermatypic frame-builder of the seaward slope in the reef-crest region. The upper fore-reef region is dominated by *Echinopora gemmacea*. The patch-reef region is dominated by *Acropora hemprichi* and *Acropora variabilis*. The lower fore-reef region is dominated by *Porites lutea*. A total of 97 scleractinian species belonging to 40 genera and 13 families were collected during the work. Each species was ranked according to its relative abundance in the different reef regions. The majority of the species recorded were rare and very few abundant or dominant. The average number of species recorded per transect increased with depth, from 11–15 species per transect in the reef-crest region to 26–29 species per transect in the *Lutea* zone. The richest zones in number of colonies per transect and percent cover of living corals are the *Millepora* zone and *Porites lutea* zone. An average of about 75% cover in the *Millepora* zone and 85% in the *Lutea* zone. These are also the zones of steepest slope along the fore-reef. The *Hemprichi–variabilis* zone is the poorest in living coral coverage (20·3% cover). This zone is characterized by wide and flat terraces subject to sediment accumulation, which may be an important factor in preventing major reef growth at this zone.

INTRODUCTION

There are very few works concerning the systematics of the scleractinian corals in the Red Sea. Earlier works are those of Ehrenberg (1834),

---

* Part of the material in this paper is taken from a Ph.D. dissertation of Yossef Loya, State University of New York at Stony Brook, entitled: "Community structure and species diversity of hermatypic corals in Eilat (Red Sea)".

Klunzinger (1878), and von Marenzeller (1906), and more recently Rossi (1954), and Scheer (1964, 1967).

This paper intends to serve as a first and preliminary list of the corals of the Gulf of Eilat (Fig. 1) and presents information on the structure and zonation of hermatypic corals in Eilat.

A thorough collection of scleractinian corals was made during the summer of 1969. The corals were collected mainly from the reefs of Eilat (northwestern Gulf of Eilat) and to a much lesser extent from the reefs of Dahab and Ras-a-Tantur, along the western shores of the Gulf

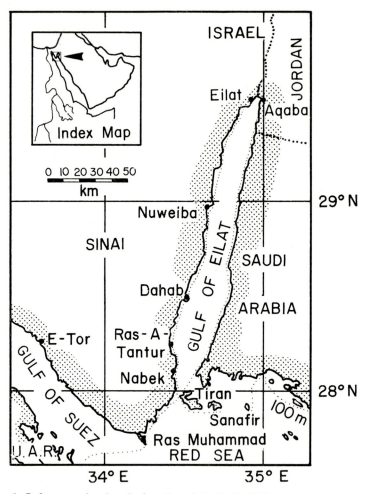

Fig. 1. Index map showing the location of the Gulf of Eilat and working area.

of Eilat, and Ras-Muhammad on the southern tip of the Sinai peninsula.

A comparison between the reefs of Eilat and those of Dahab, Ras-a-Tantur and Ras-Muhammad, as well as a study of species diversity of corals in Eilat, making use of information theory indices, will be published in subsequent papers.

DESCRIPTION OF THE LOCALITY

The Gulf of Eilat occupies part of the Great Rift Valley that extends from Turkey through the Red Sea into East Africa (Gregory, 1921).

Publications on meteorological and hydrographic research of the northern part of the Gulf of Eilat include those of Oren (1962) and Ashbel (1951, 1963). Friedman (1968) has published a detailed survey of the oceanography of the Gulf.

The Gulf is 160 km long and 5 to 26 km wide. Considering its narrow width the Gulf is very deep (average depth 650 m). The walls of the Gulf are very steep. The normal gradient ranges from 60 to 70%. The climate in this area is hot and dry. Evaporation is exceptionally intense (average 200 cm per year). Rainfall is scarce (average 22 mm per year). The mean annual temperature is 25·7°C. Winds blow predominantly from the north or northeast. Winds from the south are less frequent. The mean annual temperature of the water is 23·0°C. The water is hypersaline (41·0‰–42·0‰). Surface salinity increases progressively from south to north. No detailed information on water currents in the Gulf of Eilat is available. According to fishermen, surface currents flow counterclockwise from north to south along the Sinai coast.

METHODS

Quantitative zonation studies on coral reefs are relatively rare compared to qualitative studies. Problems of field recording arise as a result of variety of coral growth forms and bottom topography of the reef. Most of the quantitative studies record the number of species or genera per quadrat and their relative coverage (Manton, 1935; Abe, 1937; Emery, Tracey and Ladd, 1954; Odum and Odum, 1955; Kornicker and Boyd, 1962; Storr, 1964; Kissling, 1965; Stoddart, Davies and Keith, 1966). The problems of using quadrat techniques on reef-flats and reef-slopes are discussed by Pichon (1964). A brief review of different methods used in quantitative studies, and the

FIG. 2. The nature reserve of the Eilat coral reefs.

problems involved at the level of sampling unit and field recording, is given by Stoddart (1969).

The present study was carried out by means of line transects run underwater with Scuba apparatus, at three stations, in the reservation area of the Eilat reefs (Fig. 2). The transects were run along depth contours parallel to the shore at fixed intervals of 5 m, from the back-reef region through the reef-flat, to depths of 30 m. Each transect was 10 m long. Any coral species, which underlays the line, was recorded and its projected length on the line was measured to the nearest centimeter (Fig. 3). In case of two or more colonies growing one above the other and underlying the transect, the projected length of the

FIG. 3. Coverage of living corals and species abundance information were recorded by means of systematic line transects.

longest colony was recorded for the coverage analysis, and the length and species of all the overlapping colonies were recorded for the coral species abundance analysis.

RESULTS

The Eilat scleractinian corals and their abundance

The Eilat Scleractinia known to date are systematically listed in Table I. A total of 97 species belonging to 40 genera and 13 families were collected and identified, including two species. *Millepora dichotoma* and *Millepora platyphylla*, although not scleractinian corals, are included in the study as they are very important hermatypic frame-builders in the rear-reef and upper seaward slope. Out of 97 scleractinian species recorded, 93 were collected from the reefs of Eilat. Four species, *Stylophora wellsi*, *Pocillopora hemprichi*, *Acropora corymbosa* and *Tubastrea micrantha* were collected from Ras-a-Tantur and Ras-Muhammad.

Table I also summarizes the optimal depth ranges of the Eilat corals, together with their relative rank of abundance as analysed from the transects.

TABLE I

Systematic list of scleractinian corals
Gulf of Eilat, Red Sea

Classification*	Optimum depth range (m)	Relative abundance§
Class Anthozoa Ehrenberg, 1834		
Subclass Hexacorallia Haeckel, 1896		
Order Scleractinia Bourne, 1900		
Suborder Astrocoeniida Vaughan and Wells, 1943		
Family Thamnasteriidae Vaughan and Wells, 1943		
1. *Psammocora nierstraszi* van der Horst	20–40	sporadic
Family Pocilloporidae Gray, 1842		
2. *Stylophora pistillata* (Esper)	0–4	dominant
3. *Stylophora wellsi* Scheer†	0–10	?
4. *Stylophora palmata* Blainville	20–40	rare
5. *Stylophora prostrata* Klunzinger	3–40	abundant
6. *Seriatopora caliendrum* Ehrenberg	0–6	rare
7. *Seriatopora spinosa* Milne-Edwards and Haime	3–6	rare
8. *Seriatopora angulata* Klunzinger	0–30	uncommon
9. *Pocillopora danae* Verrill	0–30	sporadic
10. *Pocillopora hemprichi* Ehrenberg†	0–10	?

TABLE I (*continued*)

Family Acroporidae Verrill, 1902		
11. *Astreopora myriophthalma* (Lamarck)	0–12	sporadic
12. *Montipora lobulata* Bernard	1–40	abundant
13. *Montipora meandrina* (Ehrenberg)	0–3	rare
14. *Montipora venosa* (Ehrenberg)	3–6	rare
15. *Montipora verrucosa* (Lamarck)	0–12	uncommon
16. *Montipora tuberculosa* (Lamarck)	0–40	sporadic
17. *Montipora danae* Milne-Edwards and Haime	12–40	sporadic
18. *Montipora granulata* Bernard	0–40	common
19. *Montipora monasteriata* (Forskål)	1–6	rare
20. *Montipora erythraea* Marenzeller	1–3	rare
21. *Montipora composita* Crossland	1–3	rare
22. *Acropora nasuta* (Dana)	7–12	rare
23. *Acropora variabilis* (Klunzinger)	0–50	dominant
24. *Acropora hemprichi* (Ehrenberg)	6–50	dominant
25. *Acropora humilis* (Dana)	1–3	rare
26. *Acropora hyacinthus* (Dana)	1–3	rare
27. *Acropora corymbosa* (Lamarck)†	0–10	?
28. *Acropora eurystoma* (Klunzinger)	3–6	rare
29. *Acropora scandens* (Klunzinger)	0–3	common
Family Agariciidae Gray, 1847		
30. *Pavona varians* Verrill	1–6	common
31. *Pavona decussata* Dana	0–6	uncommon
32. *Pavona gardineri* Van der Horst	1–12	rare
33. *Pavona clavus* (Dana)	1–6	rare
34. *Pavona explanulata* (Lamarck)	7–12	rare
35. *Agariciella ponderosa* (Gardiner)	1–5	rare
36. *Leptoseris tubulifera* Vaughan	25–50	rare
37. *Leptoseris fragilis* Milne-Edwards and Haime	25–50	rare
38. *Pachyseris valenciennesi* Milne-Edwards and Haime	10–30	rare
39. *Pachyseris rugosa* (Lamarck)	10–30	rare
Family Siderastreidae Vaughan and Wells, 1943		
40. *Siderastrea lilacea* Klunzinger	20–40	rare
41. *Coscinaraea monile* (Forskål)	12–40	sporadic
Family Fungiidae Dana, 1846		
42. *Fungia fungites* (Linnaeus)	0–12	common
43. *Fungia doederleini* Marenzeller	0–20	uncommon
44. *Fungia echinata* (Pallas)	3–20	uncommon
45. *Fungia scutaria* Lamarck	0–20	uncommon
46. *Herpolitha limax* (Esper)	7–15	rare
47. *Podabacia crustacea* (Pallas)	3–30	rare
Family Poritidae, 1842		
48. *Goniopora savignyi* (Dana)	5–30	uncommon
49. *Goniopora tenella* (Quelch)	3–12	rare
50. *Goniopora lichen* (Dana)	5–30	uncommon

TABLE I (*continued*)

Classification*	Optimum depth range (m)	Relative abundance§
Class Anthozoa Ehrenberg, 1834		
Subclass Hexacorallia Haeckel, 1896		
Order Scleractinia Bourne, 1900		
Suborder Astrocoeniida Vaughan and Wells, 1943		
51. *Goniopora planulata* (Ehrenberg)	20–40	rare
52. *Porites* (*Synaraea*) *undulata* Klunzinger	7–12	rare
53. *Porites lutea* Milne-Edwards and Haime	12–40	common
54. *Porites studeri* Vaughan	12–20	rare
55. *Porites alveolata* Milne-Edwards and Haime	3–40	rare
56. *Porites mayeri* Vaughan	1–3	uncommon
57. *Porites* sp., n. sp.	25–40	rare
58. *Alveopora daedalea* (Forskål)	20–30	sporadic
Suborder Faviina Vaughan and Wells, 1943		
Family Faviidae Gregory, 1900		
59. *Plesiastrea laxa* (Klunzinger)	20–40	uncommon
60. *Plesiastrea mammillosa* (Klunzinger)	10–40	rare
61. *Favia favus* (Forskål)	0–3	abundant
62. *Favia stelligera* (Dana)	0–3	rare
63. *Favia speciosa* (Dana)	7–40	uncommon
64. *Favia doreyensis* Milne-Edwards and Haime	3–12	rare
65. *Favites pentagona* (Esper)	30–40	common
66. *Favites virens* (Dana)	0–3	uncommon
67. *Favites abdita* (Ellis and Solander)	0–40	sporadic
68. *Favites halicora* (Ehrenberg)	0–3	rare
69. *Goniastrea retiformis* (Lamarck)	0–6	common
70. *Goniastrea pectinata* (Ehrenberg)	3–12	dominant
71. *Platygyra lamellina* (Ehrenberg)	0–40	abundant
72. *Platygyra subdentata* (Milne-Edwards and Haime)	0–6	rare
73. *Platygyra rustica* (Dana)	0–2	rare
74. *Leptoria phrygia* (Ellis and Solander)	0–6	rare
75. *Hydnophora microconos* (Lamarck)	0–3	uncommon
76. *Hydnophora contignatio* (Forskål)	3–6	rare
77. *Leptastrea purpurea* (Dana)	0–12	common
78. *Leptastrea bottae* (Milne-Edwards and Haime)	0–30	sporadic
79. *Leptastrea transversa* (Klunzinger)	3–12	uncommon
80. *Cyphastrea serailia* (Forskål)	3–6	uncommon
81. *Cyphastrea microphthalma* (Lamarck)	0–6	dominant
82. *Cyphastrea chalcidicum* (Forskål)	7–12	sporadic
83. *Echinopora gemmacea* (Lamarck)	3–12	dominant
84. *Echinopora lamellosa* (Esper)	20–40	rare
85. *Echinopora gemmacea* var. *fruticulosa* Klunzinger	3–12	uncommon
Family Oculinidae Gray, 1847		
86. *Galaxea fascicularis* (Linnaeus)	0–3	sporadic

TABLE I (*continued*)

Family Mussidae Ortman, 1890			
87. *Acanthastrea echinata* (Dana)		0–40	common
88. *Lobophyllia corymbosa* (Forskål)		3–12	sporadic
89. *Lobophyllia hemprichii* (Ehrenberg)		1–10	rare
Family Pectiniidae Vaughan and Wells, 1943			
90. *Echinophyllia aspera* (Ellis and Solander)		7–12	uncommon
91. *Mycedium tubifex* (Dana)		25–40	rare
Suborder Caryophylliina Vaughan and Wells, 1943			
Family Caryophylliidae Gray, 1847			
92. *Plerogyra sinuosa* (Dana)		20–40	rare
93. *Gyrosmilia interrupta* (Ehrenberg)		0–4	sporadic
Suborder Dendrophylliina Vaughan and Wells, 1943			
Family Dendrophylliidae Gray, 1847			
94. *Balanophyllia gemmifera* Klunzinger‡		0–20	rare
95. *Tubastrea micrantha* (Ehrenberg)†		0–3	?
96. *Blastomussa* sp.		3–12	rare
97. *Turbinaria* sp.		1–3	rare
Class Hydrozoa			
Order Milleporina			
Family Milleporidae			
98. *Millepora dichotoma* Forskål		0–4	dominant
99. *Millepora platyphylla* Ehrenberg		0–1	uncommon

* Classification is according to Vaughan and Wells (1943) and Wells (1956).
† Species collected from Ras-a-Tantur and Ras-Muhammad.
‡ Ahermatypic species.
§ For relative abundance index see Table II.

Each one of the species was assigned to any one of 6 abundance categories: rare, uncommon, sporadic, common, abundant or dominant (Fig. 4). The relative abundance of each one of the species was calculated out of 84 transects surveyed. The ranks assigned to each species were given according to the number of colonies counted in each zone of the reef as shown in Table II. As expected from most of field collections, the majority of the species were rare and very few abundant or dominant (Fig. 4).

Structure and zonation

The reefs of Eilat are of the fringing type with scleractinian corals as the most important hermatypic organisms. In the lagoon and reef-flat the brown algae are common and contribute to the deposition of

TABLE II

Index table for the relative abundance of corals

Rank	Range of colonies counted	Relative abundance
1	1–10	rare
2	11–30	uncommon
3	31–50	sporadic
4	51–100	common
5	101–200	abundant
6	> 200	dominant

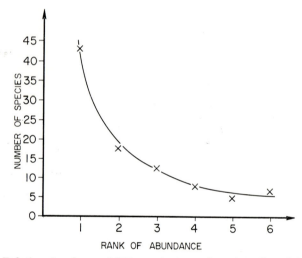

FIG. 4. Relative abundance of 95 hermatypic coral species collected from Eilat.

calcium carbonate on the reef. Friedman (1968) working on the carbonate sediments of the reefs of Eilat inferred that green algae do not contribute to the reef derived sands.

The zonal structure of the reef becomes apparent by analysing the systematic profile transects surveyed from the rear zone through the reef-table to deep water. The relative abundance and the total percent cover of living coral species were the criteria for separating different zones on the reef. The different zones and regions are named according to their most conspicuous faunal or topographical characteristic. The relationship to each other and to the reef as a whole is summarized in Table III.

TABLE III

Relationship of zones in Eilat coral reefs

Region	Zone	Width range (m)	Depth range (m)
Back reef	Shore zone	1–3	0·0–0·5
	Lagoon zone	10–50	0·5–2·0
Reef crest	Rear reef	1–3	1–2
	Reef flat	5–30	0·2–0·8
	Millepora zone	3–7	0·2–3·0
Upper fore-reef	*Gemmacea* zone	50–70	4–12
Patch reef	*Hemprichi-variabilis* zone	30–40	13–19
Lower fore-reef	*Lutea* zone	40–60	>20

The reef profile perpendicular to the shore, measured in the nature reserve of Eilat, is given in Fig. 5. The depth measurements were taken at fixed intervals of 2 m, and are represented by the black dots along the profile. Figure 5 also summarizes the depth ranges of the different regions and zones and specifies the dominant species at each zone.

The percent cover of the most important hermatypic corals of Eilat, in the different zones of the reef, is given in Table IV. The results are presented as averages, calculated from between 9 and 30 transects surveyed at each zone. The total number of species recorded in these transects was 87.

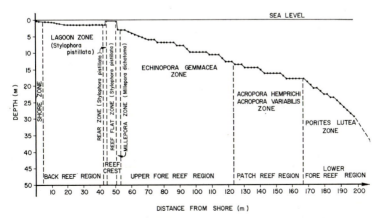

FIG. 5. Reef profile perpendicular to the shore at the nature reserve of Eilat. The black dots represent depth measurements.

TABLE IV

Percentage of the total living coral coverage represented by the 17 commonest hermatypic species, in the different zones of the reef at Eilat.*

Species	Rear zone	Reef flat	Millepora zone	Gemmacea zone	Hemprichi-variabilis zone	Lutea zone
Stylophora pistillata	22·4	25·4	1·8	4·8	11·1	2·2
Stylophora prostrata	0·0	0·0	0·8	5·2	1·6	2·5
Montipora lobulata	0·2	0·0	6·2	3·0	2·5	10·2
Montipora granulata	0·1	0·0	8·2	2·3	3·4	5·9
Acropora variabilis	5·7	4·5	1·7	8·8	12·9	5·5
Acropora hemprichi	0·4	2·2	2·8	9·5	13·1	11·1
Acropora scandens	3·8	2·5	1·6	0·1	0·0	0·0
Pavona varians	1·0	1·3	0·7	3·2	0·0	0·3
Porites lutea	0·9	6·2	1·1	0·9	3·8	12·1
Favia favus	2·4	10·7	0·0	0·2	0·3	1·0
Favites pentagona	0·6	0·3	0·7	0·5	2·1	0·9
Goniastrea pectinata	0·0	0·4	0·6	6·1	2·4	3·1
Platygyra lamellina	6·8	2·4	1·4	1·3	9·5	3·3
Cyphastrea microphthalma	12·9	14·2	1·4	2·9	1·6	1·2
Echinopora gemmacea	4·5	5·5	5·1	16·4	1·5	4·9
Acanthastrea echinata	1·0	1·3	0·7	0·2	1·8	1·4
Millepora dichotoma	9·7	9·7	36·3	3·8	0·4	0·3
Total %	72·4	86·6	71·1	69·2	68·0	65·9

* The figures given are calculated from 9–30 transects run at each zone.

TABLE V

Trends of increasing abundance of coral species with depth*

Species	Rear zone	Reef flat	Millepora zone	3–6 m	7–12 m	13–19 m	20–30 m
Psammocora nierstraszi	0·0	0·0	12·9	6·4	9·6	3·2	67·7
Montipora lobulata	0·7	0·0	21·3	13·5	9·9	4·2	50·3
Montipora granulata	1·3	0·0	12·8	7·7	17·9	6·4	53·8
Acropora hemprichi	0·4	1·3	5·2	18·7	22·7	15·5	36·2
Coscinaraea monile	6·9	0·0	0·0	3·4	20·7	24·1	44·8
Porites lutea	1·9	5·7	3·2	0·6	10·2	9·6	68·7
Alveopora daedalea	0·0	0·0	4·7	1·2	8·3	13·1	72·6
Favites pentagona	6·6	13·3	10·0	3·3	10·0	6·7	50·0

* The data are presented as percentages of the total number of colonies per transect, of each species, counted at the various zones. 9–30 transects were run at each zone.

TABLE VI

Trends of decreasing abundance of coral species with depth*

Species	Rear zone	Reef flat	Millepora zone	3–6 m	7–12 m	13–19 m	20–30 m
Stylophora pistillata	35·7	32·6	4·9	6·7	7·3	7·9	4·9
Montipora verrucosa	38·1	0·0	38·1	14·3	4·7	0·0	4·7
Acropora scandens	53·1	28·1	15·6	0·0	3·1	0·0	0·0
Favia favus	20·0	62·5	0·0	0·0	2·5	2·5	12·5
Porites mayeri	25·0	0·0	50·0	18·7	0·0	0·0	6·2
Cyphastrea microphthalma	27·0	27·0	7·3	18·4	9·2	4·9	6·1
Millepora dichotoma	25·4	14·7	40·7	14·7	0·0	1·7	2·8

* The data are presented as percentages of the total number of colonies per transect of each species, counted at the various zones. 9–30 transects were run at each zone.

Some species increased in abundance with depth (Table V) and some decreased (Table VI). Nine to 30 transects were run at each zone and the data presented in these Tables are given as percentages of the total number of colonies per transect, of each species, counted at the various zones.

The relationship between the number of species recorded per transect and the number of colonies is given in Fig. 6. The figures are calculated out of the total 84 transects surveyed at Eilat. As in most biological collections, the number of species tends to be proportional to the logarithm of the number of colonies counted at each transect (r = 0·726).

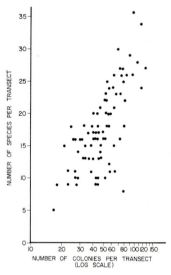

Fig. 6. The relationship between number of species and number of colonies recorded per transect, in 84 transects surveyed at Eilat.

Figure 7 summarizes in a histogram the relationship between the coral species abundance (average number of species and average number of colonies per transect), together with the percent cover of living corals, as a function of depth.

More species per transect are found at each successive depth, with the exception of the transects at 13–17 m (*Hemprichi-variabilis* zone). This trend is statistically significant, testing shallow water transects against transects surveyed at deeper water (t-tests, 0·05 level of significance). The number of colonies per transect followed, as would be expected, the percent cover of living corals in the different zones of the reef. In both cases the *Hemprichi-variabilis* zone was significantly lower in number of colonies per transect, as well as percent cover of living corals (t-tests, 0·05 level of significance). The richest zones in number of colonies per transect and percent cover of living corals are the *Millepora* zone (0·2–3·0 m depth) and *Porites lutea* zone (deeper than 20 m).

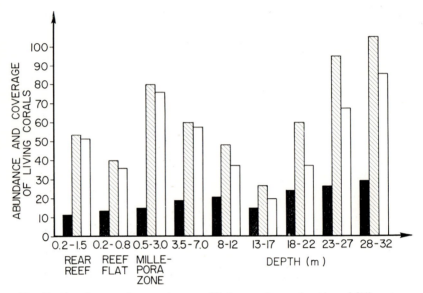

Fig. 7. Abundance and percent cover of living corals as a function of different zones at the Eilat reefs. Average number of species per transect is represented by black bars, average number of colonies per transect by hatched bars and percentage of living corals coverage by blank bars.

DISCUSSION

Quantitative methods

Greig-Smith (1964) discusses different terrestrial methods in studying plant communities. After considering different terrestrial methods and actually trying them underwater, it was found that using line transects is the most efficient method in avoiding problems that arise from variable bottom topography of the reef area. Line transects also simplify problems of field recording and are highly efficient in information per time spent underwater, which is a critical factor in deep water study. Moreover, the amount of information derived from this method is for many purposes as useful as that derived from quadrat sampling techniques.

A preliminary study was made to find out the optimal length of a transect. Analysing random transects recorded from different depths, it was found, by plotting the cumulative number of new species recorded as a function of transect length, that after 8 or 9 m of line transect, the curve levelled off, i.e., there was not any significant increase in the number of new species recorded.

The back-reef region

1. The most common material in the shore zone is beachrock. Friedman (1966) found a fossil reef in the intertidal zone of the northern Gulf, near the city of Eilat, which gave a radiocarbon age of 4770 ± 140 years.

2. Terrigenous debris from nearby wadis underlies the shallow water lagoon and decreases towards the back-reef (Friedman 1968). The width of the lagoon varies from 10–50 m and a maximum depth

FIG. 8. Patches of *Stylophora pistillata* in the shallow lagoon. This species is dominant in the reef flat, rear-reef and the lagoon.

of 2 m. The dominant coral species in this zone is *Stylophora pistillata* (Fig. 8). Other coral species which are typical to the lagoon but have much lower abundance are *Cyphastrea microphthalma*, *Millepora dichotoma*, *Platygyra lamellina*, *Favia favus*, and *Millepora platyphylla* (Fig. 9). Most of these species demonstrate trends of decreasing abundance with depth (Table VI).

Fig. 9. Typical growth form of *Millepora platyphylla*. This species can be found only in the reef crest region and particularly in the rear-reef zone.

The reef-crest region

1. The rear-reef (i.e., the inner wall of the reef-flat) is dominated by *Stylophora pistillata*. Of the "living" area about 22% of the rear-zone is covered by this species (Table IV). *Cyphastrea microphthalma* is the second most abundant species in this zone (coverage of 13%). *Millepora dichotoma* and *Millepora platyphylla*, which are hydrozoans and not true stony-corals, are very important frame-builders in this zone.

2. The reef-flat is also dominated by *Stylophora pistillata*. Of the "living" area about 25% of this zone is covered by it. Other important hermatypic species in the reef-flat are *Cyphastrea microphthalma* and *Favia favus*. These three species cover almost 50% of the "living" reef-flat. The 17 scleractinian species listed in Table IV cover approximately 87% of the reef-flat, leaving only 13% of living coral coverage to the rest of the species recorded from this zone.

3. The *Millepora* zone (i.e., the outer wall of the reef-flat) is named after the most abundant hermatypic species in this zone, namely, *Millepora dichotoma* (Fig. 10). This is, in fact, the buttress zone (Odum and Odum, 1955; Goreau, 1959) or the "spur and groove" system as

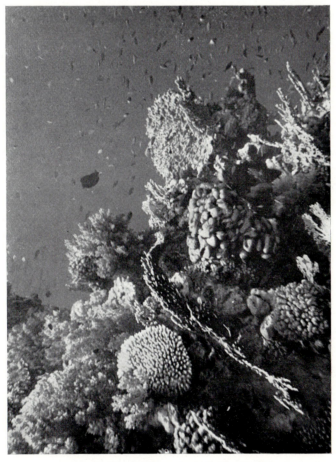

FIG. 10. The *Millepora* zone (1–3 m depth).

termed by Shinn (1963). Friedman (1968) finds that the spurs and grooves at Eilat make an angle of about 25° with the trend of the reef, which itself is almost parallel to the predominant wind direction, and therefore, the direction of maximum water agitation. *Millepora dichotoma* covers about 36% of the "living" area of this zone. Other species typical of this zone but in a much lower abundance are *Montipora granulata*, *Montipora lobulata*, and *Echinopora gemmacea*.

The upper fore-reef region

The upper fore-reef region is between 50–70 m wide and 3–12 m deep. This zone is dominated by *Echinopora gemmacea* which covers about 16% of its "living" surface. Other species typical to this zone are (in decreasing order of abundance): *Acropora hemprichi*, *Acropora variabilis*, *Goniastrea pectinata*, and *Stylophora prostrata*.

The patch-reef region

This region is between 30–40 m wide and 13–19 m deep. It is the poorest region in coral species abundance and coverage (Fig. 7). The bottom is sandy and there is correspondingly sparse coral population. Friedman (1968) finds that the most abundant reef derived sediment in Eilat is sand, although large chunks of coral debris lie scattered along the seaward side of the reef. He hypothesizes that the dark color of sand at this zone is a possible result of reducing conditions at and below the water-sediment interface.

The most abundant species in this region are *Acropora hemprichi* and *Acropora variabilis* that together cover 26% of the living area of this zone. *Stylophora pistillata* and *Platygyra lamellina* are also typical species of this zone.

The lower fore-reef region

This region is between 40–60 m wide and 20–50 m deep. The fore-reef slope with a dense population of coral growth stops at a depth of 40–50 m depth. Scattered colonies of coral may be found occasionally in deeper water, but there is no major reef building process in this area. The estimated angle of the slope below this zone is 70°–80°.

The most abundant corals in this zone, in decreasing order of abundance are: *Porites lutea*, *Acropora hemprichi* and *Montipora lobulata*. These are species which show a strong trend of increasing abundance with depth (Table V). Species which are exclusively limited to this zone are *Leptoseris tubulifera* and *Leptoseris fragilis*. Other species which are more abundant in deep water than in shallow water are *Psammocora nierstraszi*, *Alveopora daedalea*, *Favites pentagona*, *Stylophora palmata* and *Pachyseris valenciennesi*.

Sedimentation effects

Figure 7 demonstrates clearly that the *Millepora* zone, upper *Gemmacea* zone and the *Lutea* zone possess the highest precentage of living coral coverage, while the *Hemprichi-variabilis* zone is the poorest. Two main factors may be considered in explaining these phenomena: (a) the topography of the reef, (b) the sedimentation effect. The steepest zones of the reef (Fig. 5) are also the richest in living coral coverage. The lower *Gemmacea* zone and the *Hemprichi-variabilis* zone are characterized by wide and flat terraces with sparse and poor corals. It is possible that a major reef building process is prevented in this region by accumulation of sediments in flat terraces. The northern winds blowing along the Arava valley towards the Gulf of Eilat result in a southward transport of sand which is dumped into the Gulf. Other sources of heavy sedimentation are the numerous wadis which flush mud onto the reef occasionally during the winter rains. In the steep zones of the reef these sediments are washed down by water currents. However, in the flat zones they tend to accumulate and, moreover, their to-and-fro grinding movement caused by underwater currents may prevent normal development of some coral species which are abundant in other regions.

SUMMARY

1. A total of 97 scleractinian species belonging to 40 genera and 13 families (including two ahermatypic species) are reported from the Gulf of Eilat. Ninety-three of these species were collected from Eilat.

2. Eighty-four line transects, 10 m each, were surveyed at the reservation area of Eilat. The line transect method proved to be most efficient in avoiding problems of bottom topography and simplifying field recording procedures. It is also highly efficient in information recorded per time spent underwater.

3. The systematic transects, surveyed at three stations in the reefs of Eilat, demonstrate five main regions: the back reef, reef-crest, upper fore-reef and the lower fore-reef. These regions are divided into different zones named according to their most important faunal or structural characteristics. The lagoon, rear-reef and reef-flat are dominated by *Stylophora pistillata*. The rest of the zones are named after the most abundant species as follows: *Millepora dichotoma* (1–3 m depth), *Echinopora gemmacea* (4–12 m depth), *Acropora hemprichi* and *Acropora variabilis* (13–19 m depth), *Porites lutea* (deeper than 20 m).

4. Most of the species recorded were rare and very few abundant or dominant. The average number of species recorded per transect

increased at each successive depth, with the exception of the transects recorded at the *Hemprichi-variabilis* zone (13–17 m depth). This zone is also the poorest in coverage of living corals. The richest zones in coverage of living corals are the *Millepora* zone and the *Lutea* zone.

5. It is hypothesized that the *Hemprichi-variabilis* zone (13–17 m depth) is the poorest in living coral coverage and species abundance as a result of its bottom topography. This zone is characterized by wide flat terraces subject to sediment accumulation, which may be the main reason for the poor scleractinian abundance at this site.

ACKNOWLEDGEMENTS

This research has been sponsored by the Smithsonian Institution grant No. SFC-7-0074.

The authors are indebted to Prof. John Wells of Cornell University, for identifying the collection of scleractinian corals. Prof. Thomas Goreau (University of the West Indies and State University of New York at Stony Brook) contributed many useful suggestions in underwater work and actual photography of transects. We also wish to thank Dr. Lev Fishelson of Tel-Aviv University, for the use of equipment, vehicles and assistants and useful suggestions adopted in this work. Dan Popper of Tel-Aviv University assisted in underwater work and Amicam Shoob in photography. David Friedman, manager of the marine aquarium at Eilat, assisted in shallow water transects. We are particularly grateful to Nurit Gunderman of Tel-Aviv University, for her tireless assistance and interest through all the stages of this work.

REFERENCES

Abe, N. (1937). Ecological survey of Iwayama Bay, Palao, *Palao trop. biol. Stn. Stud.* **I**: 217–324.

Ashbel, D. (1951). *Bio-climatic atlas of Israel.* Jerusalem, Israel: Meteorological Dept., Hebrew University, 151 pp.

Ashbel, D. (1963). Climatic conditions of Elath. In "Elath", *Jerusalem, Israel: Israel Exploration Society,* Eighteenth Archaeological Convention, October 1962, p. 242–256.

Ehrenberg, C. G. (1834). Beitraege zur Kenntnis der Corallenthiere des Rothen Meers. *Abh. preuss. Akad. Wiss.,* 250–380.

Emery, K. O., Tracey, J. I., Jr. and Ladd, H. S. (1954). Geology of Bikini and nearby atolls. I. Geology. *Prof. Pap. U.S. geol. Surv.* **260**–A: 1–265.

Friedman, G. M. (1966). A fossil shoreline reef in the Gulf of Elat (Aqaba). *Israel J. Earth Sci.* **14**: 86–90.

Friedman, G. M. (1968). Geology and Geochemistry of reefs, carbonate sediments, and waters, Gulf of Aqaba (Elat), Red Sea. *J. sedim. Petrol.* **38**: 895–919.

Goreau, T. F. (1959). The ecology of Jamaican coral reefs. I. Species composition and zonation. *Ecology* **40**: 67–90.

Greig-Smith, P. (1964). *Quantitative Plant Ecology*. Washington, D.C., U.S.A.: Butterworth Inc. 242 p. 2nd ed.

Gregory, J. W. (1921). *The rift valleys and geology of East Africa*. London: Seeley, Service and Co. 479 p.

Kissling, D. L. (1965). Coral distribution on a shoal in Spanish Harbor, Florida Keys. *Bull. mar. Sci.* **15**: 600–611.

Klunzinger, C. B. (1879). *Die Korallthiere des Rothen Meers*. **2** und **3**. Berlin.

Kornicker, L. S. and Boyd, D. W. (1962). Shallow water geology and environments of Alacran reef complex, Campeche Bank, Mexico. *Bull. Am. Ass. Petrol. Geol.* **46**: 640–673.

Manton, S. M. (1935). Ecological surveys of coral reefs. *Scient. Rep. Gt Barrier Reef Exped.* **3**: 274–312.

Marenzeller, E., von. (1906). Riffkorallen Exped. "Pola" in das Rote Meer 1895/96–1897/98. *Denkschr. Akad. Wiss., Wien.* **80**: 27–97.

Odum, H. T. and Odum, E. P. (1955). Trophic structure and productivity of a windward coral reef community on Eniwetok Atoll. *Ecol. Monogr.* **25**: 291–320.

Oren, O. H. (1962). A note on the hydrography of the Gulf of Eylath. *Bull. Sea Fish. Res. Stn. Israel* **30**: 3–14.

Pichon, M. (1964). Contribution a l'étude de la répartition des Madréporaires sur la récif de Tuléar. *Recl Trav. Stat. mar. Endoume.* (fasc. hors-séries) Suppl. **2**: 79–203.

Rossi, L. (1954). Madreporari, Stoloniferi e Milleporini. *Riv. Biol. colon.* **14**: 23–72.

Scheer, G. (1964). Bemerkenswerte aus dem Roten Meer. *Senckenberg. biol.* **45**: 613–620.

Scheer, G. (1967). Korallen von den Sarso-Inseln im Roten Meer. *Senckenberg. biol.* **48**: 421–436.

Shinn, E. (1963). Spur and groove formation on the Florida Reef Tract. *J. sedim. Petrol.* **33**: 291–303.

Stoddart, D. R. (1969). Ecology and morphology of recent coral reefs. *Biol. Rev.* **44**: 433–498.

Stoddart, D. R., Davies, P. S. and Keith, A. (1966). Geomorphology of Addu Atoll. *Atoll Res. Bull.* **116**: 13–41.

Storr, J. F. (1964). Ecology and oceanography of the coral reef tract, Abaco Island, Bahamas. *Spec. Pap. geol. Soc. Am.* **79**: 1–98.

Vaughan, T. W. and Wells, J. W. (1943). Revision of the suborders, families and genera of the Scleractinia. *Spec. Pap. geol. Soc. Am.* No. **44**.

Wells, J. W. (1956). The Scleractinia. In *Treatise on Invertebrate Palaeontology*. Part F, Coelenterata. (R. C. Moore, ed.) Kansas, U.S.A.: Geol. Soc. Am., Univ. of Kansas Press. pp. 328–444.

Symp. zool. Soc. Lond. (1971) No. 28, 141–161.

STRUCTURE, ECOLOGY AND ZONATION OF RED SEA REEFS (IN COMPARISON WITH SOUTH INDIAN AND JAMAICAN REEFS)

HANS MERGNER

Lehrstuhl für Spezielle Zoologie an der Ruhr-Universität Bochum, West Germany

SYNOPSIS

The unusual climatic, topographic and hydrographic conditions of the Red Sea as a nearly isolated tropical sea favour the development of very rich coral reefs on both sides of the deep trench. These reefs are almost exclusively fringing reefs, but they are of a very different character and formation type according to their position in relation to the open sea and according to their geological history.

We find narrow reef fringes inside harbours and bays with calm water; typical flourishing coastal fringing reefs along the open sea; plateau-like broadened reef zones with a complicated system of inner and outer reefs and small fringing reefs composed by single reef patches along the coast or as a barrier-like series far off the main coast.

Selected examples of these different formation types with their structural, hydrographic and physiographic zonation, especially a new detailed analysis of the Eilat reef area, will be discussed and the results will be compared with those of other investigations on the Jamaican and South Indian reef areas.

INTRODUCTION

The topographic, climatic and hydrographic conditions of the Red Sea show a very unusual character: a deep and long trench with a broad and shallow shelf area on both sides is nearly isolated from the open ocean by very narrow straits, by the Suez Canal in the north and by Bab el Mandeb in the south. Furthermore, this isolated tropical sea is located between two broad deserts with a very hot and extremely dry climate. Therefore, the evaporation is intensive and temperature and salinity of the sea water are the highest throughout the oceans of the world.

The effects of these unusual conditions favour the formation and development of very rich coral reefs, which almost exclusively are fringing reefs but of very different character and formation type. This depends upon their position in relation to open sea and upon their ecological conditions, and upon their geological age and history. We find reef constructions as very narrow reef fringes inside harbours and bays with calm water; as typical coastal fringing reefs; as plateau-like broadened reef zones and as small fringing reefs composed by single reef patches of different form and dimension along the coast. Or we find barrier reef-like constructions composed by similar kinds of patches, but which are far off the main coast.

STRUCTURAL AND HYDROGRAPHIC REEF TYPES OF THE RED SEA

We now have to discuss these different structural, hydrographic and physiographic types of fringing reefs by means of some selected examples among the variety of investigated Red Sea reefs. First will be described structural types with their hydrographic conditions based on earlier investigations (Mergner, 1966, 1967) and afterwards a new detailed analysis of the structural, hydrographic and physiographic zonation of the most northern part of the Eilat reef will be given.

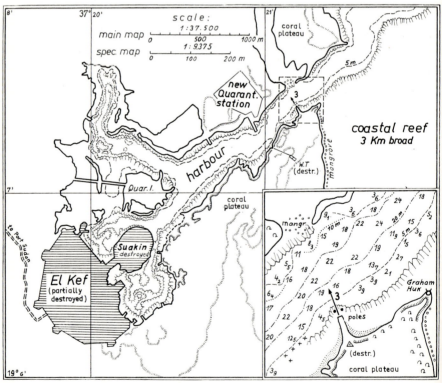

FIG. 1. Map of Suakin with its harbour. Slender reef fringes along the coast-line of the harbour channel. Inset map: Area of the investigation at the border between outer and inner channel. (From Deutsche Seekarte Nr. 331, corrected 27.IV.1963, changed by author. After Mergner, 1967.)

The narrow reef fringe inside the harbour of Suakin

The old town of Suakin was in former times a very famous centre of commerce dealing in slaves and the pilgrimages to Mecca. Nowadays however, the trade has diminished principally because the mighty coral growth of the broad coastal fringing reef has almost completely closed the mouth of the harbour. This harbour is a long narrow channel limited by an elevated fossil coral plateau and by slender living reef fringes at both sides (Fig. 1).

Close to the border between this fossil coral plateau and the recent coastal reef we find a typical biotope with calm water, with almost no water movement as surf, longreef current, rip currents or oscillation movement. In short, the water exchange with all its positive effects on coral growth is reduced by the narrowing of the channel mouth as a result of the mighty coral growth of the coastal reef.

This reduced water exchange causes a very weak coral growth of few coral species, mostly *Galaxea fascicularis* and some *Acropora*. Only rich colonies of serpulids, octocorals and actinians were found. The hydroid fauna consists of very few species of Athecata, which tolerate more mud than the Thecata, distributed throughout the whole biotope. This is typical of an area with reduced water exchange.

As an effect of the weak coral growth an old reef flat and an abrasion zone are almost missing (Fig. 2). This means, only a small slope with

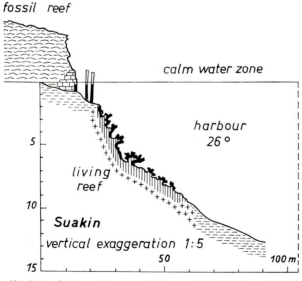

FIG. 2. Profile through the southern reef fringe of the harbour of Suakin (arrow **3** in Fig. 1). (After Mergner, 1967.)

living corals and here only small coral constructions are found. Summarising these results, we have a reef fringe with a poor coral fauna reduced by the isolation from the open sea and by the insufficient water exchange.

The typical coastal fringing reef along the coast of Jeddah

Along the sandy desert-coast to the north of Jeddah (a flourishing harbour near Mecca), especially near the bay of Sharm Bihar and northwards to the Oyster Bay, fringing reefs were found in a classic formation, which means they are constituted like reef plates. These have originated because of a stable sea level and a very rich coral growth towards the open sea (Fig. 3).

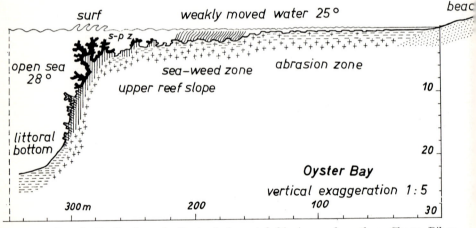

FIG. 3. Profile through the typical coastal fringing reef, northern Sharm Bihar. s-p z, small-pool zone. (After Mergner, 1967.)

Different kinds of water movement with a strong surf, large waves, sufficient oscillation movement and constant longreef current, which give a very frequent water exchange, results in the mighty and quick coral growth and a reef area with the most ideal conditions ever found.

Therefore, the structural zonation is very distinct. The beach zone is sandy, occasionally with a narrow shore channel, and it is followed outwards by a broad abrasion terrace, which represents the old reef platform covered by coral detritus and further out by sea-weed. Then we find a zone of living corals with plenty of deep wells and holes ending at the reef edge. This reef edge is formed by mighty pillars and canyons extending 10 m or more giving a buttress zone of enormous dimensions with a very intensive water exchange, which has caused the richest coral community seen by the author. The reef edge merges in a very steep and partially overhanging slope with a depth of 30–50 m or more. In the upper slope the rich coral growth within the strong light area continues with broad table-like formed *Acropora*-constructions of 3–5 m diam. The lower slope, however, is formed by a mighty scree of coral rubble, mud and organogenic sand. This scree is the underlying base of the living reef.

One of these coastal fringing reefs at the southern end of the Oyster Bay may have the richest life community of different species and individual corals, fishes, sessile animals and, including the most species and individual hydropolyps ever found within any reef area by the author. Therefore, we can signify this reef type, which grows horizontally and relatively quickly towards the open sea, as the result of its optimal ecological conditions and of the stable sea level. Finally, with increasing depth of water, the rate of lateral growth decreases because the necessary substratum basis of reef detritus is absent and the lateral growth will come to a standstill.

The plateau-like broadened reef zone of Mersa Wi Ai

The surrounding of the Flamingo Bay or Mersa Wi Ai about 5 Km north of Port Sudan (Fig. 4) shows fringing reefs, which are plateau-like, broadened and changed by different kinds of water movement to a very complicated system of outer and inner reefs separated by deep channels and lagoons. Here, the normal type of lagoon reef caused by a rising sea level, for example in Ceylon and in many regions of the Pacific, is not realized. On the contrary, the reef area of Mersa Wi Ai can only be explained by the effects of different steps in the geological history of the coastal line. It is not possible to consider this reef as a typical small barrier reef caused by slow subsiding of the coast or by a moderate rise in sea level.

According to this complicated reef system the water movement shows very different forms (Fig. 5): a strong surf with rapid rip currents and intensive oscillation movement along the outer reef combined with the intensive changing longreef current, taking place throughout the year. This longreef current dominates the channels and lagoons. The inner reefs show only a moderate surf with the depending forms of water movement. Near the shore, however, we find mostly calm water.

The coral growth and the calcium metabolism are correlated with the intensity of this water exchange. Therefore, the zonation within this reef type is very distinct. It includes a sandy shore zone, followed outwards by muddy ground with dead coral heads and sea-grass meadows, and behind it a zone with partially living coral colonies growing seawards and uniting to form miniature reefs and finally

8

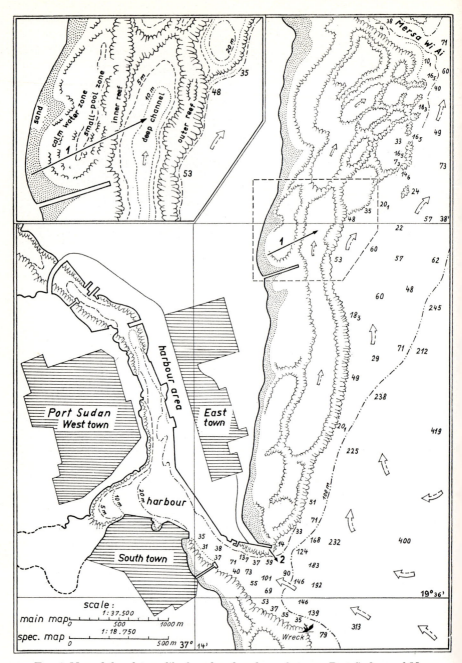

Fig. 4. Map of the plateau-like broadened reef zone between Port Sudan and Mersa Wi Ai. A complicated system of outer and inner reefs separates a number of lagoons and channels. Inside the harbour of Port Sudan slender reef fringes along the harbour-line. Special map: Area of investigation. White arrows, surface currents in the north-winter. (After Deutsche Seekarte Nr. 475, changed by the aid of author's own aerial views. After Mergner, 1967.)

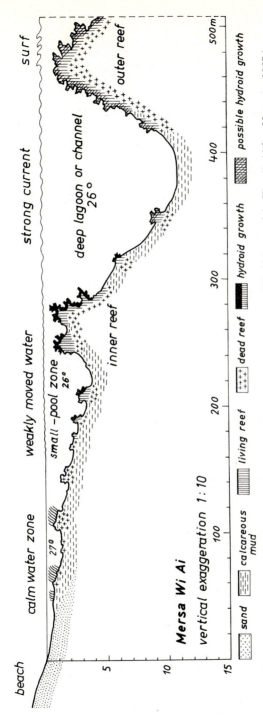

FIG. 5. Profile through the plateau-like broadened reef zone southern Mersa Wi Ai (arrow 1 in Fig. 4). (After Mergner, 1967.)

into a regular inner reef. The bottom of the channels between inner and outer reef or reefs consists of vast areas of mud and coral detritus overtopped by single living coral heads. Only the rear, the platform and the mighty and very steep outer slope of the outer reef contain living corals, while the most dense community of different species and other sessile animals is on the reef slope along the coast to the north of Jeddah.

Again summarizing the most important results of the investigation of this reef system, the similarity with a small barrier reef or with a greater lagoon reef is very noticeable. The latter normally originates from a moderately rising sea level. However, the existence of two, three or more mud flats, especially with channels or lagoons of very different depth, and with different water movement with its influence on the reef structure, allows the assumption of a more complicated case. The effects of an interesting geological history with different steps of subsiding and rising sea level have produced a very intricate reef system. This system could be explained only by the aid of aerial views made by the author in 1964 (Mergner, 1966, 1967).

The outer barrier of pillar-like reef patches at both sides of the middle Red Sea

At a distance of about 20–50 km off the main coast of the middle Red Sea, especially in front of the region around Port Sudan and Jeddah, a series of reef islets arises from the shelf floor to the sea level. These pillar-like reef patches, mostly of round or oblong shape and with steep slopes to all sides, form a long barrier along the rim of the shelf area (Fig. 6). Behind the front series we find mostly further reef patches, but these are only in an irregular pattern and not in a linear series.

It would be very interesting to explain the origin, the geological history, the structure and the zonation of these reef islets either produced by rising or subsiding shelf ground or by more complicated means. So far nobody has studied them except Einsele, Genser and Werner (1967) who investigated similar pillar-like reef islets in the Red Sea. Other investigators (Nesteroff, 1955) studied these by the means of echograms.

THE FRINGING REEF OF EILAT COMPOSED BY SINGLE PATCHES

Of the reef types so far described, different formation types are often found mixed together or specialized according to their position to the open sea, or the influence of currents or other ecological factors. These formations have been described in an earlier paper (Mergner,

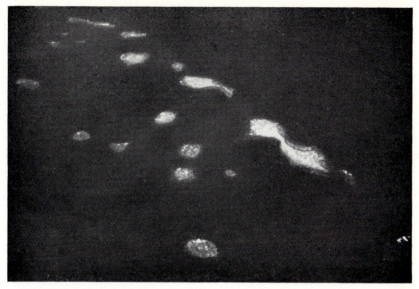

Fig. 6. Pillar-like reef islets in front of the Saudi-Arabian coast near Jeddah. A series of small reef patches arises from the shelf ground to the sea level and forms an outer barrier. Behind the front series are further reef islets forming an irregular pattern. (Aerial view by H. Mergner.)

1967), however, more detailed results of an investigation in Eilat in 1969 are given. These are in some way preliminary results because they concern only the most northern part of the Eilat reefs around the Marine Laboratory, but they may be representative for the reefs southward to the Smithsonian Bay.

The Gulf of Aqaba shows some special climatic, topographic, hydrographic and ecological conditions compared with those other regions of the Red Sea. Almost throughout the year there is a northern wind along the trench of the Jordan valley, the Dead Sea and the Gulf of Aqaba influencing the water current along the western gulf coast. Combined with this and with the deep trench formation the vertical water exchange is very intensive and causes a well-balanced water temperature of about 21–23°C, from the surface to the depth of the gulf. But the distance between the two coast lines is too small to heat the water sufficiently for a formation of mighty and flourishing coral growth. Therefore, the fringing reefs in the northern part are patchy, relatively poor in coral species, and consisting in many areas only of dead coral rock with a fragmentary covering of living corals. Probably these reefs live near the minimum conditions for existence. In spite of this, a comparison with the flourishing reef areas in the south is very interesting. This is due to the less complex physiographic zonation of the Eilat reefs, which is related to the smaller number of coral species and individuals.

First the structural and hydrographic character of these fringing reefs composed by more or less connected reef patches of different shape and length must be discussed. This means an investigation of the littoral classification together with the substratum structure as well as the coral fauna distribution within the different reef zones. These data have to be compared with the different types of water movement and the light intensity in these zones and their influence on the growth intensity, the species composition and the zonation of corals. The results of these investigations will be essential for a description of the physiographic zonation (Fig. 7).

The structural zones and their fauna

The shore zone

The beach along the Eilat reefs consists of granite sand and stones belonging to the supralittoral. The crabs *Metagrapsus mesor* and *Grapsus albilineatus* and the littorinid *Tectarius subnodosus* are found there. The eulittoral shows three subdivisions: an upper eulittoral with pure beach rock and different Littorinidae like *Littorina novae-zelandiae*; a middle eulittoral with a conglomerate of granite stones fixed by beach rock with the cirriped *Tetraclita squamosa* as the pre-dominating species and others like the molluscs *Ostrea forskali*, *Mono-donta dama*, *Cellana rota* and *Acanthopleura haddoni*; and a lower eulittoral, the pebble zone, with densely composed rounded granite stones. In this zone are found the molluscs *Nerita forskali* and *N. albicila* on the stone surface, with the littorinid *Planaxis sulcata* and the quickly running gastropod *Gena varia* found under the stones, with *Bertellina citrina* and two types of crab, the masked crab *Cryptodromia* and the interesting crab *Lybia tesselata* holding an individual of the sea anenome *Bunodeopsis prehensa* in each of the two chelae. Further animals of the lower eulittoral are the echinoderms *Asterina wega*, *Linckia multiflora*, *Ophiocoma scolopendrina*, *Echinometra matthaei* and *Nudechinus scotiopremnus*.

The lagoon or channel

The uppermost sublittoral of about 2 m depth and 25–60 m width contains the shore channel or lagoon, which is between 10 and 40 m wide and not more than 2 m deep, and the reef platform, 15–30 m wide and only 0·3–0·8 m deep.

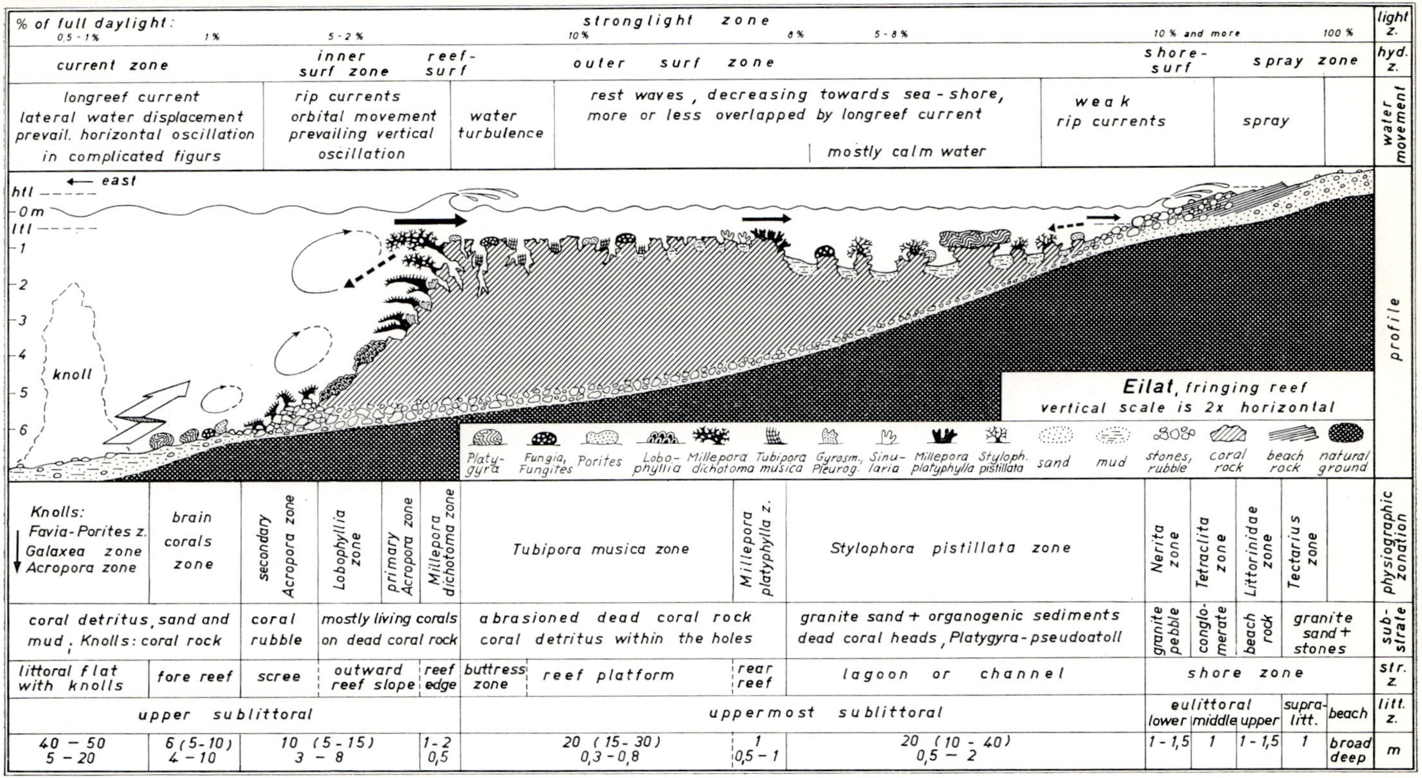

FIG. 7. Profile through the northern fringing reef of Eilat. The horizontal rows of the table from above to below show the distribution of light intensity, hydrographic zones (hyd. z.), kinds of the water movement, physiographic zones, substrate distribution, structural zones (str. z.), littoral zones (litt. z.) and width and depth of the different zones in meters. Black arrows, surf waves and their rest waves. Black broken arrows, rip currents. Rounded arrows, orbital water movement with prevailing vertical oscillation. White arrow, longreef current with prevailing horizontal oscillation and lateral water displacement. htl, high tide level. mtl, middle tide level. ltl, low tide level.

The lagoon ground is a mixture of granite sand (with its three components quartz, feldspar and mica) and of organogenic sediments (the detritus of corals, calcareous algae and of other organogenic origin). Mud, sand and rubble are well mixed. Single dead coral rocks of very different shape are covered by living coral patches of *Stylophora pistillata* and more rarely by *Favia*, *Porites* and *Platygyra*. The brain coral *Platygyra* occasionally forms so-called pseudoatolls of a mushroom shape with a dead centre and with the living coral ring directed against the longreef current.

An interesting inhabitant of *Stylophora pistillata* is a crab of the genus *Hapalocarcinus*, which is living inside galls between the coral branches. Other animals of the lagoon are the active boring sea urchin *Echinometra matthaei* living in a symbiosis with the alpheid *Arete dorsalis*, *Diadema setosum* with the ctenophore *Coeloplana*, *Echinothrix diadema*, *Tripneustes gratilla*, the crabs *Galapa hepatica* and *Trapezia* and the mullid *Parupeneus*.

The reef platform

The reef platform begins with a 0·5–1 m high step, the rear reef, and is characterized by the extended colonies of the hydrocoral *Millepora platyphylla* and the octocoral *Sinularia*. Inside galls and holes of the *Millepora*-branches are found the semiparasitic cirriped *Pyrgoma milleporae*. The reef flat is built up by dead coral rock, eroded very exactly by the effects of the water movement. It consists of more or less complicated holes and caves of different lengths. Within these holes partially filled up by coral detritus grows the octocoral *Tubipora musica* and on the flat surface small heads of *Stylophora Favia*, *Favites* and different octocoral species.

The edge of the reef platform towards the outward slope is often typically characterized by large colonies of the fire coral *Millepora dichotoma*. The fans and branches of this hydrocoral are directed with their broad side towards the longreef current, thereby gaining the best provision of plankton and oxygen. The direction of the fans shows that the surf movement is less intensive during most days of the year than that of the longreef current.

The outward slope

The upper sublittoral reaches from the reef slope to the littoral flat of the upper shelf. The outward reef slope is usually very steep and occasionally overhanging, and is composed of dead coral rock with a complicated system of deep and differentially shaped caves, holes, canyons, pillars and rips. The prevailing part of this buttress zone is covered by living corals, but partially bare dead coral rock is enclosed, on which are found calcareous algae such as *Lithothamniom* and *Halimeda*.

In the upper slope different species of *Acropora* predominate forming more or less extended tables, umbrellas and plates. In the shadowed areas of this zone, for example in caves or under the great *Acropora* tables, we find other corals like *Galaxea fascicularis*, *Gyrosmilia* and *Pleurogyra*. In the lower slope *Lobophyllia corymbosa* and other species of greenish and yellow colour predominate in the form of very extended flat colonies. Besides, also the octocorals *Sarcophyton*, *Lobophytum* and *Lithophytum* in the form of shrubs, dishes and fans occur.

The lowermost zone of the slope shows a scree with the rubble from the upper part, broken down by the effects of water movement or by the activity of boring animals like *Lithophaga* or the clionid sponges. On the surface of this scree the living pieces of *Acropora* and other corals broken down form a secondary *Acropora* zone. The rest of this gradually flattening dead zone is covered by coral detritus, rubble and mostly organogenic mud.

The fore reef and the littoral flat

The fore reef consists of a gradually outwards falling flat area with a mixture of organogenic sand, mud and coral rubble in a depth of 4–10 m. It is covered by massive coral heads of different brain corals and other corals like *Favia* and *Favites*. This fore reef leads to a vast littoral bottom or littoral flat with muddy and sandy ground of a depth from 10–20 m afterwards falling to the deep step of the trench.

In a distance of 40–50 m from the reef slope single pillar-like knolls arise from the flat. They consist of dead coral rock settled on by living corals in a similar zonation like that of the main reef slope. At the top of the knolls we find *Favia* and *Porites*, below this zone *Galaxea* and afterwards *Acropora* and *Lobophyllia*. The base of the knolls is surrounded by coral rubble like the scree of the main reef slope.

Throughout the slope, the fore reef and the knolls are numbers of the solitary coral *Fungia* in each stage of growth and many species and individuals of the sea urchins *Diadema setosum*, *Heterocentrus mammillatus* and *Tripneustes gratilla*, the crinoids *Heterometra savingii* and *Lampometra klunzingeri* and the holothuroid *Synapta*. Various molluscs live within the coral constructions, for example the lamellibranchs *Tridacna* and *Lithophaga*; the gastropods *Cypraea arabica* and, *Magilus antiquus* with its twisted tubes fixed within the coral rock. The dead coral rock especially is the habitat of many hydropolyps growing within the shadowed caves and holes with the exception of the genus *Thyroscyphus* living at the top and lighted sides of the rocks (Mergner, in preparation).

The reef fish fauna is characterized by the labrid *Coris angulata*; different Balistidae and Chaetodontidae like *Pygoplites*; parrot fishes; the fistularid *Fistularia petimba*; the scorpaenid *Pterois volitans* and, the pomacentrid fishes *Chromis, Amphiprion bicinctus, Dascyllus marginatus* and *D. aruanus*.

The hydrographic zones and their water movement

After we have observed the littoral and structural zonation with their substratum and fauna, we should now turn to the hydrographic zonation and different water movements.

The shore-surf and the spray zone

The waves along the Eilat region are usually low except for a few days during the year when stormy weather causes strong waves. Therefore, the surf in this area is not too strong. Two surf areas are found—one along the beach, "weak shore-surf" and one along the reef edge, "little stronger reef-surf". Both surfs cause an outer surf zone with rest waves decreasing landwards and an inner surf zone with water turbulence and rip currents.

However, the shore-surf with a gently marked spray zone, the supralittoral, causes only a slight oscillatory movement within the eulittoral and the close lagoon, which is sufficient for the fauna within this area.

The reef-surf and its outer surf zone

Within the lagoon the water is mostly calm and only disturbed by the rest waves of the outer reef-surf which decrease gradually towards the sea-shore. There they are overlapped by the effect of the longreef current, in the same way shown by the example of the growth-form of the *Platygyra*-pseudoatoll. This hydrographic zone from the reef edge to the beach can be designated as the outer surf zone.

On the other hand, the reef-surf is not strong enough to direct the fans of *Millepora dichotoma* parallel to the reef rim and towards the approaching waves of the open sea.

The inner surf zone along the outward reef slope

The rip currents of the reef-surf are sufficient to cause a remarkable vertical oscillation along the reef slope. For example we find an orbital water movement within the area of the upper slope decreasing towards the lower slope and leading to the prevailing horizontal oscillation of the deeper situated fore reef.

The current zone

The fore reef and the littoral flat are predominated by the longreef current expressed by prevailing lateral water displacement. But along the fore reef the vertical oscillation of the inner surf zone influences the horizontal oscillation of the longreef current, and the combination of the two causes complicated current figures of the lateral water displacement. Finally, with increasing distance down the reef slope the influence of the inner surf zone gradually decreases and the water movement will become a pure lateral displacement, taking place in the current zone.

The water exchange and its effects on the coral growth

The water exchange along the reef edge and the upper slope by the effects of the reef-surf and the turbulence of the rip currents is the most intensive within the whole reef area. It is responsible for a good plankton and oxygen supply to the reef fauna with a maximum in the *Millepora*-zone. Below this zone the *Acropora*-communities also find good ecological conditions especially with the effect of the vertical oscillation. These good conditions decrease gradually towards the shore-zone and the lower slope, where the water exchange is reduced.

Therefore, the coral growth follows the intensity of the water exchange expressed by the most dense communities along the edge and the upper slope with such species needing intensive supply of plankton and oxygen. Such corals are *Millepora dichotoma* and *Acropora*. However, within the lower slope, the fore-reef and the lagoon, are found species more easily satisfied, and often characterized by a weaker growth, such as species of *Pocillopora*, *Favia*, *Porites* and certain brain corals.

The light intensity and the light distribution

The coral distribution and the growth intensity is not only influenced by the water exchange, but also by the light intensity which depends on the incidence of light and the depth of water. The distribution of light and shadow are very important for determining these facts. The whole reef is situated within the stronglight zone with at least 10–1% of full daylight. We find about 10% light intensity at the reef platform at high tide level and even more at low tide level. Furthermore we find 5–8% light intensity within the lagoon, about 5% along the upper slope and 2–3% in the lighted parts of the lower slope. The littoral flat gets about 1% light intensity. All these percentages are only valid in calm and sunny weather with clear water for the intensity decreases with the effects of stormy and cloudy weather.

The light intensity varies throughout the day time with the movement of the sun and with clouding. Therefore, we find certain species adapted to the full light along the reef edge, on the platform and within the lagoon. Other species live within the shadowed areas of caves and holes or below the great horizontal umbrellas of *Acropora*. Areas change from deep shadow to a varying distribution of light and slight shadow.

The physiographic zones

Few investigators have reported on the physiographic zonation of Red Sea reefs (Mergner, 1967) and then often only on limited areas (Klausewitz, 1967) or on that of a certain littoral zone (Safriel and Lipkin, 1964). Safriel and Lipkin (1964) reported on the intertidal zonation of the rocky shores at Eilat, but did not give any information on the physiographic zonation of the other littoral zones. Therefore, detailed notes are given on these.

Described above were the ecological and other conditions caused by the influences of water movement, light intensity, substratum and enemies like the coral-eating parrot fishes and boring animals. Also included were the variations of the reef structure caused by storms, calcium metabolism and the local development of the coral distribution and the predomination of certain species. Considering these main factors we can define the physiographic zones within the most northern Eilat reef (Fig. 7):

The supralittoral can be termed as *Tectarius subnodosus*-zone; the upper eulittoral as Littorinidae-zone; the middle eulittoral as *Tetraclita squamosa*-zone and the lower eulittoral as *Nerita*-zone. In other words, typical mollusc-zones predominate along the shore which are influenced in their delimitation by the tide movement, light intensity and the nature of the substratum. The rest of the reef can be subdivided into various coral zones.

The lagoon can definitely be termed as *Stylophora pistillata*-zone because this coral species absolutely predominates. Next, the step region of the rear reef is a *Millepora platyphylla*-zone which leads to the reef flat. Although it is difficult to consider this reef platform as a physiographic zone, the term *Tubipora musica*-zone is proposed. More detailed investigations in all probability will reveal further subdivisions.

The reef edge is dominated by *Millepora dichotoma* and we surely cannot find a better specification than *Millepora dichotoma*-zone. Going downwards, the upper slope is occupied by a very dense community of different *Acropora* species without any one predominating. Therefore, we denote this area as a primary *Acropora*-zone. Below this zone along the lower slope we find the extended flat colonies of some species of *Lobophyllia* which predominate. Therefore, the designation *Lobophyllia*-zone is correct. At the deepest parts of the outward slope and mixed with scree of coral rubble we find a secondary *Acropora*-zone consisting of the broken down branches and tables of the primary *Acropora*-zone.

The fore reef is characterized by the abundance of massive corals of different species but mostly brain corals. This zone preliminarily is named the massive coral-zone. Finally, the knolls are subdivided from top to bottom by some more or less characteristic zones, such as an upper *Favia-Porites*-zone, with below it a *Galaxea*-zone and an *Acropora*-zone. However, a more intensive investigation would result in the description of a more detailed zonation.

COMPARISON WITH JAMAICAN AND SOUTH INDIAN CORAL REEFS

We now have discussed the influence of climate, topography, structure and hydrography on the physiographic zonation of the Red Sea fringing reefs especially the Eilat reef. While the structural and hydrographic zonation of most Red Sea reefs can be recognized easily, the great number of animal groups and coral species renders the designation of the physiographic zones more difficult. However, a few of them can be traced. For example a *Stylophora*-zone or *Pocillopora*-zone is found within the lagoon; a *Millepora dichotoma*-zone is found along the reef edge; an *Acropora*-zone is found along the upper slope, and a *Lobophyllia*-zone is found along the lower slope, sometimes forming a massive brain coral-zone, as in the case of a fore reef, still situated within the zone of strong light.

In contrast to the physiographic conditions of the Red Sea reefs, the physiographic zonation of Jamaican coral cays near Kingston Harbour and of the fringing reefs along the north coast of Jamaica is very clear and relatively easy to define. This is demonstrated by the investigations of Goreau (1959) and Zans (1958) and the author (Mergner, 1969, in press). A limited number of absolutely predominating coral species are characteristic of a series of physiographic zones, for example, the upper *Palmata*-zone within the breaker or inner surf zone; the lower *Palmata*-zone within the oscillation zone; the

Cervicornis-zone along the lower slope and the *Annularis*-zone as the fore reef within the current zone.

Moreover, the fringing reefs near to Mandapam, South India, composed of small reef patches like those near Eilat show a distinct zonation worked out by Scheer and the author. The results of this investigation will be published in the near future. The zonation of these fringing reefs is characterized by different algae and animal groups. These are not easy to recognize, since the growth of the most predominating species of the single physiographic zones is weak, or since there are several predominating species in each zone. This situation could be found especially within the reef area at the south-west coast of Ceylon. But in this region the zonation of the sublittoral lagoon area was characterized by algae, hydroids, octocorals and hexacorals. This means, it is not always possible to denote a physiographic zonation by the aid of corals as in the case of the most Red Sea reefs investigated by the author.

SUMMARY

Nearly all of the investigated reefs show a more or less broad reef platform falling gradually towards the open sea regardless of reef type and local situation (Fig. 8). The reef platform may or may not have a narrow lagoon and it is eroded by the effects of water movement following the coastal elevation. There is usually also a steep slope towards the open sea. In the case of a well-growing fringing reef at stable sea level, only those zones form the "living reef", which are affected by abundant water movement and situated closely to the reef edge. The living reef is steadily growing outwards, whereas the "dead reef" behind, continually grows broader and the sediment scree beneath the outward slope constantly grows higher.

Decisive for the above situation is the exchange of water per unit of volume and time. The intensity of water exchange is responsible for the supply of plankton-nutrition and of oxygen, also for the balance of temperature and salt concentration, as well as for the calcium metabolism and for the removal of the gathering sediments. Therefore, the most plentiful growth of corals is found in the areas of the reef edge and of the upper slope. As a result of this, a variety of densely populated miniature landscapes exists. The varying ecological conditions of these miniature landscapes satisfies the requirements of life of the various animal groups. Within this area with optimum living conditions the more delicate distribution of the distinct species is determined by their various demands on the intensity of light. On the other

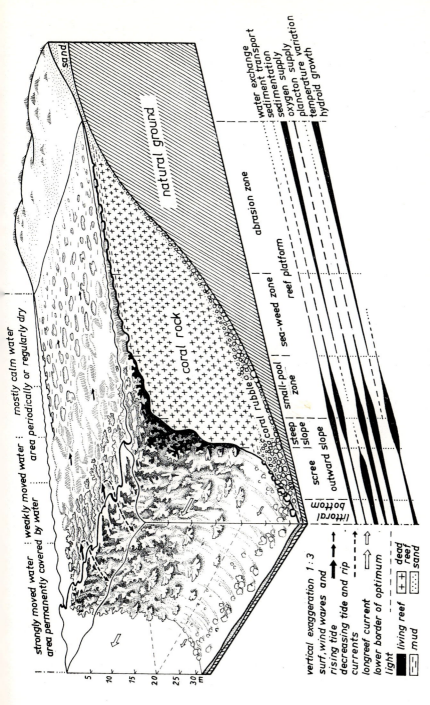

FIG. 8. Typical coastal fringing reef caused by a flourishing coral growth and by stable sea level. Three-dimensional diagram illustrating the reef structure, the reef zonation and the most important ecological conditions within the reef. (After Mergner, 1967.)

hand, the nature of the substrate is of certain but mostly of subordinate importance in the selection of the site.

A number of miniature landscapes or even only one of them represent a certain biotope with a population typically composed by algae and of mobile and sessile animals. But the population within this biotope suffers a continuously changing composition, caused by birth and death, by changes of substratum (especially by coral growth and destruction), and by changes of water movement, incidence of light and other abiotic and biotic factors.

However, in each moment a certain species or even several species predominate by their greater number, by larger structures or by more intensive growth. These predominating species may be sessile animals like lamellibranchs and bryozoans, but seldom are they mobile animals, or they may be algae especially calcareous species. But within flourishing coral reefs the predominating species are mostly corals. In nearly every case they determine the character of the physiographic zones within the reef.

ACKNOWLEDGEMENTS

The investigations concerning the reef areas of the middle Red Sea were supported by Deutsche Forschungsgemeinschaft, Bad Godesberg, B.R. Deutschland. Grateful acknowledgements are due to the following: Dr. Tsunamal and Dr. Por, both of the Hebrew University, Jerusalem, for their help and advice based on their great experience, and Dr. Holl, Justus Liebig-Universität, Giessen, for correcting this manuscript.

REFERENCES

Einsele, G., Genser, H. and Werner, F. (1967). Horizontal wachsende Riffplatten am Süd-Ausgang des Roten Meeres. *Senckenberg leth.* **48**: 359–379.

Goreau, T. F. (1959). The ecology of Jamaican reefs. I. Species composition and zonation. *Ecology* **40**: 67–90.

Klausewitz, W. (1967). Die physiographische Zonierung der Saumriffe von Sarso. *Meteor* D, **2**: 44–68.

Mergner, H. (1966). Aufgaben und Ergebnisse der Hydroidenforschung im Roten Meer. *Umschau* **24**: 814–816.

Mergner, H. (1967). Über den Hydroidenbewuchs einiger Korallenriffe des Roten Meeres. I. Die ökologischen Gegebenheiten der untersuchten Riffgebiete und ihre Auswirkungen auf Verteilung und Besiedlungsdichte des Hydroidenbewuchses. *Z. Morph. Ökol. Tiere* **60**: 35–104.

Mergner, H. (1969). The influence of several ecological factors on the hydroid growth of some Jamaican coral cays. Symposium on corals and coral reefs Mandapam Camp (Mandapam Camp: Marine Biological Association of India). In press.

Nesteroff, W. (1955). Les récifs coralliens du Banc Farsan (Mer Rouge). *Annls Inst. Océanogr., Monaco* **30**: 1–53.

Safriel, C. U. and Lipkin, Y. (1964). Note on the intertidal zonation of the rocky shores at Eilat (Red Sea, Israel). *Isr J. Zool.* **13**: 187–190.

Stoddart, D. R. (1969). Ecology and morphology of recent coral reefs. *Biol. Rev.* **44**: 433–498.

Zans, V. A. (1958). Recent coral reefs and reef environment of Jamaica. *Geonotes* **1**: 18–25.

Discussion

GUILCHER: Two of the features described in the central area of the Red Sea, around Port Sudan, Suakin and Jeddah, may have been strongly influenced by tectonic movements.

(1) The long ridges stretching along the coast of Saudi Arabia, especially in the northern part of Farsan Bank, and rising from deep water (as deep as 700 m in some places) may be termed tectonic ridges or horsts, coated by corals, the thickness of which is unknown. Geophysical investigations or borings could yield information on this point.

(2) The long narrow bays occurring on either side of the Red Sea, which are called *sherm* (plural *shurum*), as at Port Sudan and to the north of Jeddah, may have had their shapes influenced by tectonic movements, as a German geomorphologist has supposed, and have had their sides subsequently coated with corals.

In any case, tectonic influences are clear in some raised reefs, as on Abulat Island, Farsan Bank, which is cut by numerous recent faults. The fault scarps are still extremely fresh, because of the arid climate.

Symp. zool. Soc. Lond. (1971) No. 28, 163–183.

PRINCIPAL FEATURES OF REEF CORAL ECOLOGY IN SHALLOW WATER ENVIRONMENTS OF MAHE, SEYCHELLES

BRIAN R. ROSEN

Department of Geophysics and Planetary Physics, School of Physics
The University, Newcastle-upon-Tyne, England.

SYNOPSIS

The essential features of reef coral distribution on the reefs and open shores of Mahé are discussed for depths less than 10 m. By applying some of the methods and concepts of plant sociology in a largely qualitative way, coral stands can be grouped into assemblage types and hence into communities, facies and elements. Further use of plant sociological methods, quantitative and qualitative, is urged as an effective means of making local and regional comparisons of coral ecology. A schematic representation of coral assemblage distribution for Mahé is presented as a sublittoral extension of known schemes of littoral and supralittoral organic zonation of rocky shores. Representative communities are described for each assemblage type, and notable variations indicated. A discordance is recognized between the distribution of coral assemblages and their associated coastal features, and the geological implications of this are discussed. The contribution of reef corals to current reef building is briefly assessed.

INTRODUCTION*

Mahé is the principal island of the Seychelles. It is the largest in the group and consists of a granitic mass rising to nearly 1000 m altitude. A variable and irregular development of fringing reefs is present along most eastern shores of the island, while along the western side the coast is mostly free of reefs apart from occasional platforms. The prevailing winds follow a seasonally asymmetric alternation: the southeast trades are steadier and more prolonged (April to October), and the "Northwest Monsoon" (November to March) is more variable. The northwest season is wetter. The Seychelles lie beyond the usual cyclone paths. Further details of the general setting and environment of Mahé are given by Braithwaite elsewhere in this volume (pp. 39–63), and also by Taylor (1968) and Lewis (1969). The essential geological and ecological nature of the reefs and associated environments has already been described in some detail in these papers, as well as in those by Lewis (1968), Taylor and Lewis (1970) and the earlier report by Lewis and Taylor (1966).

* For localities mentioned in this account, please refer to the map in the accompanying paper by Braithwaite, p. 40.

The present writer has concentrated upon the coral ecology of the island, and two closely related problems are discussed here: (1) the sublittoral extension of universal schemes of rocky shore zonation with respect to corals, and (2) the extension of the reef front coral community subdivision first mentioned by Lewis and Taylor (1966) and subsequently described more fully by Taylor (1968). Through the discussion of these subjects, the opportunity is taken to suggest that the difficulties encountered in attempting a systematic analysis of coral communities might best be approached by drawing on the field of plant sociology.

Description of a single island contributes little to a discussion of regional variation, but the facts presented here are available for comparison. A more detailed account is in preparation.

SCHEME OF CORAL ASSEMBLAGES

Stephenson and Stephenson (1949) first pointed out the universal nature of rocky shore zonation, and their scheme has since been modified, adopted and applied by other authors (e.g. Lewis, 1964, Fig. 17; Morton and Miller, 1968, Fig. 20) for temperate waters. The Stephensons however stressed that coral reefs were no exception to the scheme, and a number of ecologists (see Taylor, 1968) have also discussed reef shores in these terms. Taylor (1968, Figs 6 and 7) presented a diagrammatic scheme for Mahé reefs analogous to those for temperate waters mentioned above. In each case, the basis of these schemes is that "physical conditions are best revealed by the organisms" (Lewis, 1964), and that the most significant controlling factors are frequency of emersion by tidal rise and fall, and vigour of water movement. For corals, emersion only determines the upper limit of growth (like the laminarian algae in temperate waters, corals serve to define the tropical sublittoral zone), and except for a very narrow uppermost zone, it exerts no direct influence on their vertical distribution. On the other hand, on Mahé at least, the main coral communities are associated with different degrees of prevailing water movement, as shown by Taylor (1968) in his discussion of "windward edges" and "sheltered edges", associated respectively with his *Acropora* and *Porites* communities. It is possible to extend and generalize this subdivision still further to cover the shallow water (i.e. uppermost 7–10 m) distribution of corals in all Mahé environments that were visited. Where water movement is most vigorous, i.e. the surf zone, the most conspicuous coral genus is *Pocillopora*; where there is water movement, but not surf action, *Acropora* is most conspicuous; and where there is

little or no tangible water movement, *Porites* predominates. This
sequence, with transitions, is therefore associated with a gradient of
decreasing water movement, and is demonstrated whenever this
gradient is traced from an exposed environment through a sequence
of less exposed environments, e.g. in passing (1) vertically downward
from the surf zone on a reef front, (2) shorewards across a reef platform, or (3) along a reef margin or reef front which passes into a more
obviously sheltered situation. Field evidence for the complete sequence
is provided by overlapping partial sequences from several localities.
The sequence is summarized for the three component directions in
the idealized scheme shown in Fig. 1.

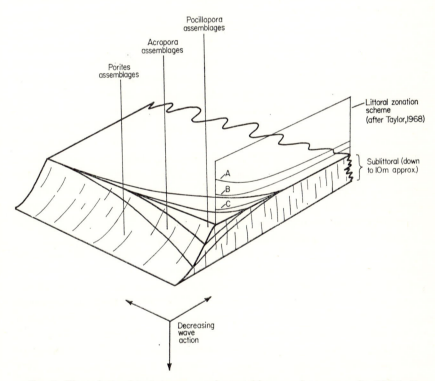

Fig. 1. The relationship between coral assemblages and exposure for Mahé, Seychelles. The scheme represents a sublittoral continuation of the littoral zonation given
by Taylor (1968) (shown in the right hand part of the diagram) and is presented here
in the form of an idealized reef section. Littoral zonation: A—upper limit of *Littorina*
and blackening organisms; B—upper limit of barnacles; C—upper limit of corals and
Sargassum algae. (Diagram not to scale.)

CORAL ECOLOGY AND THE STUDY OF PLANT COMMUNITIES:
TERMINOLOGY

Before turning to analogies with plant ecology it is first necessary to make several broader based distinctions. By confining attention to a single organic group, it is easy to give a false impression of the importance of that group in environments where it may be inconspicuous. Members of that group may still occur in definite associations with each other and other groups, but the concept of a community cannot strictly be applied. **Community** has therefore been used here for a whole fauna (i.e. biocoenosis), and the particular communities recognized on Mahé are those described by Taylor (1968). The present account thereby retains Taylor's terms of reference (with some extension for the corals). A **coral community** is one in which corals predominate. Where they occur only in local concentrations (e.g. small thickets) within a community which is otherwise made up largely of other organisms, **facies** is used; and where corals are present only as inconspicuous faunal elements, **elements** is used. A group term to cover all three levels proved necessary, and **assemblage** was adopted in preference to **fauna**, which often has regional connotations. Assemblages are grouped into the three main types shown in Fig. 1. Each of these is represented by a **principal coral community** used as a "standard", and taken to be the most representative assemblage of each assemblage type. In each case they are reef front assemblages since it is in this environment that diversities, abundances and cover are highest, presumably as a response to the most favourable conditions. There follows the deliberate implication that all other assemblages can conveniently be regarded as modifications of these principal communities by less favourable conditions.

It is a striking fact that after more than a hundred years of reef study, no really detailed comparative synthesis of coral ecology, based on representative reefs from most regions, has ever been attempted. Amongst other reasons, it has evidently proved difficult to approach the subject locally at a sufficient conceptual level to develop the kind of generalizations that are essential for effective comparisons. Advances in this field compare unfavourably with those made in the study of many non-colonial animal groups, or plants, for instance. As Stoddart (1969) has pointed out in his discussion of ecological methods applied to reef corals, the lack of consistent terminology and techniques has offset the advances made by individuals. More recently however various authors, including Scheer (1967), Barnes *et al.* (this volume, pp. 87–114) and the present author, have independently turned to plant sociology, where many of the same problems occur and have been tackled successfully, or at least consistently. This more recent trend is appropriate to hermatypic corals in view of the importance of their symbiotic algae, and the obsolete term Zoophytes, which included corals, acquires a new significance. The text book by Oosting (1956) was used during the present work, but further sources should be used in more detailed studies in the future.

It was not possible to apply any of the quantitative methods of plant sociology here, but a method of approximation was used in conjunction with a number of useful qualitative concepts, and a scheme of coral growth forms (Table I). These made it possible to define the

TABLE I

Growth form scheme

	Encrusting—Massive (EM)	Massive (M)
	Encrusting—Ramose (ER)	delicate Ramose (dR) robust Ramose (rR)
Encrusting (E)	Encrusting—Platy (EP)	delicate Platy (dP) robust Platy (rP)
	Encrusting—Columnar (EC)	Columnar (C)
	Encrusting solitary (Es)	Unattached—solitary and colonial (U)
		Fasciculate (F)

various Mahé coral assemblages. Total coral cover and relative importance was estimated subjectively and denoted by use of cover class numbers (5) and the terms discussed above: community, facies and elements. Every species (or "eco-species") present was then classed individually according to its relative abundance within the total coral biomass, this being assessed as an approximate combined estimate of frequency of occurrence and living mass. Species were classed into growth form types (Table I), this being an established environmental indicator of water movement and related factors. Class numbers of total coral cover for a given assemblage can be multiplied by class numbers of individual species abundance within that assemblage to obtain an individual rating for each species. Totals of such ratings can also be obtained to express the relative importance of a particular growth form. In this way it was possible to make comparisons between the coral populations found at different localities and in different environments, and so to recognize broader patterns.

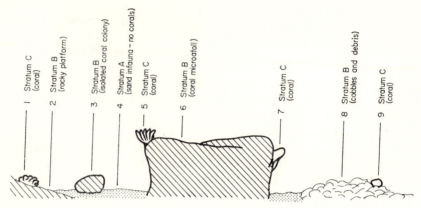

Fig. 2. Examples of stratification in coralline environments. For details see text.

Further distinctive features of a coral population, or stand, can be stressed by adopting useful descriptive terms from plant sociology. **Stratification** enabled substrate associations to be systematically recognized (Fig. 2). Stratum A denotes sandy, and other soft substrates, and a Stratum A organism is one that inhabits the sand infaunally (i.e. not usually applicable to corals). Stratum B organisms live on the sand, and can in turn provide a substrate for further organisms, i.e. those of Stratum C. Stratum B is extended to cover all hard substrates whether they overlie a soft stratum or not, and whether the B stratum is dead or alive. Subdivisions of B and C were used, though these are not referred to here. It was found that while many corals occurred indiscriminately in both B and C, certain forms were definitely restricted. The special case where a C stratum coral is consistently found on a B stratum coral (or corals) introduces the concept of **dependence,** there being an analogy in plant ecology with (e.g.) lichen-tree associations. **Dominance** is distinguished from predominance, in that a dominant species is recognized as one that determines the overall structure and stratification of a stand, rather than one that simply appears to be very abundant. In practice, predominant corals often prove to be dominant too, but the distinction is important elsewhere.

MAHÉ CORAL ASSEMBLAGES

General remarks

Mahé has a very irregular outline, and on both this account and the alternation in prevailing wind direction, precise definition of windward and leeward shores is not really possible. Prevailing swell is subjected to a great deal of refraction, as aerial photographs show. Moreover, it cannot be assumed that the broadest reefs are equivalent to windward reefs (etc.) as the wide but sheltered Victoria harbour reefs indicate. The environment pattern is correspondingly complex and irregular, and biological features must be sharply distinguished from physical features in an effort to find relationships between the two. The environmental terms used here are based on morphological features and for the reefs themselves they correspond to the zones recognized by most authors.

Pocillopora *assemblages*

True *Pocillopora* assemblages are relatively restricted in their distribution, and are associated with rough water, especially in or near the surf zone. The principal community for this group of assemblages is characterized by *Pocillopora danae-meandrina*,* *Acropora humilis* and *Millepora platyphylla*. Growth forms are characteristically encrusting or robust, an undoubted response to the potentially damaging effect of the strong water movement: encrusting corals 20%, robust ramose 10%, encrusting ramose 3%, robust platy 8%, massive corals 15%. The total for delicate forms is conspicuously low at 10%; such corals are found in well protected crevices and hollows. The general appearance of the coral assemblage is one in which robust ramose, robust platy and encrusting corals predominate visually. The substrate is consistently hard and often smooth with only a few pockets of moving sediment veneer. The whole assemblage is C stratum (Fig. 2, nos. 1 and 2). There is relatively little colonization by coral species on older growths, apart from a frequent association of *Pocillopora* growing amongst the plates of *Millepora platyphylla*. Coral cover is rather sparse (class 3, which on the basis of quadrat work is equivalent to about 15% horizontal cover). Coral colonies are rarely larger than a metre or so, and are often much smaller.

This community is typical of reef fronts of the southeast part of the island (Anse aux Pins, etc.). The reef fronts here slope gently down

* It has long been recognized by many, but not universally agreed, that *Pocillopora* species fall into two principal groups typified by *P. eydouxi* and *P. verrucosa*, and distinguished on calice details. The second group includes numerous intergradational growth forms that have been attributed to different species. They can be regarded as a series exhibiting an increasingly stout and compact branching structure from *P. damicornis* to *P. meandrina*. On Mahé, ecological evidence suggests that the series can be broken in two, with more delicate members denoted by "*P. damicornis-bulbosa*" and more robust members by "*P. danae-meandrina*". Further study and systematic treatment may eventually formalize these as two subspecies within a single species series.

beneath the water from the reef margins and consist of an irregular rocky surface in which there is an alternation of groove-and-spur like features. This can be seen in the echo-sounding profile reproduced by Lewis (1968, Fig. 2 and traverse 55 in Fig. 4; allowance should be made for the different horizontal scales between sample stations). The same community is also to be found on the reef margins adjacent to the above reef fronts. In places, especially the north end of Anse aux Pins, the occurrence of several well defined, smaller scale habitats makes it possible to distinguish a variety of coral facies within the overall community. Thus *Stylophora mordax* is an important member of the coral assemblage that is typical of surge channel margins. To seaward, where the margin platform is more dissected, and appears above low tide level as small islands, *Millepora platyphylla* and *Acropora B* (a group of species or "species" including *A. rotumana* and *A. decipiens*) are common. The shoreward side of these margins is often noticeably rich in *Acropora humilis* (up to 15% of the total hard coral cover), though it is rare or absent to seaward. *P. danae-meandrina* on the other hand increases from about 5% to 20% or more, from the shore side to the seaward side. Coral diversity usually decreases in this same direction, so that the outermost parts of the margin often bear only *Pocillopora*, *Millepora platyphylla*, *Acropora B*, and *Goniastrea retiformis*. In some places the amount of *Pocillopora* does not increase, but it becomes proportionally more important because of the diversity decrease. The shoreward part of the margin is conspicuously higher at some points on account of the *A. humilis* colonies. Dead and living colonies have built up a terrace or secondary platform above the main margin platform and corals here stand higher above mean low water in this environment than in any other. As for littoral zonation of other organisms on rocky shores, spray from the more vigorous water movement keeps emersed colonies wet. This feature is expressed on the scheme (C in Fig. 1) by the upward curve of the coral limit line at the exposed end.

Zonation within this community on reef margins is consistent with the explanation that to seaward conditions are made progressively less favourable at low water by the direct action of the surf. Only those corals which can withstand this occur there. To shoreward, ability to withstand emersion favours *Acropora humilis* in its platform sites. The zoning is probably controlled by low water conditions since at high water, the depth over the whole margin eliminates emersion as a factor and probably makes surf action less selective in its effect. Waves do not break dully here at high water. Apart from the facies and zonation on these margins, there are no significant differences between these margins and adjacent reef fronts bearing the same coral assemblage. Structurally the assemblages are the same. Substrates are similar, with surge channels on the margins passing downward into irregular grooves. On many margins however, the surge channels are very poorly developed, or even absent. Instead, the margins are uneven with irregular hollows and re-entrants. In these cases, the above facies and zonation are blurred or not evident.

Two other variations within this assemblage type are of interest. In the southern part of the island there are several bays with very small reef platforms on which corals are sparse. At Petite Police, the entire width of the reef is only about 20–30 m, and on faunal grounds it can be considered as consisting only of a reef margin without the customary flats behind. The same community can be recognized here as at Anse aux Pins, but with reduced diversity and cover. Species of *Acropora* (*Acropora B*, *A. humilis* and an encrusting form of *A. palifera*) are found closer to shore, and *Pocillopora danae-meandrina* predominates to seaward. This southern tip of Mahé is probably the most exposed part of Mahé coast on account of its headland position and aspect (but it does not face directly southeast), and this is borne out by other faunal features, e.g. the Mollusca (Taylor, 1968). The paucity of coral is possibly a consequence of excessive surf action, as is the unusually common occurrence of encrusting *A. palifera* and *Acropora B*. If this reef is taken to be the most exposed on Mahé, it is strictly a "windward" reef, and as such, it is significant that it contrasts with the conventional atoll picture in two respects: its paucity of coral and its narrowness. The geological implications of this contrast are discussed below.

The absence of a simple relationship between reef development and coral fauna is further emphasized by the features seen at Anse Takamaka on the southwest coast. Here, a coral community can be seen growing directly on steep granite surfaces and boulders of the adjacent headland. The assemblage differs only slightly from the principal assemblage already described; and this can be explained by the unusual substrate, particularly its steepness and smoothness, which is probably unfavourable to some species. Ramose corals are less evident therefore, with the notable exception of *Pocillopora eydouxi*, while encrusting, encrusting-massive and encrusting-ramose forms are relatively more important.

It seems reasonable to conclude that within a range of readily observed modifications, *Pocillopora* assemblages occur wherever rougher water conditions and a hard substrate are present. Their occurrence is independent of reef type or other morphological controls. The combination of rough water and a soft substrate, i.e. exposed sandy bays, is unfavourable to most organic groups and corals are completely absent. The apparent anomaly of Anse Takamaka and other similar instances can be accommodated into the general scheme of Fig. 1 if the steep rocky surfaces are thought of as a reef front without the reef platform behind it. It is impossible to escape from the conclusion that whatever the environmental conditions are that control the present coral assemblages, they cannot be the same as those that account for the existing shallow water coastal features, since coral ecology and coastal geomorphology are so independent of each other.

Acropora *assemblages*

The principal community for *Acropora* assemblages is found along open water reef fronts of the Victoria Harbour area (though not exclusively). These reef fronts consist of gently sloping banks of living coral and sandy sediment. The two most important corals are *Acropora A* (stagshorns, including mainly *Acropora formosa*) and *A. irregularis*, which, with other species, form dense stands of coral almost completely obscuring the substrate (i.e. cover class 5). Delicate ramose corals contribute at least 30% of the coral mass present, and most other growth forms are subsidiary (5–10% each). In places, *Acropora A* is present to the exclusion of almost all other corals, but elsewhere there are clearings of bare sandy substrate with *Fungia* or dead stagshorn rubble. Within the range of delicate ramose forms, four principal variations exist: stagshorn, the bushy and branching forms, the "terrace" forms which consist of numerous horizontal units of compactly arranged small fingers, and irregular forms with stout open branches breaking into sprays and terraces where they terminate. As far as can be seen, the substrate is an unconsolidated one. It has been widely held in the past that such substrates are unfavourable to coral growth, but it is now recognized that this must be qualified by grain size, and rates of sediment accumulation and lateral movement. In this community it is evident that accumulation and movement are insufficient to prevent young colonies from growing on debris fragments, etc., and once established they are able to maintain growth by the effect of the lower branches, which are usually dead, acting as stilts. This is especially true of stagshorn forms. In contrast to the previously described principal community, the colonization of a soft substrate places this community in the B stratum (like 3 and 6 in Fig. 2, but in stands). Branching forms afford relatively little space for colonization by other corals, and the C stratum is therefore inconspicuous. It is typified by anthocaulus stage *Fungia*, hermatypic solitaries, *Pavona varians*, *Montipora* spp. as dependents on B stratum species. Delicate ramose corals dominate, and within this group, *Acropora* A is very much the dominant species.

Although water movement is strong enough to carry a floating swimmer back and forth, it is not rough. Many of the coral growths would certainly not withstand more violent conditions, though some of the rubble may have accumulated during unusually rough periods. It is possible to trace a transition in this community as one moves from sites where the coral community is as described, to those where water movement is more vigorous, e.g. from a reef front as above to an adjacent reef margin. *Acropora* remains the most important coral genus, but *A. humilis* becomes more abundant at the expense of *Acropora* A. *A. humilis* has already been encountered as an important species on the shoreward side of rougher water reef margins, so that within the Fig. 1 scheme, it is possible to define a series of transitions which can be observed in the respective principal communities of: (1) *Pocillopora* predominant, (2) *Pocillopora* and *Acropora humilis* predominant, (3) *Acropora humilis* and *Acropora* A predominant, and (4) *Acropora* A predominant. The transitions are rarely clearly enough defined to justify their recognition as sub-assemblage types, which would in any case defeat the purpose of the scheme by complication. They do however provide additional evidence of the scheme.

Other variations within this assemblage type are also found mainly within the principal community above. They are not sufficiently distinct or well defined to be recognized as distinct assemblages. In some places for instance, *A. irregularis* and terrace-forming species like *A. cytherea* are more abundant than *Acropora* A; faviids too are more common. The precise pattern into which this particular variation fits is not yet definitely known but a certain amount of local and rather random variation is perhaps to be expected. It is sometimes encountered in association with slightly deeper calmer water. The same principal community also gives way in places to one in which poritids and faviids are more prominent, but the pattern here is more obvious in that it invariably occurs as one passes into deeper water. It does in fact represent transition in the opposite direction from that into *Pocillopora* assemblages, i.e. into *Porites* assemblages, which are associated with relatively still water.

One of the more problematic parts of the assemblage scheme is the slender evidence for an *Acropora* assemblage on the reef flat sequence. Either it is represented by the *Acropora humilis* colonies on the shoreward sides of rough water reef margins, or it is seen in the form of a

modification in which *Millepora exaesa* and *Montipora tuberculosa*
are the most important species in the coral elements of the algal
zone. In the first case, this margin zonation is not seen everywhere,
and the presence of *Pocillopora* in important amounts with the *Acropora*
suggests that this cannot be a fully developed *Acropora* assemblage.
In the second case, *Acropora* is virtually absent from the assemblage,
so forcing the scheme. Nevertheless *M. exaesa—M. tuberculosa* elements
are to be found at the point where an *Acropora* type assemblage might
be expected on other evidence; and it may be that the very shallow
Sargassum dominated environment so modifies the expected assemblage
that *Acropora* itself is eliminated. The provisional view is taken that
the *Acropora* assemblage type is represented on such reef flats in a
condensed and therefore indistinct way, associated with a rapid
change from rough to still water conditions in this region, and unusual
shallow water effects in the algal zone.

Porites *assemblages*

Porites assemblages are the most important group in areal terms.
The principal community is best seen along the deep re-entrant reef
fronts of the Victoria harbour area, together with the margins of the
associated reef channels and of the hollows completely enclosed by
reef flats in the same area. In contrast to the reef fronts colonized
by the *Acropora A—A. irregularis* Community, the present fronts are
very steep or almost vertical. The most important corals are *Porites A*
(i.e. *Porites lutea*, *P. solida* and possibly other massive *Porites* species),
and numerous faviids like *Favia favus*, *F. pallida*, *Goniastrea retiformis*
and *Favites halicora*, with *Platygyra lamellina* and *Leptoria phrygia*.
Growth forms are mostly massive (20% or more), but the still water and
large areas of dead coral surface also favour delicate and encrusting
corals (20%, 25%). The community structure is dominated by the
massive corals, which in turn provide a substrate for dependent encrusting species like *Pavona varians*, *Stylocoeniella armata* and species
of *Montipora*, delicate platy forms like *Pachyseris* and *Echinopora
lamellosa*, and ramose species, notably *Acropora humilis* (in a less compact growth form than that exhibited in previous assemblage types)
and *Pocillopora eydouxi*. Between the massive colonies are small patches
and clefts lined with soft sediment, and inhabited by *Fungia* clones.
Coral cover is extremely dense (class 5). Breakdown of the community
structure gives a B-and-C stratification (Nos. 3, 5, 6 and 7 in Fig. 2).
It is not known what substrate underlies the dominant colonies. It
may be soft where the steep margins level out, but along the edges
themselves it is difficult to envisage a nearly vertical bank of uncon-

solidated sediment being present prior to the present corals, and it must either be that the latter are growing out over previous massive coral growths in a continuous general advance of the margins (as a multiple C stratum development), or that they represent colonization of a pre-existing rocky surface. This does not alter the relationships of the present corals to each other but assigning the community to a B-and-C stratification may be an oversimplification. It is provisionally convenient however in that a considerable amount of sediment is present round the massive corals, and many species are clearly unable to survive without the hard substrate areas provided by dead areas on these massive species.

Variations within this assemblage type are numerous. As Fig. 1 suggests, reef flat environments are mostly occupied by *Porites* type assemblages, but full description is not possible here. The main point that might be made is that reef flat conditions are not favourable to corals compared with edges and margins, as diversities and coral cover indicate. Other organisms are invariably more important, e.g. algae, marine grass species, etc. The proximity to shore, the poor circulation and extreme shallowness increase the significance of factors that are probably not important elsewhere, such as salinity and temperature extremes and variation, strong insolation, terrestrial sedimentation and human interaction. Almost all reef flat environments share the common feature of reduced water movement, and *Porites* is the most common and consistent coral. Within this assemblage type there are facies and elements whose spatial relationships correspond to the zonally arranged organic communities described by Taylor (1968). At Anse aux Pins for example, the grass beds are characterized by *Porites A* and *Porites* sp. cf. *andrewsi* elements, with local patches of one of three facies: *Porites* sp. cf. *andrewsi*, *Pavona frondifera* and *Psammocora contigua*. In the sand and cobbles zone, coral ecology is complex but can be summarily described as *Porites A—Heliopora coerulea—Millepora exaesa* Facies/Elements. Density of coral growth varies a great deal, but like the dominant algae, concentrations are greater round dead coral masses, rubble patches, cobble tracts and ridges. These behave as centres of action for most organisms, since the intervening sandy areas are almost barren by comparison (on the surface). Coral roles can vary from the formation of microatolls which act as discrete ecological units (Nos. 5–7 in Fig. 2), to a very subsidiary status as inconspicuous members of a largely algal-molluscan-crustacean association on the cobble ridges (Nos. 8 and 9 in Fig. 2). Stratification is a good example of the B-and-C type, where the microatolls (e.g. of *Heliopora*) and occasional colonies (Nos. 3 in

Fig. 2, e.g. *Pocillopora damicornis-bulbosa*) form the B stratum, and
corals like *Stylocoeniella armata* and *Porites lichen* form the C stratum
as dependents. Some species like *Millepora exaesa* and *Leptastrea
purpurea* occupy both strata and cannot be regarded therefore as
dependent. The algal zone, already mentioned in connection with the
search for a reef flat representative of the *Acropora* assemblage type,
is not typified by any species of *Porites*, though *P. lichen* is quite
common. *Millepora exaesa* and *Montipora tuberculosa* are the most
important species here. Further variations within the *Porites* assemblage
type are to be found on the Victoria harbour reef flats, and also in
sheltered sandy bays like Anse à la Mouche (south) where corals are
not associated with a reef platform. It is possible to ascribe many
of these observed variations to known or assumed environmental
factors, but many assumptions remain to be proved, while other
variations remain without any satisfactory explanation. Low salinities
and very turbid water on the Victoria harbour flats may control the
occurrence of a facies in which *Stylophora pistillata* is important
alongside the poritids and faviids. On Anse aux Pins, where the water
is much shallower at low tide, but less turbid, insolation of the substrate and its fauna is probably more important. *Millepora exaesa*
seems to be able to withstand these particular conditions.

Synthesis

The complete assemblage sequence shown in Fig. 1 can be traced
in one of three component directions, laterally, radially and vertically.
For the first, a comparison of reef fronts and margins of a reef channel
in the Victoria harbour area, of an open water reef in the same area,
and the Anse aux Pins reef demonstrate the sequence from *Porites*
to *Pocillopora*. It should be possible to see this in following the reefs
from (e.g.) Cascade, round Anonyme and South East Islands to the
north end of Anse aux Pins. Radially, the sequence is shown by passing
shorewards from (e.g.) the Anse aux Pins reef front, but there is a
problem of finding a really satisfactory *Acropora* assemblage (see
above). Vertically, too, a full sequence is difficult to find in which
each assemblage is well developed. The Harbour area contains numerous
good examples of a downward change from *Acropora* to *Porites*, but
the *Pocillopora* fronts that have been studied appeared to pass down
into a zone in which *Acropora* and *Porites* together present a mixed
assemblage with elements from each. In a few instances a *Porites*
assemblage then followed, further down still. On some reef flats however, there are copious quantities of stagshorn debris, suggesting that

a good *Acropora* assemblage is to be found nearby, that is, beyond the visible reef front.

The radial and vertical components can together be used as an idealized reef profile, expressing for instance, the assemblage changes to be found in passing seawards along a reef channel (No. 3 in Fig. 3). If a broadly generalized scale is given to these components, and the reef margin assemblage of a reef is known, the other assemblages present can be predicted. In the same way, it can be shown that the Petite Police reef exhibits only a *Pocillopora* assemblage because there is insufficient width for other assemblages to be developed towards the shore (No. 5 in Fig. 3); wave action is too great over the

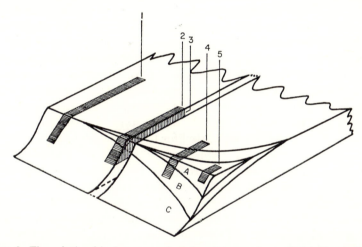

Fig. 3. The relationship between selected reef transects on Mahé, Seychelles, and the coral assemblage scheme (Fig. 1). Coral assemblages: A—*Pocillopora*; B—*Acropora*; C—*Porites*. For transects (1–5) see text. (Diagram not to scale.)

entire reef for other assemblages to thrive, this being a product both of exposure and reef width. The notion that a section of rocky shore without any platform can be regarded as a reef front without a reef, as suggested for Anse Takamaka, is consistent with this use of the scheme (i.e. just the reef front portion of No. 5 in Fig. 3). Conversely, the case of Anse à la Mouche (south) where a *Porites* assemblage occurs in a sandy bay without a reef, can be regarded as a reef flat without a front (i.e. the reef flat portion of No. 1 in Fig. 3). Sheltered reefs of the harbour area are represented by the No. 1 profile in Fig. 3, the more open reefs and a typical associated channel of the same area by Nos. 2 and 3, and a typical reef of the southeast (e.g. Anse aux Pins) by No. 4. (The gradation in reef size shown in Fig. 3 is not indicative of a general relationship.)

Although the sequence is related to prevailing water movement, as far as can be told, controls are more complex than this association would at first suggest. In the roughest water, all but the most robust corals with a strong attachment are likely to survive. In most other environments however, it is likely that most species would survive if placed there individually, but Taylor (1968) suggests that the faster growing *Acropora* prevents *Porites* and the faviids from colonization in areas of good water circulation. In very still conditions, circulation and hence oxygenation is insufficient for *Acropora*, especially the stagshorns, and the *Porites* assemblages thrive instead. He stresses that *Porites* is well known to be the most tolerant coral genus, and its absence can therefore best be explained in terms of its unsuccessful competition for space. The second conclusion is separable from the first, however, and it may be that while competition keeps poritids and faviids from *Acropora* fronts, ability to withstand sedimentation may be additionally important, or more so, than oxygenation. There is a lack of information on oxygen content of reef waters and its ecological significance but Yonge, Yonge and Nichols (1932) noted that corals are "especially well fitted for living in water of very variable oxygen content" and that respiration rate does not diminish "until the oxygen content has been reduced to one-half or less of the normal . . .". Field measurement of oxygen content is notoriously difficult, unfortunately. Sedimentation is more important in still water conditions because there is less water movement to aid the corals in clearing particles. This would operate adversely for branching corals like *Acropora*, in which the polyps themselves are not good sediment removers. Faviids and other large polyp forms are much more successful (Marshall and Orr, 1931).

GEOLOGICAL ASPECTS

It has already been mentioned in discussing *Pocillopora* assemblages that there is no direct relationship between coastal features and the distribution of the main types of coral assemblage, a fact which is emphasized if environment and community are rigorously distinguished. It is difficult to explain the presence of a consistent faunal feature in a variety of coastal features in terms of their response to the same environmental controls, and it is therefore thought that the reefs and related features owe their present form to an earlier time and different conditions from those prevailing now. This points to present coral growth as a relatively new phase of colonization on pre-existing coast forms and requires that any generalized explanation of the reefs in terms of continuous building by present communities must be viewed very critically (e.g. Lewis, 1968). It would be more sound to assume a hiatus in reef building, and search for continuous growth as an exception.

In addition to the present day distribution of coral assemblages, there are numerous local facts giving evidence of this hiatus, and also of a possible explanation. Planed-off coral colonies occur on exposed parts of the reef platforms in the southeast part of the island, and coral sections can also be seen in the rock forming the groove-like features on some reef fronts. It is possible therefore that a pre-existing reef fringe has been exposed and partially eroded subaerially. Subsequent submergence has enabled corals and other organisms to colonize the dissected platforms again, but in this way, the reefs would be expected to owe very little of their morphology to the direct contribution of present communities, except where conditions proved so favourable that new reef building could proceed rapidly enough to make a noticeable addition. A low sea level stand at -10 m (tentatively ascribed to c. 7000 years B.P.) is suggested by the submarine terrace discussed by Lewis (1968) and a relatively recent stillstand of unknown level (perhaps the same) is also the best explanation of the occurrence of subaerially weathered fluting passing continuously downward below present sea level on coastal granite masses.

It is difficult to conjecture the nature of the reefs before they were subaerially exposed, but a gently shelving basement in Victoria harbour would favour extensive development of platforms and patches, while the steeper shelving at the southern and northern ends of Mahé would give rise to slow outward growth and narrower platforms. This might have offset any windward–leeward factors that could have promoted the greatest reef development in the southeast of the island. (It is reasonable to assume that climatic conditions might not have differed greatly from those at present, since tropical conditions have remained more stable than those in high latitudes. In fact, present coral growth is most dense in the harbour area and the same may also have been true during this earlier period.) With a drop in sea level, river action would have been extended outward from the granite areas and cut courses down through the reef limestone to the new base level. The limestone would cause these valleys to have the form of small gorges, whilst karst solutioning could have given rise to enclosed depressions and hollows (recent borings in the course of airstrip construction suggest that the limestone may be largely unconsolidated beneath the present reef platform crust (C. J. R. Braithwaite, personal communication) and the gorges and hollows might be a consequence of this as well as karst processes). Present reef channels in the harbour area and elsewhere are aligned with stream courses in the granite, and this explanation may be more satisfactory than the restriction of present reef growth by stream sediment and low salinity water proposed by Lewis (1968). This latter process gives rise to broad breaches in a reef rather than narrow winding gorge-like channels. Present reef fronts and reef widths would also be expected to derive much of their character from this phase. The gently shelving fronts associated with many *Acropora* fronts could have been built originally of subaerially accumulated talus and debris away from stream courses, whereas for the *Porites* fronts the stream courses could have provided the steep features with which they are often associated. A solution is thus suggested for the substrate problem (p. 175), namely an underlying rocky substrate. In the southern part of the island, the already narrow platforms were probably eroded more rapidly and undercut more vigorously by the exposed conditions so removing them completely, or leaving them as mere remnants. To a limited extent therefore, reef form has controlled the present coral communities, rather than *vice versa*.

Subsequent submergence and recolonization by marine organisms has so far provided very little additional reef structure. The coral stands associated with granite shores and open sandy bays are incipient reef structures at places where a previous reef may have been completely removed, or even never present. *Pocillopora* assemblages have provided very little new growth, except on a small scale (e.g. the *Acropora humilis* terraces): corals are usually too small and sparse. *Acropora* assemblages provide a great deal of loose debris, which algal growth binds together in places, but their real importance is hard to assess. *Porites* assemblages are ostensibly the most important especially in the form of *Porites A*—faviid communities along channel margins. They often seem to have commenced growth on the steep sides of the river cut channels and their particular community structure has probably favoured retention of a steep feature. They are the only coral contribution of a significant scale where the corals are forming *in situ* structures; in contrast to the *Acropora* assemblages the algal contribution is relatively unimportant. As before, it is difficult to assess the amount of growth and it probably varies a great deal, but the lighthouse in Victoria harbour was originally at or close to the very edge of the reef (in the 19th century) and now stands about 3 m back from the edge. It is noticeable that the strongest reef growth is not to be found on "windward" (i.e. exposed) reefs, unlike the Pacific atolls. The absence of a substantial development of calcareous algae to seaward of the corals is undoubtedly a factor.

CONCLUSIONS

1. Application of the concepts and methods of plant sociology make it possible to compare coral stands more effectively, and hence to define assemblages and roles within the communities. Many of the concepts are useful even without full use of statistical methods. The approach outlined and applied here is useful for primary surveys.

2. Comparison of coral stands in shallow water environments (less than 10 m) round Mahé, suggests that three assemblage types exist, characterized by *Pocillopora*, *Acropora*, and *Porites* in order of decreasing water movement in their respective environments. The relationship of these assemblages to exposure can be expressed schematically as in Fig. 1, which therefore represents a sublittoral extension of the type of scheme usually used for littoral and supralittoral organisms. This scheme may only be applicable to Mahé, but it would be useful to test and extend or supplement it for other regions.

3. A **principal community** is recognizable for each coral assemblage type, this being the most representative assemblage and therefore useful as a "standard" for comparison. They are as follows:

Pocillopora: *Pocillopora danae-meandrina—Acropora humilis—*
                 Millepora platyphylla community
Acropora: *Acropora A—Acropora irregularis* community
Porites: *Porites A*—faviid community

4. Current reef growth and coral assemblage distribution is not consistently related to present coastal morphology, and the reefs themselves are considered to be remnants of earlier structures which have been subaerially dissected before being submerged again. Modern coral growth is mostly only a thin veneer over these older structures, except in the Victoria harbour area where the *Porites A*—faviid communities are making a recognizable contribution to reef building. The same community is also responsible for substantial structures in certain sheltered sandy bays of the west coast (perhaps forming incipient reefs). In general: *Porites* assemblages form *in situ* structures, *Acropora* assemblages mostly provide debris which is then algally encrusted and *Pocillopora* assemblages add to existing structures by both methods, but not in significant amounts.

ACKNOWLEDGEMENTS

Discussions with Dr. D. J. Bellamy and Mr. D. J. Jones (Dept. of Botany, University of Durham), Dr. C. J. R. Braithwaite (Dept. of Geology, University of Dundee), Dr. J. D. Taylor (Dept. of Zoology, British Museum (Natural History)) and my wife were of great help in forming and clarifying the ideas outlined in this paper. I am indebted to Dr. Braithwaite, Dr. Taylor, and Dr. M. S. Lewis (British Council), with whom the field work was carried out, as well as numerous others in this country and the Seychelles who provided assistance without which the Seychelles work would not have been possible. The work was carried out with the support of a research student grant from the Natural Environment Research Council and an equipment grant from the Royal Society (International Indian Ocean Expedition) under the late Professor J. H. Taylor, F.R.S.

REFERENCES

Barnes, J., Bellamy, D. J., Jones, D. J., Whitton, B. A., Drew, E. A., Kenyon, L., Lythgoe, J. N. and Rosen, B. R. (1971). Morphology and ecology of the reef front of Aldabra. *Symp. zool. Soc. Lond.* No. 28: 87–114.
Braithwaite, C. J. R. (1971). Seychelles reefs: structure and development. *Symp. zool. Soc. Lond.* No. 28: 39–63.
Lewis, J. R. (1964). *The ecology of rocky shores.* London: English University Press.
Lewis, M. S. (1968). The morphology of the fringing coral reefs along the east coast of Mahé, Seychelles. *J. Geol.* 76: 140–153.
Lewis, M. S. (1969). Sedimentary environments and unconsolidated carbonate sediments of the fringing coral reefs of Mahé, Seychelles. *Mar. Geol.* 7: 95–127.
Lewis, M. S. and Taylor, J. D. (1966). Marine sediments and bottom communities of the Seychelles. *Phil. Trans. R. Soc.* (A) 259: 279–290.
Marshall, S. M. and Orr, A. P. (1931). Sedimentation on Low Isles reef and its relation to coral growth, *Scient. Rep. Gt Barrier Reef Exped.* 1928–29. 1: 93–133.
Morton, J. E. and Miller, M. C. (1968). *The New Zealand sea shore.* London and Auckland: Collins.
Oosting, H. J. (1956). *The Study of plant communities: an introduction to plant ecology.* 2nd Edition, San Francisco and London: W. H. Freeman and Co.
Scheer, G. (1967). Uber die Methodik der Untersuchung von Korallenriffen. *Z. Morph. Ökol. Tiere* 60: 105–114.
Stephenson, T. A. and Stephenson, A. (1949). The universal features of zonation between tidemarks on rocky shores. *J. Ecol.* 37: 289–305.
Stoddart, D. R. (1969). Ecology and morphology of Recent coral reefs. *Biol. Rev.* 44: 433–498.
Taylor, J. D. (1968). Coral reef and associated invertebrate communities (mainly molluscan) around Mahé, Seychelles. *Phil. Trans. R. Soc.* (B) 254: 129–206.

Taylor, J. D. and Lewis, M. S. (1970). The flora, fauna and sediments of the marine grass beds of Mahé, Seychelles. *J. nat. Hist.* **4**: 199–220.

Yonge, C. M., Yonge, M. J. and Nichols, A. J. (1932). Studies on the physiology of corals, VI. The relationship between respiration in corals and the production of oxygen by their zooxanthellae. *Scient. Rep. Gt Barrier Reef Exped.* **1**: 213–251.

Symp. zool. Soc. Lond. (1971) No. 28, 185–216.

COMPARATIVE STUDY OF THE MAIN FEATURES OF SOME CORAL REEFS OF MADAGASCAR, LA REUNION AND MAURITIUS

MICHEL PICHON

Station Marine d'Endoume et Centre d'Océanographie, Marseille, France

SYNOPSIS

In this paper, the author gives the results of a comparative study of some of the coral reefs of the western Indian Ocean, with special reference to the reefs of La Réunion, Mauritius and Madagascar. In Madagascar, particular attention has been paid to the coral reefs of the northwest coast (Nossi-Bé) and of the southwest coast (Tuléar and vicinity).

The significant differences which are now observed on the reefs of these various localities take their origin in the diversity of the geologic, climatic and hydrologic conditions: La Réunion and Mauritius are high volcanic islands; Mauritius is completely reef-rimmed, whereas in La Réunion coral growth is only conspicuous on the west coast, with reefs close to the shores. In Madagascar, the reefs, including a drowned barrier reef off the northwest coast, are all established on the continental shelf. A brief comparison is made also between the conditions of sea temperature, swell and tide range (only about 0·5 m in La Réunion and Mauritius, more than 3 m in Madagascar).

These differences can be analysed in terms of morphology, sedimentology and distribution of reef fauna and flora, across each of the main conspicuous reef features: slope, reef flat and lagoon.

The outer slope has been studied with much detail in Tuléar and Nossi-Bé, while only surveyed in the two other islands. Its morphology and ecology is roughly similar in every case, except in Nossi-Bé, where the slopes are typical of sheltered reefs. On the contrary, the structure of the reef flat may vary widely from one reef to another. The width of the flat itself may extend from the narrow ribbon, only some 10 m wide of Mauritius, to the large platform of Tuléar (more than 2 km). A tentative explanation of the variations of the characteristic features of the reef flat involves: the boulder rampart (missing in La Réunion and Mauritius), the sea grass beds (restricted to the landward, inner flat in Tuléar, but also present on the outer flat, in front of the boulder rampart as well as down below the coral slope in Nossi-Bé), the coral-built tabular flat, etc. The lagoons are also very dissimilar in their morphology and ecology. The coastal fringing reefs around Nossi-Bé have no lagoon, and sedimentation of terrigenous origin mingles on the landward part of the reef flat with that of skeletal origin. Elsewhere, the lagoons vary greatly in width, depth (they are very shallow in La Réunion and Mauritius), extent of the coral growth and of the sea grass beds, and nature of the bottom deposits (muddy sand of terrigeneous origin in Tuléar).

Some biogeographical conclusions, with special emphasis on scleractinian corals are drawn from the comparison of the fauna and flora of each of these coral reefs. As far as possible, they are also compared with other coral reefs of the western Indian Ocean.

INTRODUCTION

The coral reefs of Madagascar, La Réunion and Mauritius remained unstudied for a long time—just as many other reefs of the Indian

Ocean — and above all, the researches which were undertaken had
no synthetic bearing. We must here recall that Darwin briefly
visited Mauritius, in May 1836. At the beginning of the century (1905)
a German traveller, Voeltzkow, gave a useful description of reefs of
the western coast of Madagascar. Much more recently Guilcher (1956,
1958) and Battistini (1959b) made very detailed geomorphological
studies of the reefs of the northwest coast of Madagascar, and Faure
and Montaggioni (1970) published the first paper on the reefs of La
Réunion.

During the last ten years, I have had the opportunity to gather
ecological and bionomical data on the reef structures of Madagascar,
Mauritius and La Réunion. It may prove to be interesting to try
now to define the common characters of the coral reefs of these various
regions and to clear up the particularities of each of them.

The Mascarene archipelago as a whole (that is to say Rodrigues
island also) should have been included in this study. Unfortunately
we have only very few data dealing with Rodrigues coral reefs, and
for that reason, it has not been possible to take them into account in
the present paper. Moreover, most of the reefs of Madagascar (particularly developed on the western coast of the island) are far from
being well known. In a previous paper (Pichon, 1969) I have tried,
after Guilcher (1958), to summarize the present status of knowledge
on the geomorphology and biology of the reefs of Madagascar. Nevertheless, it does not seem possible to retain for Madagascar only one
representative reef. For that reason, I will constantly refer, in the
present study to the two places which are the best known: the Bay of
Tuléar (southwest coast) and the vicinity of Nossi-Bé (northwest coast)
(Figs 1 and 2).

THE ENVIRONMENTAL FACTORS

Geological frame

In Madagascar, all the coral reefs are established on the continental
shelf. In some places, they are located on its edge. In this position is
the "drowned barrier" (Guilcher, 1956) which is more or less continuous, from the extreme northwest of Madagascar to about 19° 20'S.

The structural study of the drowned barrier has not yet been
undertaken. It is not even certain that it is a coral reef formation.
According to Guilcher (1956) it could be a cuesta, superficially covered
with a veneer of living corals. Such a cuesta would have been shaped
during a period of emersion, in rocks younger than those which constitute the emerged cuestas of the mainland.

This drowned barrier fixes the boundary of a pseudo-lagoon, extending over the whole continental shelf, on which occur various categories of reef formations (mostly reefs with sand cays and fringing reefs).

The coral reefs of Nossi-Bé, which we will take as an example, are fringing reefs located along an almost wholly volcanic coast

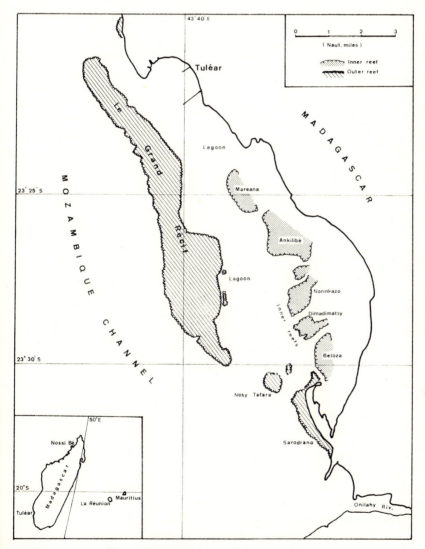

FIG. 1. The coral reefs of the bay of Tuléar.

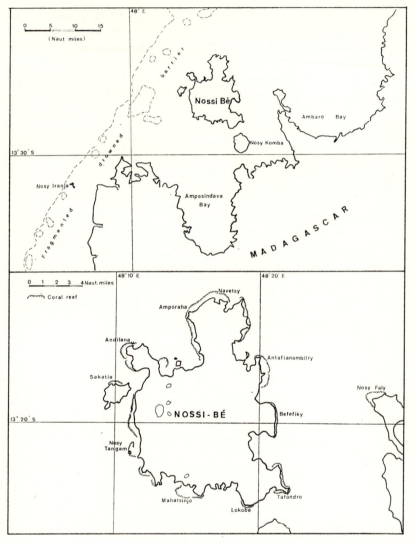

FIG. 2. Localization of Nossi-Bé and of the drowned barrier. The fringing reefs
around Nossi-Bé.

(volcanism of various ages: post-Liassic or Quaternary, sometimes very
recent). The shore itself, behind the reef, can be a rocky substrate, or
a sandy beach, or even a mangrove swamp.

On the southwest coast, where the continental shelf is everywhere
very narrow, the coral reefs are mostly of the fringing type or barrier

type, more or less distant from the shore line. On the other hand at Nossi-Bé, the coast is a low Quaternary plain, without any prominent relief. Traces of volcanic activity are occasionally related with reef formations, in that region.

La Réunion and Mauritius (Fig. 3) are entirely volcanic. La Réunion is constituted by two eruptive masses geographically distinct: the

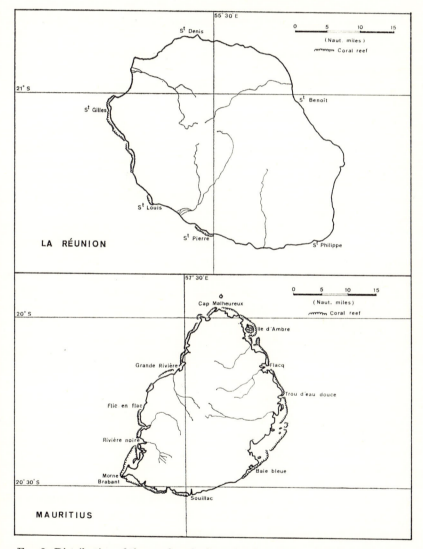

FIG. 3. Distribution of the coral reefs along the shores of La Réunion. Distribution of the coral reefs along the shores of Mauritius.

mountain of "Piton des Neiges", containing the highest summit of the Indian Ocean (3070 m) and the active volcano of "Piton de la Fournaise", which, in the southern third of the island, is composed of three concentric craters of decreasing size.

The frame of Mauritius is a series of collapsed calderas, which have been filled up, with lava (doleritic basalts) during two major volcanic phases of Quaternary age. Some of these coulées crossed the reliefs of the central caldera remnants and flowed to the sea, where they constitute a part of the coast line.

When comparing the three islands of La Réunion, Mauritius and Rodrigues one observes that:

1. The volcanism is younger westward (there is an active volcano in La Réunion).

2. The altitudes are regularly decreasing west to east.

3. The coral reefs are better developed and more distant from the shore line in the east part than in the west part of the archipelago. (There are merely a few discontinuous fringing reefs in La Réunion on the west coast only. Except on the southeast coast, coral formations almost encircle Mauritius, and in Rodrigues island the reefs are well developed with an important lagoon.)

There is, therefore, in the Mascarene archipelago a similar situation to that quoted by Guilcher et al. (1965) in the Comoro archipelago. Such a phenomenon, for the Comoro islands, can be explained by the fact that the volcanism age and the collapse of the common base are regularly increasing from west to east. In the Mascarene archipelago, the second cause is not appropriate. This archipelago, indeed, does not have structural unity, as proved by the existence of the Mauritius trench, the Rodrigues fracture zone and depths greater than 4000 m between the islands.

Climatological conditions

In Madagascar there is a great difference in the climate of the region of Nossi-Bé and of the region of Tuléar; both regions, however, are protected against the southeast trade winds. Towards Nossi-Bé, the rains are abundant during the whole hot season (southern summer), and infrequent during the cool season. Hurricanes, always accompanied with heavy rainfalls, may also occur during the hot season. The sea water around the reefs of Nossi-Bé is always turbid, even during the "dry" season. On the contrary, the coral formations off shore, as well as the drowned barrier are always surrounded by clear water.

In the region of Tuléar, the climate is arid, and the rains are scarce, even during the hot season. The rivers that debouch in this region are, however, fed during the summer, by rains falling on the highlands and the reef formations are then surrounded by turbid water.

La Réunion and Mauritius have a rather similar climate, both of these islands being located in the southeast trade winds belt. The trade winds blow most of the year, but especially during the cool season. The rainfall regularly increases with the altitude. In La Réunion, where the relief is strongly marked, there is a striking climatic contrast between the windward and leeward part of the island. In both La Réunion and Mauritius, the summer rainfalls, which are the most important, are related to thundery perturbations or to cyclonic depressions.

The sea conditions

The sea surface temperatures

The sea surface temperature of coastal waters is, in every case, subject to seasonal changes. The mean winter and mean summer temperatures are as follow:

	Summer	Winter
Nossi-Bé	29	24·5
Tuléar	27·5	22·5
Mauritius	27	22
La Réunion	27	21·5

The highest temperatures are therefore recorded in Nossi-Bé. The coasts of Mauritius and La Réunion are surrounded by oceanic waters, and that particularity explains the relatively low values found in the two islands. In Tuléar, the temperature minima may prove to be notably lower than the mean winter temperature given above. This is a result of the important diurnal air temperature variation (up to 20°C) during the cool season. This nocturnal fall in temperature influences only the surface layer of the sea and has no consequence on the coral growth.

The swell

The swell is always feeble in the region of Nossi-Bé, especially in summer, during which period the sea is particularly calm. During the southern winter alternating winds are blowing, with a land breeze at the end of the night and the first hours of the day, and a sea breeze during daytime (mostly in the afternoon). The waves raised by these winds always have a moderate amplitude. The drowned barrier has

no protective effect on the shore against offshore swells (which remain
weak and uncommon). The shorelines of Nossi-Bé and of the nearby
mainland are very irregular and particularly calm sea states are the
rule in numerous sheltered bays.

In the region of Tuléar, the southwest winds blow during the
greatest part of the year. They are frequently very strong especially
during the cool season, in the afternoon. Even when the southwest
winds are lacking, a heavy swell of remote origin is observed. In this
region the coast is relatively straight, and the few bays which occur
are themselves separated from the open sea by coral formations.
Consequently all the outer reefs, on which the heavy swell breaks are
in very exposed conditions. Only the coral reefs that are established
in the bays, sheltered by the outer barrier, will be protected against
this swell.

In La Réunion and Mauritius, the southeast swell generated by
the Trade-winds prevails. La Réunion is slightly elongated along
a NW–SE axis, and consequently the southeast swell is perceptible
on the greatest part of the coasts of the island. The coral reefs that
occur only on the western shores are therefore in very exposed conditions. (Owing to its different shape, Mauritius has a western coast,
between Le Morne Brabant and Cap Malheureux, which, on the contrary, is protected against the swells produced by the Trade-winds.)
Moreover, in La Réunion there is a heavy SW oceanic swell which
has a similar origin to that occurring in the southwest of Madagascar.

We must also point out that the four studied countries lie in the
tropical hurricanes zone. These cyclones or hurricanes are always
accompanied by strong winds, high rainfall and heavy swell, the
direction of which depends upon the hurricane trajectory. La Réunion
and Mauritius, during the hot season, are affected by these tropical
depressions every year. Their smallest consequence is an aggravation
of the heavy seas, for several days. The cyclones are less frequent in
Nossi-Bé, and they are still more exceptional in Tuléar which is not
however completely protected against their ravages.

The tides

On the western coast of Madagascar the tides are of the regula,
semi-diurnal type, and their range is important. The maximum ranger
during extreme spring tides is 3·2 m in Tuléar and 4·2 m in Nossi-Bé.
The consequences of such important tide falls are as follow:

1. The coral reef flats emerge 0·3 to 0·4 m, for a few hours at each
low water during the extreme spring tide period. This is important
for the living organisms, as the day low water occurs around noon.

2. The currents are always very strong in the vicinity of a coral reef and on the reef flat, during spring tides. These currents play an important part in sorting and spreading the sedimentary materials on the reefs and close to the reefs. Their action is reinforced, in the region of Tuléar, by the effect of the heavy southwest swell.

The tides in La Réunion and Mauritius are also of the semi-diurnal type, but with a remarkable diurnal inequality (the low water occurs in the evening during spring tide periods). The maximum range is about 0·7 m in La Réunion and 0·6 m in Mauritius. Because of the weakness of the tide range, the variations of the sea level induced by meteorological conditions (direction and force of the winds, sea state, barometric pressures) are comparatively important.

Conclusions on the environmental factors

Table I gives the most important characteristics of the environmental factors which we have previously analysed, for each of the four regions.

TABLE I

The environmental factors

	Nossi-Bé	Tuléar	La Réunion	Mauritius
Geology and coastal morphology	Drowned barrier Volcanoes of various ages or sediment., coast	Narrow cont. shelf. Low sediment., plain	Active volcano Relief very young	Recent volcanism. Relief smoothed
Climate	Humid solar breezes	Arid strong S.W. winds	Trade-winds (hurricanes)	Trade-winds (hurricanes)
Mean Winter sea surface	24·5	22·5	21·5	22
temp. Summer	29	27	27	27
Sea state	Calm	Very rough (S.W. swell)	Very rough (Trade-winds and S.W. swell)	Rough (Trade-winds)
Tides (maximum range)	4·2 m	3·2 m	0·6 m	0·6 m

We observe a great similarity in the environmental conditions of La Réunion and of Mauritius. These conditions, common to the two islands are somewhat different to those we observed in the region of Nossi-Bé and in the region of Tuléar. We can therefore assume that the four geographic localities—from a reef environment standpoint only—belong to three different regions: 1. a Mascarene region, 2. a Northwest Madagascar region and 3. a Southwest Madagascar region.

As we have already specified, both La Réunion and Mauritius consist wholly of volcanic rocks. There are nevertheless significant differences in the geological characters of the two islands. La Réunion still has an active volcano and the ground relief is very young and steep, whereas in Mauritius we find only extinct volcanoes and the relief is already smoothed by erosion. These differences are fundamental in the field of coral reefs, and it is probable that they are the major cause of the dissimilarity in the coral reef structure which we observe between the two islands.

There are few common environmental characteristics between Tuléar and Nossi-Bé. We will quote only: 1. the important tide range which contributes to the spread of the sediments on and near the coral formations and 2. the proximity of important land masses drained by rivers which play an important part in the alluvionment.

The consequence of the combined action of these two phenomena is a contamination of sediments of skeletal origin with elements of terrigenous origin.

The importance of the environmental factors is fundamental in coral reefs. Indeed slight differences in these factors will occasion considerable changes in the biology of reef building organisms, and more especially of their carbonate-deposition ability. Therefore, the whole structure of a coral reef is finally strictly dependent on the environmental factors.

COMPARATIVE ANALYSIS OF THE MAIN REEF FEATURES

I will not make in the present paper a detailed analysis of the coral reefs which we want to compare now. Such an analysis has already been published by several authors: Battistini (1959b) on the morphology of the reefs of Nossi-Bé; Pichon (1964, 1969) for Tuléar; de Baissac, Lubet and Michel (1962) and Pichon (1967) for Mauritius; Faure and Montaggioni (1970) for La Réunion.

We will only summarize here the data gathered for each of the main structural units (outer slope, reef flat, lagoon) which are to be compared.

The outer slope

The outer slope exposed to rough sea, in Tuléar, La Réunion and Mauritius

The outer slope of reefs exposed to rough sea has been studied in great detail in Tuléar (Gravier et al., 1970). We can distinguish two different zones, according to the bathymetry:

1. *The spurs and grooves zone.* From 0 to 18 m, a spurs and grooves zone has a very complex morphology which is the result of:

a. The stage of evolution (construction or degradation) of the coral reefs.

b. The local variations on the intensity of the hydrodynamic factors.

The communities are characterized by the abundance of hydrocorals (*Millepora platyphylla* in the first metres), scleractinian corals, alcyonarians and calcareous red algae. Moreover, there is a clear difference between the fauna of the wall and of the upper part of the grooves.

In the lower part of this zone, and particularly when the spurs and grooves arrangement is not very distinct, we find sometimes a thin layer of coral sediment bearing either free branching calcareous algae, with an appearance of "Maërl", or a community of the scleractinian coral *Leptoseris papyracea*, which is here free-living.

2. *The dead coral flagstone.* Deeper than 18 m we find a large even flagstone made of dead corals, slightly and regularly inclined toward the offshore. At a depth of about 50 m there is a small cliff, a few metres high, marking the end of the flagstone.

This flagstone has a very rich fauna and flora composed of algae, scleractinian corals. Porifera, hydroïds, gorgonians. In the deeper zone, we find also Antipatharia and hydrocorals. The large hollows which occur from time to time in the flagstone are filled with muddy sand of skeletal origin. In some of these hollows there is a very remarkable abundance of nodules (or "pralines") of red calcareous algae.

Lastly, we must point out the existence, in the upper part of the outer slope, of numerous tunnels, caves and crevices, with a specific sciaphilic fauna and flora.

The spurs and grooves zone has also been observed in the upper part of the outer reef slope of La Réunion and Mauritius. In both cases the vertical extent of this zone is smaller than in Tuléar.

This is a consequence of basaltic lava flows which reappear at depth of about 5 or 6 m, with the shape either of flagstones several meters wide (Mauritius) or of a terrace, gently sloping to a depth of 15 m (La Réunion).

Usually, in Mauritius as well as in La Réunion, the spurs are narrower and the grooves shallower than in Tuléar, but the fauna and flora are quite similar in every case. Particularly, the *Millepora platyphylla* community of the upper zone widespread on all these reefs. The lava flows which reappear at depths of 5 to 6 m are sometimes covered by a thin layer of organic concretion (Melobesiae) and their fauna is extremely poor.

One observes also, in La Réunion and Mauritius, when the reefs are absent, scleractinian coral growths, established on very recent volcanic coulées, with more or less vertical walls plunging into the sea. These are not true reefs, but a mere veneer of carbonate-secreting organisms. No zonation is noticeable in these first stages of coral establishment. It is not certain whether they are an embryonic stage of a future reef.

The outer slope in sheltered areas (Nossi-Bé)

The outer slopes in the region of Nossi-Bé are quite different from that of the previous regions.

The drowned barrier is always too deep and therefore there are no spurs and grooves on its outer edge. The offshore slope can have one of the following aspects:

1. More or less inclined slope (up to *ca.* 45°). There is generally a rich scleractinian coral community with tabular *Acroporas* down to 45 m. The algae belongs almost exclusively to the genera *Peyssonnelia* and *Halimeda*.

2. Almost vertical slope. In such conditions, the scleractinian corals are particularly abundant at depth less than 20 m (upper edge of the slope). Below 20 m the communities are similar to the one found on the dead coral flagstone of Tuléar, but the fauna and flora remain poorer.

At depths varying between 50 and 70 m, the walls are buried under a fine sediment composed of *Halimeda* fragments.

The vertical extension of the outer slopes of the fringing reefs around Nossi-Bé is weak: 8 to 10 m, at most. Their morphology as well as their fauna and flora are typical of sheltered areas. A rudimentary spurs and grooves structure is only discernable on the edge of the reef flat at low water of spring tides. On the outer slope itself, the spurs are, in fact, constituted by a rough alignment of scleractinian coral masses or patches. The coral species are rather numerous. The massive or foliaceous growth forms are abundant whereas *Acropora* is relatively scarce. A constant faunistic element is an antipatharian belonging to the genus *Eucirripathes*. Between the rough alignments of coral masses, series of hollows gradually disposed and filled with sediment represent groove elements. It is important to remark that this embryonic spurs and grooves zone is only conspicuous in the more exposed reefs. It is entirely lacking on the reefs of sheltered areas or on still rudimentary reefs.

In general, the outer slopes of the reefs of Nossi-Bé have no special characteristic feature. The massive scleractinian corals which are abundant on the slope are widespread species. The calcareous Algae (Melobesiae) are entirely lacking; the dominant floristic element is represented by a tall species of *Peyssonnelia* (*P.* cf. *calcea*). Sandy or muddy deposits are commonly encountered on these slopes, in all the places where the coral growth is missing. Lastly, we frequently observe growths of sea grasses on the soft bottoms lying in front of the reefs, just at the foot of the outer slopes (lower sea grass bed of Battistini).

The outer slopes which we have just described, of the fringing reefs of Nossi-Bé are quite similar to those of the inner reefs of Tuléar (which are reefs established on the landward slope of the lagoon) or to the inner slope (= backreef slope or lagoon slope) of the outer reef. In every case, indeed, the slopes have the same morphology, have little height, and bear comparable communities: the Melobesiae are lacking, and the common faunistic elements are numerous: Antipatharian *Eucirripathes* and scleractinian Fungiidae, especially colonial Fungiidae: *Halomitra, Herpolitha*. In every case also, sediments, sometimes muddy, are common on the slopes and a lower bed of sea grasses may occur (*Halophila*).

The morphological, sedimentological and ecological characters of the outer slope of the reefs of Nossi-Bé (including those which are directly exposed to wave action) are linked with the local particularities of the hydrodynamic regimen. Here, the reefs show an adaptation to the calm sea conditions which are, as shown previously, an important characteristic of the environmental conditions in the vicinity of Nossi-Bé. These conditions are also found on the inner reefs of Tuléar, which are protected against offshore swells by the Grand Récif barrier.

The reef edge

The reef edge (composed of the upper horizontal part of the spurs, at about the same level as the outer part of the reef flat) is considered here as an element related to the outer slope.

In general the communities of the reef edge are quite similar in the four studied regions. There are only a few species of scleractinian corals, alcyonarians (*Lobophytum*) and zoantharians (*Palythoa*). The

Melobesiae (*Porolithon*) are more abundant when the sea conditions become rough. Yet we find them in Nossi-Bé, where active concretion is not conspicuous. A development of calcareous Algae at the reef edge is particularly noticeable in Tuléar and La Réunion. These Algae (*Porolithon* especially) can sometimes create a slight relief, making the upper part of the spurs convex. The growth of *Porolithon* which is observed here cannot be compared with an algal ridge such as those existing in the Marshall or Tuamotu islands, for instance. It is, nevertheless, interesting to notice, in the Western Indian Ocean, a similar phenomenon, although rudimentary, caused by the same species (*Porolithon* spp.).

The true raised algal ridge is probably very scarce in the Indian Ocean.

The reef flat

Very important differences are to be observed in the morphology, sedimentology and ecology of the reef flats of Tuléar, Nossi-Bé, La Réunion and Mauritius. One of the most obvious of these differences lies in the very width of the reef flat. In Mauritius, the reef rim is extremely narrow since it scarcely goes beyond 10 m or so. At Saint Pierre (La Réunion) its mean width varies between 150 and 200 m. Some of the reef flats of Nossi-Bé (Mahatsinjo, Antafianambitry) can reach 1000 to 1500 m, and the maximum width of the Grand Récif of Tuléar is about 2900 m. The sediment deposits (on which are based the main morphological and ecological divisions of the reef flat) are greatly dependant upon these variations. The most important among these deposits are:

1. Very coarse elements (blocks) which are restricted to the seaward part of the reef flat and which constitute the boulder tracts.

2. Smaller elements (fine to coarse sands) which are transferred toward the landward part of the flat, where they can accumulate (such is the case in Tuléar). These sandy sediments are generally covered by sea grasses, as soon as they come to rest.

It is obvious that there is no possibility of sediment deposit on a very narrow reef flat. In such a case all the sediment is transferred to the lagoon, if any. This was observed in Mauritius especially. In fact, we must consider that the very narrow flat of the reefs of Mauritius corresponds in its totality to the sole reef edge, which we have included in the outer slope in the previous paragraph.

The boulder tracts

The boulder tract is a very important morphological feature. On its existence is established the division of the reef flat to an outer flat, in front of the boulder tract, and an inner flat, behind. The boulder tract is an accumulation of big coral blocks, carried by heavy swells and storms from the reef front and transferred to the reef flat, where they accumulate.

There is no true boulder tract in Mauritius. However, on the inner slope of the reef (=back reef slope) there are some dead coral blocks from the outer reef. These blocks, more or less scattered, can be considered as an equivalent of a rudimentary boulder tract, which would not have its specific morphology, and would be shifted onto the lagoon slope.

The boulder tracts are also lacking in La Réunion. We notice only, on the reef flat of Saint Pierre, about 50 m from the reef edge, a few very big blocks (a few meters long) irregularly disposed.

The boulder tracts are regularly present on the reef flats of the regions of Tuléar and Nossi-Bé. In Nossi-Bé, they are generally continuous, with a rampart shape. In Tuléar, the boulder ramparts are also present but we find more frequently a structure constituted from the juxtaposition of detrital dome-shaped accumulations, each dome being elongated perpendicularly to the reef front. The boulder tracts are generally wider (up to 100 m) and higher in Tuléar than in Nossi-Bé. In various places of Nossi-Bé, however, numerous tall-sized blocks (one meter or so) occur in the boulder tract, whereas most of the detrital elements have a centimetric size. On the contrary, in Tuléar, most of the blocks have a decimetric size, except a few "negro heads" in front of the boulder tract proper. The occurrence of boulder tracts on reefs localized in sheltered areas is seemingly surprising. Such a phenomenon can be explained by the fact that these boulder tracts are exceptionally supplied with coral blocks. The boulder supply is only effective during tempest or cyclone periods. During these periods of bad weather, which are rather scarce in that region, the boulder tracts receive only small sized detrital material, and all the detrital elements are degraded by biological and mechanical corrosion, and spread by tide currents.

In Tuléar, on the contrary, the sea state, almost permanently rough, ensures a regular replenishment of the boulder tract.

The outer reef flat

A detailed analysis of the morphology and ecology of the outer reef flats does not seem to be necessarily within the scope of this paper. We will quote only a feature characteristic of the outer flats of Nossi-Bé: the outer sea grass bed. This phanerogamic growth has the shape of an uninterrupted strip, about 20 m wide, localized just in front of the boulder tract. It is composed exclusively of *Thalassodendron ciliatum* and *Syringodium isoetifolium* taking root on a layer of sand of skeletal origin, 15 to 25 cm thick. These sediment deposits of the outer flat are always covered by sea grasses. They occur neither in La Réunion, in the corresponding zone of the reef flat (there is no individualized outer flat in La Réunion owing to the lack of a boulder tract), nor in Tuléar. In both cases the zone corresponding to the outer sea grass bed is covered with various Algae, with a summer growth of tall Phaeophyceae (*Sargassum* sp. and *Turbinaria trialata capensis* in Tuléar, *Sargassum densifolium* in La Réunion).

The inner reef flats

There are two very important communities occurring on the inner flats of the studied reefs: the scleractinian coral communities (coral-built tabular flat) and the sea grass flats (inner sea grasses).

1. The scleractinian coral communities. In La Réunion, the morphological equivalent of the inner flat (behind or landward of the algal zone) shows an important secondary growth of scleractinian corals. Several species of *Acropora* and some massive species are abundant. This coral flat, 150–200 m wide, is entirely living in its outer parts, and more and more necrotized lagoonward. In the dead parts, melobesian algae contribute to cement and to level the upper surface of the colonies. This tabular flat is here and there interrupted by irregular grooves, roughly perpendicular to the reef edge, and with a maximum depth of 30 cm. The bottom of the grooves is covered with fine sand. A few microatoll-shaped colonies can be observed in that coral built tabular flat, which, in general, comprises many species.

The scleractinian coral communities of the inner flat are not much developed in Nossi-Bé and we find them under their typical aspect on a few reefs only (Navetsy, Amporaha, Antafianambitry). In most cases the scleractinian coral communities are restricted to "islets" about 10 m wide, completely surrounded by the inner sea grasses which lie almost up to the boulder rampart. These formations are rarely very dense but have the shape of microatolls or of small tabular patches, more or less crumbly.

The inner flat of the reefs of Tuléar (especially the Grand Récif) are characterized by the occurrence at low tide of a residual sheet of water embanked between the boulder tract and the inner sea grass flat. The scleractinian coral communities of the inner flat have two main aspects.

The first aspect is a secondary flat built by scleractinian corals growing on the fundamental reef substratum. This more or less consolidated coral-built flat is perfectly horizontal because all the colonies are levelled by emersion. At very low tide they are slightly above the surface of the water sheet. This tabular formation is very dense and continuous near the boulder rampart, where it gives way rapidly to a series of coral built alignments perpendicular to the reef edge, and separated by grooves, the bottoms of which are covered by detrital sand. The width and compactness of the coral alignments regularly decrease when going toward the inner sea grass flat. Lastly, we observe only small and more or less scattered coral patches. Microatolls are also found in the inner part of this zone.

The second aspect of the scleractinian coral communities of the inner flat seems to be similar to the "inner moat" which has been described on some Indo-Pacific coral reefs. It corresponds to a depression of the inner flat which induces a greater depth of the residual pond, at low tide. In that case, the coral formations are never coalescent (isolated colonies) and rarely reach the surface of the pond. The total area covered by the scleractinian corals is therefore much smaller than in the previous case, and consequently the soft bottoms are more important.

The scleractinian fauna is probably still richer on the inner flats of Tuléar than in La Réunion although the genus *Acropora* is not so obviously dominant in Tuléar.

2. *The inner sea grass beds.* The inner sea grass beds exist only on the reefs of Tuléar and Nossi-Bé.

In Nossi-Bé they often cover the whole inner reef which has the shape of a wide but very shallow depression between the boulder tract and the shore. The phanerogams settle on the sediments lying on the bottom of this depression and there is a perfect continuity between the inner reef sea grass flats and the shore sea grass flats.

Near the boulder rampart, the dominant species is *Thalassodendron ciliatum*, fixed on coarse sand or gravel, sometimes mixed with *Syringodium isoetifolium* and *Cymodocea serrulata*. In the deeper parts of the inner flat (edge of small hollows made by erosion) these species are found again.

Most of the sea grass flats are composed of a mixed lawn including species that belong to the genera *Thalassia*, *Cymodocea*, and *Halodule*. The higher places are covered by species with very narrow leaves (*Halodule wrightii*) which, near the shore, takes the place of the mixed lawn.

A special mention must be reserved for *Enhalus acoroides*, a tall species of Hydrocharitaceae, which until now, has been recorded in Madagascar only from the region of Nossi-Bé. This phanerogam occurs in patches of approximately 100 sq. m, localized at the boundary between the *Halodule wrightii* zone and the mixed lawn or sometimes completely enclosed in the mixed lawn. *Enhalus acoroides* seems to prefer sediments which already contain elements of terrigenous origin.

In Tuléar, the sea grass beds settle on a wide sandy accumulation with a smoothed relief, stretching on the inner part (approximately the inner half) of the reef flat, between the scleractinian coral communities of the tabular flat and the backreef lagoon. The species are the same as in Nossi-Bé with the exception of *Enhalus acoroides*. Most of the sandy accumlation is covered by a mixed lawn. In the lower parts, or in those corresponding to coarse sands, *Thalassodendron ciliatum* is the dominant species, but in addition we find *Syringodium isoetifolium* and *Cymodocea serrulata*. *Halodule wrighti* is the only species remaining in the higher zones, which are completely devoid even of Phanerogams when they are much too high. The sediments deposited under special hydro-dynamic conditions, such as hydraulic dunes, submerged sand cays and sand trails are also devoid of any Phanerogamic vegetation.

On the upper part of the back-reef slope, on the edge of the lagoon, the sea grass beds show two superposed belts: a *Syringodium isoetifolium* belt and, just below, a *Thalassodendron ciliatum* belt. I have already described (Pichon, 1969) in the sea grass flats of the Grand Récif of Tuléar, some curious scleractinian coral communities (free living species on the sediment) with *Diaseris distorta*, *Diaseris* sp, *Goniopora stokesi*. When they are well developed, these communities can reduce or inhibit the phanerogam growth, in some areas of approximately 10 sq. m.

The lagoons

Except for the fringing reefs without boat channel of Nossi-Bé, the coral formations of La Réunion, Mauritius and Tuléar are separated from the shore by a depression in which the water level tends to stay the same as offshore. This we name lagoon.

In La Réunion, the reefs are usually established close to the shore and consequently the lagoons are not very developed. Their width does not exceed 300 m (150–200 m in Saint Pierre) and their maximum depth is about 2 to 3 m. They are then back-reef channels rather than true lagoons.

The reefs bounding a great part of the Mauritius coasts are discontinuous—just as in La Réunion. We must therefore consider that there is a series of lagoons, each corresponding to a separate reef, rather than a single unique lagoon. The width of the lagoons may vary greatly. They are generally wider (up to four nautical miles) on the east coast than on the west coast. Their average depth is remarkably low (1 or 2 m) except in the northern part of the island, where we record 4 m. The depth is more important locally in channels or ponds, where their origin has not been determined.

The Grand Récif of Tuléar is separated from the shore by a lagoon, the maximum width of which is about five nautical miles. The average depth is about 10 m. It is connected to the open sea through two passes, at the north and south end of the Grand Récif, with depths of 15 and 20 m respectively. The back-reef slope is steeper than the landward slope.

In the three regions, the water circulation and renewal are sufficient and the lagoon communities have nothing in common with those of almost closed sea water basins. In fact, because of the lagoons' small size and of the importance of the nearby emerged land masses, their sediments can be widely contaminated by elements of terrigenous origin. However, this does not occur in La Réunion because of the weakness of the alluvion near the reefs.

The soft bottoms and their communities

In the narrow back-reef channel of Saint Pierre (La Réunion), Faure and Montaggioni (1970) signalize three types of sediments.

1. Well sized bioclastic sands, with basaltic particles.

2. Autochthonous coral gravel, heterometric, coming from the coral patches of the lagoon.

3. Basaltic blocks, boulders and gravels, restricted to the vicinity of volcanic outcrops.

The fauna of these various sediments is extraordinarily poor.

In Mauritius the nature of the lagoon floor varies according to the local conditions of sedimentation: proximity of passes, river mouths, etc. The most characteristic bottom deposits are as follow.

1. Coarse gravel, composed of broken fragments of branching corals. The fauna is very rich, but without conspicuous species.

2. More or less fine sand (especially abundant in the lagoons of the east coast). The animal community is composed of echinoderms (mostly Ophiuroidea), Gastropods, and Crustacea.

Tall Phaeophyceae (*Turbinaria ornata* and *Sargassum* sp) which can be locally abundant, grow on large pieces of dead corals scattered on the bottom, or on basaltic outcrops when they occur.

In Tuléar, the alluvial deposits of the two rivers Fiherenana and Onilahy lead to an important sedimentation of terrigenous origin, in the lagoon. The various sedimentary stocks are distributed by tide currents, according to the bottom topography. The major sediment categories and their related communities, after Guérin-Ancey (1970) are as follows.

1. Clean coarse coral sands, influenced by bottom currents (Sands with *Asymmetron*). They are restricted to the southern part of the lagoon.

2. Sand only slightly muddy, with *Heteropsammia michelini* and *Heterocyathus aequicostatus*.

3. Muddy sands with *Ensiculus philippianus*, *Pteroides acutum* and *Lingula anatina*.

4. Muds with *Macoma hawaiiensis* and *Paphia undulata*.

The sea grass beds

There is only one species of marine phanerogam in the lagoons of La Réunion. This sea-grass is *Syringodium isoetifolium*, which constitutes small, discontinuous beds established on a coarse sand in the lagoon of Saint Gilles. The paucity of the sea grasses, in La Réunion is probably a consequence of the lack of organic matter, or even of any terrigenous particle in the sediments.

The lagoon sea grass beds of Mauritius are composed of four dominant species, which have a different distribution. These species are: *Halophila ovalis*, *Halodule uninervis*, *Syringodium isoetifolium* and *Thalassodendron ciliatum*. *Halodule uninervis* is restricted to the coastal edge of the lagoon (where this is composed of fine sand). These sea grass beds, which are not constantly present stretch towards the lagoon centre, according to the slope. On the contrary, the sea grass beds of the lagoon floor often cover large surfaces (lagoons of the east coast, for instance). They are generally composed of *Thalassodendron ciliatum* and *Syringodium isoetifolium*. The first of these two species tend to be restricted to the deeper zones. The second is very abundant in shallow water and locally constitutes a real belt on the landward boundary of the sea grass beds.

In Tuléar, the sea grass beds are essentially established on the two lagoon slopes. Towards the shore, under low tide level we find two zones, with a bathymetric superposition: a *Syringodium isoetifolium* zone and, below, a *Thalassodendron ciliatum* zone. These two belts also occur (as we have already mentioned) on the upper part of the back reef slope. On this slope, below the *T. ciliatum* belt, *Cymodocea serrulata* becomes the dominant species, but is sometimes mixed with *Halodule* cf. *beaudettei* and *Syringodium isoetifolium*. At depths greater than 4–5 m, *Cymodocea serrulata* is progressively replaced by a cover of *Halophila stipulacea*. The lagoon floor has a very reduced growth of phanerogams. We will quote only small patches of *Halophila ovalis* appearing in a few places.

The scleractinian coral communities

In very narrow and very shallow lagoons, such as in La Réunion it is difficult to make a distinction between the back reef slope and the lagoon floor. In Saint Pierre, the boundary between the reef flat and the lagoon is marked by an edge of living corals, behind which very numerous coral patches are found. These patches are essentially built by several species of *Acropora* and they show a series of stages of evolution leading to tabular constructions, with only an horizontal peripheric growth. The patches can then anastomoze and the space between the coral heads is filled up by coral sand. This formation eventually fuses with the back reef and contributes to the reduction of the lagoon. The evolution will be stopped before the lagoon is completely filled because of the occurrence of strong currents.

In the lagoons of Mauritius there are scattered coral patches similar to those of La Réunion which we described above. But the scleractinian coral growths of the shallow lagoons of Mauritius are, above all, remarkable by the great horizontal extension of the *Pavona* communities and of the branching *Acropora* communities. Because of the morphology of these species, there is no cementation of the colonies by other organisms, and we cannot speak of coral built formations. These *Pavona* and *Acropora* communities spread almost continuously over a great part of the lagoon floor.

The scleractinian coral communities of the Tuléar lagoon include:

1. the back reef slope communities,
2. the coral knoll and coral patches,
3. the inner reefs and
4. the Scleractinian coral communities on soft bottoms.

The back reef slope communities. The scleractinian corals are conspicuous on the back reef slope, only in the northern part of the Grand Récif. The slope is then almost vertical, with a height of about 6 or 7 m. The scleractinian fauna is very rich but there is no apparent zonation. We notice, however, that *Acropora pharaonis* and several Pocilloporidae are more abundant in the upper part of the slope and, that some species with massive colonies are restricted to the foot of the slope.

Coral knolls and coral patches. The dimensions of the coral knolls and coral patches hardly attain a few hundred meters. Their upper surface, when they reach the low tide level is levelled and sometimes covered with sediment. In the southern part of the lagoon, the coral knolls are numerous and they fuse together to constitute elements of reef platforms. Some of these structures, made of anastomosed knolls have been connected with the back reef, and after clogging up by sediments have been completely included in the reef frame, and sometimes even covered by the inner sea grass flats. Most of the coral species which originally constitute the knolls and patches have a massive growth form (*Diploastrea, Porites, Platygyra, Lobophyllia, Oulophyllia*). Onto these primary coral builders, numerous encrusting (*Pavona, Montipora*), foliaceous or digitate (*Acropora*) species are attached. These communities are closely related with that of the back reef slope.

The inner reefs. The "inner" reefs are small coral reefs established in the landward part of the lagoon. Their average width is about 1000 m. They are separated from the shore by a littoral channel (boat channel), the maximum depth of which is about two meters.

We have previously pointed out that the slope of such reefs was quite similar to the back reef slope of the Grand Récif, and to the outer slope of the fringing reefs of Nossi-Bé. The flats of these reefs, slightly emerged at low tide, have a conspicuous transversal zonation. From the lagoon toward the shore we find successively:

1. an *Acropora* edge, forming a rim about 20 m wide and interrupted in some places by outfalls;

2. a pond or hollow, the floor of which is covered with coarse sediment, with a growth of *Thalassodendron ciliatum*. A few colonies of small Scleractinia and tall Phaeophyceae sometimes occur. The hollow can be locally replaced by a rudimentary boulder tract made up of broken branches of *Acropora* cemented by a vermetid Gastropod (*Dendropoma*);

3. a mixed sea grass flat in which patches of scleractinian corals are sometimes enclosed. This coral community can be, in part, compared to the coral built tabular patches or "islets" of the inner reef flats of Nossi-Bé. The species are not very numerous and these formations frequently take the shape of inconspicuous microatolls of reduced vitality. On the necrotized parts alcyonarians and sponges often settle; and

4. a sandy accumulation without any phanerogamic cover, with a very poor fauna (*Echinodiscus bisperforatus, Modiolus* sp. and Gastropods). The top of this sandy accumulation is located in the inner (back) part of the reef flat. Beyond, on the slope of the littoral channel, a mixed sea grass bed occurs again.

Free living corals on soft bottoms. Free living scleractinian coral communities exist on some soft bottoms of the lagoon of Tuléar. They are:

1. a turbinolid coral—*Sphenotrochus* cf. *intermedius*, living in the clean coarse sand, influenced by bottom currents, with *Asymmetron*; and

2. the *Heteropsammia michelini* and *Heterocyathus aequicostatus* community, restricted to muddy sands. We find also *Diaseris* sp in the same environment.

Muddy sands with *Heteropsammia michelini* and *Heterocyathus aequicostatus*, together with *Trachyphyllia geoffroyi* have been recorded also from Nossi-Bé, where they stretch in front of the reef slopes. Such communities are quite similar to that described by Goreau and Yonge (1968) from Australia, and by Salvat (1964) from New Caledonia.

FAUNISTIC COMPARISONS

The faunistic and floristic inventory of the reefs of the four studied localities is far from being completed. We have provisional lists of some invertebrate groups, especially in Tuléar and Nossi-Bé, but they are too incomplete to be used for a biogeographical purpose. The problem is the same when we consider the groups which play an important part in reef building or in cementing the reef frame (scleractinian corals, melobesian algae, vermetid Gastropods).

Another difficulty in the faunistical comparisons lies in the possible occurrence, in Mauritius and La Réunion of endemic species, owing to the insularity. There are very many terrestrial endemic species (insects and vertebrates), but only a few, in the present status of our knowledge, in the sea (the echinoderm *Acanthocidaris curvatispinis*, the gastropod *Harpa costata* in Mauritius, for instance). If we consider only the coral reef environment and closely related biota, we can reasonably estimate that the endemic species play only a minor part.

Our data can only be compared for the scleractinian corals. Table II gives the list of hermatypic coral genera for each of the four localities. (The lists for Tuléar, Nossi-Bé and Mauritius have been drawn up from my own observations. The list for La Réunion has been established together with G. Faure, and from the material collected by him.)

This table shows that the scleractinian faunas of Tuléar and Nossi-Bé are practically similar. Particularly, the average sea temperatures, lower in Tuléar than in Nossi-Bé, have no effect on the hermatypic coral diversity. South of Tuléar, however, the coastal water average temperatures are still lower, and the coral fauna is notably impoverished. The faunas of La Réunion and Mauritius are somewhat less rich than those of Tuléar and Nossi-Bé, and we wonder if the relative poorness

TABLE II

Distribution of hermatypic scleractinian coral genera

	Tuléar	Nossi-Bé	La Réunion	Mauritius
Psammocora	+	+	+	+
Seriatopora	+	+	−	+
Stylophora	+	+	+	+
Pocillopora	+	+	+	+
Acropora	+	+	+	+
Astreopora	+	+	+	+
Montipora	+	+	+	+
Pavona	+	+	+	+
Pachyseris	+	+	+	+
Leptoseris	+	+	+	+
Coscinaraea	+	+	+	+
Siderastrea	+	−	−	−
Horastrea	+	−	+	−
Diaseris	+	+	−	−
Cycloseris	+	+	+	−
Fungia	+	+	+	+
Herpolitha	+	+	−	+
Herpetoglossa	+	+	−	−
Halomitra	+	+	−	−
Polyphyllia	−	+	−	−
Podabacia	+	+	−	+
Goniopora	+	+	+	+
Porites	+	+	+	+
Alveopora	+	+	−	+
Caulastrea	+	+	−	+
Plesiastrea	+	+	+	−
Favia	+	+	+	+
Favites	+	+	+	+
Oulophyllia	+	+	+	+
Goniastrea	+	+	+	+
Platygyra	+	+	+	+
Leptoria	+	+	+	+
Hydnophora	+	+	+	+
Montastrea	+	+	−	−
Diploastrea	+	+	−	−
Leptastrea	+	+	+	−
Cyphastrea	+	+	+	+
Echinopora	+	+	+	+
Trachyphyllia	−	+	−	−
Galaxea	+	+	+	+
Merulina	+	+	−	−
Acanthastrea	+	+	+	+
Lobophyllia	+	+	+	+

TABLE II (continued)

Distribution of hermatypic scleractinian coral genera

Symphyllia	+	+	—	—
Blastomussa	+	+	—	—
Parascolymia	+	+	—	—
Cynarina	+	+	—	—
Echinophyllia	+	+	+	+
Oxypora	+	+	—	+
Mycedium	+	+	—	+
Pectinia	+	+	—	—
Euphyllia	—	—	—	+
Plerogyra	+	+	—	+
Physogyra	+	+	—	—
Gyrosmilia	+	+	—	—
Turbinaria	+	+	+	+

is a consequence of the isolation of these two islands or of the present deficiency of the researches. An important point we must state however is that the difference between Madagascar and the Mascarene islands proceeds from genera of secondary importance. The occurrence of these genera of secondary importance in Madagascar is related to the great variety of reef biota, in Tuléar and Nossi-Bé. The widely distributed genera, or those playing a fundamental part in reef building are found in La Réunion as well as in Mauritius. This means that the greater richness of the coral faunas of Tuléar and Nossi-Bé has no effect on the physiognomy or the physiography of the reefs. The differences noticed in the morphology and ecology of the coral reefs of the four localities have no biogeographical origin.

DISCUSSION AND CONCLUSIONS

The reefs of Madagascar and the Mascarene Islands

The morphological, ecological and faunistic features which we have analysed in this paper are presented in Table III under a synthetic and synoptic form (see also Fig. 4).

The study of Table III indicates that the coral reefs of the four regions are dissimilar. We must however take into account the fact that the considered features do not have the same comparative value, and point out that there are some points common to Nossi-Bé and Tuléar, and to a lesser extent, to La Réunion and Mauritius.

The coral reefs of Tuléar and Nossi-Bé can be compared: by the width of their reef flats, by the importance of sediment deposits on these reef flats (boulder tract, sandy accumulation) and by the development of sea grass beds. (The width of the reef flat and the abundance

TABLE III

The compared morphological, ecological and faunistical features

		Tuléar	Nossi-Bé	La Réunion	Mauritius
Outer slope	spurs and grooves	+ + (tunnels and caves)	—	+	+
	coral flag- stone	+ +	—	—	—
Reef flat	total width	+ +	+ +	(+)	
	boulder tract	+ + (regular supply)	+ episodic supply	—	No true reef flat
	outer sea grass bed	—	+ +	—	
	scleractinian com- munities	+ +	(+)	+ +	Reef edge **only**
	inner sea grass bed	+ + on accumu- lated sediments	+ +	—	
Lagoon	width and depth	+ +	fringing reefs	+ (very shallow)	+ + (very shallow)
	scleractinian com- munities	+ +	without boat channel	+ +	+ +
	free living corals on soft bottom	+		—	—
	sea grass beds	+		(+)	+ +
Hermatypic scleractinian coral genera		53	53	30	36

Key + + very important (or very well developed)
+ present
(+) not important (or very poorly developed)
— absent

of sediments could be a result of the important tide ranges, when currents are strong enough to spread widely the detrital materials from the reef front. The development of sea grass beds is related to the sediments including elements of terrigenous origin.)

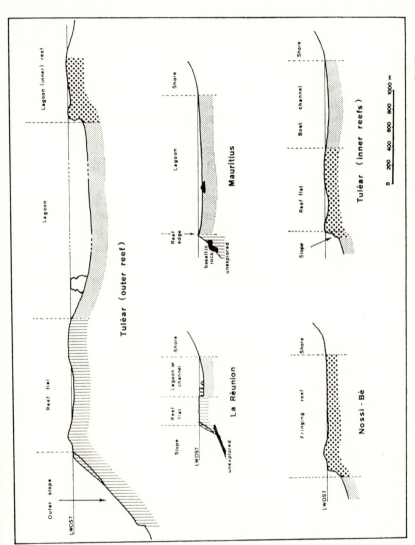

FIG. 4. Diagrammatic transversal section across some coral reefs of Madagascar and Mascarene islands (vertical exaggeration about 20 times).

We can still better compare the fringing reefs of Nossi-Bé with the inner reefs of Tuléar (which are considered as fringing reefs with a littoral—or boat—channel). We have already pointed out that the structure of the slopes of these two reef categories is similar. In both cases also, the reef flats are characterized by an important phanerogamic growth and a weak development of the scleractinian coral communities (which generally form groups of microatolls completely surrounded by the sea grass flats).

The analogy can be extended not only to the whole reefs but also to the soft bottoms lying in front of these reefs (lagoon floor, in Tuléar). In both cases, indeed, we can find on the sediments which spread in front of the reef slopes:

1. a lower sea grass bed, with *Halophila ovalis* and
2. free living scleractinian coral communities (*Heteropsammia, Heterocyathus, Trachyphyllia*).

We are therefore led to consider the fringing reefs of Nossi-Bé as "inner" reefs, and the soft bottoms in front of these reefs as those of a pseudo-lagoon, stretching between the drowned barrier (which, in that hypothesis is equivalent to the outer reef) and the coastal reefs of Nossi-Bé or of the mainland.

We would then have the following correspondence between Tuléar and Nossi-Bé:

Tuléar   Nossi-Bé

Grand Récif (= outer reef) ↔ drowned barrier

Lagoon (or back-reef channel) ↔ pseudo lagoon

Inner reefs ↔ coastal fringing reefs

In spite of the comparison which has just been made between the outer reef (Grand Récif) of Tuléar and the drowned barrier of the North-West, these two formations cannot be considered as completely similar. The coral reef origin of the drowned barrier has not been proved. Otherwise, the Grand Récif has morphological and ecological features which are not found on the drowned barrier.

The reefs of Mauritius and La Réunion have less characteristics in common than those of Tuléar and Nossi-Bé. Yet, they can be compared by the narrowness of their reef flats, their shallow lagoons, the lack of diversity of the reef biota, and a coral fauna somewhat impoverished in comparison with that of Madagascar.

The extreme reduction of the reef flat, the importance in the lagoons of scleractinian coral communities consisting of one or few species and of the sea grass beds are highly conspicuous characters of the reefs of Mauritius. In contrast, the reefs of La Réunion have a very rich reef flat fauna, lagoons with numerous polyspecific coral patches and a reduced Phanerogamic growth.

The coral formations of either of these two islands have practically no feature similar to that of the reefs of Nossi-Bé or Tuléar. In particular, there is a complete opposition between the reefs of Nossi-Bé and of La Réunion.

Comparisons with other Indo-Pacific areas

Comparison of the coral faunas

When we follow the taxonomic bases that were used by Wells (1954) in his fundamental work on the distribution of Indo-Pacific hermatypic scleractinian corals (distinction between genera and subgenera, absence of solitary Mussids), we reach the total of 55 hermatypic genera and subgenera in Madagascar and 36 in the Mascarene. These results put Madagascar first, of the Indo-Pacific areas, for richness of its hermatypic coral fauna and make two important alterations in the plotting of the isopangeneric lines proposed by Wells (1954). It is also the case when considering only the distribution of the Fungiid genera (Wells, 1966): *Pleuractis, Fungia, Podabacia, Herpolitha, Halomitra* and *Herpethoglossa* occur at Tuléar, and I have found also *Herpetoglossa* and *Polyphyllia* at Nossi-Bé.

Two conclusions can be drawn from these considerations:

1. the hermatypic coral fauna of Madagascar is very rich, and

2. the biogeographical comparisons are rendered very hazardous because of the great disparity in the present status of our knowledge in the various areas. The investigations have been more intensive in some places and less in others. It seems necessary, in any case, to revise and to complete the lists previously drawn up. For instance, there are more than 50 genera and subgenera of hermatypic corals in the Red Sea, and I have identified the genera *Leptoseris, Podabacia, Mycedium,* and *Oxypora* in material from the Gulf of Aqaba.

The investigations which have been carried out until now in the Mascarene Islands, have been too insufficient to give us an adequate idea of the real richness of the coral fauna.

It is therefore reasonable to suppose that the Indo-Malayan archipelago, centre of dispersion of the scleractinian corals, has a fauna remaining more diversified than the Madagascar coral fauna, especially at the specific level. The impoverishment of this fauna is weak, when going westward—Madagascar and the Red Sea, both have more than 50 hermatypic coral genera as we have just pointed out. Some indications lead us to think that the coral fauna reaches almost the same

level of diversity in the whole western Indian Ocean, in so far as the
temperature does not become a limiting factor (according to Boshoff,
in MacNae and Kalk, 1958, 35 hermatypic genera still occur, collected
mostly in shallow water, at Inhaca, 26°S). This very relative westward
impoverishment is partly counterbalanced by the occurrence of
endemic genera (*Gyrosmilia* in Red Sea and western Indian Ocean,
Ctenella and *Anomastraea* in the southwest Indian Ocean). It seems
to be less rapid, going the equivalent distance westward (Indian
Ocean) than it is eastward (Central Pacific) as proved by the results of
Chevalier *et al.* (1969) who have collected only 26 genera in Mururoa
(Tuamotu) after detailed and careful research.

The investigations at present in progress will allow us to confirm
that remarkable character of the distribution of Indo Pacific scleractinian corals.

*Geomorphological and bionomical comparisons in the western Indian
Ocean*

The diversity which we have already pointed out, in the four
studied reefs is so important that it is not possible to define only one
reef type representative of Madagascar or of the Mascarens. We
must therefore compare everyone of these reefs with the coral formations in other areas. Furthermore, the researches in the field of reef
ecology, not only founded on mere descriptions of the communities, but
also on a numerative characterization are still too uncommon to
authorize accurate comparisons.

We must also quote that many of the reefs (even in the western
Indian Ocean) have a geological history which strongly influences
their present structure (Red Sea and numerous islands such as Europa
and Aldabra.) In the four regions which we have compared, the reefs
are generally very young. The evidence of uplifted coral reefs (or,
more exactly, of reefs built during a period of higher sea level) is
entirely lacking in Tuléar and La Réunion, and extremely reduced
in Nossi-Bé and Mauritius.

The reef flats of Tuléar seem to be quite similar to that of Mayotte
(Comoro Islands) although no ecological data have been published
until now. In both cases, wide reef flats occur, with a boulder rampart
and sea grass beds. The coral faunas are also quite similar.

The coral formations of Nossi-Bé seem to have more in common
with those described by Taylor (1968) from Mahé, Seychelles. In both
places there are well-developed fringing reefs, with communities
showing the influence of sediments of terrigenous origin.

Little fringing reefs, with very rich flat communities and small or very small shallow lagoons, such as in Saint Pierre, La Réunion, are also to be found in areas with a weak tide range and where there is little alluvium. In that respect, some reefs from the Red Sea (Gulf of Aqaba) or from the Gulf of Tadjourah have features much like those of La Réunion. Nevertheless, we will not generalize in that way: the reef of Saint Gilles, for instance, has already a wider lagoon drawing nearer those of Mauritius. Moreover the outer slope structures are in every case different in the Red Sea (where the general reef zonation is not always noticeable) and the Mascarene.

The reef type occurring in Mauritius, the features of which are related to the characters of the volcanism, seems to be rather singular, in the whole western Indian Ocean.

The geomorphological and ecological comparisons of the reefs of Madagascar and Mascarene with others are reduced because of the lack of data dealing with a great number of coral reefs, even in the western Indian Ocean. This is only one of the arguments in favour of increased regional coral reef investigations.

Lastly, we will point out that Tuléar and Nossi-Bé are highly preferential places to carry out coral reef researches, because of the diversity and the richness of their coral biota.

REFERENCES

Baissac, J. de B., Lubet, P. and Michel, C. (1962). Les biocoenoses benthiques littorales de l'Ile Maurice. *Recl Trav. Stn Mar., Endoume* **25**, 39: 253–291.

Battistini, R. (1959a). Observations sur les récifs coralliens du Sud-Ouest de Madagascar. *Bull. Soc. géol. Fr.* (7) **1**: 341–346.

Battistini, R. (1959b). Description géomorphologique de Nosy Bé, du delta du Sambirano et de la baie d'Ampasindava. *Mém. IRSM.* F **III**: 121–343.

Chevalier, J. P., Denizot, M., Mougin, J. L., Plessis, Y. and Salvat, B. (1969). Etude géomorphologique et bionomique de l'atoll de Mururoa (Tuamotu). *Cah. Pacif.* **12**: 11–144.

Faure, G. and Montaggioni, L. (1970). Le récif corallien de Saint-Pierre de La Réunion (Océan Indien): Géomorphologie et répartition des peuplements. *Recl Trav. Stn Mar. Endoume* (H. S. Suppl.) **10**, 271–284.

Goreau, T. F. and Yonge, C. M. (1968). Coral community on muddy sand. *Nature, Lond.* **217**: 421–423.

Gravier, N. Harmelin, J. G., Pichon, M., Thomassin, B., Vasseur, P. and Weydert, P. (1970). Les récifs coralliens de Tuléar (Madagascar): morphologie et bionomie de la pente externe. *C.r. Hebd. Séanc. Acad. Sci., Paris* **270**: 1130–1133.

Guérin-Ancey, O. (1970). Etudes des intrusions terrigènes fluviatiles dans les complexes récifaux: délimitation et dynamique des peuplements des vases et des sables vaseux du chenal postrécifal de Tuléar (S.W. de Madagascar). *Recl Trav. Stn Mar. Endoume* (H. S., suppl.) **10**, 3–46.

Guilcher, A. (1956). Etude géomorphologique des récifs coralliens du nord-ouest de Madagascar. *Annls Inst. océanogr., Monaco* **33**, 2: 65–136.

Guilcher, A. (1958). Mise au point sur la géomorphologie des récifs coralliens de Madagascar et dépendances. *Mém. IRSM.* F **II**: 89–115.

Guilcher, A., Berthois, L., Le Calvez, Y., Battistini, R. and Crosnier, A. (1965). Les récifs coralliens et le lagon de l'Ile Mayotte (Archipel des Comores. Océan Indien). *Mém. ORSTOM.* **11**: 1–120.

MacNae, W. and Kalk, M. (1958). A Natural History of Inhaca Island, Moçambique. Johannesburg, South Africa: Witwatersrand University Press.

Pichon, M. (1964). Contribution à l'étude de la répartition des Madréporaires sur le récif de Tuléar, Madagascar. *Recl Trav. Stn Mar. Endoume* (hors série), suppl. **2**: 81–203.

Pichon, M. (1967). Caractères généraux des peuplements benthiques des récifs et lagons de l'Ile Maurice (Océan Indien). *Cah. ORSTOM Océanogr.* **V** (4): 31–45.

Pichon, M. (1969). Les peuplements à base de Scléractiniaires dans les récifs de la baie de Tuléar (Sud Ouest de Madagascar). *J. mar. biol. Ass. India*—Symposium on coral reefs and reef corals. Mandapam Camp. Jan. 1969.

Pichon, M. (in press). Les récifs coralliens de Madagascar in *Monographie de Madagascar*.

Salvat, B. (1964). Prospections faunistiques en Nouvelle-Calédonie dans le cadre de la mission d'étude des récifs coralliens. *Cah. Pacif.* **6**: 77–119.

Taylor, J. D. (1968). Coral reef and associated invertebrate communities (mainly molluscan) around Mahé, Seychelles. *Phil. Trans. R. Soc.* (B) **254**: 129–206.

Vasseur, P. (1964). Contribution à l'étude bionomique des peuplements sciaphiles infralittoraux de substrat dur dans les récifs de Tuléar. *Recl Trav. Stn Mar. Endoume* (hors série) suppl. no. **2**: 1–77.

Voeltzkow, A. (1905). Berichte über eire Reise nach Ost-Africa zur Untersuchung der Bildung und der Aufbaues des Riffe und Inseln des westlichen Indischen Ozeans. VI Madagascar. *Z. Ges. Erdk. Berl.*: 89–119, 184–211, 285–296.

Wells, J. W. (1954). Recent corals of the Marshall Islands. *Prof. Pap. U.S. geol. Surv.* **260–1**: 385–486.

Wells, J. W. (1966). Evolutionary development on the Scleractinian family Fungiidae. *Symp. zool. Soc. Lond.* No. **16**: 223–246.

Symp. zool. Soc. Lond. (1971) No. 28, 217–259.

REEF FORMS OF ADDU ATOLL, MALDIVE ISLANDS

P. SPENCER DAVIES

Department of Zoology, University of Glasgow, Glasgow, Scotland

D. R. STODDART

Department of Geography, University of Cambridge, Cambridge, England

and

D. C. SIGEE

Department of Botany, University College of Wales, Cardiff, Wales

INTRODUCTION

The Pacific Science Board expeditions to Pacific atolls in 1950–1954, and associated studies in the Marshall Islands, led to considerable advances in our knowledge of regional and local variations in the morphology and composition of atoll reefs. These expeditions were also concerned with the development of techniques for obtaining data in the field (Fosberg and Sachet, 1953), and with the development of a descriptive terminology and concepts for organizing the information so obtained. The purpose of the Maldive Islands Expedition of 1964 was to initiate studies on Indian Ocean reefs similar to those carried out by the Pacific Science Board in the Pacific: the aims were to identify and describe the main reef types present on Addu Atoll; to identify the taxa of scleractinian corals and benthic marine algae present on the reefs; and to describe quantitatively the zonation patterns resulting from variations in their distribution. The Expedition spent 10 weeks on the island of Gan: for political reasons it was not possible to study reefs adjacent to other islands of the atoll, and detailed observations are therefore confined to the reefs of Gan. A preliminary report on other aspects of geomorphology (Stoddart, Davies and Keith, 1966); descriptions of land and marine vegetation (Sigee, 1966); systematic lists of land plants (Fosberg, Groves and Sigee, 1966), marine algae (Tsuda and Newhouse, 1966), and scleractinian corals (Wells and Davies, 1966); with a bibliography, has already been published, and is supplementary to the account which follows.

In common with the rest of the Maldive Islands, the reefs of Addu Atoll have received scant attention. Agassiz (1903) gave a brief description of the atoll from shipboard observations. J. Stanley Gardiner's

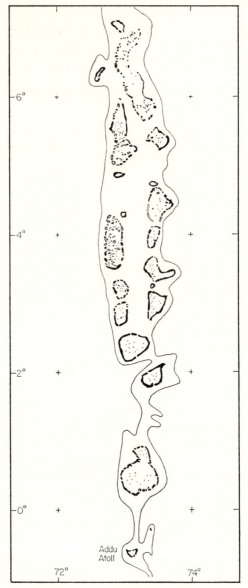

FIG. 1. The Maldive Islands, showing the location of Addu Atoll. The 1000 fathom (1830 m) depth contour is shown. After Farquharson (1936).

expedition to the Maldives and Laccadives in 1899–1900 resulted in lists of plants and animals collected and a brief description of Addu, but no detailed descriptions of reef structure or coral distribution

(Gardiner, 1903–1906). The next expedition to the Maldives was the John Murray Expedition in 1933–1934, and Sewell (1936) contributed a general description of Addu Atoll to its *Scientific Reports*. Subsequently Kohn (1964, 1968; Kohn and Robertson, 1968) described the reef Mollusca collected at Addu and elsewhere in the Maldives by the Yale Seychelles Expedition of 1957, and Hackett (1969) has studied the distribution of benthic marine algae in the Maldive Islands, including Addu, following work during the International Indian Ocean Expedition in 1964. Popular descriptions of Addu have been given by Hass (1965) and Eibl-Eibesfeldt (1966), following the *Xarifa* Expedition of 1958, when Scheer (1967, 1971) carried out important work on the zonation and field problems involved in studying the Xarifa Reef at the west side of Kudu Kanda Channel, on the northern side of Addu.

LOCATION AND ENVIRONMENT

The Maldive Islands form a double chain of atolls rising from a submarine plateau or ridge 270–380 m deep, 650 km (400 miles) long, and up to 130 km (80 miles) wide (Fig. 1). The Maldives also include the more isolated atolls of Suvadiva and Addu to the south of the main chain; these are linked to the main plateau and to one another by a ridge 1100–1650 m deep. Addu, the southernmost of the Maldive atolls, thus rises steeply from depths of 2 to 3·5 km (Gardiner, 1902, 1903–1906; Farquharson, 1936): Fig. 2, from unpublished Admiralty surveys and charts, shows the bathymetry round the atoll in detail.

Addu, situated at latitude 0°38′S and longitude 73°10′E, is separated from the nearest atoll to the north, Suvadiva, by the 70 km (45 mile) wide Equatorial Channel. It is one of the smallest of the Maldive atolls, measuring 28·3 km (17·6 miles) in maximum dimension (northwest to northeast points), and 16·5 km (10·2 miles) in transverse direction. In shape it may be termed semi-circular or triangular. The south-facing reefs are broadly convex and project northwards at each end to form prominent "horns" at the northeast and northwest corners of the atoll (Fig. 3). These reefs are broad, up to 1900 m wide in the southwest, and they have islands developed on them for most of their length. The reefs of the north side are concave in outline, narrow, and (with the exception of Bushy Islet between the two channels) do not bear islands. Of the total area of the atoll, 41% consists of reef flat and islands.

The peripheral reefs are continuous except for two gaps in the centre of the southern reef (Gan Channel, Wilingili Channel) and two in the centre of the northern reef (Kudu Kanda Channel, Man Kanda

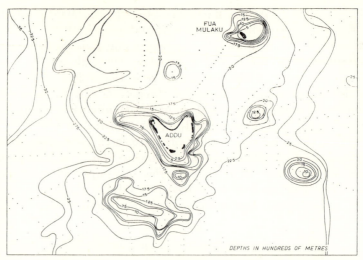

FIG. 2. Bathymetry of Addu Atoll. Reproduced from B.A. Ocean Sounding Chart No. 252 with the sanction of the Controller, H.M. Stationery Office, and Hydrographer of the Navy.

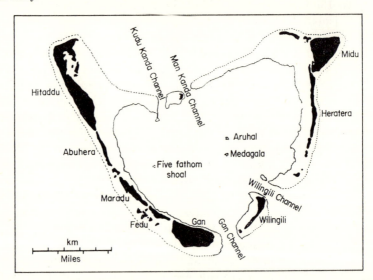

FIG. 3. Topography of Addu Atoll. Reproduced from B.A. Chart No. 2067, with the sanction of the Controller, H.M. Stationery Office and of the Hydrographer of the Navy.

Channel). Gan Channel is 950 m wide with a sill depth of 16–18 m; Wilingili Channel, 750 m wide has a sill depth of 38–57 m. In the north the channels are narrower but with similar depths: Man Kanda is

350 m wide with a 24–33 m sill, and Kudu Kanda is 250 m wide with a 24–35 m sill.

The atoll lagoon has a maximum length of 11·7 km and breadth of 9 km. Unlike the lagoons of the northern Maldive atolls there are few patch reefs and no faroes developed in the lagoon. The maximum lagoon depth is 80 m, comparable to that of Suvadiva, and considerably deeper than the lagoons of the large atolls of the northern Maldives (Fig. 4).

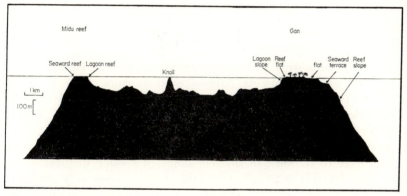

FIG. 4. North-south section through Addu Atoll showing topography and location of main reef types.

The climate of Addu differs from that of the more northern atolls, since it is too far south for the monsoon reversals to be strongly felt. During December, January and February, winds are mainly from the northern sector, but they gradually swing round in a westerly direction to blow from the south and southeast during July and August. The mean monthly air temperature is 28°C, and this is almost identical with sea temperatures.

Tidal variations are referred to the Standard Station at Madras. Admiralty Tide Tables give a range at springs of 1 m, and at neaps of 0·8 m. The flood stream sets into the lagoon through Wilingili and Kudu Kanda Channels only; the stream through Gan and Man Kanda Channels at this time is always in the outward direction. The tide ebbs from the lagoon through all four channels. Wave action at the edge of the southern reefs sends a continuous sheet of water across the reef, which passes in a flood between the islands. Current measurements in the gap between Gan and Fedu gave velocities of 0·1–1·1 m sec^{-1} (Stoddart et al., 1966).

Sea temperatures are approximately 28–29°C throughout the year. Agassiz (1903) recorded a surface temperature in the lagoon off Gan of 28·8°C (82·0°F), and the same temperature at a depth of 40 m. The lowest temperature recorded by Davies in 1964 was 27·0°C on the lagoon reef flat at Gan, following a moderate fall of rain (Stoddart *et al.*, 1966). Normal sea salinities are in the range 33·8–34·7‰. Following heavy rain the salinity of the inner zone of the seaward reef flat at Gan fell to 16·7% on one occasion, but the outer part of the reef was not affected (for details see Stoddart *et al.*, 1966).

SURVEY METHODS

The main investigations were carried out on the lagoon reefs at Gan, using quadrat transects. After a reconnaissance of the whole reef, two sites were selected as typifying the main features of coral distribution. The location of transects at these sites is shown in Fig. 5. A survey chain, in feet with tags at intervals of 10 ft (3·05 m), was laid across the reef at each transect site, from the shore to the reef edge and from the reef edge to the base of the reef slope. A wooden quadrat of 10 ft side (area 100 ft²; 9·29 m²) was laid down successively along the chain to give a continuous series of quadrats. Observation on the area within the quadrats was carried out at high tide using facemasks and snorkel tubes. In each quadrat one specimen of each coral and algal species was collected, and notes were made on the nature of the substrate, percentage cover by living coral, the dominant coral species, and other salient observations. The transects were continued down the lagoon reef slope using aqualungs.

The seaward reef flat at Gan was surveyed with Dumpy Level by wading over the reef flat during low water spring tides. Quantitative observations were made using the 10 × 10 ft quadrat laid down at intervals of 30 ft (9·1 m) on a line from the shore to the reef edge. The reef edge itself was observed during periods of low wave action but no quantitative surveys were made. Air photographs were used to interpret the broader zonation patterns on the seaward reef.

Other reefs, including the outer slopes of seaward reefs and also lagoon patch reefs, were investigated by direct observation, using aqualungs, and notes and photographs were made concurrently. Depth measurements during these observations were made using capillary type depth gauges.

The problems encountered during the quadrat surveys are briefly discussed on pp. 255–257.

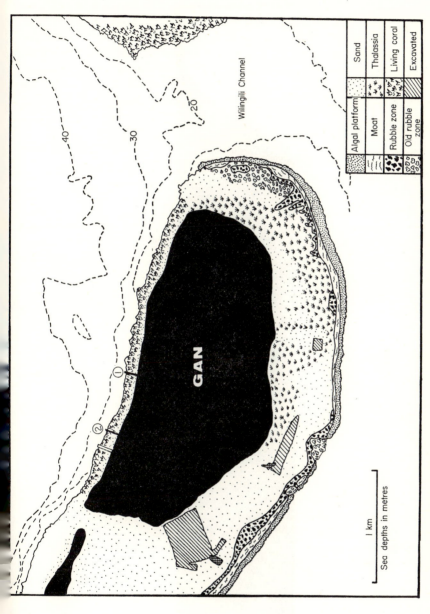

FIG. 5. Gan Island, Addu Atoll, and its surrounding reefs, showing the location of transects 1 and 2 on the lagoon reefs. After Stoddart *et al.* (1966).

Fig. 6. Profile of the Gan lagoon reef along transect 2 showing the distribution of zones.

REEFS AT GAN, WINDWARD SIDE OF ADDU

Lagoon reef at Gan

The lagoon reef at Gan is approximately 120 m wide, considerably narrower than the lagoon reefs off the more northerly islands of the atoll. It may be conveniently divided into the reef flat, a distinct reef edge, and a steep reef slope. The reef flat even at low water of spring tides carries 0·5–0·7 m of water, but at most low tides the tips of corals near the reef edge are emersed for several cm. The reef slope is inclined at an angle of about 60°, and reaches the sand floor of the lagoon at a depth of about 35 m. A profile of the reef at transect 2 is shown in Fig. 6.

Transect 1

Reef flat. For purposes of description the reef flat is divided into four fairly distinct zones, termed the Inner Zone, Mixed Coral Zone, *Acropora formosa* Zone, and Outer Zone.

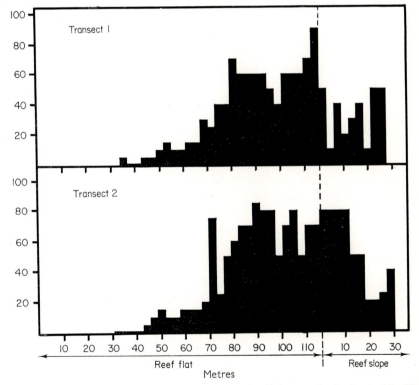

Fig. 7. Histograms showing percentage cover by living coral colonies in 10 × 10 ft quadrats laid successively along transects 1 and 2, lagoon reefs, Gan.

Inner zone. The Inner Zone extends from low water mark to a distance of approximately 35 m from the shore; it is characterized by the absence of any living corals. The first 10 m comprise loose-packed, often rippled, sand, and the continuous water motion maintains high turbidity. This is followed by an area of rubble comprising large mobile coral fragments, with larger much-eroded skeletons of massive corals firmly bonded to the substrate. Turbidity remains high, but the crevices of these coral skeletons are inhabited by gastropods such as *Conus ebraeus* and *Conus lividus* and by occasional echinoids. Near the beach the sand is colonized by the alga *Padina commersonii*, but this is replaced by *Dictyota* sp. and *Jania capillacea* on the sandy area between the dead coral boulders. Although not recorded in the transects, this zone also carries occasional swards of *Thalassia*, which become more numerous and cover a greater area northwards along the reef.

Mixed Coral Zone. The Mixed Coral Zone begins at approximately 35 m and extends to about 65 m from the shore. It is characterized by the presence of living corals which increase in number as the distance from the shore increases. The first 10 m are still dominated by large dead coral heads similar to the previous zone. The first living corals to appear are *Acropora digitifera* and the bracket form *A. convexa*, attached to the dead coral substrate. *Heliopora* is present here and in small amounts throughout this and the next zone. The number of coral species increases to about ten in passing outward over the inner subzone, the most important additions being *Pocillopora damicornis*, *Goniastrea retiformis*, *Leptoria phrygia*, *Acropora formosa*, and juvenile forms of *Fungia fungites*. The percentage cover of living corals also increases to about 15%. More massive forms such as *Leptoria* and *Goniastrea* are represented by small colonies of a few cm diameter.

Acropora formosa Zone. At about 65 m from the shore the Mixed Coral Zone gives way abruptly to the outer *Acropora* "forest", dominated by *Acropora formosa*, and 20 m wide (Fig. 8). Coral cover increases to 60–70% in passing lagoonward through this zone, partly because of the density of *A. formosa* growth but also because of the appearance of new coral species. The number of species recorded per quadrat (9·29 m^2) increases to 14–16. There is some indication of competition between *A. formosa* and the massive corals *Goniastrea* and *Leptoria*. Where the latter are present they form large boulders and the branching *Acropora* may occupy only about 5% of the coral area. In other places the massive colonies are poorly developed and *A. formosa* may account for 70% of the total coral area. Faviids such as *Favia speciosa* and *Favites abdita* and other corals of small but massive growth-form such as *Galaxea* and *Psammocora* are present in

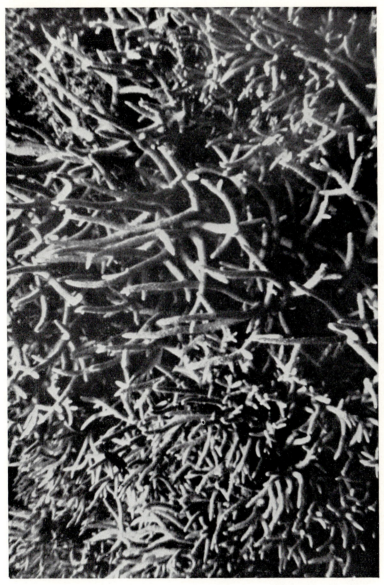

Fig. 8. Dense growth of *Acropora formosa* in the *Acropora formosa* Zone of transect 1.'

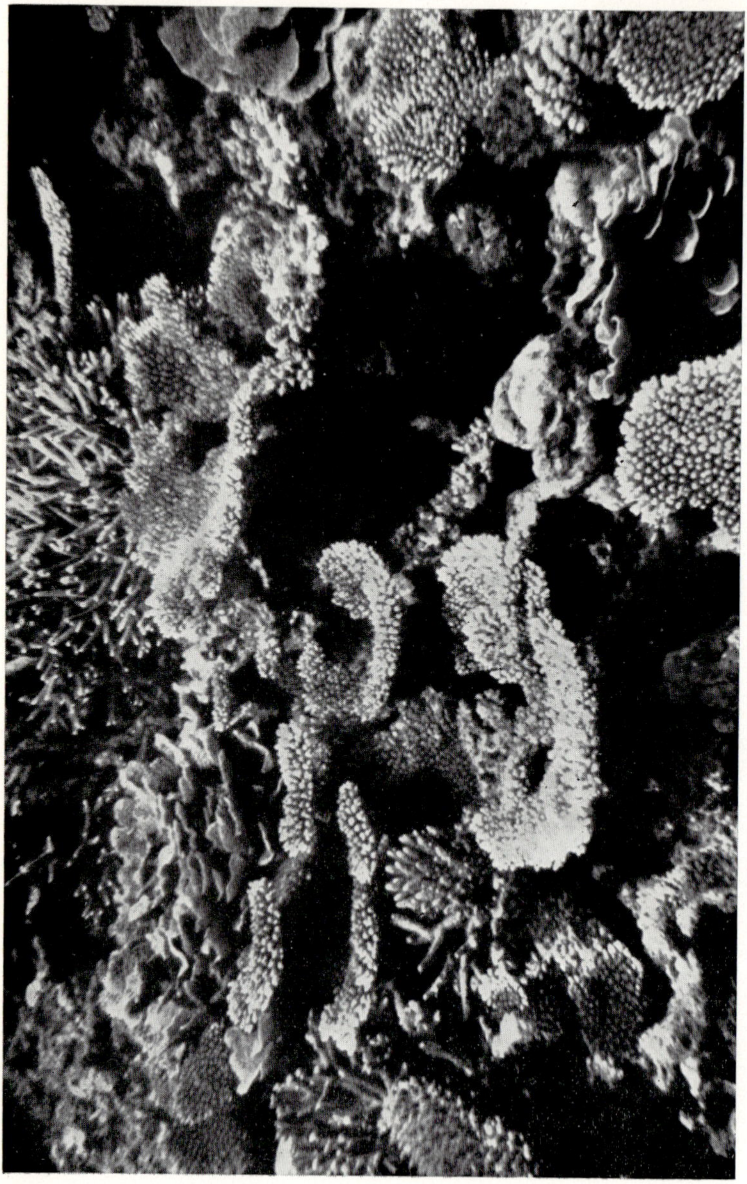

FIG. 9. Coral association at the lagoon reef edge, Gan. The dominant corals in this zone include *Acropora convexa*, *A. formosa, A. digitifera* and *Echinopora lamellosa*.

this zone, together with encrusting species such as *Pavona varians* and *Cyphastrea microphthalma*. Both stalked juveniles and adult forms of *Fungia fungites* are present, with occasional colonies of *Lobophyllia corymbosa*. Other species of *Acropora* are present, but they do not contribute significantly to the coral biomass. The surface of the reef flat between living colonies comprise dead uncemented coral fragments, sand and silt.

Outer Zone. This zone, commencing at about 85 m from the shore, is again a mixed coral association, though the massive corals are relatively more important since they are often present as large hemispherical living colonies. The number of species present in each quadrat remains fairly constant at 13–14. Of the *Acropora* species, *A. formosa* is still present, but in small amounts, as are *A. convexa* and *A. digitifera*. Other weak-framed and foliaceous corals become important in this zone, particularly *Pocillopora meandrina* (which gradually replaces *P. damicornis*) and thin plate-like growths of *Echinopora lamellosa*. Of the massive corals the meandroid *Leptoria phrygia* and the cerioid *Goniastrea retiformis* are again the most important, often forming boulders 1 m or more in diameter. Even here the percentage cover by living corals never exceeds 60%; the areas between colonies are covered with uncemented coral rubble. The outer zone slopes gradually towards the reef edge, so that at the break of slope there is a water depth of 2 m or more at low tide.

Reef edge. The reef edge, including the upper 3 m of the reef slope, is the zone of most vigorous coral growth, and is characterized by the luxuriance of the foliaceous corals (Fig. 9). *Echinopora lamellosa* is dominant, and *Acropora convexa*, *A. hyacinthus* and *A. corymbosa* are also common. Massive corals are present, including *Goniastrea*, *Leptoria* and *Galaxea*, but they do not form large colonies. Only 10% or less of the surface is not occupied by living coral.

Reef slope. The foliaceous corals characteristic of the reef edge continue to a depth of about 10 m on the reef slope. These then give way to another zone of *Acropora formosa*. Only about 10% of this is living, the dead skeletons of the remainder being covered by an unidentified sea anemone. This zone extends for about 15 m. There is some indication that the dead *Acropora* in the lower regions may have fallen down the slope rather than having grown and died *in situ*. This area of the slope comprises agglomerations of loosely packed uncemented coral fragments. Very fine sand accumulates in embayments in the slope, and in these areas there are often large numbers of colonies of *Fungia repanda*, *Herpolitha limax*, and less frequent large *Halomitra philippinensis*. Below 25 m there are large sheets of *Diploastrea heliopora*, often 4–5 m in height, forming stable outcrops and providing a substrate for encrusting corals, gorgonian sea-whips, and other organisms. The areas between the outcrops again contain fine sand populated by solitary fungiids. At a distance of 35 m and a depth of about 33 m the reef slope ends abruptly on the shallow sloping sand floor of the lagoon.

The percentage cover by living coral changes markedly in passing down the reef slope. At the reef edge 90% of the surface is covered by corals, but this decreases with increasing depth, and the middle third of the slope carries a cover of only 30%. The cover increases on the lower part of the slope to about 50%, largely because of the area covered by sheets of *Diploastrea*. The number of coral species is fairly constant, however, ranging from 10 to 16. A number of species occur only on the lower part of the slope; these include *Diploastrea heliopora*, *Favites flexuosa*, *Acropora syringodes*, *Leptoseris incrustans*, and others. The majority of the coral species of the reef slope, moreover, are not recorded from the reef flat.

The distribution of all corals, classified by growth form, which were observed on the transect, is summarized in Table I.

Transect 2

The main features of this transect are very similar to those of transect 1, and only the points of difference will be mentioned in this description.

Reef flat.

Inner Zone. This extends to 30 m from the shore. From 20–30 m there is an abundant algal growth, chiefly *Halimeda* attached to coral rubble, covering 50% of the bottom.

Mixed Coral Zone. The first corals appear at about 30 m and are represented by three species: *Favia valenciennesi*, *Pocillopora damicornis* and *Heliopora coerulea*. The number of coral species increases lagoonwards, from 3 to 8 or 9 per quadrat. Faviid corals are of greater importance, particularly *Favia doreyensis*, *Favia valenciennesi*, *Favites halicora* and *Favites abdita*.

Acropora formosa Zone. The *Acropora formosa* forest commences at about 70 m from the shore. This zone is very much wider than on transect 1 and extends to about 110 m from the shore. The associated coral fauna is similar.

Outer Zone. Because the *Acropora formosa* Zone is so extensive the Outer Zone is very compressed and occupies a narrow band some 10 m wide. The species composition and general features are similar to those of transect 1, though species of *Acropora* are of greater importance.

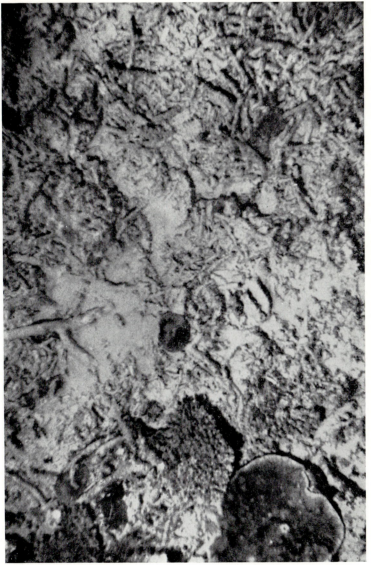

FIG. 10. Close-up of chute formation on the lagoon reef slope, Gan. The surface is of dead coral fragments overlaid with fine sand; there is a living specimen of *Fungia repanda* in the centre of the picture.

These additionally include *A. forskali*, *A. corymbosa*, *A. hemprichi* and *A. syringodes*, species which on transect 1 are confined to the reef slope.

Reef edge and reef slope. The reef edge is again dominated by a mixed community of massive and foliaceous corals which extends to 7 m on the slope. Below this depth the zone of living and dead *Acropora*

TABLE I

Distribution of coral species on lagoon reef, Gan, transect 1

(A) Mixed Coral Zone [33–66 m]

Massive	Foliaceous and branching	Encrusting	Others
Galaxea clavus	Acropora digitifera	Pavona varians	Fungia fungites
G. fascicularis	A. convexa		Symphyllia radians
Goniastrea	A. formosa		Lobophyllia
pectinata	Pocillopora		corymbosa
Hydnophora exesa	damicornis		Heliopora coerulea
Favia doreyensis	Stylophora pistillata		
F. speciosa			
Favites abdita			
Leptoria phrygia			
Psammocora			
togianensis			

(B) *Acropora formosa* Zone [66–85 m]

Massive	Foliaceous and branching	Encrusting	Others
Galaxea	Acropora digitifera	Pavona varians	Fungia fungites
fascicularis	A. convexa	Cyphastrea	Symphyllia radians
G. clavus	A. formosa	microphthalma	Lobophyllia
Goniastrea	A. eurystoma	Merulina ampliata	corymbosa
retiformis	Pocillopora		L. costata
Favia rotumana	damicornis		Euphyllia
F. hululensis	Echinopora		glabrescens
F. speciosa	lamellosa		Caulastrea furcata
F. doreyensis	Stylophora pistillata		Heliopora coerulea
Favites abdita			
Leptoria phrygia			
Psammocora			
digitata			
P. folium			
P. nierstraszi			
Leptastrea			
transversa			

TABLE I (continued)

(C) Outer Zone [85–113 m]

Massive	Foliaceous and branching	Encrusting	Others
Galaxea clavus	Acropora digitifera	Pavona varians	Fungia fungites
Goniastrea	A. convexa	Cyphastrea	F. scutaria
retiformis	A. formosa	microphthalma	Symphyllia radians
Favia speciosa	A. hemprichi	Merulina ampliata	Lobophyllia
F. doreyensis	A. hyacinthus		corymbosa
F. pallida	A. forskali		Euphyllia
Favites abdita	Pocillopora		glabrescens
F. halicora	damicornis		Millepora latifolia
Leptoria phrygia	P. meandrina		M. tenera
Psammocora	Echinopora		
nierstraszi	lamellosa		
P. haimeana	Stylophora pistillata		
P. digitata	Echinophyllia		
Leptastrea	aspera		
purpurea			
Montipora			
sinensis			

(D) Reef slope [0–30 m]

Massive	Foliaceous and branching	Encrusting	Others
Galaxea clavus	Acropora digitifera	Pavona varians	Fungia repanda
Goniastrea	A. formosa	P. planulata	Herpolitha limax
retiformis	A. hemprichi	P. acuticarinata	Halomitra
Favia speciosa	A. hyacinthus	P. maldivensis	philippinensis
F. doreyensis	A. corymbosa	Cyphastrea	Symphyllia radians
Favites halicora	A. squarrosa	microphthalma	S. valenciennesi
F. abdita	A. variabilis	Merulina ampliata	Lobophyllia
F. ehrenbergi	A. syringodes	Stylocoeniella	cristata
F. flexuosa	Pocillopora	guentheri	Oulophyllia crispa
F. pentagona	meandrina	Pachyseris	Euphyllia fimbriata
Psammocora	P. eydouxi	laevicollis	Plerogyra sinuosa
togianensis	P. ligulata	Leptoseris	Millepora latifolia
Leptastrea	P. lacera	incrustans	
purpurea	P. acuta		
Goniopora minor	Echinopora		
Porites lutea	lamellosa		
P. monticulosa	Echinophyllia		
Goniastrea	aspera		
pectinata	Oxypora lacera		
Diploastrea	Mycedium tubifex		
heliopora	Pectinia alcicornis		
Plesiastrea			
versipora			

Table II

Distribution of coral species on lagoon reef, Gan, transect 2

(A) Mixed Coral Zone [30–66 m]

Massive	Foliaceous and branching	Encrusting	Others
Galaxea clavus	Acropora digitifera	Pavona varians	Fungia fungites
Goniastrea	A. convexa		Symphyllia radians
retiformis	A. formosa		Heliopora coerulea
Favia	A. intermedia		
valenciennesi	Pocillopora		
F. speciosa	damicornis		
F. doreyensis			
Favites abdita			
F. halicora			
Leptastrea			
purpurea			
Astreopora			
ocellata			
Coscinaraea sp.			

(B) Acropora formosa Zone [66–106 m]

Massive	Foliaceous and branching	Encrusting	Others
Galaxea clavus	Acropora digitifera	avona varians	Fungia fungites
G. fascicularis	A. convexa	Cyphastrea	F. repanda
Goniastrea	A. formosa	microphthalma	Symphyllia radians
retiformis	A. corymbosa		Symphyllia nobilis
Favia speciosa	A. hyacinthus		Lobophyllia
F. doreyensis	A. conigera		costata
F. pallida	A. variabilis		L. corymbosa
F. stelligera	A. rotumana		Euphyllia
Favites abdita	A. hemprichi		glabrescens
F. hemprichi	Pocillopora		Caulastrea furcata
F. halicora	damicornis		Heliopora coerulea
F. complanata	P. eydouxi		Millepora latifolia
F. melicerum	Stylophora pistillata		
Leptoria phrygia	Echinopora		
Leptastrea	lamellosa		
purpurea			
Astreopora			
ocellata			
Coscinaraea sp.			
Platygyra			
lamellina			
Psammocora			
haimeana			
Goniopora minor			
Hydnophora			
microconos			

Table II (continued)

(C) Outer Zone [106–116 m]

Massive	Foliaceous and branching	Encrusting	Others
Galaxea clavus	*Acropora digitifera*	*Pavona varians*	*Fungia fungites*
G. fascicularis	*A. convexa*	*P. planulata*	*F. repanda*
Goniastrea	*A. formosa*	*Merulina ampliata*	*Herpolitha limax*
retiformis	*A. corymbosa*	*Pachyseris*	*Symphyllia radians*
Favia speciosa	*A. conigera*	*valenciennesi*	*Lobophyllia*
F. doreyensis	*A. hemprichi*	*P. speciosa*	*costata*
F. stelligera	*A. forskali*		*L. corymbosa*
Favites halicora	*A. syringodes*		*Millepora latifolia*
F. abdita	*Pocillopora*		*M. tenera*
Leptoria phrygia	*damicornis*		
Platygyra	*P. eydouxi*		
lamellina	*P. ligulata*		
Psammocora	*Echinopora*		
haimeana	*lamellosa*		
Montipora			
sinensis			

(D) Reef slope [0–30 m]

Massive	Foliaceous and branching	Encrusting	Others
Galaxea clavus	*Acropora digitifera*	*Pavona varians*	*Fungia repanda*
Goniastrea	*A. formosa*	*P. gardineri*	*F. echinata*
retiformis	*A. corymbosa*	*P. clavus*	*F. scutaria*
G. pectinata	*A. syringodes*	*P. planulata*	*Herpolitha limax*
Favia speciosa	*A. squarrosa*	*Merulina ampliata*	*Halomitra*
F. doreyensis	*A. variabilis*	*Pachyseris*	*philippinensis*
F. pallida	*A. hystrix*	*valenciennesi*	*Symphyllia radians*
Favites halicora	*Pocillopora ligulata*	*P. laevicollis*	*S. nobilis*
F. abdita	*P. acuta*	*P. speciosa*	*Plerogyra sinuosa*
F. flexuosa	*Echinopora*	*Cyphastrea*	*Oulophyllia crispa*
F. ehrenbergi	*lamellosa*	*microphthalma*	*Lobophyllia*
Leptoria phrygia	*Oxypora lacera*	*Stylocoeniella*	*corymbosa*
Leptastrea	*Mycedium tubifex*	*guentheri*	*L. costata*
purpurea	*Echinophyllia*		*Cynarina*
Astreopora	*aspera*		*lacrymalis*
listeri	*Stylophora*		*Millepora latifolia*
A. ocellata	*subserrata*		*M. tenera*
A. myriophthalma	*Pectinia*		
A. gracilis	*alcicornis*		
A. incrustans			
Psammocora			
togianensis			
P. haimeana			
Goniopora minor			
Porites lutea			
P. monticulosa			
P. lichen			
Diploastrea			
heliopora			

formosa begins and the number of coral species present decreases. At this position too, on this transect, commences a barren chute, some 2 m in width, floored with fine sand (Fig. 10). Such chutes, which occur along the whole length of the lagoon reef slopes off both Gan and Fedu, appear to have been formed by an avalanche of corals falling down the slope. The only living corals found in the chute are *Fungia repanda*, *F. scutaria*, *Herpolitha limax* and *Halomitra philippinensis*. The corals on either side of the chute do not appear to be affected by it. The *Acropora formosa* Zone does not extend beyond 20 m, and from here to the base of the slope at 35 m, approximately 70–80% of the surface is of fine sand. Occasional outcrops of old massive coral skeletons provide surfaces for the growth of encrusting corals such as *Pavona* and *Merulina ampliata*.

The distribution of all corals in transect 2 is summarized in Table II.

Discussion

In contrast to the seaward reef, extension of the lagoon reef is almost solely the result of coral growth. Calcareous algae are unimportant in cementing coral fragments, and this is probably one reason for the loose structural framework of the reef. The inner one-third of the reef flat, the Inner Zone, is devoid of living coral. Thereafter the number of coral species recorded in the quadrat ($9 \cdot 29$ m^2) increased steadily to reach a maximum in the Outer Zone/reef edge area (Fig. 11). The maximum number of species per quadrat recorded was 19 on transect 1 and 27 on transect 2. There is a small decrease in species abundance from the reef edge to the foot of the reef slope.

The composition of the coral species in the quadrats varies with location, certain species being confined to the reef flat while others occur only on the slope: Fig. 13 shows the distribution of the most common and important species in the transects. Species of *Acropora* form a quantitatively important constituent of the total coral biomass and are represented over the whole reef assemblage in an overlapping species series (Fig. 12). *Acropora formosa* occupies two separate zones on the reef flat and reef slope, but is excluded from the reef edge zone probably because of competition from other coral species. The importance of *Acropora* species in reef geomorphology lies in the production of fast-growing skeleton which breaks down readily into stick-like fragments. These fragments in turn form the loose structural framework of the areas between the massive corals, and the substance of the reef slope itself.

The main distinguishing features of the lagoon reefs, therefore, is the presence of a vigorous growth of weak-framed corals which are able

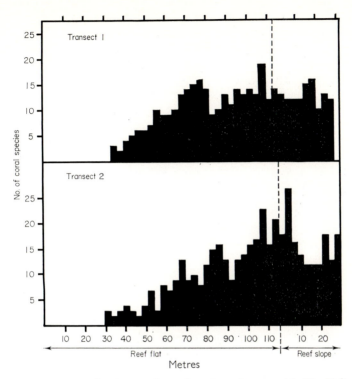

FIG. 11. Histograms showing numbers of coral species present in 10 × 10 ft quadrats on transects 1 and 2, lagoon reefs, Gan.

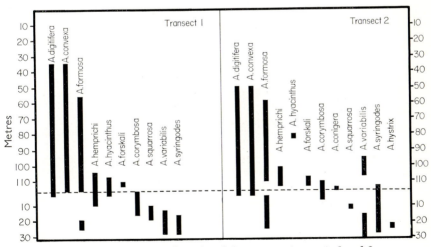

FIG. 12. Distribution of species of *Acropora* on transects 1 and 2.

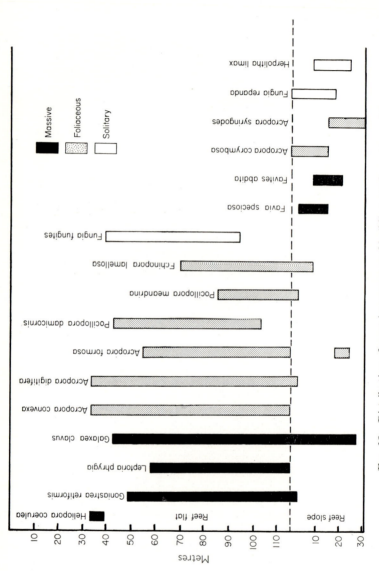

Fig. 13a. Distribution of most important reef-building corals on transect 1.

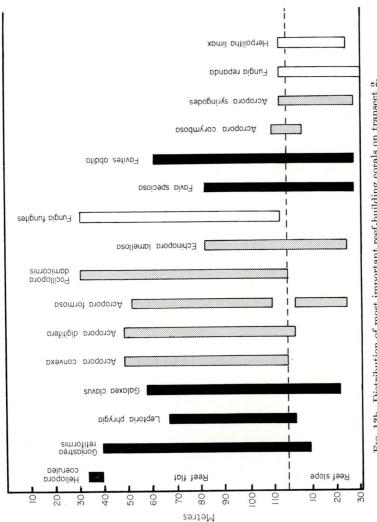

Fig. 13b. Distribution of most important reef-building corals on transect 2.

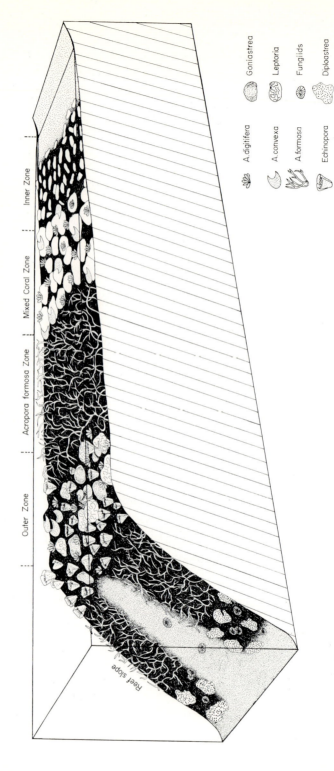

Outer Zone | Acropora formosa Zone | Mixed Coral Zone | Inner Zone

Reef slope

A. digitifera — Goniastrea
A. convexa — Leptoria
A. formosa — Fungiids
Echinopora — Diploastrea

Fig. 14. Diagram showing coral zonation on the lagoon reef, Gan. A chute formation on the reef slope is shown.

to flourish in the absence of strong wave action: the skeletal fragments produced following death are not cemented together because of the unimportance of calcareous algae. As a result the lagoon reef structure tends to be unstable, as shown by the presence of chutes on the reef slope. Hass (1965) also found evidence of instability of lagoon reefs in the Maldives: he was able to tunnel into lagoon reef slopes by lifting away uncemented coral skeletons, though this rapidly led to the collapse of the reef slope above the excavation.

Between the islands of Fedu and Gan, the lagoon reef is interrupted by a sand delta deposited by water flowing from the seaward reef flat. This flow continues southwards over the lagoon reef at Gan, carrying fine sediment in suspension: some of this sediment is deposited on the lagoon reef at Gan, particularly on the reef slope. This is probably a factor of ecological importance in determining species composition in this area. The chief zonational features of both transects are summarized in Fig. 14.

Seaward reef at Gan

Seaward reef flat

This area, extending from a narrow steep beach zone to the reef edge, comprises four distinct zones: Reef Flat Platform, Rubble Zone, Moat, and Algal Platform which is continuous with the reef edge. The total width of the seaward reef flat varies from 1500 to 2000 m.

Reef flat platform. This zone is formed of coral rock covered with a thin layer of sand; on the east side, away from the area where surface water drains through the Gan–Fedu gap, it is covered with a turf of the marine angiosperms *Thalassia hemprichii* and *Cymodocea ciliata*. South of the central part of the island of Gan the flat dries completely from the beach to the algal ridge at low spring tides. Other areas of the reef flat are covered by 0·25–1·0 m of water at low tide. In the deeper areas of the outer parts there are widely scattered colonies of *Heliopora* and *Porites*, and particularly in the deeper area between Gan and Fedu, the *Porites* forms "micro-atolls", the upper surfaces of which often support masses of the alga *Turbinaria ornata*. The algae *Jania capillacea* and *Boergenesia forbesii* are common in the sand between and within patches of the marine grasses.

Rubble Zone. This zone is at a higher level and is exposed at low tides. It is composed of small boulders, usually 0·25 m or less in diameter, with occasional boulders up to 1 m in diameter. Gravel and cobbles form irregular tongues extending inshore over the reef flat. These tongues are generally about 50 m long and only a few cm thick, but the longest, southeast of Gan, is 250 m long. There is some indication in the vegetation patterns on the reef flat of the existence of tongues of different ages, suggesting periodic storm formation. The surface of the platform in this zone is flat and irregular. Pools up to 30 cm deep are found, often containing encrusting colonies of *Acropora*, *Porites* and *Pocillopora*, with, in certain areas, high densities of the echinoid *Echinothrix diadema*.

Moat Zone. The moat zone is a deeper area, generally about 30 cm lower than the reef flat or algal ridge, and 20–70 m wide. Even at lowest tides this zone is covered with several cm of water. The floor is irregular and patchily covered with mobile rubble. Algal growth is less luxuriant than further seawards. Algae such as *Pocockiella variegata*, *Schizothrix calcicola* and *Cladophoropsis* sp. cover the rock surfaces, and there are scattered clumps of *Halimeda opuntia*, *H. discoidea* and *Jania capillacea*. Small rosettes of *Turbinaria ornata* are locally abundant towards the sea, especially near the inner ends of surge channels. Corals are present in this zone, but the percentage cover by living colonies never exceeds 5%. The corals form extremely flattened growth forms and species identification was not attempted: in many cases it was impossible to collect adequate specimens. Most common are species of *Porites*, *Millepora* and *Pocillopora*; in addition there are two species of *Acropora*, one resembling *A. digitifera* and the other of encrusting habit. Holothurians of several genera (Clark and Davies, 1966) are common beneath the stones and in crevices.

Algal ridge or platform. This, the outer zone of the reef flat, is formed by encrusting red calcareous algae of the *Porolithon* type. The zone is 30–50 m wide, rising to a level slightly above that of the main reef flat platform: it dries at extreme low water but not at other tidal stages. At low tide, waves break outside this zone where the surface curves down towards the reef slope, and each breaker sends a sheet of water over the gentle slope of the ridge, the higher parts of which remain emerged. During higher tides the platform may be covered by 1 m or more of water, and waves break over a wider area across the algal ridge itself. In places the channels of the seaward slope groove-spur system extend through the breaker zone to form surge channels through the algal ridge. Surge channels are absent over long stretches of the reef edge, however, and in such places they can only be seen where the platform descends beneath the breakers at low tide. At several locations the channels cut back into the algal ridge for 25–35 m, forming deep, steep-sided gullies with vertical or overhanging sides and floors 2 m or more below the level of the intervening ridges (Fig. 15). The channels are narrow, often less than 2 m wide, and the intervening ridges wider. Whereas breaking waves send a sheet of water across the whole length of the ridge, drainage during backwash is strongly

FIG. 15. Seaward reef edge, Gan, at low water of spring tides, showing the algal (*Porolithon*) ridge dissected by surge channels.

concentrated into the inner ends and over the sides of surge channels where these occur.

Growth of algae near the edges of surge channels is luxuriant, with compact strongly-attached clumps of *Codium edule, Halimeda opuntia* and *Jania capillacea,* and *Pocockiella variegata* between. Small flattened colonies of *Acropora* sp., with occasional *Pocillopora* and *Millepora,* occur on the walls of the channels. The intervening ridges are carpeted with sheets of a green Zoantharian, as well as *Porolithon.*

The reef edge, therefore, is formed almost entirely by the growth of calcareous algae. When fragments were removed they were found to have an open honeycomb structure, with a surprisingly high density of gastropods (e.g. *Cypraea moneta, C. isabella, C. coffia*) and decapod Crustacea. No signs of channel roofing or tunnel formation were seen, but otherwise the reef edge features are comparable to those described by Ladd, Tracey, Wells and Emery (1950) from the Marshall Islands.

Seaward reef slope

Aerial photography shows groove and spur formation to be well developed on the reef front along the whole of the southern reefs of Addu from Hitaddu to Midu. Along the reef front to the south of Gan the lineations appear to be approximately 100 m or less in length. Off Wilingili, however, they reach 250 m, and off Mulikadu they reach 300 m in length.

The zone of the reef front lying below the breakers, termed the innominate zone by Wells (1957, p. 615), remains unknown. However the seaward slope at a distance of about 150 m from the reef edge at Gan was examined briefly using aqualungs. The high bottom surge made working conditions too dangerous for more than a brief examination. The depth at this point was approximately 12 m, and the seaward beginnings of the groove and spur system could be identified. Corals, particularly massive palmate *Acropora* species, were present on the areas corresponding to the base of the spurs, reaching a height of not more than 1·5 m above the general level of the floors of the groove areas. In the grooves there was a continuous back-and-fore surge of approximately 5–7 m corresponding to the passage of each wave above. Coarse sand and fine gravel were kept in suspension, often rising to heights of 1·5 m above the floor of the channels. Although the surge also occurred over the corals forming the spurs, these areas were free of the large suspended sediment, suggesting a lower water velocity. The back-and-fore motion of the bottom water was discernible to depths of approximately 25 m on the seaward terrace.

FIG. 16. Dead coral fragments at the seaward end of grooves, groove-spur system, seaward reef front at Gan, approximately 200 m from the reef edge and at a depth of about 15 m. The fragments are coated with calcareous algae but are still mobile.

FIG. 17. *Acropora* species on the seaward reef terrace at Gan, depth about 15 m. The growing points of this massive palmate species are oriented towards the reef edge (to the left of the photograph).

A more thorough examination of the seaward reef slope was made at a distance of 200–250 m from the reef edge. At this point the seaward terrace was about 15 m deep and sloped seawards at about 10°. At a depth of 25 m there is a slight increase in the steepness of the slope to 30–40°. This steeper slope extends to a depth of about 45 m, and the floor then flattens out again.

At 200–250 m from the reef edge and a depth of 15 m there was little trace of the groove-spur system. The corals nevertheless appeared to be concentrated in bands 3–4 m wide, normal to the reef edge. Between the bands were areas of dead coral fragments, rounded and largely covered with calcareous algae, though still mobile (Fig. 16). Sand was present in places among the dead coral fragments. The living coral comprised three dominant species:

(1) a much branched *Acropora* species closely resembling *A. formosa*, growing in thickets to the exclusion of other species;

(2) a massive palmate *Acropora*, with growing tips all pointing in the direction of the reef edge (Fig. 17); and

(3) *Echinopora* sp., slightly smaller and with thicker plates but otherwise with the same open rosette growth-form as those found in the sheltered water of the lagoon reef edge.

Occasional small colonies of *Pocillopora* were present, but there were few encrusting corals. This is in marked contrast to the situation at equivalent depths on the lagoon reef slope, where encrusting corals are common. Tufts of the calcareous alga *Halimeda* were common.

At a depth of 20 m coral growth gave way to a zone of Alcyonarians, often forming masses 1·5–2 m in area. There was no trace here of the banding, and the few small corals present were randomly dispersed among the Alcyonarians, with patches of sand and small coral fragments between. There was no evidence of any cementing action by calcareous algae. At a depth of approximately 45 m, where the slope becomes flatter, the bottom material comprised largely gravel and sand.

REEFS NEAR MIDU, LEEWARD SIDE OF ADDU

The northern, leeward reefs are considerably narrower than those on the south side of the atoll, and they differ in morphology and coral species composition. No levelling or quadrat transects were carried out on these reefs, and the following descriptions are based on notes made after two observational surveys using aqualungs.

Lagoon reef

The reef surface probably carries about 0·5 m of water even at lowest tides and the circulation of water is not inhibited by the presence of islands. The surface or reef flat is characterized by the low growth forms of the corals, which rise no more than 0·5 m above the level of the surrounding sand. The area between the colonies is typically composed of coarse sand rather than coral fragments. The area occupied by living coral decreases towards the centre of the reef, where it may occupy 5–10% or less of the surface. Corals of the genus *Acropora* are dominant and comprise an estimated 95% of the total coral population. There are probably five or six species of this genus present, all tending towards a rather heavy massive growth form. Others observed include *Pocillopora* and the hydrozoan *Millepora*, but *Echinopora*, *Goniastrea*, and the massive cerioid and meandroid corals present on the lagoon reef flats of the southern reefs were not found.

The lagoon reef edge does not form a distinct zone, and the outermost area of the reef top merges with the upper area of the lagoon reef slope. It is dominated by palmate species of *Acropora*, though *Favites*, *Galaxea* and *Porites* are also present. The reef slope is less steep than at Gan, with an estimated angle of 40°. The slope merges with the lagoon floor at a depth of approximately 25 m. The cessation of coral growth is not well marked, and corals are found to depths of another 10 m on the gradually-sloping lagoon floor. Chute formations were not seen on this slope, and the overall impression was of a slow-growing and stable coral structure, lacking the weak-framed corals of the southern reefs and with the interstices filled with sand.

Seaward reef

The centre of the reef top was not observed directly, but aerial photographs indicate that there is little or no coral growth and that this area is covered with sand. Towards the seaward edge coral growth increases in abundance. *Acropora* species are again the dominant corals, particularly *A. palifera* and a branching species resembling *A. formosa* (Fig. 18). Altogether there are probably 6 or 7 species of *Acropora* composing this community; occasional species of *Pocillopora eydouxi* and *Millepora* are also present. The only common alga is a species of *Halimeda*. There are very few massive or cerioid corals. The areas between corals are again filled by sand, often consisting of flakes 1 to several mm in diam. derived from the breakdown of *Halimeda*. Toward the edge of the reef, the corals form a very close community with few gaps between the colonies. Where gaps are present they are filled with small fragments of *Acropora* cemented by encrusting calcareous algae. The dominant corals here are *A. palifera* and a massive bracket species of *Acropora*. These corals are actively growing and probably do not break surface at low water of spring tides.

FIG. 18. Seaward area of reef top, northern reefs near Midu. The dominant corals are the massive *Acropora palifera* and *A. ?formosa*. Areas between the coral colonies are filled with coarse *Halimeda* sand.

The reef edge is not distinct, but at a depth of approximately 3 m the zone of luxuriant growth gives way to a barren zone characterized by lack of vigorous coral growth. This is an area of broken coral fragments cemented into a stable structure by the growth of encrusting calcareous red algae. Very small colonies of *Acropora* and *Pocillopora*, 15–20 cm in diam., make up 10–15% of the bottom cover. This zone slopes gradually seawards to a depth of approximately 7 m, and is then replaced by a zone of very luxuriant coral growth with a steeper slope angle of approximately 30°. *Acropora* species are again dominant, but *Favia* spp., *Seriatopora*, *Millepora*, and occasional fungiids are also found. Occasional massive upgrowths, rising up to 7 m above the general surface of coral growth, were observed, and these provide niches for the establishment of several encrusting and nodular corals not otherwise seen.

At a depth of approximately 25 m a break occurs in the slope, forming a fairly distinct edge, and from here the reef slope descends at about 50–60° towards the Equatorial Channel. Beginning at depths of 12 m in the zone above, the areas between corals are filled with coarse sand similar to that on the seaward part of the reef flat above. The relative area occupied by the sand increases with increasing depth as the number of coral colonies and species decreases. At a depth of 50 m there are very few corals still present, but small colonies of *Porites* occur sporadically. The hermatypic corals are gradually replaced by large branching colonies of *Dendrophyllia* and by large gorgonian sea fans and sea whips (Fig. 19). Algae are still present at depths of 50 m, attached to the larger coral fragments.

LAGOON REEF KNOLLS

By comparison with other atolls, including those of the northern Maldives, there are few reef knolls or patches within the Addu lagoon. If patch reefs are defined as structures rising 40 m above their base and capped with wave-breaking corals, there are only three. If knolls are defined as rising 20 m above their base but failing to reach surface, there are 22. This compares with 2300 such reef structures in Eniwetok lagoon, and several hundred in other well-charted atoll lagoons. Many of the knolls which fail to reach the surface have summit elevations clustered at 30–50 m depth; most of those which reached within 20 m of the surface are small and steep-sided. The two main patch reefs, Aruhal and Medagala, are situated in the centre of the lagoon. They are topped with corals and are normally marked by breakers, peaking up to 2 m even during calm weather. These and a few other knolls have

FIG. 19. Seaward reef slope, northern reefs near Midu, depth of 50 m. Hermatypic corals are uncommon, but there are occasional colonies of ahermatypic forms such as this *Dendrophyllia* sp.

luxuriant coral growth, dominated near the surface by corymbose, vasiform and arborescent species of *Acropora*. On many other knolls, however, much of the coral growth is dead.

Underwater observations were made on Five-fathom Shoal in the western part of the lagoon, by diving on its leeward (northwestern) side to a depth of 43 m. The upper surface of the knoll lies at a depth of approximately 9 m; the minimum sounding is 8·7 m. The upper surface is flat and is characterized by almost complete absence of growing coral. There are occasional small colonies of *Pocillopora, Porites, Galaxea* and *Acropora*, but most of the surface comprises loose uncemented fragments of a branched Acropora, with individual fragments up to 0·6 m long, and of plate-like fragments of *Echinopora*. The whole is carpeted with a fine leafy alga. Below approximately 13–15 m on the northwest side, the dead coral is replaced by fine sand, and the slope is very steep to a depth of 24 m. The sand is very tightly packed, cannot readily be excavated by hand, and resembles a soft sandstone. Occasional coral colonies are found in this area, with a density which rarely exceeds one colony per 10 m^2. The most common is a loosely-branched bracket *Acropora*, but *Favia* and *Porites* were also observed. Below a depth of approximately 24 m, the slope begins to decrease in angle, and at a depth of 43 m the floor is almost flat. Between these depths reef-building corals are infrequent, although one large colony of *Porites* was seen. Small colonies of *Dendrophyllia* and occasional gorgonian sea whips were seen. Corals collected on this reef knoll were *Acropora* n.sp.?, *Astreopora myriophthalma, Caulastrea tumida, Coscinaraea monile, Favia speciosa, Fungia scutaria, Galaxea fascicularis, Goniastrea pectinata, Plesiastrea versipora*, and *Turbinaria peltata*, all between 10 and 35 m.

It is clear from these observations that reef growth within the Addu lagoon presents special problems, in the geometry of the reef knolls and patches, the relatively restricted development of luxuriant coral growth, and the widespread occurrence of dead and fragmented coral. Some of these problems are discussed in more detail by Stoddart *et al.* (1966, pp. 26–27).

DISCUSSION

In this section we summarize some of the main conclusions of the Addu survey in comparison with reefs of other oceans, and we consider some of the methodological problems raised by the survey methods used.

Zonation

Before the 1964 Expedition reef zonation patterns on Maldive reefs were very inadequately known. Gardiner (1903, pp. 314–317) described vertical zonation on outer slopes of atolls, but he gave less detailed information on the surface reefs. According to his dredging data, hermatypic corals extend to depths of about 55 m in the Maldives. At Addu he found an extensive zone of *Heliopora* with the ahermatypic coral *Dendrophyllia* at depths of 46–82 m. Our own observations extended to 45–50 m, and this *Heliopora* Zone was not observed. It is probable that there is a broad correspondence between the deeper slopes in the Maldives and the zones described in the Marshalls by Wells (1954), with *Sclerhelia* and *Dendrophyllia* below 145 m, a *Leptoseris* Zone at 90–145 m, and an *Echinophyllia* Zone at 18–90 m. Only the upper part of the seaward slope was observed in this study, and the main corals here were branching species of *Acropora* and *Echinopora*. Gardiner found that hermatypic corals on seaward slopes were most abundant between 18 and 27 m, and our observations are in accordance with this. We have no observations on the shallowest section of the seaward slope, in the Breaker Zone; coral growth is probably sparse and the surface covered with encrusting calcareous algae.

Seaward reef flats on the south side of Addu are wide and high-standing. They are generally covered with thin sheets of mobile sediment and with a turf of marine phanerogams and algae, except in deeper areas, especially between islands, where scattered microatolls are common and mobile sand sheets replace the phanerogam turf. Apart from these areas, coral growth on the seaward reef flat is restricted to the moat between the boulder zone and the algal ridge, and to the sides of surge channels through the ridge itself. The colonies are small, usually rather scattered, and often encrusting. Apart from the importance of marine phanerogams, the flats closely resemble those of the central and east Pacific, e.g. in the Tuamotus, where similar species and growth-forms of corals (mainly in the genera *Acropora* and *Pocillopora*) are common near the edges of high-standing flats. Rather different seaward flat conditions were seen further north on Addu, at Hitaddu, where there is a deeper channel between the algal ridge and the shore of the island, with large colonies of *Heliopora* and corals. The Hitaddu flat is very much narrower than that at Gan. Similar deeper flats with *Heliopora* have been described at Bikini by Emery, Tracey and Ladd (1954). In their paucity of coral growth and in the distribution of corals present, the Gan seaward flats closely resemble others subsequently studied in the Indian Ocean, at Diego Garcia in the Chagos Archipelago and further west.

The lagoon reef flat and reef slope on the southern reefs are known in much greater detail from the quadrat surveys along transects. The lagoon flats are submerged at all stages of the tide, and in this resemble other Indo-Pacific lagoon reefs and also many Caribbean reefs. The most striking feature of the Gan lagoon reefs is the abundance of fragile branching corals, especially *Acropora formosa*, and the unimportance of larger massive corals, such as the large faviid and meandrinid corals characteristic of many Caribbean reefs. It is interesting to note that *A. formosa* forms zones on the reef flat inshore from the reef edge and also at intermediate depths on the lagoon slope, a pattern similar to that described by Rosen (this volume, pp. 163–183) from the Seychelles and suggested as a general model of reef zonation in response to differences in water turbulence. One important consequence of the dominance of branching corals is the weakness of reef framework developed by them: the formation of chutes is one indicator of the resulting instability of the reef framework.

The gross zonation of the Gan (windward) reefs corresponds with that of windward reefs in the Marshall Islands (Emery *et al.*, 1954). Similarly the reefs near Midu resemble leeward reefs in the Marshalls in their generally lower level, more extensive coral cover, lack of well-defined reef edges, and absence of algal ridge and other features characteristic of windward reefs, including spur-groove systems. Again the dominance of weak-framed corals, especially species of *Acropora*, is remarkable. It is possible that in other reef areas further from the equator the growth of branching and foliaceous corals is periodically checked by major cyclones, which give the slower-growing and less easily damaged massive corals a competitive advantage. This suggestion needs to be checked by comparison of the growth-forms of corals and species-composition of reefs in the northern Maldives and Laccadives, where such storms occur.

Reef knolls and patches in Addu lagoon are few in number; most are submerged; and several, at least, are largely coated with dead coral. It is likely that the accordant summits of the knolls were developed during lower sea-level stands, but we have no explanation for their small numbers or for the paucity of reef growth on some of them, features which contrast with those of reef knolls in many Caribbean and Pacific atoll lagoons.

Morphology

The windward reefs of Addu range in width from 1·2–1·8 km, being widest in the south; this compares with a world average reef width of about 1 km. The leeward reefs on the northern side are narrower, from 0·5 to 1 km in width. Faroes, the isolated reef rings so common in the northern Maldives, are completely absent at Addu, and the reefs are thus more characteristic of Indo-Pacific atolls in general than of many Maldivian atolls. An algal ridge with surge channels and groove-spur systems are well developed around the convex south side of Addu. Elsewhere these features are characteristic of windward reefs. The designation of the Addu southern reefs as windward is perhaps misleading in meteorological terms, but heavy surf from the southern Indian Ocean is common on the southern reefs, which might better be termed swellward than windward. Similarly the protected northern reefs have many features of Pacific leeward reefs.

A terrace at 14·5–18 m has been widely described from the seaward slopes of Pacific reefs. There is some suggestion of a similar terrace at Addu. On the southern reefs there is a sloping terrace with a seaward limit at about 25 m, and on the the northern reefs there is also a distinct break of slope at 25 m. On the southern reefs there is some indication of a second terrace at 45 m. Hass (1961, p. 60) and Eibl-Eibesfeldt (1964, p. 41) have described submerged notches, attributed to erosion during low sea-level stands, at depths of 25–35 m at Addu, but such notches were not seen by us.

There are insufficient data at present on the distribution of such terraces, or on the development of groove-spur systems and algal ridges, for the Addu reefs to be compared with other Indian Ocean reefs.

Methodology

The data given in this paper were obtained either by direct visual observation or by continuous transect-surveying. The first method has the disadvantages that it depends on the experience and judgement of the observer, that important observations can be missed because of the undirected method of approach, and that observations are usually restricted to the more obvious reef features and gross zonation patterns, ignoring smaller and cryptic forms. On the other hand much larger areas can be covered and a better impression gained of local variation in reefs than if efforts are concentrated on the detailed analysis of particular reef segments. Within the limits imposed by water turbulence and accessibility, logistic problems are not significant controls of direct observation methods.

Because of the subjectivity of such methods, however, and particularly because of the field observation problems raised when dealing with a diverse and poorly known benthic biota, much of our time was spent in transect work with quadrats. Some of the problems involved have been discussed elsewhere (Stoddart, 1969, pp. 460–461; 1971). The advantages of this method are, first, that it yields results which can be compared with those from other reefs, using data objectively obtained; second, that the process of quadrat surveying directs attention to the details of the reef, and thus leads to the discovery and recording of features which might otherwise be overlooked. It is hence difficult to compare directly the results of quadrat or other quantitative surveys with those of direct observation and subjective description. The immediate criticism of quadrat or transect work is that it concentrates attention on a segment of the reef which may be unrepresentative, though in the present study the transect sites were subjectively located after a wider reconnaissance. Attempts were made to randomize the location of the transects along the lagoon reef, using random number tables, but these failed because of the results of human activity along these reefs (e.g. location of jetties, mooring buoys, etc.). Similarly attempts to locate quadrats on the seaward reef flat using random co-ordinates were unsatisfactory, partly because of the stratified nature of the populations being sampled, partly because of the logistic problems of time, tide and accessibility of points on the reef flat and the difficulties of locating pre-selected points. These problems are similar to those in plant ecology (*cf.* Greig-Smith, 1964) and could have been overcome, but the project would then have become an exercise in methodology rather than a contribution to the knowledge of Maldivian reefs.

In addition to problems of sampling design, we found considerable difficulties in field recording. Numbers of species per quadrat are relatively simple to establish; number of colonies and percentage cover are more difficult. Colony definition varies with species and growth-form, and in the case of some branching and encrusting forms must be conventionalized. Mayor (1918, 1924), in his work on Samoan and Australian reefs, gives many colony counts but does not refer to this problem; Manton (1935) at Low Isles, Great Barrier Reef, assumed that 1 sq. ft ($0 \cdot 093$ m^2) of branching coral was equivalent to one colony. Possibly because of the dominance of branching species at Gan we found it impossible to make meaningful counts of colonies during the quadrat surveying. Estimates of percentage cover are also subject to considerable variation, particularly in areas of irregular topography. Further, since colony counts and cover estimates are often obtained from quadrat records rather than directly in the field, two additional sources of error arise: one, the error inherent in the recording process, and two, the error involved in the transferral of complex three-dimensional distributions to a two-dimensional plane, particularly where the reef surface itself is not horizontal.

In retrospect it is clear that much more work is needed on the problems of quadrat surveying on reefs. Our quadrat size of $9 \cdot 29$ m^2 (100 ft^2) was selected arbitrarily. Scheer (1967, 1971) presents data on species diversity in quadrats of different sizes, ranging from 0·1 to 100 m^2, at Rasdu Atoll and elsewhere in the Maldives. He finds an increase in diversity with area up to about 50 m^2 (25 species in 10 m^2; 33 in 25 m^2; 38 in 50 m^2; 41 in 72 m^2; 44 in 100 m^2). He himself selected a quadrat of 25 m^2 for subsequent survey. His species diversities at the 9–10 m^2 level correspond reasonably well with ours (maxima of 19 and 27 species per 9·29 m^2 on the Addu transects; cf. 25 species in 10 m^2 at Rasdu). It is difficult to compare these diversity figures with those from other reef areas based on data from very different quadrat sizes. The Maldives data appear high when compared with maximum diversities of 26 species in 232·3 m^2 quadrats at Maer Island, Australia (Mayor, 1918, p. 25), and of 82 species per 232·3 m^2 on seaward reefs and 63 species/929·2 m^2 on lagoon reefs at Arno Atoll, Marshall Islands (Hiatt, 1957). Conversely they are lower than Manton's maxima of 11–22 species in 0·836 m^2 (1 yd^2) quadrats at Low Isles, Great Barrier Reef. It is clear from the available quadrat data that there are both local (cf. Hiatt's seaward and lagoon reef diversity figures) and regional (cf. Mayor's data on Torres Straits and Samoa, the former with 26 species/232·3 m^2 and the latter with 15 species/929 m^2) differences in species diversity on reefs, but much more standardization of method is required before these can be safely characterized. In addition the diversity measures, Scheer (1971) and subsequently others have used scales of coral abundance and concepts of sociability, derived from phytosociology, in describing reefs, but these were not used by us.

Finally, while measures of species diversity and cover are reasonably easy to use for comparative purposes and are capable of field determination, other measures of geological and ecological importance are less easy to obtain. These include particularly measures of colony size and growth form. In this paper we have used a simple classification of growth form, with categories such as foliaceous, branching and massive, though to have much meaning in terms of reef structure such terms need to be linked with a magnitude scale. Such measures need more work than we were able to devote to them during this survey.

Acknowledgements

This expedition was made possible by the assistance of the Ministry of Defence (Air), London, and the Royal Air Force, Gan, and by financial support from the Royal Society, the Carnegie Trust and other institutions. We particularly thank Prof. J. W. Wells, Dr. R. T. Tsuda,

Dr. J. Newhouse and other systematists who worked on our collections. We thank Miss J. Young for assistance with Fig. 14.

REFERENCES

Agassiz, A. (1903). The coral reefs of the Maldives. *Mem. Mus. comp. Zool.*, *Harvard Coll.* **29**: 1–168.
Clark, A. M. and Davies, P. S. (1966). Echinoderms of the Maldive Islands. *Ann. Mag. nat. Hist.* (13) **8**: 597–612.
Eibl-Eibesfeldt, I. (1964). Im *Reich der Tausend Atolle*: *als Tierpsychologe in den Korallenriffen der Malediven und Nikobaren*. München: R. Piper Verlag.
Eibl-Eibesfeldt, I. (1966). *Land of a thousand atolls*: *a study of marine life in the Maldive and Nicobar Islands*. London: MacGibbon and Kee.
Emery, K. O., Tracey, J. I., Jr. and Ladd, H. S. (1954). Geology of Bikini and nearby atolls. I. Geology. *Prof. Pap. U.S. geol. Surv.* **260-A**: 1–265.
Farquharson, W. I. (1936). Topography, with an appendix on magnetic observations. *Scient. Rep. John Murray Exped. 1933–34*, **1**: 43–62.
Fosberg, F. R., Groves, E. W. and Sigee, D. C. (1966). List of Addu vascular plants. *Atoll Res. Bull.* **116**: 75–92.
Fosberg, F. R. and Sachet, M.-H. (eds). (1953). Handbook for atoll research: second preliminary edition. *Atoll Res. Bull.* **17**: 1–129.
Gardiner, J. S. (1902). The formation of the Maldives. *Geogrl. J.* **19**: 277–301.
Gardiner, J. S. (1903). The Maldive and Laccadive Groups, with notes on other coral formations in the Indian Ocean. In *The fauna and geography of the Maldive and Laccadive Archipelagoes*, **1**: 12–50, 146–183, 313–346, 376–423. (J. S. Gardiner, ed.) Cambridge: University Press.
Gardiner, J. S. (ed.). (1903–1906). *The fauna and geography of the Maldive and Laccadive Archipelagoes, being the account of the work carried on and of collections made by an expedition during the years 1899 and 1900*, 2 Vols. Cambridge: University Press.
Greig-Smith, P. (1964). *Quantitative plant ecology*. 2nd Ed. London: Butterworths.
Hackett, H. E. (1969). Marine algae in the atoll environment: Maldive Islands. *Proc. VIth Int. Seaweed Symp.* (*Madrid 1968*): 187–191.
Hass, H. (1961). *Expedition ins Unbekannte*: *Bericht über die Expedition des Forschungsschiffes "Xarifa"*. Berlin: Ullstein.
Hass, H. (1965). *Expedition into the unknown*: *a report on the expedition of the research ship Xarifa to the Maldive and Nicobar Islands*. London: Hutchinson.
Hiatt, R. W. (1957). Factors affecting the distribution of corals on the reefs of Arno Atoll, Marshall Islands. *Proc. IXth Pacif. Sci. Congr.* **3A**: 929–970.
Kohn, A. J. (1964). Notes on Indian Ocean atolls visited by the Yale Seychelles Expedition. *Atoll Res. Bull.* **101**: 1–12.
Kohn, A. J. (1968). Microhabitats, abundance and food of *Conus* on atoll reefs in the Maldive and Chagos Islands. *Ecology* **49**: 1046–1062.
Kohn, A. J. and Robertson, R. (1968). The Conidae of the Maldive and Chagos Archipelagoes. *J. mar. biol. Ass. India* **8**: 273–277.
Ladd, H. S., Tracey, J. I., Jr., Wells, J. W. and Emery, K. O. (1950). Organic growth and sedimentation on an atoll. *J. Geol.* **58**: 410–425.
Manton, S. M. (1935). Ecological surveys of coral reefs. *Scient. Rep. Gt Barrier Reef Exped.* **3**: 274–312.

Mayor, A. G. (1918). Ecology of the Murray Island coral reef. *Pap. Dep. mar. Biol. Carnegie Instn Wash.* **9**: 1–48.

Mayor, A. G. (1924). Structure and ecology of Samoan reefs. *Pap. Dept. mar. Biol. Carnegie Instn Wash.* **19**: 1–25.

Rosen, B. R. (1971). Principal features of reef coral ecology in shallow water environments of Mahé, Seychelles. *Symp. zool. Soc. Lond.* No. 28: 163–183.

Scheer, G. (1967). Uber die Methodik der Untersuchung von Korallenriffen. *Z. Morph. Ökol. Tiere* **60**: 105–114.

Scheer, G. (1971). Investigation of coral reefs in the Maldive Islands, with notes on lagoon reef patches and the method of coral sociology. *Symp. Corals and Coral Reefs* (Mar. Biol. Ass. Indian): in press.

Sewell, R. B. S. (1936). An account of Addu Atoll. *Scient. Rept. John Murray Exped. 1933–1934*, 1: 63–93.

Sigee, D. C. (1966). Preliminary account of the land and marine vegetation of Addu Atoll. *Atoll Res. Bull.* **116**: 61–74.

Stoddart, D. R. (ed.). (1966). Reef studies at Addu Atoll, Maldive Islands: preliminary results of an expedition to Addu Atoll in 1964. *Atoll Res. Bull.* **116**: 1–122.

Stoddart, D. R. (1969). Ecology and morphology of Recent coral reefs. *Biol. Rev.* **44**: 433–498.

Stoddart, D. R. (1971). Field methods in the study of coral reefs. *Symp. Corals and Coral Reefs* (Mar. Biol. Ass. India): 61–68.

Stoddart, D. R., Davies, P. S. and Keith, A. C. (1966). Geomorphology of Addu Atoll. *Atoll. Res. Bull.* **116**: 13–41.

Tsuda, R. T. and Newhouse, J. (1966). Marine benthic algae from Addu Atoll, Maldive Islands. *Atoll Res. Bull.* **116**: 93–102.

Wells, J. W. (1954). Recent corals of the Marshall Islands. *Prof. Pap. U.S. geol. Surv.* No. 260–I: 385–486.

Wells, J. W. (1957). Coral reefs. *Mem. geol. Soc. Am.* No. 67 (1): 609–631.

Wells, J. W. and Davies, P. S. (1966). Preliminary list of stony corals from Addu Atoll. *Atoll Res. Bull.* **116**: 43–55.

Distribution of Corals

Symp. zool. Soc. Lond. (1971) No. 28, 263–299.

THE DISTRIBUTION OF REEF CORAL GENERA IN THE INDIAN OCEAN

BRIAN R. ROSEN

Department of Geophysics and Planetary Physics, School of Physics, The University, Newcastle-upon-Tyne, England

SYNOPSIS

Reef coral records for the Indian Ocean are presented for 57 localities, and coral distribution is discussed in terms of variations in diversity and fauna. Previous models of coral distribution are considered in the light of numerous new records, especially from the western Indian Ocean. Factors controlling reef coral distribution are reviewed and discussed, and genera grouped into provisional distribution types. Depth distribution is also discussed briefly. A bibliography of Indian Ocean reef corals is appended.

Coral records are still very incomplete for a large number of localities, but there is reasonable evidence for a western Indian Ocean subprovince based on the new high diversities discovered for this region and the presence of the characteristic genera *Siderastrea* and *Anomastraea*. Geological and oceanographic factors also favour a subprovince. This feature is of subsidiary importance to the more fundamental Indonesian-West Pacific focus, good evidence for which has been long established. Regional variation in reef coral distribution, which includes this subprovince, is not conspicuous; the predominant pattern of a homogeneous fauna diminishing radially from the principal focus is modulated rather than revised by recent additional information.

INTRODUCTION

The consistent and conspicuous presence of hermatypic corals on modern reefs, together with their important structural contribution, raises the reasonable expectation that any regional variation to be found in Indian Ocean coral reefs should be reflected, if not defined, by the corals themselves.

Regional differences in coral distribution could take at least three different forms:

1. variations in diversity, i.e. purely numerical;
2. variations in presence of given taxa at different localities, i.e. faunal, and
3. variations in relative importance of those taxa present at each locality, i.e. ecological.

Each of these in turn may be considered at various taxonomic levels. The third approach however must be omitted here and the well known severity of the species problem in corals further restricts discussion to

genera and subgenera, but its inevitable masking of distribution
patterns.

Were it not for the recent increase in knowledge of coral faunas of
the western Indian Ocean in particular, previous accounts would alone
provide an excellent basis for this review. Dependence on J. W. Wells'
substantial contribution to the subject of coral distribution must be
acknowledged at the outset. No previous account however concentrates
solely on the Indian Ocean (probably because separation from the
Pacific Ocean is mostly artificial), so that scope not only exists for a
more regional discussion, but also for presenting as complete a list of
Indian Ocean localities as possible with their fullest known coral
records (Table I–III).

CORAL COLLECTIONS OF THE INDIAN OCEAN*

Most general coral monographs contain Indian Ocean records, but
useful locality names are rare before about 1830. The first of importance
are probably those of Milne-Edwards and Haime (1848, 1849a, b,
1850, 1851a, b, 1857–60). Important lists may also be obtained from
the great generic monographs such as those by Döderlein (1902), Brook
(1893), Bernard (1896, 1897, 1903, 1905, 1906) and Boschma (1948). Material from many Indian Ocean expeditions is described in such works, but
is otherwise treated separately in monographs based solely (or nearly)
on a particular region or expedition. For the Indian Ocean, the earliest
of importance is by Forskål (1775) (Red Sea) since whose time there has
been a steady appearance of systematic works dealing with this same
region (e.g. Ehrenberg, 1834; Klunzinger, 1879; von Marenzeller, 1907;
Scheer, 1964a, 1967). Crossland's Red Sea corals were included in
Matthai's works (1914, 1928). Klunzinger's work is probably the most
complete single study of the coral fauna of an Indian Ocean locality
that has yet been published.

The most important expedition to the Indian Ocean to provide good
coral collections was the Percy Sladen Expedition led by J. Stanley
Gardiner. As with so many other collections, a complete list was never
published, but the relevant works give numerous coral records for a
wide range of localities (Matthai, 1914; 1928; Gardiner, 1909; van der
Horst, 1922; and sight records in Gardiner and Cooper, 1907; and
Gardiner, 1936). Gardiner was also responsible for an excellent Maldives
collection, but this too is incompletely described (Gardiner, 1904, 1905).
Good or reasonable lists are obtained from von Marenzeller (1901) and

* All references in this section are to be found in Appendix I, p. 289.

Ortmann (1892) for East Africa, Ortmann (1889) for southern Ceylon, Duncan (1889) and Matthai (1924) for the Mergui Archipelago, Wells (1950) for Cocos-Keeling, Crossland (1948) for Natal and Vaughan (1907) and Gravier (1910, 1911) for the Gulf of Aden. For most other regions of the Indian Ocean published lists are very obviously incomplete, or have been until recently.

The recent improvement in Indian Ocean coral data is associated in part with the International Indian Ocean Expedition. Works in which corals are described or listed, and which have mostly not previously been incorporated in previous distribution accounts include Boshoff's list in Macnae and Kalk (1958) and Wells' list in Talbot (1965) for the African coast, Wells and Davies (1966) for the southern Maldives, Wells' list in Kinsman (1964) for the Persian Gulf, Taylor (1968) for the Seychelles, Rosen (1971) for Chagos, Pillai (1967a, b, c, d, 1968) for southern India and other localities in the Indian region, Pichon (1964) for southwest Madagascar, and Scheer (1964a, b, 1967) for various Red Sea and Gulf of Aden localities. The present writer is at present engaged in a study of a number of additional collections from Aldabra, Seychelles and elsewhere, (e.g. his provisional list in Barnes et al. this volume, pp. 109–114) and his unpublished generic lists are also included here. Many useful records were obtained by reference to works dealing with other subjects, such as those by Ma (1958, 1959) on coral growth rates, and by Humes and Ho (1967a, b, 1968a, b) on coral associated organisms. Compilation from numerous works gives reasonable lists for Mauritius and Dampier Land (N. W. Australia).

Recent work very much changes the previously known pattern for the western Indian Ocean, especially for the Seychelles region, while southern Mozambique, Madagascar and Abd-el-Kuri (Scheer, 1964b) are almost entirely new localities. Little difference has been made however to regions which have always been poorly known, principally the northern Arabian Sea and the Indonesian fringe (see Fig. 1).

At the time of going to press a number of relevant publications are still not available and record lists are not quite as complete as we would have wished. Moreover, it was not possible, for obvious reasons, to incorporate most of the new records provided by other papers accompanying this review in the same volume.

PREVIOUS WORK ON REEF CORAL DISTRIBUTION

Distribution of reef corals has long been of wide interest because of its obvious implications for reef building and distribution. At the same time, search for evidence of evolution provided by geographical isolation

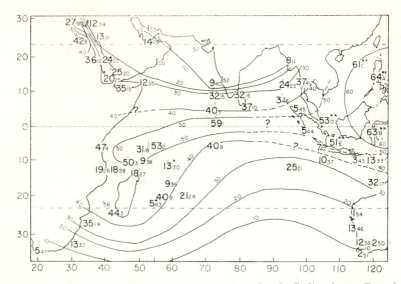

Fig. 1. Reef coral records and diversity contours for the Indian Ocean. Data from line d, Table I. Symbols: *—locality deeper than 18 m; **—data from Wells, 1954, 1966, 1968. Suffixed numbers give locality names, as in topmost line of Table I.

also stimulated interest in organic distribution in general (Darwin appropriately being responsible, in part, for both). Earliest discussions mostly concerned comparisons of species records, but Ortmann (1889, p. 538) published a table of 8 regions and 12 genera, with abundance ratings. Evolution interest in coral distribution largely foundered on the species problem, while reef interest concentrated on the limits of reef coral distribution and qualitative observations on the relative importance of one coral or another from reef to reef. The basis of current views on factors affecting reef coral distribution was established in various works by Vaughan, and by Yonge (1940) and Vaughan and Wells (1943). The mutually exclusive nature of the Atlantic and Indo-Pacific coral faunas (at species level) was not generally recognized until the early part of this century, but subsequently Gardiner (1931) recognized that the Indian Ocean coral fauna varies relatively little regionally, and that the focus of coral growth and evolution lies in the Indonesian region. Yonge (1940) and Vaughan and Wells (1943) discussed coral records for various localities. Ekman (1953) quotes coral records in his discussion of tropical zoogeographical faunas.

Recent, more detailed knowledge of coral distribution is due to Wells, especially the discussion, table and map accompanying his Marshalls coral report (1954). Stehli (1968) has pointed out that Wells' representation of regional differences in Indo-Pacific coral diversity by the use of diversity contours ("isopangeneric lines") is the earliest application of this method on this scale. Other papers by Wells have added further details to particular groups (1966 for the Fungiidae), or to particular regions (1955 for the Great Barrier Reef, 1962 for southern Australia), and in a second general discussion (1970) he has very tentatively defined a number of subprovinces within the Indo-Pacific. Maps of diversity variation in reef corals for the world have lately been published by Stehli (1968) based largely on Wells' data, and Stoddart (1969) after Stehli. These revise and extend his 1954 Indo-Pacific map. Though coral records are incomplete for a great number of localities, Wells' work provides a better overall picture for reef corals than is readily available for many other tropical marine groups. This has also enabled others to discuss various aspects of coral distribution as part of their work in other fields (Stehli, 1968; Fischer, 1960).

PRESENTATION OF DATA

In contrast to coral species, most coral genera are recognized reasonably consistently by different workers, though problems remain with rarer representatives of the Agariciidae, Siderastraeidae, Fungiidae and Pectiniidae. In assembling the generic lists, names were changed where current usage demanded this; if doubt existed, the original name was retained if valid, or omitted if invalid. Where a genus now subdivided into subgenera has been cited by an author, but the correct subgenus could not be inferred from the account, the type subgenus has been assumed. All data include the three important non-scleractinian reef corals, *Tubipora*, *Heliopora* and *Millepora* unless the contrary is indicated. Only hermatypic genera are listed, this being understood to include only those genera whose representatives always contain zooxanthellae in their tissues. Certain problems are present however, and for simplicity Wells' (1954, 1968) generic lists are followed here.

Regionally the limits of the Indian Ocean have been taken to include the Red Sea, Persian Gulf and Cape of Good Hope. To the east, where there appears to be no consistent boundary recognition, the dividing line is taken to pass across the western end of the Straits of Macassar (Malaya) along the 100°E line, through the eastern part of Sumatra, across the Sunda straits at their narrowest point, and along an imaginary median line through Java and the smaller Indonesian islands. From Alor, division follows the 125°E line southward to northwest Australia, so separating the shallower Timor Sea from the Indian Ocean. This eastern boundary is necessarily arbitrary, especially for Australia and Timor. It was found convenient to divide Indian Ocean coral records into 57 localities, as far as possible of equal extent; five Indonesian localities have also been included as essential to discussion (data from Wells, 1954, 1966, 1968). Records have been omitted where the cited locality is too large (e.g. "Madagascar" or "East Indies"), or in the very few cases where it could not be found in several large atlases.

Tabulated distribution data follow Wells' (1954) presentation (Tables I–III). Sight records and interpolated records are also indicated.

VARIATIONS IN DIVERSITY

General remarks

From Fig. 1, which is based on raw data, the following features are evident:

1) Coral records in the Indian Ocean are extremely variable over relatively short distances. While local conditions might possibly be responsible in a very few instances, this variation may be taken to represent collecting differences more than any other factor. The contours have been drawn by ignoring the most obvious anomalies (e.g. Réunion 5, Mauritius 40).

2) The northern limit of coral growth in the Indian Ocean appears to lie beyond all the northern shores, while to the south, the absence of land makes a southern limit of coral growth equally imaginary (corals have not been recorded from Amsterdam and St. Paul which lie just beyond of the southern margin of the map, 78°E).

3) Diversity decreases with increase in latitude and is highest in the Seychelles–Maldives region (more than 50 genera). It is difficult to judge whether this high diversity region is continuous with the main Indonesian focal region, there being too few records in the critical intermediate region. At high latitudes this critical area is matched by a narrowing of the diversity contours towards the equator.

4) Maximum diversity in the Indonesian region appears to be slightly higher than in the Indian Ocean maximum.

Figure 2 is based on interpolated records, sight records and uncertain records, and represents a subjective attempt to predict diversities for undersampled regions and to "smooth" the data shown on Fig. 1. The resulting pattern is similar to Fig. 1, for the most part, though generic totals are mostly greater. Data are probably least reliable for marginal regions, where interpolation is not really possible.

Figure 3 shows world variation in reef coral diversity. The revised data for the Indian Ocean has been substituted in the maps given in

TABLE III

Reef coral records for Indian Ocean localities (a) 91–146 m, (b) more than 146 m

GENERA & SUBGENERA	(a) Amirantes (18)	Farquhar–Providence (38)	Mauritius (9)	Saya de Malha (30)	Seychelles (s.s.) (2)	East Africa (4)	(b) East Africa (4)	Saya de Malha (30)	Maldives (North) (7)	details
Leptoseris	✳	✳	✳							
Psammocora (Psammocora)	✳	✳								
Cycloseris	✳			✳	✳		✳	✳		E. Africa 183–194 m, 209 m; Maldives (N) dead 832 m; dead, 1465 m; 273 m
Pachyseris		✳							✳	
Coscinaraea						|		|	|	

Note: Symbols as for Table II.

Stehli (1968) and Stoddart (1969). The Indian Ocean portion has been adapted from Fig. 1 (see below) but still shows the same broad features seen in Figs 1 and 2.

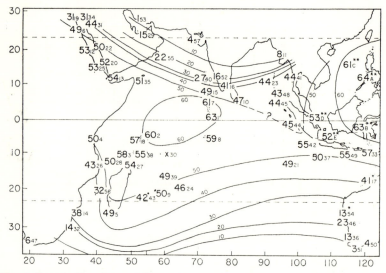

FIG. 2. Generic diversity model for reef corals in the Indian Ocean based on subjective interpolation from full records, sight records, etc. Data from line f, Table I. Symbols: *—predicted diversity takes no account of late information obtained for Houtman's Abrolhos (locality 46); **—data from Wells, 1954, 1966, 1968; x—locality not predicted because depth greater than 18 m. Suffixed numbers give locality names, as in topmost line of Table I.

Comparison with previous models

The immediate consequence of the many recent new coral records is that the western Indian Ocean now has a coral fauna very nearly as rich as that of the Indonesian focal region (Fig. 3). Adaptation of the coral records given here was necessary before constructing this particular map because previously published maps do not include the non-scleractinian corals, or take the 6 subgenera of *Fungia* (Wells, 1966) into account. They are also based on fewer, larger areas. It has already been pointed out that there is insufficient information available to be certain whether the Indian Ocean centre is continuous with the Indonesian centre, but it is now clear that the concentration of corals in the latter region is a less restricted feature than has hitherto been realized. While it is tempting to assume that a continuous high diversity belt is likely, the symmetry of the three coral foci, seen in Fig. 3, equally suggests that an element of individuality applies to the

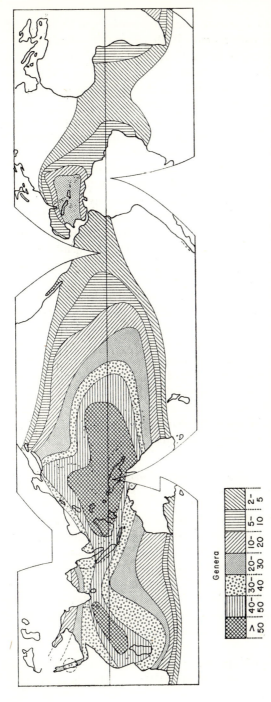

FIG. 3. World variation in reef coral diversity. Data adapted from Table I for the Indian Ocean, and from the Stehli-Wells map (Stehli, 1968) for other regions. Non-scleractinians omitted, and *Fungia* not subdivided. Based on larger regions as follows: Maldives (localities 1, 7), Mascarenes (9, 24, 39, 43), Red Sea (4 regions: 19 and 24, 6 and 31, 12 and 22, 20 and 25), Seychelles (2, 3, 18, 30, 38), Southern India (10, 16).

Indian Ocean. In each ocean, coral diversities are highest towards the west, a fact which corresponds both to reef development and (for a large part) circulation features. The densest distribution of islands is also to be found towards the west. The possibility that the Indian Ocean is to a limited extent distinctive is discussed in the light of these and other factors in subsequent discussion.

It will have been noticed that in each of the three diversity maps (Figs 1, 2 and 3) the Red Sea presents a different pattern. All three show rather lower diversities than those in Stehli's (1968) and Wells' (1954) maps. It is doubtful whether these differences represent changes in coral record interpretation, and the substantial subtraction of records that is apparently implied is obviously out of the question. The most likely reason is that different subdivisions of the Red Sea, where recorded diversities vary greatly from place to place, lead to different contour models, and the fauna for the whole area is greater than that for any of its parts. This point is made with special regard to Stehli's (1968) work, in which he tested the usefulness of organisms as indicators of the equator and rotational poles. The groups chosen, which include corals, usually provide a good, but rarely perfect fit of diversity equators with geographical equators. For corals (Stehli's Figs 45 and 46), a northward divergence from the true equator was present between the central Indian Ocean and the eastern Pacific, resulting from a northward shift of highest diversities to the Red Sea and Caribbean areas over this part of the globe. Even if the present interpretation of the Red Sea is overlooked, the new western Indian Ocean records should alone improve Stehli's fit in this region and so contribute further evidence of the accuracy of his method.

Controlling factors

Temperature

The controlling environmental conditions for reef coral survival and maximum growth have been summarized in numerous works (e.g. Vaughan and Wells, 1943; Wells, 1956, 1957b), and are well known. Kinsman's (1964) extension of the upper critical limits of temperature (to 39·5°C) and salinity (to 45‰) should be mentioned. In the Indian Ocean the limits of coral growth show no significant departure from accepted minimum temperatures: comparison of Fig. 1 with the isocrymes in Fig. 4 (after Defant, 1961) gives 15°C as the southern limit.

Temperature is widely recognized as the most important single controlling factor for organic diversity, as Hutchins (1947), Gunter

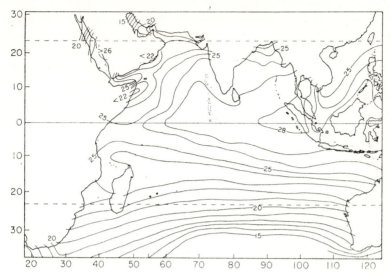

FIG. 4. Isocrymes (°C) for the Indian Ocean (based on data in Defant, 1961).

(1957), Hedgpeth (1957) and Fischer (1960) have stressed. This has long been known to be true for hermatypic corals which are frequently quoted by way of illustration. Wells (1954, pl. 186) superimposed isocrymes and coral diversity contours to present a strong visual comparison emphasizing this relationship. This can also be appreciated by comparing Fig. 1 with Fig. 4. (Recent records eliminate the conspicuous anomaly in the Seychelles region shown by Wells' map, though others remain.) Correlation is sufficiently good to bear out Yonge's (1940) view that temperature controls the horizontal distribution of reef-building corals. Nevertheless, both Gunter and Hedgpeth point out that "Although we may grant that temperature is the most significant observable factor governing distribution in the shallow sea . . . the exact manner in which temperature controls distribution is not always clear" (Hedgpeth, 1957). Correlation is not of itself an explanation, but a more intimate analysis of diversity-temperature relationships for corals requires more relevant physiological data than are at present available. Inability of reef corals to feed below a certain temperature, or to grow sufficiently vigorously to compete successfully for available space, or a temperature dependence related to the presence of zooxanthellae might all underlie temperature control of regional distribution. If so, however, they must be of secondary importance. Yonge in fact (1940) specified the influence of minimum temperatures on reproduction as the principal control of distribution, and this is widely accepted

(Wells, 1954, 1957a). Thus corals fall into Hutchins' (1947) Type 3 distribution class, i.e. minimum repopulation temperature control. Since coral genera disappear in the same sequence as one approaches the geographical limits of coral growth (Wells, 1954), it may be assumed that successive genera have successively lower temperature requirements for reproduction. It would be interesting to verify the Indo-Pacific Fungiid sequence (Wells, 1966, Fig. 5) or Crossland's (1948) Natal sequence, experimentally.

In Fig. 5, the Indian Ocean diversities indicated in Fig. 1 are plotted against the minimum prevailing sea water temperatures for each locality as obtained from the isocrymes in Fig. 4. Where an appreciable variation in minimum temperature is present within a given locality, as in the Red Sea, the recorded diversity is assumed to relate to the highest temperature. The highest diversity for each temperature is joined to present a succession of diversity histograms for each temperature. The extreme oscillations of this line certainly cannot represent a regular relationship of temperature and diversity, and a more realistic line is obtained by joining only the highest peaks. This resembles a Gaussian curve, but should be established more rigorously in the course of future work. Whatever its mathematical nature, it provides a useful criterion for assessing the numerical completeness of a given locality's record. If the same factor controls all diversities, then all localities should lie on or close to the same line. The alternative is that other factors are more significant than supposed. The latter possibility is discussed below for certain localities, but the simplest explanation is that all but the following are very much undersampled: Maldives (south) 59 genera, Seychelles 53, Aldabra 50, Madagascar (southwest) 44, Red Sea (Egypt) 42, Mauritius 40, Red Sea (Suez) 27, Houtman's Abrolhos 13, Perth 12, Cape of Good Hope 5 and Recherche Archipelago 2. It is significant that the first three are represented by the three best deeper water collections (Table II and Fig. 6) in the Indian Ocean. If undersampling is the case for most localities, it may be at least partly explained by lack of sufficient records from depths greater than 18 m.

The diversity-temperature curve becomes less steep at about 25°C and suggests a peak at about 28–30°C. The diagram therefore accords with the acknowledged optimum for coral growth (25–29°C, Wells 1957b). There are very few localities in the world in which sea water temperatures consistently reach higher temperatures, but those which do (south central Red Sea, and the Persian Gulf) should theoretically have slightly reduced diversities on this account. The diversity-temperature curve beyond the optimum would presumably be controlled by the thermal death points of different genera, i.e. maximum rather

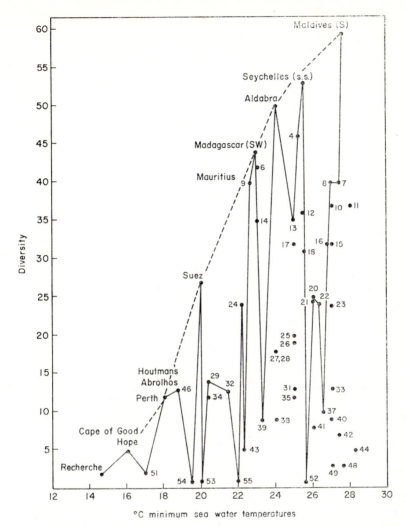

FIG. 5. Relation between reef coral diversity and minimum prevailing sea water temperatures (°C) based on coral records for the Indian Ocean as in Fig. 1. Key to locality numbers is given in topmost line of Table I. Where several isocrymes (Fig. 4) pass through a given locality, the recorded diversity is plotted against the highest value.

than minimum prevailing temperatures. Gunter (1957) has pointed out that optimum temperatures are nearer to maximum than to minimum thermal death points especially for tropical organisms, so an extended curve in Fig. 5 should be strongly asymmetric in showing a steep descent beyond 30°C. A full investigation of this region of the

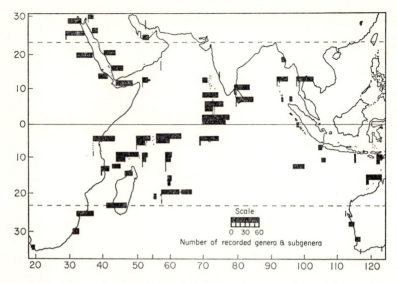

FIG. 6. Histograms of reef coral records for Indian Ocean localities. Columns represent in descending order: (1) total records (Fig. 1 and line d, Table I), (2) records for 18–91 m depth (line a, Table II), (3) records for 91–146 m depth (Table IIIa), (4) records for depths greater than 146 m depth (Table IIIb).

curve would best be done ecologically or experimentally, since regional open sea conditions rarely exceed 33°C, which is well below the coral maximum of about 39°C (Kinsman, 1964). It might be remarked that the apparent reversal in diversity gradient in the Red Sea (Fig. 3) may be genuine since the less diverse southern localities are those with the warmest maximum temperatures. Trucial Oman, Sudan, Eritrea, Jidda and southeast Red Sea may all be less undersampled than the first considerations above suggest. These same regions are also characterized by a substantial seasonal temperature range, which in itself would also inhibit diversity, particularly for stenothermic organisms like reef corals.

Though most localities are evidently undersampled, many important features of diversity variation in the Indian Ocean still correlate broadly with isocryme characteristics: the longitudinal narrowing of the coral belt in the central region, the northward decrease in diversity through the Maldives and Laccadives, and the absence or scarcity of corals along the Somali and southern Saudi Arabian coasts where cold upwelling depresses prevailing temperatures. This cooler region may possibly act as a partial barrier in cutting off the Red Sea and Gulf of Aden from the rest of the Indian Ocean.

Other factors

Of remaining sea water conditions, other than temperature, salinity is probably the most important. Over most coral regions variations in the open sea are well within the coral optimum of 34–36‰ (Wells 1957b), but the northern regions of the Indian Ocean are more divergent. Defant (1961) indicates low salinities in the Bay of Bengal (30–34‰), slightly high salinities in the Arabian Sea (36‰), and conspicuously high salinities in the Red Sea and Persian Gulf (37‰–40‰). Kinsman (1964) records even higher salinities in coastal waters in the latter area (40–45‰). By the same reasoning earlier applied to temperatures in excess of the optimum range, these high salinities should theoretically depress the diversity figures that might be expected on minimum temperature considerations alone. Since the regions of highest salinity broadly correspond to those with highest temperature maxima (and seasonal temperature range), all three factors might together operate to reduce diversity. On the other hand, the possibility of acclimatization cannot be overlooked. The slightly low salinities, and probably much more important, the high rates of sedimentation in the vicinity of the Tigris-Euphrates delta and Bay of Bengal (Ganges and Irrawaddy deltas), are probably sufficient to inhibit coral growth in these areas altogether.

Some of the diversity differences seen in Fig. 1 may be attributable to the limited areal extent of the locality concerned (e.g. Cocos-Keeling, Christmas Island, Minikoi). Referring to species, MacArthur and Wilson (1967) state that "area seldom exerts a direct effect" but "allows a large enough sample of habitats, which in turn control species occurrence". On present knowledge it would be very difficult to prove that sample area explained such examples as those above, and numerical differences moreover may be less marked at generic level. Diversity of habitats may be sufficiently reduced on coastlines without reefs to restrict coral diversity, but almost all the localities referred to here have reefs in at least a part of their areas.

On a much larger scale, a number of additional factors may underlie the present diversity pattern. Ocean currents may be of importance in transporting planktonic phases of sessile organisms to regions of settling which are otherwise too cool to sustain a locally regenerating population (Gunter, 1957). This would be especially important in the marginal areas of higher latitudes, and Wells (1954) has cited the Kuroshio Current as having the effect in Japanese waters. The less dramatic Agulhas Current might possibly have a similar role with respect to South Africa. Even within the main high diversity belt, currents may be significant when considered together with land distribution. It now appears possible that there are three foci of coral diversity whose positions are noticeably symmetrical. In each ocean, moreover, the greatest regional density and diversity of land areas lies to the west, and the ocean circulation patterns also correspond quite closely. Thus the relatively isolated eastern regions are made more so by currents which flow from cool extra tropical regions without corals, converge at the equator, and flow westwards towards more densely islanded regions. There is sufficient easterly movement as well as continental coast routes in some cases, to ensure a limited coral diversity in the east; but the net consequence of the present land and circulation pattern is one that favours the western regions by having an enriching and distributing effect on western faunas whilst having a "winnowing" (Wells, 1970) and restricting effect to the east. This in turn would depend on planulae survival, and more details are required here. The less pronounced nature of the Indian Ocean focus would follow from its interconnections with the Pacific, the easterly minimum temperature gradient, and the fact that the defining continental shores lie within the coral belt and so offset open ocean distances of land separation.

Factors such as these do not have an instantaneous role, and geological aspects are closely linked. In the first place the very relationship which is taken to be the most important in controlling distribution, that of reproduction to temperature, has probably been established for individual taxa for a substantial period of time (Gunter, 1957). There is also direct palaeontological evidence for the long-established nature of the Indonesian focus (Wells, 1970). High diversities occur not merely when conditions are favourable, but when they have remained favourable and constant over a long period of time, as Wallace first recognized. Fischer (1960) has discussed this problem in some detail. There is also an element of momentum involved, in that an existing pattern must in part be a result of earlier conditions which may have been different from those of the present. Thus a Pleistocene lowering of sea level of about 60–70 m would reveal a number of substantial land masses in the western Indian Ocean seen today as submerged banks, and would at the same time provide more of a land barrier between the Indian and Pacific Oceans within the tropics. When such considerations are added to the circulation and land mass pattern mentioned above, the possibility emerges that the Indian Ocean has been a separate focus in the recent past, although the universal nature of the Indo-Pacific coral fauna requires that effective separation could not have been for very long. Present distribution could in part be a momentum state, and in part be maintained by certain factors which operated more strongly during parts of the Pleistocene. Work on Pleistocene corals and their distribution should prove to be of great interest in this context.

VARIATIONS IN GENERIC DISTRIBUTION

General remarks

There are 92 hermatypic scleractinian genera and subgenera known from the entire Indo-Pacific region, and, at present, 76 are definitely known to occur in the Indian Ocean. The usual three non-scleractinians are also represented. It is well known that across this whole region, reef faunas are strikingly uniform generically, from which it might be thought that a discussion of regional variation within the Indian Ocean need have no reference to faunal differences at all. Aside from the variations that are present between marginal localities and regions of the main coral belt, as implied by their great differences in diversity, closer review nevertheless reveals several interesting features, including the possibility of sub-provinces as first suggested by Wells (1970). It should be stressed outright, however, that nearly every genus concerned is relatively rare or inconspicuous, and there is therefore no question of a regional variation that might be readily recognized on the basis of obvious differences in coral fauna. (This applies to presence rather than relative abundance, which is not considered here.)

In the second column of Table I, every genus has been allotted to a group, indicated by a Roman numeral, and a suffix where necessary. These are based on a classification of distribution types (Table IV and Fig. 7). This has been devised for Indian Ocean records in the first instance, and would undoubtedly require modification and expansion to make it fully applicable to the whole Indo-Pacific. Many of the groups are arbitrary, and it is anticipated that new records will make extensive changes necessary. It is principally a convenient means of discussing existing reef coral records in the Indian Ocean. It will be noticed that with a very small number of exceptions the distribution of a given genus can nearly always be expressed in terms of greater or lesser restriction to the Indo-Pacific focus. As areas peripheral to this focus are approached, "the same genera drop out in the same sequence, and the remaining peripheral faunas are of the same composition and include only genera also found more centrally" (Wells, 1954).

Genera which contribute to the main bulk of a given region's coral fauna are almost entirely contained within Groups I and II of the scheme. Thus those genera with an extensive distribution are largely those which are important reef contributors, though within this range there is evidently much local variation in importance. For the

most part, those genera which are known to be important throughout
the Indo-Pacific are of equal importance in the Indian Ocean alone,
apart from the few regionally restricted genera. Rigorous comparison
is not really possible, since Wells' (1954 and 1968) tables differ in
containing only those regions with a reasonable coral list, and by
containing more genera. For these and other reasons, simple comparison

TABLE IV

Distribution groups of reef coral genera in the Indian Ocean

	Genera occurring in more than 50% of Indian Ocean localities (as in Table I)	Genera occurring in 25–50% of Indian Ocean localities (as in Table I)	Genera occurring in fewer than 25% of Indian Ocean localities (as in Table I)
Genera distributed throughout Indo-Pacific	Group I	Group II	Group IIIa
Genera restricted to, or concentrated in particular regions of the Indo-Pacific:—			
Genera not widely distributed in the Indian Ocean and more often present in eastern localities, concentric to the Indonesian focus. Arbitrarily subgrouped on extent of Indian Ocean distribution (see Fig. 7 and text)			Groups IIIb 1, 2, 3, 4
Genera showing regional concentration discordant with the Indonesian focus			Groups
1. Western Indian Ocean			IIIc 1
2. Southern Australia			IIIc 2
3. Eastern Pacific			IIIc 3
4. irregular, includes partial concentration in the Indian Ocean			IIIc 4

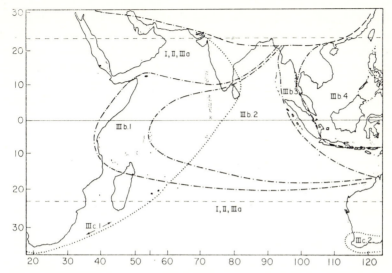

Fig. 7. Distribution groups of reef coral genera with reference to the Indian Ocean. See Table for key to groups, and second column of Table I for genera.

of position of a given genus on each table is likely to provide spurious conclusions. This can be avoided to some extent by comparing the ratio (percent) of recorded localities for a single genus to the maximum possible, with certain empirical allowances.

Common genera: Groups I and II

Group I genera occur in more than 50% of the 57 Indian Ocean localities shown in Table I and elsewhere. This is an approximate equivalent to 75% on Wells' 1968 table. *Galaxea* appears to be more consistently present in the Indian Ocean than in the Indo-Pacific overall, as to a less marked degree is *Cycloseris*. Records for *Leptastrea*, *Plesiastrea* and *Turbinaria*, on the other hand are rather low in the Indian Ocean, where Wells' data suggests a Group I distribution. (Genera which would be in separate groups in such comparisons, but are borderline in position, are not regarded as showing important differences.)

Group II genera have been recorded from proportionally fewer localities (25–50%, approximately equivalent to 40–75% on Wells' table), but are as geographically widespread, or very nearly so. Indo-Pacific data suggests that 9 further genera should belong to this group, which here are found in the lower record range of Group III: *Euphyllia*, *Stephanaria*, *Synaraea*, *Stylocoeniella*, *Echinophyllia*, *Mycedium*, *Merulina*, *Halomitra*, *Polyphyllia*. Inadequate collecting is probably the main explanation, though on current information, the last three listed appear to have a restricted distribution within the Indian Ocean and might consequently appear to fall lower in the table for this reason. Four further genera also appear to be less common in the Indian Ocean than the Indo-Pacific, though they do occur in Group II: *Astreopora*, *Leptoseris*, *Alveopora* and *Symphyllia*. The first three, like *Echinophyllia* and *Mycedium* above are associated with deeper water, for which Indian Ocean records are noticeably poor. Incomplete sampling probably explains the apparent scarcity of these four genera also. Only one genus in this group seems to be more common in the Indian Ocean than in the Indo-Pacific, this being *Echinopora*. It is very difficult to know at the present time how significant is this kind of difference (shared by *Galaxea* and possibly *Cycloseris*, as already mentioned). If it is not fortuitous, it might be a further effect of the Indian Ocean possibly having been a separate basin in the recent past (see p. 278).

Rarer genera: Groups III and IV

It is only within the lower record groups that noticeable regional differences in generic distribution occur. Group III genera are those which have so far been recorded from less than 25% of the possible localities (equivalent to 40% on Wells' tables).

Group IIIa contains genera whose overall distribution is as extensive, or very nearly, as Groups I and II, but whose records are so few that their distribution is markedly scattered in appearance. Incomplete collecting may again explain this feature, especially where a more consistent distribution is found elsewhere. The latter could equally be related to the Indonesian focus. like Group IIIb below, and more complete locality lists must be awaited. In a few instances, like *Trachyphyllia*, distribution is strikingly scattered throughout the Indo-Pacific, and this may be a genuine phenomenon. It may be controlled by unusual ecological conditions, or perhaps even represent a phase of extinction.

Table III shows that the remaining subdivisions of Group III are based on regional restriction. Group IIIb consists of a succession of genera whose present records place them in a series showing progressive restriction to the Indonesian region in a concentric pattern (Fig. 7). Group IIIc genera show restriction to regions other than this main focus, and in being very exceptional, might be thought of having a discordant distribution. Subdivisions of Group IIIb are highly arbitrary, and the genera concerned may well prove to have a wider distribution as more records are obtained. The concentric pattern seen in Fig. 7, mirrors that shown by Wells (1966, Fig. 5) for the Fungiidae alone, and may similarly hold for other families like the Faviidae. If it was a consistent feature for all coral families however, the focus implied by faunal data should correspond exactly to that defined by diversity data. Preceding sections show that the pattern is obviously more complicated, in that diversities are only slightly higher in the Indonesian region than in the western Indian Ocean. Hence reverse gradients must be present in some families. More subtle factors like a more consistent Indian Ocean distribution may also contribute (e.g. *Galaxea*?). The Indonesian focus established on diversity grounds largely corresponds to that based on considerations of the genera themselves, though many of the focal genera are found to the east (but not west) of the Indonesian 50-genera line of Fig. 3. The region of warmest seasonal minima lies to the west (Fig. 4). Such differences if significant are probably related to time lags in the relationships between climatic change, land distribution, evolution, etc. A certain lack of balance may be anticipated during a period of relatively rapid climatic change such as that suggested by recent geological history. Perfect equilibrium however is probably very rare indeed.

Of the discordantly distributed corals, four subdivisions have been made, of which Group IIIc 3 is least important here (*Cladocora* only, a largely Atlantic genus otherwise occurring only in the eastern Pacific). Group IIIc 2 is also monogeneric: *Homophyllia* is known only from the south coast of Australia (Wells, 1964) and just appears on the fringe of the Indian Ocean in southwest Australia. Together with the similarly distributed species *Plesiastrea urvillei*, this curious distribution appears to be controlled by a lower range of temperature tolerance, and the two corals may represent the only currently known exceptions to the minimum reproduction temperature rule discussed on pp. 273–274. Group IIIc 1 consists of three genera records for which are shown in Fig. 8: *Siderastrea*, *Anomastraea* and *Ctenella*. Systematic difficulties are associated with these genera, which is unfortunate in view of their significance. Two further problematic genera may also belong in this group: "*Agariciella*" and *Gyrosmilia*. Notes on these five genera are included in Appendix II.

The restriction of the above three genera to the western Indian Ocean has been pointed out previously by Wells (1954), who has subsequently (1970) defined 6 very tentative subprovinces within the Indo-Pacific based on these and similar examples. For the Indian Ocean proper, his Subprovince I is based on *Siderastrea*, and Subprovince II on *Anomastraea*. New records suggest that these are now broadly coincident, and together with *Ctenella* and diversity evidence, may be

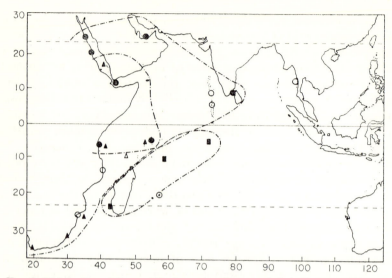

FIG. 8. Distribution of Group IIIc 1 genera. Open symbols indicate possible records. ●○—*Siderastrea* (7+6 localities), ▲△—*Anomastraea* (*Anomastraea*) (6+1 localities), ■—*Ctenella* (3 localities). Distribution areas based on definite records only.

taken to define a Western Indian Ocean Subprovince (Fig. 8). *Siderastrea* is principally an Atlantic genus, whose Indian Ocean occurrence has been attributed by Wells to post-Miocene faunal shrinkage. At this time, the distinctive nature of the Atlantic and Indo-Pacific faunas began to be established, but *Siderastrea* was left as a relic. The only other hermatypic genera common to both regions are *Acropora*, *Porites*, and *Favia*, but these show no similar restriction. Their much greater Indo-Pacific species diversity, though exaggerated by duplication of names, points perhaps to the Caribbean as the relic region. For *Anomastraea* there is no comparable palaeontological evidence, but its close systematic similarity to *Siderastrea* suggests that as a recent evolutionary descendant of that genus, it may be an indirect consequence of the same shrinkage. *Ctenella* is much rarer than either of the siderastreids, and more uncertainty surrounds it. Perhaps it is analogous with respect to the Atlantic *Meandrina*, to *Anomastraea* and *Siderastrea*.

The last subgroup of Group III, is a rather unsatisfactory mixture. Group IIIc 4 contains genera whose existing records show restriction or more consistent occurrence in the western Indian Ocean, but which are also known to occur elsewhere in the Indo-Pacific. This group is probably an important cause of diversity in the western Indian Ocean being high in spite of the typical concentric distribution pattern shown by corals as a whole. In obvious instances like *Tubipora* and *Heliopora* more records will redress the balance, and the eventual groups for such genera will probably be Group II or Group IIIa. Others are so scarce that they cannot really be said to have a distribution pattern at all (e.g. *Blastomussa* and *Barabattoia*). They could eventually prove to belong to either Group IIIa or Group IIIb. On the other hand they might conceivably prove to be valid examples of their present subgroup by showing a greater concentration in more than one region, including the western Indian Ocean (there is a suggestion of this in the more common *Oulophyllia*, as Scheer (1964) has observed). Similar explanations might be advanced here as for other evidence of an Indian Ocean subprovince. They may at the same time represent evolutionary remnants, as was tentatively proposed for *Trachyphyllia* of Group IIIa.

Finally, Group IV consists of those genera which are known from only a single specimen. Two such are from the Indian Ocean: *Astraeosmilia* (East Africa) and *Montigyra* (Dampier Land, northwest Australia). It is impossible to draw reasonable inferences from this group.

Marginal regions

The lack of truly marginal localities in the Indian Ocean gives little scope for generalization and comparison. South Africa and southwest Australia are the best examples, to which may be added the Persian Gulf. Taking sight records into account, the following genera are recorded from at least two of the three regions: *Stylophora, Seriatopora, Pocillopora, Acropora, Montipora, Coscinaraea, Porites, Plesiastrea, Favia, Favites, Platygyra, Goniastrea, Cyphastrea, Turbinaria* and *Cycloseris*. All 15 are contained within the top 25 genera in Table I, i.e. within Groups I or II. A regionally restricted genus is recorded from each locality (*Siderastrea, Anomastraea* and *Homophyllia*), but aside from these, all other genera are widespread. There is therefore no evidence for a regular, explicitly marginal fauna at generic level. The closest suggestion is given by *Homophyllia* (and the one species *Plesiastrea, purvillei*) mentioned previously, but this is found only in southern Australia. Crossland (1948) discussed the fauna of Indo-Pacific marginal areas and several genera appear quite consistently that have either not yet been recorded from the present three regions, or only recorded from one of them. They should perhaps be added to the above list: *Psammocora, Pavona* and *Leptastrea*. With more information from the northern Arabian Sea and northern Bay of Bengal, a more complete comparison might eventually be possible.

It follows that if minimum prevailing sea temperatures are a principal factor explaining current coral distribution, the genera of marginal regions must have lower critical temperatures than those which are restricted more centrally. It has already been suggested that experimental corroboration of the diminishing sequence described by Crossland (1948) for the Natal coast, or even for the transoceanic sequence implied by Group IIIb or the fungiid distribution shown by Wells (1966, Fig. 5), could prove to be of interest.

Controlling factors

As with diversity, minimum temperatures for reproduction have been shown by previous authors to control distribution. To this can be added the various reservations and additional factors already discussed in preceding sections, which mainly concern the less abundant and widespread genera.

DEPTH DISTRIBUTION

Depth records for hermatypic corals are much poorer than surface records, both in the Indian Ocean and elsewhere. No Indian Ocean locality has as full a record as that presented by Wells (1954) for Bikini Atoll, though a compilation of dredge records gives a moderately good picture for a few localities in the western Indian Ocean, as do the records obtained by diving in the Maldives (Wells and Davies, 1966) and Aldabra (Barnes, *et al.*, this volume pp. 87–114). Previous work shows that many significant variations are specific rather than generic, but there are also important changes at generic level. To review these for Indian Ocean localities, selected depths were used based on those given by Wells (1956, p. F360) which correspond metrically with those he used (1954) for zoning the seaward slope of Bikini Atoll (pl. 187): 18 m, 91 m, 146 m.

As Tables II and III and Fig. 6 show, for only 24 localities out of the total of 57 are corals recorded from depths greater than 18 m. Of these, only the Maldives, Aldabra, Amirantes and Seychelles have reasonable collections, but even here the corals are mostly recorded from within the range of Wells' *Echinophyllia* Zone (18–91 m). All but 16 of the total number of genera recorded from the Indian Ocean are recorded from this zone though nearly half of these are known from only 1 or 2 localities. Only 4 genera are known only from deeper water in the Indian Ocean: *Pseudocolumnastraea, Cynarina, Parascolymia* and *Blastomussa*. The last two are known only from single records. Comparison of Tables I and II shows that within this zone, a number of genera are far more conspicuous than they are in the total fauna: *Cycloseris, Leptoseris, Pachyseris* and *Coscinaraea*. A few genera, whilst not appearing to be of great importance are also notably higher in the Table II list: *Trachyphyllia*, *Oxypora*, *Mycedium*, *Euphyllia* and *Echinophyllia*. Comparison with Wells' (1954) list of characteristic deeper water genera suggests that *Anacropora*, *Echinophyllia* and possibly *Oxypora* should be rather more prominent than their present position in Table II, unless regional differences are responsible. This is unlikely for these genera.

Wells' next zone (*Leptoseris*, 91–146 m) is very poorly represented in the Indian Ocean, with only five definite localities and five genera (Table III(a)). Of these genera, *Leptoseris* has appropriately been recorded most often. Other genera are typical of deeper water. Wells' deepest zone (greater than 146 m depth) is really beyond the range of hermatypic corals, as the ahermatypic index corals indicate: *Sclerhelia* and *Dendrophyllia*. No hermatypes are recorded by Wells for this zone, and the two Indian Ocean records of living corals must be viewed critically (Table III(b)).

Vertical distribution of corals is attributed to control by decreasing radiation (because of the contained zooxanthellae) and depth decrease of water movements. The former controls diversity and the overall downward limits, whilst the latter affects the distribution of the genera themselves. If Bikini can be taken as a basis for generalization, it appears that temperature control does not usually apply, because diversity is invariably lower than prevailing temperatures would permit. Wells discusses these factors in his 1954 work (pp. 389 and 406). His conclusion is applicable here: "Areal variations within this [deeper water] facies, however, cannot be analysed at present because of lack of data; but from what little is known . . . it appears to vary no more and in the same fashion as the surface reef fauna".

CONCLUSIONS

Previous knowledge of reef coral distribution pointed to two centres of distribution, Caribbean and Indonesian-West Pacific. Recent increase in information for the Indian Ocean demonstrates that diversities are much higher in the western Indian Ocean than was hitherto realized, and the nature of the Indo-Pacific centre must be reviewed in this light. It is not yet clear whether the western Indian Ocean high diversity area constitutes a third centre as a separate feature or is just a western extension of an extended high diversity belt stretching from East Africa into the west Pacific. Much will depend on future work in the western Indonesian fringe region where information is noticeably lacking at present. Even if the high diversity belt model proves to be the case, rather than a separate western Indian Ocean focus, there is a reasonable amount of additional evidence pointing to this latter region as a subprovince. This consists of faunal features, environmental considerations (particularly ocean circulation, and land distribution), and geological factors. Nevertheless, it is not proposed that this focus if valid be established as a third principal centre equivalent to the other two, but that it should be recognized as a subsidiary feature superimposed on the established model. Its geological origins are probably more recent, and geographical reinforcement far less complete. For the most part the Indian Ocean is an integral part of the Indo-Pacific from the viewpoint of coral zoogeography, as the homogeneity of coral faunas suggests.

Concerning the factors controlling reef coral distribution, Yonge's (1940) conclusion is still valid: "There seems no good reason for abandoning the view that it is temperature which controls the horizontal distribution of reef-building corals, merely qualifying this by reference to the probable effect of currents in the distribution of the planulae larvae". With a very few possible exceptions, this control is exerted by influence of minimum temperatures on reproduction. Unusual conditions in the Persian Gulf and parts of the Red Sea raise the possibility of temperatures and salinities being too high for some genera, and distribution being affected accordingly. Although some emphasis has been placed here on the role of other factors in defining the western Indian Ocean subprovince, a reasonable perspective must be maintained: the overall features of coral distribution show no evident regional peculiarities, and the part played by factors other than temperature is very small. Like the few regional differences that are demonstrable, however, they are not insignificant.

It is concluded that any regional variation that is present in Indian Ocean coral reefs is not associated with conspicuous differences in coral diversities or faunas, except in the obvious cases of the marginal regions. Such differences as occur must either be sought amongst the more unusual genera, or in ecological variations.

ACKNOWLEDGEMENTS

I should particularly like to thank Professor J. W. Wells of Cornell University for generously placing at my disposal a great deal of unpublished information on Indo-Pacific coral records, and also for allowing me to refer to a manuscript still in press. Dr. D. J. Bellamy and Mr. D. J. Jones of the Botany Department, University of Durham, drew my attention to the deeper water corals collected by their group at Aldabra and together with Dr. J. D. Taylor of the Zoology Department, British Museum (Natural History), provided helpful discussion. The Library of the University College of Wales, Aberystwyth covered the costs of the large number of Xerox-copied references without which much of the information required for this paper could not have been collected in the time available. My wife has been patient and of great help on numerous matters throughout preparation of the manuscript. I should finally like to thank Dr. P. Cornelius and Mrs. M. Rowe of the Coelenterate Section, Zoology Department, British Museum (Natural History).

APPENDIX I

Bibliography of works recording reef corals from Indian Ocean localities

The bibliography consists mostly of systematic works and check lists. Many more general works contain coral sight records, and these have also been included. Works in which the localities are too broad (e.g. "western Indian Ocean") have been omitted, this often being the case for earlier monographs. In many instances, the author of a paper was not responsible for the actual identifications, especially where the coral records are presented as a check list in an ecological paper. This is usually clear from their text. The bibliography was the source of the data used in the main text, maps and Tables.

Anon. (1870). (Footnote by editor). *In* On the nature and formation of the coral islands and coral banks in the Red Sea. *J. Bombay Brch. R. Asiat. Soc.* (1841)**1**: 41. Ehrenberg, C. G., transl. Menge, C.

Baissac, J. de B., Lubet, P.-E. and Michel, C. M. (1962). Les biocénoses benthiques littorales de l'île Maurice. *Recl Trav. Stn mar. Endoume* **25**: 253–292.

Barnes, J., Bellamy, D. J., Jones, D. J., Drew, E. A., Whitton, B. A., Kenyon, L., Lythgoe J., and Rosen B. R. (1971). Morphology and ecology of the reef front of Aldabra. *Symp. zool. Soc. Lond.* No. **28**: 87–114.

Bernard, H. M. (1896). *Catalogue of the madreporarian corals in the British Museum (Natural History).* **2**: *The genus* Turbinaria, *the genus* Astreopora. London: British Museum (Natural History).

Bernard, H. M. (1897). *Catalogue of the madreporarian corals in the British Museum (Natural History).* **3**: *The genus* Montipora, *the genus* Anacropora. London: British Museum (Natural History).

Bernard, H. M. (1900). On the Madreporaria collected by Mr. C. W. Andrews at Christmas Island. *Proc. zool. Soc. Lond.* **1900**: 119–127.

Bernard, H. M. (1903). *Catalogue of the madreporarian corals in the British Museum (Natural History).* **4**: *The family Poritidae. I. The genus* Goniopora. London: British Museum (Natural History).

Bernard, H. M. (1905). *Catalogue of the madreporarian corals in the British Museum (Natural History).* **5**: *The family Poritidae. II. The genus* Porites. *Part I, Porites of the Indopacific region.* London: British Museum (Natural History).

Bernard, H. M. (1906). *Catalogue of the madreporarian corals in the British Museum (Natural History).* **6**: *The family Poritidae. II. The genus* Porites. *Part II,*

Porites *of the Atlantic and West Indies, with the European fossil forms. The genus* Goniopora, *a supplement to* 4. London: British Museum (Natural History).

Bertram, G. C. L. (1936). Some aspects of the breakdown of coral at Ghardaqa, Red Sea. *Proc. zool. Soc. Lond.* **1936**: 1011–1026.

Boschma, H. (1923). The Madreporaria of the Siboga Expedition. Part IV, *Fungia patella. Siboga Exped. Monogr.* **16d**: 129–148.

Boschma, H. (1925). Papers from Dr. Th. Mortensen's Pacific Expedition 1914– 16. 28, Madreporaria I, Fungiidae. Systematic description and biological notes from the Danish Expedition to the Kei Islands 1922, Dr. Mortensen's Pacific Expedition 1914–16, and from various other localities, in the Copenhagen Zoological Museum. *Vidensk. Meddr dansk naturh. Foren.* **79**: 184–259.

Boschma, H. (1928). An unusual manner of budding in *Echinopora lamellosa* (Esper). *Vidensk. Meddr dansk naturh. Foren.* **85**: 1–6.

Boschma, H. (1948). The species problem in *Millepora. Zool. Verh., Leiden* **1**: 1–115.

Boschma, H., (1949). Notes on specimens of the genus *Millepora* in the British Museum. *Proc. zool. Soc. Lond.* **119**: 661–672.

Boshoff, P. H. (1958). Development and constitution of the coral reef. In *A natural history of Inhaca Island, Moçambique* (W. Macnae and M. Kalk, eds). Johannesburg: Witwatersrand University Press, 49–56.

Bourne, G. C. (1888). The atoll of Diego Garcia and the coral formations of the Indian Ocean. *Proc. R. Soc.* **43**: 440–461.

Bourne, G. C. (1905). Report on the solitary corals collected by Professor Herdman, at Ceylon, in 1902. *Supplry Rep. Ceylon Pearl Fish.* **29**: 187–242.

Brook, G. (1891). Descriptions of new species of *Madrepora* in the collection of the British Museum. *Ann. Mag. nat. Hist.* (6) **8**: 458–471.

Brook, G. (1892). Preliminary descriptions of 40 new species of *Madrepora* in the collection of the British Museum—Part II. *Ann. Mag. nat. Hist.* (6) **10**: 451–465.

Brook, G. (1893). *Catalogue of the madreporarian corals in the British Museum (Natural History).* **1**: The genus Madrepora. London: British Museum (Natural History).

Brüggemann, F. (1877). Notes on stony corals in the collection of the British Museum. *Ann. Mag. nat. Hist.* (4) **19**: 415–421.

Brüggemann, F. (1878). Neue Korallen-Arten aus dem Rothen Meer und von Mauritius. *Abh. naturw. Ver. Bremen* **5**: 395–400.

Brüggemann, F. (1879). Corals. [*In* The collections from Rodriguez: Zoology] *Phil. Trans. R. Soc.* **168**: 569–579.

Carter, H. J. (1880). Report on specimens dredged up from the Gulf of Manaar and presented to the Liverpool Free Museum by Capt. W. H. Cawne Warren. *Ann. Mag. nat. Hist.* (5)**5**: 437–457.

Crossland, C. (1935). Coral faunas of the Red Sea and Tahiti. *Proc. zool. Soc. Lond.* **1935**: 499–504.

Crossland, C. (1939). Reports on the preliminary exploration of the Red Sea in the R.R.S. "Mabahith" (December 1934–February 1935). Chapter 3, some coral formations. *Publs mar. biol. Stn Ghardaqa* **1**: 21–35.

Crossland, C. (1941). On Forskål's collection of corals in the Zoological Museum of Copenhagen. *Spolia zool. Mus. haun.* **1**: 1–63.

Crossland, C. (1948). Reef corals of the South African coast. *Ann. Natal Mus.* **11**: 169–205.

Crossland, C. (1952). Madreporaria, Hydrocorallinae, *Heliopora* and *Tubipora*. *Scient. Rep. Gt Barrier Reef Exped.* **6**: 85–257.

Coutière, H. (1898a). Notes sur les récifs madréporiques observés à Djibouti. *Bull. Mus. Hist. nat., Paris* **4**: 38–41, 87–90, 155–157.

Coutière, H. (1898b). Observations sur quelques animaux des récifs madréporiques de Djibouti. *Bull. Mus. Hist. nat., Paris* **4**: 238–240, 274–276.

Dana, J. D. (1846–1849). Zoophytes. *United States Exploring Expedition during the years 1838–1842 under the command of Charles Wilkes, U.S.N.* **7**(6): 1–740, atlas.

Döderlein, L. (1901). Die Korallen-Gattung *Fungia*. *Zool. Anz.* **24**: 353–360.

Döderlein, L. (1902). Die Korallen-Gattung *Fungia*. *Abh. senckenb. naturforsch. Ges.* **27**: 1–162.

Duncan, P. M. (1883). On the madreporarian genus *Phymastraea* of Milne-Edwards and Jules Haime, with a description of a new species. *Proc. zool. Soc. Lond.* **1883**: 406–412.

Duncan, P. M. (1889). On the Madreporaria of the Mergui Archipelago collected for the Trustees of the Indian Museum, by Dr. John Anderson, F.R.S., Superintendent of the Museum. *J. Linn. Soc. (Zool.)* **21**: 1–25.

Ehrenberg, C. G. (1834). Beiträge zur physiologischen Kenntniss der Corallenthiere im allgemeinen und besonders des rothen Meeres nebst einem Versuche zur physiologischen Systematik derselben. *Akad. Abh. preuss. Wiss. (Phys.-math. tl).* **1832**: 225–380. (Separately printed and differently paged as *Die Corallenthiere des rothen Meeres: physiologisch und systematik verzeichnet.* Berlin.)

Folkeson, F. (1919). Results of Dr. E. Mjöberg's Swedish Scientific Expedition to Australia 1910–1913. XXII. Madreporaria. *K. svenska VetenskAkad. Handl.* **59**: 1–23.

Forbes, H. O. (1885). *A naturalist's wanderings in the Eastern Archipelago, a narrative of travel and exploration from 1878 to 1883.* London: Sampson Low, Marston, Searle and Rivington.

Forskål, P. (1775). *Descriptiones Animalium, Avium, Amphibiorum, Piscium, Insectorum, Vermium: quae in itinere Orientali observavit P. Forskål, post mortem auctoris editit Carsten Niebuhr.*

Friedman, G. M. (1968). Geology and geochemistry of reefs, carbonate sediments, and waters, Gulf of Aqaba (Elat), Red Sea. *J. sedim. Petrol.* **38**: 895–919.

Fryer, J. C. F. (1911). The structure and formation of Aldabra and neighbouring islands—with notes on their flora and fauna. *Trans. Linn. Soc. Lond. (Zool.)* (2)**14**: 397–442.

Gardiner, J. S. (1901–1903). The Maldive and Laccadive groups, with notes on other coral formations in the Indian Ocean. In *The Fauna and geography of the Maldive and Laccadive Archipelagoes: being an account of the work carried out on and of the collections made by an expedition during the years 1899 and 1900.* **1**(1) 1901: 12–50, (Chapters I–III), **1**(2) 1902: 146–183 (Chapters V–VII),**1**(3) 1902: 313–346 (Appendix A), **1**(4) 1903: 376–423 (Appendices B and C). (Gardiner, J. S., ed.) Cambridge: Cambridge University Press.

Gardiner, J. S. (1904). Madreporaria. I, introduction with notes on variation. II, Astraeidae. In *The fauna and geography of the Maldive and Laccadive Archi-*

pelagoes. . . **2**: 755–790. (Gardiner, J. S., ed.) Cambridge: Cambridge University Press.

Gardiner, J. S. (1905). Madreporaria. III, Fungida. IV, Turbinolidae. In *The fauna and geography of the Maldive and Laccadive Archipelagoes.* . . Supplement **1**: 933–956. (Gardiner, J. S., ed.) Cambridge: Cambridge University Press.

Gardiner, J. S. (1909). The madreporarian corals; I, family Fungidae, with a revision of its genera and species and an account of their geographical distribution. *Trans. Linn. Soc. Lond.* (Zool.) (2) **12**: 257–290.

Gardiner, J. S. (1936). The reefs of the western Indian Ocean. I, Chagos Archipelago; II, The Mascarene region. *Trans. Linn. Soc. Lond.* (Zool.) (2) **19**: 393–436.

Gardiner, J. S. (1939). Madreporaria excluding Flabellidae and Turbinolidae. *Scient. Rep. John Murray Exped.* **6**: 167–202.

Gardiner, J. S. and Cooper, C. F. (1907). Description of the Expedition. [Percy Sladen Expedition to the Indian Ocean in 1905]. *Trans. Linn. Soc. Lond.* (Zool.) (2) **12**: 1–56, 111–175.

Gideon, P. W., Menon, P. K. B., Rao, S. R. V. and Jose, K. V. (1957). On the marine fauna of the Gulf of Kutch: a preliminary survey. *J. Bombay. nat. Hist. Soc.* **54**: 690–706.

Gravier, C. (1907). Note sur quelques coraux des récifs de Tadjourah. *Bull. Mus. Hist. nat., Paris* **13**: 339–343.

Gravier, C. (1910). Sur quelques formes nouvelles de madréporaires de la Baie de Tadjourah. *Bull. Mus. Hist. nat., Paris* **16**: 273–276.

Gravier, C. (1911). Les récifs de coraux et les madréporaires de la baie de Tadjourah (Golfe d'Aden). *Annls Inst. océanogr., Monaco* **2**(3): 1–104.

Guppy, H. B. (1889) The Cocos-Keeling Islands. *Scott. geogr. Mag.* **5**: 281–297, 457–474, 569–588.

Haeckel, E. (1876). *Arabische Korallen. Ein Ausflug nach den Korallenbänke des Rothen Meeres und ein Blick das Leben der Korallenthiere.* Berlin: Georg Reimer.

Harrison, R. M. (1911). Some Madreporaria from the Persian Gulf. With a note on the memoir and some further notes on *Pyrophyllia inflata* by Sidney J. Hickson. *Proc. zool. Soc. Land.* **1911**: 1018–1044.

Harrison, R. M. and Poole, M. (1910a). Marine fauna of the Mergui Archipelago, Lower Burma, Collected by Jas. J. Simpson, M.A., B.Sc., and R.N. Rudmose-Brown, B.Sc., University of Aberdeen: Madreporaria. *Proc. zool. Soc. Lond.* **1909**: 897–912.

Harrison, R. M. and Poole, M. (1910b). Marine fauna from the Kerimba Archipelago, Portuguese East Africa, collected by Jas. J. Simpson, M.A., B.Sc., and R. N. Rudmose-Brown, B.Sc., University of Aberdeen: Madeporaria. *Proc. zool. Soc. Lond.* **1909**: 913–917.

Hodgkin, E. P., Marsh, L. and Smith G. G. (1959). The littoral environment of Rottnest Island. *J. Proc. R. Soc. West. Aust.* **42**: 85–88.

Horst, C. J. van der (1921). The Madreporaria of the Siboga Expedition. II, Madreporaria Fungida. *Siboga Exped. Monogr.* **16b**: 53–98.

Horst, C. J. van der (1922). Madreporaria: Agariciidae. *Trans. Linn. Soc. Lond.* (Zool.) (2) **18**: 417–429.

Humes, A. G. (1960). New copepods from madreporarian corals. *Kieler Meeresforsch.* **16**: 229–235.

Humes, A. G. (1962a). *Kombia angulata* n.gen., n.sp., (Copepoda, Cyclopoida), parasites in a coral in Madagascar. *Crustaceana* **4**: 47–56.

Humes, A. G. (1962b). Eight new species of *Xarifia* (Copepoda, Cyclopoida), parasites of corals in Madagascar. *Bull. Mus. comp. Zool. Harv.* **128**: 37–63.

Humes, A. G. and Ho, Ju-Shey (1967a). New cyclopoid copepods associated with the alcyonarian coral *Tubipora musica* (Linnaeus) in Madagascar. *Proc. U.S. natn. Mus.* **121**: 1–24.

Humes, A. G. and Ho, Ju-Shey (1967b). New cyclopoid copepods associated with the coral *Psammocora contigua* (Esper) in Madagascar. *Proc. U.S. natn. Mus.* **122**: 1–32.

Humes, A. G. and Ho, Ju-Shey (1968a). Lichmolgid copepods (Cyclopoida) associated with corals in Madagascar. *Bull. Mus. comp. Zool. Harv.* **136**: 353–413.

Humes, A. G. and Ho, Ju-Shey (1968b). Xarifiid copepods (Cyclopoida) parasitic in corals in Madagascar. *Bull. Mus. comp. Zool. Harv.* **136**: 415–459.

Kalk, M. (1959). A general survey of some shores in northern Moçambique. *Revta Biol.* **2**(1): 1–24.

Kent, W. S. (1897). *The naturalist in Australia.* London: Chapman and Hall.

Kinsman, D. J. J. (1964). Reef coral tolerance of high temperatures and salinities. *Nature, Lond.* **202**: 1280–1282.

Klunzinger, C. B. (1879). *Die Korallenthiere des rothen Meeres.* Berlin: Gutmann (*Zweiter Theil, Dritter Theil: Die Steinkorallen*).

Kohn, A. J. (1964). Notes on Indian Ocean atolls visited by the Yale Seychelles Expedition. *Atoll Res. Bull.* **101**: 1–12.

Kolosváry, G. (1949). Les coraux (Madreporaria) de la collection du Musée National Hongrois. *Bull. mens. Soc. linn. Lyon* **18**: 13–16.

Lewis, M. S. (1968). The morphology of the fringing coral reefs along the east coast of Mahé, Seychelles. *J. Geol.* **76**: 140–153.

Lewis, M. S. (1969). Sedimentary environments and unconsolidated carbonate sediments of the fringing coral reefs of Mahé, Seychelles. *Mar. Geol.* **7**: 95–127.

Lewis, M. S. and Taylor, J. D. (1966). Marine sediments and bottom communities of the Seychelles. *Phil. Trans. R. Soc.* (A) **259**: 279–290.

Ma, T. Y. H. (1958). The relation of growth rate of reef corals to surface temperature of sea water as basis for study of causes of diastrophisms instigating evolution of life. *Res. past. Clim. contin. Drift, Taipei* **14**: 1–60.

Ma, T. Y. H. (1959). Effect of water temperatures on growth rate of reef corals. *Oceanographia sin.* (Spec. Vol.) **1**: i–v, 1–116.

MacMunn, C. A. (1902). On the pigments of certain corals, with a note on the pigment of an asteroid. In *The fauna and geography of the Maldive and Laccadive Archipelagoes: being an account of the work carried out on and of the collections made by an expedition during the years 1899 and 1900.* **1**: 184–190. (Gardiner, J. S., ed.) Cambridge: Cambridge University Press.

Macnae, W. and Kalk, M. (1958). *A natural history of Inhaca Island, Mozambique.* Johannesburg: Witwatersrand University Press.

Marenzeller, E. von (1901). Ostafrikanische Steinkorallen. Gesammelt von Dr. Stuhlmann 1888 und 1889. *Mitt. naturh. Mus. Hamb.* **18**: 117–134.

Marenzeller, E. von (1907). Expeditionen S. M. Schiff "Pola" in das Rote Meer. Nördliche und südliche Hälfte 1895/96-1897/98. Zoologische Ergebnisse 26. Riffkorallen. *Denkschr. Akad. Wiss. Wien* **80** (Forsetzung): 27–97.

Matthai, G. (1914). A revision of the Recent colonial Astraeidae possessing distinct corallites. (Based on material from the Indo-Pacific Ocean and the collections of Paris, Berlin, Vienna, Copenhagen, London and Glasgow.) *Trans. Linn. Soc. Lond.* (Zool.) (2)**17**: 1–140.

Matthai, G. (1924). Report on the madreporarian corals in the Indian Museum, Calcutta. (1). *Mem. Indian Mus.* **8**: 1–59.

Matthai, G. (1926). Colony formation in astreid corals. *Phil. Trans. R. Soc.* (B) **214**: 313–367.

Matthai, G. (1928). *Catalogue of the madreporarian corals in the British Museum (Natural History)*. **7**. *A monograph of the Recent meandroid Astraeidae*. London: British Museum (Natural History).

Matthai, G. (1948). On the mode of growth of the skeleton in fungid corals. *Phil. Trans, R. Soc.* (B) **233**: 177–196.

Mergner, H. (1967). Über den Hydroidenbewuchs einiger Korallenriffe des Roten Meeres: I, Die ökologischen Gegebenheiten der untersuchten Riffgebiete und ihre Auswirkungen auf Verteilung und Besiedlungsdichte des Hydroidenbewuchses. *Z. Morph Ökol. Tiere* **60**: 35–104.

Milne-Edwards, H. and Haime, J. (1848). Recherches sur les polypiers; quatrième mémoire: monographie des astréides. *Annls Sci. nat. (Zool.)* (3)**10**: 209–320.

Milne-Edwards, H. and Haime, J. (1849a). Recherches sur les polypiers; quatrième mémoire: monographie des astréides (1). *Annls Sci. nat. (Zool.)* (3)**11**: 235–312.

Milne-Edwards, H. and Haime, J. (1849b). Recherches sur les polypiers: quatrième mémoire: monographie des astréides (1) (suite). *Annls Sci. nat. (Zool.)* (3)**12**: 95–197.

Milne-Edwards, H. and Haime, J. (1850). Recherches sur les polypiers; cinquième mémoire: monographie des oculinides. *Annls Sci. nat. (Zool.)* (3)**13**: 63–110.

Milne-Edwards, H. and Haime, J. (1851a). Recherches sur les polypiers: sixième mémoire: monographie des fongides. *Annls Sci. nat. (Zool.)* (3)**15**: 73–144.

Milne-Edwards, H. and Haime, J. (1851b). Recherches sur les polypiers: septième mémoire: monographie des poritides. *Annls Sci. nat. (Zool.)* (3)**16**: 21–70.

Milne-Edwards, H. and Haime, J. (1857–1860). *Histoire naturelle des coralliaires ou polypes proprement dits*. 3 volumes, atlas, La Librairie Encyclopédique de Roret, Paris. (Vols. II, III, and atlas only for Indian Ocean corals).

Möbius, K., Richters, F. and Martens E. von (1880). *Beiträge zur Meeresfauna der Insel Mauritius und der Seychelles*. Berlin: Gutmann.

Ortmann, A. (1888). Studien über Systematik und geographische Verbreitung der Steinkorallen. *Zool. Jb. (Syst.)* **3**: 143–188.

Ortmann, A. (1889). Beobachtungen an Steinkorallen von der Südküste Ceylons. *Zool. Jb. (Syst.)* **4**: 493–590.

Ortmann, A. (1892). Die Korallriffe von Dar-es-Salaam und Umgegund. *Zool. Jb. (Zool.)* **6**: 631–670.

Pichon, M. (1962). Note préliminaire sur la topographie et la géomorphologie des récifs coralliens de la région de Tuléar. *Recl Trav. Stn mar. Endoume*. Fascicule hors série. Supplément **1**: 153–168.

Pichon, M. (1964). Contribution a l'étude de la répartition des madréporaires sur le récif de Tuléar, Madagascar. *Recl Trav. Stn mar. Endoume*. Fascicule hors série. Supplément **2**: 79–204.

Pichon, M. (1967). Caractères généraux des peuplements benthiques des récifs et lagons de l'île Maurice (Océan Indien). *Cahiers O.R.S.T.O.M. Océanographie* **5**: 31–45.

Pillai, C. S. Gopinadha (1967a). Corals. In *Central Marine Fisheries Research Institute* 20th *Anniversary Souvenir* 1967. 121–124. Mandapam: Central Marine Fisheries Research Institute.

Pillai, C. S. Gopinadha (1967b). Studies on Indian corals. 1. Report on a new species of *Montipora* (Scleractinia, Acroporidae). *J. mar. biol. Ass. India* **9**: 399–401.

Pillai, C. S. Gopinadha (1967c). Studies on Indian corals. 2. Report on a new species of *Goniopora* and three new species of *Porites* (Scleractinia, Ponritidae). *J. mar. biol. Ass. India* **9**: 402–406.

Pillai, C. S. Gopinadha (1967d). Studies on Indian corals. 5. Preliminary report on new records of hermatypic corals of the suborder Astrocoeniina. *J. mar. biol. Ass. India* **9**: 412–422.

Pillai, C. S. Gopinadha (no date: 1968?). *Catalogue of corals in the reference collections of the Central Marine Fisheries Research Institute.* Mandapam: Central Marine Fisheries Research Institute.

Rehberg, H. (1892). Neue und wenig bekannte Korallen. *Abh. Geb. Naturw., Hamburg* **12**: 1–50.

Ride, W. D. L. and Serventy, D. L. (1964). The fauna of Western Australia. In *Official year book of Western Australia.* New series **4**: 68–84. (Little, R. J., ed.) Western Australia Office: Commonwealth Bureau of Census and Statistics.

Ridley, S. O. (1883). The coral-fauna of Ceylon, with descriptions of new species. *Ann. Mag. nat. Hist.* (5)**11**: 250–262.

Ridley, S. O. (1884). On the classificatory value of growth and budding in the Madreporaria, and on a new genus illustrating this point. *Ann. Mag. nat. Hist.* (5)**13**: 284–291.

Ridley, S. O. and Quelch, J. J. (1885). List of corals collected in the Keeling Islands. In *A naturalist's wanderings in the Eastern Archipelago, a narrative of travel and exploration from 1878 to 1883*: 44–47. Forbes, H. O. London: Sampson Low, Marston, Searle and Rivington.

Rosen, B. R. (1968). An account of a pathologic structure in the Faviidae (Anthozoa): a revision of *Favia valenciennesi* (Edwards and Haime) and its allies. *Bull. Br. Mus. nat. Hist.* (Zool.) **16**: 323–352.

Rosen, B. R. (1971). Annotated check list and bibliography of corals of the Chagos Archipelago (including the recent collection from Diego Garcia) with remarks on their distribution. *Atoll. Res. Bull.* **149**.

Rosen, B. R. and Taylor, J. D. (1969). Reef coral from Aldabra: new mode of reproduction. *Science, N.Y.* **166**: 119–121.

Rousseau, L. (1854). Zoophytes. In *Voyage au Pole Sûd et dans l'Océanie sur les corvettes l'Astrolabe et la Zélée: executé par ordre du Roi pendant les années 1837–1838– 1839–1840 sur le commandement de M. J. Dumont d'Urville, capitaine de vaisseau. Zoologie.* **5**: 119–124. (Hombron and Jacquinot, eds) Paris.

Scheer, G. (1959). Die Formenvielfalt der Riffkorallen. *Ber. naturw. Ver. Darmstadt* **1958/59**: 50–67.

Scheer, G. (1964a). Bemerkenswerte Korallen aus dem Roten Meer. *Senckenberg. biol.* **45**: 613–620.

Scheer, G. (1964b). Korallen von Abd-el-Kuri. *Zool. Jb. (Syst.)* **91**: 451–466.

Scheer, G. (1967). Korallen von den Sarso-Inseln im Roten Meer. *Senckenberg. biol.* **48**: 421–436.

Sewell, R. B. S. (1922). A survey season in the Nicobar Islands on the R.I.M.S. "Investigator", October 1921 to March 1922. *J. Bombay nat. Hist. Soc.* **28**: 970–989.

Sewell, R. B. S. (1932). The coral coasts of India. *Geogrl. J.* **79**: 449–465.

Sewell, R. B. S. (1935). Geographic and oceanographic research in Indian waters. Part VIII, studies on coral and coral-formations in Indian waters. *Mem. Asiat. Soc. Beng.* **9**: 461–540.

Sewell, R. B. S. (1936a). An account of Addu atoll. *Scient. Rep. John Murray Exped.* **1**: 63–93.

Sewell, R. B. S. (1936b). An account of Horsburgh or Goifurfehendu atoll. *Scient. Rep. John Murray Exped.* **1**: 109–125.

Sluiter, C. P. (1890). Einiges über die Entstehung der Korallenriffen in der Javasee und Brantweinsbai, und über neue Korallen-bildung Krakatau. *Natuurk. Tijdschr. Ned.-Indië* **49**: 360–380.

Squires, D. F. (1966). Scleractinia. *In* Port Phillip Survey 1957–1963. (Macpherson, J. H., ed.) *Mem. natn. Mus. Vict.* **27**: 167–174.

Stiasny, G. (1930). Die Madreporaria des Naturhistorischen Reichsmuseum in Leiden. I, die Genera *Porites, Goniopora, Alveopora, Montipora. Zool. Meded., Leiden* **13**: 22–52.

Stoddart, D. R. (1969). Ecology and morphology of Recent coral reefs. *Biol. Rev.* **44**: 433–498.

Stoddart, D. R. (1970). Corals from Mauritius in the Mauritius Institute. In *The Royal Society Aldabra Research Committee: projects subcommittee. Report on a visit to Mauritius*, 12–21 July 1969 (Circular ALD/2(70)), Appendix 3, pp. 18–19. London: Royal Society.

Studer, T. (1878). Übersicht der Steinkorallen aus der Familie der Madreporaria aporosa, Eupsammina und Turbinarina, welche auf der Reise S.M.S. Gazelle um die Erde gesammelt wurden. *Mber. K. preuss. Akad. Wiss.*, **1877**: 625–655.

Talbot, F. H. (1965). A description of the coral structure of Tutia reef (Tanganyika Territory, East Africa) and its fish fauna. *Proc. zool. Soc. Lond.* **145**: 431–470.

Taylor, J. D. (1968). Coral reef and associated invertebrate communities (mainly molluscan) around Mahé, Seychelles. *Phil. Trans. R. Soc.* (B) **254**: 129–206.

Taylor, J. D. and Lewis, M. S. (1970). The flora, fauna and sediments of the marine grass beds of Mahé, Seychelles. *J. nat. Hist.* **4**: 199–220.

Teichert, C. (1947). Contributions to the geology of Houtman's Abrolhos, Western Australia. *Proc. Linn. Soc. N.S.W.* **71**: 145–196.

Totton, A. K. (1952). Notes on some little-known corals from N.W. and S. Australia. *Ann. Mag. nat. Hist.* (12)**5**: 975–979.

Umbgrove, J. H. F. (1947). Coral reefs of the East Indies. *Bull. geol. Soc. Am.* **58**: 729–778.

Vaughan, T. W. (1907). Some madreporarian corals from French Somaliland, East Africa, collected by Dr. Charles Gravier. *Proc. U.S. natn. Mus.* **32**: 249–266.

Vaughan, T. W. (1918). Some shoal-water corals from Murray Island (Australia), Cocos-Keeling Islands and Fanning Island. *Pap. Dep. mar. Biol. Carnegie Instn Wash.* **9**: 51–234. (*Publs. Carnegie Instn.* **213**).

Verrill, A. E. (1864). List of the polyps and corals sent by the Museum of Comparative Zoölogy to other institutions in exchange, with annotations. *Bull. Mus. comp. Zool. Harv.* **1**: 29–60.

Verrill, A. E. (1869). Corals and polyps of the North Pacific Exploring Expedition, with descriptions of other Pacific Ocean species. *Proc. Essex Inst.* **6**: 51–104.

Verrill, A. E. (1902). Notes on corals of the genus *Acropora* (*Madrepora* Lam.) with new descriptions and figures of types, and of several new species. *Trans. Conn. Acad. Arts Sci.* **11**: 207–266.

Voeltzkow, A. (1902). Die von Aldabra bis jetzt bekannte Flora und Fauna. *Abh. senckenb. naturforsch. Ges.* **26**: 539–565.

Voeltzkow, A. (1904). Berichte über eine Reise nach Ost-Afrika zur Untersuchung der Bildung und des Aufbaues der Riffe und Inseln des westlichen Indischen Ozeans. 5, Europa-Inseln. *Z. Ges. Erdk. Berl.* **1904**: 426–451.

Wainwright, S. A. (1965). Reef communities visited by the Israel South Red Sea Expedition, 1962. *Bull. Sea Fish. Res. Stn. Israel* **38**: 40–53.

Wells, J. W. (1936). A new genus of the madreporarian family Eupsammiidae. *Ann. Mag. nat. Hist.* (10)**18**: 546–549.

Wells, J. W. (1950). Reef corals from the Cocos-Keeling atoll. *Bull. Raffles Mus.* No. 22: 29–52.

Wells, J. W. (1954). Bikini and nearby atolls: (2) oceanography (biologic). Recent corals of the Marshall Islands. *Prof. Pap. U.S. geol. Surv.* **260**(I): i–iv, 385–486.

Wells, J. W. (1962). Two new scleractinian corals from Australia. *Rec. Aust. Mus.* **25**: 239–241.

Wells, J. W. (1964). The recent solitary mussid scleractinian corals. *Zoöl. Meded., Leiden.* **39**: 375–384.

Wells, J. W. (1968). (unpublished MS table of records of reef coral genera for selected Indo-Pacific localities).

Wells, J. W. and Davies, P. S. (1966). Reef studies at Addu atoll. Preliminary results of an expedition to Addu Atoll in 1964. IV, preliminary list of stony corals from Addu Atoll. *Atoll Res. Bull.* **116**: 43–55.

Weltner, O. (1913). Anthozoa. In *Flora und Fauna der Comoren. Reise in Ostafrika in den Jahren 1903–1905. Wissenschaftliche Ergebnisse.* 3. *Systematische Arbeiten.* 479. (Voeltzkow, A., ed.) Stuttgart.

Wood Jones, F. (1907). On the growth-form and supposed species in corals. *Proc. zool. Soc. Lond.* **1907**: 518–556.

Wood Jones, F. (1910). *Coral and atolls.* London: Lovell Reeve and Co. Ltd.

Wright, E. P. (1869). Notes on the animal of the organ-pipe coral (*Tubipora musica*). *Ann. Mag. nat. Hist.* (4)**3**: 377–383.

APPENDIX II

Notes on several coral genera referred to in the main text

Three, possibly five genera are restricted in their distribution to the western Indian Ocean, and are used here to define this subprovince. Unfortunately, systematic difficulties are associated with each one, and some notes are therefore provided to explain the sense in which the names have been used.

"*Agariciella*" is an agariciid having close affinities to *Polyastra* and *Leptoseris*. It was originally described from the Maldives by Gardiner (1905) as *Agaricia? ponderosa*. Ma (1937) placed Gardiner's variety *minikoiensis* under *Agariciella*, as a new subgenus of the otherwise Atlantic distributed *Agaricia*. It still remains to be shown that Ma's name applies to the typical form as well as the variety originally described by Gardiner, though this does seem likely. The corals concerned definitely have generic or subgeneric status. Unfortunately, good figures and redescription are desirable, since there is some confusion with *Polyastra*. Apart from Ma's own records, most records are from the western Indian Ocean, where it is consistently present, but never conspicuous.

Siderastrea has in the past been confused with *Pavona*, and older records without figures have to be interpreted with caution. Horst's (1922) concept of *Siderastrea* is followed here, with the reservation that his earlier record of the genus (1921) from Aru, near New Guinea is probably *Pseudosiderastrea*, a sub-genus of *Anomastraea* (see below) not yet erected at the time. Aru is the type locality of *Pseudosiderastrea*.

Anomastraea (*Anomastraea*) has been recognized with less difficulty than the foregoing genera, but superficially resembles a small caliced *Polyastra* in some growth forms. Crossland's (1952) record from the Great Barrier Reef has been referred by Wells (1955) to *Anomastraea* (*Pseudosiderastrea*), so removing the only possible exception to the western Indian Ocean distribution of *Anomastraea* (*Anomastraea*).

Ctenella was known only from Saya de Malha and Chagos (Matthai, 1928) until Pichon (1964) recently recorded it from southwest Madagascar. A review of this genus is probably required.

Gyrosmilia was originally known only from Ehrenberg's (1834) single specimen from the Gulf of Suez. Harrison and Poole (1910b) recorded it without details or figure from northern Mozambique. A eusmiliinid coral differing from the other better known genera in this subfamily (*Physogyra* etc.) has been seen by the author in a collection from Aldabra (Barnes, *et al.* this volume, p. 113). It may represent this genus, but a redescription of the type is desirable here too.

REFERENCES

All but two of the references mentioned above are to be found in the bibliography appendix, Appendix I.

Ma, T. Y. H. (1937). On the growth rate of reef corals and its relation to sea water temperature *Palaeont. sin.* Ser. B. **16**. Fasc. 1. *China 18* : 349–418.

Wells, J. W. (1955). A survey of the distribution of reef coral genera in the Great Barrier Reef region. *Rep. Gt Barrier Reef Comm.* 6(2): 1–9.

REFERENCES

Barnes, J., Bellamy, D. J., Jones, D. J., Whitton, B. A., Drew, E. A., Kenyon, L., Lythgoe, J. N., and Rosen, B. R. (1971). Morphology and ecology of the reef front of Aldabra. *Symp. zool. Soc. Lond.* No. **28**: 87–114.

Crossland, C. (1948). Reef corals of the South African coast. *Ann. Natal Mus.* **11**: 169–205.

Defant, A. (1960–1961). *Physical oceanography.* **1** (1961) **2** (1960). Oxford: Pergamon Press.

Ekman, S. (1953). *Zoogeography of the sea.* (Palmer, E., transl.) London: Sidgwick and Jackson.

Fischer, A. G. (1960). Latitudinal variations in organic diversity. *Evolution, Lancaster, Pa.* **14**: 64–81.

Gardiner, J. S. (1931). *Coral reefs and atolls: being a course of lectures delivered at the Lowell Institute at Boston February* 1930. London: Macmillan and Co.

Gunter, G. (1957). Temperature. In *Treatise on marine ecology and paleoecology. I. Ecology.* (Hedgpeth, J. W., ed.) *Mem. geol. Soc. Am.* **67**: 159–184.

Hedgpeth, J. W. (1957). Marine biogeography. In *Treatise on marine ecology and paleoecology. I. Ecology.* (Hedgpeth, J. W., ed.) *Mem. geol. Soc. Am.* **67**: 359–382.

Hutchins, L. W. (1947). The bases for temperature zonation in geographical distribution. *Ecol. Monogr.* **17**: 325–335.

Kinsman, D. J. J. (1964). Reef coral tolerance of high temperatures and salinities. *Nature, Lond.* **202**: 1280–1282.

MacArthur, R. H. and Wilson, E. O. (1967). *The theory of island biogeography.* Princeton: Princeton University Press.

Ortmann, A. (1889) Beobachtungen an Steinkorallen von der Südküste Ceylons. *Zool. Jb. (Syst.)* **4**: 493–591.

Scheer, G. (1964). Bemerkenswerte Korallen aus dem Roten Meer. *Senckenberg. biol.* **45**: 613–620.

Stehli, F. G. (1968). Taxonomic diversity gradients in pole location: the recent model. In *Evolution and environment:* 163–227. (Drake, E. T., ed.) New Haven and London: Yale University Press.

Stoddart, D. R. (1969). Ecology and morphology of Recent coral reefs. *Biol. Rev.* **44**: 433–498.

Vaughan, T. W. and Wells, J. W. (1943). Revision of the suborders, families and genera of the Scleractinia. *Spec. Pap. geol. Soc. Am.* **44**: i–xv, 1–361.

Wells, J. W. (1954). Bikini and nearby atolls: (2) oceanography (biologic). Recent corals of the Marshall Islands. *Prof. Pap. U.S. geol. Surv.* **260** (I): i–iv, 385–486.

Wells, J. W. (1955). A survey of the distribution of reef coral genera in the Great Barrier Reef region. *Rep. Gt Barrier Reef Comm.* **6**(2): 1–9.

Wells, J. W. (1956). Scleractinia. In *Treatise on invertebrate paleontology: (F), Coelenterata:* F328–F444. (Moore, R. C., ed.) Kansas: Geological Society of America; University of Kansas Press.

Wells, J. W. (1957a). Coral reefs. In *Treatise on marine ecology and paleoecology. I. Ecology.* (Hedgpeth, J. W., ed.) *Mem. geol. Soc. Am.* **67** (1): 609–631.

Wells, J. W. (1957b). Annotated bibliography—corals. In *Treatise on marine ecology and paleoecology. I. Ecology.* (Hedgpeth, J. W., ed.) *Mem. geol. Soc. Am.* **67** (1): 1087–1104.

Wells, J. W. (1962). Two new scleractinian corals from Australia. *Rec. Aust. Mus.* **25**: 239–241.

Wells, J. W. (1964). The Recent solitary mussid scleractinian corals. *Zoöl Meded., Leiden* **39**: 375–384.

Wells, J. W. (1966). Evolutionary development in the scleractinian family Fungiidae. *Symp. zool. Soc. Lond.* No. **16**: 223–246.

Wells, J. W. (1968). (unpublished MS table of records of reef coral genera for selected Indopacific localities.)

Wells, J. W. (1970). Aspects of Pacific reef coral fauna. *Micronesica* **5**.

Wells, J. W. and Davies, P. S. (1966). Reef studies at Addu Atoll, Maldive Islands. Preliminary results of an expedition to Addu atoll in 1964. IV, preliminary list of stony corals from Addu atoll. *Atoll Res. Bull.* **116**: 43–55.

Yonge, C. M. (1940) The biology of reef-building corals. *Scient. Rep. Gt Barrier Reef Exped.* **1**: 353–391.

Symp. zool. Soc. Lond. (1971) No.28, 301–327.

COMPOSITION OF THE CORAL FAUNA OF THE SOUTHEASTERN COAST OF INDIA AND THE LACCADIVES*

C. S. GOPINADHA PILLAI

Central Marine Fisheries Research Institute, Mandapam Camp, India

SYNOPSIS

Coral reefs of fringing nature are found both in the Gulf of Mannar and Palk Bay on the southeastern coast of India. In the Gulf of Mannar, they are scattered mostly around the various islands lying between Tuticorin and Rameswaram. The reefs of Palk Bay are confined to the northern and eastern costs of Rameswaram Island and the northern side of Mandapam. Investigations on the corals of this area, between Long. 79°4′E and 79°15′E and Lat. 9°10′N and 9°18′N, have revealed the occurrence of 117 species divided among 33 genera. Of these, 110 species of 26 genera are hermatypic and the rest ahermatypic. The most conspicuous components of the coral fauna of this area are the members of the families Acroporidae, Poritidae and Faviidae. It is feared that the coral reefs of southeast India are fast deteriorating due to natural as well as artificial causes some of which are also discussed in this paper.

The scleractinia of the Laccadive Archipelago are still poorly known except for some information from Minicoy and Chetland Island. To the present a total of 69 species belonging to 26 genera are known from the archipelago, all of which are known to occur at Minicoy Atoll. A comparison of the coral faunas of southeastern India and the Laccadives is also presented.

INTRODUCTION

Coral reef formations along the coasts of peninsular India are restricted to the Gulf of Kutch on the northwestern coast and to Palk Bay and the Gulf of Mannar on the southeastern coast, where fringing or patch reefs are found. The coral formations of the southeastern coast of India extend further south, fringing the coasts of Ceylon. The major part of the Bay of Bengal and the Arabian Sea along the subcontinental coasts are devoid of reefs, which might result from the large quantity of freshwater and silt brought by the great rivers (Sewell, 1932). Further, the presence of a very high percentage of nitric acid (about 2·52 tons per square mile) in the Ganges waters, especially during the monsoon, is detrimental to any large scale reef formation at the northern sector of the Bay of Bengal (Sewell, 1935). Early references to the corals and coral reefs of the southeast coast of India are found in Thurston (1895), Foote (1888), Brook (1893), Bernard (1897, 1905), Matthai (1924, 1928), Gravely (1927) and Sewell (1932, 1935). Gardiner

---

* Published with the kind permission of the Director, Central Marine Fisheries Research Institute, Mandapam Camp, India.

has paid much attention during the beginning of this century to the corals and reefs of Minicoy Atoll in the Laccadives. There appears to be no work on the Scleractinia of the Gulf of Kutch.

Systematic and ecological investigations on the stony corals of the seas around India, mostly from Palk Bay and the Gulf of Mannar, have been carried out by the present author since 1964. Some of the results of these investigations have already been published (Pillai, 1969a, b, c). The present account is an attempt to give in brief the results so far obtained. The discussion on the Laccadive fauna is mostly confined to Minicoy, due to lack of detailed informations from other parts of the archipelago.

THE SOUTHEAST INDIAN REEFS, THEIR EXTENT AND LOCATIONS

Descriptions of a general nature of the reefs of this area are given by Foote (1888) and Thurston (1895). Sewell (1935) has paid much attention to the raised reefs of this area during his geographic and oceanographic research in Indian waters. The reefs of this area are fringing or patchy types, thriving in very shallow waters either near the shores of the mainland or encircling a few islands. Most of the reef framework is composed of dead and semifossilized *Porites*. The calcareous algae appear to play very insignificant roles in building reefs in this part of the Indian Ocean. The shallow waters with muddy or sandy surroundings considerably restrict the growth of corals and at present the reefs seem to be in a state of deterioration.

The reefs of the Gulf of Mannar

The coral reefs of the Gulf of Mannar along the Indian coast are found scattered around a large number of islands situated between Long. 79°9′E and 79°29′E and Lat. 8°45′ and 9°16′N. Rajendran and David (in press) have recently made a preliminary underwater survey on the extent of these reefs. The present author's investigations on the corals of the Gulf of Mannar are mostly confined to a few islands in the vicinity of the Central Marine Fisheries Research Institute, Mandapam Camp (Fig. 1). Shingle Island is at the eastern extremity of the chain of islands and is very close to Krusadai Island and all are surrounded by patchy coral growths. The southern, southeastern and eastern sides of Krusadai Island have well developed fringing reefs with a boulder zone. The lagoon of Krusadai becomes very shallow during low tides and has a rich assemblage of different types of corals. The Krusadai reef is mostly dead. The adjacent Pulli Island, Pullivasal Island, New Islet, Manauli Island and Hare Island all have fringing

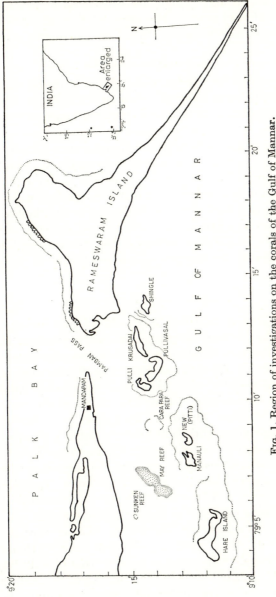

Fig. 1. Region of investigations on the corals of the Gulf of Mannar.

reefs with shallow sandy lagoons. The reefs are located 100–150 m from the shore. In listing the fauna, because of the faunal similarities and proximity, Krusadai and Shingle are considered together. The fauna of Pulli and Pullivasal are listed together while those of New Islet and Manauli are considered together. Hare Island is treated separately.

The reefs of Palk Bay

Running parallel to the mainland in an eastwest direction and located 300–600 m away from the shore in some places, there is a reef in Palk Bay at Mandapam. It extends between Long. 79°8′ and 79°12′E at a Lat. of 9°17′N. The reef is broken at Pamban Pass but continues along the northern and eastern side of Rameswaram Island. The lagoon is 1–2 m deep at low tides with a mostly sandy floor and generally devoid of any coral. The absence of corals can be due to the fact that there is hardly any hard substratum on which coral planulae can settle. A Boulder Zone is absent which might be due to the shallowness of the Bay and very little wave action during most of the months coupled with a poor growth of corals. Details of the structure and distribution of corals on this reef are presented elsewhere (Pillai, in press, a).

PHYSICAL AND HYDROBIOLOGICAL CONDITIONS OF THE AREA

The Gulf of Mannar and Palk Bay at Mandapam are separated only by a narrow strip of land having permanent connection through the Pamban Pass between Mandapam and Rameswaram Island. Palk Bay is a rather shallow basin with mostly muddy inshore regions, while the Gulf of Mannar is more open, deep and with rocky patches in the inshore regions (Jayaraman, 1954). The waters of the two mix freely at the Pamban Pass and at Adam's Bridge between Dhanushkodi and Ceylon. Both northeast and southwest monsoons prevail in this area, though the former contributes towards the major portion of the annual rainfall during which heavy winds are of common occurrence. The mean annual rainfall varies from 762–1270 mm (Tampi, 1959). No freshwater stream flows to this area. The average monthly atmospheric temperature ranges from 25° to 31°C with the maxima and minima in May and January respectively. The average temperature of the surface water varies from 25° to 30°C in different months, that of Gulf of Mannar being of a slightly higher order than that of Palk Bay (Prasad, 1957). A regular seasonal cycle in the salinities of the surface waters of this area has been observed by Prasad (1954). The salinity is low in the month of January and then gradually rises to remain high till November followed by a decline in December. In most of the months the salinity is between 33 and 36‰ with a fall between 25–27·47‰ in the month of January.

THE STRUCTURE OF THE CORAL FAUNA OF THE SOUTHEAST COAST
OF INDIA

The various localities around Mandapam from which a fairly intensive collection of corals was made are considered here as a single faunal district. The details of the occurrence of the different species at different localities are shown in Table I. An analysis of the genera of corals hitherto recorded from this place is presented below. The number of species recorded under each genus is presented in Table III. Genera are listed in alphabetical order.

TABLE I

Check-list of Scleractinia from southeast India.
The classification adopted is that of Wells, 1956

No.	Name of species	Manda-pam (Palk Bay)	Krusa-dai Island and Shingle Island	Pulli-vasal and Pulli Islands	Manauli Island and New Islet	Hare Island
		1	2	3	4	5
	Order Scleractinia Suborder Astrocoeniina Family Thamnasteriidae					
1.	*Psammocora contigua* (Esper) Family Pocilloporidae	—	×	×	—	—
2.	*Pocillopora damicornis* (Linnaeus)	×	×	×	×	×
3.	*P. danae* Verrill Family Acroporidae	—	—	—	×	—
4.	*Acropora cervicornis* (Lamarck)	—	×	—	—	—
5.	*A. ceylonica* (Ortmann)	—	—	—	×	—
6.	*A. corymbosa* (Lamarck)	×	—	×	×	×
7.	*A. digitifera* (Dana)	×	—	—	—	—
8.	*A. diversa* (Dana)	—	×	—	—	—
9.	*A. erythraeae* (Klunzinger)	—	×	×	×	×
10.	*A. exigua* (Dana)	×	—	—	—	—
11.	*A. formosa* (Dana)	×	×	×	×	×
12.	*A. haimei* (Milne-Edwards and Haime)	×	—	—	—	—

TABLE I (continued)

No.	Name of species	Manda-pam (Palk Bay)	Krusa-dai Island and Shingle Island	Pulli-vasal and Pulli Islands	Manauli Island and New Islet	Hare Island
		1	2	3	4	5
13.	A. humilis (Dana)	×	×	×	×	×
14.	A. hyacinthus (Dana)	×	—	—	—	—
15.	A. indica (Brook)	×	×	×	×	×
16.	A. intermedia (Brook)	×	—	—	—	—
17.	A. multicaulis (Brook)	—	—	×	×	—
18.	A. multiformis (Ortmann)	—	—	—	×	—
19.	A. nobilis (Dana)	—	—	—	×	×
20.	A. pharaonis (Milne-Edwards and Haime)	×	—	—	—	—
21.	A. polymorpha (Brook)	×	—	—	—	—
22.	A. obscura (Brook)	×	—	—	—	—
23.	A. spicifera (Dana)	—	×	—	—	—
24.	A. sqamosa (Brook)	×	—	—	—	—
25.	A. surculosa (Dana)	—	—	×	×	×
26.	A. thurstoni (Brook)	×	—	—	—	—
27.	A. valida (Dana)	—	—	—	—	×
28.	Montipora composita Crossland	×	—	—	—	—
29.	M. digitata (Dana)	×	×	×	×	×
30.	M. divaricata(Brüggemann)	×	×	×	×	×
31.	M. edwardsi (Bornard)	×	—	—	—	—
32.	M. elscheneri (Vaughan)	—	—	—	×	—
33.	M. explanata (Brüggemann)	×	×	—	—	—
34.	M. exserta (Quelch)	×	—	—	—	—
35.	M. foliosa (Pallas)	×	×	×	×	×
36.	M. granulosa (Bernard)	—	—	—	×	—
37.	M. informis (Bernard)	×	×	×	×	×
38.	M. manauliensis Pillai	—	—	—	×	—
39.	M. monasteriata (Forskål)	×	—	—	—	—
40.	M. spongiosa (Ehrenberg)	—	×	—	—	—
41.	M. spumosa (Lamarck)	×	—	—	×	—
42.	M. subtilis (Bernard)	—	—	—	×	—
43.	M. tuberculata (Lamarck)	—	—	—	×	—
44.	M. turgescens (Bernard)	—	—	—	×	—
45.	M. venosa (Ehrenberg)	—	×	—	—	—
46.	M. verrilli (Vaughan)	×	×	×	×	×
47.	M. verrucosa (Lamarck)	—	—	—	×	—
48.	Astreopora myriopthalma (Lamarck)	Gulf of Mannar				

TABLE I (continued)

Suborder Fungiina
Superfamily Agariciicae
Family Agariciidae

49. *Pavona decussata* (Dana)	—	—	—	×	—
50. *P. divaricata* (Lamarck)	—	×	—	—	—
51. *P. maldivensis* (Gardiner)	—	×	—	×	—
52. *P. varians* (Verrill)	×	×	—	—	—
53. *Pachyseris rugosa* (Lamarck)	—	—	—	×	—

Family Siderastreidae

54. *Siderastrea radians* (Pallas)	×	—	×	—	—
55. *S. savignyana* (Milne-Edwards and Haime)	×	—	×	—	—
56. *Coscinaraea monile* (Forskål)	×	×	—	×	×

Superfamily Poriticae
Family Poritidae

57. *Goniopora djiboutiensis* (Vaughan)	—	—	—	×	—
58. *G. duofaciata* (Thiel)	×	×	×	×	×
59. *G. lobata?*	Gulf of Mannar				
60. *G. nigra* (Pillai)	×	—	×	×	×
61. *G. stokesi* (Milne-Edwards and Haime)	×	—	—	—	—
62. *Por tes alveolata* (Milne-Edwards and Haime)	—	—	—	—	—
63. *P. compressa* (Dana)	×	×	—	—	—
64. *P. exserta* Pillai	—	—	—	×	—
65. *P. fragosa* (Dana)	—	—	—	×	—
66. *P. lichen* (Dana)	×	×	×	×	×
67. *P. lutea* (Milne-Edwards and Haime)	×	—	—	×	—
68. *P. mannarensis* (Pillai)	—	—	×	×	×
69. *P. nodifera* (Klunzinger)	×	—	—	—	—
70. *P. solida* (Forskål)	×	×	×	×	×
71. *P. somaliensis* (Gravier)	×	×	×	×	×
72. *P. thurstoni* Pillai	—	—	—	×	—
73. *Porites* sp.	—	—	—	×	—
74. *P. (Synaraea) convexa* (Verrill)	—	—	—	×	—

Suborder Faviina
Superfamily Faviicae
Family Faviidae
Subfamily Faviinae

75. *Plesiastrea versipora* (Lamarck)	×	—	—	—	—
76. *Favia favus* (Forskål)	×	—	—	—	—
77. *F. pallida* (Dana)	×	×	×	×	×
78. *F. speciosa* (Dana)	—	×	—	×	—
79. *F. stelligera* (Dana)	—	—	—	×	—
80. *F. valenciennesi* (Milne-Edwards and Haime)	×	×	×	×	×

TABLE I (continued)

No.	Name of species	Manda-pam (Palk Bay)	Krusa-dai Island and Shingle Island	Pulli-vasal and Pulli Islands	Manauli Island and New Islet	Hare Island
		1	2	3	4	5
81.	*Favites abdita* (Ellis and Solander)	×	×	×	×	×
82.	*F. halicora* (Ehrenberg)	×	—	—	—	—
83.	*F. melicerum* (Ehrenberg)	Mandapam (Gulf of Mannar)				
84.	*F. pentagona* (Esper)	—	—	—	×	—
85.	*F. virens* (Dana)	×	—	—	—	—
86.	*Goniastrea incrustans* Duncan	—	—	—	×	—
87.	*G. pectinata* (Ehrenberg)	×	×	×	×	×
88.	*G. retiformis* (Lamarck)	×	×	×	×	×
89.	*Platygyra lamellina* (Ehrenberg)	×	×	×	×	×
90.	*Leptoria phrygia* (Ellis and Solander)	—	×	—	—	—
91.	*Hydnophora exesa* (Pallas)	×	×	—	—	—
92.	*H. grandis* (Gardiner)	×	—	—	—	—
93.	*H. microconos* (Lamarck)	×	—	—	×	—
	Subfamily Montastreinae					
94.	*Leptastrea purpurea* (Dana)	×	×	×	×	×
95.	*L. transversa* (Klunzinger)	×	×	×	×	×
96.	*Cyphastrea chalcidicum* (Forskål)	×	×	—	—	—
97.	*C. microphthalma* (Lamarck)	×	—	—	—	—
98.	*C. serailia* (Forskål)	×	×	×	×	×
99.	*Echinopora gemmacea* (Lamarck)	—	×	—	—	—
100.	*E. lamellosa* (Esper)	—	×	×	×	×
	Family Rhizangiidae					
101.	*Culicia rubeola* (Quoy and Gaimard)	—	×	×	×	×
	Family Oculinidae Subfamily Galaxeinae					
102.	*Galaxea clavus* (Dana)	×	—	—	—	—
103.	*G. fascicularis* (Linnaeus)	×	×	×	×	×
	Family Merulinidae					
104.	*Merulina ampliata* (Ellis and Solander)	×	—	—	×	×
	Family Mussidae					
105.	*Symphyllia radians* (Milne-Edwards and Haime)	×	—	—	—	—

TABLE I (continued)

106. *S. recta* (Dana)	×	×	×	×	×
Family Pectiniidae 107. *Mycedium tubifex* (Dana)	×	—	—	—	—
Suborder Caryophylliina Superfamily Caryophylliicae Family Caryophylliidae 108. *Paracyathus profundus* (Duncan)	×	×	×	×	×
109. *Polycyathus verrilli* (Duncan)	×	×	×	×	×
Suborder Dendrophylliina Family Dendrophylliidae 110. *Balanophyllia affinis* (Semper)	—	—	—	×	—
111. *Endopsammia philippinensis* (Milne-Edwards and Haime)	—	—	—	×	—
112. *Tubastrea aurea* (Quoy and Gaimard)	—	—	—	×	×
113. *Dendrophyllia coarctata* Duncan	—	×	—	×	—
114. *Turbinaria crater* (Pallas)	—	×	×	—	—
115. *T. ?frondens* (Dana)	—	×	—	—	—
116. *T. mesenterina* (Lamarck)	—	—	—	×	—
117. *T. peltata* (Esper)	×	—	×	—	—

× Recorded.
— Not recorded.

Acropora

A fairly common genus exhibiting here, ramose, arborescent, tufted, digitiform, corymbose and flabellate forms of growth. Massive members are not known. *A. corymbosa*, *A. haimei A. squamosa*, *A. nobilis*, *A. erythraeae* and *A. indica* flourish in the Gulf of Mannar side. At the Palk Bay side of Rameswaram *A. formosa* shows a preponderance. Other members are occasionally met with being nowhere common. The size of the colonies varies from 15–25 cm in greater diameter, though *A. corymbosa* and *A. surculosa* may attain a greater diameter of 60–80 cm. *Acropora* is mainly a reef-dwelling genus here, being poorly represented in the lagoon. Majority of the species display a brownish corallum with pink or white axial corallites. The only exception is *A. squamosa* which has a bluish green corallum with violet axial corallites.

Astreopora

The genus is known from here by a single specimen preserved in the Government Museum, Madras with the locality marked as Gulf of

Mannar. No living colony was found during the author's investigations.

Balanophyllia

The shallow-water corals of this area include a single species of this genus known by only two specimens from Gulf of Mannar.

Coscinaraea

Very rarely seen in both Palk Bay and Gulf of Mannar. About a dozen specimens are obtained all of which are small, ranging from 8–12 cm in greater diam.

Culicia

This genus is found attached to rocks and dead *Porites*.

The small size of the calices and the raptoid nature of the corallum make the coral inconspicuous at the natural habitat. A good many of the specimens collected were found to be encrusted by Bryozoa.

Cyphastrea

This medium caliced coral is generally seen in almost all localities around Mandapam. *C. microphthalma* is the most common member of the genus in Palk Bay, where colonies generally grow to 20 cm or more in diameter. Infestation by tube-dwelling polychaetes was noticed to cause the formation of slender digitiform processes on the upper side of several colonies. *C. serailia* and *C. chalcidicum* rarely occur. The polyps are found partly expanded during day time.

Dendrophyllia

Not commonly seen in the shallow-waters of this area. Known only by a single species.

Echinopora

Two foliaceous members of this genus are known from Gulf of Mannar. *E. lamellosa* forms very large platforms in the lagoon of the various islands in the Gulf of Mannar, growing mixed with similar platforms of *Montipora foliosa*. The occurrence of a large number of stalked buds as observed by Boschma (1928) on the under side of the plates is a very common phenomenon here. Curiously enough the genus could not be collected in Palk Bay, though careful search over a period of four years was made.

Endopsammia

Seven small specimens belonging to this genus were collected from the under side of a colony of *Acropora surculosa* from Manauli Island. The living coral displayed an eosin red colour.

Favia

This genus is present in almost all localities in this area in fairly good numbers. *F. pallida* is the commonest member displaying both typical *pallida* and *hululensis* facies. It is very abundant at the shoreward side of the reef at Mandapam(Palk Bay). *F. stelligera* is very rare and could be collected only once. *F. favus* was noticed in fair numbers in Palk Bay but rarely in the Gulf of Mannar side.

Favites

This is not so important a reef-builder as *Favia*. *F. abdita* may sometimes grow to 60 or 70 cm in diameter in the Gulf of Mannar, but colonies are rare. In Palk Bay the species was observed near the Pamban Pass where some of the specimens possessed a sort of foliaceous corallum (Matthai, 1924). *F. virens* can be seen in Palk Bay but the author failed to notice any in the Gulf of Mannar. *F. halicora, F. pentagona* and *F. melicerum* are all rare and are known by a single specimen of each.

Galaxea

Not a conspicuous genus at any locality, but rarely seen under crevices of reef rocks. Individual colonies usually range from 10–20 cm in diam. The polyps are found expanded during day time with the tentacles hanging down along the thecal wall.

Goniastrea

The genus is fairly common here. Both *G. halicora* and *G. retiformis* grow to an average of 20–30 cm in size. The former species displays a wide range of skeletal variation. It is observed that specimens obtained from rocky environments and deeper waters have larger and deeper calices with thinner intercorallite walls than specimens collected from very shallow waters with sandy or muddy surroundings. Smaller colonies of *G. retiformis* are golden yellow in colour getting brown in older ones. The polyps of this genus are found partly expanded during day.

Goniopora

Nowhere in this area is it common. *G. stokesi* could be collected from the shoreward side of the reef at Palk Bay, but could not be seen on the Gulf of Mannar side. This is one of the excellent examples of coral becoming fully expanded during the day. The polyps were noticed to be expanded in the aquarium to a height of 4–5 cm completely hiding the white skeleton underneath. *G. duofaciata* is found in small patches at random. A black *Goniopora*, viz. *G. nigra*, with small polygonal calices occurs here, having remarkable affinity to certain fossil members of the genus (Pillai, 1969b).

Hydnophora

The genus, though represented by three species here, is nowhere common.

Leptastrea

This is probably the most common and successful genus of reef corals seen in rocky, sandy and muddy environments even from low water mark. It is represented by two species here. Individual colonies of this genus are seen mostly in small encrustations ranging from 5–15 cm in diam. Examination of a large number of specimens both in the field and the laboratory has revealed the existence of samples showing gradation from *L. transversa* to *L. purpurea* and as such their separate identity needs careful consideration. The polyps are partially expanded during day.

Leptoria

Very rare. No living colony could be seen during the author's investigations. A few specimens are preserved in the Museum of the Krusadai Island with the locality marked as Krusadai.

Merulina

Two live specimens of this genus were noticed in the Gulf of Mannar, one at Manauli Island and the other at Hare Island. The one at Hare Island measured nearly 50 cm in greater diameter. Dead and broken pieces of this genus are often found washed ashore in all localities around Mandapam.

Montipora

This is a very common genus inhabiting both the lagoon and the reef. Encrusting, ramose, massive and foliaceous forms occur.

M. divaricata, M. digitata and *M. foliosa* are the commonest members. Gravely (1927) has reported a papillate, ramose species (*M. spongiosa*) from Krusadai Island, remarking that it was very common. However, the present author failed to identify any specimen from Krusadai as belonging to *M. spongiosa*. The commonest member of the genus at present in Krusadai is *M. digitata*. *M. foliosa* is chiefly a lagoon form here. *M. divaricata* exhibits a wide range of skeletal variation both in the thickness of branches and calicular characters. Specimens from the deeper waters of Palk Bay showed taller coralla and more slender branches than specimens from the very shallow waters of the various lagoons of the Gulf of Mannar. Thicker coralla possess better developed papillae. One of the massive *Montipora* from the Manauli Island was found to be new and was described as such (Pillai, 1969a) under the name *M. manauliensis*. Among the encrusting species *M. verrilli* and *M. informis* are the commonest.

Mycedium

This genus is known from Palk Bay by a single specimen found washed ashore, soon after the cyclone of 1964. Living colonies were not seen in the shallow waters investigated.

Pachyseris

Very rare genus known by a single specimen from Manauli Island.

Pavona

Encrusting, hydnophoroid and foliaceous forms of this genus occur, but is not a common reef-builder of this area. *P. decussata* was found in good numbers on the northern side of Manauli Island, usually attached to the top of *M. foliosa* and *Echinopora lamellosa*. A single specimen of *P. divaricata* was noticed in the lagoon of Krusadai Island and it measured nearly 70 cm in greater diameter. *P. varians* and *P. maldivensis* are very rarely met with.

Paracyathus

A solitary, fair-sized coral with a slightly broad base, white thecal wall and purple septa is commonly seen attached to rocks and dead corals in all localities around Mandapam.

Platygyra

Though represented by only a single species it is found in all the localities in fair numbers. The size of the colonies varies from a few centimetres to rarely a metre or so. The species exhibits a wide range of skeletal variation in the thickness of the collines, length of valleys and porosity of the intercorallite walls. Polyps are found to be partly expanded during day.

Plesiastrea

Sewell (1935) has recorded the presence of this genus on the raised reef of Rameswaram Island. Skeletons preserved in a state of good condition can still be collected from there. No living colony was observed.

Polycyathus

This genus is often found attached to rocks and dead *Porites* both in the Gulf of Mannar and Palk Bay. It varies from isolated corallites to small colonies covering an area of 10–15 cm.

Pocillopora

This is the only genus of the family Pocilloporidae known to occur in this area. *P. damicornis* is the commonest and most abundant member of the genus. The sandy lagoon floor of the various islands in the Gulf of Mannar harbours a rich assemblage of this species. Colonies vary from 10–30 cm in spread, the lower part of the larger colonies being dead while the living zone extends from 10–15 cm from the top. Some of the specimens collected are very slender-stemmed approaching the condition of *P. acuta*. A few specimens of *P. danae* were noticed at the northern side of Manauli Island.

Porites

This is the most important reef-builder of this area and forms the major part of the reef framework. The majority of the colonies are dead and a good many exist in a semifossilized condition. *P. solida* and *P. somaliensis* surpass others in abundance and both the species are collected in large quantities for various economic purposes. Ramose members of this genus are so far not recorded.

Psammocora

Only *P. contigua* is recorded from here, although it is not common. A few small colonies were noticed in the lagoon of Krusadai Island and Pullivasal Island.

Siderastrea

Occasionally seen in both rocky and sandy surroundings in both lagoon and on the reef. *S. savignyana* is found in small patches while *S. radians* assume larger sizes some times as big as 30 cm in greater diameter.

Symphyllia

Not a dominant reef-builder in this part of the Indian Ocean. Both *S. recta* and *S. radians* are seen rarely in the shoreward side of the reef in Palk Bay. The polyps are found partially expanded in the day time.

Tubastrea

Rare. Sometimes seen attached to dead *Porites* from the Gulf of Mannar. Not collected from Palk Bay.

Turbinaria

T. peltata occurs both in Palk Bay and the Gulf of Mannar. Two specimens of this species from Mandapam measured nearly 50 and 60 cm in diameter and possessed elevated corallites in some parts of the corallum. *T. mesenterina* was once noticed at Manauli Island. Gravely (1927) has mentioned the presence of *T. frondens* in the Gulf of Mannar. The genus *Turbinaria* is, however, not a dominant one among the coral fauna of this place.

COMPARISON OF THE CORAL FAUNA OF PALK BAY AND GULF OF MANNAR

It seems that a comparison of the coral faunas of these two areas is not out of place here, since such a comparison yields some interesting facts on the distribution of corals even in such a limited geographic area and separated only by a narrow strip of land. The dominance of a certain coral at one place and its paucity or absence on the other side is noteworthy. Based on the field studies made by the author a few such cases can be pointed out. A typical example is *Echinopora*. This genus is found in plenty in the Gulf of Mannar but was not seen in Palk Bay. A fair number of foliaceous *Pavona* found at Manauli Island could not be seen in Palk Bay and probably do not occur there. *A. erythraeae*, *A. nobilis* and *A. surculosa* while found in plenty in the Gulf of Mannar have not been seen on the other side. *A. squamosa* flourishes towards the western side of the reef in Palk Bay but the author failed to detect any in the Gulf of Mannar. Many more such disparities in the distribution can be pointed out but the species we are concerned with, are not found in abundance to substantiate the arguments. In general it may be stated that the reefs of the Gulf of Mannar are more luxuriant both in the number of species and their abundance than the Palk Bay reef. This can be attributed to the prevalence of comparatively more adverse environmental factors in the inshore regions of Palk Bay than in Gulf of Mannar (Pillai, in press, a).

COMPOSITION OF THE SOUTHEAST INDIAN CORALS

There is a general similarity in the composition of the Scleractinia of the various parts of the Indo-Pacific region (Vaughan and Wells, 1943). However, regional variations are found both in the structure of the reef and in the composition of the fauna. Recently, Stoddart dealt with this aspect of the Indo-Pacific reef studies (Stoddart, in press). The number of genera of corals recorded from different areas in the Indo-Pacific varies considerably (Wells, 1954) and the disparity to an extent is due to insufficient collecting. It is true that some genera may not occur in some parts, but at the same time they may be abundant in another place.

At the present a total of 117 species divided among 33 genera are known from southeast India. Out of these, 110 species belonging to 26 genera are hermatypic and the other 7 species of 7 genera are ahermatypic. All these species are recorded to a depth of not more than 2 m at low tide. The deeper waters have yet to be investigated. The total number of genera (33) is less when compared to that of some other parts of the Indian Ocean where recent reports are available, such as the Red Sea (Wells, 1954) and Addu Atoll (Wells and Davies, 1966) with 47 genera each; Inhaca Island with 38 genera (Macnae and Kalk, 1958); Tuléar with 43 genera (Pichon, 1964) and Singapore with 40 genera (Purchon, 1956). At the same time it is higher than that of Tutia Reef in Tanganyika territory (Talbot, 1965) and Cocos-Keeling Island in the eastern Indian Ocean with 24 genera (Wells, 1950).

The most conspicuous elements in the coral fauna of southeastern India are the members of the family Acroporidae represented by three genera viz. *Acropora*, *Astreopora* and *Montipora*. *Montipora* and *Acropora* together constitute 39% of the total species recorded. The members of the families Poritidae and Faviidae are also rich and form the dominant reef-builders of this place. The occurrence of *Siderastrea*—a relic genus of the old Tethyan coral fauna—is also noteworthy. The extant form of a *Goniopora* viz. *G. nigra* with close affinities to some of the fossil members of this genus is interesting. The absence of certain very common Indo-Pacific genera from the faunal list of this area is conspicuous. Mentioned in this connection are *Stylophora*, *Seriatopora*, *Alveopora*, *Caulastrea*, *Diploastrea*, *Lobophyllia* and *Euphyllia* all of which are known throughout the Indo-Pacific. The paucity of the members of the family Fungiidae is another feature. *Fungia*, *Halomitra*, *Herpolitha*, *Polyphyllia* and *Podabacia* are still not known from here.

The occurrence of the various genera recorded from southeast India, in other parts of the Indian Ocean is tabulated in Table II. It is shown

TABLE II

Distribution of southeast Indian coral genera in other parts of the Indian Ocean

No.	Name of Genus	Red Sea 1	Tuléar 2	Maldives 3	Anda- mans 4	Singa- pore 5	Cocos- Keeling 6
1.	*Acropora*	×	×	×	×	×	×
2.	*Astreopora*	×	×	×	—	—	×
3.	*Balanophyllia*	×	—	×	×	×	—
4.	*Coscinaraea*	×	×	×	—	—	—
5.	*Culicia*	—	×	×	—	—	×
6.	*Cyphastrea*	×	—	×	—	×	×
7.	*Dendrophyllia*	×	×	×	×	×	×
8.	*Echinopora*	×	×	×	×	×	×
9.	*Endopsammia*	—	—	×	—	—	—
10.	*Favia*	×	×	×	×	×	×
11.	*Favites*	×	×	×	×	×	×
12.	*Galaxea*	×	×	×	×	×	—
13.	*Goniastrea*	×	×	×	×	×	—
14.	*Goniopora*	×	×	×	—	×	—
15.	*Hydnophora*	×	×	×	×	×	×
16.	*Leptastrea*	×	×	×	×	×	×
17.	*Leptoria*	×	×	×	—	×	×
18.	*Merulina*	×	×	×	×	×	—
19.	*Montipora*	×	×	×	×	×	×
20.	*Mycedium*	—	×	×	—	×	—
21.	*Pachyseris*	×	×	×	—	×	—
22.	*Pavona*	×	×	×	×	×	×
23.	*Paracyathus*	×	—	×	—	×	—
24.	*Platygyra*	×	×	×	×	×	×
25.	*Plesiastrea*	×	×	×	×	×	×
26.	*Pocillopora*	×	×	×	×	×	×
27.	*Polycyathus*	—	—	—	×	—	—
28.	*Porites*	×	×	×	×	×	×
29.	*Psammocora*	×	×	×	×	×	×
30.	*Siderastrea*	×	—	—	×	—	—
31.	*Symphyllia*	×	×	×	×	×	—
32.	*Tubastrea*	×	×	×	—	×	×
33.	*Turbinaria*	×	×	×	—	×	—

× Recorded.
— Not recorded.

that 29 genera are common to the Red Sea and southeast India, only *Mycedium* among the hermatypic forms being missing from the faunal list of the Red Sea. Tuléar in Madagascar has 26 genera in common with this area, *Siderastrea* and *Cyphastrea* among the reef-building forms are not known from Tuléar. The Maldivian fauna includes all the hermatypic genera of southeast India except *Siderastrea*. The Scleractinia of Andamans and Nicobar Islands are still not properly known but they have 21 genera in common with Palk Bay and the Gulf of Mannar. Twenty-seven genera are common to this area and Singapore while 18 are common to Cocos-Keeling and this area.

THE PRESENT CONDITION OF CORAL GROWTH IN SOUTHEAST INDIA

The effect of sedimentation

There is a wide regression of coral growth throughout the tropics (Gardiner, 1936). The reefs of southeast India are no exception to this world phenomenon. Both natural as well as artificial factors exercise their influence in the present state of deterioration of the coral growth in this area. The large degree of silt settlement has a remarkable effect. This appears to have a greater influence in the inshore regions of Palk Bay than in the Gulf of Mannar, especially during the northeast monsoon. The inshore waters of Palk Bay during the monsoon become muddy due to the presence of suspended sand and silt stirred up from the sandy shore by wave action caused by wind. This causes the death of a large number of coral colonies every year (Pillai, in press, a). The loss sustained due to this recurrent mortality is not replenished during the calm period, during which the corals of this area show a state of very active growth as evidenced by the presence of large numbers of buds in most of the living colonies. A clear case of the large scale death of corals due to the adverse effect of silt has been recently noticed at Mandapam in the Gulf of Mannar. Until recently, there was a rich coral growth of *Acropora* spp., *Montipora* spp., *Pocillopora damicornis*, *Favia pallida*, *Goniastrea retiformis* and *Porites* spp., on the granite wall of the pier at Mandapam. In October, 1969, heavy winds stirred up the protected waters making it muddy for a week. When normality was established and the water cleared, it was observed that almost all the corals had a white skeleton, a clear indication of death due to the effects of silt.

The effect of the 1964 cyclone on the coral growth

The devastating effects of cyclones on coral reefs are described by Stephenson, Endean and Bennett (1959) and Stoddart (1962, 1965) on the Great Barrier Reef and the British Honduras reefs and cays respectively. Cyclonic winds of high velocity capable of generating enough mechanical force to break corals are not usual in this area, though they are common in the Bay of Bengal, which is a potential low pressure area during a monsoon. A severe cyclone during December, 1964 brought unprecedented death and destruction to the coastal areas of southeast India and the eastern side of Ceylon. The wind speed was reported to exceed 100 k at times during the night of 22nd December, 1964. The direction of the wind was felt at Mandapam from the northeast during the night of 22nd and southwest on the morning of 23rd. Tidal waves as high as 7·6 m were caused submerging the coastal areas. As the present author was familiar with the reefs of this area prior to the cyclone, he could record some of the resulting changes that occurred to the coral fauna. The branching corals, especially the *Acropora* spp. were the worst hit and very many large colonies of *A. corymbosa* and *A. surculosa* were found uprooted and washed ashore. Several corals, both ramose and massive, were later found dead on the reefs. The alcyonarians were reduced greatly in numbers at several places. On the whole there was a reduction of corals in most of the reefs.

The effect of quarrying corals from the reef

Nowadays corals are removed on a large scale from the various reefs of southeast India, for the preparation of calcium carbide, cement, lime, etc. In the Mandapam area alone nearly 50 country boats are currently engaged in this work. Each boat is manned by 4–6 people and during days of fair weather it is capable of bringing 4–6 m³ of limestone from the reef to the shore (Pillai, in press, b). The exploited corals include different species of *Porites* and other massive corals attached to them. During seasons of peak activity approximately 250 m³ of reef are removed daily by all the boats at work. This has been in progress for most of the last decade which has at present resulted in large scale destruction of the reefs and their associated fauna. The reefs of some of the islands in the Gulf of Mannar are almost completely exploited leaving little trace of their past existence.

THE CORAL FAUNA OF THE LACCADIVE ARCHIPELAGO

Our present knowledge of the coral fauna of the Laccadives is confined to Minicoy Atoll, except for scanty information from Chetlat Island at the extreme north end of the archipelago. We have fairly good accounts of the Minicoy fauna from Gardiner (1903, 1904, 1905) and Pillai (1971). The latter has given a detailed description of the distribution of the various genera of corals in different parts of the atoll.

An enumeration of the facts presented therein will only lead to repetition and only a brief account is presented here. A list of scleractinian species so far known from the Laccadives is given in Table IV.

A total of 69* species of hermatypic corals divided among 26 genera is so far recorded from the Laccadives, of which all are known from the Minicoy Atoll. The Chetlat Island coral fauna is known to include 12 species belonging to 10 genera. The list from Chetlat is incomplete since no intensive collection has been made.

The commonest corals of Minicoy are *Acropora* spp., *Porites* spp., *Diploastrea heliopora*, *Goniastrea retifornis* and *Lobophyllia corymbosa*. The genus *Porites* is found in plenty on both lagoon shoals and on reef-flats. *Acropora* flourishes in the lagoon shoals: *A. formosa*, *A. palmata* and *A. pharaonis* are the commonest members, the first mentioned being distributed throughout while the latter two show a preponderance at the southwestern side of the lagoon. Huge colonies of *Diploastrea* measuring more than a metre in diameter are fairly common in the lagoon. This genus according to Gardiner (1904) was rare in 1899 when he visited and investigated the atoll. It seems that the colonies seen at present have grown during the last 70 years. This seems to be the case with *Lobophyllia*. *Pocillopora* occurs in fair numbers on the reef-flats but is rare in lagoon shoals. *P. damicornis* is the commonest member seen in shallow waters of Minicoy. *Fungia* was noticed in good numbers near Wiringili Island on the inner side of the lagoon reef, lying on sand or on the large colonies of *Heliopora*. *Euphyllia* occurs only near the shore at the lagoon side of the Lighthouse. The members of the Faviidae are found throughout the lagoon shoals and the reef-flats. None of the genera recorded from Minicoy are endemic, all being widely distributed throughout the Indo-Pacific. The ahermatypic forms are little investigated.

COMPARISON OF THE CORAL FAUNAS OF SOUTHEAST INDIA AND
THE MINICOY ATOLL

As listed in Table III only 18 genera of corals are found to be common to both Minicoy and southeast Indian reefs. There are certain components of the Minicoy fauna such as *Diploastrea, Fungia, Euphyllia, Lobophyllia* and *Seriatopora* that are found missing from the faunal list of southeast India. Though *Acropora* is the richest member in both places the various species occurring differ considerably. *A. echinata*,

---

* Pillai (1971) has listed 70 species. The inclusion of *Galaxea fascicularis* therein is based on an earlier erroneous identification of a specimen.

TABLE III

The occurrence of the various genera of Scleractinia in southeast India and Minicoy Atoll. The number in parentheses against each genus indicates the number of species so far recorded. Genera are listed in alphabetical order.

No.	Genus	Southeast India	Minicoy
1.	*Acanthastrea*	—	× (1)
2.	*Acropora*	× (24)	× (19)
3.	*Astreopora*	× (1)	—
4.	*Balanophyllia*	× (1)	—
5.	*Coscinaraea*	× (1)	—
6.	*Culicia*	× (1)	—
7.	*Cycloseris*	—	× (1)
8.	*Cyphastrea*	× (3)	—
9.	*Dendrophyllia*	× (1)	—
10.	*Diploastrea*	—	× (1)
11.	*Echinopora*	× (2)	—
12.	*Endopsammia*	× (1)	—
13.	*Euphyllia*	—	× (1)
14.	*Favia*	× (5)	× (3)
15.	*Favites*	× (5)	× (5)
16.	*Fungia*	—	× (3)
17.	*Galaxea*	× (2)	× (1)
18.	*Goniastrea*	× (3)	× (2)
19.	*Goniopora*	× (5)	× (2)
20.	*Hydnophora*	× (3)	× (1)
21.	*Leptastrea*	× (2)	× (3)
22.	*Leptoria*	× (1)	× (1)
23.	*Lobophyllia*	—	× (1)
24.	*Merulina*	× (1)	× (1)
25.	*Montipora*	× (20)	× (1)?
26.	*Mycedium*	× (1)	—
27.	*Pachyseris*	× (1)	—
28.	*Pavona*	× (4)	× (2)
29.	*Paracyathus*	× (1)	—
30.	*Platygyra*	× (1)	× (1)
31.	*Plesiastrea*	× (1)	× (1)
32.	*Pocillopora*	× (2)	× (3)
33.	*Polycyathus*	× (1)	—
34.	*Podabacia*	—	× (1)
35.	*Porites*	× (13)	× (6)
36.	*Psammocora*	× (1)	× (3)
37.	*Siderastrea*	× (2)	—
38.	*Stylophora*	—	× (1)
39.	*Symphyllia*	× (2)	× (2)
40.	*Tubastrea*	× (1)	—
41.	*Turbinaria*	× (4)	—

A. efflorescens, A. hemprichi, A. palifera and *A. reticulata* that are reported from Minicoy are not known from Palk Bay or the Gulf of Mannar. In this respect the Minicoy fauna has a closer affinity to the adjacent Maldives while the *Acropora* spp. of southeast India are nearer to the Malaysian region. The paucity of *Montipora* in Minicoy is a notable feature. The only record of this genus from Minicoy is that of Gardiner (1903) from the reef-flat of the Lighthouse area. The genus appears to have a tendency to become scarce towards the western sector of the Indian Ocean. While at least 20 species of this genus occur in southeast Indian reefs, only four species are known from the Addu Atoll in the Maldives (Wells and Davies, 1966) and from Tuléar in Madagascar (Pichon, 1964). Crossland (1948) has reported only one species of this genus from the Natal coast. The genera *Cyphastrea* and *Echinopora* that are found commonly in Indian Ocean reefs so far have not been recorded from Minicoy. The paucity of foliaceous corals is also worth mentioning. *Millepora* and *Heliopora* are important reef-builders in Minicoy but both are so far not known from the fringing reefs of southeast India.

SUMMARY

The extent of the coral reefs in Palk Bay and the Gulf of Mannar on the southeastern coast of India has been briefly discussed along with the physical and hydrobiological conditions of the area. A qualitative analysis of the various genera of Scleractinia hitherto recorded from the southeastern coast of India is presented with notes on their abundance. The coral fauna of this area is so far known to include 117 species divided among 33 genera, the members of the families Acroporidae, Faviidae and Poritidae forming the major components. It has been observed that the fauna of the Gulf of Mannar is richer both in the number of species and in their abundance than that of the adjacent Palk Bay.

The coral reefs of southeast India are fast deteriorating. The death of corals seems mainly to be due to the great interference of silt in the inshore waters. The large scale removal of corals for various industrial purposes is responsible for the great depletion of reef-dwelling and reef-building animals in this area. The detrimental effect of a recent cyclone on reef corals in this area has been discussed. It was noticed that the ramose types of corals were more affected by the mechanical force of waves generated by the wind than the massive and encrusting types.

The coral fauna of the Laccadive Archipelago is still poorly known. The available information is summarized. The Minicoy fauna is known

TABLE IV

Check-list of corals from Minicoy Atoll. Those marked with an asterisk are also recorded from Chetland Island

---

Order Scleractinia
Suborder Astrocoeniina
Family Thamnasteriidae
1. *Psammocora contigua* (Esper)
2. P. (*Stephanaria*) *exesa* Dana
3. P. (*Plesioseris*) *haimeana* (Milne-Edwards and Haime)

Family Pocilloporidae
4. *Stylophora mordax* Dana
5. *Pocillopora damicornis* (Linnaeus)
6. P. *verrucosa* (Ellis and Solander)
7. P. *ligulata* Dana
8. P. *eydouxi* (Milne-Edwards and Haime)

Family Acroporidae
9. *Acropora abrotanoides* (Lamarck)
10. A. *conferta* (Quelch)
11. A. *corymbosa* (Lamarck)
12. A. *echinata* (Dana)
13. A. *efflorescens* (Dana)
14. A. *formosa* (Dana)
15. A. *forskali* (Ehrenberg)
16. *A. *haimei* (Milne-Edwards and Haime)
17. A. *hemprichi* (Ehrenberg)
18. A. *humilis* (Dana)
19. A. *hyacinthus* (Dana)
20. A. *indica* (Brook)
21. A. *intermedia* (Brook)
22. A. *monticulosa* (Brüggemann)
23. A. *palifera* (Lamarck)
24. A. *pharaonis* (Milne-Edwards and Haime)
25. A. *rambleri* (Basset-Smith)
26. A. *reticulata* (Brook)
27. A. *squarrosa* (Ehrenberg)
28. *Acropora* sp.
29. *Montipora* sp.

Suborder Fungiina
Superfamily Agariciicae
Family Agariciidae
30. *Pavona maldivensis* (Gardiner)
31. *P. *varians* Verrill

Superfamily Fungiicae
Family Fungiidae
32. *Cycloseris somervillei* (Gardiner)

TABLE IV (continued)

33. *Fungia* (*Danafungia*) *danae* Milne-Edwards and Haime
34. *(*Fungia*) *fungites* (Linnaeus)
35. **F.* (*Pleuractis*) *scutaria* Lamarck
36. *Podabacia crustacea* (Pallas)

Superfamily Poriticae
Family Poritidae
37. *Goniopora minor* Grossland
38. *G. stokesi* Milne-Edwards and Haime
39. *Porites andrewsi* Vaughan
40. *P. lutea* Milne-Edwards and Haime
41. *P. minicoiensis* Pillai
42. *P. palmata* Dana
43. *P. solida* (Forskål)
44. *P. somaliensis* Gravier

Suborder Faviina
Superfamily Faviicae
Family Faviidae
Subfamily Faviinae
45. *Plesiastrea versipora* (Lamarck)
46. *Favia favus* (Forskål)
47. **F. pallida* (Dana)
48. *F. speciosa* (Dana)
49. *Favites abdita* (Ellis and Solander)
50. *F. ehrenbergi* (Klunzinger)
51. *F. halicora* (Ehrenberg)
52. *F. melicerum* (Ehrenberg)
53. *F. pentagona* (Esper)
54. *Goniastrea hombroni* (Rousseau)
55. *G. retiformis* (Lamarck)
56. **Platygyra lamellina* (Ehrenberg)
57. *Leptoria phrygia* (Ellis and Solander)
58. **Hydnophora microconos* (Lamarck)

Subfamily Monastreinae
59. *Diploastrea heliopora* (Lamarck)
60. *Leptastrea purpurea* (Lamarck)
61. *L. transversa* Klunzinger
62. *L. bottae* (Milne-Edwards and Haime)

Family Oculinidae
Subfamily Galaxeinae
63. **Galaxea hexagonalis*

Family Morulinidae
64. *Merulina ampliata* (Ellis and Solander)

TABLE IV (continued)

Family Mussidae
65. *Acanthastrea echinata* (Dana)
66. *Symphyllia radians* Milne-Edwards and Haime
67. *S. recta* Dana
68. *Lobophyllia corymbosa* (Forskål)
   Suborder Caryophylliina
   Superfamily Caryophylliicae

Family Caryophylliidae
   Subfamily Eusmiliinae
69. **Euphyllia glabrescens* (Chamisso and Eysenhardt)

---

to include 69 species belonging to 26 genera. The dominant elements in the Minicoy fauna are the members of the families Acroporidae, Faviidae and Poritidae.

A comparison of the coral faunas of southeast India and the Minicoy Atoll is made. Though *Acropora* is the richest genus at both places, the various species occurring are markedly different, those of Minicoy showing a closer affinity to those of the Maldives while the *Acropora* spp. of southeast India are nearer to those of the Malaysian region.

ACKNOWLEDGEMENTS

The author is grateful to Dr. R. V. Nair, Acting Director, Central Marine Fisheries Research Institute, Mandapam Camp, India for his kind permission to present this account at this Symposium. He also wishes to record the various help rendered by his colleagues Mr. C. Suseelan and Mr. K. Rajasekaran Nair during the preparation of this paper.

REFERENCES

Bernard, H. M. (1897). The genus *Montipora*. The genus *Astreopora*. *Catalogue of the Madreporarian corals in the British Museum* (*Nat. Hist.*), **3**: 1–192.
Bernard, H. M. (1905). *Porites* of the Indopacific region. *Catalogue of the Madreporarian corals in the British Museum.* **5**: 1–303.
Boschma, H. (1928). An unusual manner of budding in *Echinopora lamellosa* (Esper). *Vidensk. Meddr. dansk naturh. Foren.* **85**: 1–6.
Brook, G. (1893). The genus *Madrepora*. *Catalogue of the Madreporarian corals in the British Museum* (*Nat. Hist.*) **1**: 1–212.
Crossland, C. (1948). Reef corals of the South African coast. *Ann. Natal Mus.* **12**(2): 169–205, pls. 5–14.

Foote, R. B. (1888). Notes on Rameswaram Island—I. *Madras Christian College Mag.* (July): 828–840.

Gardiner, J. S. (1903). The Atoll of Minicoy. In *The fauna and Geography of the Maldive and Laccadive Archipelagoes* **1**: 27–50. London: Cambridge University Press.

Gardiner, J. S. (1904). Madreporaria Pt. I. In *The fauna and Geography of the Maldive and Laccadive Archipelagoes* **2**: 755–790. London: Cambridge University Press.

Gardiner, J. S. (1905). Madreporaria Pt. II. In *The fauna and Geography of the Maldive and Laccadive Archipelagoes* **2** (suppl): 933–957. London: Cambridge University Press.

Gardiner, J. S. (1936). The reefs of the Western Indian Ocean. I. Chagos Archipelago. II. The Mascarene region. *Trans. Linn. Soc. London.* **2**: 393–436.

Gravely, F. H. (1927). Scleractinia. *Bull. Madras Govt. Mus.* (N.S.) **I**(1): 41–51.

Jayaraman, R. (1954). Seasonal variations in the salinity, dissolved oxygen and nutrient salts in the inshore waters of the Gulf of Mannar and Palk Bay near Mandapam (S. India). *Indian J. Fish.* **I**: 345–364.

Macnae, W. and Kalk, M. (eds) (1958). *A natural history of Inhaca Island, Moçambique.* Johannesburg. Witwatersrand University Press: 1–163.

Matthai, G. (1924). Report on the collection of corals in the Indian Museum, Calcutta. Pt. I. *Mem. Indian Mus.* **8**: 1–59, pls. 1–11.

Matthai, G. (1928). A monograph of the recent Meandroid Astraeidae. *Catalogue of the Madreporarian corals in the British Museum (Nat. Hist.)* **8**: 1–288.

Pichon, M. (1964). Contribution à l'étude de la répartition des Madréporaires sur le récif de Tuléar, Madagascar. *Recl. Trav. stn mar. Endoume* (fascicule hors serie) suppl. **2**: 79–293.

Pillai, C. S. Gopinadha (1969a). Studies on Indian Corals—I. Report on a new species of Montipora (Scleractinia, Acroporidae) from Gulf of Mannar. *J. mar. biol. Ass. India.* **9**(2): 399–401.

Pillai, C. S. Gopinadha (1969b). Studies on Indian corals—II. Report on a new species of *Goniopora* and three new species of *Porites* (Scleractinia, Poritidae) from the seas around India. *J. mar. biol. Ass. India.* **9**(2): 402–406.

Pillai, C. S. Gopinadha (1969c). Studies on Indian corals—V. Preliminary report on new records of hermatypic corals from the seas around India. *J. mar. biol. Ass. India.* **9**(2): 412–422.

Pillai, C. S. Gopinadha (1971). The distribution of shallow-water stony corals in the Minicoy Atoll in the Indian Ocean with a check-list of species. *Atoll Res. Bull.* **141**: 1–12.

Pillai, C. S. Gopinadha (In press, a). Distribution of corals on a reef at Mandapam (Palk Bay), South India. *J. mar. biol. Ass. India.* **11**(1).

Pillai, C. S. Gopinadha (In press, b). The coral resources of India with special references to Palk Bay and Gulf of Mannar. *Proceedings of the Symposium on the Living Resources of the Seas around India.* C.M.F.R. Institute, Mandapam Camp, December, 1968.

Prasad, R. R. (1954). Observations on the distribution and fluctuations of planktonic larvae off Mandapam. *Proc. Symposium on the marine and fresh-water plankton in the Indo-Pacific, I.P.F.C.* Bangkok. 1954: 78–91.

Prasad, R. R. (1957). Seasonal variations in the surface temperature of sea water at Mandapam from January 1950 to December 1954. *Indian J. Fish.* **4**: 20–31.

Purchon, R. D. (1956). A list of corals collected in the vicinity of Singapore. *Proc. Linn. Soc. N.S.W.* **81**: 157–158.

Rajendran, I. and David, K. (In press). A preliminary underwater survey of the extent of the coral reefs in and around some of the islands in the Gulf of Mannar. *Proc. Symposium on corals and coral reefs. Marine Biological Association of India*, Mandapam Camp, 1969.

Sewell, R. B. S. (1932). The coral coasts of India. *Geogrl. J.* **79**: 449–465.

Sewell, R. B. S. (1935). Studies on corals and coral formations of Indian waters. *Mem. Asiat. Soc. Beng.* **9**: 461–539.

Stephenson, W., Endean, R. and Bennett, I. (1958). An ecological survey of the marine fauna of Low Isles and other reefs. *Aust. J. mar. Freshwat. Res.* **9**: 261–318.

Stoddart, D. R. (1962). Catastrophic storm effects of the British Honduras Reefs and Cays. *Nature, Lond.* **196**: 512–515.

Stoddart, D. R. (1965). Resurvey of hurricane effects on the British Honduras reefs and cays. *Nature, Lond.* **207**: 589–592.

Stoddart, D. R. (In press). Regional variation in Indian Ocean coral reefs. *Proc. Symposium on corals and coral reefs.* Marine Biological Association of India Mandapam Camp. 1969.

Talbot, F. H. (1965). A description of the coral structure of the Tutia Reef (Tanganika territory, East Africa) and its fish fauna. *Proc. zool. Soc. Lond.* **145**: 431–470.

Tampi, P. R. S. (1959). The ecological and fisheries characteristics of a salt water lagoon near Mandapam. *J. mar. biol. Ass. India.* **1**: 113–130.

Thurston, E. (1895). Rameswaram Island and the fauna of Gulf of Mannar. *Bull. Madras Govt. Mus.* (2nd Ed.): 108–112.

Vaughan, T. W. and Wells, J. W. (1943). Revision of the suborders, families and genera of the Scleractinia. *Spec. Pap. geol. Soc. Am.* **44**: 1–363.

Wells, J. W. (1950). Reef corals from the Cocos-Keeling Atoll. *Bull. Raffles Mus.* **22**: 29–52.

Wells, J. W. (1954). Recent corals from the Marshall Islands. *Prof. Pap. U.S. geol. Surv.* **260–1**: 385–479.

Wells, J. W. (1956). Scleractinia. In *Treatise on invertebrate Palaeontology*: 328–443. Edit. Moore, R. C. Pt. F. Geological Society of America and the University of Kansas Press.

Wells, J. W. and Davies, P. S. (1966). Preliminary list of stony corals from Addu Atoll. *Atoll. Res. Bull.* **116**: 43–55.

Symp. zool. Soc. Lond. (1971) No. 28, 329–367

CORAL REEFS AND CORAL GENERA IN THE RED SEA AND INDIAN OCEAN

GEORG SCHEER

Hessian State Museum, Darmstadt, Germany

INTRODUCTION

In 1957–58 the author had the opportunity to visit, as a member of the second *Xarifa* Expedition (led by Dr. Hans Hass), coral reefs in the Red Sea, at the island Abd el Kuri, in the Maldive and Nicobar Islands, and in the Strait of Malacca. At approximately 100 different places about 1400 corals were collected, 870 were in the Maldives alone. Furthermore, in 1962 the author collected corals on the Wingate Reef, Red Sea, together with members of the German Underwater Club, Darmstadt. And finally, in the last few years the Hessian State Museum at Darmstadt received a number of fairly extensive collections of Red Sea corals from Dr. Eibl-Eibesfeldt, Seewiesen; Dr. Feustel, Darmstadt; Janos Hollosi, Neu-Ulm; and Dr. Schuhmacher, Heidelberg. Altogether there are some 1900 corals at the author's disposal allowing fairly reliable statements on the distribution of the coral fauna. Although the major part of the corals has not yet been analysed (it is intended that they will be determined by the author jointly with Dr. Pillai, Cochin, in 1971), the author thinks that he can now publish data on the collected coral genera together with a brief description of the investigated reefs. He was actuated to do so by the paper of Wells (1955) on the distribution of reef coral genera in the Great Barrier Reef area, then by reef studies at Addu Atoll, edited by Stoddart (1966), including the contribution of Wells and Davies (1966) on the stony corals there, and also by Stoddart's excellent survey (1969) on the ecology and morphology of Recent coral reefs.

RED SEA

The places in the Red Sea where corals were collected are shown in Fig. 1. They are specified as given below.

Gulf of Aqaba

The corals from Eilat (Dr. Feustel, Dr. Schuhmacher) comprise 21 genera. Although Eilat is situated 29°32′N there exists a remarkably

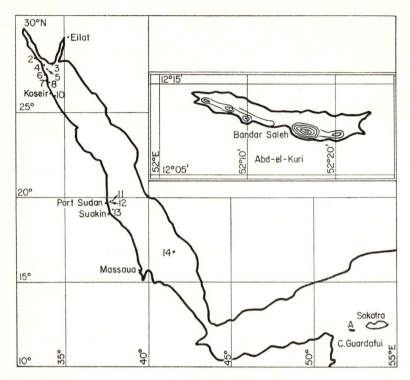

Fig. 1. Outline map of the Red Sea with collecting places. 2 = Ras Shukheir, 3 = Ras Muhammad, 4 = Gûbal Island, 5 = Shadwan Island, 6 = Ghardaqa, 7 = Ras Abu Suma, 8 = Safaga Island, 10 = Ras Abu Hagar, 11 = Sanganeb Reef, 12 = Wingate Reef, 13 = Shaab Anbar, 14 = Sarso Islands, A = Abd el Kuri. Inserted map: Abd el Kuri.

rich coral fauna due to the warm water, the reefs, however, are not very luxuriantly developed. Striking are the genera *Plerogyra* with bubble-shaped tentacles, and *Trachyphyllia*, which is firmly attached to the substratum during its youth, which occurs only in the northern part of the Red Sea and then again in the western part of the Indian Ocean, at the Nicobar Islands.

Northern Red Sea

1. In the years 1966–68 the sporting diver Janos Hollosi collected corals here at Ras Muhammad (27°43′N, 34°15′E), at the island Shadwan (27°30′N, 34°E), at Ras Abu Suma (26°51′N, 34°E), at the island Safaga (26°45′N, 33°59′E), near Koseir (26°06′N, 34°17′E), and at Ras Abu Hagar (25°58′N, 34°23′E). Remarkable are *Echinophyllia*

from the island Shadwan, *Coscinaraea* from the island Safaga as the only place where it was found, and *Pachyseris* from Koseir.

2. The second *Xarifa* Expedition dropped anchor at Ras Shukheir (28°08′N, 33°17′E), the island Gûbal (27°40′N, 33°48′E), and Hurghada (27°18′N, 33°50′E). At Ras Shukheir the sea bottom forms a very broad, flat platform which gradually descends towards the sea. After a sandy zone near the shore (Fig. 2) follows a zone with marine grasses

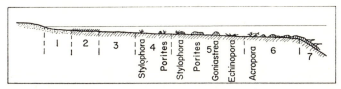

F ig. 2. Diagrammatic cross-section through the fringing reef at Ras Shukheir. 1 = Sand Zone, 2 = Zone with marine grasses, 3 = Zone with calcareous algae, 4 = Stylophora Zone, 5 = Zone with coral patches, 6 = reef flat, 7 = reef slope.

and a zone with calcareous algae, then a zone with first corals, small *Stylophora* coralla above all and some isolated *Porites*. Still farther out, at a depth of 3–4 m, the coral growth gets more intense, comprising in some scattered coral patches *Stylophora, Acropora, Porites, Goniastrea* and *Echinopora*. In the following zone up to the reef edge, lying far out, the numbers and species of corals increase continuously.

While at Ras Shukheir, mask, snorkel and fins proved sufficient for diving in the fairly shallow water of a few metres, aqualungs were necessary to collect corals at the island Gûbal. The reef dropped down extremely steeply in the bay south of Bluff Point. At a depth of 15 m lay a wreck. Here and at a depth of 9 m 25 coral genera were gathered, including among others *Echinophyllia, Mycedium* and *Plerogyra.*

Central Red Sea

1. The Wingate Reef is a barrier reef starting about 3 nautical miles off Port Sudan and first stretching to the northeast but then bending off northward. On the southeast side of the reef between 19°37′30″N, 37°17′30″E and 19°37′40″N, 37°18′E corals were collected. The top part of the reef is flat (Fig. 3), lies just below the water surface and is cemented together by calcareous algae and intersected by grooves and furrows. At the reef edge the gorges widen and deepen, thus forming isolated towers. On the reef flat only very few corals have settled; at the edges of the grooves, however, they increase in number. The towers near the reef edge and the steep, very often

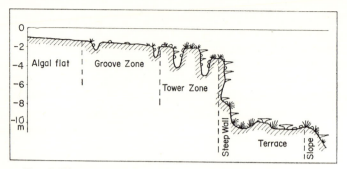

FIG. 3. Diagrammatic cross-section through the Wingate Reef.

vertical drop of the reef are densely overgrown with corals. On the whole, the genus *Acropora* is dominant. In the upper part of the reef there are low, cespitose *Acropora* species, but also *Pocillopora* is common. On the reef slope *Acropora* forms consoles, on a terrace at a depth of about 10 m broad tables and dense hedges form. Altogether 28 coral genera were collected here including *Pachyseris* and *Herpolitha;* furthermore *Podabacia, Oulophyllia* and *Diploastrea*, which were detected for the first time in the Red Sea (Scheer, 1964b), as well as *Symphyllia*. According to Vaughan and Wells (1943) *Symphyllia* does not occur in the Red Sea but Gohar (1954) found it at Al Ghardaqa.

2. Southeast of Port Sudan and east-north-east of Suakin lie the reefs of Shaab Anbar (19°18′N, 37°42′E). The northern reef in the shape of an elongated drop has the features of an atoll although it is not an atoll in the sense of Darwin. It is probably a pseudo-atoll, as described by Schäfer (1969) from the Farasan Shelf. Being better developed the outer reefs enclose a little populated lagoon with a few patch reefs. On the inner reefs 12 coral genera were collected, among them *Diploastrea*.

3. The Sanganeb Reef northeast of Port Sudan (19°45′N, 37°26′E) gives evidence of the fact that there are also genuine atolls in the Red Sea. It extends in a north-south direction over about 3 nautical miles with a maximum width of about one nautical mile. On its southern-most tip there stands a lighthouse. The southern part of the atoll is separated from the main part by a transverse reef, so that there are two lagoons of different sizes. Some corals originate from this reef, too (collected by Dr. Eibl-Eibesfeldt).

Southern Red Sea

1. In the northwest of the Farasan group lie the two Sarso Islands (16°53′N, 41°32′E), elevated reefs whose origin probably dates back

to the early Pleistocene (Fig. 4 + inserted map). On their surface there are eroded corals and their steep slopes show sub-fossil coralla still in position of growth. Before both islands there are abrasion terraces separated from each other by a channel of about 1·4 km wide and about 100 m deep. The recent reefs have developed on the terraces. The physiographic zonation of these fringing reefs has been described in detail by Klausewitz (1967). Figure 4 shows his results somewhat modified by my own records. Both he and Prof. Schäfer, as members of the *Meteor* Expedition 1964, collected corals there which have already been described together with those found by the author (Scheer 1967). There are altogether 20 genera, including *Psammocora* and *Plerogyra* which should be especially mentioned. It is striking that only a single specimen of *Pocillopora* was found, as normally it occurs very frequently on Red Sea reefs.

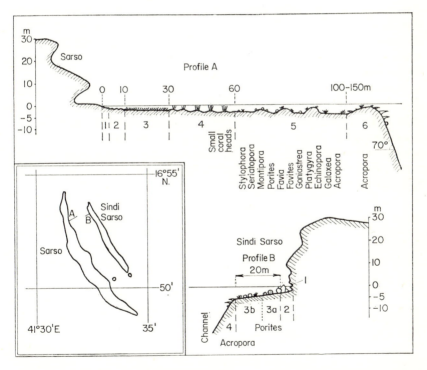

FIG. 4. Reef profiles of Sarso Islands. Section A: 1 = Sand Zone, 2 = bumpy abrasion terrace, 3 = Sand-mud Zone with marine grasses, 4 = Tang wood Zone, 5 = fore-reef with sandfields, 6 = main reef. Section B: 1 = furrow, 2 = Submerged Zone with steep wall and boulders, 3 = basic terrace, 3a = Zone with living Porites, 3b = Zone with dead Porites, 4 = outer slope. Inserted map: Sarso Islands.

2. In 1965, Hollosi collected a number of corals in the bay of Massaua, altogether there were 18 genera with *Siderastrea* and *Echinophyllia* especially conspicuous. It is remarkable that in this collection, too, there is a complete lack of *Pocillopora*.

Summary for the Red Sea

At the end of this paper the coral genera found at the various places or in the various areas are specified in a table. Altogether 39 genera were recorded from the Red Sea.

ABD EL KURI

Between the eastern point of Africa, Cape Guardafui, and the island Sokotra, Abd el Kuri (12°10′N, 52°15′E) is situated (Fig. 1 + inserted map). Both islands rise from a basement that is connected with the African mainland under the sea-bottom. On Abd el Kuri there are two mountains, Djebel Somali, 269 m, and Djebel Saleh, 743 m. These mountains as well as those of Sokotra consist of Precambrian rock similar to the rocks of the east African Somali Plateau. The rocky slope of Djebel Saleh continues under water with the same steepness in the bay Bandar Saleh on the southern side of the island. A coral reef could not develop here. The reason for this is probably cold water rising from great depths between Cape Guardafui and the equator at the Somali coast. This is why one finds only few coral genera here which grow on the rock covered with algae (Scheer 1964a). Altogether 9 genera were collected (see table at the end of this paper).

MALDIVE ISLANDS

Between the end of December, 1957 and the end of April, 1958 a number of atolls in the Maldives were visited during the second *Xarifa* Expedition (Fig. 5) starting in the south with Addu Atoll.

Addu Atoll

Fig. 6 shows the western part of Addu Atoll indicating the places where corals were found.

Inner reefs on the west side of the lagoon.

(a) The reef flat off the southern tip of Hitaddu (the partition between the two islands Hitaddu and Abuhera at 0°37′46″S could still be established quite clearly) has a width of about 1300 m. A survey along a guide-line normal to the coast resulted in the following

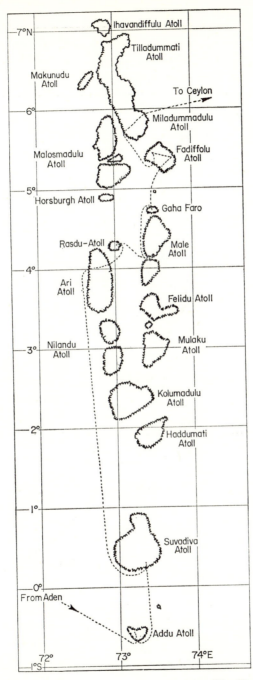

Fig. 5. Outline map of the Maldive Islands with the route of the *Xarifa* Expedition.

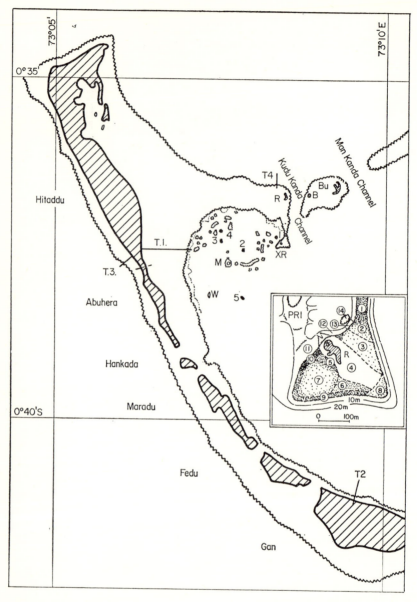

FIG. 6. Western part of Addu Atoll. T1, 2, 3, and 4 = transects 1–4; 1, 2, 3,4 , and 5 = patch reefs 1–5; M = Mini-Atoll; W = wreck; Bu = Bushy Islet; B = Bird Island; R = Rubble Island; XR = Xarifa Reef. Inserted map: Xarifa Reef with division into zones. 1–14 = zones 1–14; R = Rubble Islet; PR 1 = patch reef 1.

picture. The sandy beach skirting the island continues as a very wide sandy zone which is partly covered with marine grasses. Then coral growth starts, at first very loosely with great sandy patches in between, then getting denser and denser towards the edge of the reef flat. From the shore the sandy zone slopes gradually down to a depth of 4–5 m, where the corals start to grow the water depth decreases again to reach a depth of only about 1 m at the reef edge. The reef slope starts to slant down at an angle of about 45°, then flattens out to reach the lagoon floor at a depth of about 20 m here. The dominant coral genus is *Acropora* with several species. On the reef flat *Stylophora* and *Pocillopora* also occur frequently.

On a sandy patch there lay some *Goniopora* corals with their polyps extended even in daytime. One of them had brought forth ball-shaped structures. When touching one of these balls it became evident that within it a daughter colony was developing, the calcareous skeleton of which was not connected to the mother skeleton (Scheer, 1959, 1960). Rosen and Taylor (1969) have also reported such an "Ableger" coral in the lagoon of Aldabra.

(b) Off the island of Gan the reef flat on the lagoon side has only a width of about 100 m. The coral growth is similar to that at Hitaddu. On the reef slope, flat corals, such as *Echinopora*, *Echinophyllia*, and *Mycedium*, but also *Halomitra*, are fairly common. Altogether 26 coral genera were gathered on the western inner reefs.

Outer reef on the west side of the atoll

South of the island of Hitaddu lies a platform, 200 m wide and cemented together by calcareous algae and secreted calcium carbonate, on which some *Heliopora* and scattered corals grow. To some extent these corals are dead in their upper parts and form "micro-atolls". The platform ends with a low algal ridge. Adjacent to it is a zone with a shallow groove-and-spur system. This zone, showing only few corals, has a width of about 100 m and slopes down to 8 m. It is followed by a zone with an approximate width of 50 m, sloping down to about 18 m and bearing dispersed corals. A further somewhat more inclined zone with *Halimeda* and other calcareous algae leads to an almost flat terrace in a depth of 40–45 m.

On the western outer reefs only 9 coral genera were collected.

Outer reef on the north side of the atoll

The reef flat covered with sand and rubble and a loose overgrowth of small *Acropora* bushes and *Pocillopora*, *Porites* and *Millepora* joins, at a depth of 6 m, the reef edge that is densely overgrown with table-, hedge- and plate-shaped corals of the genera *Montipora*, *Pachyseris*, *Echinophyllia*, and *Mycedium* besides Gorgonians and Alcyonarians. (Diving descent of Hass, to a depth of 60 m.)

Northern reef flat

The northern reef flat is intersected by two channels: the Kudu Kanda Channel and the Man Kanda Channel. It is covered with sand and shows no major islands between Hitaddu in the west and Midu in the east. In its central part between the two channels lies, towards the east, "Bushy Islet". This small island, where some trees and bushes grow, is a breeding place of numerous Common Noddies and Black-Naped Terns (*Anous stolidus* and *Sterna sumatrana*). In the west of this central part the "Bird Island" is situated with a surface of only 90 × 60 m and made up exclusively of coral fragments. We called it "Bird Island" because it serves the sea swallows as a moulting place. Directly opposite, on the other side of the Kudu Kanda Channel, lies another island, elongated and hook-shaped, which we called "Rubble Island" as it consists entirely of coral debris similar to the "Bird Island". Already three bushes were growing on this island. The British Admiralty Chart No. 2067 of 1957 still shows three islets here whereas in the sea map of 1964 only one island is drawn. As this "Rubble Island" will probably be subject to many more changes I want to describe its shape as it was when I surveyed it in January, 1958 (Fig. 7). Off the northwest tip of the island there is a sandbank, 70 × 40 m, which at normal high tide remains just about dry, whereas one south of the island emerges at low tide. The southern edge of the island lies 1·40 m above mean sea level. From its western point a rubble slope descends down to a depth of 6 m. The island is surrounded by sand and coral fragments with a few fragile-branching *Acropora* hedges and *Porites* micro-atolls. Here and there on the reef flat there are reef patches with a great variety of species. In between there are also some interspersed patches overgrown with Alcyonarians. Altogether 20 coral genera were found on the reef flat.

The "Xarifa Reef"

South of the "Rubble Island" the reef flat has a peculiar hook-shaped extension into the lagoon. Its shape is due to the strong currents. At high tide, the flood stream sets into the lagoon through the Kudu Kanda Channel and hits the tip of the reef flat particularly when the northeast monsoon is blowing. At low tide the current has the opposite direction. Both the flood stream and the ebb stream set out through the Man Kanda Channel from the lagoon into the open sea. The

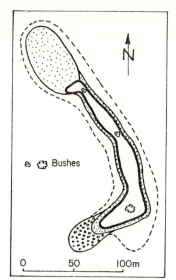

Fig. 7. "Rubble Island" on the northern reef flat of Addu Atoll, surveyed on 25th January, 1958.

southern end of the extension broadens to a triangular reef which we called "Xarifa Reef". In 1969 at the Symposium on Corals and Coral Reefs at Mandapam Camp I have already given a detailed account of this reef (Scheer, in press) so that a brief description may suffice here.

The "Xarifa Reef" (Fig. 6, inserted map) is, in its western and southern parts, densely covered with corals. The eastern and central parts consist of a rubble area made up of coral fragments blanketed with calcareous algae. The reef is connected to the reef flat through a narrow ridge, 100% overgrown with corals. In this Zone 1 *Acropora*, then *Pocillopora* and *Stylophora* are dominant. The ridge widens and continues as Zone 2 which lies 1–2 m below the water level and whose coral growth diminishes to the south from 70 to 10–20%. The adjacent Zone 3, characterized by a strong current from the channel, consists of broken corals on which a few small coralla grow. No coral fauna at all exists in Zone 4 as the coral fragments are constantly moved by breakers. In the western part of the reef the coral rubble has piled up to form the "Rubble Islet". At normal low tide its outlines correspond to those indicated in the inserted map, whereas at normal high tide it is completely submerged except for a small dome in the northwest. According to natives this island appeared for the first time only recently. The coral debris of Zone 4 advances and buries the live corals of Zones 5 and 6, thus killing them. Zone 8, constituting the east point of the reef, slopes gently down from 2 to 6 m at an angle of 8°. It is overgrown with corals to about 50% of its surface, mainly *Acropora* species with some few *Pocillopora* bushes. The marginal Zones 9 and 10 are densely overgrown, predominantly with *Acropora* species. The enclosed Zone 7 lies about 3–4 m deep, Zone 6 about 2–3 m, Zones 5 and 9 about 2 m, whereas Zone 10 reaches nearly up to the water surface. The northwest slope of the reef, extending down to a depth of 10–12 m, with Zones 11 and 12, is richly overgrown with a great variety of coral species. Zone 13 constitutes a rubble field with only half of its surface covered with small coralla. Zone 14 is a huge *Echinopora* field in a depth of about 12 m. Below the island, Zone 4 continues as a rubble slope. The reef slopes on all sides descend to the lagoon floor at an angle of about 45°. Sample plots, measuring 2 by 2 m, give information about the coral genera of the various zones:

Zone 2: rubble 40%

−1·5 m live corals 60%

Acropora, tables	30%
Acropora cf. *humilis*	10
Acropora, bushes	10
Acropora, other spec.	1
Pocillopora	7
Stylophora	
Pavona	
Goniastrea	2
Platygyra	

Acropora, bushes	10
Stylophora	1
Montipora	1
Porites	1
Psammocora	
Pavona	
Favites	
Merulina	2
Echinophyllia	
Oxypora	
Euphyllia	

Zone 3: rubble 80%

NW-edge live corals 20%

−1–2 m

Acropora, tables	10%
Acropora, bushes	6
Stylophora	2
Seriatopora	
Pocillopora	2

Zone 3: rubble 90%

centre live corals 10%

−1·5 m

Acropora cf. *humilis*	5%
Acropora, bushes	3
Acropora, other spec.	1
Pocillopora	1

Zone 3: rubble 70%

E-edge live corals 30%

−1–2 m *Acropora*, tables 15%

Zone 4: rubble; coral fragments encrusted with calcareous algae 100%

Zone 5: sand 10%

−2 m live corals 90%

Acropora cf. *humilis*	30%
Acropora, elkhorn	20
Acropora, tables	15
Acropora, bushes	5
Acropora hemprichi	5
Acropora palifera	2
Millepora	5
Stylophora	2
Pocillopora	2

Pavona	
Fungia	
Porites	
Favia	
Goniastrea	4
Leptoria	
Hydnophora	
Cyphastrea	
Galaxea]	
Lobophyllia	

Zone 6: rubble and sand 30 %
−3 m live corals 70 %

Acropora, elkhorn	20 %
Acropora hemprichi	15
Acropora, tables	10
Acropora cf. humilis	5
Acropora, bushes	5
Acropora, other spec.	5
Pocillopora	4
Echinopora	3
Stylophora	2
Seriatopora	1

Zone 7: rubble 40 %
−4 m sand 10 %
live corals 50 %

Acropora, elkhorn	18 %
Acropora, tables	18
Acropora cf. humilis	5
Acropora hemprichi	3
Acropora, bushes	2
Psammocora	
Pocillopora	
Montipora	
Porites	
Favia	
Goniastrea	4
Platygyra	
Leptoria	
Echinopora	
Galaxea	
Lobophyllia	

Zone 7: rubble 30 %
−4 m sand 20 %
live corals 50 %

Acropora, tables	20 %
Acropora, elkhorn	12
Acropora hemprichi	5
Acropora, bushes	5
Acropora cf. humilis	3
Stylophora	
Pocillopora	
Montipora	
Pavona	
Fungia	5
Goniastrea	
Platygyra	
Echinopora	
Galaxea	
Millepora	

Zone 8: rubble 50 %
−5 m live corals 50 %

Acropora, hedges	35 %
Acropora, tables	10
Acropora hemprichi	3
Pocillopora	2

Zone 9: dead corals 10 %
S-side live corals 90 %
−1·5 m

Acropora, hedges	50 %
Acropora, tables	15
Acropora, elkhorn	10
Acropora hemprichi	5
Acropora cf. humilis	5
Acropora palifera	2
Pocillopora	3
Psammocora	+

Zone 10: live corals 100 %
−0·5 m

Acropora, elkhorn	40 %
Acropora, hedges	20
Acropora, tables	15
Acropora cf. humilis	15
Acropora, other spec.	5
Pocillopora	2
Goniastrea	2
Leptoria	1

Zone 12: live corals 100 %
−2–3 m

Acropora, hedges	60 %

Acropora, hemprichi	15
Acropora, elkhorn	10
Acropora, bushes	4
Acropora cf. humilis	3
Acropora, tables	3
Acropora palifera	1
Echinopora	2
Stylophora	1
Pocillopora	1

| Zone 12: | dead corals | 10% |
| −6 m | live corals | 90% |

Echinopora	35%
Acropora, elkhorn	15
Acropora, hedges	14
Acropora, tables	7
Acropora hemprichi	5
Acropora cf. humilis	4
Acropora, other spec.	2
Seriatopora	2
Stylophora *Pocillopora*	2
Psammocora *Fungia* *Goniastrea* *Platygyra* *Galaxea*	4

| Zone 12: | dead corals | 10% |
| −7 m | live corals | 90% |

Echinopora	25%
Acropora, elkhorn	20
Acropora, hedges	15
Acropora, tables	10
Acropora hemprichi	5
Acropora, other spec.	5
Stylophora *Seriatopora* *Pocillopora*	5
Pavona *Fungia* *Goniopora* *Porites* *Oulophyllia* *Favia* *Goniastrea* *Platygyra* *Hydnophora* *Galaxea*	5

Zone 12:	dead corals	15%
−12 m	rubble and sand	15%
	live corals	70%

Acropora	30%
Porites	10
Echinopora	10
Stylophora	5
Pocillopora	5
Montipora	5
Fungia	5
Favia	5
Favites	5
Goniastrea	5
Platygyra	5
Lobophyllia	5
Pavona *Hydnophora* *Echinophyllia* *Mycedium* *Plerogyra*	5

Zone 12:	rubble	40%
below	live corals	60%
rubble		
slope	*Acropora,* hedges	25%
−10 m	*Acropora,* tables	10
	Acropora hemprichi	10
	Acropora palifera	5
	Echinopora	3
	Stylophora	1
	Fungia	1
	Goniastrea	1
	Seriatopora *Pavona* *Porites* *Platygyra* *Galaxea*	4

| Zone 13: | rubble | 50% |
| −3 m | live corals | 50% |

Acropora	40%
Pocillopora	6
Stylophora *Porites* *Goniastrea* *Platygyra* *Mycedium*	4

| Zone 14: | live corals | 100% |
| −12 m | | |

Echinopora	100%

Altogether 29 coral genera were collected on the "Xarifa Reef".

Patch reefs

The coral knolls, occuring at Addu Atoll in the northeast and especially the northwest of the lagoon, are highly interesting reef formations. They rise from the bottom of the lagoon and reach the surface only in rare cases. Generally they are a little below it. Their tops are often flattened (platform reefs). Coral knolls in greater depths usually have an arched surface (knoll reefs). Investigations were carried out on patch reefs Nos. 1, 2, 3, 4 and 5 (Fig. 6) as well as on a bigger reef, measuring about 120 by 90 m, with a flattened top and a lagoon-like depression, which was not covered with corals and measured about 60 m in diam. This reef was called "mini-atoll". As I have already spoken about this mini-atoll and about patch reefs at the Symposium at Mandapam Camp I want to describe here as an example of patch reefs only No. 2 (Fig. 8).

The reef extends in a north/south direction, has a length of about 20 m and a width of about 8 m, and its top lies in a depth of 6–7 m. Its surface Zone 1 is only sparsely covered with corals, less in the centre, more towards the edge. The inclinations of the reef slopes can be seen from the cross-section and the longitudinal section which were surveyed by Hass. Zone 2 of the west slope is covered with sand and coral fragments and overgrown with corals to only about 15%, namely with *Acropora hemprichi*, small bush-shaped *Acropora* and *Porites*. Along the cross-section coral growth increases slightly in a depth of 12 m, between 12 and 16 m there are bigger *Acropora* hedges. Between 16 and 28 m no corals could be found. At a depth of 28 m, at the beginning of the flat part of the slope, one *Lobophyllia* was growing, another one on the even oozy ground at a depth of 32 m. This specimen measured 1·5 m in diam. Zone 3 is a little more overgrown than the upper part of Zone 2, above all table-shaped *Acropora* appear additionally. Zone 4 is covered to 70% with different *Acropora* species. Zone 5 corresponds roughly to Zone 3 with 60% sand and rubble and about 40% *Acropora* at a depth of 6 to 14 m; below are sand and debris. At a depth of 12 m there is a small terrace which stretches around the southern part of the patch reef and is covered with some *Echinopora* plates. In Zone 6, down to the small terrace in 12 m, there grow *Acropora hemprichi* and other *Acropora* species. On the terrace there is *Echinopora*. Below it, down to 18 m, the slope descends somewhat more steeply and is bare. At a depth of 18 m a flat platform, 26 m long and 90% populated with corals, extends towards the south. The coral fauna here includes *Acropora* tables and various *Acropora* species, furthermore *Fungia*, *Porites*, *Favia*, *Platygyra*, *Lobophyllia*, *Pectinia* and *Euphyllia*. Remarkable were two *Cycloseris* which appeared

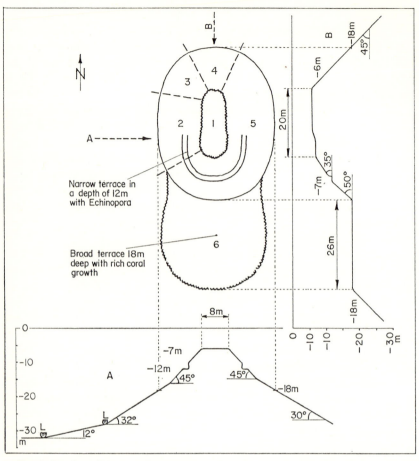

Fig. 8. Patch reef No. 2 in the northwest of the lagoon of Addu Atoll. 1–6 = Zones of different coral growth, L = *Lobophyllia*.

brilliant red under water, a fact which we noticed only when diving up to the surface again due to the absorption of the long-wave colours. The slope of this reef flat towards the lagoon floor was not surveyed.

Altogether 24 coral genera were collected on the various patch reefs and the mini-atoll.

Wrecked tanker

Mention should be made of a wrecked tanker at Addu Atoll that was sunk in 1944. The wreck lies off the island Abuhera and is remarkable for its coral growth. The tanker rests on its starboard side, its bottom forming an angle of 78° with the lagoon floor. In this some-what darker region *Dendrophyllia* and *Plerogyra* were found besides Gorgonians. The light-coloured top part and the super-structures of the wreck were overgrown to a greater extent. Conspicuous were large goblet-shaped *Turbinaria*, one of them measuring 18 cm in length and weighing 1000 g, and *Plerogyra* the tentacles of which looked like ball-shaped bubbles. Remarkable, too was a table-shaped *Acropora* with a diameter of 90 cm. This coral could not be more than 14 years old. Furthermore the following genera were collected: *Psammocora, Pocillopora, Acropora, Fungia, Porites, Favia, Favites, Goniastrea, Platygyra, Acanthastrea, Parascolymia (Acanthophyllia)* and *Euphyllia*, altogether 15 genera.

Summary for Addu Atoll

This is to conclude the survey on Addu Atoll where the *Xarifa* anchored from 21st December, 1957 to 8th February, 1958. In total, 42 coral genera were gathered at Addu Atoll.

Suvadiva Atoll

For a short time only the *Xarifa* dropped anchor at Suvadiva Atoll, which is one of the largest atolls with a diameter of 65 km. While flying over the Maldive Islands, Dr. Hass discovered a wreck on the reef flat in the south of the atoll (Hass, 1961, page 84). The surge channels intersecting the reef flat were of a black colour between wreck and lagoon and white between wreck and open sea. As we found out when diving the sunken ship had carried granite stones as ballast. These stones were pushed in the surge channels towards the lagoon by the approaching waves, while the channels towards the open sea remained clear and showed a light-coloured sandy surface.

Comparatively few corals were found near the wreck at a depth of 4–5 m. *Pocillopora elegans* and *damicornis* dominated, then *Acropora cf. humilis, A. hemprichi* and other species; finally, there were also *Montipora, Leptoseris, Favia, Favites, Goniastrea, Platygyra* and *Leptastrea*, altogether 9 genera.

Ari Atoll

The next anchoring place of the *Xarifa* was Ari Atoll. The reef flat, which in the case of Addu Atoll leads right round the lagoon only intersected by four channels, is in the case of Ari Atoll split into many small atolls surrounding the lagoon. Gardiner (1903, page 155) proposed to call these miniature atolls "faros". Both "faro" and "atoll" are Maldivian expressions. The lagoon of a faro is termed "velu".

A great number of such faros exists also in the lagoon of Ari Atoll. Figure 9 shows a section of the northern part of the atoll.

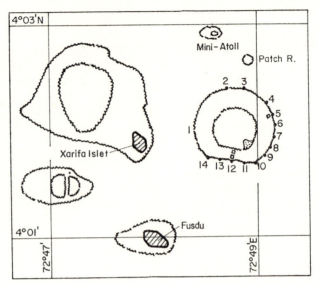

FIG. 9. Faros in the lagoon of Ari Atoll. 1–14 = observing points on the slope of the circular Faro.

(a) I have already reported on the elongated faro with its cross-divided lagoon at the Symposium at Mandapam Camp. The almost circular faro with a diameter of about 1·4 km was investigated in the following way. We drove slowly along the edge of the reef in a boat. Hass, in the water, clung to the boat and reported on the state of the reef slope. I was in the boat, operating the engine, steering and taking notes. At specific points we dropped anchor and I went into the water as well. We moved round the faro in a clockwise direction, starting from the west. Here is a concise summary of the results:

1. West slope covered with broken coral and sand, about 15% live corals, above all *Porites* and *Millepora*. Gradient of the slope about 40°.

2. Coral fragments of *Acropora*. *Millepora* increasing.

3. Dead *Acropora* hedges with sandy patches in between. Live *Porites* and *Millepora*. Gradient about 40°.

4. Live *Porites* and *Millepora* only very rarely. Apart from that only dead *Acropora* hedges with sandy areas in between.

5. Slope still dead. Gradient about 35°. At reef edge sample plot 5 × 5 m, depth 2 m:

dead corals	50%
live corals	50%
Millepora, branching	20%
Millepora, flat	10
Pocillopora	7
Goniastrea	4
Porites	3
Acropora cf. *humilis*	3
Psammocora	
Acropora	
Fungia	
Goniopora	
Platygyra	3
Leptoria	
Galaxea	
Lobophyllia	
Turbinaria	

6. Slope as before, at 20 m big *Porites* specimen.

7. More *Millepora*.

8. Small local rubble slope; otherwise as before, dead *Acropora* with live *Millepora* and *Porites* in between. A few *Porites* coralla, 3 m high and hollowed out from below.

9. No more *Acropora*, only *Porites* and *Millepora*.

10. Gradient 45°. *Porites* and *Millepora*.

11. Steep drop. In its upper part *Porites*, *Millepora* and dead *Acropora*.

Between 11 and 12 small gorge.

12. Steep drop with grotto. Survey of the profile. Gradient to 9 m 75°, then vertical wall to 20 m. At a depth of 18 m a 4 m high and 2·8 m deep grotto, to 30 m 40° slope with rubble, sand and some coralla, then sandy slope of 20°, finally 10° to the lagoon floor at a depth of 45 m. Corals from this and a neighbouring grotto at a depth of 15 m: *Montipora*, *Leptoseris*, *Pachyseris*, *Goniastrea*, *Leptastrea*, *Cyphastrea*, *Echinopora*, *Physogyra*, *Balanophyllia*, *Dendrophyllia*, *Tubastrea*.

Distribution of corals in a sample plot, 5 × 5 m, at the reef edge, depth 1·5 m:

dead corals	80%
live corals	20%

Pocillopora	6%
Porites	5
Acropora, elkhorn	5
Acropora cf. humilis	1
Goniastrea	1
Millepora	1
Psammocora	
Parahalomitra	1
Platygyra	

The distance between reef edge and velu, that is the lagoon of the faro, is about 150 m here in the south. About 30 m away from the lagoon another sample plot of 5 × 5 m, depth 1·5 m:

sand	20%
dead corals	30%
live corals	50%
Acropora, hedges	20%
Acropora hemprichi	5
Acropora, elkhorn	5
Acropora cf. humilis	5
Acropora palifera	5
Pocillopora	4
Porites	3
Montipora	
Fungia	
Parahalomitra	3
Goniastrea	
Platygyra	

The lagoon has a depth of approximately 14 m and a diameter of about 800 m. On its southeast side sand has accumulated.

13. Steep drop. Further grottoes.

14. End of steep drop, beginning of normal slope with a gradient of 45°. Presumably the whole southern part of the faro between 10 and 14 had once broken off and slid down into the depth.

(b) North of the circular faro there is a small faro which would better be termed mini-atoll. Perhaps it is useful here to comment briefly on the order of magnitude of diameter of atoll-like formations: micro-atoll 1 m, patch reef 10 m, mini-atoll 100 m, faro 1000 m, atoll 10 000 m.

The mini-atoll to be considered now has a size of about 400 × 200 m and extends in an east/west direction (Fig. 10). It was roughly surveyed by Hass and me swimming along in different directions.

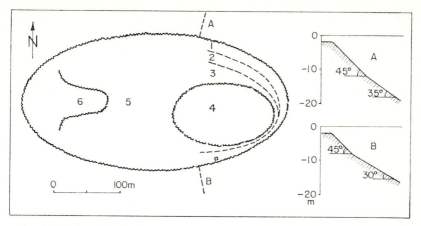

Fig. 10. Mini-atoll in the lagoon of Ari Atoll. 1 = Zone with living corals, 2 = plate, cemented through calcareous algae, 3 = Zone with coral debris, 4 = Velu with big *Porites* in the centre, 5 = Zone with live and dead corals, 6 = tongue of coral debris; A = profile north slope, B = profile south slope.

The 5·5 m deep velu or lagoon, measuring 150 × 90 m, is located to the southeast. Zone 1 consists of living corals, Zone 2 is a platform cemented together by calcareous algae, whereas Zone 3 shows coral fragments. Zone 4 is constituted by the lagoon, Zone 6 is a 30–50 m wide tongue consisting of coral fragments coated with calcareous algae and partly cemented together, which advances over the live and dead corals of Zone 5. In the south of the mini-atoll a sample plot of 5 × 5 m at a depth of 1·5 m was examined:

dead corals	20%
live corals	80%
Acropora, hedges	40%
Acropora cf. humilis	10
Pocillopora	10
Porites	5
Platygyra	5
Goniastrea	4
Favia	3
Acropora, elkhorn	2
Psammocora *Pavona*	1

Summary for Ari Atoll

A total of 32 coral genera was collected at Ari Atoll.

Rasdu Atoll

Rasdu Atoll is situated east of the northern point of Ari Atoll. It possesses an ideal circular reef shape and has a diameter of about 9 km. In its south there are three islands, two of them are inhabited. A fourth island, Weligandu, lies in the east and is narrow and elongated and uninhabited. On the lagoon reef as well as on the seaward reef at Weligandu, sample plots were investigated with methods taken from phytosociology.

1. Plant sociologists characterize a plant species within a community by two figures, the first indicating the abundance or dominance or, in brief, the quantity; the second, separated from the first by a point, the sociability. In order to examine a plant community sample quadrats are chosen. The same procedure was adopted for the investigation of a coral reef.

(a) To determine the size of the sampling plot the number of coral species was counted in an area with progressively increasing size. There were in $0 \cdot 1 \, \mathrm{m}^2$: 0 species; $0 \cdot 25 \, \mathrm{m}^2$: 2 species; $0 \cdot 5 \, \mathrm{m}^2$: 3 species; $1 \, \mathrm{m}^2$: 7; $2 \, \mathrm{m}^2$: 12; $4 \, \mathrm{m}^2$: 17; $10 \, \mathrm{m}^2$: 25; $25 \, \mathrm{m}^2$: 33; $50 \, \mathrm{m}^2$: 38; $72 \, \mathrm{m}^2$: 41; $100 \, \mathrm{m}^2$: 44 species. Expressed in a graph, that is plotting species number against quadrat size, these data produce a curve which approaches asymptotically a final value. From this curve it may be concluded that a sampling plot of $25 \, \mathrm{m}^2$ is most suitable, best in the shape of a square of 5×5 m.

(b) The quantity of the different coral species in the sample plot is estimated according to the following classification:

r a few isolated specimens, coverage negligible

+ sparsely present, coverage low

1 more frequently present though covering less than 5% of sample plot (i.e. $1 \cdot 25 \, \mathrm{m}^2$), or only isolated with the same coverage

2 abundant, or covering 5–25% of sample plot ($1 \cdot 25$–6 m^2)

3 any number of specimens, covering 25–50% of sample plot

4 any number, covering 50–75% of sample plot

5 any number, covering 75–100% of sample plot.

(c) For the sociability the following classification was chosen:

1 small isolated coralla or isolated solitary corals

2 small coralla or solitary corals growing in small groups or forming patches of the size of a hand (about 10×20 cm or circle with 16 cm diameter)

3 small coralla growing in troops, forming small hedges or patches of $0 \cdot 20$–$0 \cdot 4 \, \mathrm{m}^2$ (up to 65×65 cm or 70 cm diameter)

4 coralla of $0 \cdot 7$–2 m diameter, or hedges and patches of $0 \cdot 4$–4 m^2

5 coralla larger than 2 m diameter, or hedges and patches bigger than 4 m².

Such a coral sociology is discussed in detail by Scheer (in press), see also Vasseur (1964).

2. First of all the inner reef off Weligandu was examined. On the almost level reef flat (inclination 5°) six sample squares were selected near the reef edge at a depth of 1–2 m. The corals found there were entered in a table together with their characteristic values and arranged according to their abundance-dominance. As could be expected the six plots showed very similar results both in terms of composition and species number. The following coral genera and species, in the order of their frequency, were found: *Acropora* cf. *humilis*, *Acropora hemprichi*, other *Acropora* species, *Porites*, *Echinopora*, *Goniastrea*, *Pavona*, *Pocillopora*, *Psammocora*, *Leptoria*, *Fungia*, *Galaxea*, *Favites*, *Platygyra*, *Favia*, *Lobophyllia*, *Cyphastrea*, *Stylophora*, *Goniopora*, *Astreopora*, *Montipora*, *Merulina*, *Leptastrea*.

Two further sample plots, a little deeper (3–4 m) and somewhat more inclined (15–20°), yielded, however, slightly different results. The order of coral genera is now as follows: *Porites*, *Echinopora*, elkhorn-*Acropora*, *Acropora* cf. *humilis*, *Acropora hemprichi*, other *Acropora* species, *Pavona*, *Favites*, *Pocillopora*, *Goniastrea*, *Fungia*, *Lobophyllia*, *Cyphastrea*, *Favia*, *Symphyllia*, *Stylophora*, *Platygyra*, *Diploastrea*, *Montipora*, *Hydnophora*, *Caulastrea*.

3. In the same way four sample squares were investigated at the reef edge of the outer reef off Weligandu at a depth of 1–2 m. Again, the genera of the collected corals in the order of their frequency are: *Porites*, *Pocillopora*, *Acropora* cf. *humilis*, *Millepora*, *Acropora palifera*, other *Acropora* species, *Leptoria*, *Favites*, *Lobophyllia*, *Goniastrea*, *Psammocora*, *Galaxea*, *Fungia*, *Favia*, *Hydnophora*, *Echinopora*, *Platygyra*, *Pavona*, *Montipora*, *Astreopora*, *Leptastrea*.

By the way, the outer reef dropped down very steeply here and was only interrupted between 40 and 45 m by a terrace measuring about 30 m in width.

4. A collection of corals from the lagoon bottom at a depth of 35 m, which was 85% covered with sand and mud and bore coral patches, showed completely different results. According to their frequency, the following coral genera were found in a sampling plot of 20 × 20 m: *Leptoseris*, *Echinophyllia*, *Goniopora*, *Mycedium*, *Pachyseris*, *Acropora*, *Caulastrea*, *Alveopora*, *Symphyllia*, *Turbinaria*, *Oxypora*, *Pocillopora*, *Pavona*, *Herpolitha*, *Halomitra*, *Favia*, *Favites*, *Galaxea*, *Acanthastrea*, *Parascolymia*, *Physophyllia*, *Euphyllia*, *Plerogyra*.

The *Goniopora* collected proved to be again "Ableger" corals like those from the inner reef at Hitaddu. The formation of "Ableger" is likely to be a means of adaptation to life on sandy and oozy grounds. Another interesting fact is that one of the coral patches, measuring 5 m in height, thus already forming a knoll reef, consisted of 50% *Halomitra*.

Summary for Rasdu Atoll

Altogether 39 coral genera were found at Rasdu Atoll.

Gaha Faro

North of Male Atoll, separated by a channel, the small atoll Gaha Faro is situated. Its size is 8 × 15 km, its largest extension is in an east/west direction. On the reef flat, across which run two narrow channels, one in the northeast, the other in the northwest, there lies only one island, Gafaru, which is inhabited.

At this atoll some corals were collected at a wreck on the seaward reef; above all, however, a patch reef in the lagoon was surveyed, and the most important corals were identified (Fig. 11). The flattened surface of the patch reef measures 12 × 17 m. The edge of this surface is covered with 80% living corals and it lies 1·5 m deep. It contains a field of about 8 m diameter which shows only 30% live corals, the other 70% are dead corals, coral fragments and sand. The sandy ground lies at a depth of 2·5 m. The reef gives the impression of a minute atoll with a lagoon.

At areas 1–8 the following coral genera were collected:

Area 1: *Porites*
—1·5 m table-shaped *Acropora*
       Acropora cf. humilis
       Pocillopora
Area 2: table-shaped *Acropora*
—3 m   *Echinopora*
       Lobophyllia
       Podabacia

Area 3: elkhorn-*Acropora*
—2 m   *Leptoria*
       Platygyra
       Favites
       Millepora

Area 4: *Porites*
—1·5 m *Acropora*
       Favia
       Goniastrea

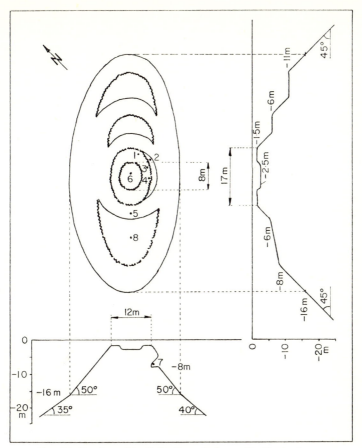

FIG. 11. Patch reef in Gaha Faro. 1–8 = collecting points.

Area 5: *Diploastrea,* covering a great area
−3 m table-shaped *Acropora*
   Porites
   Goniastrea
   Echinopora
   Symphyllia

Area 6: *Acropora palifera*
−2·5 m *Acropora* cf. *humilis*
   Acropora, small tables
   Platygyra
   Leptoria
   Pocillopora
   Porites
   Fungia

Lobophyllia
Symphyllia
Goniopora

Area 7: *Dendrophyllia*
−7 m

Area 8: area overgrown to 90%,
−7 m   *Acropora* species dominant
        Pocillopora
        Fungia
        Halomitra
        Parahalomitra
        Porites
        Favia
        Favites
        Goniastrea
        Platygyra
        Leptorir
        Leptastrea
        Echinopora
        Lobophyllia
        Plerogyra

Altogether 22 coral genera were found at the atoll Gaha Faro.

Fadiffolu Atoll

The next anchorage-ground of the *Xarifa* Expedition was
Fadiffolu Atoll north of Gaha Faro. At the island Madewaru in the
west of the atoll, some growth records were made on the inner reef,
using the method of coral sociology. The reef of a width of about
300 m presents the usual zonation. From island to lagoon first a
sandy zone, then sand with marine grasses, then first corals in small
patches on the sand, finally increasing coral growth up to the edge of
the reef.

A sample plot of 5 × 5 m on the reef flat at a depth of 1–2 m
and at a distance from the reef edge of 20 m produced the following
result (Fig. 12):

dead corals	30%
Alyconarians	10%
live corals	60%
Acropora palifera	2·4
elkhorn-*Acropora*	2·4
Leptoria	2·3
Pocillopora	2·3
Acropora cf. humilis	2·3
table-*Acropora*	1·4

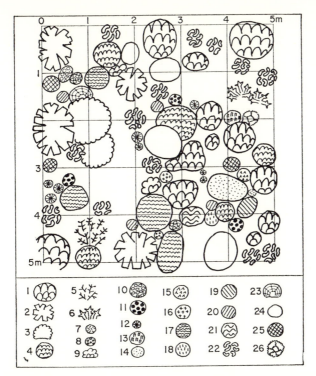

FIG. 12. Sample quadrat 5 × 5 m at the lagoon reef flat of the Fadiffolu Atoll at a depth of 1–2 m. Dead corals and alcyonarians are not plotted.
1 = *Acropora palifera*; 2 = *Acropora*, elkhorn; 3 = *Acropora*, tables; 4 = *Acropora cf. humilis*; 5 = *Acropora*; 6 = *Acropora hemprichi*; 7 = *Alveopora*; 8 = *Astreopora*; 9 = *Echinopora*; 10 = *Favia* 1; 11 = *Favia* 2; 12 = *Fungia*; 13 = *Galaxea*; 14 = *Goniastrea*; 15 = *Hydnophora*; 16 = *Leptastrea*; 17 = *Leptoria*; 18 = *Montipora*; 19 = *Pavona*; 20 = *Pavona repens*; 21 = *Platygyra*; 22 = *Pocillopora*; 23 = *Podabacia*; 24 = *Porites*; 25 = *Psammocora*; 26 = *Symphyllia*.

Porites	1·3
bush-*Acropora*	+.3
Acropora hemprichi	+.3
Psammocora	+.2
Pavona repens	+.2
Favia 1	+.2
Favia 2	+.2
Fungia	+.2
Goniastrea	r.3
Pavona	r.3
Montipora	r.2
Platygyra	r.2
Echinopora	r.2
Symphyllia	r.2

Podabacia	r.2
Hydnophora	r.1
Galaxea	r.1
Astreopora	r.1
Alveopora	r.1

Another sample plot of 5 × 5 m, nearer to the island, on a coral patch in the sand about 70 m away from the reef edge and 2–2·5 m deep showed:

dead corals	10%
live corals	90%
about 10 different	
Acropora species	70%
Leptoria	10
Pocillopora	4
Pavona	4
another 10 genera	2

A sample plot of 5 × 5 m at a depth of about 5 m on the densely populated reef slope towards the lagoon produced the following result:

dead corals	10%
live corals	90%
Porites	35%
4 *Acropora* species	25
Pavona	15
Montipora	10
Seriatopora	3
another 13 genera	2

A total of 26 coral genera was found on the lagoon reef of Madewaru at Fadiffolu Atoll.

Miladummadulu Atoll

This was the last Maldive atoll where the *Xarifa* dropped anchor because the passage to Ceylon followed and the corals had to be packed and stored away in a seaworthy manner. Therefore there was little time to collect corals at this atoll, but six specimens were found. One each of *Psammocora*, *Acropora*, *Montipora*, *Parahalomitra*, *Tubastrea* and *Heliopora* were collected.

When swimming along the reefs round the island Kuludu in the southeast of the atoll, at least a rough zonation could be established.

Inner reef

Next to the beach of the island the Wide Sandy Zone, then big *Heliopora* coralla, and furthermore a few corals, then coral patches, and finally dense population, of almost 100% coverage. The reef edge was 5 m deep. The reef slope towards the lagoon descended at an angle of 45° down to about 15 m.

Channel reef

Northwest of the island channel between lagoon and open sea. 40–50% dead corals with large sandy areas and numerous rays in between. Towards the shore turbid water on account of sand stirred up by the surf. Many corals were more or less buried under sand and partly dead.

Outer reef

At the shore first of all a boulder rampart. Then indistinct grooves and spurs, getting flatter towards the open sea. Then a few dead coralla encrusted with calcareous algae. The reef flat sloped down steadily from the shore over a width of 150–200 m to the reef edge at a depth of 20 m. Here dense overgrowth with living corals, but still many dead coralla.

Summary for the Maldive Islands

Again, the coral genera collected at the various places have been entered in the table at the end of the paper. There were collected at

A.	Addu Atoll	42 genera
B.	Suvadiva Atoll	9 genera
C.	Ari Atoll	32 genera
D.	Rasdu Atoll	39 genera
E.	Gaha Faro	22 genera
F.	Fadiffolu Atoll	26 genera
G.	Miladummadulu Atoll	5 genera
	and altogether in the Maldives	51 genera

NICOBAR ISLANDS

From 30th June until 9th September, 1958 the *Xarifa* visited the Nicobars, that is to say the islands Great Nicobar and Tillanchong

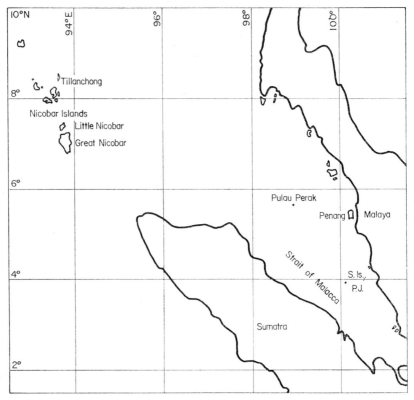

FIG. 13. The Nicobar Islands and the Strait of Malacca. S. Is. = Sembilan Islands,
P. J. = Pulau Jarak.

(Fig. 13). The islands are mountainous and covered with thick forest.
The coast, apart from some sandy bays, is steep and rocky.

Great Nicobar

Great Nicobar is the largest and southernmost island of the group.
The *Xarifa* anchored at the north coast in a bay of Ganges Harbour
between the west cape and a land projection near the mouth of the
Jubilee River (Fig. 14). The official permit for our stay had not arrived,
so we were under the supervision of Indian policemen who were
stationed on the small island Kondul between Great Nicobar and
Little Nicobar. Thus we were considerably hampered in our work.
Our anchoring bay was sandy with few corals. 500 m away from the
beach there was pure ooze at a depth of 12 m. Only before the steep
coasts of the west cape and the projecting land east of the mouth of

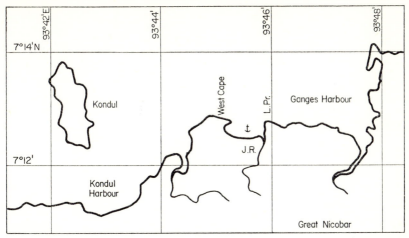

FIG. 14. Ganges Harbour with anchorage bay of the *Xarifa* at the north coast of Great Nicobar. L. Pr. = land projection, J. R. = Jubilee River.

the river Jubilee, reefs could develop on a rocky foundation. At these two points corals were collected. To a certain extent, the reefs were densely covered with *Acropora* tables and hedges. Where the *Acropora* species did not grow quite so densely, many other species could be found and above all *Pocillopora*. The rocky surface was partially coated with big sea anemones of the genera *Radianthus* and *Discosoma*. With retracted tentacles *Radianthus* was the size of a head, and *Discosoma* measured up to 1 m in diam.

Altogether 32 coral genera were collected, 30 at the west cape and 16 at the land projection. All of them are listed in the Table.

Tillanchong

The *Xarifa* cast anchor in the Castle Bay. This bay is surrounded by steep mountains in the north and west, and has a fringing reef lying at its shores (Fig. 15).

Fringing reef

After a narrow sandy beach which continued as a sandy zone in the water and was replaced by sea-grass fields at certain points, the coral reef started. It had a width of about 300 m in the northern part of the bay and about 200 m in the western part. The waves, approaching from the southeast, broke over the reef which was covered with white crests for at least half of its width. It was difficult and dangerous to move about by boat here or to swim and to dive. The corals formed

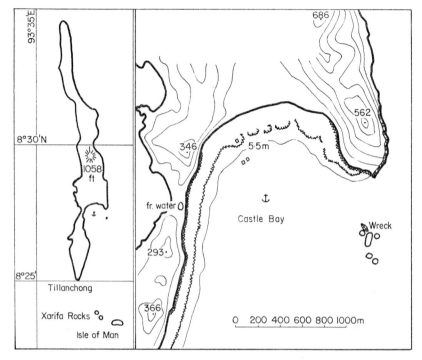

FIG. 15. Tillanchong Island and Castle Bay.

towers and knolls measuring 4–5 m in height and almost reaching up to the water surface. Between them were canyons with sandy floors or low corals. Eight coral genera were found at a depth of 4m. Here, too *Acropora* species dominated. Remarkable were thick stout *Acropora cf. palifera* specimens with branch ends ramified in the form of lobes.

A little nearer to the centre of the bay, at a depth of about 10 m, further corals were collected, and 16 coral genera were found. Here there were also huge *Porites* coralla. One of them formed a knoll, 6 m high, with an oval ground plan of 6 × 8 m. Another one had the shape of a mushroom, its 4 m high "cap" with a diameter of 6 m resting on a 2 m tall "stem" with a diameter of 2 m. In a larger sandy area there was a reef patch of 13 m² (Fig. 16). All corals growing there were surveyed according to their coverage. The result was as follows:

Acropora palifera   26%
Porites, finger-shaped   23

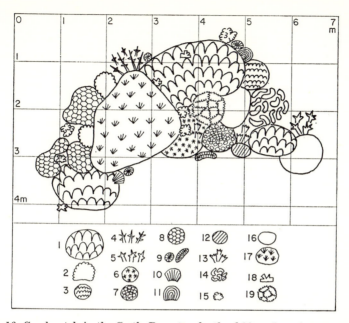

FIG. 16. Coral patch in the Castle Bay at a depth of 10 m. 1 = *Acropora palifera*; 2 = *Acropora*, tables; 3 = *Acropora cf. humilis*; 4 = *Acropora*; 5 = *Acropora hemprichi*; 6 = *Diploastrea*; 7 = *Favia*; 8 = *Favites*; 9 = *Fungia*; 10 = *Merulina*; 11 = *Pachyseris*; 12 = *Pavona repens*; 13 = *Pectinia*; 14 = *Pocillopora*, broad; 15 = *Pocillopora damicornis*; 16 = *Porites*; 17 = *Porites*, finger-shaped; 18 = *Stylophora*; 19 = *Symphyllia*.

Favites	9
Porites, solid	6
Pocillopora, broad	5
Diploastrea	5
Pocillopora damicornis	3
Acropora, thick and long	3
Acropora cf. humilis	3
Favia	3
Symphyllia	3
Acropora, tables	2·5
Acropora hemprichi	2
Pectinia	2
Stylophora	1·5
Fungia	1
Pavona	1
Merulina	0·5
Pachyseris	0·5

altogether 13 coral genera.

Rock cliffs

As a southern continuation of the cape which bordered Castle Bay to the east, some steep cliffs rose from the sea bottom at a depth of 25 m. In this area lay a wreck, the *Elphinstone*, a ship of the Royal Indian Navy, which in 1925 had run into the cliffs and sunk. On the wreck and on the cliffs in depths of 5–10 m and at another place, 10–12 m deep, 19 coral genera were collected. *Trachyphyllia*, which had not been found since the Gulf of Aqaba, Red Sea, originated from the sea bottom by the wreck.

Bottom of the bay

A descent to the sea bottom round the anchoring place of the *Xarifa*, in a depth of 26 m and covered with sand and ooze, resulted in some few, though highly interesting corals: bright red *Cycloseris*; *Goniopora* with "Ableger" in their balls as at Rasdu Atoll and on the inner reef of Hitaddu; *Trachyphyllia*; and finally *Heterocyathus* and *Heteropsammia*, living in symbiosis with a Sipunculid of the genus *Aspidosiphon* (Schindewolf, 1958; Feustel, 1965).

Further corals

These were gathered south of the island on the fringing reef and in a channel between two cliffs which we called *Xarifa* Rocks. Conspicuous is a *Turbinaria* resembling a flat dish with its edge arching down, and lying loose on the sandy surface.

Summary for the Nicobar Islands

30 coral genera were found on the reefs at the island Tillanchong, and altogether in the Nicobars 40 genera.

STRAITS OF MALACCA

1. When sailing from the Nicobars to the island of Penang off the Malayan coast the *Xarifa* called at Pulau Perak, a steep and completely bare rocky island (5°41'40''N, 98°56'20''E). It has a diameter of 100 m and is about 100 m high. The island looks as if whitewashed on account of the droppings of the many sea swallows and boobies breeding there. Under water the steep walls of the rocks continue to drop down to a depth of about 50 m, where a less steep rubble slope begins. At the walls there lived numerous sea anemones the size of a head, and at certain points the precipice was covered with red *Tubastrea* corals. *Pocillopora* also occurred fairly frequently while

Acropora was lacking completely. The coral fauna was not very abundant; only 10 genera were collected.

2. Approximately 85 nautical miles south of Penang lie the Sembilan Islands (around 4°01′N, 100°33′E). Here the water was very turbid. No reefs have developed at the islands, and only few corals inhabited the partly sandy, partly rocky ground. Corals were collected in the channel between both Lalang Islands and also at Pulau Saga and then in a bay at the west coast of Pulau Rumbia, the biggest island of this group (Fig. 17). At all three places a total of only 8 coral genera were found.

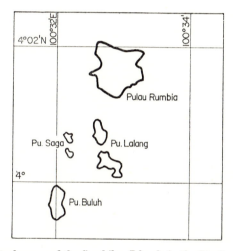

FIG. 17. Central group of the Sembilan Islands in the Straits of Malacca.

3. The situation was a little better at Pulau Jarak (3°58′30″N, 100°05′45″E), a small island 27 nautical miles to the west of the Sembilan Islands. Pulau Jarak is about 1 km long, 150 m high, covered with thick forest and has steep slopes down to the sea. There is no sandy beach here, but massive granite blocks lie on the shore. Here a fringing reef could develop, the water is relatively clear. Big *Porites* coralla were dominant, *Acropora* was represented by comparatively little growth, while *Montipora* occurred fairly frequently. The reef reached down to a depth of about 15 m, there a rubble slope began on which only a few *Fungia* lay. At three places southeast of the island, in depths of 3–6 m, 10 m and 15 m corals were collected, altogether 13 genera.

Summary for the Straits of Malacca

This was the last place where corals were gathered. A total of 19 genera were found in the Straits of Malacca.

CONCLUSION AND ACKNOWLEDGEMENTS

All 58 of the coral genera found are listed in Table I, systematically arranged according to Wells (1956). Those genera that have been collected at different places are so indicated.

Genera present in all regions, that is to say in the Red Sea, at Abd el Kuri, in the Maldive and Nicobar Islands, and in the Straits of Malacca are: *Pocillopora, Acropora, Pavona, Porites, Favia, Hydnophora* and *Leptastrea*.

Genera occurring in all regions with the exception of Abd el Kuri are: *Montipora, Fungia, Favites, Goniastrea, Diploastrea, Symphyllia, Plerogyra, Balanophyllia, Dendrophyllia* and *Tubastrea*.

Stylophora was found everywhere except in the Straits of Malacca, and *Psammocora* was absent from the Nicobars only.

Genera which were collected in the Red Sea, in the Maldive and Nicobar Islands, but which were not represented at Abd el Kuri and in the Straits of Malacca, are: *Seriatopora, Astreopora, Pachyseris, Herpolitha, Goniopora, Oulophyllia, Platygyra, Leptoria, Echinopora, Galaxea, Mycedium* and *Turbinaria*.

In the Red Sea only were found: *Coscinarea* at the island Safaga and *Siderastrea* at Massaua.

In the Maldives only were found: *Leptoseris, Halomitra, Parahalomitra, Caulastrea, Acanthastrea, Cynarina, Parascolymia, Oxypora, Physophyllia* and *Physogyra*.

In the Nicobars only were found: *Coeloseris, Heterocyathus, Flabellum* and *Heteropsammia*.

It should always be borne in mind that if a coral was not found at a certain place this does not mean that it does not exist there. The number of corals found increases asymptotically with the number of collectors and with the number of hours spent with collecting. This should be considered when looking at Table I.

The reefs, which were visited during the *Xarifa* Expedition 1957–58 from the Red Sea to the Strait of Malacca and which have been described here in a rather matter-of-fact language, come to life through the profusely illustrated books on the expedition by Hass (1961) and Eibl-Eibesfeldt (1964). Here, too, I want to express my gratitude to Dr. Hans Hass for enabling me to participate in the *Xarifa* Expedition.

Furthermore, I thank Dr. Eibl-Eibesfeldt, Seewiesen, Dr. Feustel, Darmstadt, Diplom-Sportlehrer Hollosi, Neu-Ulm, and Dr. Schuhmacher, Heidelberg, for having placed coral collections at the disposal of the Hessian State Museum, Darmstadt. I owe thanks also to Dr. Klausewitz and Prof. Dr. Schäfer of the Senckenberg Research Institute, Frankfurt, for letting me have their corals from the Sarso Islands for determination.

SUMMARY

1. During the *Xarifa* Expedition 1957–1958 the author collected about 1400 corals in the Red Sea, at Abd el Kuri, in the Maldive Islands, in the Nicobar Islands, and in the Straits of Malacca by aqualung diving. A further 500 corals were put at the disposal of the Darmstadt museum by different collectors.

2. A brief description is given of the Red Sea reefs visited by the author, and the coral genera collected there by him and others are arranged in Table I.

3. The island Abd el Kuri off the eastern point of Africa has no reefs and only few corals.

4. Of the Maldive Islands, a most detailed account is given of Addu Atoll. The individual reefs (inner reef, outer reefs, reef flat) are described, and the coral genera collected there are recorded. A reef, partly covered with fractured corals, with a newly-developed small island, is divided into zones according to coral growth. Furthermore, a patch reef in the lagoon is described, and mention is made of corals from a wreck.

5. A faro and a mini-atoll are described from Ari Atoll. The corals found there are recorded.

6. At Rasdu Atoll a coral sociological method to investigate coral reefs according to the model of phytosociology is elaborated. With its aid the corals on the inner and outer reef as well as on the lagoon floor are made out according to their quantity and "sociability" and registered in accordance with their frequency.

7. A patch reef at Gaha Faro and a fringing reef at Fadiffolu Atoll is described as well as reefs of Miladummadulu Atoll.

8. In the Nicobar Islands corals were collected in a bay at the north coast of Great Nicobar and in a bay of the island Tillanchong. Fringing reef, cliffs and the bottom of the bay were investigated.

9. In the Straits of Malacca only few corals could be found due to the steep rocky shores on the one hand and the turbid water on the other.

10. All collected coral genera are systematically arranged in a table (Table I), and the genera are marked under the different places where they were found. It is pointed out that corals, which could not be found on a certain reef, need not necessarily be absent.

REFERENCES

Eibl-Eibesfeldt, I. (1964). *Im Reich der tausend Atolle.* München: Piper.

Feustel, H. (1965). Anatomische Untersuchungen zum Problem der Aspidosiphon-Heterocyathus-Symbiose. *Verh. dt. zool. Ges.:* 131–143.

Gardiner, J. S. (1903). *The Fauna and Geography of the Maldive and Laccadive Archipelagoes.* **1.** Cambridge: University Press.

Gohar, H. A. F. (1954). The Place of the Red Sea between the Indian Ocean and the Mediterranean. *Istanb. Univ. Fen. Fak. Hidrobiol.* (B). **2:** 47–82.

Hass, H. (1961). *Expedition ins Unbekannte.* Berlin, Frankfurt, Wien: Ullstein.

Klausewitz, W. (1967). Die physiographische Zonierung der Saumriffe von Sarso. *Meteor Forsch. Ergebn.* R.D., No. 2. Biol.: 44–68.

Rosen, B. R. and Taylor, J. D. (1969). Reef coral from Aldabra: New mode of Reproduction. *Science, N.Y.* **166:** 119–121.

Schäfer, W. (1969). Sarso, Modell der Biofazies-Sequenzen im Korallenriff-Bereich des Schelfs. *Senckenberg. marit.* (1) **50:** 165–188.

Scheer, G. (1959). Die Formenvielfalt der Riffkorallen. *Ber. naturw. Ver. Darmstadt* **1958/59:** 50–67.

Scheer, G. (1960). Viviparie bei Steinkorallen. *Naturwissenschaften.* **47:** 238–239.

Scheer, G. (1964a) Korallen von Abd-el-Kuri. *Zool. Jb.* (Syst.) **91:** 451–466.

Scheer, G. (1964b). Bemerkenswerte Korallen aus dem Roten Meer. *Senckenberg. biol.* **45:** 613–620.

Scheer, G. (1967). Korallen von den Sarso-Inseln im Roten Meer. *Senckenberg. biol.* **48:** 421–436.

Scheer, G. (in press). Investigations of coral reefs in the Maldive Islands with notes on lagoon patch reefs and the method of coral sociology. Proc. Symp. Corals and Coral Reefs at Mandapam Camp, 1969.

Schindewolf, O. H. (1958). Würmer und Korallen als Synöken. Zur Kenntnis der Systeme Aspidosiphon/Heterocyathus und Hicetes/Pleurodictum. *Abh. Akad. Wiss.* Mainz *math. naturw. Kl.* **6:** 1–70.

Stoddart, D. R., Edit. (1966). Reef Studies at Addu Atoll, Maldive Islands. *Atoll Res. Bull.* **116:** 1–122.

Stoddart, D. R. (1969). Ecology and morphology of recent coral reefs. *Biol. Rev.* **44:** 433–498.

Vaughan, T. W. and Wells, J. W. (1943). Revision of the suborders, families, and genera of the Scleractinia. *Spec. Pap. geol. Soc. Am.* **44:** 363 pp.

Vasseur, P. (1964). Contribution à l'étude bionomique des peuplements sciaphiles infralittoraux de substrat dur dans les Récifs de Tuléar. *Recl Trav. Stn. mar. Endoume* (fasc. hors-sér.) Suppl. **2:** 1–77.

Wells, J. W. (1955). A survey of the distribution of reef coral genera in the Great Barrier Reef region. *Rep. Gt. Barrier Reef Comm.* **6:** 1–9.

Wells, J. W. (1956). Scleractinia. In: *Treatise on Invertebrate Paleontology.* (Moore, R. C., ed.), pt. F., Coelenterata. Geol. Soc. America and University of Kansas, 238–444.

Wells, J. W. and Davies, P. S. (1966). Preliminary list of stony corals from Addu Atoll. *Atoll Res. Bull.* **116**: 43–55.

DISCUSSION

GUILCHER: Concerning the area south of Cape Guardafui and between Cape Guardafui and Socotra, the very strong upwelling of cold water during the southwest monsoon, described by Dr Swallow following the International Indian Ocean Expedition, must normally result in the absence or reduction of coral growth in at least some parts of this area. It would be interesting to know to what extent this is reflected in the coral diversity data.

Other Reef Invertebrate Communities

Symp. zool. Soc. Lond. (1971) No. 28, 371–396.

LES FACIES D'EPIFAUNE ET D'EPIFLORE DES BIOTOPES SEDIMENTAIRES DES FORMATIONS CORALLIENNES DANS LA REGION DE TULEAR (SUD-OUEST DE MADAGASCAR)

BERNARD A. THOMASSIN

Station Marine d'Endoume et Centre d'Océanographie, Marseille, France

SYNOPSIS

Epifaunal and epiflora faciès enumerated in the biodetrital sedimentary biotopes on the coral reefs of the Tulear area are presented in the different reef "Ensembles".

Epifaunal facies are specially made by Scleractinian communities, which free individuals, established on soft bottoms, are more or less closed: *Diaseris distorta* and *Goniopora stokesi* in the Epirecifal "Ensemble" (on the reef flat), *Heteropsammia michelini* and *Heterocyathus aequicostatus* in the Postrecifal "Ensemble" (on the inner reef flat or in the lagoon).

Epifloral facies are made by free Melobesian Algae rhodoliths, sprinkled upon the bottoms of the Frontorecifal and Epirecifal "Ensembles", and by marine Phanerogams (Hydrocharitacae and Zanicheliacae) in the Epirecifal and Postrecifal "Ensembles".

The endofauna of these bottoms is not specially modified by these epibiotic facies; yet, a quantitative enriching of the species is observed in the bottoms having a high organic matter content.

RESUME

Les faciès d'épifaune et d'épiflore rencontrés dans les biotopes sédimentaires des formations coralliennes de la région de Tuléar sont passés en revue dans les différents "Ensembles" récifaux.

Les faciès d'épifaune (les phénomènes de foule étant considérés comme d'autres particularités) sont essentiellement représentés par des peuplements plus ou moins denses de Scléractiniaires libres: *Diaseris distorta* et *Goniopora stokesi* dans l'Ensemble épirécifal, *Heteropsammia michelini* et *Heterocyathus aequicostatus* dans l'Ensemble postrécifal.

Les faciès d'épiflore sont représentés par des développements d'Algues Mélobésiées libres dans les Ensembles frontorécifal et épirécifal, et de Phanérogames marines (Hydrocharitacae et Zanicheliacae) dans les Ensembles épirécifal et postrécifal.

L'endofaune des sédiments n'est pas essentiellement modifiée par la présence de des faciès d'épibiose; cependant, on note un enrichissement quantitatif des espèces dans les sédiments à la forte teneur en matière organique.

INTRODUCTION

Les faciès d'épifaune et d'épiflore rencontrés dans les biotopes sédimentaires des formations coralliennes n'avaient, jusqu'alors, pas été individualisés des peuplements endopsammiques. Au cours de l'étude plus générale des biotopes de sables coralliens dérivant des appareils récifaux de la région de Tuléar (Thomassin, 1969a, b), il nous est apparu que divers peuplements de Scléractiniaires libres, de Mélobésiées libres et de Phanérogames marines, représentaient de véritables faciès d'épibioses des peuplements benthiques (Fig. 1).

D'aprés Pérès (1961), Pérès et Picard (1964), une "biocoenose présente un **faciès** particulier lorsque la prédominance locale de certains facteurs écologiques entraine l'exubérance d'une, ou d'un petit nombre, d'espèces (que cette ou ces espèces soient ou non caractéristique(s) de la biocoenose), sans que pour cela la composition qualitative de la biocoenose en soit affectée". Ces mêmes auteurs désignent par **épibiose** (**épifaune** ou **épiflore**) "la totalité des espèces sessiles ou vagiles qui se trouvent à la surface du substrat"; cette notion s'opposant à celle d'**endobiose**.

La répartition des divers faciès d'épibiose des substrats meubles rencontrés sur les récifs coralliens de la région de Tuléar est présentée en suivant la classification horizontale en "Ensembles", mise au point Picard (1967) pour les grands types de peuplements benthiques tropicaux.

LES FACIES D'EPIFAUNE DES SEDIMENTS CORALLIENS

Les faciès d'épifaune des substrats meubles coralliens, exceptés les phénomènes de foule observés chez certains Gastéropodes (*Strombus gibberulus gibberulus* Linné, *Monetaria annulus harmandiana* (Rochebrune), *Nassarius albescens* (Dunker)), Echinodermes (*Diadema setosum* (Leske), *Tripneustes qratilla* (Linné)), Crustacés Amphipodes (*Siphonoecetes erythraeus* Ruffo), ou Pycnogonides (*Anoplodactylus arescus*) ou les faciès de l'endofaune en surface (banquettes à Phyllochaetopterinae, à *Modiolus*), sont surtout représentés par des peuplements de Scléractiniaires libres (Pichon, 1969).

Dans l'Ensemble épirécifal: les fonds à Diaseris distorta, Diaseris *sp.
et à* Goniopora stokesi (*Fungiidae et Poritidae*)

Dans la partie postérieure du platier interne du Grand Récif se développe sur les sables grossiers envasés, situés dans l'axe de dépressions draînant aux basses mers de vive-eau les herbiers de Phanérogames, un peuplement épibenthique très dense de petits Fungiidae: *Diaseris distorta* (Michelin) et *Diaseris* sp. (plus de 1000 individues par m^2). Le surface du sédiment laissée libre est généralement graveleuse, tandis qu'en profondeur les sédiments sont sablo-vaseux. Quelques touffes de Phanérogammes peuvent s'y rencontrer.

Toujours sur le Grand Récif, mais au voisinage de la Pointe du Serpent, en bordure du chenal postrécifal (ou lagon), au niveau des

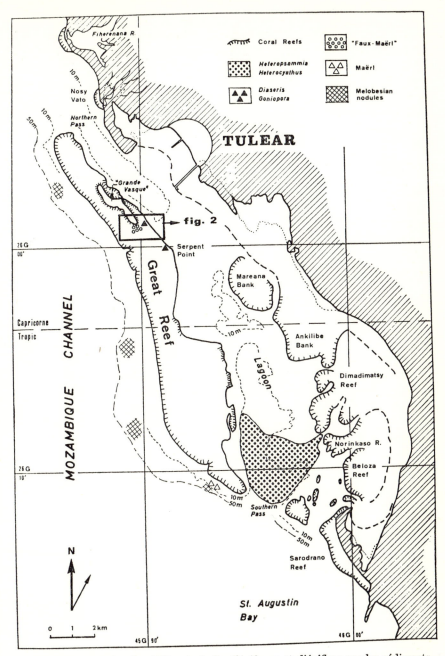

FIG. 1. Localisation des différents faciès d'épifaune et d'épiflore sur les sédiments coralliens des récifs de la Baie de Tuléar.

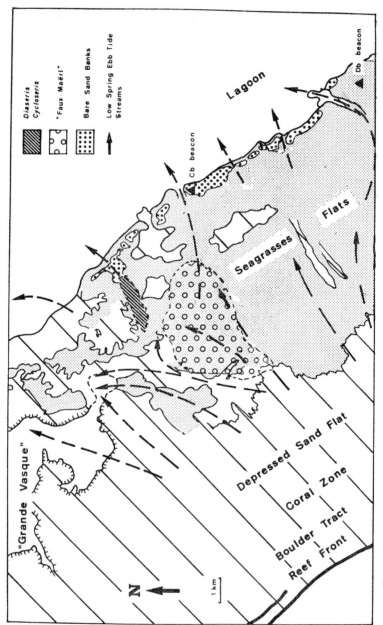

Fig. 2. Détail de la localisation des fonds à "faux-Maërl" et à *Diaseris* spp. sur le Grand Récif de Tuléar.

ceintures de Phanérogames *Cymodocea ciliata* et *Syringodium isoetifolium* marquant la limite entre les Ensembles épirécifal et postrécifal, se rencontre, en taches de plusieures dizaines de m², le peuplement épibenthique, quasi monospécifique, à *Goniopora stokesi* Milne-Edwards et Haime. Les zones où se développe ce faciès, bien que n'étant pas dans des dépressions, sont toujours dans des zones de courants de marée assez vifs, d'où des individus parfois sphériques. Le substrat, recouvert à 90% par les *Goniopora*, est un sable grossier, meuble et peu envasé.

Dans l'Ensemble postrécifal: les fonds à Heteropsammia michelini, Heterocyathus aequicostatus (*Dendrophylliidae et Caryophylliidae*)

Dans le chenal postrécifal (ou lagon) du Grand Récif se poursuit l'envasement progressif, récent, des sables grossiers coralliens propres, constituant les dépôts primitifs. Cet apport de particules fines, terrigènes, se fait par la passe Nord, à partir des alluvions du fleuve Fiherenana, soit par décantation directe lors des crues, soit par remise en suspension et transports par les courants de marée à partir des fonds de décantation situés sur le plateau continental en face de l'embouchure (Picard, 1967; Guérin-Ancey, 1970). Actuellement, la résultante hydrodynamique des houles de S.S.W. pénétrant par la passe Sud et des courants de marée limite, en retrait des sédiments biodétritiques, grossiers, propres, du seuil de la passe, la contamination à un apport de sables fins qui s'envasent progressivement vers l'intérieur du lagon.

Sur ces sédiments de développe un peuplement épibenthique de Scléractiniaires libres: *Heterocyathus aequicostatus* (Milne-Edwards et Haime), jusqu'à 38 individus par 50 dm³ de sédiment dragué, et *Heteropsammia michelini* (Milne-Edwards et Haime), jusqu'à 93 individus par 50 dm³ de sédiment dragué; tous deux associés au Sipunculide commensal *Aspidosiphon corallicola* Sluiter. Quelques individus de *Diaseris distorta* les accompagnent dans les secteurs les plus envasés. Ce faciès à Scléractiniaires libres représente environ 20% du peuplement macrobenthique général.

En même temps que se développent en épibiose les Scléractiniaires, s'installent les colonies cupuliformes du Bryozoaire libre *Anoteropora magnicapitata* Canu et Bassler, dont la densité peut atteindre une valeur importante, jusqu'à 50 colonies par 50 dm³ de sédiment dragué. Il ne semble pas qu'il y ait un parallélisme entre le développement des Scléractiniaires libres et celui du Bryozoaire libre (Tableau I).

L'endofaune de ces sables grossiers, très peu envasés, est à dominante d'espèces gravellicoles (84·8% du peuplement général), parmi lesquelles dominent les Pélécypodes et les Scaphopodes (*Merethrix*

TABLEAU I.

Abondance (A) et Dominance (D) des Scléractiniaires libres et du Bryozoaire libre dans cinq stations, au Sud du lagon du Grand Récif (d'après les chiffres de Guérin-Ancey, 1970)

	A	D	A	D	A	D	A	D	A	D
Heterocyathus aequicostatus	16	5·37%	1	0·69%	—	—	38	9·69%	—	—
Heteropsammia michelini	67	22·48%	2	1·39%	1	2·44%	93	23·73%	2	1·61%
Anoteropora magnicapitata	38	12·75%	2	1·39%	—	—	2	0·51%	50	40·32%

habraea Lamarck, *Circe scripta* (Donovan), *Leucoma japonica* Kira, *Solen roseomaculatus* Pilsbry, *Dentalium octangulatum* Donovan), suivis des Polychètes (*Arabella mutans* (Chamberlin), *Nephthys dibranchis* Grube, *Onuphis quinquedens* Audouin et Milne-Edwards), des Echinides (*Echinodiscus auritus* (Leske)) et des Céphalocordés (*Asymmetron lucayanum* (Andrews)). Les Crustacés n'y sont représentés que par des Brachyoures, en petit nombre.

LES FACIES D'EPIFLORE DES SEDIMENTS CORALLIENS

Les faciès d'épiflore des substrats meubles coralliens, dans les Etages infralittoral et circalittoral, ne sont représentés dans la région de Tuléar que par des Mélobésiées,* dont les thalles libres recouvrent les sédiments et par des Phanérogames marines, dont les rhizomes tendent à fixer ces sédiments†. On n'y rencontre pas, comme sur les platiers récifaux de Nossi-Bé (N.W. de Madagascar), de véritables faciès à *Halimeda* (Masse, 1970).

Dans l'Ensemble frontorécifal

Les fonds de nodules de Mélobésiées sur la dalle corallienne des récifs de mode battu

Sur le front externe, de mode battu, du Grand Récif, en dessous de 18 m, les structures éperons-sillons, qui caractérisent le haut de

---

* Les Mélobésiées dont il est question dans cette note sont en cours de détermination par Mme J. Cabioch, Station biologique, Roscoff, France.

† Les banquettes de vases sableuses, fixées saisonnièrement par un feutrage d'Algues filamenteuses du genre *Lyngbia*, ne représentent pas, bien que situées sur certains platiers récifaux, un faciès d'épiflore des sédiments coralliens; ces dépots résultant d'apports terrigènes turbides.

la pente récifale, s'adoucissent et finissent par laisser place à une dalle corallienne, solide, plus ou moins régulière (Gravier, et al., 1970) Cette dalle, en pente douce vers le large, présente dans les horizons les plus profonds, à partir de 34–36 m jusqu'au rebord du tombant récifal (50 m), des cuvettes de grandes étendues, remplies de sables grossiers plus ou moins vaseux généralement recouverts de galets et de nodules de Mélobésiées vivantes, disposées par endroits en trainées parallèles.

La fraction sableuse du sédiment, plus ou moins grossière et très roulée, est de nature corallienne; par contre. la fraction vaseuse paraît être de nature hétérogène et résulterait d'une décantation terrigène.

Ces fonds à nodules de Mélobésiées semblent liés à un régime de courants particuliers, l'Algue étant vivante sur toute la surface du nodule: elle doit pour ce faire rouler à périodes rapprochées sous l'influence de courants de fond (influence des houles, courants de décharge, courants parallèles au front récifal).

L'endofaune, actuellement en cours d'étude, est référable à: une biocoenose de type détritique, avec parmi les grosses espèces *Strombus decorus* Röding, *Lambis digitata* (Perry), *Conus tessulatus* Born, et dans certains secteurs un peuplement d'Ophiures endopsammiques.

Les fonds de Maërl, en arrière de la dalle corallienne

Au Sud du Grand Récif, à la profondeur de 17 m, se développe un fond de Lithothamniées branchues, sorte de Maerl, reposant sur des sables grossiers biodétritiques.

L'endofaune est composée de nombreuses espèces gravellicoles, parmi lesquelles les Mollusques *Venus lamellaris* (Schumacher), Merethrix *habraea*, *Mactra olorina* Philippi, *Psammobia squamosa* Lamarck, *Pyramidella sulcata* (Adams), et les Céphalocordés *Branchiostoma* sp., *Asymmetron lucayanum*.

Dans l'Ensemble épirécifal: les fonds de "faux-Maërl"

Sur le Grand Récif, au Sud de la Grande Vasque (Fig. 2), dans la partie postérieure du platier récifal, habituellement colonisé par les herbiers de Phanérogames, se développe dans une grande dépression un peuplement de Mélobésiées branchues. Les thalles, de forme subsphérique, peuvent atteindre 7 à 8 cm de diamètre; ils recouvrent le substrat sablo-vaseux. Leur densité, ainsi que la superficie de la zone dans laquelle ils prospèrent, est assez fluctuante selon les années. En 1963 et 1965, cette Lithothamniée formait un faciès d'épiflore très dense, recouvrant par endroit le substrat à 70%, au point de gêner la croissance des herbiers de *Cymodocea ciliata* et de *Syringodium*

isoetifolium. Depuis le passage du cyclone "Georgette" (fin janvier
1968), qui entraina un remodelage de l'accumulation de sédiments
fins formant la partie postérieure du platier récifal, ensablant les
herbiers de Phanérogames, cette zone à "faux-Maërl" occupe une
superficie restreinte à des taches éparses. De plus, les thalles semblent
être dans un état de vitalité réduite (communication de J. Picard,
observations faites en 1968, 1969).

L'endofaune des sédiments sablo-vaseux, recouverts par ce faciès
d'épiflore, paraît être celles des sédiments colonisés par les herbiers
de Phanérogames.

*Dans les Ensembles épirécifal et postrécifal: les herbiers de Phanérogames
marines*

Les herbiers de Phanérogames marines se développent dans tout
l'Etage infrallitoral, aussi bien sur des sédiments biodétritiques dérivant
des appareils récifaux que sur ceux terrigènes des atterrissements
frontolittoraux. Toutefois, sur les côtes de Madagascar, il semble,
d'après les observations de nombreux auteurs (Petit, 1930; Poisson,
1949; Guilcher, 1958; Pichon, Mireille, 1964; Battistini, 1966), qu'ils
ne prospèrent que dans les régions soumises à des influences fluviatiles
importants. Ce n'est pas tant la teneur en matières humiques dans
les sédiments qui favoriserait leur implantation, mais les apports en
sels minéraux nutritifs dissous. Ainsi, sur les récifs coralliens, qu'ils
se situent au large (I. Europa) ou à la côte (récifs d'Itampolo), mais
localisés en dehors de ces zones "enrichies", les herbiers de Phanérogames sont absents ou chétifs.

Dans les complexes récifaux, de mode battu à moyennement battu,
les herbiers de Phanérogames tendent à coloniser (à l'exception des
secteurs d'hypersédimentation vaseuse, d'où ils sont éliminés):—toute
la zone de rétention des sédiments fins de l'Ensemble épirécifal—et
une partie de l'Ensemble postrécifal (Picard, 1967; Thomassin, 1969b).
Sur les récifs coralliens de mode abrité (récifs internes dans le chenal
de Tuléar), en plus des localisations citées ci-dessus, les herbiers,
notamment ceux de *Cymodocea ciliata*, s'implantent fréquemment sur
des bancs de gravelles du platier interne (dans la zone des formations
organogènes construites) en arrière des levées détritiques ou au fond
des criques du front externe. Parfois même, ils colonisent dans la
partie antérieure de l'Ensemble épirécifal les gravelles du platier
externe (herbiers de *Cymodocea ciliata* et de *Syringodium isoetifolium*
installés en avant des levées détritiques sur les récifs coralliens du
N.W. de Madagascar, Nossi-Bé) ou l'ensemble de la pente externe,

dans ce cas beaucoup plus apparentée à l'Ensemble postrécifal qu'à l'Ensemble frontorécifal.

Sur les récifs coralliens de la région de Tuléar, douze espèces de Phanérogames marines sont rencontrées:*

Hydrocharitacae: *Thalassia hemprichii* (Ehrenb.) Ascherson
Halophila balfourii Solered. (ex. *H. cf. stipulacea*, Pichon, Mireille, 1964; Picard, 1967; Thomassin, 1969b.)
Halophila minor (Zoll.) den Hartog
Halophila ovalis (R. Br.) Hooker fils

Zanicheliacae: *Halodule* (*Diplanthera*) *wrightii* Ascherson
Halodule (*Diplanthera*) *tridentata* (Steinheil)
(= *H. madagascariensis* Doty et Stone)
Halodule (*Diplanthera*) *uninervis* (Forsk.) Ascherson
Halodule (*Diplanthera*) *cf. beaudettei* den Hartog
Cymodocea rotundata (Ehrenb. et Hemprich.) Ascherson et Schweinf
Cymodocea serrulata Ascherson et Magnus
Cymodocea (*Thalassodendron* den Hartog) *ciliata* Ehrenb.
Syringodium isoetifolium (Acherson) Dandy

Les exigences des diverses espèces varient en fonction de leur physiologie; elles concernent: —l'état de fractionnement du sédiment, —la proportion de matières humiques, —l'intensité des radiations lumineuses, —la résistance à l'exondation.

La présence des herbiers de Phanérogames constitue un facteur biotique, qui, en fonction de la morphologie des espèces:

—crée un nouveau milieu épibenthique dans la frondaison; chez les grandes espèces (*Cymodocea spp.*, *Thalassia hemprichii*), ce milieu joue un rôle important dans la sédimentation, la rétension de particules fines, et les apports de tests provenant de l'épifaune des feuilles.

—modifie quelque peu la structure du substrat et la teneur en matière organique, selon l'importance du système radiculaire.

Les herbiers de Phanérogames sur les sédiments non stabilisés

Toutes les espèces d'*Halophila* se localisent sur des sédiments non stabilisés et souvent remaniés.

* Les herbiers d'*Enhalus acoroïdes* (L.f.) Roem et Schultes (= *E. Koenigii* Richard) n'existent que dans le N. de Madagascar (région de Nossi-Bé). Il semble que la température des eaux plus basse dans le région de Tuléar soit un facteur limitant pour leur extension (Pichon, 1964).

Halophila minor se situe dans les hauts niveaux, mélangée ou non, sur les substrats sableux terrigènes à *Halodule tridentata*.

Halophila ovalis pousse sur les platiers récifaux, plus rarement sur les atterissements, à un niveau légèrement inférieur à celui d'*Halophila minor*. On la retrouve fréquemment, en mode calme, au pied de la pente externe des récifs (6 à 10 m) sur des sédiments très vaseux et pulvérulents (récifs de Beloza, de Norinkaso dans le chenal).

Halophila balfourii est l'espèce pionnière de fixation des sédiments grossiers, très légèrement envasés. Sur les platiers récifaux elle se localise à un niveau plus bas qu'*Halophila ovalis*; de même que cette dernière espèce, on la trouve fréquemment dans les niveaux les plus profonds des chenaux postrécifaux ou des pentes externes envasées.

L'endofaune des herbiers d'*Halophila balfourii* et d'*Halophila minor* renferme encore de nombreux représentants soit de la faune des sables grossiers peu ou pas envasés (Actiniaire Edwarsiidae sp., Gastéropode *Nassarius albescens*, Amphipode *Lysianassa* cf. *variegata* (Simpson), Céphalocorde *Asymmetron lucayanum*), soit des "groupements permanents" des dunes hydrauliques (Opistobranche *Bulla ampulla* Linné, Anomoure Hippide *Albunea microps* Miers, Echinide *Echinodiscus auritus*) (Thomassin, 1969b), auxquels s'ajoutent des espèces sablo-vasicoles, telles les Mollusques *Solen roseomaculatus*, *Solemya occidentalis* Deshayes, *Loripes globosus*, *Tellina rostrellum*, *Polinices pyriformis* (Récluz), *Natica* sp.2, les Crustacés *Ampelisca brevicornis* (Costa), *Gomeza bicornis* Gray, *Callianassa* sp., une espèce de Synapte, et l'Entéropneuste *Balanoglossus studiosorum* v.d. Horst.

Les herbiers de Cymodocea ciliata, *plus ou moins associés à ceux de* Syringodium isoetifolium

Cymodocea ciliata est la Phanérogamme marine la plus tolérante envers les sédiments de taille centimétrique, mais elle supporte mal les exondations prolongées (les feuilles perdent leur chlorophylle et prennent une teinte rouge), c'est pourquoi sur les platiers récifaux exondables on la trouve principalement dans les creux. Elle est la première espèce à coloniser un platier, s'implantant sur les bancs de gravelles et les sables grossiers. Elle est très fréquente dans les déversoirs de platier (Récifs de Nosy Vé, de Nosy Tafara—région de Tuléar), les fonds de chenaux d'herbiers épirécifaux et les pentes du lagon. Sur les récifs coralliens de mode abrité (bancs coralliens de Mareana, d'Ankilibé) des herbiers de *Cymodocea ciliata* recouvrent en partie les sédiments grossiers, plus ou moins envasés de la pente externe, prolongeant ainsi les herbiers épirécifaux jusqu'aux fonds terrigènes envasés.

Syringodium isoetifolium est l'espèce la plus tolérante envers une teneur élevée en matière organique dans les sédiments, aussi est-elle la seule espèce à coloniser des milieux très réduits (fonds de cuvettes d'érosion dans les herbiers, bords de chenaux). Sur les platiers récifaux ou dans les fonds de chenaux sableux, on la retrouve mélangée à d'autres espèces de Phanérogames marines; mais, les sédiments grossiers étant très souvent enrichis en matière organique par colmatage, *Syringodium isoetifolium* est ainsi fréquemment associée à *Cymodocea ciliata*.

Sur le haut des pentes des chenaux postrécifaux ou des lagons, *Syringodium isoetifolium* forme une ceinture au niveau des basses mers de vive-eau, tandis que *Cymodocea ciliata*, immédiatement en dessous, en forme une autre plus ou moins discontinue. Lorsque le fond du lagon est comblé par un sédiment biogène grossier (au droit de la passe d'Ifaty—région N. de Tuléar), *Cymodocea ciliata* forme des taches subcirculaires ou des couronnes, de dimensions variables, dont le centre peut être occupé par *Syringodium isoetifolium* (Chassé, 1962; Picard, 1967).

Les sédiments des herbiers de *Cymodocea cialiata* renferment, outre les espèces sablo-vasicoles des herbiers d'*Halophila*, un grand nombre de Sipunculides (genre *Siphonosoma*), des Pélécypodes (*Arca scapha, Codakia exasperata*), une Ophiure (genre *Ophiotela*). La Crevette *Alpheus crassimanus* y creuse ses terriers, habités par des Gobiidae commensaux.

Les herbiers mixtes, composés d'espèces diverses en mosaïque

Les hauts niveaux des herbiers de Phanérogames (dôme des herbiers sur les platiers récifaux, hauts niveaux des atterissements littoraux), à l'exception des hyperaccumulations de sédiments vaseux (banquettes à *Modiolus* ou à *Lyngbia*), sont toujours occupés par *Halodule wrightii*, qui apparaît comme la vicariante, en milieu tropical, de *Zostera capensis* Setchell des côtes d'Afrique du Sud ou de *Zostera nana* Roth des côtes européennes.

Sur les substrats sablo-vaseux, *Halodule uninervis, Halodule cf. beaudettei, Cymodocea rotundata, Cymodocea serrulata, Thalassia hemprichii*, associées en une mosaïque complexe, composent les herbiers épirécifaux ou postrécifaux, toujours localisées entre les niveaux à *Halophila* et ceux à *Syringodium isoetifolium—Cymodocea ciliata*.

Originalités faunistiques des herbiers

Dans tous les herbiers récifaux se retrouvent dispersées les grosses Holothuries fouisseuses : *Halodeima atra* (Jaeger), *Holothuria arenicola*

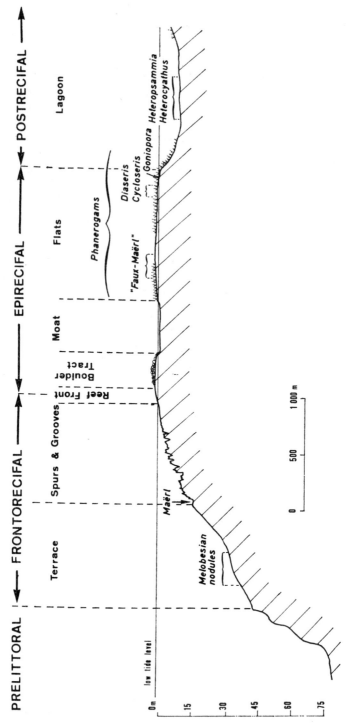

Fig. 3. Répartition schématique des divers faciès d'épibiose des sédiments coralliens sur une coupe théorique du Grand Récif de Tuléar.

Jaeger, *Holothuria scabra* Jaeger (la seule à peupler les herbiers terrigènes), *Actinopyga plebeja* (Selenka), *Holothuria impatiens* Forskål.

A la surface des sédiments on rencontre dans les herbiers de Cymodocées une faune de gros Gastéropodes carnivores: *Fasciolaria trapezium* (Linné) (prédateur de Pélécypodes fouisseurs), de très nombreux *Conus*: *Conus betulinus* Linné, *C. lividus* Bruguière, *C. miles* Linné, *C. tessulatus* (tous prédateurs de Sipunculides ou de Polychètes).

Les grosses Actinies pivotantes *Cryptodendron* sp., *Thalassodendron* sp., ainsi que les Pélécypodes Pinnidae (*Pinna muricata* Linné, *P. bicolor* Gmelin, *Atrina vexillum* (Born)) sont localisés sur les platiers récifaux aux zones d'herbiers mixtes.

La fronde des feuilles est un excellent refuge en sous-strate pour des espèces se nourrissant, soit du feutre épiphytique des feuilles ou du sédiment, soit de la faune vagile de la frondaison, soit des organes végétatifs. Ce sont de nombreux Gastéropodes (*Mitra flammigera* Reeve, *M. interlirata* Reeve, *Pusia aureolata*, *Vexillum pacificum* (Reeve), *Cypraea annulus*, *Strombus gibberulus* Linné, *Strombus floridus* Lamarck, *Tonna canaliculata* (Linné)), de nombreux Echinodermes (Echinides: *Tripneustes gratilla* (Linné), *Toxopneustes pileolus* (Lamarck); Stellérides: *Culcita schmideliana* (Retzius), *Pentaceros renhardti*, *Pentaceraster mammillata*, *Protoreaster lincki*, *P. nodosus*; Holothurides: *Synapta maculata* Chamisso et Eysenhart), de nombreux Brachyoures (*Calappa hepatica* (Linné), *Monoethius monoceros*, *Carcinoplax longimanus* (de Haan), *Huenia proteros* de Haan, *Thalamita chaptali* Audouin et Savigny, *Thalamita integra* Dana, *Macrophthalmus millioti* Crosnier, *Rhinolambrus gracilis* Dana).

DISCUSSION

Les faciès d'épibiose à Scléractiniaires libres, à Mélobésiées libres ou à Phanérogames marines semblent représenter divers aspects à partir des sables grossiers sous influence de courants de fond, dont ils matérialiseraient ainsi les stades progressifs d'envasement. De tels types de faciès d'épibioses ont déjà été signalés dans les milieux tropicaux, coralliens ou terrigènes.

Les faciès d'épifaune à Scléractiniaires libres

Les graviers et sables grossiers sous influence de courants de fond, caractérisés par une biocenose édaphique dont les espèces principales sont déjà bien connus dans la région de Tuléar (Thomassin, 1969a, b), renferment un Scléractiniaire libre *Sphaenotrochus* sp. De petite taille et de forme pivotante, cette espèce n'est jamais distingués de l'endofaune. L'extension de ce genre n'est pas du tout liée aux complexes récifaux, mais à un milieu sédimentaire particulier; ainsi on trouve *Sphaenotrochus intermedius* (Münster) dans les sables grossiers sous influence de courants de fond, en Méditerranée (Picard, 1965) et en Atlantique Nord (Glémarec, 1969), *Sphaenotrochus auritus* Pourtalès sur les côtes du Brésil (Kempf, 1970).

Les fonds à *Heterocyathus aequicostatus* et *Heteropsammia michelini* du lagon de Tuléar représenteraient un faciès de transition entre les sédiments grossiers propres des passes, peuplés par une biocoenose des sables et graviers sous influence de courants de fond (à *Venus lamellaris* et Céphalocordés), et les sédiments plus ou moins envasés de l'intérieur du lagon, peuplés par la biocoenose à *Ensiculus philippianus* (Dunker). L'existence de diverses espèces, telles les Polychètes *Ophelia peresi* Bellan et Picard, *Armandia leptocirrus* Grube, l'Anomoure Hippide *Albunea thurstoni* Henderson, montre des relations avec les "groupements permanents" des dunes hydrauliques édifiées au droit des passes (Thomassin, 1969b). L'important développement pris par le Bryozoaire *Anoteropora magnicapitata*, espèce récoltée dans l'Indopacifique sur des fonds de sables grossiers, coquilliers, ou de vases (Cook, 1966) et caractéristique des fonds détritiques prélittoraux dans la région de Tuléar (Picard, 1967; Guérin-Ancey, 1970), montre un autre lien avec cette biocoenose à *Turritella gracillima*.

Les fonds à *Heteropsammia michelini* ou à *Heterocyathus aequicostatus* étaient déjà connus dans l'Indopacifique, des milieux récifaux de mode abrité. Certains d'entre eux montrent une analogie parfaite avec ceux observés dans le chenal de Tuléar.

Dans le N.W. de Madagascar, des fonds détritiques peu envasés à *Heterocyathus aequicostatus* et *Heteropsammia* ont été reconnu au Sud de Nossi-Bé. L'endofaune renferme soit, divers Lucinidae, l'Echinide *Fibularia ovulum*, et des petits Bryozoaires libres (Pichon, 1969; Masse, 1970); soit un peuplement dominé par une espèce de *Callianassa*, associée à de nombreux autres Décapodes (*Leucosia, Areania, Podophthalmus, Cosmonotus*, Alphaeidae, *Processa*), le restant de l'endofaune étant pauvre (présence d'*Asymmetron lucayanum*), que Plante (1967) apparente aux communautés à "petits crabes", citées par Thorson (1957) dans le Golfe Persique.

A l'extérieur des récifs de Mahé (I. Seychelles), Taylor (1968) trouve par 25 m un fond du même type. Des sables moyens, coquilliers, y renferment, outre les *Heteropsammia* et les *Heterocyathus* associés au Sipunculide commensal *Aspidosiphon corallicola*, l'Echinide *Maretia planulata* (Lamarck), les Pélécypodes *Parvicardium sueziense* (Issel), *Ervilia bisculpta* (Gould), *Corbula subquadrata* Melvill, et les Gastéropodes *Fenella scabra* Adams, *Leptothyra candida* Pease, *Triphora monolifera* (Hinds).

Sur les fonds du Golfe de Tadjourah (Mer Rouge), Jousseaume (*in*: Bouvier, 1895) avait récolté de nombreux *Heteropsammia michelini*.

Dans le S. du Golfe d'Oman (Ras al Hadd), la "John Murray Expedition" (1933–1934) découvre par 16 m de fond (Station 80) un fond à *Heteropsammia cochlea* Spengler et *Heterocyathus aequicostatus* dont le peuplement est composé de *Dentalium octangulatum, Penoeopis vaillanti* Nobili, *Branchiostoma arabiae* Webb et *Branchiostoma lanceolatum* (Pallas).

Aux I. Maldives, Agassiz (1903) signale dans le lagon de Gan (Addu), dans de sables grossiers coquilliers à Corallines, des *"Balanophyllia"* avec Sipunculide commensal qui doivent être des *Heteropsammia*. D'ailleurs, Gardiner et Waugh (1939) y draguent des fonds de sables grossiers à *Diaseris* et *Cycloseris* à Malakadu Atoll (44 m), ainsi que des fonds de sables grossiers à *Heteropsammia michelini* et *H. cochlea* Spengler à Malosmadulu Atoll (75 et 16–22 m).

Dans le Sud du Japon (région d'Amakusa), Kikuchi et Araga (1968) rencontrent à proximité des récifs coralliens des fonds à *Cycloseris cyclolites* entre 7–10 m et à *Heterocyathus japonicus* (Verrill) entre 3–80 m.

Les fonds décrits du S.W. du Pacifique par Salvat (1964, 1965) et par Goreau et Yonge (1968), bien que très apparentés à ceux connus de Tuléar, montreraient des aspects déjà plus envasés.

Dans un lagon de la Grande Barrière d'Australie, à proximité de l'île granitique de Lizard Island, Goreau et Yonge (1968) décrivent, par 12 m, un fond mixte, coquillier et terrigène, dont la surface est recouverte de colloïdes et d'un peuplement d'*Heteropsammia michelini, Diaseris distorta, Cycloseris cyclolites*, avec quelques rares *Trachyphyllia geoffroyi* (Audouin), L'endofaune riche y est constituée d'espèces fouisseuses, parmi lesquelles des Cérianthaires, des Pennatulaires, des Echinodernes et des Pélécypodes (*Pinna ?carnea*). Des Algues caractéristiques de milieux de mode calme s'y rencontrent (*Caulerpa, Avrainvillea, Udotea, Halimeda, Penicillus*).

Le fond à *Heterocyathus* sp., *Cycloseris* sp. et *Trachyphyllia geoffroyi*, signalé par Salvat (1964, 1965) d'un chenal postrécifal aux eaux turbides de la Baie de St. Vincent (Nouvelle-Calédonie), paraît encore plus enrichi en fraction fine. Outre la présence d'un herbier d'*Halophila ovalis* et de *Cymodocea serrulata*, l'endofaune semble être celle de sédiments plus envasés (présence d'un Pennatulaire Ptéroïde). Ce type de fond montre un gradient d'envasement; il serait plus comparable aux fonds à *Diaseris* décrits de Tuléar, dans certains secteurs des herbiers épirécifaux (avec faciès à *Goniopora stokesi*) ou dans des zones déjà bien envasées du chenal postrécifal.

Rosen et Taylor (1969) signalent un fond à *Goniopora stokesi* dans le lagon de l'I. Aldabra, juste en arrière d'une passe (passe Gionnet). Les colonies y recouvrent à 80% un sable biodétritique propre, mélangées à des *Halophila*, des *Caulerpa* et des *Halimeda*. Ce faciès à *Goniopora* est toutefois quelque peu différent de celui reconnu à Tuléar. Alors que sur le Grand Récif de Tuléar, les colonies sont de forme subsphérique et subissent une exondation aux basses mers de vive-eau, dans le lagon d'Aldabra elles sont de forme hémisphérique, immergées dans 1 m d'eau aux basses-mers, et elles peuvent subir l'ombrage de la mangrove voisine. Par contre, la densité du recouvrement et la nature du substrat sont semblables dans les deux localités.

Les faciès d'épiflore à Mélobésiées libres

Les fonds de Maërl

Dans l'Ensemble frontorécifal de mode battu du Grand Récif de Tuléar, les fonds de Maërl paraissent représenter un faciès d'épibiose des sables grossiers sous influence de courants de fond et de la biocoenose caractéristique à *Venus lamellaris* et Céphalocordés qui les peuple.

Les fonds de Maërl étaient déjà connus de Madagascar. Ainsi, Berthois, Battistini et Crosnier (1964) en ont dragué sur les sables grossiers calcaires du plateau continental au S. de Madagascar (travers de Lavanoro, W. du Cap Ste. Marie, E. de Faux Cap; de 35 à 100 m). Au S. de Nossi-Bé (passe entre le Lokobé et Nossi-Komba), des fonds de Lithothamniées branchues prospèrent sur des sédiments mixtes, terrigènes et coralliens (Masse, 1970; M. Pichon et R. Plante, communications personnelles).

Dans les régions tropicales, de tels types de fond à *Lithothamnium* ramifiées sont actuellement connus des côtes du Brésil, en avant des récifs coralliens (Kempf, 1970), et le long des côtes W. africaines (Crossland, 1905; Longhurst, 1958; Masse, 1968; Morgans, 1962).

En général, les peuplements infralittoraux de Lithothamniées branchues, libres, associées à des sédiments grossiers propres ou très légèrement enrichis en fraction fine, pourraient représenter un terme de passage des peuplements référables à une biocoenose du type "sables grossiers sous influence de courants de fond" vers les peuplements des fonds détritiques prélittoraux.

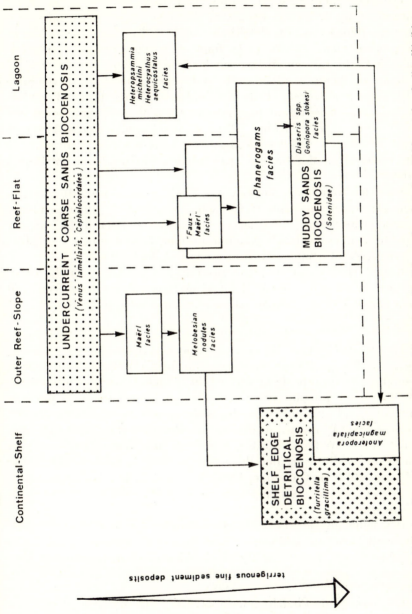

FIG. 4. Relation dynamiques entre les diverses biocoenoses benthiques de substrats meubles et les faciès d'épibiose des sédiments coralliens dans la région de Tuléar. (L'orientation des flèches indique le sens de succession réversible ou non et les parentés faunistiques entre les diverses biocoenoses et les faciès d'épibiose).

Les fonds à nodules de Mélobésiées

Dans la région de Tuléar, les fonds à nodules de Mélobésiées représenteraient un faciès de transition entre les fonds détritiques prélittoraux (biocoenose du détritique côtier à *Turritella gracillima* et *Anoteropora magnicapitata*) et les fonds de graviers propres frontorécifaux. Ils sont situés en enclave sur les fonds de type "coralligène" de la dalle corallienne profonde. Ils font partie d'un horizon référable à l'Etage circalittoral, et ils matérialiseraient un faciès d'épibiose frontorécifal transgressant par endroits des sédiments renfermant une endobiose de type prélittoral. D'après Picard (1967), Pérès (1967), ce faciès d'épiflore à nodules de Mélobésiées libres serait équivalent de celui présenté, en Méditerranée, par la biocoenose des fonds détritiques côtiers.

Dans les complexes récifaux, ces fonds à nodules de Mélobésiées n'ont été signalé que très récemment. Barnes *et al.* (1970) semblent en avoir découvert d'analogues à ceux du Grand Récif de Tuléar, sur la pente récifale N. de l'I. Aldabra, à 30 m de profondeur ("substrat . . . composed of compacted coral sands and rhodoliths").

Kempf (1970), sur la pente précontinentale des côtes du Brésil signale des fonds à nodules de Mélobésiées, en grandes taches, recouvrant des fonds détritiques peuplés par une communauté circalittorale.

Les fonds de "faux-Maërl"

Le terme de "faux-Maërl" a été pour la première fois employé par de Gaillande (1968) pour décrire un fond à Mélobésiées calcifiées, recouvrant la totalité de la surface du sédiment, par 2–3 m de fond, dans la zone la plus interne d'une calanque des environs de Marseille (France); fond très différent du Maërl classique. Ce "faux-Maërl", rencontrés en certains points des côtes de Provence et de Corse (Méditerranée), dans des fonds abrités, représente un faciès d'épiflore de la biocoenose méditerranéenne des sables vaseux de mode calme (Pérès et Picard, 1964; de Gaillande, 1968); les herbiers de *Zostera nana* et de *Cymodocea nodosa*, ainsi que ceux de *Caulerpa prolifera*, constituant les autres faciès.

Il semble que le "faux-Maërl" rencontré sur le Grand Récif de Tuléar ait la même signification écologique, et constitue un des faciès des sables vaseux, fixés ou non par les herbiers de Phanérogames marines.

Les herbiers de Phanérogames marines

Les herbiers de Phanérogames paraissent être un élément constant de la plupart des platiers récifaux indopacifiques (Pichon, 1964; Stoddart, 1969).

Sur les côtes de Madagascar, les herbiers de Phanérogames représentent de façon marquée des faciès d'épiflore des substrats meubles, biogènes ou terrigènes. Ceci résulte du fait que les Phanérogames marines considérées ont, en général, de larges tolérances vis-à-vis du substrat sur lequel elles poussent. L'endofaune du sédiment n'est pas essentiellement modifiée par la présence des herbiers ; cependant, on note un enrichissement quantitatif des espèces dans les sédiments à forte teneur en matières organiques (augmentation des Polychètes et des Sipunculides).

A Madagascar, les herbiers d'*Halophila*, du fait de leur couverture et de leur système radiculaire, sont des faciès d'épiflore locaux ; ils ne prennent jamais l'extension signalées dans le lagon de Tahiti.

Comme *Halophila stipulacea* (den Hartog, 1957), avec laquelle elle est parfois confondue (Isaac, 1968), *Halophila balfourii* croîtrait sur des fonds soumis à de vifs courants. D'ailleurs, l'endofaune de pelouses d'*H. balfourii* renferme encore de nombreuses espèces des dunes hydrauliques épirécifales (communauté assimilable à l' *"Astropecten association"* de Macnae et Kalk, 1962, à l'I. Inhaca, Mozambique) et de la biocoenose des sables grossiers sous influence de courants de fond. Elle serait très apparentée à l' *"Halophila stipulacea-Asymmetron cf. lucayanum* community", mise en évidence sur les fonds sablo-vaseux du Golfe d'Eilat (Mer Rouge), par 5 à 30 m de fond (Fishelson, 1968).

L'endofaune des herbiers d'*Halophila ovalis* et d'*H. minor*, au contraire, comprendrait de nombreuses espèces sablo-vasicoles. D'ailleurs, *Halophila ovalis* est souvent signalée de milieux vaseux, exondés ou non (Isaac, 1968). Elle serait très tolérante à la pollution (den Hartog, 1957) et semblerait associée aux vases réduites contenant un taux sulfures importants (Ferguson Wood, 1959).

Halophila minor est très répandue dans les milieux de mode calme, sur fonds sableux. Elle tolère bien une exondation porlongée aux basses mers et elle est souvent associée à *Halodule uninervis* den Hartog, 1957—en Malaisie ; Cohen, 1939—à l'I. Inhaca).

Les herbiers d'*Halodule wrightii*, de même qu'à Madagascar, occupent toujours sur les côtes E. africaines (Kenya, Tanzanie) les hauts niveaux du littoral (Isaac, 1968). En taches isolées, ces herbiers n'atteignent jamais dans l'Océan Indien l'extension qu'ils occupent aux Caraïbes (O'Gower et Wacasey, 1967).

Dans les autres herbiers de la région de Tuléar, lorsque ceux-ci ne sont pas implantés sur du matériel trop hétérogène, l'endofaune est constituée d'espèces sablo-vasicoles, dont les peuplements sont caractérisés par la présence de Pélécypodes Solenidae. Ces peuplements de sables vaseux à Solenidae se situeraient à mi-chemin dans la succession conduisant des sables grossiers sous influence de courants de fond (biocoenose à *Venus lamellaris*) vers les vases (biocoenose à *Macoma hawaiiensis* Sowerby, dans le lagon; Guérin-Ancey, 1970). Il semble d'ailleurs qu'il existerait trois modalités de cette succession, avec trois types de peuplements à *Solenidae* pouvant s'individualiser en biocoenoses ou en facies de l'endofaune:

1. le peuplement des sables coralliens grossiers envasés, à *Solen roseomaculatus*,

2. le peuplement des sables vaseux mixtes, à *Ensiculus philippianus* (Guérin-Ancey, 1970),

3. le peuplement des sables vaseux terrigènes, frontolittoraux, à *Solen corneus* (Pichon, Mireille, 1967).

Ces types de faciès à Solenidae remplaceraient dans les sables fins infralittoraux de mode plus calme les peuplements à dominance de *Donax* ou de *Tellina* (Pérès, 1961).

A l'I. Inhaca, Cohen (1939) distinguait deux niveaux dans les herbiers de Phanérogames, celui à *Diplanthera uninervis, Cymodocea rotundata, C. serrulata* dans les niveaux émergeant à peine aux basses mers, celui à *Cymodocea ciliata* et *Syringodium isoetifolium* dans les niveaux plus profonds. Macnae et Kalk (1962) individualisent deux communautés des herbiers: la *"Diplanthera-Thalassia* association" et la *"Cymodocea* association", toutes deux bien différentes de la *"Macrophthalmus grandidieri* association", cette dernière étant équivalente de la biocoenose des sables vaseux à *Solen corneus, Macoma dubia*, décrite de Tuléar par Pichon, Mireille (1967).

Sur les récifs coralliens de Mahé (I. Seychelles), Taylor (1968) ne considère par contre qu'une seule communauté dans les herbiers de Phanérogames: la *"Thalassia-Codakia-Holothuria* community". De la même façon qu'à Nossi-Bé, les herbiers d'*Enhalus acoroïdes*, en taches, n'y poussent qu'à la limite de cette communauté et des vases sableuses terrigènes (caractérisée par la *"Uca annulipes-Gafrarium tumidum* community", apparentée à la biocoenose des vases médiolittorales inférieures de Tuléar—Dérijard, 1965).

Dans le lagon des récifs coralliens de l'I. Maurice, Baissac *et al.* (1962) retrouvent les deux grands types de communauté des herbiers; au niveau des basses mers de vive-eau, les pelouses à *Diplanthera uninervis* et *Halophila ovalis*, dans les niveaux les plus profonds, les herbiers de *Cymodocea ciliata* et de *Syringodium isoetifolium* (cette espèce formant une ceinture au dessus des *C. ciliata*). Fait original, des pelouses algales mixtes (*Caulerpa, Laurencia, Gracilaria*) remplacent les herbiers de *Diplanthera*, sur les fonds plus envasés.

Sur les récifs de l'I. de La Réunion, Faure et Montaggioni (1970) précisent que *Syringodium isoetifolium* est la seule espèce de Phanérogames rencontrée; elle y constitue les herbiers postrécifaux.

Aux Low Isles (Grande Barrière d'Australie), d'après les récultats de Stephenson, Endean et Bennett (1958), les herbiers de *Thalassia hemprichii* et d'*Halophila ovalis* apparaissent comme des faciès d'épiflore des sables et des graviers moyennement stabilisés des retenues d'eau (moats). Les espèces fouisseuses sont les mêmes (notamment les Holothuries) ou les vicariantes de celles trouvées à Madagascar. La faune de surface est caractérisée de façon analogue par une abondance de Gastéropodes et de crabes.

En effet, la grande particularité présentée par les herbiers de Phanérogames est qu'au milieu épibenthique de la frondaison sont liés divers compartiments faunistiques très riches:

1. des espèces épiphytes, sessiles et sédentaires: le film de Bactéries et de Diatomées, des Mélobésiées (*Melobesia Lejolisii* Rosan; Hariot, 1902), de nombreux Hydroïdes (Gravier, 1970), des Gastéropodes divers (*Ischiocerithium rostratum* Sowerby, *Cantharides suarezensis* Fischer, *Phasianella* sp., *Smaragdia rangiana* (Récluz) *Smaragdia sowerbyana* (Monrouzier), des Crustacés Amphipodes (*Cymadusa filosa* (Savigny), *Lembos teleporus* Barnard; Ledoyer, 1969), des Ascidies (Vasseur, 1970).

2. des espèces nageuses: des Mollusques Opistobranches (*Aplysia petiti* Risbec, *Dolabella gigas* Rang) et Céphalopodes, de très nombreux Crustacés, Isopodes (*Paracilicea mossambica* Barnard,*Synidotea variegata* Collinge; Roman, 1970), Amphipodes (*Tulearogammarus peresi* Ledoyer, *Cerapus tubularis* Say; Ledoyer, 1967), Caridae (*Hyppolyte kraussiana* (Stimpson), *Leander tenuicornis* (Say), *Periclimenes seychellensis* Borraidaille, *Latreudes pygmaeus* Nobili, *L. mucronatus* (Stimpson); Ledoyer, 1968), de nombreux Poissons (Maugé, 1967).

En fonction de la surface portante, de la taille et de la densité de la frondaison (chez les *Cymodocea*, notamment *C. ciliata*), on note des variations faunistiques importantes.

CONCLUSIONS

L'inventaire des principaux faciès d'épibiose rencontrés dans les biotopes de sédiments coralliens, dérivant des appareils récifaux de la région de Tuléar, est donné en suivant la classification par "Ensemble" définie par Picard (1967).

Les rapports entre chaque faciès d'épibiose et l'endofaune connue des sédiments sont analysés. Ils permettent de définir les grands types de relations dynamiques à partie des sables grossiers sous influence de courants de fond vers les fonds enrichis en fraction sableuse et vaseuse, dans les Ensembles considérés.

Dans l'Ensemble frontorécifal

1. les fonds de Maërl représentent un aspect des sables grossiers sous influence de courants de fond,

2. les fonds de nodules de Mélobésiées apparaissent comme un facies d'épibiose frontorécifal transgressant une endobiose de type prélittoral.

Dans les Ensembles épirécifal et postrécifal

1. les fonds de "faux-Maërl",
2. les herbiers de Phanérogames marines,
3. les fonds à *Diaseris distorta*, *Diaseris* sp., *Cycloseris cyclolites*,
4. les fonds à *Goniopora stokesi*,

sont divers aspects d'épiflore et d'épifaune de mode calme, des sédiments sableux, plus ou moins envasés et stabilisés, de l'accumulation sableuse en arrière du platier récifal ou des fonds de lagon.

Dans l'Ensemble postrécifal

Les fonds à *Heterocyathus aequicostatus* et *Heteropsammia michelini* représentent un faciès d'ensablement de la biocoenose des sables grossiers sous influence de courants de fond. La tendance au développement d'un faciès à *Anoteropora magnicapitata* montre une parenté avec les fonds détritiques prélittoraux propres.

Ces divers faciès d'épibiose sont comparés à ceux connus des milieux tropicaux, coralliens ou terrigènes, plus particulièrement de l'Indopacifique, et exceptionnellement à ceux décrits des milieux tempérés-chauds (Mer Méditerranée).

BIBLIOGRAPHIE

Agassiz, A. (1903). The coral reefs of the Maldives. *Mem. Mus. comp. Zool. Harv. Coll.* **29**: 168p.

Baissac, J. de B., Lubet, P. E. et Michel, C. M. (1962). Les biocoenoses benthiques littorales de l'Ile Maurice. *Recl Trav. Stn mar. Endoume* **25**: 253–291.

Barnes, J., Bellamy, D. J., Jones, D. J., Whitton, B. A., Drew, E. and Lythgoe, J. (1970). Sublittoral Reef phenomena of Aldabra. *Nature, Lond.* **225**: 268–269.

Battistini, R. (1966). La morphologie de l'Ile Europa. *Mém. Mus. natn. Hist. nat. Paris* (n.s.) (A) **41**: 7–17.

Berthois, L., Battistini, R. et Crosnier, A. (1964). Recherches sur le relief et la sédimentologie du plateau continental de l'extrème Sud de Madagascar. *Cah. Océanogr. C.C.O.E.C.* **1964** (7): 511–527.

Bouvier, E.-L., (1895). Le commensalisme de certains polypes Madréporaires. *Annls Sci. nat.* (Pris) **20**: 1–32.

Chassé, C. (1962). Remarque sur la morphologie et la bionomie des herbiers de Monocotylédones marines tropicales de la province de Tuléar (République Malgache). *Recl Trav. Stn mar. Endoume* (fasc. hors sér.) Suppl. **6**: 25–35.

Cohen, E. (1939). The marine Angiosperms of Inhaca Island. *S. Afr. J. Sci.* **36**: 246–256.

Cook, P. L. (1966). Some "sand fauna" Polyzoa (Bryozoa) from Eastern Africa and the Northern Indian Ocean. *Cah. Biol. mar.* **7**: 207–223.

Crossland, C. (1905). Ecology and deposits of the Cape Verde marine fauna. *Proc. zool. Soc. Lond.* **1905** (1): 170–186.

Derijard, R. (1965). Contribution à l'étude des peuplements des sédiments sablo-vaseux ou vaseux intertidaux, compactés ou fixés par la végétation dans la région de Tuléar (S.W. de Madagascar). *Recl Trav. Stn mar. Endoume* (fasc. hors sér.) Suppl. **3**: 83 p.

Faure, G. et Montaggioni, L. (1970). Le récif corallien de Saint-Pierre de la Réunion (Océan Indien): géomorphologie et répartition des peuplements. *Recl Trav. Stn mar. Endoume* (fasc. hors sér). Suppl. **10**: 271–284

Ferguson Wood, E. J. (1959). Some East Australian sea-grass communities. *Proc. Linn. Soc. N.S.W.* **84**: 218–226.

Fishelson, L. (1968). Marine biological and oceanographical research in the Red Sea. *Final Report for Contract N 62558-4556 and Contract F 671052 67C 0043 between The Office of Naval Research and Tel-Aviv University, Department of Zoology*: 65 p.

Gaillande, D. de (1968). Monographie des peuplements benthiques d'une calanque des côtes de Provence: Port-Miou. *Recl Trav. Stn mar. Endoume* **44** (60): 357–401.

Gardiner, J. S. and Waugh, P. (1939). Madreporaria excluding Flabellidae and Turbinolidae. *Scient. Rep. John Murray Exped.* **6** (5): 225–242.

Glémarec, M. (1969). *Les peuplements benthiques du plateau continental Nord-Gascogne.* Thèse Doctorat Sci. nat., Paris, n° C.N.R.S. AO 3422.

Goreau, T. F. and Yonge, C. M. (1968). Coral community on muddy sand. *Nature, Lond.* **217**: 421–423.

Gravier, N. (1970). Etude des Hydraires épiphytes des Phanérogames marines de la région de Tuléar, Sud-Ouest de Madagascar. *Recl Trav. Stn mar. Endoume* (fasc. hors sér.) Suppl. **10**: 111–161.

Gravier, N., Harmelin, J.-G., Pichon, M., Thomassin, B., Vasseur, P. et Weydert, P. (1970). Les récifs coralliens de Tuléar (Madagascar): morphologie et bionomie de la pente externe. *C.r. Hebd. Séanc. Acad. Sci. Paris* (D) **270**: 1130–1133.

Guérin-Ancey, O. (1970). Etude des intrusions terrigènes fluriatiles dans les complexes récifaux: délimitation et dynamique des peuplements des vases et des sables vaseux du chenal postrécifal de Tuléar (S.W. de Madagascar). *Recl Trav. Stn mar. Endoume* (fasc. hors sér.) Suppl. **10**: 3–46.

Guilcher, A. (1958). Mise au point sur la géomorphologie des récifs de coralliens de Madagascar et dépendances. *Mém. Inst. Sci. Madagascar* (F) **2**: 89–115.

Hariot, P. (1902). Quelques Algues de Madagascar. *Bull. Mus. Hist. nat. Paris* **8**: 470–472.

Hartog, C., den (1957). Hydrocharitaceae. *Flora Malesiana Bull.* (1) **5**: 381–413.

Isaac, F. M. (1968). Marine botany of the Kenya coast. 4. Angiosperms. *J. E. Afr. nat. hist. Soc. Nat. Mus.* **37**: 29–47.

Kempf, M. (1970). Notes on the benthic bionomy of the N.-N.E. Brazilian shelf. *Mar. Biol.* **5**: 213–224.

Kikuchi, T. and Araga, C. (1968). Description of the area studied and outline of the survey. In *Report of the underwater survey on the coastal area proposed for Marine Park, Kumamoto Prefecture. Contr. Amakusa mar. biol. Lab.*, Kyushu Univ. 208.

Ledoyer, M. (1967). Amphipodes Gammariens des herbiers de Phanérogames marines de la région de Tuléar (République Malgache). Etude systématique et écologique. *Recl Trav. mar. Endoume* (fasc. hors sér.) Suppl. **7**: 1–56.

Ledoyer, M. (1968). Les Caridea de la frondaison des herbiers de Phanérogames de la région de Tuléar. Etudes systématique et écologique. *Recl Trav. Stn mar. Endoume* (fasc. hors sér.) Suppl. **8**: 63–115.

Ledoyer, M. (1969). Amphipodes tubicoles des feuilles des herbiers de Phanérogames marines de la région de Tuléar. *Recl Trav. Stn mar. Endoume* (fasc. hors sér.) Suppl. **9**: 179–182.

Longhurst, A. R. (1958). An ecological survey of the West African marine benthos. *Fishery Publs colon. Off.* (11): 102 p.

Macnae, W. and Kalk, M. (1962). The fauna and flora of sand flats at Inhaca Island, Moçambique. *J. anim. Ecol.* **31**: 93–128.

Masse, J.-P. (1968). Contribution à l'étude des sédiments actuels du plateau continental de la région de Dakar (République du Sénégal). *Rep. Lab. Géol. Fac. Sci. Univ. Dakar* (23): 81 p.

Masse, J.-P. (1970). Contribution à l'étude des sédiments bioclastiques actuels du complexe récifal de l'île de Nossi-Bé (N.W. de Madagascar). *Recl Trav. Stn mar. Endoume* (fasc. hors sér.) Suppl. **10**: 229–251.

Maugé, A. (1967). Contribution préliminaire à l'inventaire ichtyologique de la région de Tuléar. *Recl Tarv. Stn mar. Endoume* (fasc. hors sér.) Suppl. **7**: 101–132.

Morgans, J. F. C. (1962). The benthic ecology of False bay. II. Soft and Rocky bottoms observed by diving and sampled by dredging, and the recognition of grounds. *Trans. R. Soc. S. Afr.* **36**: 287–334.

O'Gower, A. K. and Wacasey, J. W. (1967). Animal communities associated with *Thalassia, Diplanthera*, and sand beds in Biscayne Bay. I. Analysis of communities in relation to water movements. *Bull. Mar. Sci.* **17**: 175–210.

Pérès, J.-M. (1961). *Océanographie biologique et biologie marine.* I. *La vie benthique.* Paris: Presses Univ. France.

Pérès, J.-M. (1967). Les biocoenoses benthiques dans le système phytal. *Recl Trav. Stn mar. Endoume* **42** (58): 3–113.

Pérès, J.-M. et Picard, J. (1964). Nouveau manuel de bionomie benthique de la Méditerranée. *Recl Trav. Stn mar. Endoume* **31** (47): 137 p.

Petit, G. (1930). *L'industrie des pêches à Madagascar.* Paris: Soc. Edit. Géogr. Mar. Col.

Picard, J. (1965). Recherches qualitatives sur les biocoenoses marines des substrats meubles draguables de la région de Marseillaise. *Recl Trav. Stn mar. Endoume* **36** (52): 1–160.

Picard, J. (1967). Essai de classement des grands types de peuplements marins benthiques tropicaux d'après les observations effectuées dans les parages de Tuléar. *Recl Trav. Stn mar. Endoume* (fasc. hors sér.) Suppl **6**: 3–24.

Pichon, Michel (1964). Contribution à l'étude de la répartition des Madréporaires sur le récif de Tuléar. *Recl Trav. Stn mar. Endoume* (fasc. hors sér.) Suppl. **2**: 84–200

Pichon, Michel (1969). Les peuplements à base de Scléractiniaires dans les récifs de la baie de Tuléar (Sud-Ouest de Madagascar). *Symposium "Coral and coral reefs"* jan. 1969 Mandapam Camp India.

Pichon, Mireille (1964). Aperçu préliminaire des peuplements sur sables et sables vaseux, libres ou couverts par des herbiers de Phanérogames marines, de la région de Nosy-Bé. *Cah. O.R.S.T.O.M.* (océanogr.) **2** (4): 5–15.

Pichon, Mireille (1967). Contributions à l'étude des peuplements de la zone intertidale sur sables fins et sables vaseux non fixés dans la région de Tuléar. *Recl Trav. Stn mar. Endoume* (fasc. hors sér.) Suppl. **7**: 57–100.

Plante, R. (1967). Etude quantitative du benthos dans la région de Nosy-Bé: Note préliminaire. *Cah. O.R.S.T.O.M.* (océanogr.) **5** (2): 95–108.

Poisson, H. (1949). Le biotope à Cymodocées à Madagascar. *Naturaliste malgache* **I** (1): 11–25.

Roman, M.-L. (1970). Ecologie et répartition de certains groupes d'Isopodes dans divers biotopes de la région de Tuléar (Sud-Ouest de Madagascar). *Recl Trav. Stn mar. Endoume* (fasc. hors sér.) Suppl. **10**: 163–208.

Rosen, R. R. and Taylor, J. D. (1969). Reef coral from Aldabra: new mode of reproduction. *Science, N.Y.* **166**: 119–121.

Salvat, B. (1964). Prospections faunistiques en Nouvelle-Calédonie, dans le cadre de la Mission d'études des récifs coralliens. *Cah. Pacif.* **6**: 77–119.

Salvat, B. (1965). Etude préliminaire de quelques fonds meubles du lagon calédonien. *Cah. Pacif.* **7**: 101–106.

Stoddart, D. R. (1969). Ecology and morphology of recent coral reefs. *Biol. Rev.* **44**: 433–498.

Stephenson, W., Endean, R. and Bennett, I. (1958). An ecological survey of the marine fauna of Low Isles, Queensland. *Aust. J. mar. Freshwat. Res.* **9** (2): 261–318.

Taylor, J. D. (1968). Coral reef and associated invertebrate communities (mainly Molluscan) around Mahé, Seychelles. *Phil. Trans. R. Soc.* (B) **254** (793): 129–206.

Thomassin, B. A. (1969a). Peuplements de deux biotopes de sables coralliens sur le Grand Récif de Tuléar (S.W. de Madagascar). *Recl Trav. Stn mar. Endoume* (fasc. hors sér.) Suppl. **9**: 59–133.

Thomassin, B. A. (1969b). Les biotopes de sables coralliens dérivant des appareils récifaux de la région de Tuléar (S.W. de Madagascar). *Symposium "Coral and coral reefs"*, jan. 1969, Mandapam Camp, India.

Thorson, G. (1957). Bottom communities (sublittoral or shallow shelf). In *Treatise on Marine Ecology and Paleocology.* **1**: 461–534. Hedgpeth, J. W. *Mem. geol. Soc. Am.* No. 67.

Vasseur, P. (1970). Contribution à l'étude des Ascidies de Madagascar (région de Tuléar). III. La faune ascidiologique des herbiers de Phanérogames marines. *Recl Trav. Stn mar. Endoume* (fasc. hors sér.) Suppl. **10**: 209–221.

DISCUSSION

GUILCHER: I am impressed by the development of sea-grass meadows in many places in the Indian Ocean, in strong contrast to their scarcity in the Pacific Ocean. What are the causes of this difference?

STODDART: We need more information on the distribution of sea-grasses in the Indian Ocean. Thus only two species have been recorded from the

Maldive Islands, and those not until 1964. We have very little information indeed on the sea-grasses of the more isolated islands and reefs of the western and central Indian Ocean. It does seem to be the case that the greatest diversity is found in the southwest Indian Ocean. The contrast with the Pacific is most marked with the eastern Pacific, where with the exception of *Halophila*, sea-grasses are apparently absent from the Cook Islands and the Tuamotus. They are abundant, however, in the southeast Asian area. Den Hartog's recent monograph (*Verh. kon. Ned. Akad. Wet. Nat.* **59** (1970), 1–275) provides a great deal of distributional and ecological data on the sea-grasses of the world.

Symp. zool. Soc. Lond. (1971) No. 28, 397–431.

COMPARISON OF SPECIES DIVERSITY AND ECOLOGY OF REEF-LIVING INVERTEBRATES ON ALDABRA ATOLL AND AT WATAMU, KENYA

K. M. BRANDER*,

and

A. A. Q. R. McLEOD

Marine Science Laboratories, Menai Bridge, Anglesey, Wales

and

W. F. HUMPHREYS†

Department of Zoology, University College of North Wales, Bangor, Wales

SYNOPSIS

Extensive quantitative samples of components of the invertebrate fauna (Errant Polychaeta, Decapod and Stomatopod Crustacea, and Echinodermata) associated with intertidal and subtidal reef areas on Aldabra and at Watamu, Kenya are analysed statistically to give estimates of population sizes, species diversity, dominance and distribution. A brief description of the topography and general ecology of the reefs studied is given and the two areas are compared. Techniques for sampling reef fauna are discussed and a method of obtaining quantitative samples of the infauna of hard substrates is described. Results are given for several "habitats" (e.g. channel, subtidal coral platform, intertidal cobble ridge) and for different substrates within the same "habitat" e.g. live coral, dead coral) in order to test the validity of existing "habitat" classifications and to determine which factors may account for species diversity. In a section on the breakdown and colonization of dead coral, the action of boring organisms is considered and also their interaction with subsequent colonizers. It is concluded that, in general, hard substrates support a larger and more varied infauna than soft substrates; that biotic interactions play a very important part in determining species diversity (a measure of the importance is given in the section on colonization of coral) and that reef areas at Watamu support a greater diversity of species than similar "habitats" and substrates on Aldabra.

INTRODUCTION

Much work has been carried out, particularly in recent years, to establish why tropical regions support a greater diversity of species than regions of higher latitude (MacArthur, 1965; Lowe-McConnell,

---

* Present address: Fisheries Laboratory, Ministry of Agriculture, Fisheries and Food, Lowestoft, England.

† Present address: Department of Zoology, Australian National University, Canberra, Australia.

1969), but although some of it has been concerned with the theoretical aspects of species diversity in marine tropical communities (Thorson, 1957; Dunbar, 1960; Connell and Orias, 1964) there has been very little practical work (Parker, 1963; Paine, 1966). Several studies of reef environments and reef-living invertebrates have described the major types of "community" or "habitat" (Yonge, 1963a; Scheer, 1967; Taylor, 1968) and a few have attempted to describe the trophic structure (Odum and Odum, 1955). The "biomorphology" of Solomon Island shores is described in great detail by Morton and Challis (1969) and they have proposed a new terminology for the various components. Papers by Sanders (1968) on the marine benthic diversity of soft substrates in tropical and temperate seas and by Kohn (1967, 1968) on the diversity and distribution of *Conus* on reef platforms in the Indo-West Pacific have added a great deal to our knowledge of the subject and to the methods for studying it. Species diversity and the origin of species are interesting in their own right and also for the part they play in an understanding of community organization.

This paper describes our attempts to discover why certain "habitats", areas or substrates will support a high diversity of species, while others have few. We hope to show how the present ecological structure is able to support the number of species which it does, rather than to postulate how such a level has been attained, although the two are ultimately inseparable.

The groups dealt with in this contribution are the errant polychaetes, Decapod and Stomatopod Crustacea and Echinodermata. It has not been possible to include all the data on the detailed distribution of the animals of each phylum and the data on the sedentary polychaetes, Isopoda, Amphipoda, Cirrepedia, Mollusca, Sipunculida, and Pycnogonida have yet to be worked up. Fauna lists and further publications, which will treat the special features and adaptations of the major phyla are in preparation.

A very large proportion of the time was spent in the identification of the collections and the authors are responsible for all the identifications (Brander—Polychaeta; Humphreys—Echinodermata; McLeod—Crustacea).

TOPOGRAPHY, CLIMATE AND PHYSICAL CONDITIONS

General description of Aldabra

Aldabra is an elevated limestone atoll (9°24'S, 46°20'E; Fig. 1) 650 km off the African mainland. It is separated from all land, save

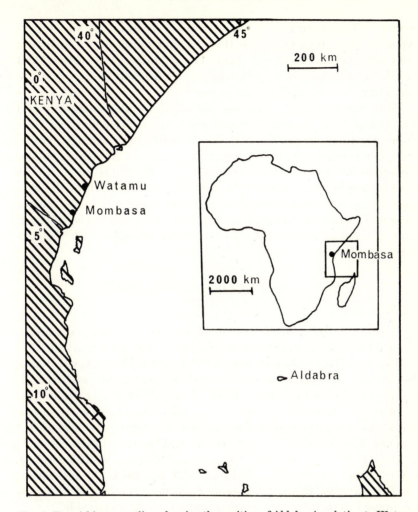

FIG. 1. East African coastline, showing the position of Aldabra in relation to Watamu.

for Cosmoledo and Assumption, by an oceanic basin of between 2 and 3 thousand fathoms.

The morphology of recent and fossil reefs has been reviewed by Stoddart (1969); that of Aldabra by Stoddart *et al.* (1971) and Barnes *et al.* (1970). The raised limestone rises to a general level of around 3 m and reaches a maximum of 10 m. Stoddart (1967) reviews and supplements previous work on the atoll.

The atoll is surrounded by a moderate to extensive reef flat of varying level and the rim is penetrated by a series of shallow and deep channels. The nature of the shore varies according to the degree of exposure, from high energy in the east and southeast to medium and low energy in the north and west. The characteristics of the Aldabra reefs have been discussed by Barnes *et al.* (1970) and their work suggests that the reef is advancing only to the west.

The seasons on Aldabra are governed by the migration of the subtropical high pressure belt and the intervening equatorial trough. From April to October the S.E. Trade-winds blow strongly, bringing negligible rainfall. During the summer months of November to March the monsoon season brings moderate N.N.W. winds and with them the major rainfall. Farrow (1971) has shown that much of the annual rainfall can fall within a few days and that Aldabra is in the most arid section of the Indian Ocean. His work indicates potential lagoon surface temperatures of 35°C if extreme low water coincides with the middle of the day in summer.

Description of the sampling areas on Aldabra

Passe du Bois

Figure 2 is a map of the Western Channels and Settlement area and the positions of the profiles shown in Figs 3 and 4 are marked.

Passe du Bois is the only one of the Western Channels which deeply dissects the reef platform and as such is comparable with the other major channels of the atoll: Grande Passe, Passe Houareau and Passe Gionnet. It is bounded by low energy cliffs with a deep solution notch, which rise from the *Cymodocea*-covered intertidal flats bordering the channel. The flats drop off very steeply and the sides of the channel are lined with a variety of corals and coral rubble (Fig. 5). The coral cover is fairly low—about 20%—and a notable feature is the presence of a black *Dendrophyllia* sp. This occurs from near the bottom right up to the lower intertidal and is more abundant on the north side.

The bottom of the channel (Fig. 6) is composed of mobile sand and rubble and supports no live coral, except at the seaward end, where it becomes wider and shallower, before falling again to the sandy fan just beyond the edge of the intertidal boulder ridge. Lagoonwards the channel is soon lost amongst the *Cymodocea* flats and coral growth.

Tidal records and current measurements made during the course of our work in Passe du Bois are fully described in Farrow and Brander (1971). Temperature and salinity records were also kept and between 12th August and 8th September they show a mean temperature of 25·3°C, with a maximum of 28·5°C (at the end of the ebb period) and a minimum of 23·0°C (during the inflowing tide). The mean salinity

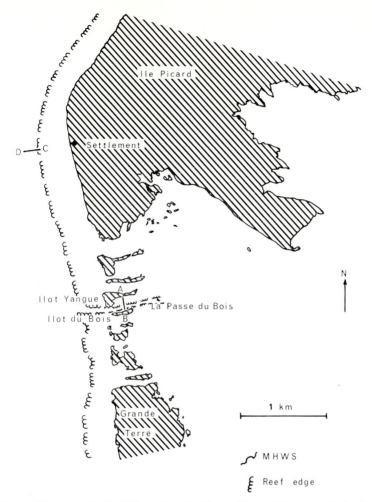

Fig. 2. Western end of Aldabra, showing the position of the transects in Passe du Bois and off Settlement.

for the period was $35 \cdot 16^\circ/_{00}$ with a maximum of $35 \cdot 64^\circ/_{00}$ and a minimum of $33 \cdot 24^\circ/_{00}$. Thirteen out of eighteen readings fell within the range $35–35 \cdot 5^\circ/_{00}$. Measurements made over a complete tidal cycle and analysis of other records indicate highest salinities at the end of the ebb period and the fluctuation over the cycle is about $1^\circ/_{00}$.

Settlement reef

The beach at Settlement is the only extensive one on the island. It is a steeply shelving low energy beach, due to its leeward position

17

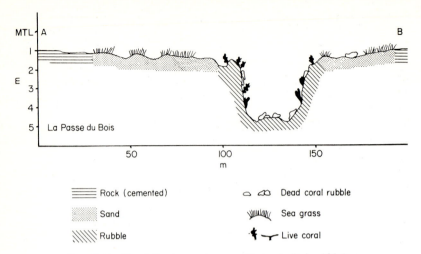

FIG. 3. Profile of the transect across Passe du Bois, Aldabra.

during the dominant S.E. Trades. An inshore rock platform fringes part of the beach, but is only extensive immediately north of the landing. The reef flats are intertidal at Settlement, but slope down into the shallow sublittoral to the south. They are sparsely covered with marine angiosperms, chiefly *Cymodocea* sp., which is progressively eroded and covered by sand to the north during the S.E. Trades. The flats are pitted with erosion hollows up to one meter deep and lined with sand and rubble.

At the seaward limit of the intertidal flats there is a well defined boulder ridge, beyond which a gently shelving rock platform merges into sand patches, *Cymodocea* beds and millepore corals (Fig. 3). Barnes *et al.* (this volume, pp. 87–114) have outlined a zonation scheme for this reef front, based on a photographic transect. Our sampling was carried

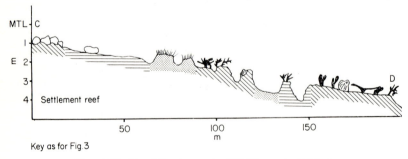

FIG. 4. Profile of the transect off Settlement, Aldabra.

Fig. 5. Side of Passe du Bois, showing a diver sampling a one meter square quadrat.

FIG. 6.   Wire mesh shark cage on the bottom of Passe du Bois. The mesh has been undercut by the current over a period of two weeks and some small stones have been carried on top of it.

FIG. 7. Profuse coral growth 4 m below MTL in the sampling area off Settlement, Aldabra.

out on the boulder ridge and subtidally on the coral area at a depth of 3–5 m below Mean Tide Level (MTL) (Fig. 4). A narrow sandy channel runs parallel to the boulder ridge about 100 m out from it, and at a depth of 3–4 m below MTL. This divides the coral terrace into an area of predominantly branching acroporan corals on the landward side and an area of mixed, small corals on the seaward side. Most of our sampling was carried out on the latter, where the diversity of corals is very high and the cover of live coral about 50% (Fig. 7). Beyond this terrace there is a shelf break at a depth of 4–5 m below MTL, below which is a belt of predominantly soft corals and below which we were unable to dive.

Sea temperature records kept from the beginning of October to the end of November showed an increase over that period, from an average of 25·2°C for the first half of October to just over 26°C for November. One also found a thermocline, particularly at low tide on calm days, with temperatures in the surface layer 0·6–1·0°C higher than on the bottom. No current speeds of over one knot were recorded during this period and observations while diving and from R.V. "Manihine" using a Carruthers totalizing current meter showed a prevailing northerly or northeasterly drift, with occasional changes to southerly. Surge has a much stronger influence on the coral area and made diving impossible on several occasions. It is likely to be even more important during the N.W. monsoon.

General description of the Watamu area

The Watamu Marine National Park is situated on the coast of Kenya (40°00′E, 3°20′S; Fig. 1) 22·5 km S.S.W. of Malindi and 960 km N.W. of Aldabra.

The past and present reefs of the East African coast have been studied at points ranging from the Sudan to Moçambique (Table I) and the Malindi area in particular by Thompson (1956). The coastal plain of Kenya is generally below 33 m and is 11 km wide in the Watamu area. The coast here is backed by a wide band of raised fossil reef and coral breccia, which shows little dolomitization. It is overlain by sands and sandstone and gypsum belts around Mida Creek and Kibirijini Point. Thompson further recognizes several marine transgressions and coastal terraces which are summarized in Table II.

The coast is fringed by a reef platform up to 1·75 km wide and patch reef development occurs immediately southeast of Malindi. Resistant coquinas form a series of champignon islets on the reef flats around Watamu. At Kibirijini and Watamu headlands these are joined to the shore by sands, forming tombolos.

TABLE I

Previous workers on the reefs of the east coast of Africa

S. Africa:	Boshoff, 1958
Tanzania:	Cox, 1927
	Crossland, 1902, 1903
	Ortmann, 1892
	Talbot, 1965
	Werth, 1901
Kenya:	Caswell, 1953, 1956
	Crossland, 1903
	Lawson, 1969
	McKinnon Wood, 1930
	Thompson, 1956
Sudan:	Berry, Whiteman and Bell, 1966
	Crossland, 1907
	Veeh and Giegengack, 1970

There is little continental shelf and consequently the water is deep fairly close offshore, although not as close in as around Aldabra. Thompson recognizes submarine terraces at -8 m and -35 m.

The weather on the Kenya coast is governed by the same seasonal factors as at Aldabra. During the S.E. Trades from April to October the winds blow strongly with great constancy and bring the main rainfall, which reaches a maximum in May. The "short rains" occur during the calmer N.E. monsoon from November to March. As with Aldabra the rainfall can be torrential and much of a month's rainfall can occur within a few days. Comparative meteorological data for Malindi and Aldabra are given in Table III.

Neither Aldabra nor Watamu come under the influence of a major drainage system. The nature of the terrain on Aldabra mitigates against any large scale run-off across the reef flats. The catchment area of Mida Creek is very restricted and the sands inland lead to slow percolation drainage rather than rapid surface run-off (Thompson, 1956). Hence the main rainfall effects in both areas can be expected when monsoonal rainfall coincides with extreme low water. At such times considerable damage to exposed corals can be expected (Taylor, 1968).

Turtle Bay (Fig. 8) is bounded in the north by a raised limestone platform with characteristic medium energy cliffs and adjacent reef flats. To the south the bay ends with the channel of Mida Creek. The

TABLE II

Recent earth movements and events in the Malindi area

Period	Local representatives	Earth movements and events	Pluvials etc.
Recent	Wind blown sands Marine sands	Sea level as at present day. Silting up of Mida Creek etc.	
Pleistocene	Upper	Silting up of Mida Creek starts. Sea level rises to present day. Terrace cut. Sea-level drops to about −25′ O.D. Coquinas accumulate. Sea level rises to about +25′ O.D. Wind blown sands accumulate on coastal plain.	Post-pluvial Gamblian 3rd Inter-pluvial
	Middle	Wind blown sands start to accumulate. Sea level drops. Platform cut about −130′ O.D. Coquinas accumulate as off-shore bars. Wind blown sands accumulate as dunes. Lagoonal sands accumulate. Corals grow. Sea level rises to about +120′ O.D.	 2nd Inter-pluvial
	Lower	Marine platform cut on which corals grow. Marine recession. Marine recession.	Kamasian Kageran
Pliocene	Lower	Uplift.	
Miocene	Lower	Marine invasion.	
Cretaceous		Uplift.	
Jurassic	Upper	Fluctuations in sea level.	
Triassic	Upper Karroo Lower	Uplift. Uplift.	

From Thompson, 1956.

TABLE III

Meteorological data for Aldabra (Settlement) and Malindi (22·5 km N.E. of Turtle Bay)

	Aldabra	Malindi
Rainfall mean	670 mm	1020 mm
Rainy days	112	105
Max. annual rainfall	1192 mm	
Min. annual rainfall	349 mm	
Mean humidity 0800	No data	80%
1400	See Farrow, 1971	72%
Temperature		
extreme max.	36·3°C	36·2°C
min.	19·5°C	15·6°C
Mean summer max.	32°C	30°C
Mean winter min.	22°C	22·8°C
Annual mean temp. fluctuations	4°C	
Mean diurnal temp. fluctuations	6·5°C	
Extreme diurnal range	11°C	
Mean wind speed (Beaufort Scale)	2·9	
Month max. rain	Variable	May
Mean rainy days		
March, Nov., Dec.	See Farrow, 1971	3
Jan., Feb.		1
May		19
Wind constancy April to October	91·8	

Sources: Aldabra—Farrow, 1971.
Malindi—Meteorological Office.

predominantly sandy beach is backed by low stabilized dunes overlying raised reef limestone, which occasionally outcrops on the beach. During the S.E. Trades the beach is exposed to the full force of the waves at high spring tides. Jones (1970) has shown, by particle size analysis, that the beach is increasingly sheltered to the north of Turtle Rock.

The beach and cliffs drop to a rock platform about one meter above datum. This platform occurs at a uniform level throughout the park and is characteristic of many parts of the coast to the north and south. A remnant of it forms the roof of the Big Three Caves in the middle of Mida Channel.

The most widespread bottom community in Turtle Bay is that dominated by beds of marine angiosperms, particularly *Cymodocea ciliata*. The flora of the coast has been described by Graham (1929),

Isaac (1967, 1968) and that of Turtle Bay in particular by Kay (1970). The grass beds extend from 0·5 m below MTL to 5 m below and those in shallow water are extensively eroded during the S.E. monsoon. To the south the grass beds are increasingly broken by sand channels and coral growth, ending in the mobile sands and coral areas of Mida Creek.

To seaward a poorly developed rocky ridge diverges slightly from the coast, to which it is attached by the peninsula at the northern end of the park. At its northern end it emerges on low spring tides, but to the south it gradually shelves down and is broken by surge channels up to 1·5 m deep. There are several lines of sunken reefs running parallel to the coast beyond this "inner reef".

The physical features, conditions and the principal animal and plant communities of the park are described in some detail in the Preliminary Report of the 1969 Bangor Watamu Expedition (Jones, 1970).

Description of the sampling areas at Watamu

Most of our rock samples from Turtle Bay were taken in the region of the coral heads (Figs 8, 9) at a depth of about 5 m below MTL. The coral here is mainly in the form of massive heads of *Porites*, with a fair diversity of other species and a cover of about 50% live coral. The heads border a deep sandy channel running parallel to the beach, but there are no currents along it. A few of the samples came from an area of dense coral growth near the Big Three Caves in Mida Creek, from an area which may in many ways be compared with the sides of Passe du Bois. Currents of up to four knots run through the channel, but the cover of hard and soft corals is high, even on the floor of the channel.

SAMPLING METHODS

The transect and quadrat method

The initial approach was to follow the kind of "habitat" classification widely used in work on coral reefs (Kohn 1967, 1968; Taylor, 1968) and attempts were made to obtain quantitative samples of the invertebrate fauna of intertidal and subtidal "habitats" in Passe du Bois, using a transect and quadrat method. A chain was laid across the channel floor and quarter meter square quadrats were sampled at regular intervals of 4 m or 8 m.

The method followed was for two divers to dig up the substrate to a depth of about 10 cm and put it in large polythene bags underwater. The volume of substrate obtained from each quadrat varied a great deal, depending on whether the frame encompassed coral heads or a

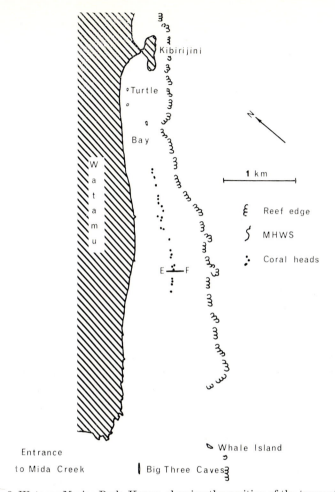

FIG. 8. Watamu Marine Park, Kenya, showing the position of the transect.

flat bottom (Fig. 5). Shovels, hammers, crowbars and a suction pump were used to complete the sampling. The samples were roughly subdivided into sand-and-gravel, coral rock (dead) and live coral. The average volume of material extracted from each quadrat was 18·8 l, made up of 7·0 l of coral rock, 3·7 l of gravel, 7·6 l of sand and 0·5 l of live coral. Figure 10 shows the percentage of each fraction in the samples from the three "habitats". The animals were extracted by breaking up the rocks into small pieces with a hammer and chisel and sorting by hand. In some cases the samples were so large that they had to be subdivided.

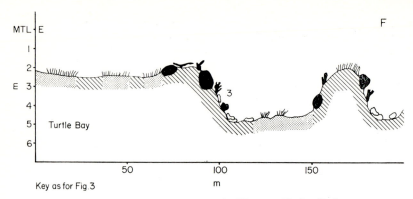

FIG. 9. Profile of the transect in Watamu Marine Park.

It rapidly became apparent that, although this method is suitable for sampling the larger elements of the fauna, particularly molluscs and echinoderms, it would not work with the small and infaunal elements. There are two reasons for this. In the first place the small animals are not sampled efficiently, since the volume of material to be examined is too large and the substrate composition too mixed. This point is illustrated in Table IV, which compares the numbers extracted per litre of coral rock by this method (Method 1) and by the method subsequently adopted (Method 2). Since the latter method has been shown to be only 58% efficient for polychaetes and only 81% efficient for Crustacea, it follows that extraction efficiency by the quadrat method is of the order of 5% efficient for polychaetes and 25% for Crustacea. The second, more important, difficulty encountered with the quadrat method is one of "within-sample heterogeneity". As may be seen from Fig. 10 the

TABLE IV

Numbers of animals per litre extracted from coral rock and sand in Passe du Bois. (1, by the quadrat method; 2, by the rock method) ± twice the standard error

	Errant Polychaetes	Decapod + Stomatopod Crustacea	Echinoderms
Method 1 Gravel/sand	$0\cdot5 \pm 1\cdot58$	$3\cdot0 \pm 2\cdot50$	$0\cdot4$
Coral rock	$3\cdot5 \pm 0\cdot87$	$1\cdot6 \pm 3\cdot97$	$0\cdot71$
Method 2 Coral rock	$35\cdot1 \pm$	$5\cdot26 \pm 2\cdot35$	$1\cdot7$

composition of the substrate within any quadrat from a particular "habitat" may vary considerably and it was found that the numbers of animals and the species composition of the different fractions within the same quadrat showed even greater variations. Table IV shows that the number of polychaetes per litre in the sand fraction was well below the number found in coral rock. A reasonable analogy might be to sample the animals of mixed woodland and heath with a large quadrat. It might give good results for deer, but would be impossible for counts of small arthropods. This is partly a question of choosing the right size of sample for a particular job, but it also raises the question of how widely applicable the existing kinds of "habitat" classification are in such a heterogeneous area. The infauna of a rock from a subtidal coral area may show greater faunistic affinities to nearby beachrock than to the sand on which it rests. In this context Hiatt's assertion (Hiatt, 1953) that the transect method is the only method by which a quantitative analysis can be made and that "any other means of collecting data will fall short of the critical analyses made possible by the transect method" must be denied.

A further difficulty encountered with all sampling methods is that of quantifying the data, as this can either be per unit of area or per unit of volume. It is common practice to give population densities in units of area, particularly in productivity studies, since this is the only basis on which incident light can be measured, but for infauna in an area of three dimensional complexity such as a coral reef this measure is unsuitable. Quantifying by volume is not ideal either, since the

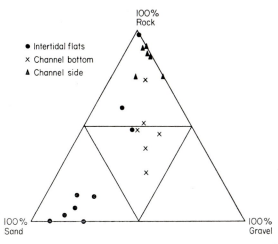

Fig. 10. Triangular diagram of substrate composition in Passe du Bois.

number of animals tends to decrease towards the centre of the rock. Correlations of numbers of animals with volume and area were calculated, but gave no conclusive results, because the numbers were too small. Our approach has been to give numbers per unit of volume, but we also made notes on the nature of each sample, including its surface area and on this basis we have been able to show that for certain groups, particularly Crustacea, numbers are related to surface area.

The rock sampling method

The method of sampling subsequently adopted was to pick rocks or pieces of coral of approximately one litre volume (Fig. 7) and to extract the animals by smashing the rock into small pieces, leaving the pieces in a flat gravel tray containing 5 l of seawater and 20 ml of 4% formalin overnight and hand sorting the following day. Fifteen samples were minutely re-sorted to test the efficiency of the method and it was found to be about 37·5% efficient for sipunculids, 58% efficient for polychaetes, 81% efficient for Crustacea, 93% for molluscs and 100% for echinoderms. Only animals which could be seen with the naked eye were dealt with. The efficiency of this method is much higher than the quadrat method for small animals and sampling and processing are much easier. We found that two people could take 6 replicate samples from a particular area or of a species of coral and process them in one day. Working with a quarter meter quadrat only one sample was possible, the extraction efficiency was low and replication of the samples was unsatisfactory. The problem of quantifying remains, but the variability in the volume and surface area of each sample is greatly reduced, which makes estimation of population densities far more accurate. The disadvantages of the method are that sampling is more subjective, because one is selecting rocks or heads of about the right size and one is only sampling a part of the "habitat". The method provides an index of the numbers of species and their abundance, rather than an absolute value. It is interesting to note that a similar method has been found useful in studying the ecology of the fauna of stones in a South African river (Chutter, 1968).

The echinoderms, errant polychaetes and decapod and stomatopod Crustacea have been identified to species and work is continuing on the remaining groups of these phyla, plus the sipunculids and molluscs. It is not possible to give full details of the distribution of animals within each phylum in this contribution, but fauna lists and detailed analyses are in preparation. Tables V–VII give the number of samples, animals and species for each area or type of coral sampled.

Table V

Sample sizes and numbers of errant polychaetes, decapod and stomatopod Crustacea and echinoderms
(nos per litre ± twice the standard error)

	No. of rocks	Total volume	Polychaeta Nos per litre	Crustacea Nos per litre	Echinodermata Nos per litre
ALDABRA					
Intertidal:					
Boulder ridge	14	14·9	7·45 ± 5·25	7·25 ± 2·39	0
Subtidal:					
Coral area	17	13·0	30·23 ± 6·04	4·77 ± 2·23	0·4
PdB side	12	11·9	28·51 ± 7·00	7·39 ± 3·25	1·7
PdB bottom	10	7·9	28·73 ± 11·0	2·04 ± 1·38	0
WATAMU					
Subtidal:					
Coral area	14	17·4	9·49 ± 4·62	5·92 ± 2·93	

TABLE VI

Comparison of numbers of species per 100 (or per 50) individuals as calculated by the rarefaction method

	Polychaeta			Crustacea			Echinodermata	
	No. of animals	No. of species	Species per 100	No. of animals	No. of species	Species per 50	No. of animals	No. of species
ALDABRA								
Intertidal:								
Boulder ridge	120	13	12·3	108	18	14·3	0	0
Subtidal:								
Coral area	393	33	20·9	62	17	15·3	5	3
PdB side	336	37	25·9	88	26	22·1	20	10
PdB bottom	227	19	15·4	16	7		0	0
WATAMU								
Subtidal:								
Coral area	219	50	38·0	106	30	22·3		

TABLE VII

Sample sizes and numbers of errant polychaetes, decapod and stomatopod Crustacea and echinoderms in coral samples from the Settlement coral area (nos per litre ± twice the standard error)

	No. of rocks	Total volume	Polychaeta Nos per litre	Crustacea Nos per litre	Echinodermata Nos per litre
Rock					
Coral area	17	13·0	30·23 ± 6·04	4·77 ± 2·21	0
Coral					
Pocillopora	6	4·5	4·44 ± 3·19	28·40 ± 11·28	0·9
Stylophora	6	7·4	11·80 ± 6·25	24·04 ± 10·94	1·8
Porites	6	3·6	5·00 ± 3·42	3·63 ± 1·94	1·1
Millepora	6	2·7	9·26 ± 9·63	12·39 ± 9·10	1·5
Acropora A	6	8·6	0·58 ± 0·57	0·61 ± 0·64	0·2
Acropora B	6	5·0	0·60 ± 0·83	54·81 ± 10·86	0·4
Leptoria	6	11·9	2·02 ± 1·89	1·92 ± 1·72	0

In order to permit direct comparison of species diversity between samples of different sizes, we have used the rarefaction method described by Sanders (1968) in his comparative study of within-habitat diversity of temperate and tropical marine benthic communities. Each group of samples is used to generate a line representing the number of species which would be found in a sample containing any particular number of animals (Figs 11, 12). Since the method depends on the shape of the species abundance curve, rather than the absolute number of specimens per sample, it is independent of sample size, however when the sample is very small, it is not worth applying the method and we have only given total numbers of animals and numbers of species. It is only possible to extrapolate for numbers smaller than the size of the sample by the rarefaction method. Even with our larger samples it has not been possible to give confidence limits for the curves and while we regard the general form and separation of the curves as significant we have not attempted to interpret the detail.

Sanders compares the rarefaction methodology with other commonly used measures of diversity. He finds good agreement with the Shannon–Wiener information function.

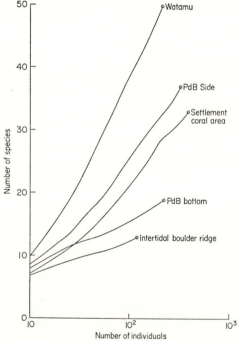

FIG. 11. Rarefaction curves for errant polychaetes.

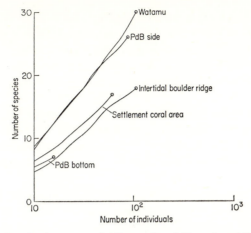

FIG. 12. Rarefaction curves for Decapod and Stomatopod Crustacea.

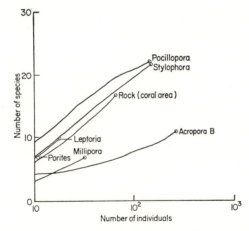

FIG. 13. Rarefaction curves for Decapod and Stomatopod Crustacea on live corals.

RESULTS

Comparison of species diversity on Aldabra and at Watamu

Preliminary surveys of the subtidal grass beds and coral areas at Watamu showed us that, as expected, the diversity of species is greater there than on Aldabra. This increased diversity was most apparent for the echinoderms, particularly asteroids and echinoids, but rock sampling revealed that the diversity of polychaetes and Crustacea was also higher, although only marginally so for the latter (Figs 11, 12).

The fact that the small units of sampling which we were using showed this difference is of particular interest when considering the hypotheses to account for the differences in diversity. Although it is impossible to select samples which are in every way similar from the two areas, our method does allow a high degree of confidence in the comparability of the samples.

The rock samples from Watamu may be most closely compared with those from the coral area at Settlement, Aldabra, which they resembled in type of rock, depth at which found, nature of the surrounding "habitat" and, as described in the "Introduction", physical environment.

There are two hypothetical patterns to account for a greater diversity of species in one region than another. In the first, each small component of one region has x times as many species as each equivalent area of the other. In the second, equivalent areas have equal numbers of species, but there is a greater variety of components in the former region. Our data supports the first hypothesis, although there may also be a greater number of different "habitats" on the East African coast than on Aldabra.

Kohn (1967) discusses similar data for the genus *Conus* in relation to "species diversity gradients" in the Indo-West Pacific from the Indonesian "faunistic centre" (Ekman, 1953) or "centre of dispersal" (Ladd, 1960). Until we can use our methods to obtain data from many more localities, our own views on the question must remain speculative. The diversity of the reef-living invertebrates which we have studied is higher on the mainland than on Aldabra and this is a "within-habitat" difference.

Comparison of the species diversity of intertidal and subtidal rocks

The intertidal samples, taken from the boulder ridge on the edge of the intertidal flats at Settlement, Aldabra, show the lowest diversity of any group of samples. There is however a difference between the polychaetes and the Crustacea in this respect, as the former show a far lower diversity in the intertidal than on adjacent subtidal areas, while for the latter the difference is small (Figs 11, 12). Most of the polychaetes live within the rock and one finds much larger aggregations of one species in the intertidal than in subtidal rocks. The Crustacea tend to be more mobile and scavenging and the dense mat of small green algae, mussels, detritus and sand found on the surface of intertidal rocks provides a suitable habitat. The Isopoda and Amphipoda are particularly numerous, but are difficult to sample accurately.

Topographically, the boulder ridge is very similar in appearance to the subtidal coral area and apart from surface cover, rocks from the two areas are identical. Thus topographic diversity cannot be responsible *per se* for differences in species diversity.

It seems likely that the intertidal ridge represents a community of the type which Sanders (1968) describes as "physically controlled", in which the physical conditions fluctuate widely and the animals are exposed to severe physiological stress, while the subtidal rocks come from a "biologically accomodated" community, which is a more stable, complex and buffered assemblage, characterized by a large number of stenotopic species. This is borne out by the presence of a few abundant and highly aggregated species in the samples from the boulder ridge and the more equable, but spotty distribution of subtidal species.

Table VIII gives the indices of species overlap for the chief sampling areas, using R_o (Horn, 1966). The intertidal polychaete samples resemble the samples from the bottom of Passe du Bois most closely. A possible explanation for this may be that both have lost the fraction of the fauna normally found on the surface of the rock; in the case of the intertidal sample due to wave action and extreme physiological stress and in the channel sample due to current action and abrasion.

The origin of the rocks on the intertidal boulder ridge may be of importance in determining the type of fauna they support. Those examined appeared to be of the same origin as the coral rocks and rubble of the subtidal coral areas. In many cases it was possible to determine the species of coral of the rock and the intertidal and subtidal rocks came from the same species. An experiment to find out how much movement rocks on the boulder ridge undergo showed that little movement took place during the two and a half months of the experiment. This period included some very rough weather and there was considerable movement of nearby sand banks, but none of the experimental rocks had moved more than 7 m.

Comparison of the species diversity of subtidal rocks from the Settlement coral area, Passe du Bois side and Passe du Bois bottom

Of the three subtidal areas sampled on Aldabra the coral and rubble sides of Passe du Bois showed the highest diversity and the bottom of the channel the lowest, with the coral area off Settlement intermediate. The sides of Passe du Bois have a much lower coral cover than the Settlement coral area and there is more loose coral and rubble. Physical conditions in the Passe are described in the "Introduction" and in Farrow and Brander (1971). The high species diversity here may be

TABLE VIII

Indices of species overlap for the chief sampling areas, using R_o (Horn, 1966)

Polychaeta

	Passe du Bois side	Passe du Bois bottom	Settlement coral area	Settlement intertidal
Passe du Bois bottom	0·8974	—	—	—
Settlement coral area	0·8607	0·8791	—	—
Settlement intertidal	0·4962	0·6778	0·6179	—
Watamu	0·5508	0·5249	0·5234	0·4781

Crustacea

	Passe du Bois side	Passe du Bois bottom	Settlement coral area	Settlement intertidal
Passe du Bois bottom	0·0428	—	—	—
Settlement coral area	0·5574	0·2509	—	—
Settlement intertidal	0·2003	0·0691	0·2128	—
Watamu	0·3868	0·2536	0·3060	0·1469

Total overlap = 1
Zero overlap = 0

due to components of the lagoonal fauna being present as well as the oceanic species. There is some evidence for this among the polychaetes, particularly Amphinomidae, but until the lagoon samples are worked up fully, the extent of the lagoonal contribution cannot be assessed quantitatively.

The contrast between the samples from the sides of Passe du Bois and the bottom is particularly striking, since they are in physical respects almost identical. The one important exception is current speed. Detailed measurements of the flow of water through the channel, using fluorescein (described in Farrow and Brander, 1971) have shown that flow along the sides of the channel and among the coral heads is extremely turbulent and the current speed is greatly reduced. Rocks on the bottom of the channel tend to be smaller and flat and are frequently covered with sand and moved by the current (Fig. 6). They often lack a surface cover of calcareous or filamentous algae and the surfaces are smooth and scoured. The numbers of surface living animals, particularly Crustacea, are correspondingly reduced.

Comparison of the species diversity of the fauna of subtidal rocks from the Settlement coral area and seven species of live coral from the same area

Tables VII, IX give the numbers of animals per litre and the numbers of species per 25 individuals and Fig. 13 gives the rarefaction curves for the Decapod and Stomatopod Crustacea for the corals and the "dead" rock samples from the same area. The coral species are:

Pocillopora eydouxi, a branching species, which forms small heads;

Stylophora mordax, similar to the latter;

Porites nigrescens, a grey branching species;

Millepora platyphylla, forming large upright plates, with numerous barnacles (*Pyrgoma* sp.) on them;

Acropora palifera (= *Acropora A*), a massive species, forming fingers 5–10 cm wide;

Acropora tubicinaria, (= *Acropora B*) a highly branching species forming extensive heads;

Leptoria sp., a "meandrine" brain coral.

The numbers of polychaetes to be found in the live corals is extremely low and those present were generally found near the base of the coral, where it becomes difficult to separate "live" from "dead" coral. A noteable exception to this is a large species of serpulid, which is fairly common on many live corals, particularly *Acropora palifera*. The numbers of Crustacea on live corals varies a great deal and there are often more of them than on the coral rock. The high numbers appear to be correlated with the degree of branching, or surface area of the coral and the brain coral and massive *Acropora* support very low numbers.

The rarefaction curves for the Crustacea show that the species diversity varies a great deal between the different species of live coral. *Pocillopora* and *Stylophora* have extremely high diversities and also show a high degree of species overlap (Table X). *Millepora* and *Acropora tubicinaria* show a much lower diversity of Crustacea and are in effect dominated by two or three abundant species. However, they show a very low degree of overlap. The reasons for these similarities are not at present known, but may become apparent in a closer examination of the species involved. There may be physiological and morphological adaptations to living on live coral.

TABLE IX

Comparison of numbers of species per 25 individuals as calculated by the rarefaction method

	Polychaeta			Crustacea			Echinodermata	
	No. of animals	No. of species	Species per 25	No. of animals	No. of species	Species per 25	No. of animals	No. of species
ROCK								
Settlement coral area	393	33	11·2	62	17	10·5	5	3
CORAL								
Pocillopora	20	12	12	146	22	14·68	4	4
Stylophora	72	18	12·17	159	22	11·92	11	4
Porites	18	6	—	11	7	—	4	2
Millepora	25	11	11	32	7	5·91	4	3
Acropora A	5	5	—	6	5	—	2	2
Acropora B	3	3	—	271	11	5·01	2	1
Leptoria	24	12	12	18	10	—	0	0

TABLE X

Indices of species overlap for some of the corals sampled, using R_o
(Horn, 1966)

Polychaeta

	Pocillopora eydouxi	Stylophora mordax	Millepora platyphylla	Leptoria sp.
Stylophora mordax	0·6012	—	—	—
Millepora platyphylla	0·6773	0·7719	—	—
Leptoria sp.	0·6664	0·6742	0·6475	—
Settlement coral area	0·9422	0·6141	0·7809	0·7744

Crustacea

	Pocillopora eydouxi	Stylophora mordax	Millepora platyphylla	Acropora tubicinaria
Stylophora mordax	0·8008	—	—	—
Millepora platyphylla	0·1122	0·1204	—	—
Acropora tubicinaria	0·0587	0·0571	0·0880	—
Settlement coral area	0·0642	0·0775	0·5482	0·0225

Total overlap = 1
Zero overlap = 0

The degree of overlap between the samples from live coral and from coral rock is very low. This suggests that, unlike the polychaetes, there is a change in the crustacean species composition when the coral dies.

Other animals found in the live coral include various boring sponges, Sipunculida and various boring bivalves, including *Lithophaga* sp. They all bore into the rock and make cavities, which are then occupied by other species. Most of the original colonizers of live coral are relatively large species, compared with the small polychaete and crustacean species which then move in. The breakdown is offset by the growth of a layer of calcareous algae, or even other encrusting corals, but these also produce "microhabitats" for other species to colonize.

An interesting contrast to the rich infauna of coral rock was provided by three rocks from Mida Creek, two composed of granite and one of sandstone. These had the usual profusion of species on the surface, but no boring species at all.

The relationship between the fauna of coral rock and the "habitat" as a whole

We have largely ignored the problem of relating our findings for coral rocks to the "habitat" as a whole, in the present paper. This can be partly justified because in the "habitats" investigated, coral rock made up at least 50% of the substrate. However in order to give some idea of population sizes per unit of area and per unit of volume for the whole "habitat" and to estimate the numbers of the larger animals— particularly molluscs and echinoderms, for which the rock method is inadequate—we have carried out a variety of quadrat counts and searches, the results of which will be published separately.

The validity and usefulness of trying to calculate population densities and diversities of small invertebrates for large scale "habitats" such as "smooth intertidal limestone platforms" and "subtidal coral reef platforms" is in any case doubtful. "Habitat" classifications based on characteristic organisms must also be treated with caution when trying to apply them to organisms for which they were not originally intended. As Stoddart (1969) puts it: "The description of zones by characteristic organisms fails to aid in reef comparisons, because of the wide variations in species composition and colony density within them."

DISCUSSION AND SUGGESTIONS FOR FURTHER WORK

In this study of differences in species diversity between coral rock samples (i.e. "within-habitat" samples) from different areas we have made three main comparisons (i) we have compared rocks from widely separate geographical areas, (ii) rocks from areas of differing physical conditions and (iii) live and dead coral, which may be described as rocks at different stages in an ecological succession. Although it is possible to establish differences in species diversity and abundance between samples, one may only guess at the reasons for such differences, since none of the factors held to be responsible was open to manipulation under controlled conditions.

The differences in diversity between Aldabra and Watamu are probably due largely to historical processes and to differing rates of colonization and extinction in the two areas. Beyond recording that such differences exist there is little we can add.

Differences due to physical factors may be open to experiment, such as moving rocks from the side of Passe du Bois to the channel floor and studying changes in the fauna. Our results indicate that species diversity is higher in areas where physical conditions are stable and not liable to great fluctuations. It has often been claimed (Sanders, 1968; MacArthur, 1969) that where conditions are stable marginal ways of life become possible and highly specialized forms of mutualism, symbiosis and "biotic interaction" evolve. This argument runs the risk of becoming circular, but if one looks at the present ecological structure and at the progressive breakdown of live coral by invertebrates, it does seem that "biotic interactions" play an important part in the structure. Whether the present-day ecological succession mirrors the evolution of such marginal ways of life is a different matter. We do not propose an extension of Haeckel's Biogenetic Law.

There have been a number of accounts of rock-boring organisms and of the breakdown of coral (Otter, 1931; Bertram, 1936; Yonge, 1963b; Neumann, 1966), but as far as we are aware no one has studied this from the point of view of an ecological succession, although Morton and Challis (1969) do give some details. The works of Thorson (1955, 1964, 1966) have dealt with many aspects of the establishment of marine benthic communities, principally on soft substrates. A paper by Kensler and Crisp (1965) describes the crevice fauna in temperate waters and the establishment of colonies in artificial crevices. We carried out two experiments to investigate the colonization of coral rock and building blocks and interesting results were obtained within a very short space of time.

Comparisons between the coral rock community and similar temperate communities have not been possible as we know of no study similar to this one from temperate waters with which to make comparisons. Laminarian holdfasts might provide a similar biotope. A study of the "community organization" of coral rock, including productivity measurements to show the trophic structure of the community would make direct comparison between the trophic levels and between this and other communities possible. As Dickman (1968) has pointed out, an index of diversity sensitive to changes in the relative abundance of all trophic levels can be obtained by using relative productivity rather than numerical abundance as a measure.

SUMMARY

The position, topography, general structure and physical environment of reef areas on Aldabra and at Watamu, Kenya are compared. A method of obtaining reasonably accurate estimates of components of the infaunal invertebrate populations of coral rock and live coral is described and compared with a transect and quadrat method. It is shown that for Polychaeta and Crustacea the extraction efficiency of the former method is much higher and where the substrate is heterogeneous it provides a more consistent index of species diversity.

Species diversities of errant polychaetes, Decapod and Stomatopod Crustacea and Echinodermata are determined for subtidal samples of coral rock from Watamu, Kenya and Aldabra, plus one intertidal sample from Aldabra and seven species of live coral from subtidal coral areas on Aldabra.

The highest diversities, as calculated by the rarefaction method, of both Crustacea and Polychaeta were found in the sample from Watamu and it is concluded that this falls in with the general pattern of higher species diversity on mainlands than on isolated islands. Of the subtidal samples from Aldabra, those from the side of Passe du Bois showed the highest diversities and this may be because both oceanic and lagoonal fauna are present here. The adjacent channel floor showed the lowest diversity, which is ascribed to the unstable, current swept nature of the substrate. The sample from the intertidal boulder ridge at Settlement showed the lowest diversity for both polychaetes and crustacea, but a few of the species present were abundant. This falls into the pattern of a "physically controlled" habitat, in which conditions of physiological stress determine the level of diversity.

The live coral samples gave mixed results, which will ultimately have to be interpreted for individual species. They show that there is an ecological succession as the coral is penetrated by various boring organisms, which in turn create "microhabitats" for further colonizers. Some organisms tend to break down the coral rock (sponges, bivalves, sipunculids), while others form encrusting layers which build it up (calcareous algae, other corals). As this process continues the diversity and numbers of polychaetes increases, but for the Crustacea the situation is complicated by the presence of large numbers of surface living species, which may either feed on the live coral or have some sort of symbiotic relationship with it. As the coral dies off many of these species disappear and are replaced by others. Thus the overall diversity of the Crustacea may not change, although the species composition will. Such biotic interactions play an extremely important part in determining the faunistic composition and diversity of this kind of community.

ACKNOWLEDGEMENTS

This work was carried out during Phase V of the Royal Society Expedition to Aldabra and during the 1969 Bangor Watamu Expedition.

We gratefully acknowledge assistance with fieldwork from all the members of the Watamu Expedition and from G. E. Farrow and J. Gamble on Aldabra. Our special thanks are due to C. J. Bayne, who took part in the first half of the project and gave us valuable advice and help.

References

Barnes, J., Bellamy, D. J., Jones, D. J., Whitton, B. A., Drew, E. and Lythgoe, J. (1970). Sublittoral reef phenomena of Aldabra. *Nature, Lond.* **225**: 268–269.

Berry, L., Whiteman, A. J. and Bell, S. V. (1966). Some radiocarbon dates and their geomorphological significance, emerged reef complex of the Sudan. *Z. Geomorph.* N. F. **10**: 119–143.

Bertram, G. C. L. (1936). Some aspects of the Breakdown of Coral at Ghardaqa, Red Sea. *Proc. zool. Soc. Lond.* **1936**: 1011–1026.

Boshoff, P. H. (1958). Development and constitution of the coral reefs. In *A Natural History of Inhaca Island Moçambique.* 49–56. (Macnae, W. and Kalk, M., eds). Johannesburg: Witwatersrand U.P.

Caswell, P. V. (1953). Geology of the Mombasa–Kwale area. *Rep. geol. Surv. Kenya,* **24**.

Caswell, P. V. (1956). Geology of the Mombasa–Kwale area. *Rep. geol. Surv. Kenya,* **34**.

Chutter, F. M. (1968). On the ecology of the fauna of stones in the current in a South African river. *J. appl. Ecol.* **5**: 531–563.

Connell, J. H. and Orias, E. (1964). The ecological regulation of species diversity. *Am. Nat.* **98**: 399–414.

Cox, L. R. (1927). *Report on the palaeontology of Zanzibar Protectorate.* Govt. Printer, Zanzibar.

Crossland, C. (1902). The coral reefs of Zanzibar. *Proc. Camb. phil. Soc.* **11**: 493–503.

Crossland, C. (1903). The coral reefs of Pemba Island and of the East African mainland. *Proc. Camb. phil. Soc.* **12**: 36–43.

Crossland, C. (1907). Reports on the marine biology of the Sudanese Red Sea. IV, The recent history of the coral reefs of the mid-west shores of the Red Sea. *J. Linn. Soc. Lond.* (Zool.) **31**: 14–30.

Dickman, M. (1968). Some indices of diversity. *Ecology* **49**: 1191–1193.

Dunbar, M. J. (1960). The evolution of stability in marine environments. *Am. Nat.* **94**: 129–136.

Ekman, S. (1953). *Zoogeography of the Sea.* Sidgwick and Jackson, London.

Farrow, G. E. (1971). The climate of Aldabra Atoll. *Phil. Trans. R. Soc.* (B). **260**: 67–91.

Farrow, G. E. and Brander, K. M. (1971). Tidal studies on Aldabra Atoll. *Phil. Trans. R. Soc.* (B). **260**: 93–121.

Graham, R. W. (1929). Notes on the Mangrove Swamps of Kenya. *Jl E. Afr. Uganda nat. Hist. Soc.* **36**: 157–164.

Hairston, N. G. (1959). Species abundance and community organization. *Ecology* **40**: 404–416.

Hiatt, R. W. (1953). Instructions for Marine Ecological work on Coral Atolls. *Atoll Res. Bull.* **17**: 100–108.

Horn, H. S. (1966). Measurement of "overlap" in comparative ecological studies. *Am. Nat.* **100**: 419–424.

Isaac, F. M. (1968). Marine Botany of the Kenyan coast (4). Angiosperms. *Jl E. Afr. nat. Hist. Soc. Natn. Mus.* **27**: 29–47.

Isaacs, W. E. (1967). Marine Botany of the Kenyan coast (1). A first list of Kenya Marine Algae. *Jl E. Afr. nat. Hist. Soc. Natn. Mus.* **26**: 75–83.

Isaacs, W. E. (1968). Marine Botany of the Kenya coast (2). A second list of Kenya Marine Algae. *Jl E. Afr. nat. Hist. Soc. Natn. Mus.* **27**: 1–16.

Isaacs, W. E. and Isaac, F. M. (1968). Marine Botany of the Kenyan coast (3). General account of the Environment, flora and vegetation. *Jl E. Afr. nat. Hist. Soc. Natn. Mus.* **27**: 7–28.

Jones, D. A. (1970). (ed.) *Preliminary Report of the 1969 Bangor Watamu Expedition.* Univ. Coll. N. Wales Press.

Kay, Q. (1970). In *Preliminary Report of the 1969 Bangor Watamu Expedition.* (Jones, D. A., ed.) Univ. Coll. N. Wales Press.

Kensler, C. B. and Crisp, D. J. (1965). The colonization of artificial crevices by marine invertebrates. *J. Anim. Ecol.* **34**: 507–516.

Kohn, A. J. (1967). Environmental complexity and species diversity in Conus on Indo-West Pacific reef platforms. *Am. Nat.* **101**: 251–259.

Kohn, A. J. (1968). Microhabitats, Abundance and Food of Conus on Atoll Reefs in the Maldive and Chagos Islands. *Ecology.* **49**: 1046–1062.

Ladd, H. S. (1960). Origin of the Pacific island molluscan fauna. *Am. J. Sci.* **258A**: 137–150.

Lawson, G. W. (1969). Some observations on the littoral ecology of rocky shores in East Africa (Kenya and Tanzania). *Trans. R. Soc. S. Afr.* **38**: 329–340.

Lowe-McConnell, R. H. (1969) (ed.). Speciation in Tropical Environments. *Biol. J. Linn. Soc.* **1.**

MacArthur, R. H. (1960). On the relative abundance of species. *Am. Nat.* **94**: 25–36.

MacArthur, R. H. (1965). Patterns of species diversity. *Biol. Rev.* **40**: 510–534.

MacArthur, R. H. (1969). Patterns of communities in the tropics. *Biol. J. Linn. Soc.* **1**: 19–30.

MacArthur, R. H. and MacArthur, J. W. (1961). On Bird Species Diversity *Ecology.* **42**: 594–598.

McKinnon Wood, M. (1930). Reports on Geological Collections from the coastlands of Kenya Colony. *Mon. Geol. Dept. Hunterian Mus. Glasgow Univ.* **IV.**

Morton, J. E. and Challis, D. A. (1969). The biomorphology of Solomon Island shores with a discussion of zoning patterns and ecological terminology. *Phil. Trans. R. Soc.* (B) **255**: 459–516.

Neumann, A. C. (1966). Observations on coastal erosion in Bermuda and measurements of boring rates of the sponge, *Cliona lampas. Limnol. Oceanogr.* II: 92–109.

Odum, H. T. and Odum, E. P. (1955). Trophic structure and productivity of a windward coral reef community on Eniwetok Atoll. *Ecol. Monogr.* **25**: 291–320.

Ortmann, A. E. (1892). Die Korallenriffe von Dar-es-Salaam und Umgegend. *Zool. Jb.* **6**: 631–670.

Otter, G. W. (1931). Rock destroying organisms in relation to coral reefs. *Scient. Rep. Gt Barrier Reef Exped.* 1928–1929. **1**: 323–352.

Paine, R. T. (1966). Food web complexity and species diversity. *Am. Nat.* **100**: 65–75.

Parker, R. H. (1963). Zoogeography and ecology of some macroinvertebrates, particularly Mollusks, in the Gulf of California and the Continental Slope off Mexico. *Vidensk. Meddr. Dansk naturh. Foren.* **126**.

Pielou, E. C. (1966). Shannon's Formula as a measure of species diversity: its use and misuse. *Am. Nat.* **100**: 463–465.

Sanders, H. L. (1960). Benthic Studies in Buzzards Bay. III The Structure of the Soft Bottom Community. *Limnol. Oceanogr.* **5**(2): 138–153.

Sanders, H. L. (1968). Marine benthic diversity: a comparative study. *Am. Nat.* **102**: 243–282.

Scheer, G. (1967). Uber die Methodik der Untersuchung von Korallenriffen. *Z. Morph. Ökol. Tiere* **60**: 105–114.

Stoddart, D. R. (1967) (ed.). Ecology of Aldabra Atoll, Indian Ocean. *Atoll. Res. Bull.* **118**: 1–141.

Stoddart, D. R. (1969). Ecology and morphology of Recent coral reefs. *Biol. Rev.* **44**: 433–498.

Stoddart, D. R., Taylor, J. D., Fosberg, F. R. and Farrow, G. E. (1971). Geomorphology of Aldabra Atoll. *Phil. Trans. R. Soc.* (B). **260**: 31–65.

Talbot, F. H. (1965). A description of the coral structure of Tutia Reef (Tanganyika Territory, East Africa) and its fish fauna. *Proc. zool. Soc. Lond.* **145**: 431–470.

Taylor, J. D. (1968). Coral reefs and associated invertebrate communities (mainly molluscan) around Mahé, Seychelles. *Phil. Trans. R. Soc.* (B) **254**: 129–206.

Thompson, A. O. (1956). Geology of the Malindi area. *Rep. Geol. Surv. Kenya* **36**.

Thorson, G. (1955). Modern Aspects of Marine Level-Bottom Animal Communities. *J. Mar. Res.* **14**: 387–397.

Thorson, G. (1957). Bottom Communities (Sublittoral and Shallow Shelf) In *Treatise on Marine Ecology and Palaeoecology.* (Hedgpeth, J., ed.) *Mem. geol. Soc. Am.* **67**(1): 461–534.

Thorson, G. (1964). Light as an ecological factor in the dispersal and settlement of larvae of marine bottom invertebrates. *Ophelia* **1**: 167–208.

Thorson, G. (1966). Some factors influencing the recruitement and establishment of marine benthis communities. *Neth. J. Sea Res.* **3**: 267–293.

Veeh, H. H. and Giegengack, R. (1970). Uranium-Series Ages of Corals from the Red Sea. *Nature, Lond.* **226**: 155–156.

Werth, E. (1901). Lebende und jungfossile Korallenriffe in Ost-Africa. *Z. Ges. Erdk. Berl.* **36**: 115–144.

Yonge, C. M. (1963a). The biology of coral reefs. *Adv. mar. Biol.* **1**: 209–260.

Yonge, C. M. (1963b). Rock-boring organisms. *Publs. Am. Ass. Advmt Sci.* **75**: 1–24.

DISCUSSION

Gibbs (The Marine Laboratory, Plymouth): J. Stanley Gardiner considered that the polychaetes constituted the prime and most effective agents in the destruction of coralline rocks. From his work on Aldabra, would Mr. Brander agree with this opinion?

Brander: No. Our impression was that sponges and molluscs are the most important agents of coral erosion, particularly in dead coral. Polychaetes are less important, and echinoderms even less.

Symp. zool. Soc. Lond. (1971), No. 28, 433–454.

OBSERVATIONS ON *ACANTHASTER PLANCI* AND OTHER CORAL REEF ECHINODERMS IN THE SUDANESE RED SEA

R. F. G. ORMOND

Physiological Laboratory, University of Cambridge, Cambridge, England

and

A. C. CAMPBELL

Department of Zoology, Oxford University, Oxford, England

SYNOPSIS

Plague numbers of *Acanthaster planci* (the Crown-of-Thorns Starfish) have been recorded in the last six years in an increasing number of places in the Pacific, and recently perhaps off the east coast of Malaysia and in the Indian Ocean. In the Sudanese Red Sea. *A. planci* were found at approximately normal or pre-plague rates, and equal numbers of two year olds and three or more year olds were found. The population of *Charonia tritonis* (the Giant Triton) seems too low to be an important factor in controlling the *A. planci* population, but a quarter of the *A. planci* found had missing or damaged arms. *A. planci* favoured areas that were not sandy, not too exposed, and where there was a high density of coral, and they tended to travel further between meals in unfavourable areas. Comparison of the genera of coral predated in different situations suggested that the difficulty of holding on to different coral growth forms while attacking them is important in determining which forms are predated and in producing the low numbers of *A. planci* in exposed areas. *A. planci* were found down to depths of 16 m and signs of predation by them to depths of 20 m; smaller *A. planci* were found in shallower water and near Port Sudan, in two more limited areas, including zones of reef with a high proportion of bare coral rock. Specimens of *A. planci* found in the Red Sea have fewer arms than those described from the Pacific.

Of the echinoids found in the area, *Echinostrephus molare* was locally observed boring into the coral limestone of the more sheltered reefs. It may assist coral reef erosion. Grazing echinoids were commonly met with, and it is likely that they help to restrict the growth of algae on the reefs.

The ophiuroids *Ophiocoma pica* and *O. erinaceus* were plentiful in the branches of corals near the water surface.

INTRODUCTION AND REVIEW

During 1968–1969 our group has been studying the biology of *Acanthaster planci*, the "Crown-of-Thorns" starfish, in the Red Sea, and at the same time gathering comparative data on the other coral reef echinoderms. The information that is available on the echinoderms of the Red Sea depends largely on the work of Clark (1952, 1962) and on that of Tortonese (1960). Most records come from collections made in the Gulf of Aqaba, the Gulf of Suez and in the area of the Dahlak Archipelago.

A. planci has recently become notorious as a coral predator, especially in the Pacific, where since 1966, plagues of these starfish have been found in an increasing number of areas. *A. planci* feeds by embracing a chosen living coral with its arms and then everting its stomach on the prey. The digestive epithelium is applied to the polyps, and its enzymes break down the living tissues. The products of digestion are absorbed, leaving behind a whitened coral skeleton. *A. planci* generally feeds at night, hiding by day in holes or crevices in the reef (Goreau, 1964; Barnes, 1966).

The effects of a large population of starfish feeding on the coral are dramatic. There is widespread destruction of living coral, rendering the exposed skeletons liable to erosion, and a breakdown of all animal communities that depend on the coral either for food or for shelter, Chesher, 1969a; Endean, 1969; Weber, 1969). Numbers of starfish were first reported near Cairns in 1963, and widespread destruction was recorded in the Green Island area of the Great Barrier Reef (Barnes, 1966); now a great portion of the coral has been killed in some areas, especially between Cairns and Townsville (Endean, 1969). Elsewhere infestations were recorded early from Guam (Chesher, 1969a), and the Westinghouse survey of summer 1969 (Chesher, 1969b), and other reports show plagues to be present in places widely scattered over the western Pacific (Fig. 1). The chequerboard distribution of these sites argues against the spread of any more viable strain of *A. planci* from one area across the Pacific. Previously *A. planci* had been recorded rather uncommonly in the Indo-Pacific, from the Red Sea and East Africa to Hawaii and Tuamoto, its northern and southern limits being those of the coral reefs. In the Indian Ocean, particularly, there had been records of *A. planci* from the Cocos-Keeling Islands (Clark, 1950); the Maldive Islands (Clark and Davies, 1965); the Seychelles (where C. J. R. Braithwaite reports very small numbers); the Andaman Islands, Ceylon, East Africa, Java, the Laccadive Islands, and Mauritius (Madsen, 1955); and Aldabra (D. R. Stoddart, personal communication, again in very small numbers). *A. planci* has been found throughout the Red Sea, from the Gulf of Eilat (Y. Loya, personal communication) to the Dahlak archipelago (Goreau, 1964).

In the past year we have had initial reports of large numbers of *A. planci* from several localities of the Indian Ocean. Those from the Seychelles and Addu Atoll were probably not in fact of plague numbers, although there may have been some increase in the population. A

Fig. 1. Pacific Ocean showing location of places where infestations have been reported. Data principally from Chesher, 1969b. Circled areas where Infestation reported; but note may only indicate large numbers within small portion of area named.

report of plague numbers in some islands off the east coast of Malaysia is perhaps well founded.

Chesher (1969b) in the Westinghouse Report classifies *A. planci* population densities under 6 separate conditions:—

1) The normal condition—less than 20 *A. planci* observed during a 20 min survey period towing divers behind boats. This corresponds to 4 or 5 *A. planci* per km of reef length.

2) 500 to 10 000 *A. planci* concentrated in a small area, suggested seed populations of a plague.

3) Increased plague numbers spread over several km. Up to 5000+ *A. planci* have been counted in such areas in a 20 min period.

4) The animals have spread out forming a front over many km.

5) Where *A. planci* have grazed most of the coral in the area. If the condition is recent, large numbers may still remain; otherwise an

equilibrium may have been reached where there are still more *A. planci* than normal and the amount of living coral remains small. Chesher suggests this is the situation described by Goreau (1964) at Dahlak.

6) A tentatively identified condition where the numbers of *A. planci* have increased towards condition 2, but recruitment has been insufficient for a plague to result.

So far the exact causes and significance of these outbreaks remains uncertain. Such plagues might still have occurred naturally before, and indeed some Pacific Islanders claim to remember such occurrences (Chesher, 1969b; P. Vine, personal communication). Whether or not this is the case, they present a problem of peculiar interest to the coral reef scientist, since if they were to reach catastrophic proportions his livelihood would perhaps be the foremost threatened! As to the cause, Endean (1969) has suggested that the collection of the major known predator, the giant triton, *Charonia tritonis*, may be the reason. This is a favourite shell with collectors. Very large numbers of this mollusc have been taken from the Great Barrier Reef of Australia in the last 20 years; its ability to destroy *A. planci* has been demonstrated although one *C. tritonis* can deal with only one adult *A. planci* in a week (Chesher, 1969b; Endean, 1969). Chesher (1969a) has suggested that the bare rock surfaces created by man's mechanical interference with the reefs might allow unusually large numbers of larvae to settle successfully, freed from the danger of being killed by the carnivorous activities of coral polyps. He noticed the tendency of seed populations to occur in such places in Guam, Rota and Johnston Island. The predatory activities of the starfish themselves, leaving a trail of dead coral skeletons fit for successful settlement would in either case accelerate the process. Other suggestions have also been made; that accumulation of chemical pollutants in the sea might have altered the balance of the plankton, and hence the rate of larval survival; or that a possible slight temperature shift in the Pacific in recent years could have had a similar effect. We hope that by determining what factors could control the populations of a non-plague area, the Red Sea, it might be possible to assess what factors are no longer operating in plague areas.

Of the other echinoderms we shall discuss, the echinoid *Echinostrephus molare* is of interest because it is not included in the lists of animals collected in the Red Sea, apart from one specimen reported by Mortensen (1943). *E. molare* is not described by Otter (1932) in his survey of boring echinoids. This species makes conical burrows, which enlarge as they deepen due to the growth of the urchin (Hyman, 1955). When present in quantities, the bore-holes affect the reef structure, possibly rendering it more liable to mechanical damage.

Diadema setosum and *Echinothrix diadema* are grazing species, and their feeding activities have been described by Mortensen (1940), Thornton (1956) and Lewis (1964). Bertram (1936) describes how the grazing activities of echinoids are important in controlling the development of algae on the coral limestone. These species of sea urchin were frequently found on the more sheltered areas of the reefs.

The commonest echinoderms in most marine communities are ophiuroids. Their influence on the ecology of coral communities is not well understood. It seems likely that they either use the coral as a feeding platform to support them while they feed either on detritus, or gather food from the surface film suspension; or that they scavenge upon dead or dying organic material (Nagabhushanam and Colman, 1959; Roushdy and Hansen, 1960; Fontaine, 1965).

AREA

The study area on the Sudanese coast was centred on Port Sudan and reefs were visited up to Mohammed Qol and Mayetib Island 120 km to the north, and Suakin and Qad Eitwid 60 km to the south (Fig. 2). Most of the detailed work, however, was carried out on the Wingate, Towartit and other reefs, within a 10 km radius of Port Sudan itself. Port Sudan is situated on the edge of a coastal semi-desert plane which is up to 30 km wide, and runs from the Red Sea Hills, over 2000 m high, to the Red Sea.

The reefs of the area were described by Darwin (1842). Subsequently their geomorphology has been investigated by Crossland (1907, 1911, 1913) and by Berry, Whiteman and Bell (1966). They consist of an almost continuous fringing reef, rarely interrupted by freshwater entrances. Along the coast are thirty or more Marsas or inlets, extending up to several kms inshore, which would appear to be valley courses incised during the lower sea levels and then flooded (Berry *et al.* 1966). The fringing reef, although poorly developed, extends along much of the sides of these Marsas.

Outside the fringing reefs is a series of banks and barrier reef complexes, widening in the south of the region to form the Suakin archipelago which extends up to 50 km from the coast. The barrier reef complexes cover intermittently about two-thirds of the coast and each is from 2–10 km wide. They are formed of barrier reefs along the outside edge and much of the other edges of large submarine banks. Within the barrier reefs are large numbers of patch reefs and knolls. Beyond the main banks are some smaller ones, up to 20 km from the shore.

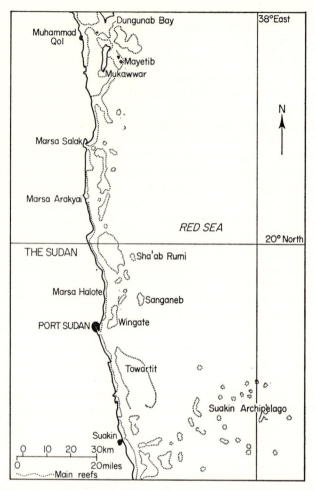

Fɪɢ. 2. A general outline map of the central area of the Sudanese Red Sea Coast showing main reefs visited.

The outline of these banks suggests that block faulting has been involved in the production of at least some of them (Berry *et al.*, 1966) and to the north the peaks of the series form Mukkawar and Mayetib Islands and are continuous with the peninsula surrounding Dungunab Bay.

Emerged reefs form an extensive coastal feature and five well defined, apparently untilted bench levels have been recognized at 2, 3·5, 7–8, 11–12 and 16 m above high water mark (Berry *et al.*, 1966).

Between the shore and fringing reef is a boat channel, up to several hundred metres wide, and three or four metres deep. It is generally sandy bottomed and in these calm conditions, some coral colonies actually grow freely on the bottom. In the gaps between the outer banks, deep water comes inshore and here, (e.g. Port Sudan) the fringing reef may be well developed. Elsewhere (e.g. Mohammed Qol) the reef may consist only of a band of knolls and coral masses in between one and 20 m of water, on a gently sloping floor.

Between the fringing reef and barrier reef complexes is a deep channel up to 100 m deep and 1–5 km wide, probably mainly structural in origin but accentuated by drainage along structurally controlled lines during lower sea levels (Berry *et al.* 1966). The submarine banks beyond rise from deep water of 600–1000 m to within 10–80 m of the surface and are surmounted by the barrier reefs and patch reefs. The barrier reefs and deep water fringing reefs (Wingate, Port Sudan) have a well developed terrace at about 10–20 m; sometimes up to 60 m or more wide, and the richest coral faunas occur on the face of these deep water reefs, above the 10–20 m terrace, and on the sides of the patch reefs.

The area is hot and there is little rain. The air temperatures average from 26°C in February to 32°C in August, and can reach 45°C. The sea temperatures average 25–26°C in February and 29–30°C in August, being cooler to the north. The annual rainfall averages less than 25 mm in the north of the region, but increases to perhaps 50 mm or more to the south. The prevailing winds are northeasterly all the year round in the northern part, but there is an appreciable portion of southeasterly winds during October to January, in the southern part. The winds are rarely strong, being less than force three (3·4–5·5 m/sec), for over 80% of the time, and over force seven (13·9–17·2 m/sec) (gale force) for less than 1% of the time, and no tropical storm has been officially recorded in the area. The tidal range is rarely more than 0·5 m (Red Sea and Gulf of Aden Pilot, 1967).

METHOD

The reefs were visited by inflatable boats, and up to seven divers searched the chosen length of reef for *A. planci*, or signs of its feeding activities. Both snorkels and aqualungs were used. Normal searches were considered to be effective down to about 12 m, but in addition a limited number of dives were made down to depths of 70 m. Signs of predation of coral by *A. planci* were an invaluable aid to finding the starfish. The predation was apparent as patches of whitened coral, usually occurring in groups where a single *A. planci* has been active.

The patches when new were a conspicuous clean white, and were easily visible from the surface. On closer examination some partly digested polyps were often still found on the coral skeleton, and with time the patches were covered with an increasingly dense layer of algae. On the more rounded corals the patches were almost circular, about two-thirds of the diameter of a starfish in size save where several adjacent patches overlapped. The boundaries of the patches were quite distinct, in contrast with patches of coral that were dying for other reasons, e.g. predation by other animals, or infection. Furthermore, the areas of white coral skeletons caused by the feeding of the starfish did not increase in size, while those due to coral dying as a result of other agencies did. Storm damage can also produce small white patches, particularly in the arborescent corals, but these were usually pieces that had been broken off their parent colonies. The only confusing instances of identification of corals that had been killed by *A. planci* rather than by other means, were very small colonies that were completely dead. Where such patches occurred in the region of more typical *A. planci* predated coral patches, *A. planci* was assumed to be the cause. Where one or a few of these patches occurred in isolation, they were ascribed to another. Wherever predated coral indicated the presence of an *A. planci* it was found if possible; some *A. planci* were found without any signs of predation having previously been noticed. The *A. planci* found were examined before release, and details of predated coral and habitat were recorded.

BIOLOGY OF *Acanthaster planci*

Abundance and distribution

During July and September 1969, reef areas were searched at 19 sites for *A. planci* or signs of its feeding activities. The areas searched are shown in the map of the Sudanese coast (Fig. 2) and results of the searches and brief descriptions of the areas given in Table I. Time searching per *A. planci* found, and length of reef searched per *A. planci* found, have been used to indicate relative abundance. The overall figures obtained were one *A. planci* found per 10 man-hours of searching or one group of patches of coral predated by *A. planci* (i.e. one *A. planci* actually present) per $5\frac{1}{4}$ man-hours of search or per 220 m of reef. The values per hour of search are not directly comparable with Chesher's (1969b) because of the different search procedure employed. Chesher's figures are per 20 min tow of a team of divers behind a boat, counting the immediately obvious *A. planci*, or groups of predated patches. Our figures per man-hour of search, even when several divers searched together; and whenever predated corals were found a considerable amount of time was always spent trying to find the starfish responsible. The values per length of reef match better the subjective impressions obtained for the varying population densities, and the overall value corresponds surprisingly well with Chesher's figures for the normal condition of four or five *A. planci* per km of reef. Hence the size of the population of *A. planci* in this area of the Red Sea would seem to be quite normal.

In considering the distribution of *A. planci* in the areas searched the following tendencies were apparent:

1) *A. planci* was not found in many of the most exposed places.

2) On the lengths of the more exposed barrier reefs, *A. planci* was concentrated at points which were more sheltered, to the leeward of spurs in the line of the reef, or at some depths on the terraces.

3) *A.planci* was often not found in comparatively sandy or seemingly stagnant areas.

Similarly it was noticed on the Great Barrier Reef (Endean, 1969) that *A. planci* appeared to avoid the weathered sides of reefs, and was virtually absent from many exposed outer areas; and in Guam the spreading of groups of *A. planci* into some areas was delayed or prevented by rough conditions (Chesher, 1969a).

Population structure and breeding

In the histogram (Fig. 3) showing data from the *A. planci* found in the summer of 1969, two size groups are apparent, distributed about animals of maximum diameters 22·5 and 32·5 cm. It seems likely that these are consecutive year groups so that the larger animals would have grown about 10 cm in the previous year. This correlates well with the growth rate of about 1 cm per month for the first year found in

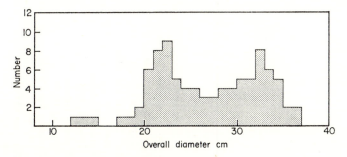

Fig. 3. Numbers of *A. planci* found of different sizes; overlapping histogram, number in 3 cm groups centred on overall diameter given.

TABLE I

Areas searched and finds of Acanthaster planci

Location	Sandiness	Coral abundance	Exposure	A. planci found	Other predated areas	Man hours of search	Hours per find	Reef length in metres	Length per find in metres
1. Port Sudan Lagoon or Boat Channel	S	CS	—	0	0	22	—	—	—
2. Port Sudan Fringing Reef	NS	CR	E	4	3	30	4	1700	240
3. Wingate Outside Barrier Reef	NS	CR	SE–E	6	5	41	3	1470	130
4. Wingate Inside Barrier Reef	MS	—	P	1	0	11	11	1110	1110
5. Wingate NE Patch Reefs	NS	CR	SE	1	1	11	5	590	300
6. Wingate SW Patch Reefs	NS	CR	P–SE	7	7	61	4	1670	120
7. Towartit Outside Barrier Reef	NS	—	E	0	0	11	—	490	—

#	Reef	Substrate	Coral	Exposure						
8.	Towartit Inside Barrier Reef	MS	—	P	3	2	17	3	1050	210
9.	Towartit NE Patch Reefs	NS–MS	CR	P–SE	5	2	28	4	1380	230
10.	Mohammed Qol Fringing Reef	MS	—	SE–E	2	0	9	4	540	270
11.	Mayetib Island Lagoon	S	CS	—	0	0	7	—	—	—
12.	Mayetib Island Fringing Reef	S	—	P–SE	0	0	11	—	—	—
13.	Mayetib Island Barrier Reef	NS	CR	E	0	4	18	4	1080	270
14.	Marsa Arakiyai Barrier Reef	—	—	SE	1	2	12	4	490	160
15.	Small Mayetib Island Fringing Reef	S	—	—	0	0	4	—	400	—
16.	Mayetib Mid-Channel Reef	MS	—	E	0	0	4	—	300	—
17.	Mesharifa Fringing Reef	S	—	—	0	0	4	—	440	—
18.	Marsa Salak Barrier Reef	—	—	—	1	1	2	1	290	150
19.	Reef 12 miles South of Marsa Salak	—	—	—	0	2	3	1	200	100
	Totals:				31	29	313			
	Averages:							5		220

The amount of searching in areas 15–19 is regarded as insufficient for the results to be very significant.

Abbreviations:

S = Sandy	MS = Moderately sandy	NS = Not sandy
CR = Coral rich	CS = Coral sparse	E = Exposed
P = Protected	SE = Semi-exposed	

The hours of search include a portion of those spent on subsidiary work. The portion is equal to the ratio of the average number of *A. planci* found per hour of subsidiary work to the average for ordinary number of *A. planci* found during ordinary searches.

Queensland (Endean, 1969) as the growth rate might be expected to decrease with age. The groups probably represent animals of the order of two and three years old. We do not yet know how old the animals may live to be, and up to eight years has been suggested (Chesher, 1969a). However, the second size group may include several year groups, but no animals of more than 39 cm in diam were found although animals of up to 60 cm in diam have been found in the Pacific. Thus so far it is difficult to deduce anything about rates of adult mortality, but comparison with population structures in plague areas might be instructive.

We are unable to state the breeding season of *A. planci* in the Red Sea, but for Queensland it is between mid-December and mid-January (Pearson, personal communication) and in Java ripe gonads were found in late April (Mortensen, 1931). It might be possible to deduce indirectly from our observations a certain amount of information about sites of larval settlement. *A. planci* were found at depths between 1·3 and 16 m, and signs of predation by them down to 20 m. The graph of depth against size (Fig. 4) shows the recorded positions for animals

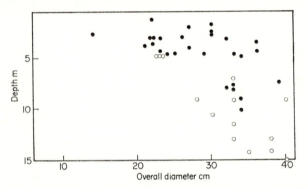

Fig. 4. Depth of *A. planci* of different sizes. ● size of *A. planci* found; ○ size of *A. planci* estimated from size of predicted coral patches.

that were actually found, and the mean depths of predation by animals that were not found, the size of the latter being estimated by the size of the predated patches they produced. The graph shows that the smaller animals were found in shallow waters, suggesting that larval settlement might occur there. This correlates with the finding of juvenile *A. planci* amongst the branches of *Acropora* and *Pocillopora* spp. of coral in 5 m or less of water in plague areas (Pearson, personal communication). Thus it seems likely that settlement is restricted to these shallow areas.

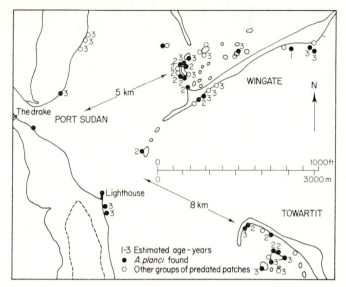

FIG. 5. Map of position of *A. planci* in Port Sudan Area.

The map (Fig. 5) showing the position and age of the *A. planci* found in the Port Sudan area indicates that the two-year-old animals were generally limited to two small areas, with the three-year-old animals more widely distributed. The authenticity of this appearance is disputable, but it might be that the animals are spreading out from areas where successful larval settlement has occurred, and it is of interest that these areas are those near Port Sudan with the highest proportions of bare coral limestone, and the greatest numbers of *A. planci*. They are those which would perhaps approach most closely the equilibrium condition (condition 5) defined by Chesher.

Behaviour and feeding

The favoured and unfavoured environmental conditions described above occur in close proximity, suggesting that the differing population densities result from an effect on adult behaviour. Even if larval and juvenile starfish had survived to different extents in closely adjacent areas, should these be equally favourable to the adults, then the adults would be expected to obscure this original difference by distributing themselves equally in the several areas. The starfish might actively avoid and turn away from unsuitable conditions, and descriptions from Guam of the movement of animals into new areas being delayed by rough conditions (Chesher, 1969a), suggest that this type of behaviour does occur. Likewise reports of groups of *A. planci* moving up and down with the tide, keeping clear of the rough surf zone (P. Goreau, personal communication) also support this idea. Another strong effect of environment was however apparent from the nature of the trails of patches of predated coral left by individual *A. planci*. In the least favourable situations the individual patches comprising the trail tended to be fewer and further apart so that it seemed that either the starfish ate less often or moved more rapidly across the reef areas. To assess this effect the number of predated patches produced within 30 m of reef by *A. planci* in different environments was compared. It is suggested that differences in this number represent differences in overall rate of movement rather than in feeding, simply because it seems likely that there was usually sufficient coral for an animal to find a suitable piece within a relatively short time of being hungry. In any case the ratios do give some idea of the relative rates of overall movement in different situations.

A total of 47 *A. planci* was involved showing an average of 6.2. Each situation, where a group of patches of predated coral was found, was assigned to one of the ranks under each of the headings Exposure, Coral abundance, and Sandiness and Table II gives the mean values calculated for reef situations classified as described. The first row of figures (a) compares the means for all the cases falling within each rank under the headings concerned. In the sub-tables (b) the values are compared for situations which differ in their classification within only one of the three headings. Finally in line (c) the mean values are calculated for the ratio of the values obtained in (b) and is the most accurate assessment of the starfish behaviour we have estimated this way.

Comparison of the figures in (a) and (c) indicate the inter-relationships between the apparent effects of exposure, coral abundance and sandiness. Thus it would appear that the lower value for protected situations than for semi-protected situations simply reflects the tendency for the protected situations to be more sandy and to have less coral. Thus when in (b) and (c) situations with similar sand and coral abundance, ratings are compared this difference becomes much smaller. When the effect of exposure in situations in the same coral abundance rank only are compared, the levelling out is not so great, suggesting that the tendency for protected situations to be sandy as well as to have less coral is important. This correlation could, in fact, explain the difference in values of protected and semi-protected situations completely, for as only two ranks have been used within each of the other categories, there still remains a degree of variability among situations classified under the same ranks.

TABLE II

Mean values of numbers of predated patches produced by one A. planci per 30 m of reef

	Moder-ately sandy	Not sandy	Coral sparse	Coral not sparse	Ex-posed	Semi-exposed	Pro-tected
a) All observa-tions	5·3	6·9	2·4	7·1	3·7	9·2	5·4
standard error	0·8	0·9	0·7	0·8	0·4	1·4	0·9
ratio	1·0	1·3	1·0	3·0	1·0	2·5	1·5
b) One variable only							
only coral abundant and exposed	3·0	3·8					
	0·0	0·5					
	1·0	1·3					
coral abund-ant and semi-protected	8·0	9·2					
	0·0	1·4					
	1·0	1·1					
coral abund-ant and protected	5·7	8·3					
	1·2	1·9					
	1·0	1·5					
coral abund-and moder-ately sandy					3·0	8·0	5·7
					0·0	0·0	1·2
					1·0	2·7	1·9
coral abund-ant and not sandy					3·8	9·2	8·3
					0·5	1·4	1·9
					1·0	2·4	2·2
coral abund-ant sub totals	5·4	7·3			3·7	9·2	6·5
	0·9	1·0			0·4	1·4	1·0
	1·0	1·4			1·0	2·5	1·8
c) Average of ratios ob-tained with one variable only	1·0	1·3	1·0	3·0	1·0	2·5	1·8

Too few situations were classified as coral sparse for valid comparisons to be made among such situations.

Below each mean value is given the standard error and the ratio of the means.

The figures obtained suggest that the starfish move across sandy, or coral sparse, or exposed areas of reef at respectively about 1·3 or 3 or 2·5 times the total average rates for more acceptable areas. Thus on an hypothetical small reef of which one side was comparatively protected, sand free, and rich in coral, and the other side exposed, sandy, and coral sparse we might expect that, if these were the only important factors involved, an average starfish would spend over 9 times (1·3 × 3 × 2·5 = 9·75) as much time on the former side as on the latter. Consequently if on this reef there were 10 starfish we would expect to find, on average, 9 of these on the one side and only one on the other.

This conclusion suggests how within restricted localities A. planci will tend to concentrate themselves into the more favourable areas. The mechanisms by which these factors produce this effect remains to be discussed. Coral scarcity would clearly act by making it necessary for the starfish to move further to find coral to feed on. It is difficult to say to what extent sandy conditions might act independently of their effect on coral growth, or how they might act. The starfish cannot cross sandy areas in rough weather conditions, and some areas may be protected in this way (Chesher, 1969b). Exposure might act by forcing the starfish to search further for a suitably protected resting place, but probably its strongest effect is that which emerges from a consideration of the starfish's food preferences. Of the instances of predation on corals, Acropora and Pocillopora species account for 31% of those recorded, Goniastrea and Goniopora species for 47%, Porites species 9% and a variety of other corals, including in two instances a species of soft coral, for the remaining 13%.

It seems that the ease with which A. planci can maintain a hold on corals of different growth form varies, so that in the more exposed areas it is difficult for the animal to predate some corals. This idea is supported by comparing the numbers of corals of the different genera predated in situations subject to varying degrees of exposure. This is done in Table III, in which the sites where the starfish were found are ranked as described above. The trend is very apparent, the smoother rounder genera being predated principally in the less exposed situations, and mainly the branched forms in the most exposed situations. The effect of the preference of different corals for different situations has not been allowed for, but probably would not alter the conclusions.

Other observations correlate with this. It has been observed in Guam that animals feeding on the larger round massive corals are fairly easily dislodged, especially if much mucus is produced during the feeding, and that the tops of these corals are often still alive while much of the sides has been killed: whereas in comparison feeding

TABLE III

Exposure and genera of corals predated

Situation	Numbər of predated patches *Acropora* and *Pocillopora*	*Goniastrea*	*Porites*	Number of sites recorded
Exposed	32	11	5	13
Ratio	6·4	2·2	1	
	2·9	1		
Semi-protected	43	56	11	16
Ratio	3·9	5·1	1	
	0·8	1		
Protected	19	39	10	11
Ratio	1·9	3·9	1	
	0·5	1		

A. planci are not easily dislodged from branched corals (Chesher, 1969b). *A. planci* have also been closely observed while feeding, and during the initial stages there is much movement of the tube feet as if they were reacting to being stung by the nematocysts of the coral (Woodley, personal communication). These enforced movements would increase for the starfish the difficulty of holding on. Thus a principal cause of the greater overall rates of movement in exposed areas would be the need for the starfish to travel further to find either branched or rough textured corals or corals in such a position that the starfish could still somehow maintain its hold.

Predation of A. planci

Charonia tritonis is the main known significant predator of the adult *A. planci*, but only two *C. tritonis* were found during the three months. Five are known to have been collected by local shell collectors, but the general opinion is that they are only found very occasionally. Signs of injury to the *A. planci* found were recorded and of 31 animals, nine had one or two arms shortened or reduced to stumps. These injuries might be due in whole or in part to other causes, but they do suggest that attack by some predator might be quite widespread. If however the number of *C. tritonis* found is a true indication of that animals population, it is difficult to believe that it is the principal factor keeping the *A. planci* population in check, but *C. tritonis* is very strictly nocturnal and well camouflaged so that it is difficult to be sure of its real population.

External morphology and venom

Detailed descriptions of each *A. planci* were recorded since it seemed possible that the Red Sea *A. planci* might show morphological differences, indicative of possible ecological differences, on comparison with Pacific forms. The overall body colouring tended towards two extreme varieties, dark grey-blue and light grey-green, although there were many intermediate forms. The arms are often rather darker than the body, though at a distance the red-brown colouring of the papullae and pedicellariae is the prominent one. Mortensen (1931) commented on the similar existence of two varieties in Java, together with intermediate and mixed forms.

The only obvious apparent difference on comparison with descriptions of Pacific animals is in the number of arms. Endean (1969) describes the Australian animals as having 13 to 17 arms, with juveniles averaging 16. Chesher describes it in Guam as ordinarily having 16 arms. In the Red Sea however the mean number of arms was just over 13, and none had more than 15. The major/minor radius was very similar, 0·57 in Guam, and 0·54 in the Red Sea. Madsen (1955) examined specimens collected from throughout the Indo-Pacific, and drew the conclusion that the number of arms and madreporites increased with the size of the starfish. He therefore suggested that *A. planci* started life as a five-armed starfish and increased its arms and madreporite numbers as it grew. However, we know that this is not the case, as immature starfish in plague areas have many arms, and our data shows no correlation between size and arm number. Perhaps a cline of increasing size, arm and madreporite numbers, across the Indo-Pacific, would explain these factors, and why the largest *A. planci* found by our expedition was rather smaller than some of those found in the Pacific.

Most of the divers had single *A. planci* spines penetrate their skin on more than one occasion, but there was no evidence of any strong venom. In the Pacific however, injuries have produced severe effects of poisoning (Barnes and Endean, 1964), though generally when the injuries have been more extensive than a mere pin-prick. The degree of poisoning might also depend on the particular *A. planci*, its food and the sensitivity of the victim.

THE INFLUENCE OF ECHINOIDS ON REEF BREAKDOWN AND ALGAL GROWTH

Echinostrephus molare

Echinostrephus molare was common on locally sheltered sites of the fringing reefs both to the north and south of the harbour at Port Sudan.

It was found to a lesser extent on the sheltered sides of the barrier reefs, and was absent from any exposed surfaces. On a small outcrop of the fringing reef at Flamingo Bay, the burrows of this animal were very frequent, especially on the top and leeward side. In certain places there were up to eight burrows in the coral limestone per square yard. Approximately 30% of these animals were albinos, being either grey or greenish grey.

E. molare builds characteristic burrows, probably using its lantern of Aristotle. Otter (1932) suggests this as a burrowing mechanism for *Strongylocentrotus lividus*. As the urchin burrows the test grows in diameter and the bore-hole becomes conical so that the urchin is imprisoned. When the holes were broken open to extract the urchins, there was always a certain amount of calcareous matter in the form of granules. These probably resulted from drilling activities.

Empty, but intact, holes were never seen. This suggests that burrows may be taken over by other urchins if there is a death. These would have to be of another species because *E. molare* cannot change its burrow, and small individuals were always found in small holes. The echinoid *Echinometra matthaei*, which is a crevice dweller may take over the holes of *E. molare*, wearing these to a new shape by the action of its spines. Near the edge of the reef, broken pieces of limestone were occasionally seen, where the fracture had passed through a burrow. Possibly the greater wave action in this area might effect the limestone structure that had been weakened by the boring activities of *E. molare*. Certainly the activities of this animal severely sculpture the reefs at some localities near Port Sudan.

Diadema setosum *and* Echinothrix diadema

The diadematids, *Diadema setosum* and *Echinothrix diadema*, were very common on the less sheltered faces of the fringing reefs, and on most surfaces of the barrier reefs. By day *Diadema setosum* hid in crevices at about four metres depth, and could only be made out by a few of its primary spines showing through the entrance to its retreat (Thornton, 1956). At night it emerged in great flocks and moved actively over the face of the reef to graze on encrusting organisms, in particular algae. It appeared to move vertically as well as horizontally. *Echinothrix diadema*, is also nocturnal, but hid under flat coral tables rather than in crevices. It dwells in very shallow water, and was frequently seen in depths less than a metre. By night it emerged to browse on algae and other encrusting growth on the top of the reef.

In the reefs visited by the expedition, it was very noticeable that the only areas that showed a rich development of algae were those where no trace was to be seen of either of these echinoids. This applied to both coralline and non-coralline algae. Such areas were limited to the sheltered aspects of fringing reefs. On the barrier reefs where these echinoids were most common, the development of algal mats on the tops and sides of the reefs was almost nil. The coral limestone showed clean and unencrusted for the greater part. Probably the echinoids *Heterocentrotus mammillatus* and *Echinometra matthaei*, which were also very common in these areas, also graze in this fashion, but there are no records of their feeding habits.

It is likely that these echinoids, particular *Diadema setosum* and *Echinothrix diadema*, with their long and fragile spines, could not survive in the rough conditions of the surf zones of oceanic reefs, and this would contribute to the comparative success of growth of algae in such places.

THE OPHIUROIDS

In most marine communities the ophiuroids are the predominant echinoderms. In the coral communities of the Sudanese Red Sea at Port Sudan, two species of the genus *Ophiocoma* were very common. Most heads of species of the corals *Acropora* and *Montipora* contained at least two individuals, and in many cases the number was as high as seven. This produces a population, e.g. for the fringing reef at Flamingo Bay, of 45 ophiocomas per sq. m. The two species were *O. pica* and *O. erinaceus* which were present in equal densities, and were always found in the coral heads just below the surface of the water. Magnus (1962) explains that *O. scolopendrina*, a sand dwelling species, feeds on the water surface film suspension. Possibly these other two species do likewise, and they may take up their positions in these corals so as to be in a convenient position for this sort of feeding activity, using the coral as a support platform.

CONCLUSION

In conclusion we have shown that the population of *A. planci* in the Sudanese Red Sea is very similar to that for normal non-plague areas of the Pacific. In some very limited areas forming foci of local *A. planci* populations, *A. planci* may have some small effect in limiting coral growth. The echinoids, *Echinostrephus molare*, and *Diadema setosum* and *Echinothrix diadema* may respectively assist in the breakdown of coral limestone and control the level of algal growth.

The fact that this normal population occurs in the area of the hottest sea temperature suggests that temperature is not limiting the *A. planci* population but increases the likelihood that the factors involved are similar to those in the Pacific. We have demonstrated some factors which affect the local distribution patterns of *A. planci* and something of the mechanisms by which they are effective. As regards the central problem, our results are so far equivocal. Quite possibly both of the two major theories of plague outbreak are relevant in different situations, for although rare *A. planci* previously had a super-abundant food supply, and few natural enemies as an adult. It was therefore in an especially favourable situation to exploit many of the changes in environment which man might produce.

ACKNOWLEDGEMENTS

This work was supported by a grant-in-aid from the Royal Society and carried out while R.F.G.O. was receiving a grant from the Medical Research Council.

We wish to acknowledge the vital role of the other members of our group in carrying out this work, Dr C. H. Roads, E. M. Maxim, G. W. Lewis, I. D. Lindsay, J. W. C. Ward, N. A. Peacock, P. R. Fickling, and N. V. C. Polunin, and to thank all those who have helped the group in so many ways, especially Sir Maurice Yonge for his valuable support and encouragement.

Note added in proof on page 554.

REFERENCES

Barnes, J. H. (1966). The Crown-of-Thorns Starfish as a destroyer of coral. *Aust. Nat. Hist.* **15**: 257–261.

Barnes, J. H. and Endean, R. (1964). A dangerous starfish—*Acanthaster planci* (Linne). *Med. J. Aust.* **1**: 592–593.

Berry, L., Whiteman, A. J. and Bell, S. V. (1966). Some radiocarbon dates and their geomorphological significance on the emerged reef complex of the Sudan. *Z. Geomorph* (N.F.) **10**: 119–143.

Bertram, G. C. L. (1936). Some aspects of the breakdown of coral at Ghardaqa, Red Sea. *Proc. zool. Soc. Lond.* **1936**: 1011–1026.

Chesher, R. H. (1969a). Destruction of Pacific Corals by the Sea-Star *Acanthaster planci*. *Science, N.Y.* **165**: 280–283.

Chesher, R. H. (1969b). *Acanthaster planci*. Impact on Pacific Coral Reefs. Westinghouse Report to the U.S. Department of the Interior.

Clark, A. H. (1950). Echinoderms from the Cocos-Keeling Islands. *Bull. Raffles Mus.* **22**: 53–67.

Clark, A. M. (1952). The "Manihine" Expedition of the Gulf of Aqaba 1948–1949. VII Echinodermata. *Bull. Brt. Mus.* (*nat. Hist.*) *Zool.* **1**: 203–214.

Clark, A. M. (1962). Echinoderms from the Red Sea. Part 2. Crinoids, Ophiuroids, Echinoids and more Asteroids. *Bull. Sea Fish. Res. Stn Israel* **41**: 26–58.

Clark, A. M. and Davies, P. S. (1965). Echinoderms of the Maldive Islands. *Ann. Mag. nat. Hist.* (13) **8**: 597–612.

Crossland, C. (1907). Reports on marine biology of the Sudanese Red Sea. IV, The recent history of the coral reefs of the mid-west shores of the Red Sea. *J. Linn. Soc. (Zool.)* **31**: 14–30.

Crossland, C. (1911). Reports on the marine biology of the Sudanese Red Sea. A physical description of Khor Dungunab. *J. Linn. Soc. (Zool.)* **31**: 265–286.

Crossland, C. (1913). *Desert and water gardens of the Red Sea.* London: Cambridge University Press.

Darwin, C. (1842). *The structure and distribution of coral reefs.* London: Smith, Elder and Co.

Endean, R. (1969). Report on investigations made into aspects of the current *Acanthaster planci* infestations of certain reefs of the Great Barrier Reef. Fisheries Branch, Queensland Department of Primary Industries, Brisbane. 37pp. Mimeographed.

Fontaine, T. R. (1965). The feeding mechanism of the ophiuroid *Ophiocomina nigra. J. mar. biol. Ass. U.K.* **45**: 373–385.

Goreau, T. F. (1964). On the predation of coral by the spiny starfish *Acanthaster planci* (L.) in the southern Red Sea. *Bull. Sea Fish. Res. Stn Israel* **35**: 23–26.

Hyman, L. H. (1955). *The Invertebrates.* IV. *Echinodermata.* New York: McGraw-Hill.

Lewis, J. B. (1964). Feeding and digestion in the tropical sea-urchin *Diadema antillarum* (Philippi). *Can. J. Zool.* **42**: 549–557.

Madsen, F. J. (1955). A note on the sea-star genus *Acanthaster. Vidensk. Meddr. dansk naturh. Foren.* **117**: 179–92.

Magnus, D. B. E. (1962) Über das "Abweiden" der Flutwasseroberfläche durch den-Schlangenstern *Ophiocoma scolopendrina. Verh. dtsch. zool. Ges.* **1962**. *Zool. Anz. suppl.* **26**: 471–481.

Mortensen, T. (1931). Contributions to the study of the larval forms of echinoderms. *Kong. Dansk. Vidensk. Skrifter,* **9** (4) 4: 1–39.

Mortensen, T. (1940). A monograph of the Echinoidea **3**. 1. Copenhagen: Reitzel.

Mortensen, T. (1943). A monograph of the Echinoidea. Copenhagen: Reitzel.

Nagabhushanam, A. K. and Colman, J. S. (1959). Carrion-eating by ophiuroids. *Nature, Lond.* **184**: 285.

Otter, G. W. (1932). Rock-burrowing echinoids. *Biol. Rev.* **7**: 89–107.

Red Sea and Gulf of Aden Pilot (1967). 11th Edition. London: Hydrographer of the Navy.

Roushdy, H. M. and Hansen, V. K. (1960). Ophiuroids feeding on phyto-plankton. *Nature, Lond.* **188**: 517–518.

Thornton, I. W. B. (1956). Diurnal migrations of the echinoid *Diadema setosum. Br. J. Anim. Behav.* **4**: 143–146.

Tortonese, E. (1960). Echinoderms from the Red Sea. Part 1 Asteroidea. *Bull. Sea Fish. Res. Stn Israel* **29**: 17–23.

Weber, J. N. (1969). Disaster at Green Island. *Bull. P St. Univ., Earth Miner. Sci.* **38**: 37–41.

Symp. zool. Soc. Lond. (1971) No. 28, 455–500.

BACK-REEF AND LAGOONAL ENVIRONMENTS OF ALDABRA ATOLL DISTINGUISHED BY THEIR CRUSTACEAN BURROWS

GEORGE E. FARROW

*Department of Geology, University of Hull, Hull, England**

SYNOPSIS

Aldabra is an excellent natural laboratory for the investigation of the development of sedimentary facies in relation to environmental energy levels, since it lies in the belt of strong Trade-winds, possesses a high tidal range and a very shallow lagoon. As a basis for the facies interpretation of elevated Pleistocene reef limestones and earlier Mesozoic and Caenozoic sediments, where biogenic sedimentary structures are of widespread significance, the burrow forms and associated surface traces characteristic of the commoner littoral and immediately sub-littoral Crustacea were determined by epoxy resin casting. Burrow form varies between habitats, being determined both by an endogeneous burrowing pattern and by an exogeneous substrate control. Variations in the thickness, mobility and consistency of the bottom sediments are chiefly responsible for observed modifications to basic styles.

Eight reef environments may be identified by their biogenic sedimentary structures. These are all dealt with in the following sections. Many burrows disappear into crevices in the underlying champignon, particularly those of *Uca*, *Callianassa* and *Neaxius*. In the lagoon, areas of very highly burrowed sediment are found in localized depressions and solution holes: original structures are destroyed and individual burrow forms rarely determinable.

When compared with the diversity of burrowing crustaceans recorded from mainland reefs, atoll communities are somewhat restricted. They nevertheless include two facies—*Callianassa* sandsheets and *Alpheus* mudflats—which are very widespread today and which have had an important geological history since the early Mesozoic.

INTRODUCTION

Background of previous work

As facies indicators in British Mesozoic and Caenozoic strata, crustacean burrows have already proved their worth (Farrow, 1966; Bromley, 1967; Kennedy and MacDougall 1969). By comparison, present-day arthropod structures are perhaps less well known. Most papers refer to the burrowing habits of single species, such as *Ocypode* spp. (Takahashi, 1932; Utashiro and Horii, 1965) or *Callianassa* spp., on which a bulky literature has been built up (Stevens, 1929; MacGinitie, 1930; 1934; Weimer and Hoyt, 1964). Recently, however, a number of more geologically biased studies have appeared, treating communities of burrowing crustaceans in the context of their lateral facies relationships. The most pertinent in terms of reef environments is probably Shinn's

* Present address: Department of Geology, University of Glasgow, Glasgow, Scotland.

(1968) treatment of burrowing in recent lime sediments of Florida and the Bahamas, where the technique of resin casting used in the present study was first applied. Frey and Howard (1969) also employed resin casting in their field studies on the development of biogenic sedimentary structures in the barrier island—salt marsh complex of Georgia. Ohshima (1963, 1967) has recently demonstrated the control of sedimentary setting on the distribution of infaunal Crustacea in Japanese bays, though decades earlier the strong influence of tidal cover had been stressed both for open ocean beaches (Hayasaka, 1935) and for mangrove swamps (Verwey, 1930).

A sound framework of sedimentological and ecological studies exists on back-reef and lagoonal carbonates, largely stemming from the classical work of Black (1933) on the Great Bahama Bank. Concentration of work on extensive shallow platforms such as the Bahamas (Illing, 1954; Newell, Imbrie, Purdy and Thurber, 1959; Cloud, 1961; Purdy, 1963; Ball, 1967) was influenced by the impressive development there of oolitic and pelletal sediments which are such a conspicuous feature of ancient limestones. Sedimentological data for atolls are more restricted, however, since they are not so obviously relevant to the interpretation of fossil epicontinental deposits, being made up of skeletal rather than oolitic material (Wiens, 1962, pp. 77–84). In the Pacific, Ladd, Tracey, Wells and Emery (1950), McKee (1958) and McKee, Chronic and Leopold (1959) have described atoll sediments from relatively deep lagoons. In the Atlantic, Milliman (1967) has described the sediments from Hogsty Reef, a Bahaman atoll with an unusual grapestone facies: Stoddart (1962) has noted the curious absence of certain grades of carbonate detritus from Caribbean atolls, which is a widely recorded phenomenon (Sorby, 1879; Jindrich, 1969). In the Indian Ocean good accounts exist of the soft sediments associated with fringing reefs (Lewis and Taylor, 1966; Lewis, 1969) and barrier reefs (Guilcher, 1965), but descriptions of atoll sediments are scarcer (Stoddart, Taylor, Fosberg and Farrow, 1971).

Sediment accumulation on Aldabra

The significance of Aldabra Atoll as an environment of formation of carbonate sediments lies in its geomorphology and tidal range relative to other atolls. For its large size the lagoon is extremely shallow, averaging about 3 m and never exceeding 6 m. In the Marshall and Caroline Islands of the Pacific, atolls of comparable size possess lagoons 60 m deep (Wiens, 1962, p. 32). Tidally, Aldabra's mean spring-tide range of 2·74 m is far greater than the normal 0·5 m for truly oceanic atolls (Farrow and Brander, 1971), with the result that much of the lagoon is swept by strong tidal currents which may reach seven knots in the tortuous Passe Gionnet (Fig. 1). In consequence much of the lagoon, particularly the central part, consists of scoured rock pavement. Sediment bodies are associated with the channel areas, occurring at the eastern and western ends of the lagoon. Along the protected southern shore of the lagoon the rock pavement is covered with a mantle of fine calcareous silt forming wide intertidal flats normally less than 0·3 m thick. Nowhere on the atoll does soft sediment thickness exceed 1 m, and this exerts considerable control on the burrowing patterns of many of the infaunal crustaceans. This makes comparison with the burrows of Bahaman Crustacea the more illuminating, for there the thickness of unconsolidated carbonates may reach 5 m (Shinn, 1968).

Outside the lagoon sediment is accumulating in the lee of the atoll under the influence of the strong westward-drifting ocean currents, forming a long back-reef sandbar (broken by Passe bu Bois) extending from south of Anse Mais to West Point (Fig. 1). On the windward coast of Grande Terre there appears to be little sediment overlying the reef platform, but on northern and western coasts much sediment is trapped by marine grass beds. Beaches are only extensive on the west coasts of Picard and Grande Terre.

Scope and objective of present paper

With extensive areas of sediment forming under extreme régimes of current activity, Aldabra has proved to be a fine natural laboratory for investigating the development of biogenic sedimentary structures in relation to environmental energy levels. The recognition in the present study of burrow forms controlled by both thickness and mobility of the substrate should open the way to detailed facies interpretations for many trace fossils, which have hitherto received only taxonomic study.

This work was undertaken with a particular hope that it might help towards delineating back-reef and lagoonal facies in the elevated Pleistocene limestones, not only on Aldabra and neighbouring atolls, but also on the African mainland where a sequence of shallow water marine carbonates extending back to the Miocene is preserved (Thompson, 1956).

METHOD

Resin casting of burrows under natural conditions

The resin casting method of Shinn (1968, p. 881) was adopted and because polyester resin was not immediately available for use on the

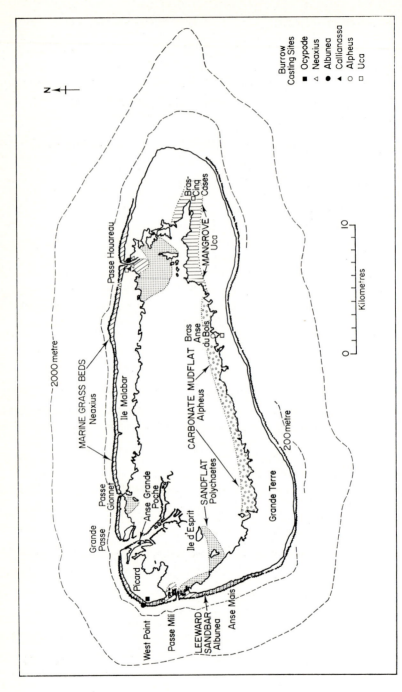

Fig. 1. Map of Aldabra Atoll showing the broad distribution of bottom facies and crustacean burrow casting sites.

atoll epoxy resin was substituted. Polyester casts have the distinct advantage that should fracturing occur they can be repaired more easily than epoxy resin casts. Any resin casts, however, are superior to those made of Plaster of Paris, especial virtues being:

i) greater strength, with less risk of brittle fracture both on retrieval from sediment and in transit:

ii) controllable viscocity for substrates with wide ranges of porosity:

iii) possibility of elegant "freezing" of burrow producers and commensals in "life position":

iv) impregnation of substratum enclosing burrow may "fossilize" sedimentary structures:

v) resin will harden under water, so that sublittoral communities can be studied, whereas previous investigations involving Plaster of Paris were automatically confined to the intertidal zone.

A total of 40 gallons of resin was used in the study. The large number of burrow casts resulting from each habitat enabled variation in burrow form to be assessed semi-quantitatively. Burrow openings were mapped and resin casts orientated in the field before retrieval so that in the laboratory original densities and alignment could be reconstructed accurately. Figure 2 illustrates the technique, and shows dense *Uca marionis* burrows from the mangrove mud of Bras Cinq Cases.

FIG. 2. Burrow casts of *Uca marionis* from the Mangrove Mud of Bras Cinq Cases reconstructed in their original density.

The most successful casts obtained were those of lined burrows such as are produced by the thalassinids *Neaxius* and *Callianassa*. The mole crab *Albunea*, being incredibly mobile, tended to escape the advancing resin. Casting *Ocypode* burrows presented problems because of the highly porous nature of the beach sand which it inhabits. Excessive wastage caused by resin infiltrating pore space was avoided by preparing a very viscous mixture which began setting within minutes. In contrast, *Alpheus* burrows form extensive horizontal networks of narrow diameter tunnels which can only be filled completely by a mixture of low viscosity. Greatest difficulty was experienced in extracting the basal portions of *Uca*, *Neaxius* and *Callianassa* burrows from beneath large coral boulders, platin ledges or champignon crevices, whence the majority disappeared. Under these conditions 100% retrieval was seldom possible even with the use of 10 lb sledge hammer and crowbar.

Impregnation of enclosing sediments

In order to place each burrow in its geological perspective the physical structures of the sediment surrounding it were "fossilized" by allowing surplus resin to seep through the unlined walls or to escape around the opening of the burrow. Figure 3 illustrates the alternative methods: *A* shows typical beach sand lamination (*cf.* McKee, 1957, pl. 1, p. 1710) broken by a "U"-shaped *Ocypode ceratophthalma* burrow: *B* shows a partially infilled "J"-shaped burrow of the same species, where the homogeneous fill contrasts sharply with the beach lamination: *C* shows the sediment surrounding the funnel-shaped opening of a *Callianassa* burrow system, the structure being caused by alternating, partially erosive, ebb and flow tidal currents which produce small scale cross-bedded accretion sets (Imbrie and Buchanan, 1965).

Not all sediments could be impregnated successfully, and in these instances loose sediment samples were taken for analysis. Marine grass beds and muddy silts proved most difficult. Only limited soft sediment samples were taken during the present study, the main account of which should be available later through the quantitative studies of J. C. Gamble and R. Hughes.

Recognition and distribution of bottom facies with distinctive crustacean burrows

The present paper does not document the whole range of back-reef and lagoonal environments present on Aldabra, neither does it take into account the use of any invertebrate group other than Crustacea in identifying the facies described, which were determined on the atoll without prior reference to existing descriptions of atoll ecosystems. Subsequently, comparable facies were easily recognized from the extensive literature on carbonate sedimentation, even though very few papers refer specifically to atolls. Following Ginsburg and

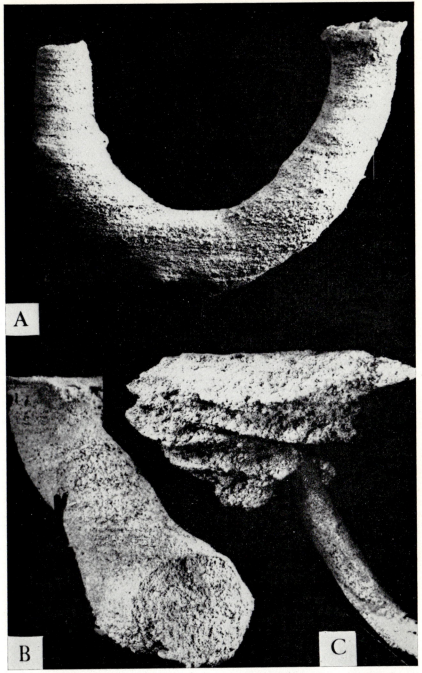

Fig. 3. Sedimentary structures revealed by resin impregnation. (A) "U"-shaped *Ocypode* burrow penetrating laminated beach sand; (B) Homogeneous fill of abandoned "J"-shaped *Ocypode* burrow; (C) Small scale cross-bedded accretion sets surrounding funnel-shaped opening of *Callianassa* burrow.

Lowenstam (1958) and Lewis (1969) I regard biological zones on the reef-flat and in the lagoon as separate sedimentary environments. Facies are distinguished by:—

  i) Geomorphological Setting—areal distribution on the atoll.
  ii) Geometry—shape of sand or mud body in relation to setting.
  iii) Internal Structure—biological (chiefly characteristic crustacean burrows) and physical (bedding and ripple types).
  iv) Texture—limited use of grain-size and sorting properties.
No mention is made of sediment composition and provenance, which is outside the scope of this paper.

The following sections describe certain sections with their diagnostic burrowing crustaceans.

Differences in the lateral variation of environments are illustrated between the moderate energy northern coast with deep eastern channel Passe Houareau (Fig. 4) and the relatively low energy western leeward coast with shallow passes (Fig. 5). Typical sediment analyses for the major facies are plotted in Fig. 6.

LEEWARD OCEANIC COASTS

Upper beach—Ocypode ceratophthalma *burrows*

Voeltzkow (1897, p. 68) remarked that "the well-known sand crabs, *Ocypoda* etc., are practically conspicuous by their absence on the sea shore of Aldabra." In 1968 a population of thousands was present along the extensive Picard beach, especially in the vicinity of the boathouse where the dominant species *O. ceratophthalma* feeds nocturnally on discarded fish. This species also occurs on more remote beaches such as Anse Grande Poche, where feeding and burrowing were observed during the day. On the stretch of Picard beach studied new burrows were constructed within 2 h of each spring high tide (*c.* 21.00 h). Burrow openings are limited to a narrow zone just above H.W.N.T. The other species of *Ocypode* present on Aldabra have different distributions with respect to tidal height. *O. kuhli*, probably the small form which Voeltzkow (1897) observed, extends a little lower down the beach. *O. cordimanus* in contrast is dominantly supratidal, making very deep burrows in the sand of the hurricane beach. This species seems comparable in habits to *O. albicans*, which extends at least 40 m above high water mark (Phillips, 1940) but is not supratidal everywhere (Sawaya, 1939). Milne and Milne (1946, p. 368) record only adult *O. quadrata* from supratidal dunes, younger crabs staying closer to shore.

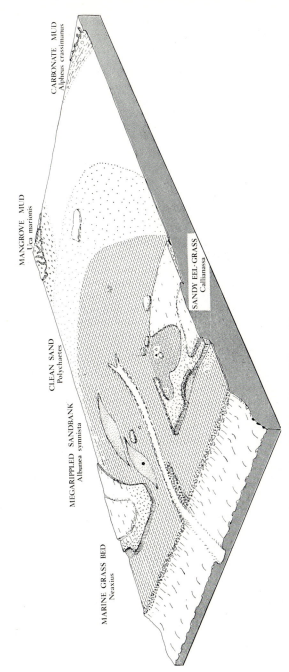

Fig. 4. Lateral facies variation in the region of Passe Houareau: moderate energy coast with deep channel.

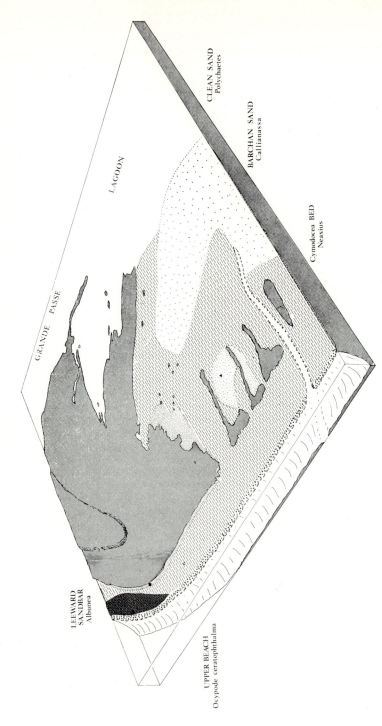

LAGOON

GRANDE PASSE

LEEWARD
SANDBAR
Albunea

UPPER BEACH
Ocypode ceratophthalma

CLEAN SAND
Polychaetes

BARCHAN SAND
Callianassa

Cymodocea BED
Neaxius

FIG. 5. Lateral facies variation to the lee of the atoll: moderate to low energy coast with shallow passes.

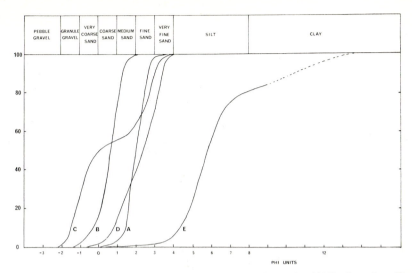

Fig. 6. Cumulative soft sediment analyses for the major facies. (A) Back-reef sandbar, Picard; (B) Megarippled sandbank, Passe Houareau; (C) Channel sandsheet, Anse Grande Poche; (D) Polychaete sandflat, Ile d'Esprit; (E) Carbonate mudflat, Bras Anse duBois.

The burrows of *Ocypode ceratophthalma* are strikingly dimorphic. The male, with its enlarged cheliped, invariably produces a spiral burrow. On the night of 12–13th August, 1968, after a spring high tide at 20.00 h, I observed 48 male *Ocypode* constructing their burrows. Twenty-one possessed an enlarged right chela, and produced a clockwise spiral: 27 possessed an enlarged left chela, and produced an anti-clockwise spiral. The sense of orientation of these crabs is very strong. They direct the initial spiral up the beach, loads of sand being deposited in piles obliquely downbeach by the smaller chela which also does the digging (Fig. 7). One round trip takes only 10–15 s, with greatest activity between 1 and $1\frac{1}{2}$ h after high water. By 22.30 h, $2\frac{1}{2}$ h later, the whole population had finished burrowing and was feeding. Burrowing with the small chela ensures that the large chela always emerges first and is therefore an effective defensive device.

Female burrows are usually in the form of a "U" which may be either simple (Fig. 3A) or multiple (Fig. 8A). Abandoned apertures and deepened basal portions of some burrows (Fig. 8B) indicate modification of existing structures rather than construction of new ones. Certain burrows with a "J" shape seem to represent incomplete "U"s which were blocked before being finished (Fig. 3B), while others show the effects of finer wind-blown sand forming a passive lining to the

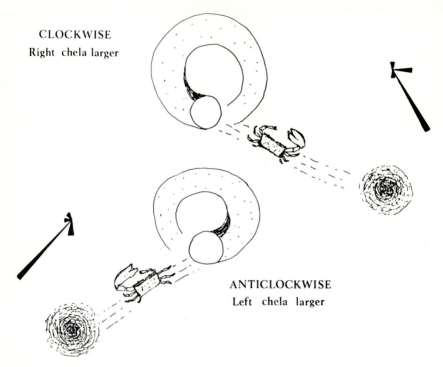

CLOCKWISE
Right chela larger

ANTICLOCKWISE
Left chela larger

Fig. 7. Male *Ocypode ceratopthalma* burrows and the distribution of sand piles, Picard Beach.

burrow. Hayasaka (1935) has illustrated both "U" (pl. 2, Fig. 1) and "J" (pl. 1, Fig. 1) shaped plaster casts of *Ocypode ceratophthalma* burrows from northwest Formosa, but the associated crab *Ilyoplax* is absent from Aldabra. The "Y"-shaped form commonly cast on Formosa (Takahashi, 1932) is not seen, though small subsidiary burrow branches are sometimes found.

The well-laminated nature of the upper beach sand may be seen from Fig. 3B. The coarse laminae, deposited at spring tides, consist of polished, well-rounded fragments of reef organisms varying in size from granule gravel to very coarse sand on the Wentworth (1922) scale. On Picard beach the fine laminae are dominantly of aeolian origin, being derived by ablation from the hurricane beach.

Marine grass beds—Neaxius *burrows*

Along the leeward coast of Aldabra a narrow rippled sand zone characterized by large, sharp-crested oscillation ripples exists at the

FIG. 8. Female *Ocypode ceratophthalma* burrows, Picard Beach. (A) Compound "U"-shaped burrow; (B) Burrow with abandoned aperture and deepened basal portion.

base of the beach. It is reworked by worms and strongly resembles the analogous zone on Mahé figured by Lewis (1969, p. 101, Fig. 4B). Resin casting techniques proved unsatisfactory in this zone, where burrowing crustaceans seem to be subordinate to bivalves and poly-chaetes. Seawards, and relatively emergent, lie the marine grass beds of poorly sorted conglomeratic sand. A very prolific fauna is present here, including many burrowing forms (see Taylor, 1968 for a representative list from the equivalent facies in the Seychelles), but the most con-spicuous open burrows are those of a bright red anomuran *Neaxius* sp., a common form on Mauritius. These thalassinideans are widespread around the leeward coasts of the atoll and also extend in to channel platforms. They are most abundant (more than one opening per square metre) in sandy *Cymodocea serrulata* beds. Burrows were cast in four areas (Fig. 1) which served to demonstrate the remarkably constant form of the *Neaxius* burrow.

The opening of the burrow remains cylindrical to the surface and is lined with a thick brown material apparently composed of finely macerated eel-grass blades. Several swollen chambers at depths of from 15 to 45 cm are linked by a succession of subvertical shafts averaging 17 mm in diam. (Fig. 9A). The burrows are characteristically simple, only one burrow out of the twenty cast showing any trace of branching, which was confined to the basal chamber. The swollen chambers probably function as somersaulting areas, as in the burrows of *Callianassa* and *Upogebia* (MacGinitie, 1934), since captive *Neaxius* specimens placed in aquaria will automatically perform a somersault after turning over several superficial stones in the laboratory sediment. Once an optimum depth of about 45 cm is attained a very large basal chamber is produced, usually under a coral boulder, platin ledge or champignon crevice: thereafter no attempt is made to extend the burrow. Normally resin fails to fill the basal chambers completely because of air blockage, but one filled example from within Passe Houareau had a volume of 1700 cc.

The red shrimps live in pairs in the burrows (*cf. Callianassa affinis* and *Upogebia pugettensis*, MacGinitie and MacGinitie, 1968, pp. 288–291) one of which can be seen at low water hovering in the entrance. Feeding is largely from suspension, though this is interrupted if a particle of any description (usually eel-grass) drifts across the opening, when it is seized and transported below. Such trapping of extraneous particles is not observed, however, if the creature is currently engaged in smoothing the lining of its burrow, which is done so effectively that only the most delicate of scratch markings can be seen on resin casts. The collecting habit implies that the large basal chamber is used as a

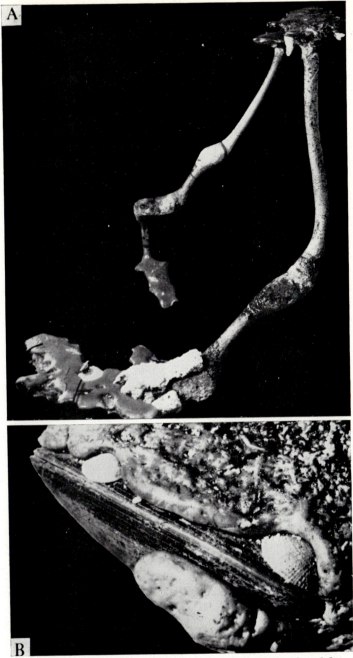

FIG. 9. *Neaxius* burrows from *Cymodocea serrulata* Bed, Picard reef flat. (A) Two resin casts showing the simple, chambered structure (basal chamber incompletely filled); (B) commensal molluscs *Erycina* and *Capulus* from the burrow lining of a chamber.

store from which eel-grass fragments and the like may possibly be used
in the production of lining material.

Commensals

Thalassinidean burrows offer classic examples of commensalism
(MacGinitie and MacGinitie, 1968, pp. 287–290). On Aldabra *Neaxius*
is no exception. A small grapsid crab was captured from one burrow
on the Picard reef-flat, but I have not seen gobies in red shrimp
burrows, though they are very common in alpheid systems. By far the
most common commensal was the ciliary feeding bivalve *Erycina* sp.,
always situated on the lateral margin of a swollen chamber. Taylor
(1968, p. 163) records *Erycina* in *Alpheus rapax* burrows. Commonly the
bivalve carried secondary commensals in the form of a species of the
mesogastropod genus *Capulus*, attached in twos or threes along the
ventro-lateral margin (Fig. 9B). Out of the 7 casts recovered from the
Picard flats 4 contained the commensal bivalve, sometimes in each of
the three chambers of the system. It was also widely recorded around
the atoll, from the Malabar Platform and Passe Houareau. This particular commensal association is of interest for two main reasons. First,
since both forms are shelly they would be well preserved in fossil
Neaxius burrows, which would aid recognition in elevated Pleistocene
limestones: (even pinnotherid crabs are preserved in Miocene burrows;
MacGinitie and MacGinitie, 1968, p. 94). Second, it is a very different
molluscan associate from that described in American callianassid and
Urechis burrows where *Cryptomya californica* is situated not within the
burrow but in the surrounding sediment with its short siphons penetrating the lining (Yonge, 1951). Since this form, like *Neaxius*, is a
suspension feeder it would probably not be expected as a commensal.

Back-reef sandbar—Albunea *burrows*

Immediately shoreward of the algal cobble zone along the western
reef lies an extensive sandbar (Fig. 5) composed of well-sorted fine–
medium sand (Fig. 6). Faunally the environment is strikingly poor
compared with the zones on either side, though at spring low tide
occasional stellate castings reveal a deeply burrowing infauna. The
producers of the casts are extremely agile, and it took several days of
digging before it could be established that they are the work of the mole
crab *Albunea* (*A. steinitzsi* or *A. thurstoni:* according to Dr. Thomassin).
Except for short vertical shafts it proved impossible to cast the burrows,
for the animal rapidly disappears ahead of the resin, the thixotropic
sand collapsing behind it. Similarly other burrowing structures in the

form of a broad "U" with apertures 25 cm apart produced by large *Balanogossus* are obliterated by sediment thixotropy, so that this facies in elevated limestones would probably appear homogeneous or with only the haziest of biogenic structures (*cf.* Hamblin, 1962, 1965). This is in marked contrast to burrows in eel-grass sands which are lined and of a more permanent nature. The associated fauna, though patchy, would give a clearer indication of facies, for it includes many mobile forms such as a box crab *Calappa* sp., the gastropods *Oliva episcopalis* and *Polinices* sp. (often puncturing valves of *Codakia punctata* and *Ctena divergens*) and maldanid polychaetes. Frey and Howard (1969, p. 429) have described a very similar, slightly more prolific, fauna from the lower foreshore of Sapelo Island dominated by active species of *Oliva* and *Polinices* and the mole crab *Lepidopa websteri*.

CHANNEL PLATFORMS

Megarippled sandbank—Albunea *burrows*

Farrow and Brander (1971, p. 115 and Fig. 16) have figured and briefly discussed the transient nature of the sandbanks along the eastern platform of Passe Houareau (Fig. 1) which is caused by strong tidal scour. In faunal and sedimentary terms they have much in common with the back-reef sandbar described above, but the sand is coarser, slightly less well-sorted (Fig. 6) and less thixotropic, as a result of which it is possible to obtain casts of the mole crab burrows. These are simple vertical tubes of elliptical cross section and very great depth, usually in excess of 60 cm: one burrow shows periodic globular offshoots (Fig. 10). That casts of this length were obtained at all in such a pervious substratum seem remarkable, but an explanation can be offered by comparison with the known mode of life of the closely related mole crab *Lepidopa myops* which burrows deeply in sand, maintaining a water current to the surface by means of a "tube" created by its extremely long antennules (MacGinitie and MacGinitie, 1968, p. 305).

The mobility of this environment is extreme. The bottom is constantly shifting to-and-fro with the alternating tidal currents as trains of megaripples pass over the bank, and becomes static only when water level has dropped below L.W.N.T. From day to day the limits may vary by 4 m, while at times of the major spring tides the entire 400 m long seaward bank may be eroded, leaving scoured, cobble-covered rock pavement. A sparse, specialized fauna exists, all highly mobile: *Mitra mitra*, *Terebra* sp., *Oliva* sp. (not *episcopalis*), *Albunea* sp. and the spatangoid *Metalia* sp.

FIG. 10. *Albunea* burrows from megarippled sandbank, Passe Houareau.

The origin of such sandbanks has been attributed by Macnae and Kalk (1962, p. 119) to the death of neighbouring *Cymodocea* beds consequent upon subaerial exposure at extreme low tides. This causes removal of plant cover, alters the tidal current pattern, thereby initiating a sandbank. Thomassin (1969, p. 87) has noted the rapidity with which such "dunes hydrauliques" are recolonized. Following the cyclone "Georgette", which nearly obliterated the structures on the Tuléar reef, the characteristic fauna of predatory gastropods and burrowing echinoids re-established itself in two months.

The internal sedimentary structure of the bank was difficult to establish since trenches could not be dug into the unstable waterlogged sand. In view of the warning of Imbrie and Buchanan (1965, p. 167) that surface form commonly bears a complex relation to internal features it is possibly unwise to speculate as to its form, though reversing megaripples would be expected to produce partially erosive cross-ripple structure. Megaripples are widely recorded in channel areas of carbonate deposition, though in the Lower Florida Keys their location is **within** channels, especially on point bars and tidal delta-mouth bars (Jindrich, 1969, pp. 546–548) rather than on platforms bordering the channel, as on Aldabra. Intertidal channel-edge sandbars constitute an important facies in the Bahamas (Imbrie and Buchanan, 1965), though since Aldabran sands are skeletal not oolitic, detailed comparison is inapposite.

The presence of this facies in elevated reef deposits would seem unlikely in view of its transitory nature and manifestly low "fossilization potential" (*sensu* Goldring, 1965) which is less than that of any other back-reef environment. Gross features of the sand body—its elongation normal to the atoll rim, sigmoidal outline and limited areal extent—would identify the facies more easily than either the fauna, which is sparse, or smaller scale sedimentary structures, which could conceivably be confused with the leeward coast sandbar facies if studied in isolation from its geomorphological setting.

Current-swept sandsheets—Callianassa *burrows*

Conspicuous sand volcanoes associated with funnel-shaped craters occur on the surface of sandsheets at several points around the atoll, all within channel areas. Normally they occur in relative isolation, either on coarse, mobile, barchan-like sands as in Passe Mili (Fig. 11A), or within sandy eel-grass in more protected areas as in Passe Houareau (Fig. 11B). Occasionally they are found amongst mangrove roots in very quiet regions, where the volcanoes are larger (Fig.11 C). In Grande Passe, at the foot of Anse Grande Poche, a wide expanse of sand shows

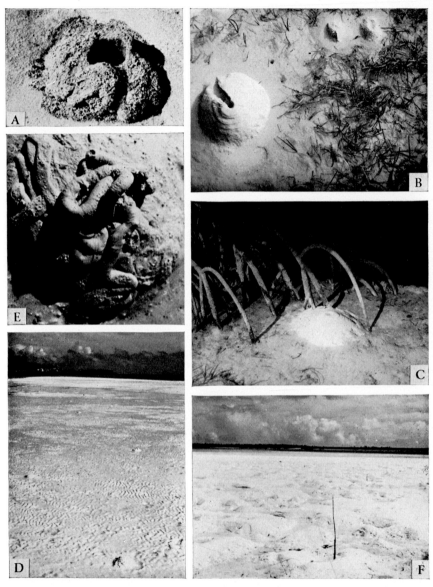

FIG. 11. Channel sandsheets with *Callianassa* volcanoes. (A) Coarse sand volcano on Passe Mili barchan; (B) Coalescing sand volcanoes smothering *Cymodocea*, Passe Houareau; (C) Large isolated volcano amongst *Rhizophora*; (D) Bottom topography of bare sandsheet with low density *Callianassa*, Grande Poche (seaward); (E) Associated casting of *Balanoglossus studiosorum*; (F) Chaotic bottom topography produced by high density *Callianassa*.

the effect of varying volcano density on bottom topography. At the seaward end of the sands is a region dominated by small current ripples with sporadic volcanoes (Fig. 11D) and large "worm casts" probably produced by *Balanoglossus studiosorum* (Fig. 11E): at the southern end the sediment surface is thrown into a confused mass of ridges and hollows produced by the coalescence of adjacent volcanoes (Fig. 11F). This area is very intensely burrowed and the sediments appear quite dissimilar to their lateral equivalents 50 m distant, deposited under the same environmental conditions. In these areas the organisms complicate the usual environmental interpretation of grain-size parameters by acting as efficient sorting agents themselves. Warme (1967, p. 545) has described graded bedding produced by very dense *Callianassa* volcanoes in Mugu Lagoon, California, and MacGinitie (1934) has calculated that the substratum to a depth of 75 cm may be completely reworked in only 8 months. The marked bimodal sorting of the Anse Grande Poche sediments (Fig. 6) cannot easily be explained otherwise.

The density of surface volcanoes thus varies widely in different areas of sand, but subsurface resin casts have shown the number of openings to be a misleading reflection of true burrow density below ground. This was discovered by casting volcano systems in two contrasted areas of sand deposition: Passe Mili, one of the shallow western channels, an expanse of coarse, migrating barchan-like sand; and Anse Grande Poche, an area of relatively thick and less mobile sand. Between the two, environmentally induced differences in burrowing style are striking.

Burrow form in relation to substrate thickness and mobility

Resin casts prepared of Grande Poche burrows reveal a very distinctive arrangement of galleries on four or even five levels (Fig. 12A). Each system appears quite separate from that of its neighbours and is of only limited lateral extent, unlike *Alpheus* burrows (p. 484). Such a geometric form reflects maximum utilization of a unit volume of sediment, clearly of some benefit to a deposit feeder. The sand here is relatively thick (50 cm +) and the whole thickness down to bedrock is exploited. The depth below surface of the first gallery is always between 21 and 25 cm, lower galleries forming at intervals as close as 4 cm. In Passe Mili, where the sediment is thickest towards the higher parts of the barchan structure (Fig. 13) *Callianassa* may form galleries like those in Grande Poche but of greater lateral extent (Fig. 12B) since there is less competition for space. These structures are incredibly similar to the casts figured by Shinn (1968, pl. 110) from the Florida Keys, testifying to the constancy of burrowing style in this species-

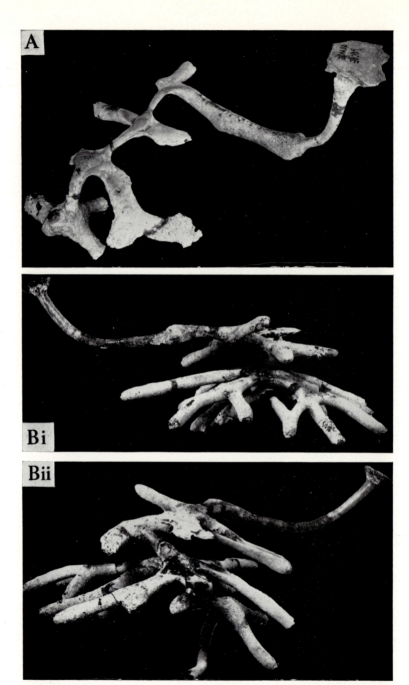

Fig. 12. *Callianassa* burrows from thick channel sands. (A) Galleried structure from high density population, Grande Poche; (B) Highly branched, galleried system from top of sand barchan, Passe Mili; pictured from both sides: the steeply descending basal limb disappears into champignon.

group of *Callianassa*. However, the pattern is an ideal one which is rarely obtained elsewhere in Passe Mili, especially around the margins of the sandsheet where the environment is unstable and sediment cover often thin. Here burrow apertures are liable to be overrun by up to 20 cm of sediment or else eroded by migration of the channel shown in Fig. 13. The result of this mobility on the burrowing pattern of *Callianassa* is shown by resin casts from marginal areas: Fig. 14A shows the great horizontal extent of the system and the absence of distinct galleries. Clear indication of the organism's response to being overrun with sand is given by abandoned apertures grouped at one horizon, with one tube extended obliquely upwards from this level to re-establish an excurrent opening.

Frequently when casting the burrows, resin will fill only the proximal portion of the system. This is caused by either sediment or gastropods completely blocking the tube. Some are water-worn and clearly derived, such as *Cypraea*, *Bulla* and *Tonna*: others are fresh and belong to species which habitually graze on the sand surface, such as *Laevistrombus cf. gibberulus* and *Conus arenatus*, and can be seen accidentally disappearing into *Callianassa* craters. Happenings of this kind are of interest to the paleontologist, who should take note that if fossilized, the presence of such gastropods would not indicate that they were responsible for producing the burrow. Such blocking provides further motivation for horizontal burrowing in order to create a new incurrent opening for the maintenance of the respiratory current.

Certain aspects of *Callianassa's* burrowing are most curious. Some tunnels are conspicuously packed with gravelly débris (Fig. 14B) while others are stuffed with eel-grass blades, giving a meniscus structure when tunnels are split along their length (Fig. 14C). Shinn (1968, pl. 110) has reported identical fillings in Floridan burrows, but no satisfactory explanation has been given for such fastidious sorting. It is noticeable that both size fractions packed into the tunnels represent the very material which would be most difficult for the organism to flush out. By emplacing such material in pre-existing tunnels *Callianassa* is thus able to extend its system without ever being forced to carry material to the surface. Why the débris is subsequently sorted may be connected with the use of eel-grass blades in manufacturing the thick brown lining material (*cf. Neaxius*, p. 468).

The ability to close off certain sections of the burrow and to reopen the whole system when overrun with sediment must give this species of *Callianassa* distinct adaptive advantages over other burrowers which may accompany it in more stable substrata but which are absent from Passe Mili. The molluscan fauna is richer than in the Megarippled

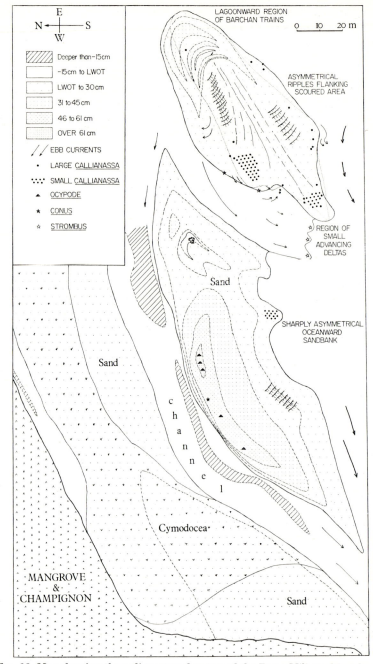

FIG. 13. Map showing the sedimentary features of the Passe Mili sand barchan.

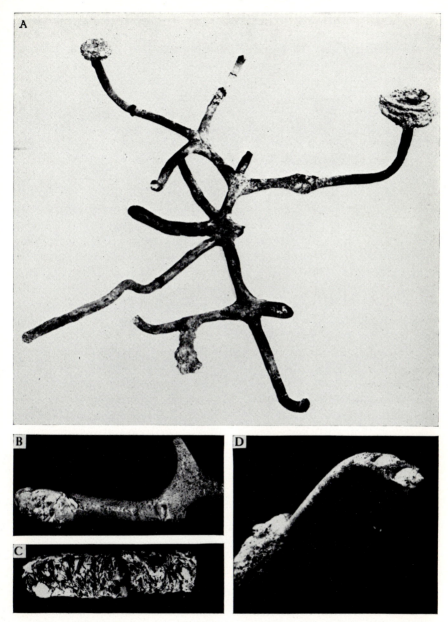

FIG. 14. *Callianassa* burrows from thin, mobile channel sands and grass beds. (A) Dominantly horizontal system from margin of Passe Mili barchan, with abandoned apertures marking former sediment surface; (B) Gravel-filled branch; (C) Eel-grass packed into branch giving meniscus structure; (D) Gastropods blocking proximal shaft of Passe Houareau system from sandy *Cymodocea* bed.

Sandbank facies, though still sparse compared with marine grass beds. The commoner living forms recorded were *Laevistrombus cf. gibberulus*, *Conus tessulatus* and the terebrid *Acuminia lanceata*, of which the first produce long trails on the surface of deltaic lobes at the end of the bank (Fig. 13). The presence of abundant fresh, undamaged, dead shells as part of the sedimentary fraction would cause problems for the palaeoecologist. Many fragile forms such as small species of *Pinna*, *Turritella* and *Bulla* could not have been transported far, but this need not be so for such commonly found shells as *Fragum fragum*, *Chlamys* spp., species of *Arca* and *Trochus*, *Harpa conoidalis* and *Conus litoglyphus*.

In terms of the recognition in elevated reef limestones of various types of channel sands, deposited under widely varying energy conditions, the gross morphology of *Callianassa* burrow systems may thus be most useful. Strongly current-swept areas with relatively thin sediment cover possess dominantly horizontal systems where the number of branches at each junction is restricted, often to dichotomy (Fig. 15). Cross-bedded accretion sets of small scale characterize the sedimentary structures (Fig. 3C): grain size is coarse, with imbrication, and derived molluscs common. In quieter areas, often protected by Pleistocene promontories, thicker expanses of finer sediment possess vertically developed *Callianassa* systems forming galleries like the various levels in a coal-mine (Fig. 12A). Internally these sands are more massive, with anomalous sorting characteristics produced by the abundant burrowers. In that they lack an eel-grass covering they are less prolific faunally than sandy eel-grass beds, where *Callianassa* burrows are associated with rare *Neaxius* and stomatopod structures. This channel eel-grass habitat has much in common with that of oceanic coasts, but the species of *Callianassa* clearly seems to prefer conditions of reduced wave action, for it does not extend outside the atoll; though considerable current activity seems necessary since it does not extend far into the lagoon where the water is more stagnant.

LAGOON PLATFORMS

Sandflats—polychaete dominated

Lagoonwards of each of the channel areas lies a belt of clean sand which is dominated by polychaetes (Fig. 1): conspicuous permanent crustacean burrows are lacking. Other areas of sand accumulation tend to occur where tidal régimes from two channels meet, as in the vicinity of Île d'Esprit. Here, on the southeast coast of the island, is a wide expanse of fairly well-sorted fine–medium sand (Fig. 6) sharply

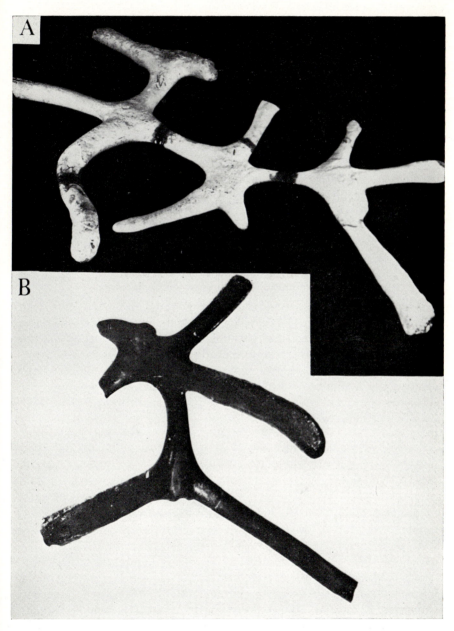

Fig. 15. Horizontal elements of *Callianassa* burrows from thin, migrating sand, Passe Mili. (A) Floored with rod-like anomuran faecal pellets; (B) Branching reduced to dichotomy.

delineated on all sides by tidal currents (Fig. 16A). A species of *Arenicola* is extremely abundant on the sandflats, which bear small sharp-crested oscillation ripples (Fig. 16B). Trenching proved most of the burrows to be "U"-shaped, with radiating feeding trails associated with many openings. Although the traces illustrated on Fig. 16C, D were both produced by the same species of *Arenicola* it is doubtful if palaeontologists would recognize the fact, for such trace fossils are classified on geometric form and would undoubtedly be described as separate "ichnospecies". Such recent examples as these argue strongly against too inflexible a system of nomenclature for trace fossils.

In emerged limestones this facies would be recognizable from its numerous "U" burrows and small oscillation ripples, an association not known from other facies. Although oscillation ripples occur in sublittoral sands offreef, lagoonal examples are of much shorter wavelength and cover wider areas. The molluscan fauna recorded was not prolific: live specimens of *Cypraea lynx*, *Pleuroploca trapezium*, and several dead *Cypraea tigris*.

Carbonate mudflats—Alpheus—goby burrows

Along the protected southern shore of the Aldabra Lagoon is an area of extensive intertidal carbonate mudflats (Fig. 1). The sediments are white-grey, extremely heavily burrowed muddy silts (Fig. 6). The region is one of reduced tidal amplitude and pronounced lag (Farrow and Brander, 1971, p. 107) though, unlike the *Uca* community at the head of the mangrove creeks, the *Alpheus crassimanus* community is situated nearer extreme low water and is probably covered at neap high tides. Thousands of small burrow openings may be seen at low tide, many with small gobies. Resin casting was very successful, striking similarities to the burrows of *Alpheus floridanus* (Shinn, 1968, p. 882) becoming apparent. The entrances to each complex are paired, forming a series of "Y"'s which lead to the main dominantly horizontal part of the system at a depth of 8–13 cm, where branching is dichotomous (Fig. 17A). Tube diameter usually varies from 13 to 20 mm, is unlined, and rather trigonal in cross section, with smooth concave floor and somewhat pointed scratched roof (Fig. 17B). Shinn has explained this by watching *Alpheus* burrowing in aquaria.

In contrast to the *Callianassa* systems seen on Aldabra, *Alpheus* burrows branch with very regular dichotomy. Out of 63 junctions examined from four alpheid burrows, 57 were dichotomous: angles measured are plotted on Fig. 18A and compared with the corresponding values for *Callianassa*. Frequency of branching is also compared (Fig. 18B) by measuring the distance between junctions. By using such

FIG. 16. Lagoon sandflat, southeast of Île d'Esprit. (A) Aerial view, showing sharp delineation by conflicting tidal currents; (B) Bottom topography with small oscillation ripples and abundant polychaete burrow openings; (C), (D) Two surface traces produced by the same species of *Arenicola*.

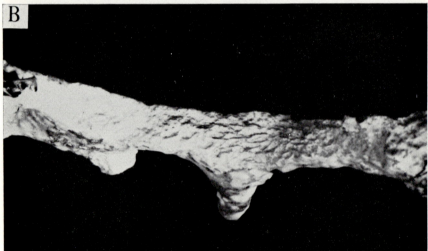

FIG. 17. *Alpheus crassimanus* burrows from carbonate mudflat, Bras Anse du Bois.
(A) Paired "Y"-shaped openings leading to horizontal, dichotomously branched system;
(B) scratch markings on burrow wall revealed by resin cast.

statistics as these on fossil material it should be possible to differentiate
an alpheid from a callianassid origin for Mesozoic *Thalassinoides*,
which often occur with widely different tunnel diameters, and may be
lined or unlined. At present an anomaly exists whereby the criterion
for identifying fossil callianassid burrows (*Thalassinoides*) is taken to

be "Y"-shaped forking (Häntzschel, 1962, W. 218) while recent callianassids may not demonstrate this nearly as consistently as do alpheids. It is likely that many of the smaller *Thalassinoides*, especially those from the English Chalk (Kennedy, 1967), may be the work of alpheids rather than Anomura.

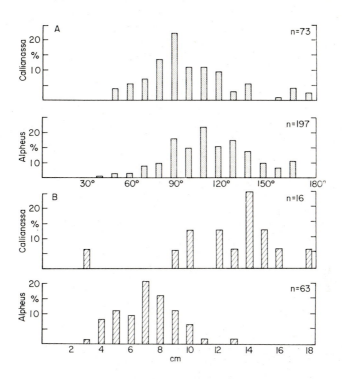

FIG. 18. Branching characteristics of *Alpheus* compared with *Callianassa*. (A) Angle of branching; (B) Distance between junctions.

Snapping shrimp—goby commensalism

Association between alpheids and gobioid fishes is common in the Indian Ocean. On the sandflats of Inhaca Island, Moçambique, Macnae and Kalk (1958, p. 43) record pairs of gobies, either *Crypto-centrus octofasciatus* or *Gobius inhacae*, in the burrows of *Alpheus rapacida* from areas of wet, consolidated sand with a sparse *Diplanthera* covering. The common alpheid from Aldabran mudflats, *A. crassimanus*, is associated with *Gobius nudiceps* at Zwartkops mudflat near Port Elizabeth, though no commensal gobies have been seen with this species at Inhaca Island (Macnae and Kalk, 1962, p. 117). In the muds of Saco da Inhaca *A. malabaricus* is found with the small skipping gobies *Butis butis*. Evidently snapping shrimp—goby commensalism is common all along the east coast of Africa (Mrs. J. L. B. Smith in Macnae and Kalk, 1958, p. 75) and is also reported from the Red Sea and Persian Gulf, where *A. djiboutensis* harbours *Cryptocentrus lutheri* (Luther, 1958, pp. 175–177; Palmer, 1963, pp. 447–450).

On Aldabra it was impractical to study the relationship in Bras Anse du Bois, the burrow casting site, where the population is lower midlittoral. In sheltered embayments on the western platform of Passe Houareau (Fig. 4) shrimp-goby burrows are common sublittorally in the fine muddy sand surrounding *Seriatopora* heads. This is an environment of such tranquillity that great care is taken in the placing of material around the burrow opening. The alpheids use their large claws as trays to convey piles of mud to the surface: this mud is subsequently searched for food by the goby. Periodically the shrimps carefully arrange broken twiglets of coral around the aperature, which effectively prevents mud from slurrying back into the burrow. From the frequency at which alpheids appeared in any one opening it seemed that at least two individuals were involved in constructing any one system. Of the several hundred burrow openings examined in the area 75% had goby associates, one-or-two of whom could be seen assisting with the burrowing by taking mouthfuls of mud from within the burrow and ejecting them around the periphery. Territorialism was strong; attempts by surrounding gobies to capture a neighbour's burrow entrance being met with violence. Resin casts of these sublittoral burrows were prepared in 0·5 m of water by guiding the resin from a champignon overhang through metal guttering and into burrows via a small funnel. They show far greater irregularity than examples from Bras Anse du Bois owing to obstructions in the path of burrowing, such as large *Fungeia* and *Seriatopora* twiglets. That area of the burrow occupied by the goby is however very clear (in the form of a "U" connecting two apertures), for it is much wider than the alpheid zone which extends beneath it.

The only other abundant burrower on the alpheid mudflats is *Macrophthalmus*. In very highly churned areas their burrows may penetrate those of shrimp-goby origin, apparently forming part of the same system, but normally they occur separately as simple spirals with a single swollen chamber (Fig. 19). It is of interest that *Macrophthalmus* and *Alpheus* species accompany one another in several of the facies described from Inhaca Island by Macnae and Kalk (1958). In the swamp interior *M. depressus* and *A. crassimanus*

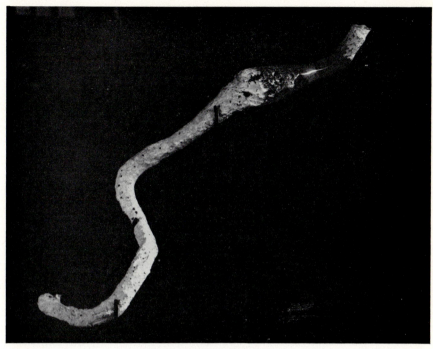

FIG. 19. Isolated spiral burrow of *Macrophthalmus* with swollen chamber, from *Alpheus* mudflat.

occur together in waterlogged muds, though subordinately to *Upogebia africana* (Macnae and Kalk, 1958, p. 39).

Mangrove creeks and mudflats—Uca *burrows*

Landwards of the *Alpheus* carbonate mudflats along the southern shore of the lagoon a series of creeks extend into the mangrove (Fig. 20A), on the sides of which occur very distinctive mud chimneys (Fig. 20B) produced by *Uca*, while on the floor are abundant faecal pyramids associated with stellate grazing trails (Fig. 20C). In contrast to the adjacent environment, the fine white mud is pelleted, either in coarse form up to 5 mm by *Uca* (Fig. 20D) or in tiny ovoid pellets (Fig. 20C). The producer of the latter type was not captured in the field, but comparisons with known lime mud pellet producers (Cloud, 1961, pp. 27–29) suggest a polychaete rather than a gastropod origin. Though *Cerithium morum* is very abundant locally its pellets would probably be rather longer than those commonly observed, as are those of *Batillaria minima* described from the northern extremity of Bimini Lagoon, where the sediment is 90% of faecal origin (Kornicker and Purdy, 1957). Dessication of the substratum during emergence causes a permanent hardening of the pellets, and since large areas of the mangrove probably dry out for several days during each tidal cycle (Farrow and Brander, 1971, p. 107) they would be most likely to be preserved and correspondingly recognizable in thin sections of elevated calcilutites.

The redolent brown gelatinous mangrove muds tend to be confined to the most protected regions of the atoll where production of organic matter far exceeds the supply of fine aragonitic detritus. This facies is typically seen in the southeast of the lagoon at the heads of creeks such as Bras Cinq Cases (Fig. 1) where an algal film is commonly plastered over the mud surface. The simple, unlined, vertical *Uca* burrows are again very abundant, though pellets of other creatures are not conspicuous as in the carbonate mud mangrove regions: polychaetes are also extremely rare from brown mangrove muds (Macnae and Kalk, 1958, p. 41). The gastropod *Terebralia palustris* is strikingly common, browsing over the algal mats and wet mud surface where it is thought to feed on diatoms (Macnae and Kalk, 1958, p. 41). The acid environment frequently corrodes the shells of these molluscs to such an extent that their columellas are visible even during life. The forms of *Uca* burrow cast in Bras Cinq Cases show considerable diversity (Fig. 2), "Y" and "U" shaped varieties accompanying the more common simple structures. In Passe Houareau, where sandy mangrove mud only thinly overlies the platin, many burrows of *Uca marionis* disappear inextricably into bedrock (Fig. 20E).

DISCUSSION

Environmental control on basic burrowing patterns:
palaeoecological implications

Various aspects of the environment may be determined from an analysis of burrow form. These range from gross features such as the energy level to smaller details such as the role of sediment consolidation. Viewed in their geographical context, burrows are very rare in sediments accumulating around the atoll rim compared with their abundance in sheltered regions of the lagoon. Not only are oceanic sediments deposited at a high energy level, they are also poor in contained organic detritus and so becomes inhabited by a relatively sparse, highly adapted fauna which leaves largely ephemeral structures. It is only the development of marine grass beds which makes possible the establishing of permanent lined burrows, occupied throughout life. These are typical

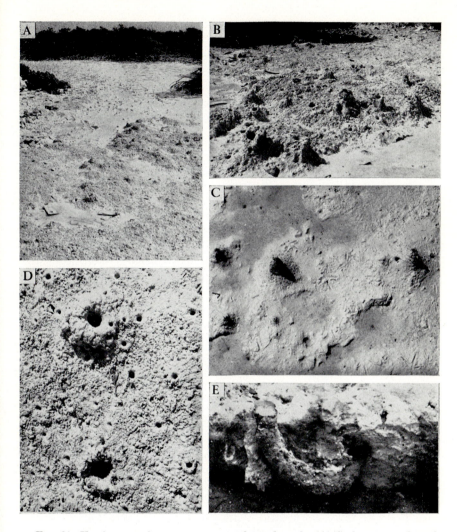

FIG. 20. *Uca* burrows from mangrove creeks and muds. (A) Carbonate mud creek at the head of Bras Anse du Bois; (B) Mud chimneys formed by *Uca*; (C) Faecal pyramids on the creek floor; (D) Pseudo-faecal pellets of *Uca*; (E) Burrow of *Uca marionis* disappearing into platin bedrock, Passe Houareau.

of areas stabilized by *Cymodocea* (Fig. 9): they are simple, the extensive branched systems of deposit feeders being confined to channel and lagoon areas. In low energy lagoonal substrates where sediment accumulation is very slow relative to biological activity, original depositional structures become obliterated. Complex burrows utilize the maximum available thickness of soft sediment and may remain open for thousands of years (Shinn, 1968).

Between these two extremes of environmental energy a number of more subtle distinctions can be made, whereby certain characteristic patterns of burrowing are produced by different facets of the contemporary environment. Used in reverse when dealing with fossil reef carbonates such controls could have widespread palaeoecological implications: these I have grouped into seven categories.

Depth of burrows related to water table

Takahashi (1932) and Hayasaka (1935) have pointed out that whether erect or inclined the bases of *Ocypode* burrows always reach ground water level. Thus the higher above H.W.N.T. a burrow is constructed the deeper it is likely to be, and measurements of the depth of penetration of burrows in elevated beach calcarenites could provide information on tidal range and position with respect to former high water levels. Present day species of *Ocypode* are strictly governed in their distribution by tidal height (p. 462) and the recognition of diagnostic burrow forms of certain species (e.g. Fig. 8) could pinpoint quite precisely the height of any raised beach. Stephenson (1965, p. 881) has observed that many recent *O. kuhli* on the east African coast near Malindi construct burrows 1 m deep at neap tides, and has found Pleistocene equivalents at least 70 cm deep: at spring tides the structures are shallower.

Burrowing patterns necessitated by thin sediment cover

Most sediment feeding organisms attempt to utilize the maximum available thickness of sediment, normally constructing deep burrow networks (Fig. 12). On Aldabra, however, many regions possess only a thin sediment cover. *Alpheus* burrows which in other reef areas may be more than 1 m in depth (Shinn, 1968, p. 882) may be abnormally shallow (Fig. 17) and more horizontal than vertical. Similarly *Uca* burrows often disappear into crevices in the platin; *Neaxius* and *Callianassa* into champignon, even where the cover is relatively thick (for Aldabra).

Burrow modification caused by erosion of contemporary sediment surface

Since most burrowers possess an optimum depth to which they habitually tunnel it follows that erosion frequently causes deepening of an existing structure to the new, lower, sedimentary surface. This is seen in the lowering of the floors of several *Ocypode* burrows from the upper beach (Fig. 8B) resulting from tidal scour, though this was not a discernible feature of lined thalassinidean burrows from other scoured environments, for these are more permanent in character.

Burrow modification induced by sand deposition over original surface

In current-swept channel areas, migration of the lateral margins of a sandsheet may inundate a previously stable habitat, raising the sedimentary surface by up to 20 cm in a single event. *Callianassa* burrow systems faithfully record such happenings by leaving a series of abandoned apertures all at the same horizon, where a change in inclination of the new excurrent tunnel also occurs (Fig. 14A). Abandoned apertures are likewise to be found in *Ocypode* burrows (Fig. 8B), where responses to both erosion and sedimentation may even be seen in the same burrow, giving an indication of the typical mode of formation of beach sands.

Blocked apertures

The openings of individual burrows may be overrun with sediment on a more localized scale. *Ocypode*, for example, may be forced to re-bore because of the continued accumulation in its burrow of either wind-blown or tidally derived sand, which produces a "pseudo-lining". Occasional incomplete "U" burrows in the form of a "J" partially infilled with coarse sand, represent abandoned attempts (Fig. 3B). Incurrent funnels of *Callianassa* systems may be obstructed adventitiously by surface-grazing gastropods such as *Laevistrombus* (Fig. 14D), which causes them to be abandoned and the system extended horizontally to maintain the respiratory current.

Burrow forms associated with obstructions in the substratum

Abnormalities may be produced when burrows encounter bulky objects in the sediment. In white carbonate mud *Uca* burrows possess a smooth simple outline bearing clear scratch markings, but in tough brown mangrove mud the outline is rough and varied burrow forms occur, including a doughnut shape where one crab tunnelled on both sides of a large mangrove twig (Fig. 2). Curiously, the lined burrows of *Neaxius* from conglomeratic eel-grass sands are most consistent in their form. Only basal chambers show the effect of obstructions (Fig. 9A), the tunnel cross section being accurately circular throughout its length. In contrast, *Alpheus*-Goby systems are highly irregular in sublittoral sandy muds containing *Fungia* and also *Seriatopora* sticks, though the regularity of their dichotomous branching in pure carbonate silts is most noticeable (Fig. 18).

Population density as a control on burrow form

Some channel sandsheets are inhabited by very dense populations of *Callianassa* whose coalescing sand volcanoes and funnel-shaped apertures produce a characteristic hummocky bottom topography (Fig. 11E; *cf.* Warme, 1967, Fig. 4). Below ground, resin casts show a very distinctive galleried structure to each burrow system which is of only limited horizontal extent (Fig. 12A). This pattern is functionally most efficient for large numbers of sediment feeders, whose activities cause anomalous sorting characteristics of the sediment (Fig. 6).

Atoll sedimentary facies and burrowing crustacean communities compared with those of other reef areas

Taken individually, each of the environments described above has a close equivalent in some other region of carbonate sedimentation. Thus, the *Ocypode* Upper Beach and Marine Grass Bed facies are virtually pantropical: even *Axius*, the dominant burrowing crustacean in sandy *Cymodocea serrulata* Beds, has a very wide distribution in the southwestern Indian Ocean (Macnae and Kalk, 1962, p. 121). Ball (1967, p. 573) has described Platform Interior Sand Blankets from the Bahamas which resemble some of the sandsheets described from Aldabra, especially inasmuch as their internal structure reflects the work of burrowing organisms rather than the depositing agency. Jindrich (1969), in analysing the carbonate sand bodies forming in tidal channels, notes many phenomena such as the development of megaripples which can be paralleled on Aldabra. Shinn (1968) has studied burrowing in lime muds very similar to those now forming on the atoll.

In isolation, then, none of the facies is especially remarkable, nor peculiar to atolls: many can be related to the communities and bottom facies of Newell *et al.* (1959) described from the Grand Bahama Bank, which is in reality a gigantic atoll, devoid of terrigenous clastics. This makes it closer in some respects to Aldabra than neighbouring Indian Ocean reefs which are affected by terrestrial detritus. What is unique to the atoll environment is the areal extent of particular facies and their geomorphological relationship to the reef front (Figs 4, 5). Beaches and marine grass beds occur only on leeward coasts and in channels, back-reef sandbars being even more restricted.

The distribution of the burrowing Crustacea on Aldabra reveals some interesting subtleties. The first concerns the ghost crab *Ocypode ceratophthalma*, which Voeltzkow (1897, p. 68) described as absent from the island. It must therefore be either a recent introduction or else the population must fluctuate widely in numbers from year to year. The fact that this crab is confined to western coastal and channel beaches supports Macnae and Kalk's observations at Inhaca Island (1958, p. 38) that it is confined to areas with reduced wave action. Further east along the leeward northern coast beaches may be deserted, for even *O. kuhli* is not abundant there though it tolerates considerable wave action on Inhaca beaches. In Florida and the Bahamas *Callianassa* and *Alpheus* evidently occur together (Shinn, 1968, p. 884), though on Aldabra they characterize separate environments; the former preferring current-swept channel sands, the latter quiescent lagoonal silts. They appear to form distinct communities in Usu Bay, Hokkaido; *Callianassa* tending to concentrate at around mid-tide level, with *Alpheus* dominating near low-tide mark (Ohshima, 1963, p. 39, Fig. 8). On Aldabra, substrate type and current activity seem to exert a stronger control than tidal level.

SUMMARY

The accompanying Table summarizes the faunal and sedimentary characteristics of the soft sediment facies. For the purposes of assessing whether any particular bottom facies is likely to exist in elevated reef limestones I have allotted it an "Index of Fossilization Potential" (Goldring, 1965): this is directly related to the mobility of the environment. A rating "A" denotes high probability that a given habitat will be preserved and eventually lithified: a rating "D" low probability, associated with demonstrably transient structures. Equivalent facies are tabulated from three contrasted reef areas: the Bahama Banks (Newell *et al.*, 1959), notably for lagoonal sediments: Inhaca Island (Macnae and Kalk, 1962), the southern limit of reef growth on the African mainland. Seychelles (Lewis, 1969), for oceanic coastal environments.

It must be difficult for any scientist who has undertaken prolonged fieldwork during the Trades not to conclude that they are instrumental in shaping not only the atoll perimeter but also the sedimentary environments and their communities. On the atoll of Aldabra the strong SE Trades combine with a formidable tidal range to produce a prodigious environmental energy gradient which is paralleled by the distribution of benthic facies, each closely dependent upon régimes of wave and current activity.

ACKNOWLEDGEMENTS

This paper represents part of a marine ecological and palaeoecological study of Aldabra Atoll undertaken from July to December,

SUMMARY TABLE

Back-reef and lagoonal environments of Aldabra Atoll

Environment	Dominant burrowing crustacean	Burrow type	Burrow density	Sediment grain size	Sorting	Sedimentary structures
LEEWARD OCEANIC COASTS						
Upper beach	Ocypode ceratophthalma	Spiral	Moderate	coarse–fine sand	Bimodal	Parallel lamination
Marine grass bed	Neaxius sp.	"U", "J" simple chambered	Low	conglomeratic fine sand	Poor	Massive with rhizomes
Back-reef sandbar	Albunea sp.	vertical deep	Very low	medium–fine sand	Good	Massive with air heave and thixotropic structures
CHANNEL PLATFORMS						
Megarippled sandbank	Albunea sp.	vertical deep	Very low	coarse sand	Good	Partially erosive cross ripples
Migrating sandsheets	Callianassa sp.	branching horizontal	Moderate	coarse sand	Good	Cross ripples
Sandy eel-grass or stable sandsheets	Callianassa sp.	branching galleries	High	coarse–fine sand	Bimodal	Massive with rhizomes
LAGOON PLATFORMS						
Polychaete sandflats	(Arenicola sp.)	"U" with surface trials	High	medium–very fine sand	Fair	Small oscillation ripples
Carbonate mudflats	Alpheus crassimanus	extensive horizontal networks	Very high	silt	Fair–poor	Destroyed
Mangrove muds	Uca marionis	simple, "U" or "Y"	High	highly organic mud	—	Algal mats, mangrove roots

Environment	Tidal range (springs) m	Tidal height	Wave action	Current activity	Associated fauna*
LEEWARD OCEANIC COASTS					
Upper beach	3·0	HWOT	Moderate	Swash	*Ocypode kuhli*; **Erycina*
Marine grass bed	2·8	LWOT	Moderate to high	Slight	**Capulus*; *Codakia tigerina*
Back-reef sandbar	3·0	LWNT–LWOT	High	Slight	*Oliva espiscopalis*; Maldanid polychaetes; *Ochetostoma erythrogramma*; *Polinices* sp.; *Calappa* sp.
CHANNEL PLATFORMS					
Megarippled sandbank	2·1	LWNT–LWST	High	High	*Mitra mitra*; *Oliva* sp.; *Metalia* sp.
Migrating sandsheets	1·6	LWNT–LWST	Low	Moderate	*Terebra* spp.; *Conus tessulatus*; *C. arenatus*; *Laevistrombus* sp.
Sandy eel-grass or stable sandsheets	1·1–2·5	LWOT	Low	Moderate	*Laevistrombus gibberulus*; *Conus* spp.; *Fragum fragum*; *Balanoglossus studiosorum*
LAGOON PLATFORMS					
Polychaete sandflats	1·6	LWNT–LWST	Slight	Slight	*Cypraea* spp.; *Macrophthalmus*
Carbonate mudflats	1·2	ELW	Nil	Nil	**Gobioid fishes*
Mangrove muds	1·0	HWOT	Nil	Nil	*Terebralia palustris*; *Cerithium morum*

* = Commensals from crustacean burrows

(Table continued on next page)

SUMMARY TABLE (continued)

Environment	Newell et al. 1959	Equivalent facies Macnae and Kalk, 1962	Lewis, 1969	Index of fossilization potential
LEEWARD OCEANIC COASTS				
Upper beach		Protected beach	Beach	C
Marine grass bed		Cymodocea serrulata Zone	Marine grass bed	A
Back-reef sandbar		Astropecten Association	Sands of Radial Zone	C
CHANNEL PLATFORMS				
Megarippled sandbank	Unstable oolite sand	Dune Hydraulique (Thomassin, 1969)		D
Migrating sandsheets		Coarse sandbank with Callianassa kraussi	? ex-Mangrove Fringe	C
Sandy eel-grass of stable sandsheets	Stable sand Strombus costatus community	Platform interior sand blankets (Ball, 1967)		B
LAGOON PLATFORMS				
Polychaete sandflats				B
Carbonate mudflats	Muddy sediment of Shelf lagoon			A
Mangrove muds	Mangrove	Swamp interior	Mangrove	A

1968 while I was a member of the Royal Society Expedition. Dr. J. C. Gamble has generously made available his sediment analyses, and Mr. A. A. Q. R. McLeod kindly identified many of the Crustacea. Dr. A. Wheeler drew my attention to the widespread nature of alpheid-goby commensalism, and Dr. W. J. Kennedy to current Japanese literature.

The field assistance of Harry Charles and Georges Larou enabled many more resin casts to be retrieved than would have been expected, and without the technical skills of Mr. K. G. Walker in reassembly and Mr. H. Chamberlain in mounting many would have been valueless. Field photography is my own: laboratory photography the work of Mr. B. Nettleton. Advice on the quantity of resin necessary for the study, and its use in the field, was supplied by Dr. Eugene Shinn; cost being borne by the Royal Society: to both I am most grateful.

In conclusion I thank Prof. M. R. House and the Natural Environment Research Council for granting leave of absence, and Dr. J. D. Taylor for first arousing my interest in working on Aldabra.

REFERENCES

Ball, M. M. (1967). Carbonate sand bodies of Florida and the Bahamas. *J. sedim. Petrol.* **37**(2): 556–591.

Black, M. (1933). The algal sediments of Andros Island, Bahamas. *Phil. Trans. R. Soc.* (B) **122**: 165–192.

Bromley, R. G. (1967). Some observations on burrows of thalassinidean Crustacea in chalk hardgrounds. *Q. Jl geol. Soc. Lond.* **123**: 157–182.

Cloud, P. E. (1961). Environment of calcium carbonate deposition west of Andros Island, Bahamas. *Prof. Pap. U.S. geol. Surv.* no. **350**, 138 pp.

Farrow, G. E. (1966) Bathymetric zonation of Jurassic trace fossils from the coast of Yorkshire, England. *Palaeogeography, Palaeoclimatol., Palaeoecol.* **2**: 103–151.

Farrow, G. E. and Brander, K. M. (1971). Tidal studies on Aldabra. *Phil. Trans. R. Soc.* (B) **260**: 93–121.

Frey, R. W. and Howard, J. D. (1969). A profile of biogenic sedimentary structures in a Holocene barrier island—salt marsh complex, Georgia. *Trans. Gulf Cst. Ass. geol. Socs.* **19**: 427–444.

Ginsburg, R. N. and Lowenstam, H. A. (1958). The influence of marine bottom communities on the depositional environments of sediments. *J. Geol.* **66**: 310–318.

Goldring, R. (1965). Sediments into rock. *New Scient.* **28**: 863–865.

Guilcher, A. (1965). Coral reefs and lagoons of Mayotte Island, Comoro Archipelago, Indian Ocean, and of New Caledonia, Pacific Ocean. In *Submarine Geology and Geophysics*: 21–45. (Whittard, W. F. and Bradshaw, R., eds). London: Butterworths.

Hamblin, W. K. (1962). X-ray radiography in the study of structures in homogeneous sediments. *J. sediment. Petrol.* **32**(2): 201–210.

Hamblin, W. K. (1965). Internal structures of "homogeneous" sandstones. *Bull. Kans. Univ. geol. Surv.* **175**: 1–37.

Häntzschel, W. (1962). Trace fossils and problematica. In *Treatise on Invertebrate Paleontology*. **W**: 177–245. (Moore, R. C., ed.) New York: Geol. Soc. Am. and Kansas: Univ. Kansas Press.

Hayasaka, I. (1935). The burrowing activities of certain crabs and their geologic significance. *Am. Midl. Nat.* **16**: 99–103.

Illing, L. V. (1954). Bahaman calcareous sands. *Bull. Am. Ass. Petrol. Geol.* **38**: 1–95.

Imbrie, J. and Buchanan, H. (1965). Sedimentary structures in modern carbonate sands of the Bahamas. In *Primary Sedimentary Structures and their Hydrodynamic Interpretation:* 149–172. (Middleton, G. V., ed.). *Spec. Publs. Soc. econ. Paleont. Miner. Tulsa.* No. 12, 265 pp.

Jindrich, V. (1969). Recent carbonate sedimentation by tidal channels in the lower Florida Keys. *J. sediment. Petrol.* **39**: 531–553.

Kennedy, W. J. (1967). Burrows and surface traces from the Lower Chalk of southern England. *Bull. Br. Mus. nat. Hist.* (Geol.) **15**(3): 125–167.

Kennedy, W. J. and MacDougall, J. D. S. (1969). Crustacean burrows in the Weald Clay (Lower Cretaceous) of south-eastern England and their environmental significance. *Palaeontology* **12**(3): 459–471.

Kornicker, L. S. and Purdy, E. G. (1957). A Bahamian faecal pellet sediment. *J. sediment. Petrol.* **27**: 126–128.

Ladd, H. S., Tracey, J. I., Wells, J. W. and Emery, K. O. (1950). Organic growth and sedimentation on an atoll. *J. Geol.* **58**: 410–425.

Lewis, M. S. (1969). Sedimentary environments and unconsolidated carbonate sediments of the fringing coral reefs of Mahé, Seychelles. *Marine Geol.* **7**: 95–127.

Lewis, M. S. and Taylor, J. D. (1966). Marine sediments and bottom communities of the Seychelles. *Phil. Trans. R. Soc.* (A) **259**: 279–290.

Luther, W. (1958). Symbiose von Fischen (Gobiidae) mit einem Krebs (*Alpheus djiboutensis*) im Roten Meer. *Z. Tierpsychol.* **15**: 175–177.

MacGinitie, G. E. (1930). The natural history of the mud shrimp *Upogebia pugettensis* Dana. *Ann. Mag. nat. Hist.* (10) **6**: 36–44.

MacGinitie, G. E. (1934). The natural history of *Callianassa californiensis* Dana. *Am. Midl. Nat.* **15**: 166–177.

MacGinitie, G. E. and MacGinitie, N. (1968). *Natural History of Marine animals.* New York; Mcgraw–Hill. 523 pp.

Macnae, W. and Kalk, M. (1958). *A Natural History of Inhaca Island, Moçambique.* Johannesburg: Witwatersrand Univ. Press.

Macnae, W. and Kalk, M. (1962). The fauna and flora of sand flats at Inhaca Island, Moçambique. *J. anim. Ecol.* **31**: 93–128.

McKee, E. D. (1957). Primary structures in some Recent sediments. *Bull. Am. Ass. Petrol. Geol.* **41**: 1704–1747.

McKee, E. D. (1958). Geology of Kapingamarangi Atoll, Caroline Islands. *Bull. geol. Soc. Am.* **69**: 241–278.

McKee, E. D., Chronic, J. and Leopold, E. B. (1959). Sedimentary belts in the lagoon of Kapingamarangi Atoll. *Bull. Am. Ass. Petrol. Geol.* **43**: 501–562.

Milliman, J. D. (1967). Carbonate sedimentation on Hogsty Reef, a Bahamian Atoll. *J. sediment. Petrol.* **37**: 658–676.

Milne, L. J. and Milne, M. J. (1946). Notes on the behaviour of the ghost crab. *Am. Nat.* **80**: 362–380.

Newell, N. D., Imbrie, J., Purdy, E. G. and Thurber, D. L. (1959). Organism communities and bottom facies, Great Bahama Bank. *Bull. Am. Mus. nat. Hist.* **117**: 177–228.

Ohshima, K. (1963). Ecological studies of Usu Bay, Hokkaido, Japan. Part 1. Bottom materials and benthic fauna. *Bull. Hokkaido reg. Fish. Res. Lab.* **27**: 32–51.

Ohshima, K. (1967). Some burrowing crustaceans and shape of their burrows from the Usu Bay, Hokkaido. *Jubilee Publ. Commem., Prof. SASA, 60th Birthday*: 241–265.

Palmer, G. (1963). A record of the gobiid fish *Cryptocentrus lutheri* Klausewitz from the Persian Gulf, with notes on the genus *Cryptocentrus*. *Senckenberg. biol.* **44**: 447–450.

Phillips, A. M. (1940). The ghost crab. *Nat. Hist., N.Y.* **46**(1): 36–41.

Purdy, E. G. (1963). Recent calcium carbonate facies of the Great Bahama Bank. Part II. Sedimentary facies. *J. Geol.* **71**: 472–497.

Sawaya, P. (1939). Animais cavadores da Práia arenosa. *Archos Inst. biol. S. Paulo* **10**: 319–326.

Shinn, E. A. (1968). Burrowing in Recent lime sediments of Florida and the Bahamas. *J. Paleont.* **42**: 878–894.

Sorby, H. C. (1879). The structure and origin of limestones. *Proc. geol. Soc. Lond.* **25**: 56–95.

Stephenson, D. G. (1965). Fossil burrows on the coast of Kenya. *Nature, Lond.* **207**: 850–851.

Stevens, B. A. (1929). Ecological observations on the Callianassidae of Puget Sound. *Ecology* **10**: 399–405.

Stoddart, D. R. (1962). Three Caribbean Atolls: Turneffe Islands, Lighthouse Reef, and Glover's Reef, British Honduras. *Atoll Res. Bull.* **87**: 1–151.

Stoddart, D. R., Taylor, J. D., Fosberg, F. R. and Farrow, G. E. (1971). The Geomorphology of Aldabra Atoll. *Phil. Trans. R. Soc.* (B). **260**, 31–65.

Takahashi, S. (1932). On the burrows of *Ocypoda ceratophthalma* Fabricius. *Kwagaku* **2**: 329–335. (in Japanese).

Taylor, J. D. (1968). Coral reef and associated invertebrate communities (mainly molluscan) around Mahé, Seychelles. *Phil. Trans. R. Soc.* (B) **254**: 129–206.

Thomassin, B. (1969). Peuplements de deux biotopes de sables coralliens sur le grand récif de Tuléar, sud-ouest de Madagascar. *Recl. Trav. Stn. mar. Endoume* (Fasc. hors série) Suppl. No. **9**: 59–133.

Thompson, A. O. (1956). *Geology of the Malindi Area. Rep. geol. Survey Kenya* No. 36.

Utashiro, T. and Horii, Y. (1965). Some knowledges on the ecology of *Ocypoda stimpsoni* Ortmann and on its bubbows. *Res. Rep. Takada Branch Fac. Educ. Niigata Univ.* No. 9: 121–141. (in Japanese).

Verwey, J. (1930). Einiges über die Ost-Indischer Mangrove-krabben. *Treubia* **12**: 167–261.

Voeltzkow, A. (1897). Aldabra, Indische Ocean, 1895. *Abh. senckenb. naturforsch. Ges.* **21**: 40–76.

Warme, J. E. (1967). Graded bedding in the Recent sediments of Mugu Lagoon, California. *J. sediment. Petrol.* **37**: 540–547.

Weimer, R. J. and Hoyt, J. H. (1964). Burrows of *Callianassa major* Say, geologic indicators of littoral and shallow neritic environments. *J. Paleont.* **38**: 761–767.

Wentworth, C. K. (1922). A scale of grade and class terms for clastic sediments
J. Geol. **30**: 377–392.
Wiens, H. J. (1962). *Atoll environment and ecology.* New Haven and London:
Yale Univ. Press.
Yonge, C. M. (1951). Studies on Pacific Coast Molluscs. I. On the structure and
adaptations of *Cryptomya californica* (Conrad). *Univ. Calif. Publs Zoöl.* **55,**
395–400.

Symp. zool. Soc. Lond. (1971) No. 28, 501–534.

REEF ASSOCIATED MOLLUSCAN ASSEMBLAGES IN THE WESTERN INDIAN OCEAN

JOHN D. TAYLOR

Department of Zoology, British Museum (Natural History), London, England

SYNOPSIS

The islands of the western Indian Ocean have a very uniform fauna comprising species which have larvae capable of surviving pelagic transport. The continental margins have the same species but more are found at any one locality. In addition they have a set of species which are confined to continental margins and some endemic species. Isolated areas of the fringes of the Indian Ocean show a higher degree of endemicity and a latitudinal decrease in diversity. The importance of studying fossil assemblages is stressed. The molluscan assemblage comprising part of the biomorphological communities of reef areas exhibit a remarkable uniformity throughout the area. Those of continental areas are more complex. The main features of assemblages inhabiting the various hard, soft and mangrove substrates are described and variation around the area discussed. In the shallow sublittoral, communities are biologically accommodated, in the intertidal there is an upward transition to physically controlled communities. In the biologically accommodated communities interactions reduce competition. The more important of the factors are considered to be space and food, and the ways in which these interactions occur in various families, genera and species are examined.

INTRODUCTION

This paper reviews some aspects of the composition, distribution and structure of shallow water reef associated molluscan assemblages of the islands and continental margins of the western Indian Ocean. The conclusions are based upon field observations in the Seychelles, Addu Atoll, Diego Garcia, Coetivy, Platte, Aldabra and the east African Coast during the period 1963–1969 and by reference to published work in the area. Before discussing the composition of the assemblages it is worthwhile examining larger scale effects influencing the faunal composition of the area which may explain some of the smaller scale differences in assemblage constituents from place to place and help to ascertain how much similarity we might expect.

ZOOGEOGRAPHIC CONSIDERATIONS

It has been established for the terrestrial biota of islands that there is a positive correlation between the size of the island and the number of species occurring upon it (MacArthur and Wilson, 1967; Peake, 1969, 1970). Island size may also be considered an approximate measure of habitat diversity. Although data are at present limited a similar positive correlation seems to exist between the numbers of shallow water Mollusca and the area of shallow water around an island. Thus for bivalves where there are reasonable faunal lists from several localities 87 species are recorded from Cocos-Keeling (Maes, 1967), 54 species from Diego Garcia (J. D. Taylor, unpublished), 104 species from Aldabra (J. D. Taylor, unpublished); these compare with 224 species from Dar es Salaam (Spry, 1964) and 167 from Inhaca, an island on the Mozambique coast (Boshoff, 1965). The granitic Seychelles which lie on an extensive shallow water bank support 176 species (Taylor, 1968 and unpublished), a faunal size more comparable with that of the continental margins than the low coralline islands. Further analysis of the faunal lists shows that the species lacking on the islands are mainly burrowing species from the Veneracea and Tellinacea. This might suggest a lack of suitable substrates on the smaller islands.

Thorson (1963) has pointed out that marine larvae tend to travel in swarms and if an island is very small a swarm may easily miss it. A whole swarm may reach a continental coast and with favourable conditions found a population; the chances of this occurring on an oceanic island are far less.

Certain genera and species are absent from the islands altogether but have ranges extending all around the continental margins of the Indian Ocean. Probably because of its size the west coast of Madagascar at least, supports a fauna similar to that of the mainland. A good example of this continental distribution is the buccinid gastropod genus *Bullia* which ranges from the Cape of Good Hope to Burma and the only island record is from southern Madagascar (Fig. 1). The arcid bivalve genus *Trisidos* exhibits a similar but more widespread distribution. In some genera, certain species may have wide distributions including the oceanic islands and other species are restricted to the mainland. Examples are *Phalium faurotis* (Abbott, 1968), *Strombus terebellatus* (Abbott, 1960), *Pinna bicolor* (Rosewater, 1961), and *Tellina capsoides* (Boss, 1969). In the case of *Bullia* this phenomenon can be directly related to the type of larval development. Barnard (1959, Fig. 26) shows an attached egg capsule of *Bullia* with a single larval shell of very large size within. The free swimming stage is obviously very short or completely suppressed. Therefore, short of rafting of the egg capsules dispersal will be entirely along continental margins.

Thorson (1940) has shown in a widespread Indo-Pacific gastropod *Planaxis sulcata* which normally has a pelagic stage in its development (Risbec, 1935) that in the Persian Gulf the populations have the pelagic stage suppressed.

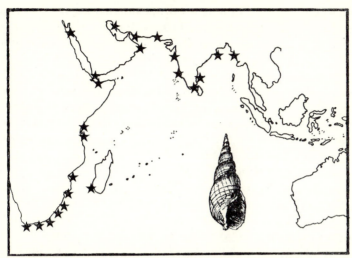

FIG. 1. The distribution of the genus *Bullia* showing the restriction to continental margins characteristic of a number of Indo-Pacific genera and species.

The concentration of species with short or suppressed pelagic larval stages will encourage the development of endemism along continental margins as opposed to islands where most of the species which arrive have pelagic larval stages. Of course, with extreme isolation of an island one might expect the appearance of non-pelagic reproductive stages but this does not seem to happen for islands in the tropical Indian Ocean.

Study of ocean current maps shows that the major movement in the equatorial region is towards the east African coast. Here the currents divide and move either northwards or southwards along the African coast. The northbound current follows a clockwise movement along the northern fringes of the Indian Ocean back to Indonesia. The southerly current passes down through the Mozambique Channel and into the colder southerly waters. This current movement will thus encourage the continental distribution of species arising on the African coast.

For marine molluscs dispersal is far easier than for terrestrial species and the fauna shows very little endemism. Indeed, as opposed to terrestrial faunas the endemism is on the continental margins rather than the islands. This endemism is most marked in the case of isolated sections of continental margins such as the Red Sea and Persian Gulf.

As well as the continental margins other places such as the southern Mascarenes, on the fringes of the main circulation show a fauna with a higher degree of endemism,

From island to island differences of the dominance of certain species in assemblages is very apparent. Thus, in Mahé in the *Thalassia* beds bivalves such as *Codakia*, *Anodontia* and *Quidnipagus* are very abundant (Taylor, 1968). On Aldabra there are extensive *Thalassia/Cymodocea* beds apparently similar to those of Mahé but supporting virtually no bivalves. This is not a reflection of the difference between high and low islands because the low coralline island of Coetivy supports large numbers of bivalves in the grass beds. Similarly the intertidal gastropod *Monodonta* is common on Mahé but only a single specimen was found on Aldabra. On coralline islands many species are rare and for some species only a single or a few specimens may be found in months of collecting. This might mean that although larvae may be arriving at islands they do not always arrive in sufficient numbers to found a population. Abbott (1968) has shown that for *Cassis* the relative abundance over a range may vary considerably; this may not always be due to a lack of suitable habitats but because a species may be just arriving and dying out in any particular area.

Study of Pleistocene fossil assemblages shows that interpretation of dispersal routes on the basis of present day distribution patterns could be most unreliable. Preliminary work on the faunas from the raised limestone of Aldabra shows that there have been remarkable changes in the distribution of species within the last 125 000 years. For instance in the youngest limestone of Aldabra five species of the bivalve family Tridacnidae are found, only two of these *T. maxima* and *T. squamosa* inhabit the waters today. The other three, *Hippopus hippopus*, *Tridacna gigas* and *T. crocea*, are restricted in distribution to Indonesia and the west Pacific arc (Rosewater, 1965). This region has frequently been considered the centre of dispersal for the Indo-Pacific fauna (Ekman, 1953; Kohn 1967). However for the Tridacnidae at least it could possibly be considered as an accumulation area resulting from the retraction of ranges of the species. During the Pleistocene the reduction in sea level during periods of glacial advance will have considerably increased the areas of shallow water available for colonization in the western Indian Ocean. Thus the Seychelles Bank, and the Cargados Carajos shoals will have been very shallow water. The present lower diversity of the western Indian Ocean fauna compared with that of Indonesia may thus have been a result of a reduction in the number of available habitats in the western Indian Ocean.

This is supported by Kohn (1967) who examined the diversity of *Conus* on a uniform habitat across 160 degrees of longitude and found no diversity gradient towards Indonesia, concluding that habitat complexity was a greater determinant of species diversity than isolation or distance from a faunistic centre. Discontinuous distribution patterns, variations in relative abundance and diversity may result from present day distributive forces, but the faunal history of an area must also be taken into account where possible.

Stehli (1968) in a study of faunal diversity has shown that diversity gradients in all widely distributed major groups of organisms studied exhibited a form which is latitude dependant. Thus for *Strombus* and *Cypraea*, (the two gastropod genera examined) there is a rapid attenuation in species diversity both in the northern and particularly the southern part of the Indian Ocean in the region of south Madagascar, and the southern Mascarenes. In the north there is a less marked gradient in the Red Sea and the Persian Gulf. In the genus *Strombus* there is, superimposed upon the latitudinal diversity gradient, some degree of longitudinal variation. Although there is a high diversity in the Indonesian/N. Australian area there is a low in the middle of the Indian Ocean with a subsidiary diversity high in the east African area. In *Cypraea*, species are more widespread and although the Indonesian area shows a diversity high the rest of the Indian Ocean shows more uniform diversity, but with a steep diversity gradient at the southern margin.

In summary, the islands of the western Indian Ocean have a very uniform fauna comprising species which have larvae capable of surviving pelagic transport. The continental margins have these same species but more of them are found at any one locality. In addition they have a set of species which are confined to the continental margins and some endemic species. Isolated areas on the fringes of the Indian Ocean show a higher degree of endemicity whilst experiencing a latitudinal decrease in diversity (Fig. 2).

MOLLUSCAN ASSEMBLAGES

Introduction

Until about twelve years ago most of the work concerning molluscs in this area had been of an inventory nature. In recent years there has been an enormous increase in the amount of ecological work particularly in the description of coral communities. This work has been carried out at a few centres, beginning at Inhaca (Kalk, 1958; Macnae and Kalk, 1958, 1962a, b). The overwhelmingly greatest contribution has come from the large group of workers at Tuléar, summarized by Picard (1967) but including notably Pichon (1964), Plante (1964), Dérijard (1965), Mirielle Pichon (1967) and Thomassin (1969). Other ecological work mentioning molluscs has been at Mauritius (Baissac, Lubet and

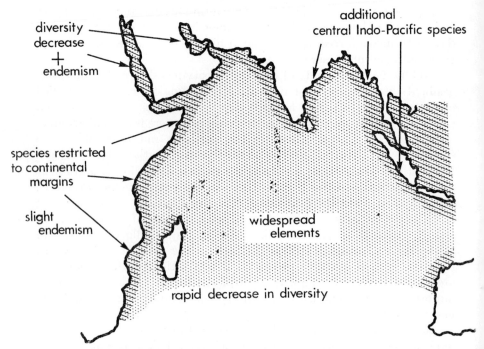

FIG. 2. Generalized diagram attempting to summarize the major distributive features of the molluscan fauna of the Indian Ocean. There is a dominant widespread element; a group of species more or less confined to continental margins supplemented in the east by central Indo-Pacific species and by endemics around the fringes. Superimposed is a latitudinal diversity gradient.

Michel, 1962; Hodgkin and Michel, 1963), Mahé (Taylor, 1968), Maldives and Chagos (Kohn, 1968), Diego Garcia (Stoddart and Taylor, in press) and recently at Aldabra of which little is yet published (Taylor, 1971).

There is a large gap in our knowledge of the East African coast, a few molluscs are mentioned in Lawson (1969) and some brief habitat notes by Spry (1964, 1968), but apart from these there are no ecological accounts mentioning molluscs. Although sedimentological and geomorphological work has been carried out in N. Madagascar (Guilcher, 1955; Guilcher, Berthois, Battistini and Fourmanoir, 1958) and in the Comoros (Guilcher, 1965) no molluscs have been recorded.

It is obvious from the preceding remarks that there are enormous gaps in our basic knowledge of the area both in faunal composition and communities and any attempt to generalize is full of uncertainties.

However molluscan assemblages inhabiting the various biomorphological zones of the reefs exhibit a remarkable similarity over this wide area and some of the main features of these assemblages are described below.

The mangrove assemblage

The mangrove community is exposed to variable salinities and very restricted circulation in the quiet waters where they flourish. This allows the accumulation of large amounts of organic detritus and the associated sediments are frequently fine and show blackened reducing conditions immediately beneath the surface.

The mangrove assemblage may be divided into two components, one component is that colonizing the actual mangrove trees and the other those species living on and in the sediment below and around the mangroves.

Mangroves are not uniformly distributed around the Indian Ocean and they are rare or absent in the atolls of the Chagos group, Addu and Cocos Keeling where conditions are apparently favourable for their colonization. They are also absent from the non-atoll coralline islands of the Seychelles and Amirantes where conditions for their colonization are unfavourable. The mangrove molluscan assemblages largely follow this distribution, but for instance on Diego Garcia virtually all the species of the mangrove assemblage are present but not associated into a single assemblage.

The fauna of the mangrove trees is fairly uniform throughout the area. The littoral fringe zone of the high trunks, branches and leaves is colonized by *Littorina scabra* alone. The eulittoral zone of the trunks, prop roots and pneumatophores is colonized typically by *Crassostrea cucullata* and *Isognomon dentifer*. Other species such as *Planaxis sulcata* and *Brachidontes variabilis* may be locally present (Baissac et al., 1962; Taylor, 1971). On the African mainland and in parts of Madagascar *Cerithidea decollata* is very common on the trunks of mangroves, however this species is absent from all the other Indian Ocean Islands.

The fauna of the mangrove sediment ranges into more open areas of the muddy sands of sheltered shores. The composition of this assemblage depends upon the degree of circulation around the base of the mangroves; for instance at Aldabra the fauna of the mangroves found near the lagoon channels is a typical marine fauna of good circulation sites (Taylor, 1971). The most characteristic inhabitant of poor circulation sites is the large herbivorous gastropod *Terebralia palustris* which can occur in vast numbers. Lower on the shore usually in channels within the mangroves the gastropod species belonging to the *Cerithium morum* group are extremely abundant. Other mangrove associated species inhabiting the substrate surface are *Nassarius*, and at the landward fringes *Cassidula* and *Assiminea*. Some bivalves are found in the sediment but these can be regarded as the more tolerant of the muddy-sand sheltered shore assemblage; these species are *Quidnipagus palatam*, *Gafrarium tumidum*, *G. pectinatum*, *Anadara antiquata* and *Ctena divergens*.

Plante (1964) records different faunas from different genera of mangroves but this is probably a reflection of the different situations occupied by the mangroves rather than any micro-substrate differences between them. The mangrove fauna of the Indo-Pacific has recently been reviewed by Macnae (1968). Dérijard (1965) has described the mangrove communities of Tuléar and Macnae and Kalk (1962a) those from Inhaca. The general features of the mangrove assemblage are thus low species diversity, high species abundance and the preponderance of herbivorous gastropods and suspension feeding bivalves. The only non-herbivorous gastropod is *Nassarius*. Species found in mangroves are usually not completely restricted to them.

Soft substrates of reef platforms

Various facies of soft substrates may be found on reef platforms, each is deposited under different physical conditions and each supports a characteristic molluscan assemblage. The main facies are discussed in approximate order of distance from the shore.

Beaches

Beaches in the true sense are found at the land-sea interface and span the littoral fringe and eulittoral zones. The base of the beach and change in slope of the reef platform usually demarcates the eulittoral and the change in slope of the reef platform usually demarcates the eulittoral/sublittoral zone boundary.

Clean washed, calcareous sandy beaches are found throughout the region. In general seaward or exposed sites have a coarse medium grade sand and lagoons or sheltered shores are fine grained.

Throughout the region this habitat is occupied by only a very few molluscs and the only apparently successful species are of two genera of suspension feeding bivalves *Atactodea* and *Donax*. *Atactodea glabrata* has a much greater range than any of the species of *Donax* and is the only sandy beach inhabitant found on some of the islands such as Aldabra (Taylor, 1971) or Diego Garcia (Stoddart and Taylor, in press). At Mauritius and Mahé (Baissac *et al.* 1962; Taylor, 1968) *Atactodea glabrata* and *Donax faba* occupy the same beaches but

Atactodea occupies a slightly higher position and ranges into more sheltered waters than *Donax*. At Tuléar (Mirielle Pichon, 1967) there is a more complex zonation with *Donax faba* and *Atactodea glabrata* having similar ranges and abundances in the lower part of the eulittoral zone but a third species of *Atactodea* (*Tiara*) inhabiting the higher part of the beach. At Inhaca only *Donax faba* has been recorded (Macnae and Kalk, 1962b). On many beaches molluscs are apparently absent.

Soft substrates of very sheltered sites

Very sheltered shores are often clothed in mangroves. In front of the mangrove fringes there are accumulations of muddy sand rich in organic detritus. They may occupy the eulittoral and shallow sublittoral zones, and experience variable salinities and high turbidities. This facies is a transition from the mangrove sediment on the landward side to the better oxygenated grass beds or open sands to the seaward. The sediment surface is frequently coated with green algae but beneath the surface the sediment is blackened and fetid and conditions are reducing. Habitats such as this have been described from most of the high islands, in Mauritius (Baissac *et al.*, 1962), Tuléar (Dérijard, 1965; Pichon, 1967) and Mahé (Taylor, 1968). A similar habitat is found on the lower islands in lagoons where circulation is very restricted, such as the Barachois of Diego Garcia and parts of Aldabra lagoon.

In general the fauna is very limited in numbers of species but large numbers of individuals can be present. These relatively stable sands support a fauna of burrowing bivalves, including deposit feeders *Quidnipagus palatam*, *Psammotea radiata* and in more oxygenated sites *Asaphis deflorata*. Shallow burrowing suspension feeders include *Anadara antiquata* and in particular *Gafrarium tumidum* which occurs in high densities (Taylor, 1968). The sediment surface and the algae are colonized in particular by large numbers of *Cerithium morum*; species of *Nassarius* are also common and occasionally the bivalve feeding *Natica marochiensis*.

At Tuléar close to the mangroves a rather different assemblage of molluscs is found (Dérijard, 1965). This includes the bivalves *Angulus iridescens*, *Thracia* sp., *Quadrans pristis*, *Loripes clausus* and the gastropods *Nassarius* sp. and *Terebralia palustris*. On other muddy shores (Pichon, 1967) an assemblage including *Macoma dubia*, *Solen corneus*, *Dosinia hepatica* and *Mysella* sp. is found; sands rich in organic detritus support *Quidnipagus palatam*, *Loripes clausus*, *Mactra aequisulcata* and *Tellinimactra* sp.

Spry (1964) notes that the "sand and sludge" of the creeks around Dar es Salaam supports a bivalve fauna including *Solen, Dosinia, Macoma, Psammotea* and *Loripes*, a community similar to that above from Tuléar. All these forms are recorded from muddy sand at Inhaca (Macnae and Kalk, 1962b).

The centre of Aldabra lagoon is floored by rock bottom with a thin veneer of fine grey silt. The surface of the silt is colonized by masses of *Cerithium morum*.

Beds of marine phanerogams (grass beds)

Beds of marine phanerogams of the genera *Thalassia, Cymodocea Halodule, Halophila, Enhalus, Zostera* and *Syringodium* are a common feature of reef platforms throughout the area. They occur on all but the most exposed shores and on some reefs occupy the entire width of the platform. They have an important and well documented role in stabilizing the accumulations of sand grade sediments on reef flats (Ginsburg and Lowenstam, 1958; Lewis, 1969; Taylor and Lewis, 1970). The boundaries and areal extent of these grass beds appear stable over a number of years and they offer the thickest, most stable sediment accumulation in shallow water reef areas.

Within the apparently uniform grass beds there is a very distinct stratification of the fauna into sub-habitats showing very different constituents. Thus there are sand-burrowing, substrate surface, foliage and coral debris sub-assemblages (Fig. 3).

The thick sand accumulation offers a suitable habitat for the more sedentary members of the molluscan infauna. Thus we find a very characteristic infauna dominated by lucinoid bivalves which are suspension feeders but burrow deeply, forming a semi-permanent mucous lined tube connecting to the surface. These include genera such as *Codakia* (2 species), *Anodontia*, and *Ctena*. Other sedentary forms are the buried byssate pinnas *Altrina vexillum* and *Pinna muricata*. Other suspension feeders are represented by species of *Gafrarium, Pitar* and *Vasticardium* which are restricted to the top few centimetres by their short siphons. Deposit feeders are generally deeper burrowers and include *Tellinella staurella, Quidnipagus palatam, Scissulina dispar* and *Leptomya*.

Burrowing gastropods are less common, the most important are species of *Natica* which feed upon bivalves.

On the sediment surface and amongst the rhizomes and stem bases of the grasses a different assemblage is found. Apart from a few byssate bivalves, particularly *Modiolus auriculatus*, the fauna is gastropod dominated. Grazing species predominate and the most abundant are

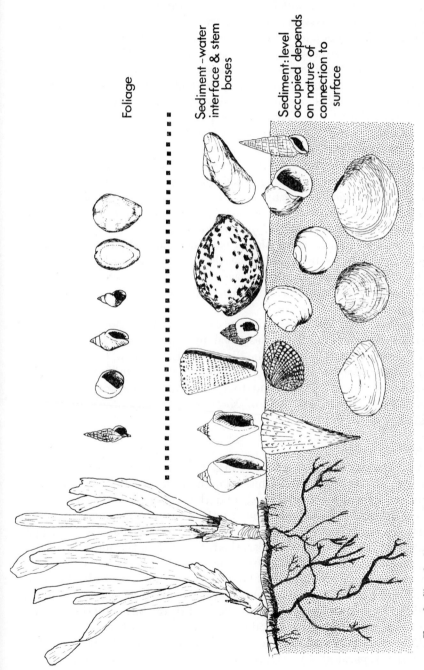

Foliage

Sediment–water interface & stem bases

Sediment: level occupied depends on nature of connection to surface

Fig. 3. Sketch diagram showing stratification in the grass beds assemblage into foliage, sediment—water interface and sediment sub-assemblages.

Strombus gibberulus, S. mutabilis and other *Strombus* species. In non-human populated areas the large *Lambis lambis* and *L. truncata* may be found. The Cypraeidae are general grazers and three species in particular are associated with grass beds, these are *Cypraea annulus*, *C. moneta* and *C. tigris*. Scavenging *Nassarius* are abundant throughout the area, the species concerned varying around the region. On continental margins the mollusc feeding *Melongena paradisiaca* is abundant but absent from the islands. Large *Conus* are also typical of this habitat, particularly *C. litteratus, C. leopardus, C. betulinus, C. quercinus* and *C. virgo*. The large opisthobranch *Dolabella auricularia* is common.

The stems and leaves of the grasses support another sub-assemblage of dominantly grazers feeding upon the epiphytic growths on the leaves. Two species of a tiny neritid *Smaragdia* are ubiquitous, and other commonly occurring species are *Cerithium rostratum, Phaseanella aethiopica, Pyrene azora* and *Cypraea annulus*.

Limestone or dead coral blocks may be found scattered over the surface of the grass beds and beneath these hard substrates species are found which are usually associated with more extensive hard substrates; typical are *Morula margariticola* and several *Cypraea* and *Conus* species.

The grass beds fauna is similar in character throughout the region, (personal observation). That described by Macnae and Kalk (1962b) from Inhaca is remarkable for the diversity of the fauna, however most of the species are uncommon and the dominants resemble those found elsewhere. There does not seem to be any extensive account of the grass beds at Tuléar and those of Mauritius are only briefly described (Baissac *et al.*, 1962).

Unvegetated sands

Apart from the grass beds there may be accumulations of unvegetated sand on the reef flats. This accumulation may be more or less extensive, depending upon depth and the degree of wave action. In general, narrow exposed reefs have only a very thin veneer of sand, sometimes confined to pockets whilst sheltered reefs may have thicker deposits which are largely undisturbed. On all but the most sheltered or deeper shores the sand is shifting and frequently rippled. Thomassin (1969) has described shifting sand bodies moving over grass beds at Tuléar and a similar phenomenon may be seen at the western end of Aldabra. The sands are usually in the sublittoral but sometimes as in the case of the shifting sand bodies they may be eulittoral.

A commonly recurring facies is that of coral colonies (usually *Acropora*) separated by greater or lesser extents of open sands.

Thomassin (1969) has described such a community from Tuléar, Taylor from Mahé (1968) and Aldabra lagoon (unpublished) and Baissac *et al.* (1962) and Pichon, M. M. (1967) from Mauritius. The only accounts of sand facies in the area giving details of the molluscan fauna are Thomassin (1969), Taylor (1968) and Macnae and Kalk (1962).

The mollusc fauna is predominantly infaunal and only a few gastropods are found on the sediment surface. The shifting sands of seaward reefs are obviously not a suitable habitat for sedentary species and most of the species found in this assemblage are fairly active. In medium grade sands on shores of fairly good circulation burrowing deposit bivalves *Tellinella crucigera*, *Quadrans gargadia*, *Scutarcopagia scobinata* and *Fabulina clathrata* are common. Suspension feeders are *Fragum fragum* and *Timoclea marica*.

With few exceptions the gastropods are all burrowers and particularly abundant are species of *Terebra*, a toxoglossan which probably feeds upon polychaetes. Many species may be present at any one site and up to ten species were found within a few square metres on Aldabra and Mahé. Two *Conus* species particularly are characteristic of this habitat, *Conus arenatus* and *C. tessulatus*; both are polychaete feeders. Other species of *Conus* which have a wider range of habitat preferences may occur. Other predators are *Vexillum*, *Natica*, *Polinices*, *Harpa*, *Gutturnium* and *Pleuroploca*. Scavengers are represented by species of *Oliva* and by *Nassarius*. Herbivores and general browsers are obviously less common but a few species, particularly *Rhinoclavis asper*, *R. articulatum* and *Strombus lentiginosus* are frequent. *Pyramidella terebellum* and *P. maculosa* are found in close association with ptychoderid worms (Macnae and Kalk, 1962b; Taylor, 1968).

On deeper or more sheltered sites the sand accumulations are thicker, finer and less disturbed. The fauna of these facies is similar to that of the grass beds with *Codakia* common and *Terebra* less common or absent.

The very active shifting sand bodies described by Thomassin (1969) and on Aldabra (J. D. Taylor, unpublished) extend upwards into the eulittoral zone and are subject to desiccation. They are largely bare of molluscs but on the damper slopes a normal sand fauna may be found. Macnae and Kalk (1962b) and Thomassin (1969) have described from sand banks an "*Astropecten* association" of which the most important molluscs are naticids, *Terebra* and tellinid bivalves. On very exposed shores where the sand accumulation on the reef platform is very limited only a few species occur, the most usual being *Terebra affinis* and *Conus arenatus*.

22

Deeper soft substrates outside the reefs

In some areas, particularly around the higher islands the fringing reefs are fronted by deeper platforms at about 20–30 m which may be sediment covered. This platform is particularly well developed around the granitic Seychelles (Taylor, 1968) where it is extended outwards as the Seychelles Bank. Deeper sandy areas have been surveyed in northwest Madagascar (Pichon, 1966).

In the Seychelles the fauna is bivalve dominated and the majority of species found were rare or absent from the shallow sands of the reef platforms. Medium grade sands were dominated by venerid and cardiid bivalves, the more important species being *Dosinia histrio*. *Lioconcha picta, Pitar affinis, Periglypta puerpera, Laevicardium australe, Hemicardia hemicardia* and *Anadara clathrata*. Gastropods are less abundant but include species of *Nassarius, Strombus, Phos, Vexillum, Xenuroturris* and *Terebra*.

In the very find sand of deeper or quieter areas a different assemblage is found which includes more deposit feeders such as *Fabulina clathrata, Arcopagia robusta* and *Gari* sp. The only common gastropods abundant in this fine sediment are *Terebellum terebellum, Vexillum deshayesi*, and species of *Fenella, Scaliola* and *Nassarius*.

The shallow (40–60 m) Seychelles Bank supports a different fauna again but this will not be considered here.

Hard substrates

The intertidal rocky shore

Throughout the region the nature of the rocky shore substrate is variable and thus affects the composition and distribution of the intertidal rocky shore assemblage. The major substrate categories are:

1. The low coralline islands usually only have low beach rock exposures available for colonization. These can be regarded as only ephemeral in nature as the beachrock is frequently entirely covered or scoured by migrating sand, or the exposure may be broken up in storms. Some low islands have no intertidal hard substrates at all.

2. The raised coralline islands such as Aldabra, Cosmoledo, Assumption and the East African coast have solid, fairly continuous limestone cliffs of variable height. The limestone cliffs of the East African coast stretch for many hundreds of miles and provide a very uniform habitat of wide lateral extent. The height of the cliffs means that they are exposed to both marine and subaerial weathering producing a wide variety of micromorphological variations. The older limestone shores such as the Eocene limestones at Tuléar may be included in this category.

3. The rocky shore may be formed by igneous rocks; these may be granite as in the Seychelles or basalts as in the Comoros, Mauritius, Reunion or Rodriguez. These rocks have very different substrate properties than the limestones. Igneous islands can of course also have superimposed raised limestone and beach rock shores.

There is very obviously a great difference in faunal diversity between the sparse fauna of a scoured beachrock and the diverse abundant faunas of high limestone or igneous shores. There are also substrate character differences between limestone and igneous shores which cause differences in the distribution of species. For instance boring bivalve genera such as *Lithophaga* and *Gastrochaena* common on limestone shores are excluded from igneous shores because of the resistance of the rock to acid boring. The higher porosity of the limestone substrate appears less favourable than igneous shores to macro-algal colonization.

Rocky shores in the area have received some detailed study by Kalk (1958) at Inhaca, Plante (1964) at Tuléar, Baissac *et al.* (1962) and Hodgkin and Michel (1963) at Mauritius, Taylor (1968) at Seychelles, Taylor (1971) at Aldabra, and Stoddart and Taylor (*in press*) at Diego Garcia. Even so there are vast areas for which we have very little information such as most of the East African coast, the Comoros and most of Madagascar.

Studies have usually been based upon a tripartite zonal scheme such as that evolved by the Stephensons and elaborated by Lewis (1964). The three zones recognized are a littoral fringe, a eulittoral zone and a sublittoral zone with sometimes a division into a sublittoral fringe. French workers refer to these as "l'étage supralittoral" "l'étage mediolittoral" and "l'etage infralittoral".

The littoral fringe zone

Throughout the region, as indeed throughout the world, this zone is occupied almost exclusively by species of Littorinacea.

At Tuléar five species of *Littorina* were found (Plante, 1964) which show very different tolerances of wave action and substrate characters. Four species are found on very exposed shores, two species on moderately exposed shores and only one, *Littorina scabra*, on mangrove fringed shores with extreme shelter. On exposed shores at Inhaca (Kalk, 1958) three species are found each having slightly different but overlapping vertical ranges. On Mauritius (Baissac *et al.*, 1962) *Littorina mauritiana* and *Tectarius granularis* are common on exposed shores with *Littorina scabra* and *L. mauritiana* on sheltered shores.

On the other islands only two species are common, for example on Aldabra (Taylor, 1971) *Littorina scabra* is confined to the mangrove fringed lagoon whereas *L. glabrata* is found all round the seaward shore on both exposed and sheltered shores. However although the same two species are found on Mahé, *Littorina scabra* was common at an exposed site (Taylor, 1968). In Mahé, Aldabra, Diego Garcia and Mombasa, *Nerita plicata* may bridge the littoral fringe and eulittoral zones.

The littoral fringe is thus very much a fringe of the marine environment and only exploited to any extent by a single molluscan family. Most species graze on blue-green algal encrustations, but *Littorina scabra* appears able to eat mangrove leaves. The zone shows a low species diversity and high abundances. Nonetheless the continental margin and large islands such as Madagascar show a higher diversity.

The eulittoral

The molluscan assemblages of this zone are much more varied than in the littoral fringe. It is difficult to generalize about the assemblages throughout the region as exposure, substrate, tidal and microclimatic conditions vary independently from place to place each imposing limitations on the fauna. Some species tolerate a wide range of exposure conditions whilst others are found exclusively upon either exposed or sheltered shores.

The typical inhabitants of the Eulittoral Zone may be considered in terms of their trophic position. On the upper part of the zone algal grazers predominate and are represented by several families of gastropods, amongst the most important of which are the limpets. These may be from the Patellacea, genera such as *Cellana*, *Acmaea*, *Scutellastra* and *Patella* or species of the pulmonate genus *Siphonaria*. An important functional difference between the two limpet groups is that members of the Patellacea mentioned all have part of the radula formed of teeth capped with iron oxide (Lowenstam, 1962; Runham, Thornton, Shaw and Wayte, 1969) enabling actual scraping and removal of the rock surface to extract endolithic algae. Another group of exclusively rocky shore species is *Nerita* and about 8 species are found in the western Indian Ocean; several species may occur at the same site but show marked zonal separation. Two species of *Monodonta* occur in the Seychelles. The only other macro-grazer is the large chiton *Acanthopleura brevispinosa* (a number of species are recorded around the area but they are probably all synonymous). This chiton possesses some very large magnetite capped teeth and scrapes deep into limestone substrates.

Suspension feeders are represented predominantly by cemented and byssate bivalves. The oyster *Crassostrea cucullata* is found throughout the region and tolerates a wide range of exposure conditions. Where particularly abundant as at Inhaca (Kalk, 1958) the oyster forms a broad band in the middle of the Eulittoral Zone. As on all shores, members of the Mytilacea are common and two species in particular in this region; *Brachidontes variabilis* may be extremely abundant on sheltered shores forming tightly packed byssate crusts and very low in the eulittoral *Septifer bilocularis* may be locally dominant (Kalk, 1958). Two species of Pteriacea occur, one, *Isognomon dentifer* occupies crevices high in the Eulittoral Zone (Taylor, 1968, 1970; Spry, 1964 as *Melina dentifera*; Plante, 1964 as *Pedalion nucleus*) the other species *Isognomon ephippium* occurs at the very lowest parts of the zone in Tuléar (Plante, 1964) and Mauritius (Baissac *et al.*, 1962). Other byssate bivalves are *Barbatia helbingi* in the low eulittoral, and *Lasaea rubra* in the higher parts.

On calcareous shores the lower parts of this zone may be inhabited by the boring bivalve *Lithophaga* and several species are found for instance *L. nasuta* at Aldabra (Taylor, 1971) and *L. teres* at Dar es Salaam (Spry, 1964).

Predatory gastropods form the only other feeding category of any importance. Several families (Muricacea, Buccinacea, Mitridae and Conidae) occur in the zone, but by far the most successful are the Muricacea. The main items in the diets of the predators are barnacles, polycheates and other molluscs.

Species of Muricacea which appear common throughout the area are *Purpura rudolphi*, *Thais aculeata*, *T. armigera*, *Drupa marginatra*, *D. morum*, *D. ricinus*, *Morula granulata* and *M. anaxeres*. Each species has a slightly different vertical range, exposure tolerance or diet.

The Conidae which are so common in the sublittoral are not very successful in the eulittoral and only two species *Conus ebraeus* and *C. sponsalis* are found at this level, both being polychaete feeders. They are more abundant on gently sloping rocky shores such as beachrock, but they seem unable to climb steeply sloping cliffs.

Other common predators are *Strigatella litterata* which feeds on sipunculids (Kohn *in* Houbrick and Fretter, 1969) and *Engina mendicaria* which appears to feed upon ascidians. The main characters of the assemblage in this zone are summarized in Fig. 4.

On very sheltered shores the diversity is much reduced and in particular the predatory gastropods are uncommon. Two algal feeders *Planaxis sulcata* and *Cerithium morum* are particularly diagnostic of these shores and both may occur in vast numbers; the other constituents of very sheltered shores are frequently the more tolerant of those species found on more exposed sites.

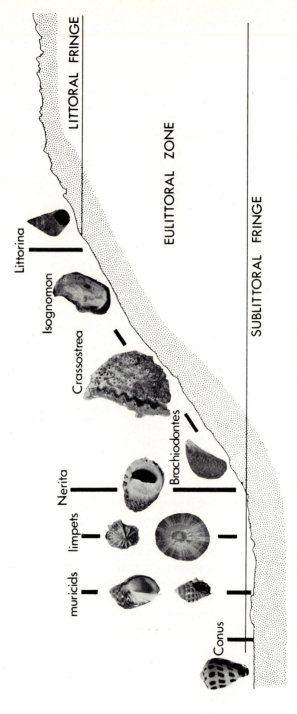

FIG. 4. Diagram of the distribution of the main elements in the intertidal rocky shore fauna. Each group having a wide vertical range is represented by several species having narrower ranges. Limpets occur in two unrelated groups the Patellacea and the pulmonate *Siphonaria*.

Sublittoral non-coralline hard substrates

The major part of the reef platforms fall within the upper part of the Sublittoral Zone. A variety of non-coral hard substrate habitats are found often in close proximity on the same platform. These habitats include flat pavement, deposits of cor-algal cobbles, dead coral, boulders, cavernous calcareous algal growths and surge channels. Reef platforms are then topographically diverse and each of these substrate categories may be separated by soft substrate deposits or be continuously gradational.

Although the habitats are apparently complex, the molluscan fauna is remarkably uniform. The greatest diversity of molluscs is found at the seaward edge of reef platforms where generally high energy conditions prevail and where limiting conditions such as high insolation and deoxygenation experienced upon the reef platforms are least. In this situation the habitat is at its most complex with boulders superimposed upon a cavernous topography. Also, as Vasseur (1964) has described, the density and diversity of encrusting animals are at their greatest in this situation.

A broad diversion may be made into species which occur on open surfaces and those which are restricted to shelter beneath boulders, and cobbles and in crevices. The position of some species on the substrate is shown in Fig. 5.

The bivalve fauna is limited to suspension feeding byssate and cemented forms. *Modiolus auriculatus* may occur as a byssate crust on platforms and *Tridacna maxima* and *Pinctada margaritifera*, byssate on open surfaces and crevices. Other species *Cardita variegata*, *Arca avellana*, *Barbatia helblingi*, *Acar plicata*, *Ostrea numisma* and *Chama asperella* occur cemented or byssally attached beneath boulders and cobbles. The cemented gastropods *Cheila equestris* and *Vermetus* spp. can also be included in this last category.

The gastropod fauna is extremely diverse and the greatest proportion of species are predators or grazers upon encrusting animals. Algal grazers are not abundant and are largely restricted to the seaward edge of the platform where circulation is at its optimum. The species *Turbo argyrostmous*, *T. setosus*, *Trochus flammulatus*, *T. maculatus* and *Tectus mauritianus* occur on open surfaces. Other grazers include small species of *Cerithium* and *Rissoina* which occur in the algal mat around the base of boulders. There do not appear to be any molluscan grazers upon the larger growths of *Sargassum* and *Turbinaria* characteristic of many areas.

Reef platforms support a large number of species of the predatory genus *Conus* the habits of which have been discussed in some detail

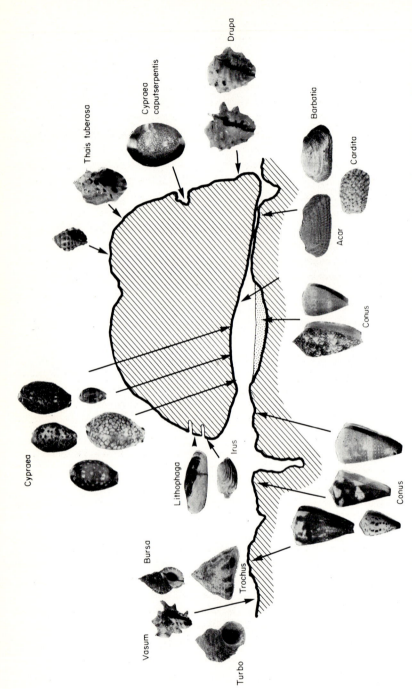

FIG. 5. Diagram illustrating sub-division of the boulder zone hard substrates at the seaward edge of reef platforms. Most *Cypraea* and most bivalves live beneath the boulders; muricids prefer the outside of the boulders and *Conus*, *Turbo*, *Trochus*, *Bursa* and *Vasum* prefer the open hard substrate.

by Kohn (1959, 1960, 1967, 1968). Most species can occur on open hard surfaces but some such as *Conus textile* and *C. coronatus*, are found in sand pockets, trapped beneath boulders. Common species in open habitats are *C. lividus, flavidus, ebraeus, chaldeus, coronatus, sponsalis, catus* and *litoglyphus*. Different species have slightly varying habitat preferences, thus *C. ebraeus* is more common in inshore sites and *C. chaldeus* prefers the seaward bouldered sites.

As on rocky intertidal shores the Muricacea are again abundant. Some species prefer the open surfaces and are typically found upon the upper surfaces of boulders and cobbles; these species are *Drupa morum, D. ricinus, Thais tuberosa* and *Morula granulata*. Other species, particularly *Morula margariticola, M. uva* and *Maculotriton digitalis*, are found on the damp shaded undersides of boulders.

Other common predators are members of the Tonnacea, *Bursa granularis, Cymatium nicobaricum* and *C. pileare* which feed upon polychaetes, gastropods and bivalves respectively (Houbrick and Fretter, 1969), *Vasum turbinellus*, the mitrids *Strigatella litterata* and *Mitra cucumerina*, and the buccinids *Leucozonia smaragdula* and *Latirus craticulatus*.

Many species which graze upon encrusting animals but may also take algae are abundant in this habitat. Species of *Cypraea* show great diversity on the hard reef platform; they are largely photonegative and during the day are restricted to the undersides of boulders. On the Boulder Zones at platform edges *Cypraea histrio, C. vitellus, C. lynx, C. fimbriata, C. carneola*, are typical. *Cypraea caputserpentis* is found in crevices in the side of boulders and in the open calcareous algal surface. Other species, *C. helvola, C. isabella* and *C. caurica*, are most characteristic of mid-reef platforms. Other general grazing genera are *Triphora, Pyrene* and *Engina*.

Few molluscs are found in surge channels and on the smooth calcareous algae coated surfaces at the reef edge. There may be a few *Tridacna maxima* and gastropods *Turbo* and *Trochus, Lambis scorpio* and *Vasum turbinellus*.

Coral substrates

It is difficult to generalize about coral associated assemblages as corals are found in many different habitats and some of the species found living upon them are refugees from the surrounding substrate. However most coral growth takes place at platform fronts and knolls in the sublittoral, although not necessarily in the most exposed situation.

Coral assemblages can be divided into two distinct divisions; there are those species which use the coral as a convenient hard substrate and others which feed upon or have a close association with the coral. The first category varies according to the habitat in which the coral is found, the second is largely independent of the surrounding habitat.

Recently Robertson (1970) has reviewed the molluscan predators and parasites of stony corals. Most coral feeders in the western Indian Ocean are muricids and most belong to the family Coralliophilidae. The most abundant are *Coralliophilia costularis*, *C. violacea* and *Quoyula madreporarum* which show a progressive morphological trend towards a limpet-like form. They seem to prefer the corals *Porites*, *Pocillopora*, *Stylophora* and *Seriatopora*. Two forms in the area, *Magilopsis lamarkii* and *Magilus antiquus*, bore and live inside living coral (Soliman, 1969) and prefer massive corals such as *Platygyra*, *Favia*, *Porites* and *Symphyllia*. *Magilus* seems to be the most abundant.

Other muricids associated with and feeding upon corals are *Drupella cornus* and possibly *D. ochrostoma* which prefer branching corals. Both species may be found away from corals but they are difficult to distinguish.

The scallop *Pedum spondyliodeum* is strongly associated with massive *Porites* (Yonge, 1967) but it does not seem to spread further west than Diego Garcia.

As a substrate, coral colonies are very complex and the dead undersides and branches offer shelter and protection for large numbers of animals. There are obvious differences in the type of substrate provided by various growth form categories of the corals, for instance branching corals are better for byssate forms and massive corals for boring bivalves.

Tridacna maxima and *T. squamosa* are byssate in crevices between colonies on the dead upper surface. A wide range of byssate bivalves are attached to the dead part of branches of the undersides of massive corals. Typical species are *Barbatia helblingi*, *B. fusca*, *Septifer bilocularis*, several species of *Chlamys*, *Pteria* and *Pinctada*, *Isognomon ephippium*, *Streptopinna saccata*, *Cardita variegata* and *Trapezium oblongum*; these represent practically all the byssate groups of bivalves. Other forms are cemented to the branches or undersides, these are *Spondylus aurantius*, *S. hystrix*, species of *Chama* and several oysters particularly *Ostrea frons* and *O. hyotis*. Borers are also common particularly *Lithophaga*, *Botula* and *Gastrochaena*; these have been the subject of a recent review (Soliman, 1969).

On reef platforms the undersides of corals support a gastropod fauna largely similar to that of surrounding hard substrates, that is rich in *Cyprea, Conus, Bursa* etc. In deeper water of coral areas species such as *Trochus maculatus, Lambis crocata, Turbo marmoratus, Clanculus, Vanikoro, Bursa rubeta, Latirus craticulatus, Vasum turbinellus,* and *Conus vexillum* are characteristic. Some species of *Cypraea*, particularly *C. scurra* are strongly associated with corals.

Pichon (1964) has recorded a few molluscs from the coral of the reef front at Tuléar; these are *Charonia tritonis, Lambis scorpio* and *Cypraea isabella.* On the edge of the platform he found species of *Turbo, Cypraea caputserpentis, Cassis rufa, Vasum turbinellus, Tridacna maxima* and *Lambis crocata.*

On the whole the diversity of molluscs inhabiting coral areas is less than on the boulder zone at the edge of the platform.

SPECIES INTERACTIONS

Many workers have discussed the high diversity of animals in tropical areas as compared with higher latitudes (Fischer, 1960; MacArthur, 1965; Sanders, 1968; Stehli, 1968). Most authors attribute this diversity in part to the temporal stability of the warm tropics. Valentine (1969) has argued that stable, shallow, tropical waters have been enriched in species by a latitudinal climatically controlled "diversity pump". Sanders (1968) concludes that the critical factors appear to be time and environmental stability. A largely similar view is taken by Bakus (1969) who relates species diversity to biological interactions, habitat complexity, generation time and geological history.

TABLE I

Number of mollusc species in various habitats around Mahé, Seychelles (Taylor, 1968 and additions). Numbers of prosobranchs and bivalves also shown.

Habitat	No. of species	Prosobranchs	Bivalves
Mangroves	9	5	4
Sandy beach	3	0	3
Muddy sands	33	19	14
Grass beds	75	49	26
Unvegetated sands	62	41	21
Deeper water sands	109	49	60
Intertidal rocky shore	39	34	5
Cobble ridges	50	43	7
Algal ridge-boulder Zone	77	64	13
Coral Substrates	51	27	24

Although diversity is high in reef areas close study shows widely varying diversities between habitats. Table I shows the number of mollusc species in various habitats of reefs around Mahé, Seychelles

(Taylor, 1968 with additions). This shows that sublittoral habitats support more species than those of the inter-tidal. With the exceptions of the deeper water habitats the number of species on reef platforms is broadly similar from habitat to habitat; grass beds and the algal ridge boulder zone show the highest number of species and coral communities rather less. The high value for deeper water assemblages may represent a sampling of more than one community. This diversity pattern is discussed by Sanders (1968) who carefully distinguishes between physically controlled and biologically accommodated communities. In the former adaptations are to a variable physical environment and populations are genetically variable and occupy rather broad niches. This type of community is characterized by a small number of species but a high individual abundance. The biologically accommodated community is present where physical conditions are constant and hence not a critical control. With time, biological stresses are accommodated by biological interactions to produce a stable complex community characterized by a large number of species having relatively narrow niches. What is the nature of these interactions and how are species packed together in the reef assemblages? Grant (1968) has suggested that the two most important resources which might be competed for are food and space. Four main methods are employed for reducing competition between related or functionally similar species; a) species may occupy different habitats, b) species may occupy the same habitat but different parts of it, c) species occupy the same habitat but take food of different sizes, d) species occupy the same habitat but take different foods. The importance of the food niche and feeding interactions in tropical shallow waters is stressed by Bakus (1969).

Spatial separation is seen in many species groups. Almost complete geographical separation is effected by species of *Littorina* at Aldabra (Fig. 6); *Littorina scabra* is confined to lagoon, mangrove-fringed

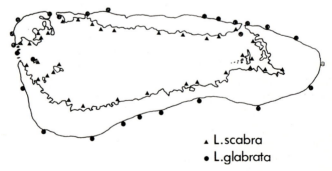

▲ L.scabra
● L.glabrata

Fɪɢ. 6. Distribution of *Littorina scabra* and *Littorina glabrata* at Aldabra.

shores and *Littorina glabrata* virtually restricted to the seaward cliffs. Within-habitat separation is shown by species of *Nerita*; at any particular intertidal site several species may be found but they are spatially separated by sharp vertical zonation or in *Nerita polita* by behavioural differences (Taylor, 1968, 1971).

On the broad scale at familial and generic level there is a spatial separation into different types of habitat; for instance the Terebridae and Olividae are confined to sandy habitats, *Nerita* to the intertidal rocky shore, most *Conus* and the Thaidae to hard substrates (the latter mainly intertidal), the Coralliophilidae to living coral and the Turbinidae to sublittoral hard substrates.

Various types of interaction are seen amongst the predatory intertidal Muricacea of which 13 species have been recorded around Aldabra (Taylor, 1971). In some cases species are separated geographically, thus *Purpura rudolphi* is found only upon the exposed southeast shore and *Morula anaxeres* only upon the more sheltered northern and western shores. In other cases species are segregated by vertical zonation, for example *Morula uva* occurs in the sublittoral fringe, *Morula granulata* in the mid-low eulittoral and *Morula anaxeres* in the high eulittoral. Overlapping ranges are found in between some species and in these situations analysis of feeding shows that each feeds upon different prey or different proportions of the same prey (Fig. 7). *Purpura rudolphi* and *Thais aculeata* are both large species which feed respectively upon the large barnacle *Tetraclita squamosa* and upon the limpets *Acmaea* and *Siphonaria*. Smaller species are *Drupa marginatra* which feeds upon limpets and the small barnacles *Tetrachthamalus* and *Morula granulata* which feeds predominantly upon tubiculous eunicid worms. At other sites where the usual prey is absent they may feed upon other items, showing that the diets are not as specialized as might be thought.

In some situations there may be functionally similar but unrelated species inhabiting the same place. On rocky intertidal shores at Aldabra several algal grazers, *Nerita textilis*, the patellacean limpets *Acmaea profunda* and *Cellana cernica*, the pulmonate limpet *Siphonaria* and the large chiton *Acanthopleura brevispinosa* may co-occur. At these sites the diversity of intertidal algae is very low and most are endolithic blue greens. Examination of radular teeth shows that *Acanthopleura*, *Acmaea* and *Cellana* all have some iron mineralization of the teeth (Lowenstam 1962; Towe and Lowenstam, 1967) thus enabling them to scrape away the rock surface and remove the endolithic algae. The other species do not have this type of radula and are restricted to scraping surface coatings. Apart from the basic radula division there are further separations by size. The large *Acanthopleura* feeds upon

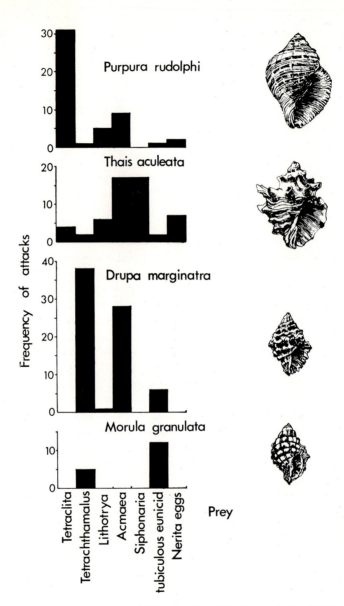

Fig. 7. Major items in the diet of four species of Muricacea in the Eulittoral Zone, Dune Jean-Louis, Aldabra (September, 1969).

smoother areas of rock than *Acmaea* which prefers more highly dissected microtopography. The larger radula teeth of *Acanthopleura* can penetrate the substrate deeper than *Cellana*, which in turn has a bigger radula than *Acmaea*. In the surface scrapers there are again differences in the size and type of radula indicating differences in feeding. There is, therefore, in a seemingly simple habitat a stratification of feeding areas which is possibly a mechanism allowing several algal grazers to co-exist.

Shallow water reef platforms are well known for the great diversity shown in some genera of prosobranchs, for instance 27 species of *Conus*, 23 *Cypraea* and 20 species of *Terebra* have been recorded from the platforms of Aldabra. The detailed work of Kohn (1959, 1968) has shown how species of *Conus* which are members of the same assemblage and which have overlapping microhabitats differ in the food items or proportions of the same food items taken.

In another toxoglossan genus *Terebra* detailed feeding data are not available but species exhibit an extremely high degree of habitat overlap and up to ten species may be found in apparently uniform small sand patches in Aldabra channels. Some idea of species interactions may be obtained by comparing the relative species abundance with that expected from the MacArthur (broken stick) model of relative abundance (MacArthur, 1957, 1960). This model estimates the expected abundance of the rarest species in a mixed population of species of similar size and physiology and occupying a single adequately sampled habitat and whose ecological niches are contiguous. The outcome is an expected result of interspecific competition (Kohn, 1968). If the relative abundance of *Terebra* in an Aldabra sand patch is compared with the expected abundance, (Fig. 8a) then a wide divergence is seen with the most abundant species being far more abundant than expected. This species is *Terebra affinis* which on Aldabra is about half the size of the other *Terebra* species; if this species is ignored (Fig. 8b) then there is a very close fit between the observed and expected abundances. This strongly suggests that there is less interaction between *Terebra affinis* and the other species than there is between the other species. By its smaller size *Terebra affinis* may be able to take advantage of some unexploited character in the habitat.

At Mahé a large number of bivalve species are found in the grass beds of the reef platform (Taylor, 1968). If the observed abundance is compared with the expected abundance then in most cases a close fit is obtained (J. D. Taylor, unpublished). There is some degree of spatial separation amongst the bivalve species (Fig. 9); *Quidnipagus palatam*, *Gafrarium pectinatum* and *Ctena fibula* are more abundant near the

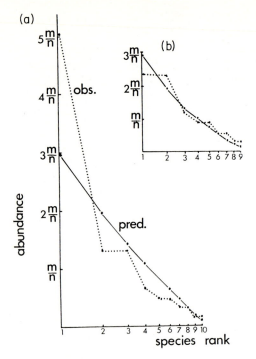

Fig. 8. (a) Relative abundance of *Terebra* species in sand patch (Passe Gionnet, Aldabra, October, 1967). Dotted lines = observed abundance, solid lines = predicted abundance, from MacArthur Model I. Species rank: 1 = *T. affinis*, 2 = *T. babylonia*, 3 = *T. subulata*, 4 = *T. argus*, 5 = *T. cingulifera*, 6 = *T. maculata*, 7 = *T. albula*, 8 = *T. monilis*. 9 = *T. guttata*, 10 = *T. solida*. (b) As above but without *Terebra affinis*, each ranking one higher than in (a).

shore whilst *Codakia tigerina* and *C. punctata* are more abundant some distance from the shore. Possibly amongst these suspension feeding bivalves competition for space is more important than feeding.

Much more work such as that by Kohn (1959, 1960, 1967 and 1968) on the detailed ecology of reef dwelling molluscs is needed before we will be able to understand the composition and distribution of the molluscan assemblages.

SUMMARY

1. The islands of the western Indian Ocean have a very uniform fauna comprising species which have larvae capable of surviving pelagic transport. The continental margins have the same species but more are found at any one locality. In addition they have a set of

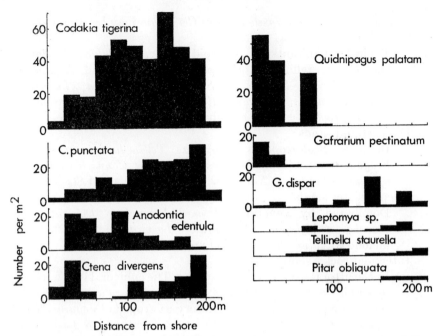

Fig. 9. Frequency per m² of bivalves in grass beds Anse aux Pins, Mahé, Seychelles, showing changes in assemblage composition with increasing distance from the shoreline. Composite of 5 transects (1964–5).

species which are confined to continental margins and some endemic species. Isolated areas of the fringes of the Indian Ocean show a higher degree of endemicity and a latitudinal decrease in diversity. The importance of studying fossil assemblages for the interpretation of present day distribution patterns is stressed.

2. The molluscan assemblages comprising part of the bio-morphological communities of reef areas exhibit a remarkable uniformity throughout the area. Those of continental areas are more complex. The most commonly recurring assemblages and their main constituents are:

Mangroves:
  Littorina scabra, *Cerithidea* and *Crassostrea* on the trees; *Terebralia palustris*, *Nassarius* and *Cerithium* on the substrate.
Beaches:
  The bivalves *Donax* and *Atactodea*.
Sheltered soft substrates:
  Variable throughout the region but *Quidnipagus palatam*, *Psammotea*, *Gafrarium*, *Anadara*, *Loripes*, *Dosinia*, *Solen*,

23

Macoma, Natica, Nassarius and *Cerithium* may be common.
Grass beds:
    Typical inhabitants are lucinoid bivalves *Codakia, Anodontia*
and *Ctena*; tellinids *Quidnipagus, Tellinella* and *Leptomya*;
Pinna, Atrina. Species of *Strombus, Melongena, Nassarius,
Cypraea annulus, moneta* and *tigris, Conus litteratus* and *Smarag-
dia rangiana*, occur on the substrate surface and foliage.
Unvegetated sands:
    Bivalves *Scutarcopagia scobinata, Tellinella crucigera* and
Fragum fragum. Many species of *Terebra; Conus arenatus, C.
tessulatus, Polinices, Natica, Oliva, Rhinoclavis* and *Strombus.*
Deeper water sands:
    Dominated by venerid and cardiid bivalves *Dosinia, Lio-
choncha, Periglypta, Hemicardia, Laevicardium.* Gastropods
include *Vexillum, Terebra, Xenuroturris* and *Terebra.*
Intertidal rocky shores:
    In the littoral fringe *Littorina* species. The eulittoral is dominated
by species of *Nerita*, the limpets *Cellana, Acmaea* and *Siphonaria,*
the chiton *Acanthopleura*, predatory gastropods *Purpura, Thais,
Drupa, Morula* and *Conus.* Common bivalves are *Isognomon,
Crassostrea, Brachidontes* and *Lithophaga. Planaxis* and *Cerithium* common on sheltered shores.
Sublittoral non-coralline hard substrates:
    Very variable microhabitats and a very diverse fauna. Species
of *Conus* and *Cypraea* very common, *Bursa, Cymatium* and
Vasum. Turbo and *Trochus* at exposed sites. Bivalves byssate
or cemented, *Barbatia, Pinctada, Ostrea* and *Chama.*
Coral substrates:
    Gastropods in the family *Coralliophilidae* and *Drupella* feed
upon living coral. Other species use coral as complex substrate
including a host of byssate cemented and boring bivalves *Barbatia, Septifer, Spondylus, Ostrea, Tridacna, Trapezium* and
Cardita. Gastropods include *Turbo, Cypraea, Bursa, Conus* and
Charonia.

3. Species diversity in the shallow reef areas is high but there are
widely varying diversities between assemblages. Those assemblages
which are to some extent physically controlled, as in the intertidal are
low in species compared with the sublittoral where communities are
biologically accommodated and characterized by high species diversity
and relatively narrow niches. Various examples of spatial and feeding
interactions are examined to show how partitioning of the niche may
have taken place to accommodate more species.

ACKNOWLEDGEMENTS

I am grateful to the Trustees of the British Museum (Natural History), The Royal Society and the late Professor J. H. Taylor for the opportunity of carrying out this work over the last seven years. Discussion with Mr. J. F. Peake has been most useful.

REFERENCES

Abbott, R. T. (1960). The genus *Strombus* in the Indo-Pacific. *Indo-Pacif. Mollusca* **1**: 33–144.

Abbott, R. T. (1968). The helmet shells of the world (Cassidae). Pt. 1. *Indo-Pacif. Mollusca* **2**: 7–201.

Baissac, J. de B., Lubet, P. E. and Michel, C. M. (1962). Les biocoenoses benthiques littorales de l'Ile Maurice. *Recl. Trav. Stn. Mar. Endoume.* **25**: 253–291.

Bakus, G. J. (1969). Energetics and feeding in shallow marine waters. In. Felts, W. J. L. and Harrison, R. J. *General and Experimental Zoology.* **4**: 275–369 London and New York: Academic Press.

Barnard, K. H. (1959). Contributions to the knowledge of South African marine molluscs. Part II. Gastropoda; Prosobranchiata; Rachiglossa. *Annls, S. Afr. Mus.* **45**: 1–237.

Batzli, G. O. (1969). Distribution of biomass in rocky intertidal communities on the Pacific coast of the United States. *J. anim. Ecol.* **38**: 531–546.

Boshoff, P. H. (1965). Pelecypoda of Inhaca Island, Moçambique. *Mems. Inst. Invest. cient. Moçamb.* A.**7**: 65–206.

Boss, K. J. (1969). The sub family Tellininae in South African waters (Bivalvia) Mollusca. *Bull. Mus. comp. Zool. Harv.* **138**: 81–162.

Caye, G. and Thomassin, B. (1967). Note préliminaire à une étude ecologique de la levée détritique et du platier friable du grand récif de Tuléar: Morphologie et hydrodynamismo. *Recl. Trav. Stn. Mar. Endoume Suppl.* **6**: 25–35.

Dérijard, R. (1965). Contribution a l'étude du peuplement des sédiments sablo-vaseux et vaseux intertidaux, compactés ou fixés par la végétation de la region de Tuléar (Madagascar). *Recl. Trav. Stn. Mar. Endoume* (hors ser.) suppl. **3**: 1–94.

Ekman, S. (1953). *Zoogeography of the Sea.* London: Sidgwick and Jackson.

Fischer, A. G. (1960). Latitudinal variations in organic diversity. *Evolution* **14**: 14–81.

Ginsburg, R. N. and Lowenstam, H. A. (1958). The influence of marine bottom communities on the depositional environments of sediments. *J. Geol.* **66**: 310–318.

Grant, P. R. (1968). Bill size, body size and the ecological adaptations of bird species to competitive situations on islands. *Syst. Zool.* **17**: 319–333.

Guilcher, A. (1955). Etude geomorphologique des récifs coralliens du nord-ouest de Madagascar. *Annls Inst. oceanogr* (Paris) **33**: 65–136.

Guilcher, A. (1965). Coral reefs and lagoons of Mayotte Island, Comoro Archipelago, Indian Ocean, and of New Caledonia, Pacific Ocean. *In*: *Submarine Geology and Geophysics* (W. F. Whittard and R. Bradshaw, eds). London: Butterworths. pp. 21–45.

Guilcher, A., Berthois L., Battistini, R. and Fourmanoir, P. (1958). Les récifs coralliens des Iles Radama et de la Baie Ramanetaka (Cote nord-ouest de Madagascar), étude geomorphologique et sedimentologique. *Mém. Inst. scient. Madagascar* (Sér. F.) **2**: 117–199.

Hodgkin, E. P. and Michel, C. (1963). Zonation of plants and animals on the rocky shores of Mauritius. *Proc. R. Soc. Arts Sci. Mauritius* **11**: 121–145.

Houbrick, J. R. and Fretter, V. (1969). Some aspects of the functional anatomy and biology of *Cymatium* and *Bursa. Proc. malac. Soc. Lond.* **38**: 415–429.

Kalk, M. (1958). The intertidal fauna of rocks at Inhaca Island, Moçambique. *Ann. Natal Mus.* **13**: 189–242.

Kohn, A. J. (1959). The ecology of *Conus* in Hawaii. *Ecol. Monogr.* **29**: 47–90.

Kohn, A. J. (1960). Ecological notes on *Conus* (Mollusca: Gastropoda) in the Trincomallee region of Ceylon. *Ann. Mag. nat. Hist.* (13) **2**: 309–320.

Kohn, A. J. (1967). Environmental complexity and species diversity in the gastropod genus *Conus* on Indo-West Pacific reef platforms. *Am. Nat.* **101**: 251–259.

Kohn, A. J. (1968). Microhabitats, abundance and food of *Conus* on atoll reefs in the Maldive and Chagos Islands. *Ecology* **49**: 1046–1062.

Lawson, G. W. (1969). Some observations on the littoral ecology of rocky shores in East Africa (Kenya and Tanzania). *Trans. R. Soc. S. Afr.* **38**: 329–340.

Lewis, J. R. (1964). *The ecology of rocky shores*. London: English Universities Press.

Lewis, M. S. (1969). Sedimentary environments and unconsolidated carbonate sediments of the fringing coral reefs of Mahé, Seychelles. *Marine Geol.* **7**: 95–127.

Lewis, M. S. and Taylor, J. D. (1966). Marine sediments and bottom communities of the Seychelles. *Phil. Trans. R. Soc.* (A) **259**: 279–290.

Lowenstam, H. A. (1962). Goethite in the radular teeth of some recent marine gastropods. *Science, N.Y.* **137**: 279–280.

MacArthur, R. H. (1957). On the relative abundance of bird species. *Proc. natn. Acad. Sci., U.S.A.* **43**: 293–295.

MacArthur, R. H. (1960). On the relative abundance of species. *Am. Nat.* **94**: 25–36.

MacArthur, R. H. (1965). Patterns of species diversity. *Biol. Rev.* **40**: 510–533.

MacArthur, R. H. and Wilson, E. O. (1967). *The Theory of island biogeography*. New Jersey: Princeton.

Macnae, W. (1963). Mangrove swamps in South Africa. *J. Ecol.* **51**: 1–25.

Macnae, W. (1968). A general account of the fauna and flora of mangrove swamps and forests in the Indo-West-Pacific region. *Adv. Mar. Biol.* **6**: 73–270.

Macnae, W. and Kalk, M. (1958). *A natural history of Inhaca Island, Moçambique* Johannesburg: Witwatersrand University Press.

Macnae, W. and Kalk, M. (1962a). The ecology of the mangrove swamps at Inhaca Island, Moçambique. *J. Ecol.* **50**: 19–34.

Macnae, W. and Kalk, M. (1962b). The fauna and flora of sand flats at Inhaca Island, Moçambique. *J. anim. Ecol.* **31**: 93–128.

Maes, V. (1967). The littoral marine mollusks of Cocos-Keeling Islands (Indian Ocean). *Proc. Acad. nat. Sci. Philad.* **119**: 93—217.

Paine, R. T. and Vadas, R. L. (1969). Calorific values of benthic marine algae and their postulated relation to invertebrate food preference. *Mar. Biol.* **4**: 79–86.

Peake, J. F. (1969). Patterns in the distribution of Melanesian land Mollusca. *Phil. Trans. R. Soc.* (B) **255**: 285–306.

Peake, J. F. (1970). The evolution of terrestrial faunas in the Western Indian Ocean. *Phil. Trans. R. Soc. Lond.* (B) **260**: 581–610.

Pérès, J. M. and Picard, J. (1962). Note préliminaire generale sur le benthos littoral de la region de Tuléar (Madagascar) *Recl. Trav. Stn. Mar. Endoume.* Suppl. **1**: 146–151.

Picard, J. (1967). Essai de classement des grands types de peuplements marins benthiques tropicaux, d'après les observations effectuées dans les parages de Tuléar (S. W. de Madagascar). *Recl. Trav. Stn. Mar. Endoume* Suppl. **6**:3–24.

Pichon, Michel (1964). Contribution a l'étude de la répartition des Madréporaires sur le récif de Tuléar. *Recl. Trav. Stn. Mar. Endoume.* **2**: 81–203.

Pichon, Michel (1966). Note sur la faune des substrates sablo-vaseux infra-littoraux de la baie d'Ambara (Côte N. W. Madagascar). *Cah. O.R.S.T.O.M. Oceanogr.* **4**: 78–94.

Pichon, M. M. (1967). Caractères généraux des peuplements benthiques des récifs et lagons de l'Île Maurice. *Cah. O.R.S.T.O.M.* (Oceanogr.) **5**: 31–45.

Pichon, Mireille (1967). Contribution a l'étude des peuplements de la zone inter-tidale sur sables fins et sables vaseux non fixés dans la région de *Tuléar. Rec. Trav. Stn. Mar. Endoume Suppl.* **7**: 57–100.

Plante, R. (1964). Contribution à l'étude des peuplements de hauts niveaux sur substrats solides non récifaux dans la region de Tuléar. *Recl. Trav. Stn. Mar. Endoume* Suppl. **2**: 205–315.

Risbec, J. (1935). Biologie et ponte de Mollusques gastéropodes Neo-Caledoniens. *Bull. Soc. zool. Fr.* **60**: 387–417.

Robertson, R. (1970). Review of the predators and parasites of stony corals with special reference to symbiotic prosobranch gastropods. *Pacif. Sci.* **24**: 43–54.

Rosewater, J. (1961). The family Pinnidae in the Indo-Pacific. *Indo-Pacif. Mollusca* **1**: 175–185.

Rosewater, J. (1965). The family Tridacnidae in the Indo-Pacific. *Indo-Pacif. Mollusca* **1**: 347 396.

Runham, N. W., Thornton, P. R., Shaw, D. A. and Wayte, R. C. (1969). The mineralization and hardness of the radular teeth of the limpet *Patella vulgata* L. *Z. Zellforsch, mikrosk. Anat.* **99**: 608–626.

Sanders, H. L. (1968). Marine benthic diversity: a comparative study. *Am. Nat.* **102**: 243–282.

Soliman, G. N. (1969). Ecological aspects of some coral boring gastropods and bivalves of the north western Red Sea. *Am. Zool.* **9**: 887–894.

Spry, J. F. (1964). The sea shells of Dar es Salaam pt. II Pelecypoda (Bivalves). *Tanganyika Notes Rec.* **63**: 41 pp.

Spry, J. F. (1968). The sea shells of Dar es Salaam *Tanganyika Notes Rec.* **56**: 40pp. 2nd revision 1968.

Stehli, F. G. (1968). Taxonomic diversity gradients in pole location: the recent model. p. 163–227. *In Evolution and Environment.* edited E. T. Drake, Yale Univ. Press. pp. 470.

Stoddart, D. R. and Taylor, J. D. (eds) (In press.) The ecology and Geography of Diego Garcia atoll. *Atoll. Res. Bull.* **149**: 1–237

Taylor, J. D. (1968). Coral reef and associated invertebrate communities (mainly molluscan) around Mahé Seychelles. *Phil. Trans. R. Soc.* (B.) **254**: 129–206.

Taylor, J. D. (1970). Intertidal zonation at Aldabra Atoll. *Phil Trans. R. Soc. Lond.* (B). **260**: 173–213.

Taylor, J. D. and Lewis, M. S. (1970). The flora, fauna and sediments of the marine grass beds of Mahé, Seychelles. *J. Nat. Hist.* **4**: 199–220.

Thomassin, B. (1969). Peuplements de deux biotopes de sables coralliens sur le grand récif de Tuléar, sud ouest de Madagascar. *Recl. Trav. Stn. Mar. Endoume* Suppl. **9**: 59–133.

Thorson, G. (1940). Studies on the egg masses and larval development of gastropoda from the Iranian Gulf. *Dan. scient. Invest. Iran.* **2**: 159–238.

Thorson, G. (1963). Length of pelagic larval life in marine bottom invertebrates as related to larval transport by Ocean currents. *Publs. Am. Ass. Advmt. Sci.* **67**: 455–473.

Towe, K. M. and Lowenstam, H. A. (1967). Ultrastructure and development of iron mineralization in the radular teeth of *Cryptochiton stelleri. J. Ultrastruct. Res.* **17**: 1–13.

Valentine, J. W. (1969). Niche diversity and niche size patterns in marine fossils. *J. Palaeont.* **43**: 905–915.

Vasseur, P. (1964). Contribution a l'étude bionomique des peuplements sciaphiles infralittoraux de substrat dur dans les récifs de Tuléar, Madagascar. *Recl. Trav. Stn. Mar. Endoume* Suppl. **2** 1–77.

Yonge, C. M. (1967). Observations on *Pedum spondyloideum* (Chemnitz) Gmelin, a scallop associated with reef building corals. *Proc. malac. Soc. Lond.* **37**: 311–323.

Symp. zool. Soc. Lond. (1971) No. 28, 535–539.

THE CORAL GARDENS OF SHADWAN*

HELMUT FLEISSNER

Unterwasser- und Dokumentarfilm für Wissenschaft und Bildung, Bad Nauheim, Steinfurther Str. 33, West Germany

and

GUENTHER FLEISSNER

Zoologisches Institut der Universität Frankfurt/M, Siesmayerstr. 70, West Germany

This documentary film tries to give a comprehensive report on the biology of coral reefs in the Red Sea. While producing the film it was the authors' aim to design it for teaching students at university as well as pupils at school or adults by television. Although some other short film sequences on coral reefs had already appeared (Hass, 1961) no film synopses of coral reef biology have so far been available.

The film was made in the north of the Red Sea, in the coastal regions of different islands in the strait of Gubal, mainly in those of Shadwan, and along the coast from Hurghada to Koseir, from summer 1964 until spring 1967. In spite of their geographical position these reefs are astonishing well developed fringing reefs.

In this paper we would like to describe briefly the contents of the film and some technical details, which are of general interest.

The film story is determined by the corals and the members of the reef community alone. No human being is acting. The film tries to answer many questions by using many different methods and experiments: filming under water as well as microscopic views (e.g. at the zooxanthellae and cnidia), behavioral studies in the reef as well as electrophysiological experiments (such as exploding the cnidia, etc.). Some of the main problems and questions the film is dealing with are mentioned here.

The coral reef, so populous as to have no parallel in any other environment on earth, provokes the question, how the coral substrate supports such a concentrated biomass, and what are the relationships of corals, fish, and other organisms in the reef community? After learning by close-up photography and animation how a coral colony with its thousands of polyps is organized, how coral polyps are built (Kaestner,

* 16-mm sound colour film—48 min—English and German.

1965), how they produce their skeletons, and seeing the enormous lime-stone masses laid down by corals for miles along the shore, the viewer follows the problem how the coral, though being a very simple organized animal, can manage such an enormous metabolism. One can detect zooanthellae and green algae within the coral colony. It has been shown that the biomass of these primary producers is about three times the amount of animal tissue, a fact which fits very well into the ecologist's food pyramid (Odum and Odum, 1955). The symbiosis between algae and coral tissue explained in this film in its essential details by anima-tion, corresponds very well with the modern findings about the metabolic relationships (Odum and Odum, 1955; Goreau, 1959; Goreau and Goreau, 1959, 1960a, b; Yonge, 1963; Muscatine and Hand, 1958; L. Muscatine, personal communication, 1969): not only does the plant tissue use the carbon dioxide and other important compounds from corals, but also the animal tissue is well supported by the plants, i.e. with organic material deriving from photosynthesis by zooxanthellae.

The viewer can observe how the coral polyps catch small amphipoda in order to obtain their nitrogen and phosphorous compounds. At a high magnification he can follow in slow-motion how single cnidia explode (Weill, 1964) and how the tiny cilia transport the prey towards the polyp's mouth. The next sequences of the film demonstrate how the different types of coral growth have built up the whole reef (Scheer, 1959, 1960) into a labyrinthine structure, how corals although incapable of locomotion have spread out over a large area by sexual reproduction, what animals are living in the dark cavities of the reef, and how the reef supports growing animal life because it is a shelter for many animals against predators like sharks and groupers (Eibl-Eibesfeldt, 1962, 1964), and because it offers a rich source of food for many different specialized feeders (Abel, 1960; Hiatt and Strasburg, 1960). Furthermore the viewer can see the big turtles coming to the reef and the giant manta-rays dancing their courtship dance in the shallow water. In the sandy area between the reefs one can detect interesting adaptations to the special conditions of the environment. Nearly blind prawns of the genus *Alpheus* are living commensally with gobiids: deriving shelter from their piscine mentor, they spend their lives continually dredging out the fish's cave in the sandy sea bed (Luther, 1958; Magnus, 1967). Besides showing how the coral's limestone is laid down the film demon-strates to the viewer how the coral skeletons degenerate into sand, and brings a time-lag sequence of the sand-cleaning mechanism performed by polyp colonies. Then the film finishes with a short review.

Since some technical details might be of general interest too, they are mentioned as follows.

First of all to show the corals' life means to show original scenes of the tiny polyps of the stony corals, and not to restrict oneself to the big polyps of sea-anemones. However, this is quite a difficult undertaking, because most of the coral polyps are irritated by light and retract quickly as soon as the film light is turned on, for example species of *Goniastrea*. Many polyps are also sensitive to stimulation other than lighting so one needs a lot of experience to get their tentacles to expand at all. Therefore it is a great advantage or even necessary to be very close to sea, i.e. to have fresh sea water running through the aquarium as well as to have fresh animals at your disposal. For that reason we built a camp on Shadwan island which included many laboratory facilities where we took most of the microscopic and close-up photography. To demonstrate how a coral polyp feeds on plankton shrimps, we needed a very insensitive polyp. The best results we have obtained were with the trophozooids of *Fungia* sp. when they were fixed as little discs on the trophozooid stump. They were more insensitive to the bright film light, and for many weeks we kept them alive with well expanded tentacles. They are also very suitable for studying sand-cleaning mechanisms in corals, and they have the advantage of growing in abundance in some places of the reef, and can be collected in depths of less than 1 or 2 m where they are usually hidden in cavities between the other coral skeletons. To show single nematocysts shooting out their inverted threads is quite a problem too. The methods worked out by R. Weill (personal communication, 1964) were used rather successfully. Definite groups of many nematocysts or even the majority of them in one end of the tentacle explode simultaneously when the tentacle is stimulated by an electric voltage of some 1–6 volts. One electrode is put into the tentacle and the other one is surrounding it. You can even observe without using slow motion picture how a single nematocyst explodes quite slowly if a pressed piece of tentacle smeared on a glass is completely dried and than wetted again. Very big nematocysts (for example longer than $200\,\mu$) were found in polyps of *Goniopora* sp. We have used the same animals to photograph their zooxanthellae. The time-lag sequences showing the coral sand-cleaning mechanism have been taken from *Fungia* polyps. One polyp completely covered by sand takes about half an hour to clean itself.

Many underwater scenes could only be filmed by the help of transportable underwater lamps. For close-up shootings in the aquarium as well as under water it was necessary to use reflex cameras with a special light metre measuring through the lenses, because the depth of focus, the parallax, and the film exposure are quite critical. Furthermore we used spotlights for concentrating light on the little specimens. In order to solve such problems we constructed and developed—from our own experience—all special equipment such as underwater lamps, light metre, reflex camera housings, etc. The original film was made with 16 mm Ektachrome commercial colour material. The film shown at the Symposium was finished in 1967 and published for the first time in April, 1968 by West German Television.

REFERENCES

Abel, E. (1960). Zur Kenntnis des Verhaltens und der Ökologie von Fischen an Korallenriffen bei Ghardaqa. *Z. Morph. Ökol. Tiere* **49**: 430–503.

Darwin, C. (1876). *Über den Bau und die Verbreitung der Corallenriffe.* Stuttgart. (übersetzt v.I.v. Carus).

Eibl-Eibesfeldt, I.v. (1962). Freibeobachtungen zur Deutung des Schwarmverhaltens verschiedener Fische. *Z. Tierpsychol.* **19**: 165–182.

Eibl-Eibesfeldt, I.v. (1964). *Im Reich der tausend Atolle.* München: Piper-Verlag.

Gerlach, S. A. (1958). Das tropische Korallenriff als Lebensraum. *Verh. dt. zool. Ges.* 356–363.

Goreau, T. F. (1959). The physiology of skeleton formation in corals. I.A method for measuring the rate of calcium deposition by corals under different conditions. *Biol. Bull. mar. biol. Lab. Woods Hole.* **116**: 59–75.

Goreau, T. F. (1961). Problems of growth and calcium deposition in reef corals. *Endeavour* **20**: 32–39.

Goreau, T. F. and Goreau, N. I. (1959). The physiology of skeleton formation in corals. II. Calcium deposition by hermatypic corals under various conditions in the reef. *Biol. Bull. mar. biol. Lab. Woods Hole.* **117**: 239–250.

Goreau, T. F. and Goreau, N. I. (1960a). The physiology of skeleton formation in corals. III. Calcification rate as a function of colony weight and total nitrogen content in the reef coral *Manicina areolata* (Linnaeus). *Biol. Bull. mar. biol. Lab. Woods Hole.* **118**, 419–429.

Goreau, T. F. and Goreau, N. I. (1960b). The physiology of skeleton formation in corals. IV. On isotopic equilibrium exchanges of calcium between corallum and environment in living and dead reef-building corals. *Biol. Bull. mar. biol. Lab. Woods Hole.* **119**: 416–427.

Hass, H. (1961). *Expedition ins Unbekannte.* Berlin: Ullstein.

Hiatt, R. W. and Strasburg, D. W. (1960). Ecological relationships of the fish fauna on coral reefs of the Marshall Islands. *Ecol. Monogr.* **30**: 65–127.

Kaestner, A. (1965). *Lehrbuch der speziellen Zoologie.* Stuttgart: Fischer. **1**: 118–216.

Lorenz, K. (1965). Naturschönheit und Daseinskampf. In "Darwin hat recht gesehen". *Opuscula in Wissenschaft und Dichtung* **20**: 9–23.

Luther, W. (1958). Symbiose von Fischen (Gobiidae) mit einem Krebs (*Alpheus djiboutensis*) im Roten Meer. *Z. Tierpsychol.* **15**: 175–177.

Magnus, D. B. E. (1967). Zur Ökologie sedimentbewohnender Alpheus–Garnelen (Decapoda, Natantia) des Roten Meeres. *Helgoländer wiss. Meeresunters.* **15**.

Muscatine, L. and Hand, C. (1958). Direct evidence for the transfer of materials from symbiontic algae to the tissues of a coelenterate. *Proc. natn. Acad. Sci. U.S.A.* **44**: 1259–1263.

Odum, H. T. and Odum, E. P. (1955). Trophic structure and productivity of a windward coral reef community on Eniwetok *Atoll Ecol. Monogr.* **25**: 291–320.

Scheer, G. (1959). Die Formenvielfalt der Riffkorallen. *Ber. natur. Ver. Darmstadt* **58/59**: 115–177.

Scheer, G. (1960). Der Lebensraum der Riffkorallen. *Ber. natur. Ver. Darmstadt* **59/60**: 29–44.

Wickler, W. (1963). Zum Problem der Signalbildung am Beispiel der Verhaltens-mimikry zwischen Aspidontus und Labroides. *Z. Tierpsychol.* **20**: 657–668.

Yonge, C. M. (1930). *A Year on the Great Barrier Reef*. London: Putnam.

Yonge, C. M. (1963). The biology of coral reefs. *Adv. mar. Biol.* **1**: 209–260.

Conclusion

Conclusion

Symp. zool. Soc. Lond. (1971) No. 28, 543–547.

REMARKS

K. G. McKENZIE

British Museum (Natural History), London, England

Some of the descriptive studies reported to this meeting have been oriented spatially, often in great detail, and have neglected the time component; others, which recognize the significance of time, as does Dr. Stoddart's paper on the development of geomorphic features of some Indian Ocean coral reefs, have been concerned mainly with a relatively short time span—the Pleistocene. It seems to me necessary also to consider the Indian Ocean coral reefs in the perspective of a longer history, from the upper Mesozoic onwards, especially in view of the significant impetus given by plate tectonics studies to ideas on the relative movements of continental masses which are embodied in the Continental Drift hypothesis. This hypothesis is now firmly established as viable—sufficiently respectable indeed to appear on the cover of each issue of *Palaeogeography, Palaeoclimatology, Palaeoecology*. In the context of Drift, the Indian Ocean as we see it today, a water body representing a sizable percentage of the world's oceans and extending over about 50 degrees of latitude and 70 degrees of longitude, did not exist in the Upper Cretaceous. Instead, if we accept a recent computer-generated map of the southern continents and India prior to break-up fitted at the 1000 m (approx.) depth contour, the Cretaceous "Indian Ocean" consisted of long relatively narrow marine channels between Africa-Madagascar and India, India-Malaysia and Antarctica and Malaysia-Indonesia and Western Australia (Smith and Hallam, 1970). There was a contemporary, markedly latitudinal, world ocean to the north of these channels (which led into it) and its name was Tethys.

The physical fit of the southern continents (into Gondwanaland) has long been argued—and is still being refined (Burton, 1970). Thus, more than a decade before the Smith and Hallam synthesis very similar reconstructions had been proposed by South African and Australian geologists, principally L. C. King and S. W. Carey. The evidence in favour of Drift, however, is much more than the, in part subjective, good fit of shelf lines which is common to all these reconstructions.

Contributory, too, is the igneous and sedimentary record in the southern continents. Some evidence from the volcanic record is given in Smith and Hallam (1970, Table 2). It also seems significant that there are no islands in the Indian Ocean—Madagascar not considered in this context—with a continental (granitic) basement with the exception of the Seychelles. The Seychelles alone are not an adequate argument against shifts of the magnitude sponsored here. Considering the distribution of sedimentary rocks, in Australia the major Lower Cretaceous marine incursion did not affect the western coast of Western Australia except marginally. Yet eastwards it developed the vast Artesian Basin, taking in much of Queensland and western New South Wales, continuing into South Australia (the Murray Basin) and even into Western Australia (the Eucla Basin). The faunas indicate that this incursion came more from the tropical north, from Tethys. In the next period of interest, the Upper Cretaceous, shelf sediments are known in the Perth Basin, Western Australia, where the sequence is relatively thin. It thickens somewhat further to the north in the Carnarvon Basin but the outcrop pattern remains longitudinal and marginal along the western coast and near hinterland of the State. No inland deposits are known. In the Palaeocene and Upper Eocene there were further major transgressions and the first definite evidence of a continuous seaway along the southern coast of Australia. In Western Australia, sediments indicative of a warm marginal nearshore and shelf facies were deposited during the Upper Eocene as far inland as Norseman. Along the western coast of Western Australia, however, the Eocene transgression did not extend as far inland as it did in the south of the State. It is not until the Oligocene that there is evidence of a seaway through Bass Strait.

In India, outcrops of post-Jurassic marine sediments fringe the southern margins of the subcontinent while the principal marine sequences are all in the north along what formed part of the Tethyan Corridor before the abutment of insular India against the Himalayas during the mid-Tertiary. The earliest marine sediments along the coast of southeast India are Lower Cretaceous in age (Bhalla, 1970).

A similar synthesis can be arrived at for the Cretaceous and Tertiary of South Africa as a glance at a geological map should make clear.

There is solid biological evidence in favour of the existence of Tethys but that in support of Drift in the Indian Ocean region during the Cainozoic may be considered more tenuous. Fossil faunal distributions may be difficult to interpret because of bad preservation, because they are rare anyway (e.g. the organisms of interest may have soft skeletons), because of a lack of sufficient, comparative Recent studies, and because of such taxonomic problems as homeomorphy and such biological problems as changes in the biological continuity of the study organisms (e.g. any drastic alterations in their environmental tolerances). Assuming that these difficulties are met, and they are simply met by selecting groups with a good fossil record in warm shallow waters environments and reasonably well understood Recent distributions—suitable groups would include corals, molluscs, foraminiferans and ostracodes—then the interpretations are relatively straightforward.

Before looking at some Recent distributions, it is important to recall that Tethys became disrupted by the closure of the Middle East corridor in the mid-Tertiary so that following the Vindobonian (Miocene) there was little opportunity for faunal and floral exchange between the Caribbean, Mediterranean and Indo-West Pacific.

With this in mind, the present distribution of some marine angiosperms (Good, 1964) seems to me to be a relict of a typical Tethyan pattern and indicative of the extent of Tethys in the late Mesozoic—early Cainozoic when, on the limited fossil evidence, marine angiosperms underwent their initial radiation. A similar interpretation is then mandatory with regard to organisms which prefer a phanerogamic niche, e.g. some paradoxostomatid ostracodes (McKenzie, 1969). Earlier, I interpreted the presence of a continuous marine corridor (Tethys) from the Gulf of Mexico to Australasia throughout much of the early Cainozoic on the basis of distributions of many marine ostracode genera (McKenzie, 1967). Such work is confirmative of a general view expressed, for example, by Ekman (1953, p. 44) as follows, ". . . both the West Indies and the Indo-West Pacific fauna were formerly part of the same original fauna, namely that of the Tethys Sea . . .".

On the other hand, comparative ostracode studies are now available on the Cretaceous faunas of South Africa (Dingle, 1969a, b), East Africa (Bate and Bayliss, 1970) and Western Australia (Bate, in press) which indicate the presence in these areas at that time of some endemic component. More significantly, this recent work shows that the faunas have a non-Tethyan aspect, i.e. they differ from those of West Africa (Reyment, 1960) and Egypt (van den Bold, 1964). The hypothesized marine channels leading off Tethys—separated from each other by continental blocks—in which the oceanic circulation was much different from that today, would favour the development of some local endemism. Indeed, endemism in the belemnite fauna at least had developed in the region bordered by East Africa Madagascar and Cutch even in Jurassic times (Stevens, 1965).

Recent distributions of benthic animals may show some traces of this endemism, i.e. faunas along the coasts which once bounded these channels may differ significantly from the Tropical Tethyan fauna. The echinoderm distributions of Australia monographed by Clark (1946) are a case in point. The Western Australia fauna forms part of his distinct Dampieran Province while the South Australian fauna, quoting Ekman again, is, ". . . characterized partly in its pronounced independence,

24

particularly in species, and partly also, as far as the origin of the fauna is concerned, by a strong affinity with the tropical fauna . . ." (Ekman, 1953, p. 200). Among tropical spiny lobsters, the species from Western Australia, *Panulirus cygnus* George, is an Australian endemic whereas the northern Australian species belong to the Indo-West Pacific fauna and occur throughout the Indian Ocean region (George, 1968, 1969).

In part, the uniformity of the Indo-West Pacific fauna is attributable to organisms with long distance larvae (in the sense of Thorson, 1961). The tropical spiny lobsters are one example, cowries are another. However, I believe that much of this uniformity is due to a common Tethyan ancestry. I found the Tethyan element to predominate over the austral element even in the Cainozoic ostracode faunas of south-eastern Australia (McKenzie, in press, a) and Fleming (1962) reached a similar conclusion earlier via a more general palaeontological approach with respect to the faunas of New Zealand.

Finally, when one considers the distributions of land faunas several of them seem inexplicable unless viewed in terms of the Drift hypothesis. Thus, the distribution of phreatoicid isopods appears fragmented until the Indian wedge is fitted into a reassembled Gondwanaland and, to my mind, Drift theory best explains the distributions of several groups of freshwater ostracodes (McKenzie, in press b).

References

Bate, R. H. (in press). *Upper Cretaceous Ostracoda from the Carnarvon Basin, Western Australia.*

Bate, R. H. and Bayliss, D. D. (1970). An outline account of the Cretaceous and Tertiary Foraminifera and of the Cretaceous ostracods of Tanzania. *Proc. 3rd afr. micropaleont. Colloq., Cairo* (1968): 113–164.

Bhalla, S. N. (1970). Marine invasions and oil possibilities in Andhra Pradesh, India. *Palaeogeogr. Palaeoclimat. Palaeoecol.* **7**: 61–67.

van den Bold, W. A. (1964). Ostracoden aus der Oberkreide von Abu Rawash, Agypten. *Palaeontographica* a **123**: 111–136.

Burton, C. K. (1970). The palaeotectonic status of the Malay Peninsula. *Palaeogeogr. Palaeoclimat. Palaeoecol.* **7**: 51–60.

Clark, H. L. (1946). The echinoderm fauna of Australia. *Publs Carnegie Instn.* No. **566**.

Dingle, R. V. (1969a). Marine Neocomian Ostracoda from South Africa. *Trans R. Soc. S. Afr.* **38**: 139–163.

Dingle, R. V. (1969b). Upper Senonian ostracods from the coast of Pondoland, South Africa. *Trans R. Soc. S. Afr.* **39**: 347–385.

Ekman, S. (1953). *Zoogeography of the sea.* London: Sidgwick and Jackson.

Fleming, C. A. (1962). New Zealand biogeography a palaeontologist's approach. *Tuatara* **10**: 53–108.

George, R. W. (1968). Tropical spiny lobsters, *Panulirus* spp., of Western Australia (and the Indo-West Pacific). *Jl R. Soc. W. Aust.* **51**: 33–38.

George, R. W. (1969). Natural distribution and speciation of marine animals *Jl R. Soc. W. Aust.* **52**: 33–40.

Good, R. D'o. (1964). *The geography of the flowering plants.* London: Longmans.

McKenzie, K. G. (1967). The distribution of Caenozoic marine Ostracoda from the Gulf of Mexico to Australasia. In *Aspects of Tethyan biogeography*, Adams, (C. G. and Ager, D. V. eds.), *Publs. Syst. Ass.* **7**: 219–238.

McKenzie, K. G. (1969). Notes on the Paradoxostomatids. In *The taxonomy, morphology and ecology of Recent Ostracoda:* 48–66. (Neale, J. W., ed.) Edinburgh: Oliver and Boyd.

McKenzie, K. G. (in press a). Cainozoic Ostracoda of southeastern Australia with the description of *Hanaiceratina* new genus. In (van den Bold, W. A., ed.) Baton Rouge: La. State Univ. Press.

McKenzie, K. G. (in press b). Palaeozoogeography of Freshwater Ostracoda. *Proceedings of the* 1970 *Colloquium on the Palaeoecology of Ostracods at Pau, France.*

Reyment, R. A. (1960). Studies on Nigerian Upper Cretaceous and Lower Tertiary Ostracoda. Part 1: Senonian and Maestrichtian Ostracoda. *Stockh. Contr. Geol.* **8**: 1–238.

Smith, A. G. and Hallam, A. (1970). The fit of the southern continents. *Nature, Lond.* **225**: 139–144.

Stevens, G. R. (1965). The Jurassic and Cretaceous belemnites of New Zealand and a review of the Jurassic and Cretaceous belemnites of the Indo-Pacific Region. *Palaeont. Bull. Wellington* **36**.

Thorson, G. (1961). Length of pelagic larval life in marine bottom invertebrates as related to larval transport by ocean currents. In *Oceanography* (Sears, M. ed.), *Publs Am. Ass. Advmt Sci.* **67**: 455–474.

Sym. zool. Soc. Lond. (1971) No. 28, 549–553

PROBLEMS AND PROSPECTS IN INDIAN OCEAN REEF STUDIES

D. R. STODDART

Department of Geography, University of Cambridge, Cambridge, England

SYNOPSIS

In addition to bringing together a great deal of new information about the coral reefs of the Indian Ocean, the discussions during this Symposium have focussed attention on a number of problems. In drawing the Symposium to a close, I propose, rather than reviewing the present state of knowledge, to consider some of the problems raised, under the general headings of substantive, conceptual and operational problems. To some extent each of these groups of problems corresponds with particular scales of enquiry, and each spans the old divisions of reef study into geological and biological studies. Their recognition suggests priorities for future work in this area.

SUBSTANTIVE PROBLEMS

Most of the papers given during this Symposium have been primarily concerned with western Indian Ocean reefs, and, within this area, with intensive investigations in the Red Sea, at Tuléar and elsewhere in Madagascar and the Comoros, in the Seychelles, and at Aldabra. There are fewer studies of the great reefs of the Chagos and Maldive Islands, or of the mainland reefs of East Africa, the Persian Gulf and India. The reefs of the eastern Indian Ocean are even less well known, with the exception of the long series of studies at Cocos-Keeling Atoll. There is an urgent need for work on high-island reefs in the Andamans and Nicobars, to compare with high-island reefs in the granitic Seychelles and volcanic Mascarenes and Comoros. We also need investigations of mainland reefs of the eastern Indian Ocean, in the Mergui Archipelago, Malaya, Sumatra and northwest Australia. Rosen has pointed out that there is considerable zoogeographic interest in the composition of reef faunas in this area intermediate between the western Indian Ocean and the western Pacific.

The need for additional data on the reefs themselves is thus geographically extensive, but it is also possible to indicate specific problems on which work is needed. One, discussed by Guilcher, is the origin of faros, classically described from and best developed in the Maldive Islands, where they have never been properly studied. A second concerns the status of benthic communities on the great submerged banks of the west-central Indian Ocean, and the reasons why these

549

areas, great reefs in the past, have not developed surface reefs during the Holocene. A third concerns the history of the reefs as geological structures, their changes in form during recurrent Pleistocene changes in sea-level and their earlier history in the context of the development of the Indian Ocean itself. All of these will throw light on the development of modern reefs in the comparatively brief span of post-Wisconsin time. Such investigations will lead not only to a greater understanding of Indian Ocean reefs, but to a refinement of the classical models of general reef development proposed by Darwin, Daly, and others, mostly before 1930.

CONCEPTUAL PROBLEMS

Conceptual problems are at present most acute at an intermediate scale. Whereas models of reef evolution over geological time, such as Darwin's, and of sea-level change associated with the Pleistocene glaciations assist in the organization of data at the regional level, models at the level of reef zonation and detailed morphology (i.e. at linear scales of 10^2–10^4 m) are less developed. The complexity of reefs at this scale only really became apparent with the development of aerial photography and of detailed reef surveys: the complexity is such that organizing concepts are required to enable us to perceive broad regional gradients through the often high local variability. The concept most frequently used, particularly in descriptive work, has been that of zonation, but because of biotic diversity, both on individual reefs and within broader zoogeographic distribution patterns, zonation studies have usually been of local rather than general applicability. In their work on the Seychelles reefs, Rosen (pp. 163–183) and Taylor (1968) have distinguished ecologically and physiographically distinct communities of reef corals, in particular a shallow *Pocillopora*, a *Porites*, and a deeper *Acropora* community. Rosen has suggested that this pattern, in response to changing exposure conditions, may have wider application in interpreting reef patterns. A similar pattern of communities dominated by *Acropora formosa* has been described at this Symposium from the lagoon reefs of Addu Atoll by Davies, Stoddart and Sigee (pp. 217–259). Clearly the concept would have to be extended to incorporate the reef variations which are already known to exist, perhaps utilizing the concept of vicarious species. Thus in Mauritius Pichon (pp. 185–216) has described *Porites* and *Acropora* communities on fringing reefs. Generalizing concepts of this kind are important in helping to reduce the complexity of observations on individual reefs and in aiding the comparison of reefs in different areas. Their development raises interesting problems concerning what it is useful to measure and record on reefs. It may, for example, be too readily assumed that Linnaean taxa are the only useful units for recording coral distributions, since much of the discussion during this Symposium has concentrated on groupings defined in terms of growth form and magnitude of colony.

Once concepts and models have been developed, we can then proceed to test them in the field. Some experimental work has already been carried out, particularly on the ecological tolerances of individual species, and Rosen has suggested that such work might be extended to the Indian Ocean to test hypotheses concerning present coral distributions. Most hypothesis-testing in reef work, however, is likely to be non-experimental, and concerned either with testing the inferences made from particular deductive models, or sorting out the interrelationships of factors in multivariate situations. In the first class, for example, the testing of geological inferences by deep boring provides a notable example: the Indian Ocean is in fact the only major reef area where we have no direct knowledge of reef foundations resulting from deep boring operations. In the second class, a variety of simple models for testing can be readily conceived. Thus we could test the effects on reef growth and island structure of catastrophic storms by comparative studies within and outside the hurricane seas; or we could test the effects of rainfall on both present reef growth and on inherited karst erosion forms by sampling along rainfall gradients at the present time.

OPERATIONAL PROBLEMS

Operational problems become particularly acute at the level of field survey, in the recording of local variability on reefs. A number of contributors to this Symposium (particularly Scheer, pp. 329–367; Davies, Stoddart and Sigee, pp. 217–259; Barnes et al., pp. 87–114; and Loya and Slobodkin, pp. 117–139) have been concerned with problems of data recording, and the relative advantages and disadvantages of using quadrat and line-transects and other field recording methods. In the Indian Ocean, as elsewhere (Stoddart, 1971), the recording methods used have been extremely diverse, to the extent that quantitative distribution data are rarely comparable from one reef area to another. Logistic problems of time and tide are particularly acute in the reef environment, and it may be that the range of exposure conditions experienced on reefs, together with the diverse scales of reefs themselves, will rule out any universally applicable survey methods.

Too little attention has certainly been given in the past, when designing field measuring procedures, to the use to which the data will be put. The significance of the paper by Loya and Slobodkin on the reefs of the Gulf of Eilat surely lies in the fact that here field procedures were specifically designed to yield data for specific methods of analysis. As Scheer (1967) and other later workers have suggested, there is great scope for the application of the concepts, methods and techniques of quantitative plant ecology to the reef environment. Thus the analysis of the Aldabra reefs by Barnes *et al.* applies the plant-sociological concepts of the Braun-Blanquet school. Field methods, however, are not independent of the conceptual framework within which they are used, and there is an urgent need for a critical review of community concepts in reef ecology. McIntosh (1967) and Whittaker (1962, 1967) have reviewed a wide and diverse literature on the nature of terrestrial vegetation, where many of the problems encountered are comparable to those found in the study of benthic marine organisms on reefs. In vegetation studies, different techniques have become associated with different concepts of the nature of vegetation itself, and though, as Langford and Buell (1969) point out, confusions associated with differences in scale of study have occurred, reef students cannot afford to ignore the experience gained by plant ecologists. We need, therefore, to look not only at our so far inadequately defined concepts of reef organization, but also at the range of techniques made available by plant ecologists for survey and analysis, and at the literature, mainly in forestry, on the field efficiency—in terms of time and effort—of particular survey techniques (Greig–Smith, 1964; Kershaw, 1964).

<h3 style="text-align:center">FUTURE WORK</h3>

I conclude, therefore, that future reef studies in the Indian Ocean fall largely into two types. On the one hand there are the relatively extensive studies which are required to provide us with data on the many unstudied and almost unknown reefs, particularly of the central and eastern Indian Ocean, and to broaden our knowledge of those areas where studies have already begun. And on the other there is the prospect of more intensive work, yielding insights not only in the context of the Indian Ocean but for reef understanding generally, and for this it is clear that a great deal of basic work has yet to be done, if efforts, particularly in quantitative surveys, are not to be wasted.

In the Indian Ocean we are perhaps fortunate in the availability of marine stations at which such basic investigations can take place: at Tuléar in Madagascar, at Eilat in the Red Sea, at Mandapam in India, at Aldabra, at Zanzibar, and elsewhere. I believe our first priority in reef work should be to use the opportunities provided by these stations to attack the conceptual and technical problems to which I have referred. A number of further symposia when these issues were discussed again have already taken place: on the Indian Ocean itself at Cochin in January 1971 and at Kiel, Germany, in March 1971. Another symposia has been announced on coral reefs generally to be held at Heron Island, Australia, in May 1973.

Finally, in drawing this Symposium to a close, I would like to thank the Zoological Society of London and the Royal Society for sponsoring the meeting, the Zoological Society and its staff for organizing it and for their most generous hospitality, and our overseas visitors, both for coming to London to tell us of their work and for speaking in English. I hope we can all have the opportunity to continue these discussions on a reef itself at some time in the future.

REFERENCES

(These do not include references to papers in the present volume)

Greig-Smith, P. (1964). *Quantitative plant ecology.* 2nd edition. London: Butterworths.

Kershaw, K. A. (1964). *Quantitative and dynamic ecology.* London: Arnold.

Langford, A. N. and Buell, M. F. (1969). Integration, identity and stability in the plant association. *Adv. ecol. Res.* **6**: 83–135.

McIntosh, R. P. (1967). The continuum concept of vegetation. *Bot. Rev.* **33**: 130–187.

Scheer, G. (1967). Uber die Methodik der Untersuchung von Korallenriffen. *Z. Morph. Ökol. Tiere* **60**: 105–114.

Stoddart, D. R. (1971). Field methods in the study of coral reefs. *Symposium on Corals and Coral Reefs* (Marine Biological Association of India): 61–68.

Taylor, J. D. (1968). Coral reef and associated invertebrate communities (mainly molluscan) around Mahé, Seychelles. *Phil. Trans. R. Soc.* (B) **254**: 129–206.

Whittaker, R. H. (1962). Classification of natural communities. *Bot. Rev.* **28**: 1–239.

Whittaker, R. H. (1967). Gradient analysis of vegetation. *Biol. Rev.* **42**: 207–264.

Note Added in Proof

Further work in the summer of 1970 has confirmed that most reefs in this area have small populations of scattered *A. planci* averaging between one and twenty per km length of reef. Parts of Wingate and Towartit previously visited showed a consistent population increase by a factor of about three. But in addition on a few occasional previously unvisited reefs in both the Port Sudan and Suakin areas concentrations of up to 1500 were found. At the three sites with more than 100 *A. planci*, dense aggregations of the starfish had formed within a small area. Several lines of evidence suggest chemoattraction between feeding animals may be important in bringing these animals together. We favour the suggestion that such concentrations, presumably corresponding to Chesher's condition 6, are an equally normal and more important condition of the usual low level population, and that successful breeding is probably limited to these concentrations. Many of the apparent plague reports outside the main plague areas of the central Great Barrier Reef and Micronesia may only have been observations of such normal concentrations. Gonad index determinations suggest the breeding season for *A. planci* in the area is centred on July and August, and more extensive size-frequency data shows significant classes that are assumed to represent yearly age groups as follows: 1·2 years = 15 cm overall diameter, 2·2 years = 22 cm, 3·2 years = 28 cm, 4·2 plus years = 32 plus cm. Some evidence suggests that the major predator of the adult *A. planci* in the area is *Cheilinus undulatus*, the hump-headed wrasse.

AUTHOR INDEX

Numbers in Italics refer to page in the References at the end of each article.

SYSTEMATIC INDEX

Asterisks refer to folding tables placed after the indicated page:
e.g. 268** = Table II after page 268; 364* = Table I after page 364

A

Abudefduf, 98, 99

Abudefduf septemfasciatus, 99

Abudefduf sexfasciatus, 99

Acanthaster planci, 433–436, 439–445, 448–450, 452–454

Acanthastrea, 112, 208, 268*, 268**, 321, 345, 351, 364, 364*

Acanthastrea echinata, 103, 112, 125, 128, 325

Acanthocidaris curvatispinis, 207

Acanthophyllia, 268*, 345

Acanthopleura, 527, 530

Acanthopleura brevispinosa, 516, 525

Acanthopleura haddoni, 150

Acanthurus leucosternon, 98–100

Acanthurus lineatus, 98

Acanthurus triostegus, 98

Acar, 520

Acar plicata, 519

Acmaea, 516, 525–527, 530

Acmaea profunda, 525

Acrhelia, 268*

Acropora, 14, 39, 42–44, 46, 47, 50, 52–55, 59, 94, 102, 103, 110, 143, 151, 153, 155–157, 164, 165, 171–173, 176–178, 180, 181, 196, 200, 201, 205, 206, 208, 224, 229, 230, 239, 242, 244, 246, 247 248, 250, 252–254, 268*, 268**, 284, 285, 296, 309, 316–322, 325, 331–333, 337–343, 345–349, 351–356, 359–361, 363–364, 364*, 417, 424, 444, 448, 449, 452, 512, 550

Acropora abrotanoides, 323

Acropora cervicornis, 157, 305

Acropora ceylonica, 305

Acropora conferta, 323

Acropora conigera, 234, 235, 237

Acropora convexa, 226, 228, 229, 232, 233, 234, 235, 237, 238–240

Acropora corymbosa, 122, 123, 228, 229, 230, 233, 234, 235, 237, 238, 239, 305, 309, 319, 323

Acropora cytherea, 173

Acropora decipiens, 170

Acropora digitifera, 42, 43, 46, 226, 228, 229, 232, 233, 234, 235, 237, 238–240, 242, 305

Acropora diversa, 43, 103, 110, 305

Acropora echinata, 320, 323

Acropora efflorescens, 322, 323

Acropora erythraeae, 305, 309, 315

Acropora eurystoma, 123, 232

Acropora exigua, 305

Acropora formosa, 42, 172, 224–230, 232–237, 238–240, 248, 249, 254, 305, 309, 320, 323

Acropora forskali, 230 233, 235, 237, 323

Acropora glochiclados, 101, 102, 107, 110

Acropora haimei, 305, 323

Acropora hemprichi, 117, 127–129, 131, 136–138, 230, 233, 234, 235, 237, 322, 323, 340–343, 345, 348, 351, 355, 361

Acropora humilis, 42, 43, 46, 50, 51, 123, 169–171, 173, 174, 180, 181, 306, 323, 340, 341, 345, 347–349, 351–355, 361

Acropora hyacinthus, 43, 123, 229, 233, 234, 237, 306, 323

Acropora hystrix, 235, 237

Acropora indica, 306, 309, 323

Acropora intermedia, 234, 306, 323

Acropora irregularis, 42–44, 54, 102, 110, 172–174, 181

Acropora monticulosa, 103, 110, 323

Acropora multicaulis, 306

Acropora multiformis, 306

Acropora nasuta, 123

Acropora nobilis, 306, 309, 315

Acropora obscura, 306

Acropora palifera, 102, 110, 171, 248, 249, 322, 323, 340–342, 351, 353–355, 360, 361, 423,

Acropora palmata, 157, 320

Acropora pharaonis, 42, 43, 107, 205, 306, 320, 323

SUBJECT INDEX

Note: An asterisk or double asterisk after a page number denotes the folding table after that page, e.g.—364* = Table I after p. 364, 268** = Table II after p. 268